My Utmost for His Highest

UPDATED EDITION

ALSO BY OSWALD CHAMBERS

Biblical Ethics

Biblical Psychology

Christian Disciplines

The Complete Works of Oswald Chambers

Conformed to His Image and *The Servant as His Lord*

If You Will Ask

Knocking at God's Door

The Love of God

Our Brilliant Heritage with *If You Will Be Perfect* and *Disciples Indeed*

Our Ultimate Refuge

The Quotable Oswald Chambers

So Send I You and *Workmen of God*

Studies in the Sermon on the Mount

Oswald Chambers—Abandoned to God: The Life Story of the Author of My Utmost for His Highest
by David McCasland

A Daily Companion to My Utmost for His Highest
by Jed and Cecilie Macosko

My Utmost for His Highest®

UPDATED EDITION

Oswald Chambers

EDITED BY James Reimann

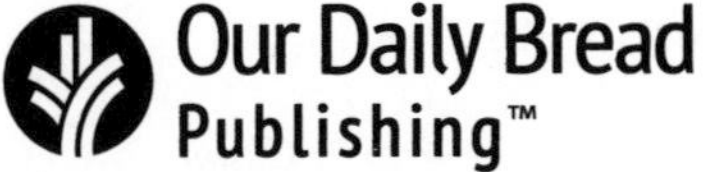

Authorized by the Oswald Chambers Publications Association, Ltd.

ISBN: 978-1-62707-875-7

Printed in China

22 23 24 25 26 27 / 10 9 8 7 6

Introduction

My Utmost for His Highest has been a close companion to me through most of my Christian life. It was first recommended to me by my pastor, Charles Stanley, who has often expressed his love for its powerful content. It is a work that has endured far beyond the author's death in 1917. Oswald Chambers, who died at the age of 43, originally shared these thoughts as lectures at the Bible Training College in Clapham, England, from 1911 to 1915, and as devotional talks while serving with the Young Men's Christian Association from 1915 to 1917. The YMCA had appointed him to serve in Egypt with the Australian and New Zealand troops who were guarding the Suez Canal during World War I. These lectures and talks were later compiled by Chambers's wife and published in book form in 1927 in England, and in 1935 in the United States. It has since become the best-selling devotional book of all time.

The idea of a new edition was prompted by the changes in the English language over the last century. As owner of a Christian bookstore, I have sold thousands of copies of *My Utmost for His Highest* through the years. However, because of these language changes, I have had an ever-increasing concern that readers were not gleaning all they could from the book. One morning, after reading the devotional selection for that day, I asked the Lord to impress on someone a burden to write a new edition. Much to my surprise, I immediately sensed God's directive to write it myself. I began that same day.

What you hold in your hand is the culmination of approximately 1,800 hours of research and editing. It is not a paraphrase of the original work, but could be considered a translation of it. Thousands of word studies have been done to render an accurate yet readable edition. This edition also includes the reference for every Scripture quotation to allow the reader to further his or her study of the biblical passage. (Note: Scripture quotations without references are passages that have been referred to earlier in the selection.) I encourage you to read with this book in one hand and your Bible in the other.

This book is not the Bible—it is intended to point you to the Bible. The desire of my heart is that this work will unlock for you the treasure of the truth of God's Word and the insights into that truth that Oswald Chambers explored. May you use this book as a help in meditating on God's Word, and as a help in applying it to your life.

James Reimann (1950–2013)
Joshua 1:8

A Word about Oswald and Biddy Chambers

Oswald Chambers was not famous during his lifetime. At the time of his death in 1917, at the age of forty-three, only three books bearing his name had been published. Among a relatively small circle of Christians in Britain and the U.S., Chambers was much appreciated as a teacher of rare insight and expression, but he was not widely known.

His wide-ranging influence came during the decades following his death as his widow compiled Oswald's spoken words into thirty published books, many of which have become Christian classics: *Baffled to Fight Better, If Ye Shall Ask, Studies in the Sermon on the Mount*, and of course, *My Utmost for His Highest*.

Oswald Chambers was born in Aberdeen, Scotland, on July 24, 1874, the eighth of nine children of Rev. Clarence Chambers, a rather stern Baptist minister, and his gracious wife, Hannah. During Oswald's boyhood years in Perth, he first exhibited his keen talent in art. When he was fifteen, the family moved to London where Oswald made his public profession of faith in Christ and became a member of Rye Lane Baptist Church. This marked a period of rapid spiritual growth, along with an intense struggle to find God's will and way for his life.

As a gifted artist and musician, Chambers trained at London's National Art Training School, later named the Royal Academy of Art. He sensed God's call to be an ambassador for Christ in the world of art, music, and aesthetics. But while studying at the University of Edinburgh (1895–96), he experienced a major redirection in life. Following an agonizing internal battle, he decided to train for the Christian ministry, a profession he said he would never enter "unless God takes me by the scruff of the neck and throws me in." He left the university and entered Dunoon College, near Glasgow, where he spent nine years, first as a theological student, then as a tutor of philosophy. Under the wise guidance of Rev. Duncan

MacGregor, his mentor and friend, Oswald matured greatly and came through a long "dark night of the soul" into a deeper and more joyful knowledge of Christ.

In 1906 and 1907 Oswald spent six months teaching at God's Bible School in Cincinnati, Ohio. From there he went to Japan, visiting the Tokyo Bible School, founded by Charles and Lettie Cowman. This journey around the world marked his transition from Dunoon College to full-time work with the London-based Pentecostal League of Prayer.

While serving as a travelling speaker and representative of the League of Prayer in Britain, Oswald met Gertrude Hobbs. Their friendship blossomed during a voyage to the United States in the summer of 1908, and two years later they were married. Oswald called her "Beloved Disciple," shortened to the initials B.D., and spoken as "Biddy." For the rest of her life, she was known by this affectionate nickname.

A longtime dream of Oswald's became reality in January 1911 with the opening of the Bible Training College (BTC) near Clapham Common in London. Sponsored by the League of Prayer, it housed twenty-five residential students and reached hundreds more through evening classes and Bible correspondence courses. Oswald served as Principal and main teacher while Biddy filled the role of Lady Superintendent, overseeing a myriad of logistical details, from the preparation of meals to temporary housing for missionary families in transit through London.

During Oswald's lectures Biddy sat in the back of the room recording his words verbatim in her precise Pitman's shorthand. Trained as a court stenographer, she could take dictation rapidly while remaining engaged with her husband's purpose as he taught. Biddy's storehouse of notes grew as Oswald taught Biblical Psychology, Studies in Genesis, Biblical Ethics, and a host of other classes. Of special significance were her records of the sermon class and the weekly devotional hour when Oswald spoke to the residential students from his heart.

Their only child, Kathleen, was born in May 1913, and promptly began her reign as queen of the BTC. Oswald found himself completely charmed by this new arrival. He had always loved children, but the feelings produced by his own daughter were something entirely new. When she cried at the top of her lungs during a meal at the college, Oswald would say, "And now my daughter will sing." But the happy days of a settled life in London were soon to end.

The outbreak of World War I in August 1914 changed Britain dramatically and led to the closing of the BTC within a year. Oswald volunteered as a YMCA secretary in Egypt, where Biddy, Kathleen, and several former students from the BTC joined him to assist in the work. At Zeitoun Camp, near Cairo, Oswald quickly established himself as a friend of the troops and a man of uncommon spiritual insight. One soldier described him as "the personification of the Sherlock Holmes of fiction—tall, erect, virile, with clean-cut face, framing a pair of piercing bright eyes . . . a detective of the soul."

Biddy continued to fill shorthand notebooks with Oswald's talks to the troops, including "The Shadow of an Agony," "Shade of His Hand" (Studies in Ecclesiastes), and "Baffled to Fight Better" (Studies in Job). Against the formidable foes of heat, insects, and blowing sand, she continued a ministry of hospitality that produced the special touches of home for the troops so far from their families.

In a letter to Biddy's mother, Oswald freely praised his wife: "As for Biddy I love her and I am her husband but I do not believe it is possible to exaggerate what she has been in the way of a Sacrament out here—God conveying His presence through the common elements of an ordinary life. The letters she has received from mothers and wives and sisters and fathers and brothers are in themselves a deep testimony to a most unconscious ministry of wife and mother and woman."

In the desert camp Oswald supervised the construction of rock-lined walkways and a myriad of flower beds. Some critics said it was a waste of time, but Chambers believed that if physical improvements were not made and new touches occasionally given to the huts, they would reflect slovenly care, unpleasing to God. "A grave defect in much work of today," he said, "is that men do not follow Solomon's admonition, 'Whatsoever thy hand findeth to do, do it with thy might.' The tendency is to argue, 'It's only for so short a time, why trouble?' If it is only for five minutes, let it be well done."

In late October 1917 Oswald underwent an emergency appendectomy and appeared to be recovering. But two weeks later, while still in Gizeh Red Cross Hospital, he suffered a relapse and died early in the morning on November 15. All those who knew and loved him were stunned.

Dazed with disbelief and sorrow, Biddy began dealing with the numbing tasks facing a young widow with a four-year-old daughter. Her telegram to family and friends in Britain said simply, "Oswald in His Presence." The next afternoon, Chambers was buried with full military honors in the British Military Cemetery in Old Cairo.

For the next two years, Biddy and Kathleen continued to work among the troops at Zeitoun. In the ways of God's providence, which Oswald frequently referred to as "the haphazard," Biddy's personal sending of one of his sermons as a Christmas gift to the troops in Egypt mushroomed into a monthly printing and mailing of 10,000 copies by the YMCA. Gradually it became clear to Biddy that her calling in life was to give her husband's words to the world. In so doing, she continued the dream she and Oswald had shared of working together to help others.

Upon her return to England in 1919, Biddy continued transcribing her shorthand notes and preparing them for publication. She worked to support herself and Kathleen, using any money from sales to help finance the next book.

While maintaining a boarding house for students in Oxford, Biddy compiled a book of daily readings which she titled *My Utmost for His Highest*. Since it was first published in 1927, *My Utmost* has been continuously in print and has sold millions of copies. It exists today in more than forty different languages, and every day, multiplied thousands of people around the world open its pages seeking a word from the Lord through His servant Oswald Chambers.

From the earliest days of publication after World War I, Mrs. Chambers was advised and assisted by a small group of personal friends. In later years, this group became known as the Oswald Chambers Publications Association. It was incorporated in 1942, and exists today as a Registered British Charity overseeing the publication and distribution of Oswald Chambers's material around the world. Royalties are used to help fund new translations of Chambers's books in developing nations and to provide gift copies of the OC books to students and pastors.

My Utmost for His Highest, along with all the other OC books, sprang from the shared life and vision of two remarkable people—Oswald and Biddy Chambers. The books are the result of their love for God, for each other, and for people everywhere. Together Oswald and Biddy touched individuals from varied backgrounds and many nations through hospitality, biblical teaching, encouragement, and joyful good humor. The pages of *My Utmost* are infused with their belief that taking the gospel to the whole earth involves following God's example of "keeping open house for the universe."

Kathleen described her mother as always having time for people. A knock at the door would take her from the typewriter to the teakettle. She considered it just as important to chat with a child from the neighborhood as it was to prepare the next book for publication. Biddy personally answered the hundreds of letters that came to her, and often included a complimentary copy of one of Oswald's books with her reply.

By the time Biddy Chambers died in 1966, she had compiled and published some fifty books that bore the name of Oswald Chambers but never mentioned her own. Occasional words of greeting at the beginning of a volume, followed by her initials "B.C.," were the only evidence of her role.

In the weeks just after Oswald's death in Egypt, Biddy wrote to her mother of a friend whose life had been radically changed by reading some of Oswald's sermons. "It confirms me so much in the assurance I have that I am to go on getting everything I can printed," Biddy said. "It will be like casting bread upon the waters and we'll know someday all it has meant in people's lives." To her sister, she wrote: "Living with Oswald and seeing his faith in God and knowing that 'by his faithfulness he is speaking to us still' is the secret of life these days, and I feel as if it will be overwhelming to one day see what God has wrought, and one will only be sorry not to have trusted more utterly. So just go on praying and believing and we will surely find that God is doing His wondrous things all the time."

By their faithfulness in the ordinary circumstances of each unfolding day, Oswald and Biddy Chambers have demonstrated the significance and power of giving our utmost for God's highest.

David McCasland

My Utmost for His Highest

Let Us Keep to the Point

". . . my earnest expectation and hope that in nothing I shall be ashamed, but with all boldness, as always, so now also Christ will be magnified in my body, whether by life or by death." **Philippians 1:20**

My Utmost for His Highest. ". . . my earnest expectation and hope that in nothing I shall be ashamed." We will all feel very much ashamed if we do not yield to Jesus the areas of our lives He has asked us to yield to Him. It's as if Paul were saying, "My determined purpose is to be my utmost for His highest—my best for His glory." To reach that level of determination is a matter of the will, not of debate or of reasoning. It is absolute and irrevocable surrender of the will at that point. An undue amount of thought and consideration for ourselves is what keeps us from making that decision, although we cover it up with the pretense that it is others we are considering. When we think seriously about what it will cost others if we obey the call of Jesus, we tell God He doesn't know what our obedience will mean. Keep to the point—He does know. Shut out every other thought and keep yourself before God in this one thing only—my utmost for His highest. I am determined to be absolutely and entirely for Him and Him alone.

My Unstoppable Determination for His Holiness. "Whether it means life or death—it makes no difference!" (see 1:21). Paul was determined that nothing would stop him from doing exactly what God wanted. But before we choose to follow God's will, a crisis must develop in our lives. This happens because we tend to be unresponsive to God's gentler nudges. He brings us to the place where He asks us to be our utmost for Him and we begin to debate. He then providentially produces a crisis where we have to decide—for or against. That moment becomes a great crossroads in our lives. If a crisis has come to you on any front, surrender your will to Jesus absolutely and irrevocably.

Will You Go Out Without Knowing?

"He went out, not knowing where he was going."
Hebrews 11:8

Have you ever "gone out" in this way? If so, there is no logical answer possible when anyone asks you what you are doing. One of the most difficult questions to answer in Christian work is, "What do you expect to do?" You don't know what you are going to do. The only thing you know is that God knows what He is doing. Continually examine your attitude toward God to see if you are willing to "go out" in every area of your life, trusting in God entirely. It is this attitude that keeps you in constant wonder, because you don't know what God is going to do next. Each morning as you wake, there is a new opportunity to "go out," building your confidence in God. "Do not worry about your life . . . nor about the body" (Luke 12:22). In other words, don't worry about the things that concerned you before you did "go out."

Have you been asking God what He is going to do? He will never tell you. God does not tell you what He is going to do—He reveals to you who He is. Do you believe in a miracle-working God, and will you "go out" in complete surrender to Him until you are not surprised one iota by anything He does?

Believe God is always the God you know Him to be when you are nearest to Him. Then think how unnecessary and disrespectful worry is! Let the attitude of your life be a continual willingness to "go out" in dependence upon God, and your life will have a sacred and inexpressible charm about it that is very satisfying to Jesus. You must learn to "go out" through your convictions, creeds, or experiences until you come to the point in your faith where there is nothing between yourself and God.

"Clouds and Darkness"

"Clouds and darkness surround Him . . ." **Psalm 97:2**

A person who has not been born again by the Spirit of God will tell you that the teachings of Jesus are simple. But when he is baptized by the Holy Spirit, he finds that "clouds and darkness surround Him." When we come into close contact with the teachings of Jesus Christ we have our first realization of this. The only possible way to have full understanding of the teachings of Jesus is through the light of the Spirit of God shining inside us. If we have never had the experience of taking our casual, religious shoes off our casual, religious feet—getting rid of all the excessive informality with which we approach God—it is questionable whether we have ever stood in His presence. The people who are flippant and disrespectful in their approach to God are those who have never been introduced to Jesus Christ. Only after the amazing delight and liberty of realizing what Jesus Christ *does*, comes the impenetrable "darkness" of realizing who He *is*.

Jesus said, "The words that I speak to you are spirit, and they are life" (John 6:63). Once, the Bible was just so many words to us—"clouds and darkness"—then, suddenly, the words become spirit and life because Jesus re-speaks them to us when our circumstances make the words new. That is the way God speaks to us; not by visions and dreams, but by words. When a man gets to God, it is by the most simple way—words.

"Why Can I Not Follow You Now?"

"Peter said to Him, 'Lord, why can I not follow You now?'" **John 13:37**

There are times when you can't understand why you cannot do what you want to do. When God brings a time of waiting, and appears to be unresponsive, don't fill it with busyness, just wait. The time of waiting may come to teach you the meaning of sanctification—to be set apart from sin and made holy—or it may come after the process of sanctification has begun to teach you what service means. Never run before God gives you His direction. If you have the slightest doubt, then He is not guiding. Whenever there is doubt—wait.

At first you may see clearly what God's will is—the severance of a friendship, the breaking off of a business relationship, or something else you feel is distinctly God's will for you to do. But never act on the impulse of that feeling. If you do, you will cause difficult situations to arise which will take years to untangle. Wait for God's timing and He will do it without any heartache or disappointment. When it is a question of the providential will of God, wait for God to move.

Peter did not wait for God. He predicted in his own mind where the test would come, and it came where he did not expect it. "I will lay down my life for Your sake." Peter's statement was honest but ignorant. "Jesus answered him, '. . . the rooster shall not crow till you have denied Me three times'" (John 13:38). This was said with a deeper knowledge of Peter than Peter had of himself. He could not follow Jesus because he did not know himself or his own capabilities well enough. Natural devotion may be enough to attract us to Jesus, to make us feel His irresistible charm, but it will never make us disciples. Natural devotion will deny Jesus, always falling short of what it means to truly follow Him.

The Life of Power to Follow

"Jesus answered him, 'Where I am going you cannot follow Me now, but you shall follow Me afterward.'" **John 13:36**

"And when He had spoken this, He said to him, 'Follow Me'" (John 21:19). Three years earlier Jesus had said, "Follow Me" (Matthew 4:19), and Peter followed with no hesitation. The irresistible attraction of Jesus was upon him and he did not need the Holy Spirit to help him do it. Later he came to the place where he denied Jesus, and his heart broke. Then he received the Holy Spirit and Jesus said again, "Follow Me" (John 21:19). Now no one is in front of Peter except the Lord Jesus Christ. The first "Follow Me" was nothing mysterious; it was an external following. Jesus is now asking for an internal sacrifice and yielding (see 21:18).

Between these two times Peter denied Jesus with oaths and curses (see Matthew 26:69–75). But then he came completely to the end of himself and all of his self-sufficiency. There was no part of himself he would ever rely on again. In his state of destitution, he was finally ready to receive all that the risen Lord had for him. "He breathed on them, and said to them, 'Receive the Holy Spirit'" (John 20:22). No matter what changes God has performed in you, never rely on them. Build only on a Person, the Lord Jesus Christ, and on the Spirit He gives.

All our promises and resolutions end in denial because we have no power to accomplish them. When we come to the end of ourselves, not just mentally but completely, we are able to "receive the Holy Spirit." *"Receive the Holy Spirit"*—the idea is that of invasion. There is now only One who directs the course of your life, the Lord Jesus Christ.

Worship

"He moved from there to the mountain east of Bethel, and he pitched his tent with Bethel on the west and Ai on the east; there he built an altar to the LORD and called on the name of the LORD." **Genesis 12:8**

Worship is giving God the best that He has given you. Be careful what you do with the best you have. Whenever you get a blessing from God, give it back to Him as a love-gift. Take time to meditate before God and offer the blessing back to Him in a deliberate act of worship. If you hoard it for yourself, it will turn into spiritual dry rot, as the manna did when it was hoarded (see Exodus 16:20). God will never allow you to keep a spiritual blessing completely for yourself. It must be given back to Him so that He can make it a blessing to others.

Bethel is the symbol of fellowship with God; Ai is the symbol of the world. Abram "pitched his tent" between the two. The lasting value of our public service for God is measured by the depth of the intimacy of our private times of fellowship and oneness with Him. Rushing in and out of worship is wrong every time—there is always plenty of time to worship God. Days set apart for quiet can be a trap, detracting from the need to have daily quiet time with God. That is why we must "pitch our tents" where we will always have quiet times with Him, however noisy our times with the world may be. There are not three levels of spiritual life—worship, waiting, and work. Yet some of us seem to jump like spiritual frogs from worship to waiting, and from waiting to work. God's idea is that the three should go together as one. They were always together in the life of our Lord and in perfect harmony. It is a discipline that must be developed; it will not happen overnight.

JANUARY 7

Intimate with Jesus

"Jesus said to him, 'Have I been with you so long, and yet you have not known Me, Philip?'" **John 14:9**

These words were not spoken as a rebuke, nor even with surprise; Jesus was encouraging Philip to draw closer. Yet the last person we get intimate with is Jesus. Before Pentecost the disciples knew Jesus as the One who gave them power to conquer demons and to bring about a revival (see Luke 10:18–20). It was a wonderful intimacy, but there was a much closer intimacy to come: "I have called you friends" (John 15:15). True friendship is rare on earth. It means identifying with someone in thought, heart, and spirit. The whole experience of life is designed to enable us to enter into this closest relationship with Jesus Christ. We receive His blessings and know His Word, but do we really know Him?

Jesus said, "It is to your advantage that I go away" (John 16:7). He left that relationship to lead them even closer. It is a joy to Jesus when a disciple takes time to walk more intimately with Him. The bearing of fruit is always shown in Scripture to be the visible result of an intimate relationship with Jesus Christ (see John 15:1–4).

Once we get intimate with Jesus we are never lonely and we never lack for understanding or compassion. We can continually pour out our hearts to Him without being perceived as overly emotional or pitiful. The Christian who is truly intimate with Jesus will never draw attention to himself but will only show the evidence of a life where Jesus is completely in control. This is the outcome of allowing Jesus to satisfy every area of life to its depth. The picture resulting from such a life is that of the strong, calm balance that our Lord gives to those who are intimate with Him.

Is My Sacrifice Living?

"Abraham built an altar . . . ; and he bound Isaac his son and laid him on the altar." **Genesis 22:9**

This event is a picture of the mistake we make in thinking that the ultimate God wants of us is the sacrifice of death. What God wants is the sacrifice *through* death which enables us to do what Jesus did, that is, sacrifice our lives. Not—"Lord, I am ready to go with You . . . to death" (Luke 22:33). But—"I am willing to be identified with Your death so that I may sacrifice my life to God."

We seem to think that God wants us to give up things! God purified Abraham from this error, and the same process is at work in our lives. God never tells us to give up things just for the sake of giving them up, but He tells us to give them up for the sake of the only thing worth having, namely, life with Himself. It is a matter of loosening the bands that hold back our lives. Those bands are loosened immediately by identification with the death of Jesus. Then we enter into a relationship with God whereby we may sacrifice our lives to Him.

It is of no value to God to give Him your life for death. He wants you to be a "*living* sacrifice"—to let Him have all your strengths that have been saved and sanctified through Jesus (Romans 12:1). This is what is acceptable to God.

JANUARY 9

Prayerful Inner-Searching

"May your whole spirit, soul, and body be preserved blameless." **1 Thessalonians 5:23**

"Your whole spirit . . ." The great, mysterious work of the Holy Spirit is in the deep recesses of our being which we cannot reach. Read Psalm 139. The psalmist implies—"O Lord, You are the God of the early mornings, the God of the late nights, the God of the mountain peaks, and the God of the sea. But, my God, my soul has horizons further away than those of early mornings, deeper darkness than the nights of earth, higher peaks than any mountain peaks, greater depths than any sea in nature. You who are the God of all these, be my God. I cannot reach to the heights or to the depths; there are motives I cannot discover, dreams I cannot realize. My God, search me."

Do we believe that God can fortify and protect our thought processes far beyond where we can go? *"The blood of Jesus Christ His Son cleanses us from all sin"* (1 John 1:7). If this verse means cleansing only on our conscious level, may God have mercy on us. The man who has been dulled by sin will say that he is not even conscious of it. But the cleansing from sin we experience will reach to the heights and depths of our spirit if we will "walk in the light as He is in the light" (1:7). The same Spirit that fed the life of Jesus Christ will feed the life of our spirit. It is only when we are protected by God with the miraculous sacredness of the Holy Spirit that our spirit, soul, and body can be preserved in pure uprightness until the coming of Jesus—no longer condemned in God's sight.

We should more frequently allow our minds to meditate on these great, massive truths of God.

JANUARY 10

The Opened Sight

"I now send you, to open their eyes . . . that they may receive forgiveness of sins." **Acts 26:17–18**

This verse is the greatest example of the true essence of the message of a disciple of Jesus Christ in all of the New Testament.

God's first sovereign work of grace is summed up in the words "that they may receive forgiveness of sins." When a person fails in his personal Christian life, it is usually because he has never *received* anything. The only sign that a person is saved is that he has received something from Jesus Christ. Our job as workers for God is to open people's eyes so that they may turn themselves from darkness to light. But that is not salvation; it is conversion—only the effort of an awakened human being. I do not think it is too broad a statement to say that the majority of so-called Christians are like this. Their eyes are open, but they have received nothing. Conversion is not regeneration. This is a neglected fact in our preaching today. When a person is born again, he knows that it is because he has received something as a gift from Almighty God and not because of his own decision. People may make vows and promises, and may be determined to follow through, but none of this is salvation. Salvation means that we are brought to the place where we are able to receive something from God on the authority of Jesus Christ, namely, forgiveness of sins.

This is followed by God's second mighty work of grace: "an inheritance among those who are sanctified." In sanctification, the one who has been born again deliberately gives up his right to himself to Jesus Christ, and identifies himself entirely with God's ministry to others.

What My Obedience to God Costs Other People

"As they led Him away, they laid hold of a certain man, Simon . . . , and on him they laid the cross that he might bear it after Jesus." **Luke 23:26**

If we obey God, it is going to cost other people more than it costs us, and that is where the pain begins. If we are in love with our Lord, obedience does not cost us anything—it is a delight. But to those who do not love Him, our obedience does cost a great deal. If we obey God, it will mean that other people's plans are upset. They will ridicule us as if to say, "You call this Christianity?" We could prevent the suffering, but not if we are obedient to God. We must let the cost be paid.

When our obedience begins to cost others, our human pride entrenches itself and we say, "I will never accept anything from anyone." But we must, or disobey God. We have no right to think that the type of relationships we have with others should be any different from those the Lord Himself had (see Luke 8:1–3).

A lack of progress in our spiritual life results when we try to bear all the costs ourselves. And actually, we cannot. Because we are so involved in the universal purposes of God, others are immediately affected by our obedience to Him. Will we remain faithful in our obedience to God and be willing to suffer the humiliation of refusing to be independent? Or will we do just the opposite and say, "I will not cause other people to suffer"? We can disobey God if we choose, and it will bring immediate relief to the situation, but it will grieve our Lord. If, however, we obey God, He will care for those who have suffered the consequences of our obedience. We must simply obey and leave all the consequences with Him.

Beware of the inclination to dictate to God what consequences you would allow as a condition of your obedience to Him.

Have You Ever Been Alone with God?

"When they were alone, He explained all things to His disciples." **Mark 4:34**

Our Solitude with Him. Jesus doesn't take us aside and explain things to us all the time; He explains things to us as we are able to understand them. The lives of others are examples for us, but God requires us to examine our own souls. It is slow work—so slow that it takes God all of time and eternity to make a man or woman conform to His purpose. We can only be used by God after we allow Him to show us the deep, hidden areas of our own character. It is astounding how ignorant we are about ourselves! We don't even recognize the envy, laziness, or pride within us when we see it. But Jesus will reveal to us everything we have held within ourselves before His grace began to work. How many of us have learned to look inwardly with courage?

We have to get rid of the idea that we understand ourselves. That is always the last bit of pride to go. The only One who understands us is God. The greatest curse in our spiritual life is pride. If we have ever had a glimpse of what we are like in the sight of God, we will never say, "Oh, I'm so unworthy." We will understand that this goes without saying. But as long as there is any doubt that we are unworthy, God will continue to close us in until He gets us alone. Whenever there is any element of pride or conceit remaining, Jesus can't teach us anything. He will allow us to experience heartbreak or the disappointment we feel when our intellectual pride is wounded. He will reveal numerous misplaced affections or desires—things over which we never thought He would have to get us alone. Many things are shown to us, often without effect. But when God gets us alone over them, they will be clear.

JANUARY 13

Have You Ever Been Alone with God?

"When He was alone . . . the twelve asked Him about the parable." **Mark 4:10**

His Solitude with Us. When God gets us alone through suffering, heartbreak, temptation, disappointment, sickness, or by thwarted desires, a broken friendship, or a new friendship—when He gets us absolutely alone, and we are totally speechless, unable to ask even one question, then He begins to teach us. Notice Jesus Christ's training of the Twelve. It was the disciples, not the crowd outside, who were confused. His disciples constantly asked Him questions, and He constantly explained things to them, but they didn't understand until after they received the Holy Spirit (see John 14:26).

As you journey with God, the only thing He intends to be clear is the way He deals with your soul. The sorrows and difficulties in the lives of others will be absolutely confusing to you. We think we understand another person's struggle until God reveals the same shortcomings in our lives. There are vast areas of stubbornness and ignorance the Holy Spirit has to reveal in each of us, but it can only be done when Jesus gets us alone. Are we alone with Him now? Or are we more concerned with our own ideas, friendships, and cares for our bodies? Jesus cannot teach us anything until we quiet all our intellectual questions and get alone with Him.

Called by God

"I heard the voice of the Lord, saying: 'Whom shall I send, and who will go for Us?' Then I said, 'Here am I! Send me.'" **Isaiah 6:8**

God did not direct His call to Isaiah—Isaiah overheard God saying, "Who will go for Us?" The call of God is not just for a select few but for everyone. Whether I hear God's call or not depends on the condition of my ears, and exactly what I hear depends upon my spiritual attitude. "Many are called, but few are chosen" (Matthew 22:14). That is, few prove that they are the chosen ones. The chosen ones are those who have come into a relationship with God through Jesus Christ and have had their spiritual condition changed and their ears opened. Then they hear "the voice of the Lord" continually asking, "Who will go for Us?" However, God doesn't single out someone and say, "Now, *you* go." He did not force His will on Isaiah. Isaiah was in the presence of God, and he overheard the call. His response, performed in complete freedom, could only be to say, "Here am I! Send me."

Remove the thought from your mind of expecting God to come to force you or to plead with you. When our Lord called His disciples, He did it without irresistible pressure from the outside. The quiet, yet passionate, insistence of His "Follow Me" was spoken to men whose every sense was receptive (Matthew 4:19). If we will allow the Holy Spirit to bring us face-to-face with God, we too will hear what Isaiah heard—"the voice of the Lord." In perfect freedom we too will say, "Here am I! Send me."

Do You Walk in White?

"We were buried with Him . . . that just as Christ was raised from the dead . . . even so we also should walk in newness of life." **Romans 6:4**

No one experiences complete sanctification without going through a "white funeral"—the burial of the old life. If there has never been this crucial moment of change through death, sanctification will never be more than an elusive dream. There must be a "white funeral," a death with only one resurrection—a resurrection into the life of Jesus Christ. Nothing can defeat a life like this. It has oneness with God for only one purpose—to be a witness for Him.

Have you really come to your last days? You have often come to them in your mind, but have you *really* experienced them? You cannot die or go to your funeral in a mood of excitement. Death means you stop being. You must agree with God and stop being the intensely striving kind of Christian you have been. We avoid the cemetery and continually refuse our own death. It will not happen by striving, but by yielding to death. It is dying—being "baptized into His death" (Romans 6:3).

Have you had your "white funeral," or are you piously deceiving your own soul? Has there been a point in your life which you now mark as your last day? Is there a place in your life to which you go back in memory with humility and overwhelming gratitude, so that you can honestly proclaim, "Yes, it was then, at my 'white funeral,' that I made an agreement with God."

"This is the will of God, your sanctification" (1 Thessalonians 4:3). Once you truly realize this is God's will, you will enter into the process of sanctification as a natural response. Are you willing to experience that "white funeral" now? Will you agree with Him that this is your last day on earth? The moment of agreement depends on you.

JANUARY 16

The Voice of the Nature of God

"I heard the voice of the Lord, saying: 'Whom shall I send, and who will go for Us?'" **Isaiah 6:8**

When we talk about the call of God, we often forget the most important thing, namely, the nature of Him who calls. There are many things calling each of us today. Some of these calls will be answered, and others will not even be heard. The call is the expression of the nature of the One who calls, and we can only recognize the call if that same nature is in us. The call of God is the expression of God's nature, not ours. God providentially weaves the threads of His call through our lives, and only we can distinguish them. It is the threading of God's voice directly to us over a certain concern, and it is useless to seek another person's opinion of it. Our dealings over the call of God should be kept exclusively between ourselves and Him.

The call of God is not a reflection of my nature; my personal desires and temperament are of no consideration. As long as I dwell on my own qualities and traits and think about what I am suited for, I will never hear the call of God. But when God brings me into the right relationship with Himself, I will be in the same condition Isaiah was. Isaiah was so attuned to God, because of the great crisis he had just endured, that the call of God penetrated his soul. The majority of us cannot hear anything but ourselves. And we cannot hear anything God says. But to be brought to the place where we can hear the call of God is to be profoundly changed.

JANUARY 17

The Call of the Natural Life

"When it pleased God . . . to reveal His Son in me." **Galatians 1:15–16**

The call of God is not a call to serve Him in any particular way. My contact with the nature of God will shape my understanding of His call and will help me realize what I truly desire to do for Him. The call of God is an expression of His nature; the service which results in my life is suited to me and is an expression of my nature. The call of the natural life was stated by the apostle Paul—"When it pleased God . . . to reveal His Son in me, that I might *preach* Him [that is, *purely and solemnly express* Him] among the Gentiles."

Service is the overflow which pours from a life filled with love and devotion. But strictly speaking, there is no *call* to that. Service is what I bring to the relationship and is the reflection of my identification with the nature of God. Service becomes a natural part of my life. God brings me into the proper relationship with Himself so that I can understand His call, and then I serve Him on my own out of a motivation of absolute love. Service to God is the deliberate love-gift of a nature that has heard the call of God. Service is an expression of my nature, and God's call is an expression of His nature. Therefore, when I receive His nature and hear His call, His divine voice resounds throughout His nature and mine and the two become one in service. The Son of God reveals Himself in me, and out of devotion to Him service becomes my everyday way of life.

"It Is the Lord!"

"Thomas answered and said to Him, 'My Lord and my God!'" **John 20:28**

"Jesus said to her, 'Give Me a drink'" (John 4:7). How many of us are expecting Jesus Christ to quench our thirst when we should be satisfying Him! We should be pouring out our lives, investing our total beings, not drawing on Him to satisfy us. "You shall be witnesses to Me" (Acts 1:8). That means lives of pure, uncompromising, and unrestrained devotion to the Lord Jesus, which will be satisfying to Him wherever He may send us.

Beware of anything that competes with your loyalty to Jesus Christ. The greatest competitor of true devotion to Jesus is the service we do for Him. It is easier to serve than to pour out our lives completely for Him. The goal of the call of God is His satisfaction, not simply that we should do something *for* Him. We are not sent to do battle for God, but to be used by God in His battles. Are we more devoted to service than we are to Jesus Christ Himself?

Vision and Darkness

"When the sun was going down, a deep sleep fell upon Abram; and behold, horror and great darkness fell upon him." **Genesis 15:12**

Whenever God gives a vision to a Christian, it is as if He puts him in "the shadow of His hand" (Isaiah 49:2). The saint's duty is to be still and listen. There is a "darkness" that comes from too much light—that is the time to listen. The story of Abram and Hagar in Genesis 16 is an excellent example of listening to so-called good advice during a time of darkness, rather than waiting for God to send the light. When God gives you a vision and darkness follows, wait. God will bring the vision He has given you to reality in your life if you will wait on His timing. Never try to help God fulfill His word. Abram went through thirteen years of silence, but in those years all of his self-sufficiency was destroyed. He grew past the point of relying on his own common sense. Those years of silence were a time of discipline, not a period of God's displeasure. There is never any need to pretend that your life is filled with joy and confidence; just wait upon God and be grounded in Him (see Isaiah 50:10–11).

Do I trust at all in the flesh? Or have I learned to go beyond all confidence in myself and other people of God? Do I trust in books and prayers or other joys in my life? Or have I placed my confidence in God *Himself*, not in His blessings? "I am Almighty God"—El-Shaddai, the All-Powerful God (Genesis 17:1). The reason we are all being disciplined is that we will know God is real. As soon as God becomes real to us, people pale by comparison, becoming shadows of reality. Nothing that other saints do or say can ever upset the one who is built on God.

Are You Fresh for Everything?

"Jesus answered and said to him, 'Most assuredly, I say to you, unless one is born again, he cannot see the kingdom of God.'" **John 3:3**

Sometimes we are fresh and eager to attend a prayer meeting, but do we feel that same freshness for such mundane tasks as polishing shoes?

Being born again by the Spirit is an unmistakable work of God, as mysterious as the wind, and as surprising as God Himself. We don't know where it begins—it is hidden away in the depths of our soul. Being born again from above is an enduring, perpetual, and eternal beginning. It provides a freshness all the time in thinking, talking, and living—a continual surprise of the life of God. Staleness is an indication that something in our lives is out of step with God. We say to ourselves, "I have to do this thing or it will never get done." That is the first sign of staleness. Do we feel fresh this very moment or are we stale, frantically searching our minds for something to do? Freshness is not the result of obedience; it comes from the Holy Spirit. Obedience keeps us "in the light as He is in the light" (1 John 1:7).

Jealously guard your relationship with God. Jesus prayed "that they may be one just as We are one"—with nothing in between (John 17:22). Keep your whole life continually open to Jesus Christ. Don't pretend to be open with Him. Are you drawing your life from any source other than God Himself? If you are depending on something else as your source of freshness and strength, you will not realize when His power is gone.

Being born of the Spirit means much more than we usually think. It gives us new vision and keeps us absolutely fresh for everything through the never-ending supply of the life of God.

Recall What God Remembers

"Thus says the Lord: 'I remember . . . the kindness of your youth.'" **Jeremiah 2:2**

Am I as spontaneously kind to God as I used to be, or am I only expecting God to be kind to me? Does everything in my life fill His heart with gladness, or do I constantly complain because things don't seem to be going my way? A person who has forgotten what God treasures will not be filled with joy. It is wonderful to remember that Jesus Christ has needs which we can meet—"Give Me a drink" (John 4:7). How much kindness have I shown Him in the past week? Has my life been a good reflection on His reputation?

God is saying to His people, "You are not in love with Me now, but I remember a time when you were." He says, "I remember . . . the love of your betrothal" (Jeremiah 2:2). Am I as filled to overflowing with love for Jesus Christ as I was in the beginning, when I went out of my way to prove my devotion to Him? Does He ever find me pondering the time when I cared only for Him? Is that where I am now, or have I chosen man's wisdom over true love for Him? Am I so in love with Him that I take no thought for where He might lead me? Or am I watching to see how much respect I get as I measure how much service I should give Him?

As I recall what God remembers about me, I may also begin to realize that He is not what He used to be to me. When this happens, I should allow the shame and humiliation it creates in my life, because it will bring godly sorrow, and "godly sorrow produces repentance" (2 Corinthians 7:10).

Am I Looking to God?

"Look to Me, and be saved." **Isaiah 45:22**

Do we expect God to come to us with His blessings and save us? He says, "*Look to Me*, and *be* saved." The greatest difficulty spiritually is to concentrate on God, and His blessings are what make it so difficult. Troubles almost always make us look to God, but His blessings tend to divert our attention elsewhere. The basic lesson of the Sermon on the Mount is to narrow all your interests until your mind, heart, and body are focused on Jesus Christ. "Look to Me . . ."

Many of us have a mental picture of what a Christian should be, and looking at this image in other Christians' lives becomes a hindrance to our focusing on God. This is not salvation—it is not simple enough. He says, in effect, "Look to Me and you are saved," not "You will be saved someday." We will find what we are looking for if we will concentrate on Him. We get distracted from God and irritable with Him while He continues to say to us, "Look to Me, and be saved." Our difficulties, our trials, and our worries about tomorrow all vanish when we look to God.

Wake yourself up and look to God. Build your hope on Him. No matter how many things seem to be pressing in on you, be determined to push them aside and look to Him. "Look to Me . . ." Salvation is yours the moment you look.

Transformed by Beholding

"We all, with unveiled face, beholding as in a mirror the glory of the Lord, are being transformed into the same image." **2 Corinthians 3:18**

The greatest characteristic a Christian can exhibit is this completely unveiled openness before God, which allows that person's life to become a mirror for others. When the Spirit fills us, we are transformed, and by beholding God we become mirrors. You can always tell when someone has been beholding the glory of the Lord, because your inner spirit senses that he mirrors the Lord's own character. Beware of anything that would spot or tarnish that mirror in you. It is almost always something good that will stain it—something good, but not what is best.

The most important rule for us is to concentrate on keeping our lives open to God. Let everything else including work, clothes, and food be set aside. The busyness of things obscures our concentration on God. We must maintain a position of beholding Him, keeping our lives completely spiritual through and through. Let other things come and go as they will; let other people criticize us as they will; but never allow anything to obscure the life that "is hidden with Christ in God" (Colossians 3:3). Never let a hurried lifestyle disturb the relationship of abiding in Him. This is an easy thing to allow, but we must guard against it. The most difficult lesson of the Christian life is learning how to continue "beholding as in a mirror the glory of the Lord."

God's Overpowering Purpose

"I have appeared to you for this purpose." **Acts 26:16**

The vision Paul had on the road to Damascus was not a passing emotional experience, but a vision that had very clear and emphatic directions for him. And Paul stated, "I was not disobedient to the heavenly vision" (Acts 26:19). Our Lord said to Paul, in effect, "Your whole life is to be overpowered or subdued by Me; you are to have no end, no aim, and no purpose but Mine." And the Lord also says to us, "You did not choose Me, but *I chose you* and appointed you that you should go" (John 15:16).

When we are born again, if we are spiritual at all, we have visions of what Jesus wants us to be. It is important that I learn not to be "disobedient to the heavenly vision"—not to doubt that it can be attained. It is not enough to give mental assent to the fact that God has redeemed the world, nor even to know that the Holy Spirit can make all that Jesus did a reality in my life. I must have the foundation of a personal relationship with Him. Paul was not given a message or a doctrine to proclaim. He was brought into a vivid, personal, overpowering relationship with Jesus Christ. Acts 26:16 is tremendously compelling "to make you a minister and a witness." There would be nothing there without a personal relationship. Paul was devoted to a Person, not to a cause. He was absolutely Jesus Christ's. He saw nothing else and he lived for nothing else. "For I determined not to know anything among you except Jesus Christ and Him crucified" (1 Corinthians 2:2).

Leave Room for God

"When it pleased God . . ." **Galatians 1:15**

As servants of God, we must learn to make room for Him—to give God "elbow room." We plan and figure and predict that this or that will happen, but we forget to make room for God to come in as He chooses. Would we be surprised if God came into our meeting or into our preaching in a way we had never expected Him to come? Do not look for God to come in a particular way, but *do look for Him*. The way to make room for Him is to expect Him to come, but not in a certain way. No matter how well we may know God, the great lesson to learn is that He may break in at any minute. We tend to overlook this element of surprise, yet God never works in any other way. Suddenly—God meets our life—"when it pleased God . . ."

Keep your life so constantly in touch with God that His surprising power can break through at any point. Live in a constant state of expectancy, and leave room for God to come in as He decides.

Look Again and Consecrate

"If God so clothes the grass of the field . . . , will He not much more clothe you . . . ?" **Matthew 6:30**

A simple statement of Jesus is always a puzzle to us because we will not be simple. How can we maintain the simplicity of Jesus so that we may understand Him? By receiving His Spirit, recognizing and relying on Him, and obeying Him as He brings us the truth of His Word, life will become amazingly simple. Jesus asks us to consider that "if God so clothes the grass of the field . . ." how "much more" will He clothe you, if you keep your relationship right with Him? Every time we lose ground in our fellowship with God, it is because we have disrespectfully thought that we knew better than Jesus Christ. We have allowed "the cares of this world" to enter in (Matthew 13:22), while forgetting the "much more" of our heavenly Father.

"Look at the birds of the air" (6:26). Their function is to obey the instincts God placed within them, and God watches over them. Jesus said that if you have the right relationship with Him and will obey His Spirit within you, then God will care for your "feathers" too.

"Consider the lilies of the field" (6:28). They grow where they are planted. Many of us refuse to grow where God plants us. Therefore, we don't take root anywhere. Jesus said if we would obey the life of God within us, He would look after all other things. Did Jesus Christ lie to us? Are we experiencing the "much more" He promised? If we are not, it is because we are not obeying the life God has given us and have cluttered our minds with confusing thoughts and worries. How much time have we wasted asking God senseless questions while we should be absolutely free to concentrate on our service to Him? Consecration is the act of continually separating myself from everything except that which God has appointed me to do. It is not a onetime experience but an ongoing process. Am I continually separating myself and looking to God every day of my life?

Look Again and Think

"Do not worry about your life." **Matthew 6:25**

A warning which needs to be repeated is that "the cares of this world and the deceitfulness of riches," and the lust for other things, will choke out the life of God in us (Matthew 13:22). We are never free from the recurring waves of this invasion. If the frontline of attack is not about clothes and food, it may be about money or the lack of money; or friends or lack of friends; or the line may be drawn over difficult circumstances. It is one steady invasion, and these things will come in like a flood, unless we allow the Spirit of God to raise up the banner against it.

"I say to you, do not worry about your life." Our Lord says to be careful only about one thing—our relationship to Him. But our common sense shouts loudly and says, "That is absurd, I *must* consider how I am going to live, and I *must* consider what I am going to eat and drink." Jesus says you must not. Beware of allowing yourself to think that He says this while not understanding your circumstances. Jesus Christ knows our circumstances better than we do, and He says we must not think about these things to the point where they become the primary concern of our life. Whenever there are competing concerns in your life, be sure you always put your relationship to God first.

"Sufficient for the day is its own trouble" (6:34). How much trouble has begun to threaten you today? What kind of mean little demons have been looking into your life and saying, "What are your plans for next month—or next summer?" Jesus tells us not to worry about any of these things. Look again and think. Keep your mind on the "much more" of your heavenly Father (6:30).

How Could Someone So Persecute Jesus!

"Saul, Saul, why are you persecuting me?" **Acts 26:14**

Are you determined to have your own way in living for God? We will never be free from this trap until we are brought into the experience of the baptism of "the Holy Spirit and fire" (Matthew 3:11). Stubbornness and self-will will always stab Jesus Christ. It may hurt no one else, but it wounds His Spirit. Whenever we are obstinate and self-willed and set on our own ambitions, we are hurting Jesus. Every time we stand on our own rights and insist that this is what we intend to do, we are persecuting Him. Whenever we rely on self-respect, we systematically disturb and grieve His Spirit. And when we finally understand that it is Jesus we have been persecuting all this time, it is the most crushing revelation ever.

Is the Word of God tremendously penetrating and sharp in me as I hand it on to you, or does my life betray the things I profess to teach? I may teach sanctification and yet exhibit the spirit of Satan, the very spirit that persecutes Jesus Christ. The Spirit of Jesus is conscious of only one thing—a perfect oneness with the Father. And He tells us, "Take My yoke upon you and learn from Me, for I am gentle and lowly in heart, and you will find rest for your souls" (Matthew 11:29). All I do should be based on a perfect oneness with Him, not on a self-willed determination to be godly. This will mean that others may use me, go around me, or completely ignore me, but if I will submit to it for His sake, I will prevent Jesus Christ from being persecuted.

How Could Someone Be So Ignorant!

"Who are You, Lord?" **Acts 26:15**

"The Lord spoke thus to me with a strong hand" (Isaiah 8:11). There is no escape when our Lord speaks. He always comes using His authority and taking hold of our understanding. Has the voice of God come to you directly? If it has, you cannot mistake the intimate insistence with which it has spoken to you. God speaks in the language you know best—not through your ears, but through your circumstances.

God has to destroy our determined confidence in our own convictions. We say, "I know that this is what I should do"—and suddenly the voice of God speaks in a way that overwhelms us by revealing the depths of our ignorance. We show our ignorance of Him in the very way we decide to serve Him. We serve Jesus in a spirit that is not His, and hurt Him by our defense of Him. We push His claims in the spirit of the devil; our words sound all right, but the spirit is that of an enemy. "He . . . rebuked them, and said, 'You do not know what manner of spirit you are of'" (Luke 9:55). The spirit of our Lord in His followers is described in 1 Corinthians 13.

Have I been persecuting Jesus by an eager determination to serve Him in my own way? If I feel I have done my duty, yet have hurt Him in the process, I can be sure that this was not my duty. My way will not be to foster a meek and quiet spirit, only the spirit of self- satisfaction. We presume that whatever is unpleasant is our duty! Is that anything like the spirit of our Lord—"I *delight* to do Your will, O my God" (Psalm 40:8).

JANUARY 30

The Dilemma of Obedience

"Samuel was afraid to tell Eli the vision." **1 Samuel 3:15**

God never speaks to us in dramatic ways, but in ways that are easy to misunderstand. Then we say, "I wonder if that is God's voice?" Isaiah said that the Lord spoke to him "with a strong hand," that is, by the pressure of his circumstances (Isaiah 8:11). Without the sovereign hand of God Himself, nothing touches our lives. Do we discern His hand at work, or do we see things as mere occurrences?

Get into the habit of saying, "Speak, Lord," and life will become a romance (1 Samuel 3:9). Every time circumstances press in on you, say, "Speak, Lord," and make time to listen. Chastening is more than a means of discipline—it is meant to bring me to the point of saying, "Speak, Lord." Think back to a time when God spoke to you. Do you remember what He said? Was it Luke 11:13, or was it 1 Thessalonians 5:23? As we listen, our ears become more sensitive, and like Jesus, we will hear God all the time.

Should I tell my "Eli" what God has shown to me? This is where the dilemma of obedience hits us. We disobey God by becoming amateur providences and thinking, "I must shield 'Eli,'" who represents the best people we know. God did not tell Samuel to tell Eli—he had to decide that for himself. God's message to you may hurt your "Eli," but trying to prevent suffering in another's life will prove to be an obstruction between your soul and God. It is at your own risk that you prevent someone's right hand being cut off or right eye being plucked out (see Matthew 5:29–30).

Never ask another person's advice about anything God makes you decide before Him. If you ask advice, you will almost always side with Satan. "I did not immediately confer with flesh and blood" (Galatians 1:16).

Do You See Your Calling?

"*. . . separated to the gospel of God . . .*" **Romans 1:1**

Our calling is not primarily to be holy men and women, but to be proclaimers of the gospel of God. The one all-important thing is that the gospel of God should be recognized as *the* abiding reality. Reality is not human goodness, or holiness, or heaven, or hell—it is redemption. The need to perceive this is the most vital need of the Christian worker today. As workers, we have to get used to the revelation that redemption is the only reality. Personal holiness is an effect of redemption, not the cause of it. If we place our faith in human goodness we will go under when testing comes.

Paul did not say that he separated himself, but "when it pleased God, who separated me" (Galatians 1:15). Paul was not overly interested in his own character. And as long as our eyes are focused on our own personal holiness, we will never even get close to the full reality of redemption. Christian workers fail because they place their desire for their own holiness above their desire to know God. "Don't ask me to be confronted with the strong reality of redemption on behalf of the filth of human life surrounding me today; what I want is anything God can do for me to make me more desirable in my own eyes." To talk that way is a sign that the reality of the gospel of God has not begun to touch me. There is no reckless abandon to God in that. God cannot deliver me while my interest is merely in my own character. Paul was not conscious of himself. He was recklessly abandoned, totally surrendered, and separated by God for one purpose—to proclaim the gospel of God (see Romans 9:3).

The Call of God

"Christ did not send me to baptize, but to preach the gospel." **1 Corinthians 1:17**

Paul states here that the call of God is to preach the gospel. But remember what Paul means by "the gospel," namely, the reality of redemption in our Lord Jesus Christ. We are inclined to make sanctification the goal of our preaching. Paul refers to personal experiences only by way of illustration, never as the end of the matter. We are not commissioned to preach salvation or sanctification—we are commissioned to lift up Jesus Christ (see John 12:32). It is an injustice to say that Jesus Christ labored in redemption to make *me* a saint. Jesus Christ labored in redemption to redeem the whole world and to place it perfectly whole and restored before the throne of God. The fact that we can experience redemption illustrates the power of its reality, but that experience is a by-product and not the goal of redemption. If God were human, how sick and tired He would be of the constant requests we make for our salvation and for our sanctification. We burden His energies from morning till night asking for things for ourselves or for something from which *we* want to be delivered! When we finally touch the underlying foundation of the reality of the gospel of God, we will never bother Him anymore with little personal complaints.

The one passion of Paul's life was to proclaim the gospel of God. He welcomed heartbreak, disillusionment, and tribulation for only one reason—these things kept him unmovable in his devotion to the gospel of God.

The Compelling Force of the Call

"Woe is me if I do not preach the gospel!"
1 Corinthians 9:16

Beware of refusing to hear the call of God. Everyone who is saved is called to testify to the fact of his salvation. That, however, is not the same as the call to preach, but is merely an illustration which can be used in preaching. In this verse, Paul was referring to the stinging pains produced in him by the compelling force of the call to preach the gospel. Never try to apply what Paul said regarding the call to preach to those souls who are being called to God for salvation. There is nothing easier than getting saved, because it is solely God's sovereign work—"Look to Me, and be saved" (Isaiah 45:22). Our Lord never requires the same conditions for discipleship that he requires for salvation. We are condemned to salvation through the Cross of Christ. But discipleship has an option with it—"*If* anyone . . ." (Luke 14:26).

Paul's words have to do with our being made servants of Jesus Christ, and our permission is never asked as to what we will do or where we will go. God makes us as broken bread and poured-out wine to please Himself. To be "separated to the gospel" means being able to hear the call of God (Romans 1:1). Once someone begins to hear that call, a suffering worthy of the name of Christ is produced. Suddenly, every ambition, every desire of life, and every outlook is completely blotted out and extinguished. Only one thing remains—"*separated to the gospel.*" Woe be to the soul who tries to head in any other direction once that call has come to him. The Bible Training College exists so that each of you may know whether or not God has a man or woman here who truly cares about proclaiming His gospel and to see if God grips you for this purpose. Beware of competing calls once the call of God grips you.

Becoming the "Filth of the World"

"We have been made as the filth of the world."
1 Corinthians 4:13

These words are not an exaggeration. The only reason they may not be true of us who call ourselves ministers of the gospel is not that Paul forgot or misunderstood the exact truth of them, but that we are too cautious and concerned about our own desires to allow ourselves to become the refuse or "filth of the world." "Fill up in my flesh what is lacking in the afflictions of Christ" (Colossians 1:24) is not the result of the holiness of sanctification, but the evidence of consecration—being "separated *to* the gospel of God" (Romans 1:1).

"Beloved, do not think it strange concerning the fiery trial which is to try you" (1 Peter 4:12). If we do think the things we encounter are strange, it is because we are fearful and cowardly. We pay such close attention to our own interests and desires that we stay out of the mire and say, "I won't submit; I won't bow or bend." And you don't have to—you can be saved by the "skin of your teeth" if you like. You can refuse to let God count you as one who is "separated to the gospel." Or you can say, "I don't care if I am treated like 'the filth of the world' as long as the gospel is proclaimed." A true servant of Jesus Christ is one who is willing to experience martyrdom for the reality of the gospel of God. When a moral person is confronted with contempt, immorality, disloyalty, or dishonesty, he is so repulsed by the offense that he turns away and in despair closes his heart to the offender. But the miracle of the redemptive reality of God is that the worst and the vilest offender can never exhaust the depths of His love. Paul did not say that God separated him to show what a wonderful man He could make of him, but "*to reveal His Son in me*" (Galatians 1:16).

The Compelling Majesty of His Power

"The love of Christ compels us . . ."

2 Corinthians 5:14

Paul said that he was overpowered, subdued, and held as in a vise by "the love of Christ." Very few of us really know what it means to be held in the grip of the love of God. We tend so often to be controlled simply by our own experience. The one thing that gripped and held Paul, to the exclusion of everything else, was the love of God. "The love of Christ compels us . . ." When you hear that coming from the life of a man or woman it is unmistakable. You will know that the Spirit of God is completely unhindered in that person's life.

When we are born again by the Spirit of God, our testimony is based solely on what God has done for us, and rightly so. But that will change and be removed forever once you "receive power when the Holy Spirit has come upon you" (Acts 1:8). Only then will you begin to realize what Jesus meant when He went on to say, "You shall be *witnesses to Me*." Not witnesses to what Jesus can do—that is basic and understood—but "witnesses to Me." We will accept everything that happens as if it were happening to Him, whether we receive praise or blame, persecution or reward. No one is able to take this stand for Jesus Christ who is not totally compelled by the majesty of His power. It is the only thing that matters, and yet it is strange that it's the last thing we as Christian workers realize. Paul said that he was gripped by the love of God and that is why he acted as he did. People could perceive him as mad or sane—he did not care. There was only one thing he lived for—to persuade people of the coming judgment of God and to tell them of "the love of Christ." This total surrender to "the love of Christ" is the only thing that will bear fruit in your life. And it will always leave the mark of God's holiness and His power, never drawing attention to your personal holiness.

Are You Ready to Be Poured Out as an Offering?

"If I am being poured out as a drink offering on the sacrifice and service of your faith, I am glad and rejoice with you all." **Philippians 2:17**

Are you willing to sacrifice yourself for the work of another believer—to pour out your life sacrificially for the ministry and faith of others? Or do you say, "I am not willing to be poured out right now, and I don't want God to tell me how to serve Him. I want to choose the place of my own sacrifice. And I want to have certain people watching me and saying, 'Well done.'"

It is one thing to follow God's way of service if you are regarded as a hero, but quite another thing if the road marked out for you by God requires becoming a "doormat" under other people's feet. God's purpose may be to teach you to say, "I know how to be abased" (Philippians 4:12). Are you ready to be sacrificed like that? Are you ready to be less than a mere drop in the bucket—to be so totally insignificant that no one remembers you even if they think of those you served? Are you willing to give and be poured out until you are used up and exhausted—not seeking to be ministered to, but to minister? Some saints cannot do menial work while maintaining a saintly attitude, because they feel such service is beneath their dignity.

Are You Ready to Be Poured Out as an Offering?

"I am already being poured out as a drink offering."
2 Timothy 4:6

Are you ready to be poured out as an offering? It is an act of your will, not your emotions. *Tell* God you are ready to be offered as a sacrifice for Him. Then accept the consequences as they come, without any complaints, in spite of what God may send your way. God sends you through a crisis in private, where no other person can help you. From the outside your life may appear to be the same, but the difference is taking place in your will. Once you have experienced the crisis in your will, you will take no thought of the cost when it begins to affect you externally. If you don't deal with God on the level of your will first, the result will be only to arouse sympathy for yourself.

"Bind the sacrifice with cords to the horns of the altar" (Psalm 118:27). You must be willing to be placed on the altar and go through the fire; willing to experience what the altar represents—burning, purification, and separation for only one purpose—the elimination of every desire and affection not grounded in or directed toward God. But *you* don't eliminate it, God does. You "bind the sacrifice . . . to the horns of the altar" and see to it that you don't wallow in self-pity once the fire begins. After you have gone through the fire, there will be nothing that will be able to trouble or depress you. When another crisis arises, you will realize that things cannot touch you as they used to do. What fire lies ahead in your life?

Tell God you are ready to be poured out as an offering, and God will prove Himself to be all you ever dreamed He would be.

Spiritual Dejection

"We were hoping that it was He who was going to redeem Israel. Indeed, besides all this, today is the third day since these things happened." **Luke 24:21**

Every fact that the disciples stated was right, but the conclusions they drew from those facts were wrong. Anything that has even a hint of dejection spiritually is always wrong. If I am depressed or burdened, I am to blame, not God or anyone else. Dejection stems from one of two sources—I have either satisfied a lust or I have not had it satisfied. In either case, dejection is the result. *Lust* means "I must have it at once." Spiritual lust causes me to demand an answer from God, instead of seeking God Himself who gives the answer. What have I been hoping or trusting God would do? Is today "the third day" and He has still not done what I expected? Am I therefore justified in being dejected and in blaming God? Whenever we insist that God should give us an answer to prayer we are off track. The purpose of prayer is that we get ahold of God, not of the answer. It is impossible to be well physically and to be dejected, because dejection is a sign of sickness. This is also true spiritually. Dejection spiritually is wrong, and we are always to blame for it.

We look for visions from heaven and for earth-shaking events to see God's power. Even the fact that we are dejected is proof that we do this. Yet we never realize that all the time God is at work in our everyday events and in the people around us. If we will only obey, and do the task that He has placed closest to us, we will see Him. One of the most amazing revelations of God comes to us when we learn that it is in the everyday things of life that we realize the magnificent deity of Jesus Christ.

FEBRUARY 8

The Cost of Sanctification

"May the God of peace Himself sanctify you completely." **1 Thessalonians 5:23**

When we pray, asking God to sanctify us, are we prepared to measure up to what that really means? We take the word *sanctification* much too lightly. Are we prepared to pay the cost of sanctification? The cost will be a deep restriction of all our earthly concerns, and an extensive cultivation of all our godly concerns. Sanctification means to be intensely focused on God's point of view. It means to secure and to keep all the strength of our body, soul, and spirit for God's purpose alone. Are we really prepared for God to perform in us everything for which He separated us? And after He has done His work, are we then prepared to separate ourselves to God just as Jesus did? "For their sakes I sanctify Myself" (John 17:19). The reason some of us have not entered into the experience of sanctification is that we have not realized the meaning of sanctification from God's perspective. Sanctification means being made one with Jesus so that the nature that controlled Him will control us. Are we really prepared for what that will cost? It will cost absolutely everything in us which is not of God.

Are we prepared to be caught up into the full meaning of Paul's prayer in this verse? Are we prepared to say, "Lord, make me, a sinner saved by grace, as holy as You can"? Jesus prayed that we might be one with Him, just as He is one with the Father (see John 17:21–23). The resounding evidence of the Holy Spirit in a person's life is the unmistakable family likeness to Jesus Christ, and the freedom from everything which is not like Him. Are we prepared to set ourselves apart for the Holy Spirit's work in us?

Are You Exhausted Spiritually?

"The everlasting God . . . neither faints nor is weary."
Isaiah 40:28

Exhaustion means that our vital energies are completely worn out and spent. Spiritual exhaustion is never the result of sin, but of service. Whether or not you experience exhaustion will depend on where you get your supplies. Jesus said to Peter, "Feed My sheep," but He gave him nothing with which to feed them (John 21:17). The process of being made broken bread and poured-out wine means that *you* have to be the nourishment for other people's souls until they learn to feed on God. They must drain you completely—to the very last drop. But be careful to replenish your supply, or you will quickly be utterly exhausted. Until others learn to draw on the life of the Lord Jesus directly, they will have to draw on His life through you. You must literally be their source of supply, until they learn to take their nourishment from God. We owe it to God to be our best for His lambs and sheep, as well as for Him.

Have you delivered yourself over to exhaustion because of the way you have been serving God? If so, then renew and rekindle your desires and affections. Examine your reasons for service. Is your source based on your own understanding or is it grounded on the redemption of Jesus Christ? Continually look back to the foundation of your love and affection and remember where your Source of power lies. You have no right to complain, "O Lord, I am so exhausted." He saved and sanctified you to exhaust you. Be exhausted for God, but remember that He is your supply. "All my springs are in you" (Psalm 87:7).

Is Your Ability to See God Blinded?

"Lift up your eyes on high, and see who has created these things." **Isaiah 40:26**

The people of God in Isaiah's time had starved their imagination by looking on the face of idols. But Isaiah made them look up at the heavens; that is, he made them begin to use their imagination correctly. If we are children of God, we have a tremendous treasure in nature and will realize that it is holy and sacred. We will see God reaching out to us in every wind that blows, every sunrise and sunset, every cloud in the sky, every flower that blooms, and every leaf that fades, if we will only begin to use our starved imagination to visualize it.

The real test of spiritual focus is being able to bring your thoughts and imagination under control. Is your mind focused on the face of an idol? Is the idol yourself? Is it your work? Is it your idea of what a servant should be, or maybe your experience of salvation and sanctification? If so, then your ability to see God is blinded. You will be powerless when faced with difficulties and will be forced to endure in darkness. If your power to see has been blinded, don't look back on your own experiences, but look to God. It is God you need. Go beyond yourself and away from the faces of your idols and away from everything else that has been blinding your thinking, your imagination. Wake up and accept the ridicule that Isaiah gave to his people, and deliberately turn your thoughts and your eyes to God.

One of the reasons for our sense of futility in prayer is that we have lost our power to visualize. We can no longer even imagine putting ourselves deliberately before God. It is actually more important to be broken bread and poured-out wine in the area of intercession than in our personal contact with others. The power of imagination is what God gives a saint so that he can go beyond himself and be firmly placed into relationships he never before experienced.

FEBRUARY 11

Is Your Mind Stayed on God?

"You will keep him in perfect peace, whose mind is stayed on You, because he trusts in You." **Isaiah 26:3**

Is your mind stayed on God or is it starved? Starvation of the mind, caused by neglect, is one of the chief sources of exhaustion and weakness in a servant's life. If you have never used your mind to place yourself before God, begin to do it now. There is no reason to wait for God to come to you. You must turn your thoughts and your eyes away from the face of idols and look to Him and be saved (see Isaiah 45:22).

Your creative mind is the greatest gift God has given you and it ought to be devoted entirely to Him. You should seek to be "bringing every thought into captivity to the obedience of Christ" (2 Corinthians 10:5). This will be one of the greatest assets of your faith when a time of trial comes, because then your faith and the Spirit of God will work together. When you have thoughts and ideas that are worthy of credit to God, learn to compare and associate them with all that happens in nature—the rising and the setting of the sun, the shining of the moon and the stars, and the changing of the seasons. You will begin to see that your thoughts are from God as well, and your mind will no longer be at the mercy of your impulsive thinking, but will always be used in service to God.

"We have sinned with our fathers . . . [and] did not remember" (Psalm 106:6–7). Then prod your memory and wake up immediately. Don't say to yourself, "But God is not talking to me right now." He ought to be. Remember whose you are and whom you serve. Encourage yourself to remember, and your affection for God will increase tenfold. Your mind will no longer be starved, but will be quick and enthusiastic, and your hope will be inexpressibly bright.

Are You Listening to God?

"They said to Moses, 'You speak with us, and we will hear; but let not God speak with us, lest we die.'" **Exodus 20:19**

We don't consciously and deliberately disobey God—we simply don't listen to Him. God has given His commands to us, but we pay no attention to them—not because of willful disobedience, but because we do not truly love and respect Him. "If you love Me, keep My commandments" (John 14:15). Once we realize we have constantly been showing disrespect to God, we will be filled with shame and humiliation for ignoring Him.

"You speak with us, . . . but let not God speak with us." We show how little love we have for God by preferring to listen to His servants rather than to Him. We like to listen to personal testimonies, but we don't want God Himself to speak to us. Why are we so terrified for God to speak to us? It is because we know that when God speaks we must either do what He asks or tell Him we will not obey. But if it is simply one of God's servants speaking to us, we feel obedience is optional, not imperative. We respond by saying, "Well, that's only your own idea, even though I don't deny that what you said is probably God's truth."

Am I constantly humiliating God by ignoring Him, while He lovingly continues to treat me as His child? Once I finally do hear Him, the humiliation I have heaped on Him returns to me. My response then becomes, "Lord, why was I so insensitive and obstinate?" This is always the result once we hear God. But our real delight in finally hearing Him is tempered with the shame we feel for having taken so long to do so.

The Devotion of Hearing

"Samuel answered, 'Speak, for Your servant hears.'"
1 Samuel 3:10

Just because I have listened carefully and intently to one thing from God does not mean that I will listen to everything He says. I show God my lack of love and respect for Him by the insensitivity of my heart and mind toward what He says. If I love my friend, I will instinctively understand what he wants. And Jesus said, "You are My friends" (John 15:14). Have I disobeyed some command of my Lord's this week? If I had realized that it was a command of Jesus, I would not have deliberately disobeyed it. But most of us show incredible disrespect to God because we don't even hear Him. He might as well never have spoken to us.

The goal of my spiritual life is such close identification with Jesus Christ that I will always hear God and know that God always hears me (see John 11:41). If I am united with Jesus Christ, I hear God all the time through the devotion of hearing. A flower, a tree, or a servant of God may convey God's message to me. What hinders me from hearing is my attention to other things. It is not that I don't want to hear God, but I am not devoted in the right areas of my life. I am devoted to things and even to service and my own convictions. God may say whatever He wants, but I just don't hear Him. The attitude of a child of God should always be, "Speak, for Your servant hears." If I have not developed and nurtured this devotion of hearing, I can only hear God's voice at certain times. At other times I become deaf to Him because my attention is to other things—things which I think I must do. This is not living the life of a child of God. Have you heard God's voice today?

FEBRUARY 14

The Discipline of Hearing

"Whatever I tell you in the dark, speak in the light; and what you hear in the ear, preach on the housetops." **Matthew 10:27**

Sometimes God puts us through the experience and discipline of darkness to teach us to hear and obey Him. Song birds are taught to sing in the dark, and God puts us into "the shadow of His hand" until we learn to hear Him (Isaiah 49:2). "Whatever I tell you in the dark"—pay attention when God puts you into darkness, and keep your mouth closed while you are there. Are you in the dark right now in your circumstances, or in your life with God? If so, then remain quiet. If you open your mouth in the dark, you will speak while in the wrong mood—darkness is the time to listen. Don't talk to other people about it; don't read books to find out the reason for the darkness; just listen and obey. If you talk to other people, you cannot hear what God is saying. When you are in the dark, listen, and God will give you a very precious message for someone else once you are back in the light.

After every time of darkness, we should experience a mixture of delight and humiliation. If there is only delight, I question whether we have really heard God at all. We should experience delight for having heard God speak, but mostly humiliation for having taken so long to hear Him! Then we will exclaim, "How slow I have been to listen and understand what God has been telling me!" And yet God has been saying it for days and even weeks. But once you hear Him, He gives you the gift of humiliation, which brings a softness of heart—a gift that will always cause you to listen to God *now*.

"Am I My Brother's Keeper?"

"None of us lives to himself." **Romans 14:7**

Has it ever dawned on you that you are responsible spiritually to God for other people? For instance, if I allow any turning away from God in my private life, everyone around me suffers. We "sit *together* in the heavenly places" (Ephesians 2:6). "If one member suffers, all the members suffer with it" (1 Corinthians 12:26). If you allow physical selfishness, mental carelessness, moral insensitivity, or spiritual weakness, everyone in contact with you will suffer. But you ask, "Who is sufficient to be able to live up to such a lofty standard?" "Our sufficiency is from God" and God alone (2 Corinthians 3:5).

"You shall be witnesses to Me" (Acts 1:8). How many of us are willing to spend every bit of our nervous, mental, moral, and spiritual energy for Jesus Christ? That is what God means when He uses the word *witness*. But it takes time, so be patient with yourself. Why has God left us on the earth? Is it simply to be saved and sanctified? No, it is to be at work in service to Him. Am I willing to be broken bread and poured-out wine for Him? Am I willing to be of no value to this age or this life except for one purpose and one alone—to be used to disciple men and women to the Lord Jesus Christ. My life of service to God is the way I say "thank you" to Him for His inexpressibly wonderful salvation. Remember, it is quite possible for God to set any of us aside if we refuse to be of service to Him—"lest, when I have preached to others, I myself should become disqualified" (1 Corinthians 9:27).

FEBRUARY 16

The Inspiration of Spiritual Initiative

"Arise from the dead." **Ephesians 5:14**

Not all initiative, the willingness to take the first step, is inspired by God. Someone may say to you, "Get up and get going! Take your reluctance by the throat and throw it overboard—just do what needs to be done!" That is what we mean by ordinary human initiative. But when the Spirit of God comes to us and says, in effect, "Get up and get going," suddenly we find that the initiative is inspired.

We all have many dreams and aspirations when we are young, but sooner or later we realize we have no power to accomplish them. We cannot do the things we long to do, so our tendency is to think of our dreams and aspirations as dead. But God comes and says to us, "Arise from the dead." When God sends His inspiration, it comes to us with such miraculous power that we are able to "arise from the dead" and do the impossible. The remarkable thing about spiritual initiative is that the life and power comes after we "get up and get going." God does not give us overcoming life—He gives us life *as we overcome.* When the inspiration of God comes, and He says, "Arise from the dead," we have to get ourselves up; God will not lift us up. Our Lord said to the man with the withered hand, "Stretch out your hand" (Matthew 12:13). As soon as the man did so, his hand was healed. But he had to take the initiative. If we will take the initiative to overcome, we will find that we have the inspiration of God, because He immediately gives us the power of life.

Taking the Initiative Against Depression

"Arise and eat." **1 Kings 19:5**

The angel in this passage did not give Elijah a vision, or explain the Scriptures to him, or do anything remarkable. He simply told Elijah to do a very ordinary thing, that is, to get up and eat. If we were never depressed, we would not be alive—only material things don't suffer depression. If human beings were not capable of depression, we would have no capacity for happiness and exaltation. There are things in life that are designed to depress us; for example, things that are associated with death. Whenever you examine yourself, always take into account your capacity for depression.

When the Spirit of God comes to us, He does not give us glorious visions, but He tells us to do the most ordinary things imaginable. Depression tends to turn us away from the everyday things of God's creation. But whenever God steps in, His inspiration is to do the most natural, simple things—things we would never have imagined God was in, but as we do them we find Him there. The inspiration that comes to us in this way is an initiative against depression. But we must take the first step and do it in the inspiration of God. If, however, we do something simply to overcome our depression, we will only deepen it. But when the Spirit of God leads us instinctively to do something, the moment we do it the depression is gone. As soon as we arise and obey, we enter a higher plane of life.

FEBRUARY 18

Taking the Initiative Against Despair

"Rise, let us be going." **Matthew 26:46**

In the Garden of Gethsemane, the disciples went to sleep when they should have stayed awake, and once they realized what they had done it produced despair. The sense of having done something irreversible tends to make us despair. We say, "Well, it's all over and ruined now; what's the point in trying anymore." If we think this kind of despair is an exception, we are mistaken. It is a very ordinary human experience. Whenever we realize we have not taken advantage of a magnificent opportunity, we are apt to sink into despair. But Jesus comes and lovingly says to us, in essence, "Sleep on now. That opportunity is lost forever and you can't change that. But get up, and let's go on to the next thing." In other words, let the past sleep, but let it sleep in the sweet embrace of Christ, and let us go on into the invincible future with Him.

There will be experiences like this in each of our lives. We will have times of despair caused by real events in our lives, and we will be unable to lift ourselves out of them. The disciples, in this instance, had done a downright unthinkable thing—they had gone to sleep instead of watching with Jesus. But our Lord came to them taking the spiritual initiative against their despair and said, in effect, "Get up, and do the next thing." If we are inspired by God, what is the next thing? It is to trust Him absolutely and to pray on the basis of His redemption.

Never let the sense of past failure defeat your next step.

Taking the Initiative Against Drudgery

"Arise, shine . . ." **Isaiah 60:1**

When it comes to taking the initiative against drudgery, we have to take the first step as though there were no God. There is no point in waiting for God to help us—He will not. But once we arise, immediately we find He is there. Whenever God gives us His inspiration, suddenly taking the initiative becomes a moral issue—a matter of obedience. Then we must act to be obedient and not continue to lie down doing nothing. If we will arise and shine, drudgery will be divinely transformed.

Drudgery is one of the finest tests to determine the genuineness of our character. Drudgery is work that is far removed from anything we think of as ideal work. It is the utterly hard, menial, tiresome, and dirty work. And when we experience it, our spirituality is instantly tested and we will know whether or not we are spiritually genuine. Read John 13. In this chapter, we see the Incarnate God performing the greatest example of drudgery—washing fishermen's feet. He then says to them, "If I then, your Lord and Teacher, have washed your feet, you also ought to wash one another's feet" (John 13:14). The inspiration of God is required if drudgery is to shine with the light of God upon it. In some cases the way a person does a task makes that work sanctified and holy forever. It may be a very common everyday task, but after we have seen it done, it becomes different. When the Lord does something through us, He always transforms it. Our Lord takes our human flesh and transforms it, and now every believer's body has become "the temple of the Holy Spirit" (1 Corinthians 6:19).

Taking the Initiative Against Daydreaming

"Arise, let us go from here." **John 14:31**

Daydreaming about something in order to do it properly is right, but daydreaming about it when we should be doing it is wrong. In this passage, after having said these wonderful things to His disciples, we might have expected our Lord to tell them to go away and meditate over them all. But Jesus never allowed idle daydreaming. When our purpose is to seek God and to discover His will for us, daydreaming is right and acceptable. But when our inclination is to spend time daydreaming over what we have already been told to do, it is unacceptable and God's blessing is never on it. God will take the initiative against this kind of daydreaming by prodding us to action. His instructions to us will be along the lines of this: "Don't sit or stand there, just go!"

If we are quietly waiting before God after He has said to us, "Come aside by yourselves," then that is meditation before Him to seek His will (Mark 6:31). Beware, however, of giving in to mere daydreaming once God has spoken. Allow Him to be the source of all your dreams, joys, and delights, and be careful to go and obey what He has said. If you are in love with someone, you don't sit and daydream about that person all the time—you go and do something for him. That is what Jesus Christ expects us to do. Daydreaming after God has spoken is an indication that we do not trust Him.

Do You Really Love Him?

"She has done a good work for Me." **Mark 14:6**

If what we call love doesn't take us beyond ourselves, it is not really love. If we have the idea that love is characterized as cautious, wise, sensible, shrewd, and never taken to extremes, we have missed the true meaning. This may describe affection and it may bring us a warm feeling, but it is not a true and accurate description of love.

Have you ever been driven to do something for God not because you felt that it was useful or your duty to do so, or that there was anything in it for you, but simply because you love Him? Have you ever realized that you can give things to God that are of value to Him? Or are you just sitting around daydreaming about the greatness of His redemption, while neglecting all the things you could be doing for Him? I'm not referring to works which could be regarded as divine and miraculous, but ordinary, simple human things—things which would be evidence to God that you are totally surrendered to Him. Have you ever created what Mary of Bethany created in the heart of the Lord Jesus? "She has done a good work for Me."

There are times when it seems as if God watches to see if we will give Him even small gifts of surrender, just to show how genuine our love is for Him. To be surrendered to God is of more value than our personal holiness. Concern over our personal holiness causes us to focus our eyes on ourselves, and we become overly concerned about the way we walk and talk and look, out of fear of offending God. "But perfect love casts out fear" once we are surrendered to God (1 John 4:18). We should quit asking ourselves, "Am I of any use?" and accept the truth that we really are not of much use to Him. The issue is never of being of use, but of being of value to God Himself. Once we are totally surrendered to God, He will work through us all the time.

The Discipline of Spiritual Perseverance

"Be still, and know that I am God." **Psalm 46:10**

Perseverance is more than endurance. It is endurance combined with absolute assurance and certainty that what we are looking for is going to happen. Perseverance means more than just hanging on, which may be only exposing our fear of letting go and falling. Perseverance is our supreme effort of refusing to believe that our hero is going to be conquered. Our greatest fear is not that we will be damned, but that somehow Jesus Christ will be defeated. Also, our fear is that the very things our Lord stood for—love, justice, forgiveness, and kindness among men—will not win out in the end and will represent an unattainable goal for us. Then there is the call to spiritual perseverance. A call not to hang on and do nothing, but to work deliberately, knowing with certainty that God will never be defeated.

If our hopes seem to be experiencing disappointment right now, it simply means that they are being purified. Every hope or dream of the human mind will be fulfilled if it is noble and of God. But one of the greatest stresses in life is the stress of waiting for God. He brings fulfillment, "because you have kept My command to persevere" (Revelation 3:10).

Continue to persevere spiritually.

The Determination to Serve

"The Son of Man did not come to be served, but to serve." **Matthew 20:28**

Jesus also said, "Yet I am among you as the One who serves" (Luke 22:27). Paul's idea of service was the same as our Lord's—"ourselves your bondservants for Jesus' sake" (2 Corinthians 4:5). We somehow have the idea that a person called to the ministry is called to be different and above other people. But according to Jesus Christ, he is called to be a "doormat" for others—called to be their spiritual leader, but never their superior. Paul said, "I know how to be abased" (Philippians 4:12). Paul's idea of service was to pour his life out to the last drop for others. And whether he received praise or blame made no difference. As long as there was one human being who did not know Jesus, Paul felt a debt of service to that person until he did come to know Him. But the chief motivation behind Paul's service was not love for others but love for his Lord. If our devotion is to the cause of humanity, we will be quickly defeated and brokenhearted, since we will often be confronted with a great deal of ingratitude from other people. But if we are motivated by our love for God, no amount of ingratitude will be able to hinder us from serving one another.

Paul's understanding of how Christ had dealt with him is the secret behind his determination to serve others. "I was formerly a blasphemer, a persecutor, and an insolent man" (1 Timothy 1:13). In other words, no matter how badly others may have treated Paul, they could never have treated him with the same degree of spite and hatred with which he had treated Jesus Christ. Once we realize that Jesus has served us even to the depths of our meagerness, our selfishness, and our sin, nothing we encounter from others will be able to exhaust our determination to serve others for His sake.

The Delight of Sacrifice

"I will very gladly spend and be spent for your souls." **2 Corinthians 12:15**

Once "the love of God has been poured out in our hearts by the Holy Spirit," we deliberately begin to identify ourselves with Jesus Christ's interests and purposes in others' lives (Romans 5:5). And Jesus has an interest in every individual person. We have no right in Christian service to be guided by our own interests and desires. In fact, this is one of the greatest tests of our relationship with Jesus Christ. The delight of sacrifice is that I lay down my life for my Friend, Jesus (see John 15:13). I don't throw my life away, but I willingly and deliberately lay it down for Him and His interests in other people. And I do this for no cause or purpose of my own. Paul spent his life for only one purpose—that he might win people to Jesus Christ. Paul always attracted people to his Lord, but never to himself. He said, "I have become all things to all men, that I might by all means save some" (1 Corinthians 9:22).

When someone thinks that to develop a holy life he must always be alone with God, he is no longer of any use to others. This is like putting himself on a pedestal and isolating himself from the rest of society. Paul was a holy person, but wherever he went Jesus Christ was always allowed to help Himself to his life. Many of us are interested only in our own goals, and Jesus cannot help Himself to our lives. But if we are totally surrendered to Him, we have no goals of our own to serve. Paul said that he knew how to be a "doormat" without resenting it, because the motivation of his life was devotion to Jesus. We tend to be devoted, not to Jesus Christ, but to the things which allow us more spiritual freedom than total surrender to Him would allow. Freedom was not Paul's motive at all. In fact, he stated, "I could wish that I myself were accursed from Christ for my brethren" (Romans 9:3). Had Paul lost his ability to reason? Not at all! For someone who is in love, this is not an overstatement. And Paul was in love with Jesus Christ.

The Destitution of Service

". . . though the more abundantly I love you, the less I am loved." **2 Corinthians 12:15**

Natural human love expects something in return. But Paul is saying, "It doesn't really matter to me whether you love me or not. I am willing to be completely destitute anyway; willing to be poverty-stricken, not just for your sakes, but also that I may be able to get you to God." "For you know the grace of our Lord Jesus Christ, that though He was rich, yet for your sakes He became poor" (2 Corinthians 8:9). And Paul's idea of service was the same as our Lord's. He did not care how high the cost was to himself—he would gladly pay it. It was a joyful thing to Paul.

The institutional church's idea of a servant of God is not at all like Jesus Christ's idea. His idea is that we serve Him by being the servants of others. Jesus Christ actually "out-socialized" the socialists. He said that in His kingdom the greatest one would be the servant of all (see Matthew 23:11). The real test of a saint is not one's willingness to preach the gospel, but one's willingness to do something like washing the disciples' feet—that is, being willing to do those things that seem unimportant in human estimation but count as everything to God. It was Paul's delight to spend his life for God's interests in other people, and he did not care what it cost. But before we will serve, we stop to ponder our personal and financial concerns—"What if God wants me to go over there? And what about my salary? What is the climate like there? Who will take care of me? A person must consider all these things." All that is an indication that we have reservations about serving God. But the apostle Paul had no conditions or reservations. Paul focused his life on Jesus Christ's idea of a New Testament saint; that is, not one who merely proclaims the gospel, but one who becomes broken bread and poured-out wine in the hands of Jesus Christ for the sake of others.

Our Misgivings About Jesus

"The woman said to Him, 'Sir, You have nothing to draw [water] with, and the well is deep.'" **John 4:11**

Have you ever said to yourself, "I am impressed with the wonderful truths of God's Word, but He can't really expect me to live up to that and work all those details into my life!" When it comes to confronting Jesus Christ on the basis of His qualities and abilities, our attitudes reflect religious superiority. We think His ideals are lofty and they impress us, but we believe He is not in touch with reality—that what He says cannot actually be done. Each of us thinks this about Jesus in one area of our life or another. These doubts or misgivings about Jesus begin as we consider questions that divert our focus away from God. While we talk of our dealings with Him, others ask us, "Where are you going to get enough money to live? How will you live and who will take care of you?" Or our misgivings begin within ourselves when we tell Jesus that our circumstances are just a little too difficult for Him. We say, "It's easy to say, 'Trust in the Lord,' but a person has to live; and besides, Jesus has nothing with which to draw water—no means to be able to give us these things." And beware of exhibiting religious deceit by saying, "Oh, I have no misgivings about Jesus, only misgivings about myself." If we are honest, we will admit that we never have misgivings or doubts about ourselves, because we know exactly what we are capable or incapable of doing. But we do have misgivings about Jesus. And our pride is hurt even at the thought that He can do what we can't.

My misgivings arise from the fact that I search within to find how He will do what He says. My doubts spring from the depths of my own inferiority. If I detect these misgivings in myself, I should bring them into the light and confess them openly—"Lord, I have had misgivings about You. I have not believed in Your abilities, but only my own. And I have not believed in Your almighty power apart from my finite understanding of it."

The Impoverished Ministry of Jesus

"Where then do You get that living water?" **John 4:11**

"The well is deep"—and even a great deal deeper than the Samaritan woman knew! (John 4:11). Think of the depths of human nature and human life; think of the depth of the "wells" in you. Have you been limiting, or impoverishing, the ministry of Jesus to the point that He is unable to work in your life? Suppose that you have a deep "well" of hurt and trouble inside your heart, and Jesus comes and says to you, "Let not your heart be troubled" (John 14:1). Would your response be to shrug your shoulders and say, "But, Lord, the well is too deep, and even You can't draw up quietness and comfort out of it." Actually, that is correct. Jesus doesn't bring anything up from the wells of human nature—He brings them down from above. We limit the Holy One of Israel by remembering only what we have allowed Him to do for us in the past, and also by saying, "Of course, I cannot expect God to do this particular thing." The thing that approaches the very limits of His power is the very thing we as disciples of Jesus ought to believe He will do. We impoverish and weaken His ministry in us the moment we forget He is almighty. The impoverishment is in us, not in Him. We will come to Jesus for Him to be our comforter or our sympathizer, but we refrain from approaching Him as our Almighty God.

The reason some of us are such poor examples of Christianity is that we have failed to recognize that Christ is almighty. We have Christian attributes and experiences, but there is no abandonment or surrender to Jesus Christ. When we get into difficult circumstances, we impoverish His ministry by saying, "Of course, He can't do anything about this." We struggle to reach the bottom of our own well, trying to get water for ourselves. Beware of sitting back, and saying, "It can't be done." You will know it can be done if you will look to Jesus. The well of your incompleteness runs deep, but make the effort to look away from yourself and to look toward Him.

"Do You Now Believe?"

"'By this we believe . . . .' Jesus answered them, 'Do you now believe?'" **John 16:30–31**

"Now we believe . . ." But Jesus asks, "Do you . . . ? Indeed the hour is coming . . . that you . . . will leave Me alone" (John 16:31–32). Many Christian workers have left Jesus Christ alone and yet tried to serve Him out of a sense of duty, or because they sense a need as a result of their own discernment. The reason for this is actually the absence of the resurrection life of Jesus. Our soul has gotten out of intimate contact with God by leaning on our own religious understanding (see Proverbs 3:5–6). This is not deliberate sin and there is no punishment attached to it. But once a person realizes how he has hindered his understanding of Jesus Christ, and caused uncertainties, sorrows, and difficulties for himself, it is with shame and remorse that he has to return.

We need to rely on the resurrection life of Jesus on a much deeper level than we do now. We should get in the habit of continually seeking His counsel on everything, instead of making our own commonsense decisions and then asking Him to bless them. He cannot bless them; it is not in His realm to do so, and those decisions are severed from reality. If we do something simply out of a sense of duty, we are trying to live up to a standard that competes with Jesus Christ. We become a prideful, arrogant person, thinking we know what to do in every situation. We have put our sense of duty on the throne of our life, instead of enthroning the resurrection life of Jesus. We are not told to "walk in the light" of our conscience or in the light of a sense of duty, but to "walk in the light *as He is in the light*" (1 John 1:7). When we do something out of a sense of duty, it is easy to explain the reasons for our actions to others. But when we do something out of obedience to the Lord, there can be no other explanation—just obedience. That is why a saint can be so easily ridiculed and misunderstood.

What Do You Want the Lord to Do for You?

"'What do you want Me to do for you?' He said, 'Lord, that I may receive my sight.'" **Luke 18:41**

Is there something in your life that not only disturbs you, but makes you a disturbance to others? If so, it is always something you cannot handle yourself. "Then those who went before warned him that he should be quiet; but he cried out all the more" (Luke 18:39). Be persistent with your disturbance until you get face-to-face with the Lord Himself. Don't deify common sense. To sit calmly by, instead of creating a disturbance, serves only to deify our common sense. When Jesus asks what we want Him to do for us about the incredible problem that is confronting us, remember that He doesn't work in common-sense ways, but only in supernatural ways.

Look at how we limit the Lord by only remembering what we have allowed Him to do for us in the past. We say, "I always failed there, and I always will." Consequently, we don't ask for what we want. Instead, we think, "It is ridiculous to ask God to do this." If it is an impossibility, it is the very thing for which we have to ask. If it is not an impossible thing, it is not a real disturbance. And God will do what is absolutely impossible.

This man received his sight. But the most impossible thing for you is to be so closely identified with the Lord that there is literally nothing of your old life remaining. God will do it if you will ask Him. But you have to come to the point of believing Him to be almighty. We find faith by not only believing what Jesus says, but, even more, by trusting Jesus Himself. If we only look at what He says, we will never believe. Once we see Jesus, the impossible things He does in our lives become as natural as breathing. The agony we suffer is only the result of the deliberate shallowness of our own heart. We *won't* believe; we *won't* let go by severing the line that secures the boat to the shore—we prefer to worry.

MARCH 1

The Piercing Question

"Do you love Me?" **John 21:17**

Peter's response to this piercing question is considerably different from the bold defiance he exhibited only a few days before when he declared, "Even if I have to die with You, I will not deny You!" (Matthew 26:35; also see verses 33–34). Our natural individuality, or our natural self, boldly speaks out and declares its feelings. But the true love within our inner spiritual self can be discovered only by experiencing the hurt of this question of Jesus Christ. Peter loved Jesus in the way any natural man loves a good person. Yet that is nothing but emotional love. It may reach deeply into our natural self, but it never penetrates to the spirit of a person. True love never simply declares itself. Jesus said, "Whoever *confesses* Me before men [that is, confesses his love by everything he does, not merely by his words], him the Son of Man also will confess before the angels of God" (Luke 12:8).

Unless we are experiencing the hurt of facing every deception about ourselves, we have hindered the work of the Word of God in our lives. The Word of God inflicts hurt on us more than sin ever could, because sin dulls our senses. But this question of the Lord intensifies our sensitivities to the point that this hurt produced by Jesus is the most exquisite pain conceivable. It hurts not only on the natural level, but also on the deeper spiritual level. "For the Word of God is living and powerful, piercing even to the division of soul and spirit"—to the point that no deception can remain (Hebrews 4:12). When the Lord asks us this question, it is impossible to think and respond properly, because when the Lord speaks directly to us, the pain is too intense. It causes such a tremendous hurt that any part of our life which may be out of line with His will can feel the pain. There is never any mistaking the pain of the Lord's Word by His children, but the moment that pain is felt is the very moment at which God reveals His truth to us.

Have You Felt the Pain Inflicted by the Lord?

"He said to him the third time, '. . . do you love Me?'"
John 21:17

Have you ever felt the pain, inflicted by the Lord, at the very center of your being, deep down in the most sensitive area of your life? The devil never inflicts pain there, and neither can sin nor human emotions. Nothing can cut through to that part of our being but the Word of God. "Peter was grieved because He said to him the third time, 'Do you love Me?'" Yet he was awakened to the fact that at the center of his personal life he was devoted to Jesus. And then he began to see what Jesus' patient questioning meant. There was not the slightest bit of doubt left in Peter's mind; he could never be deceived again. And there was no need for an impassioned response; no need for immediate action or an emotional display. It was a revelation to him to realize how much he did love the Lord, and with amazement he simply said, "Lord, You know all things." Peter began to see how very much he did love Jesus, and there was no need to say, "Look at this or that as proof of my love." Peter was beginning to discover within himself just how much he really did love the Lord. He discovered that his eyes were so fixed on Jesus Christ that he saw no one else in heaven above or on the earth below. But he did not know it until the probing, hurting questions of the Lord were asked. The Lord's questions always reveal the true me to myself.

Oh, the wonder of the patient directness and skill of Jesus Christ with Peter! Our Lord never asks questions until the perfect time. Rarely, but probably once in each of our lives, He will back us into a corner where He will hurt us with His piercing questions. Then we will realize that we do love Him far more deeply than our words can ever say.

MARCH 3

His Commission to Us

"Feed My sheep." **John 21:17**

This is love in the making. The love of God is not created—it is His nature. When we receive the life of Christ through the Holy Spirit, He unites us with God so that His love is demonstrated in us. The goal of the indwelling Holy Spirit is not just to unite us with God, but to do it in such a way that we will be one with the Father in exactly the same way Jesus was. And what kind of oneness did Jesus Christ have with the Father? He had such a oneness with the Father that He was obedient when His Father sent Him down here to be poured out for us. And He says to us, "As the Father has sent Me, I also send you" (John 20:21).

Peter now realizes that he does love Him, due to the revelation that came with the Lord's piercing question. The Lord's next point is—"Pour yourself out. Don't testify about how much you love Me and don't talk about the wonderful revelation you have had, just 'Feed My sheep.'" Jesus has some extraordinarily peculiar sheep: some that are unkempt and dirty, some that are awkward or pushy, and some that have gone astray! But it is impossible to exhaust God's love, and it is impossible to exhaust my love if it flows from the Spirit of God within me. The love of God pays no attention to my prejudices caused by my natural individuality. If I love my Lord, I have no business being guided by natural emotions—I have to feed His sheep. We will not be delivered or released from His commission to us. Beware of counterfeiting the love of God by following your own natural human emotions, sympathies, or understandings. That will only serve to revile and abuse the true love of God.

Is This True of Me?

"None of these things move me; nor do I count my life dear to myself." **Acts 20:24**

It is easier to serve or work for God without a vision and without a call, because then you are not bothered by what He requires. Common sense, covered with a layer of Christian emotion, becomes your guide. You may be more prosperous and successful from the world's perspective, and will have more leisure time, if you never acknowledge the call of God. But once you receive a commission from Jesus Christ, the memory of what God asks of you will always be there to prod you on to do His will. You will no longer be able to work for Him on the basis of common sense.

What do I count in my life as "dear to myself"? If I have not been seized by Jesus Christ and have not surrendered myself to Him, I will consider the time I decide to give God and my own ideas of service as dear. I will also consider my own life as "dear to myself." But Paul said he considered his life dear so that he might fulfill the ministry he had received, and he refused to use his energy on anything else. This verse shows an almost noble annoyance by Paul at being asked to consider himself. He was absolutely indifferent to any consideration other than that of fulfilling the ministry he had received. Our ordinary and reasonable service to God may actually compete against our total surrender to Him. Our reasonable work is based on the following argument which we say to ourselves, "Remember how useful you are here, and think how much value you would be in that particular type of work." That attitude chooses our own judgment, instead of Jesus Christ, to be our guide as to where we should go and where we could be used the most. Never consider whether or not you are of use—but always consider that "you are not your own" (1 Corinthians 6:19). You are His.

Is He Really My Lord?

". . . so that I may finish my race with joy, and the ministry which I received from the Lord Jesus." **Acts 20:24**

Joy comes from seeing the complete fulfillment of the specific purpose for which I was created and born again, not from successfully doing something of my own choosing. The joy our Lord experienced came from doing what the Father sent Him to do. And He says to us, "As the Father has sent Me, I also send you" (John 20:21). Have you received a ministry from the Lord? If so, you must be faithful to it—to consider your life valuable only for the purpose of fulfilling that ministry. Knowing that you have done what Jesus sent you to do, think how satisfying it will be to hear Him say to you, "Well done, good and faithful servant" (Matthew 25:21). We each have to find a niche in life, and spiritually we find it when we receive a ministry from the Lord. To do this we must have close fellowship with Jesus and must know Him as more than our personal Savior. And we must be willing to experience the full impact of Acts 9:16—"I will show him how many things he must suffer *for My name's sake*."

"Do you love Me?" Then, "Feed My sheep" (John 21:17). He is not offering us a choice of how we can serve Him; He is asking for absolute loyalty to His commission, a faithfulness to what we discern when we are in the closest possible fellowship with God. If you have received a ministry from the Lord Jesus, you will know that the need is not the same as the call—the need is the opportunity to exercise the call. The call is to be faithful to the ministry you received when you were in true fellowship with Him. This does not imply that there is a whole series of differing ministries marked out for you. It does mean that you must be sensitive to what God has called you to do, and this may sometimes require ignoring demands for service in other areas.

Taking the Next Step

". . . in much patience, in tribulations, in needs, in distresses." **2 Corinthians 6:4**

When you have no vision from God, no enthusiasm left in your life, and no one watching and encouraging you, it requires the grace of Almighty God to take the next step in your devotion to Him, in the reading and studying of His Word, in your family life, or in your duty to Him. It takes much more of the grace of God, and a much greater awareness of drawing upon Him, to take that next step, than it does to preach the gospel.

Every Christian must experience the essence of the incarnation by bringing the next step down into flesh-and-blood reality and by working it out with his hands. We lose interest and give up when we have no vision, no encouragement, and no improvement, but only experience our everyday life with its trivial tasks. The thing that really testifies for God and for the people of God in the long run is steady perseverance, even when the work cannot be seen by others. And the only way to live an undefeated life is to live looking to God. Ask God to keep the eyes of your spirit open to the risen Christ, and it will be impossible for drudgery to discourage you. Never allow yourself to think that some tasks are beneath your dignity or too insignificant for you to do, and remind yourself of the example of Christ in John 13:1–17.

The Source of Abundant Joy

"In all these things we are more than conquerors through Him who loved us." **Romans 8:37**

Paul was speaking here of the things that might seem likely to separate a saint from the love of God. But the remarkable thing is that nothing *can* come between the love of God and a saint. The things Paul mentioned in this passage can and do disrupt the close fellowship of our soul with God and separate our natural life from Him. But none of them is able to come between the love of God and the soul of a saint on the spiritual level. The underlying foundation of the Christian faith is the undeserved, limitless miracle of the love of God that was exhibited on the Cross of Calvary; a love that is not earned and can never be. Paul said this is the reason that "in all these things we are more than conquerors." We are super-victors with a joy that comes from experiencing the very things which look as if they are going to overwhelm us.

Huge waves that would frighten an ordinary swimmer produce a tremendous thrill for the surfer who has ridden them. Let's apply that to our own circumstances. The things we try to avoid and fight against—tribulation, suffering, and persecution—are the very things that produce abundant joy in us. "We are more than conquerors through Him" "*in* all these things"; not in spite of them, but in the midst of them. A saint doesn't know the joy of the Lord in spite of tribulation, but *because* of it. Paul said, "I am exceedingly joyful in all our tribulation" (2 Corinthians 7:4).

The undiminished radiance, which is the result of abundant joy, is not built on anything passing, but on the love of God that nothing can change. And the experiences of life, whether they are everyday events or terrifying ones, are powerless to "separate us from the love of God which is in Christ Jesus our Lord" (Romans 8:39).

MARCH 8

The Surrendered Life

"I have been crucified with Christ." **Galatians 2:20**

To become one with Jesus Christ, a person must be willing not only to give up sin, but also to surrender his whole way of looking at things. Being born again by the Spirit of God means that we must first be willing to let go before we can grasp something else. The first thing we must surrender is all of our pretense or deceit. What our Lord wants us to present to Him is not our goodness, honesty, or our efforts to do better, but real solid sin. Actually, that is all He can take from us. And what He gives us in exchange for our sin is real solid righteousness. But we must surrender all pretense that we are anything, and give up all our claims of even being worthy of God's consideration.

Once we have done that, the Spirit of God will show us what we need to surrender next. Along each step of this process, we will have to give up our claims to our rights to ourselves. Are we willing to surrender our grasp on all that we possess, our desires, and everything else in our lives? Are we ready to be identified with the death of Jesus Christ?

We will suffer a sharp painful disillusionment before we fully surrender. When people really see themselves as the Lord sees them, it is not the terribly offensive sins of the flesh that shock them, but the awful nature of the pride of their own hearts opposing Jesus Christ. When they see themselves in the light of the Lord, the shame, horror, and desperate conviction hit home for them.

If you are faced with the question of whether or not to surrender, make a determination to go on through the crisis, surrendering all that you have and all that you are to Him. And God will then equip you to do all that He requires of you.

Turning Back or Walking with Jesus?

"Do you also want to go away?" **John 6:67**

What a penetrating question! Our Lord's words often hit home for us when He speaks in the simplest way. In spite of the fact that we know who Jesus is, He asks, "Do you also want to go away?" We must continually maintain an adventurous attitude toward Him, despite any potential personal risk.

"From that time many of His disciples went back and walked with Him no more" (John 6:66). They turned back from walking with Jesus; not into sin, but away from Him. Many people today are pouring their lives out and working for Jesus Christ, but are not really walking with Him. One thing God constantly requires of us is a oneness with Jesus Christ. After being set apart through sanctification, we should discipline our lives spiritually to maintain this intimate oneness. When God gives you a clear determination of His will for you, all your striving to maintain that relationship by some particular method is completely unnecessary. All that is required is to live a natural life of absolute dependence on Jesus Christ. Never try to live your life with God in any other way than His way. And His way means absolute devotion to Him. Showing no concern for the uncertainties that lie ahead is the secret of walking with Jesus.

Peter saw in Jesus only someone who could minister salvation to him and to the world. But our Lord wants us to be fellow laborers with Him.

In verse 70 Jesus lovingly reminded Peter that he was chosen to go with Him. And each of us must answer this question for ourselves and no one else: "Do you also want to go away?"

Being an Example of His Message

"Preach the word!" **2 Timothy 4:2**

We are not saved only to be instruments for God, but to be His sons and daughters. He does not turn us into spiritual agents but into spiritual messengers, and the message must be a part of us. The Son of God was His own message—"The words that I speak to you are spirit, and they are life" (John 6:63). As His disciples, our lives must be a holy example of the reality of our message. Even the natural heart of the unsaved will serve if called upon to do so, but it takes a heart broken by conviction of sin, baptized by the Holy Spirit, and crushed into submission to God's purpose to make a person's life a holy example of God's message.

There is a difference between giving a testimony and preaching. A preacher is someone who has received the call of God and is determined to use all his energy to proclaim God's truth. God takes us beyond our own aspirations and ideas for our lives, and molds and shapes us for His purpose, just as He worked in the disciples' lives after Pentecost. The purpose of Pentecost was not to teach the disciples something, but to make them the incarnation of what they preached so that they would literally become God's message in the flesh. "You shall be witnesses to Me" (Acts 1:8).

Allow God to have complete liberty in your life when you speak. Before God's message can liberate other people, His liberation must first be real in you. Gather your material carefully, and then allow God to "set your words on fire" for His glory.

Obedience to the "Heavenly Vision"

"I was not disobedient to the heavenly vision." **Acts 26:19**

If we lose "the heavenly vision" God has given us, we alone are responsible—not God. We lose the vision because of our own lack of spiritual growth. If we do not apply our beliefs about God to the issues of everyday life, the vision God has given us will never be fulfilled. The only way to be obedient to "the heavenly vision" is to give our utmost for His highest—our best for His glory. This can be accomplished only when we make a determination to continually remember God's vision. But the acid test is obedience to the vision in the details of our everyday life—sixty seconds out of every minute, and sixty minutes out of every hour, not just during times of personal prayer or public meetings.

"Though it tarries, wait for it" (Habakkuk 2:3). We cannot bring the vision to fulfillment through our own efforts, but must live under its inspiration until it fulfills itself. We try to be so practical that we forget the vision. At the very beginning we saw the vision but did not wait for it. We rushed off to do our practical work, and once the vision was fulfilled we could no longer even see it. Waiting for a vision that "tarries" is the true test of our faithfulness to God. It is at the risk of our own soul's welfare that we get caught up in practical busywork, only to miss the fulfillment of the vision.

Watch for the storms of God. The only way God plants His saints is through the whirlwind of His storms. Will you be proven to be an empty pod with no seed inside? That will depend on whether or not you are actually living in the light of the vision you have seen. Let God send you out through His storm, and don't go until He does. If you select your own spot to be planted, you will prove yourself to be an unproductive, empty pod. However, if you allow God to plant you, you will "bear much fruit" (John 15:8).

It is essential that we live and "walk in the light" of God's vision for us (1 John 1:7).

MARCH 12

Total Surrender

"Peter began to say to Him, 'See, we have left all and followed You.'" **Mark 10:28**

Our Lord replies to this statement of Peter by saying that this surrender is "for My sake and the gospel's" (10:29). It was not for the purpose of what the disciples themselves would get out of it. Beware of surrender that is motivated by personal benefits that may result. For example, "I'm going to give myself to God because I want to be delivered from sin, because I want to be made holy." Being delivered from sin and being made holy are the result of being right with God, but surrender resulting from this kind of thinking is certainly not the true nature of Christianity. Our motive for surrender should not be *for* any personal gain at all. We have become so self-centered that we go to God only for something from Him, and not for God Himself. It is like saying, "No, Lord, I don't want You; I want myself. But I do want You to clean me and fill me with Your Holy Spirit. I want to be on display in Your showcase so I can say, 'This is what God has done for me.'" Gaining heaven, being delivered from sin, and being made useful to God are things that should never even be a consideration in real surrender. Genuine total surrender is a personal sovereign preference for Jesus Christ Himself.

Where does Jesus Christ figure in when we have a concern about our natural relationships? Most of us will desert Him with this excuse—"Yes, Lord, I heard You call me, but my family needs me and I have my own interests. I just can't go any further" (see Luke 9:57–62). "Then," Jesus says, "you 'cannot be My disciple'" (see Luke 14:26–33).

True surrender will always go beyond natural devotion. If we will only give up, God will surrender Himself to embrace all those around us and will meet their needs, which were created by our surrender. Beware of stopping anywhere short of total surrender to God. Most of us have only a vision of what this really means, but have never truly experienced it.

God's Total Surrender to Us

"For God so loved the world that He gave . . ." **John 3:16**

Salvation does not mean merely deliverance from sin or the experience of personal holiness. The salvation which comes from God means being completely delivered from myself, and being placed into perfect union with Him. When I think of my salvation experience, I think of being delivered from sin and gaining personal holiness. But salvation is so much more! It means that the Spirit of God has brought me into intimate contact with the true Person of God Himself. And as I am caught up into total surrender to God, I become thrilled with something infinitely greater than myself.

To say that we are called to preach holiness or sanctification is to miss the main point. We are called to proclaim Jesus Christ (see 1 Corinthians 2:2). The fact that He saves from sin and makes us holy is actually part of the effect of His wonderful and total surrender to us.

If we are truly surrendered, we will never be aware of our own efforts to remain surrendered. Our entire life will be consumed with the One to whom we surrender. Beware of talking about surrender if you know nothing about it. In fact, you will never know anything about it until you understand that John 3:16 means that God completely and absolutely gave Himself to us. In our surrender, we must give ourselves to God in the same way He gave Himself for us—totally, unconditionally, and without reservation. The consequences and circumstances resulting from our surrender will never even enter our mind, because our life will be totally consumed with Him.

Yielding

"You are that one's slaves whom you obey . . ." **Romans 6:16**

The first thing I must be willing to admit when I begin to examine what controls and dominates me is that I am the one responsible for having yielded myself to whatever it may be. If I am a slave to myself, I am to blame because somewhere in the past I yielded to myself. Likewise, if I obey God I do so because at some point in my life I yielded myself to Him.

If a child gives in to selfishness, he will find it to be the most enslaving tyranny on earth. There is no power within the human soul itself that is capable of breaking the bondage of the nature created by yielding. For example, yield for one second to anything in the nature of lust, and although you may hate yourself for having yielded, you become enslaved to that thing. (Remember what lust is—"I must have it now," whether it is the lust of the flesh or the lust of the mind.) No release or escape from it will ever come from any human power, but only through the power of redemption. You must yield yourself in utter humiliation to the only One who can break the dominating power in your life, namely, the Lord Jesus Christ. "He has anointed Me . . . to proclaim liberty to the captives" (Luke 4:18 and Isaiah 61:1).

When you yield to something, you will soon realize the tremendous control it has over you. Even though you say, "Oh, I can give up that habit whenever I like," you will know you can't. You will find that the habit absolutely dominates you because you willingly yielded to it. It is easy to sing, "He will break every fetter," while at the same time living a life of obvious slavery to yourself. But yielding to Jesus will break every kind of slavery in any person's life.

The Discipline of Dismay

"As they followed they were afraid." **Mark 10:32**

At the beginning of our life with Jesus Christ, we were sure we knew all there was to know about following Him. It was a delight to forsake everything else and to throw ourselves before Him in a fearless statement of love. But now we are not quite so sure. Jesus is far ahead of us and is beginning to seem different and unfamiliar—"Jesus was going before them; and they were amazed" (Mark 10:32).

There is an aspect of Jesus that chills even a disciple's heart to its depth and makes his entire spiritual life gasp for air. This unusual Person with His face set "like a flint" (Isaiah 50:7) is walking with great determination ahead of me, and He strikes terror right through me. He no longer seems to be my Counselor and Friend and has a point of view about which I know nothing. All I can do is stand and stare at Him in amazement. At first I was confident that I understood Him, but now I am not so sure. I begin to realize that there is a distance between Jesus and me and I can no longer be intimate with Him. I have no idea where He is going, and the goal has become strangely distant.

Jesus Christ had to understand fully every sin and sorrow that human beings could experience, and that is what makes Him seem unfamiliar. When we see this aspect of Him, we realize we really don't know Him. We don't recognize even one characteristic of His life, and we don't know how to begin to follow Him. He is far ahead of us, a Leader who seems totally unfamiliar, and we have no friendship with Him.

The discipline of dismay is an essential lesson which a disciple must learn. The danger is that we tend to look back on our times of obedience and on our past sacrifices to God in an effort to keep our enthusiasm for Him strong (see Isaiah 50:10–11). But when the darkness of dismay comes, endure until it is over, because out of it will come the ability to follow Jesus truly, which brings inexpressibly wonderful joy.

MARCH 16

The Master Will Judge

"We must all appear before the judgment seat of Christ." **2 Corinthians 5:10**

Paul says that we must all, preachers and other people alike, "appear before the judgment seat of Christ." But if you will learn here and now to live under the scrutiny of Christ's pure light, your final judgment will bring you only delight in seeing the work God has done in you. Live constantly reminding yourself of the judgment seat of Christ, and walk in the knowledge of the holiness He has given you. Tolerating a wrong attitude toward another person causes you to follow the spirit of the devil, no matter how saintly you are. One carnal judgment of another person only serves the purposes of hell in you. Bring it immediately into the light and confess, "Oh, Lord, I have been guilty there." If you don't, your heart will become hardened through and through. One of the penalties of sin is our acceptance of it. It is not only God who punishes for sin, but sin establishes itself in the sinner and takes its toll. No struggling or praying will enable you to stop doing certain things, and the penalty of sin is that you gradually get used to it, until you finally come to the place where you no longer even realize that it is sin. No power, except the power that comes from being filled with the Holy Spirit, can change or prevent the inherent consequences of sin.

"If we walk in the light *as He is in the light*" (1 John 1:7). For many of us, walking in the light means walking according to the standard we have set up for another person. The deadliest attitude of the Pharisees that we exhibit today is not hypocrisy but that which comes from unconsciously living a lie.

The Call of the Natural Life

"We make it our aim . . . to be well pleasing to Him." **2 Corinthians 5:9**

"We make it our aim . . ." It requires a conscious decision and effort to keep our primary goal constantly in front of us. It means holding ourselves to the highest priority year in and year out; not making our first priority to win souls, or to establish churches, or to have revivals, but seeking only "to be well pleasing to Him." It is not a lack of spiritual experience that leads to failure, but a lack of working to keep our eyes focused and on the right goal. At least once a week examine yourself before God to see if your life is measuring up to the standard He has for you. Paul was like a musician who gives no thought to audience approval, if he can only catch a look of approval from his Conductor.

Any goal we have that diverts us even to the slightest degree from the central goal of being "approved to God" (2 Timothy 2:15) may result in our rejection from further service for Him. When you discern where the goal leads, you will understand why it is so necessary to keep "looking unto Jesus" (Hebrews 12:2). Paul spoke of the importance of controlling his own body so that it would not take him in the wrong direction. He said, "I discipline my body and bring it into subjection, lest . . . I myself should become disqualified" (1 Corinthians 9:27).

I must learn to relate everything to the primary goal, maintaining it without interruption. My worth to God publicly is measured by what I really am in my private life. Is my primary goal in life to please Him and to be acceptable to Him, or is it something less, no matter how lofty it may sound?

Will I Bring Myself Up to This Level?

". . . perfecting holiness in the fear of God."
2 Corinthians 7:1

"Therefore, having these promises . . ." I claim God's promises for my life and look to their fulfillment, and rightly so, but that shows only the human perspective on them. God's perspective is that through His promises I will come to recognize His claim of ownership on me. For example, do I realize that my "body is the temple of the Holy Spirit," or am I condoning some habit in my body which clearly could not withstand the light of God on it? (1 Corinthians 6:19). God formed His Son in me through sanctification, setting me apart from sin and making me holy in His sight (see Galatians 4:19). But I must begin to transform my natural life into spiritual life by obedience to Him. God instructs us even in the smallest details of life. And when He brings you conviction of sin, do not "confer with flesh and blood," but cleanse yourself from it at once (Galatians 1:16). Keep yourself cleansed in your daily walk.

I must cleanse myself from all filthiness in my flesh and my spirit until both are in harmony with the nature of God. Is the mind of my spirit in perfect agreement with the life of the Son of God in me, or am I mentally rebellious and defiant? Am I allowing the mind of Christ to be formed in me? (see Philippians 2:5). Christ never spoke of His right to Himself, but always maintained an inner vigilance to submit His spirit continually to His Father. I also have the responsibility to keep my spirit in agreement with His Spirit. And when I do, Jesus gradually lifts me up to the level where He lived—a level of perfect submission to His Father's will—where I pay no attention to anything else. Am I perfecting this kind of holiness in the fear of God? Is God having His way with me, and are people beginning to see God in my life more and more?

Be serious in your commitment to God and gladly leave everything else alone. Literally put God first in your life.

Abraham's Life of Faith

"He went out, not knowing where he was going."
Hebrews 11:8

In the Old Testament, a person's relationship with God was seen by the degree of separation in that person's life. This separation is exhibited in the life of Abraham by his separation from his country and his family. When we think of separation today, we do not mean to be literally separated from those family members who do not have a personal relationship with God, but to be separated mentally and morally from their viewpoints. This is what Jesus Christ was referring to in Luke 14:26.

Living a life of faith means never knowing where you are being led. But it does mean loving and knowing the One who is leading. It is literally a life of *faith*, not of understanding and reason—a life of knowing Him who calls us to go. Faith is rooted in the knowledge of a Person, and one of the biggest traps we fall into is the belief that if we have faith, God will surely lead us to success in the world.

The final stage in the life of faith is the attainment of character, and we encounter many changes in the process. We feel the presence of God around us when we pray, yet we are only momentarily changed. We tend to keep going back to our everyday ways and the glory vanishes. A life of faith is not a life of one glorious mountaintop experience after another, like soaring on eagles' wings, but is a life of day-in and day-out consistency; a life of walking without fainting (see Isaiah 40:31). It is not even a question of the holiness of sanctification, but of something which comes much farther down the road. It is a faith that has been tried and proved and has withstood the test. Abraham is not a type or an example of the holiness of sanctification, but a type of the life of faith—a faith, tested and true, built on the true God. *"Abraham believed God"* (Romans 4:3).

Friendship with God

"Shall I hide from Abraham what I am doing . . . ?" **Genesis 18:17**

The Delights of His Friendship. Genesis 18 brings out the delight of true friendship with God, as compared with simply feeling His presence occasionally in prayer. This friendship means being so intimately in touch with God that you never even need to ask Him to show you His will. It is evidence of a level of intimacy which confirms that you are nearing the final stage of your discipline in the life of faith. When you have a right-standing relationship with God, you have a life of freedom, liberty, and delight; you *are* God's will. And all of your commonsense decisions are actually His will for you, unless you sense a feeling of restraint brought on by a check in your spirit. You are free to make decisions in the light of a perfect and delightful friendship with God, knowing that if your decisions are wrong He will lovingly produce that sense of restraint. Once He does, you must stop immediately.

The Difficulties of His Friendship. Why did Abraham stop praying when he did? He stopped because he still was lacking the level of intimacy in his relationship with God, which would enable him boldly to continue on with the Lord in prayer until his desire was granted. Whenever we stop short of our true desire in prayer and say, "Well, I don't know, maybe this is not God's will," then we still have another level to go. It shows that we are not as intimately acquainted with God as Jesus was, and as Jesus would have us to be—"that they may be one just as We are one" (John 17:22). Think of the last thing you prayed about—were you devoted to your desire or to God? Was your determination to get some gift of the Spirit for yourself or to get to God? "For your Father knows the things you have need of before you ask Him" (Matthew 6:8). The reason for asking is so you may get to know God better. "Delight yourself also in the Lord, and He shall give you the desires of your heart" (Psalm 37:4). We should keep praying to get a perfect understanding of God Himself.

Identified or Simply Interested?

"I have been crucified with Christ." **Galatians 2:20**

The inescapable spiritual need each of us has is the need to sign the death certificate of our sin nature. I must take my emotional opinions and intellectual beliefs and be willing to turn them into a moral verdict against the nature of sin; that is, against any claim I have to my right to myself. Paul said, "I have been crucified with Christ." He did not say, "I have made a determination to imitate Jesus Christ," or, "I will really make an effort to follow Him"—but—"I have been *identified* with Him in His death." Once I reach this moral decision and act on it, all that Christ accomplished *for* me on the Cross is accomplished *in* me. My unrestrained commitment of myself to God gives the Holy Spirit the opportunity to grant to me the holiness of Jesus Christ.

". . . it is no longer I who live . . ." My individuality remains, but my primary motivation for living and the nature that rules me are radically changed. I have the same human body, but the old satanic right to myself has been destroyed.

". . . and the life which I now live in the flesh . . . ," not the life which I long to live or even pray that I live, but the life I now live in my mortal flesh—the life which others can see, "I live by faith in the Son of God." This faith was not Paul's own faith in Jesus Christ, but the faith the Son of God had given to him (see Ephesians 2:8). It is no longer a faith in faith, but a faith that transcends all imaginable limits—a faith that comes only from the Son of God.

The Burning Heart

"Did not our heart burn within us . . . ?" **Luke 24:32**

We need to learn this secret of the burning heart. Suddenly Jesus appears to us, fires are set ablaze, and we are given wonderful visions; but then we must learn to maintain the secret of the burning heart—a heart that can go through anything. It is the simple, dreary day, with its commonplace duties and people, that smothers the burning heart—unless we have learned the secret of abiding in Jesus.

Much of the distress we experience as Christians comes not as the result of sin, but because we are ignorant of the laws of our own nature. For instance, the only test we should use to determine whether or not to allow a particular emotion to run its course in our lives is to examine what the final outcome of that emotion will be. Think it through to its logical conclusion, and if the outcome is something that God would condemn, put a stop to it immediately. But if it is an emotion that has been kindled by the Spirit of God and you don't allow it to have its way in your life, it will cause a reaction on a lower level than God intended. That is the way unrealistic and overly emotional people are made. And the higher the emotion, the deeper the level of corruption, if it is not exercised on its intended level. If the Spirit of God has stirred you, make as many of your decisions as possible irrevocable, and let the consequences be what they will. We cannot stay forever on the "Mount of Transfiguration," basking in the light of our mountaintop experience (see Mark 9:1–9). But we must obey the light we received there; we must put it into action. When God gives us a vision, we must transact business with Him at that point, no matter what the cost.

We cannot kindle when we will
The fire which in the heart resides,
The spirit bloweth and is still,
In mystery our soul abides;
But tasks in hours of insight willed
Can be through hours of gloom fulfilled.

Am I Carnally Minded?

"Where there are envy, strife, and divisions among you, are you not carnal . . . ?" **1 Corinthians 3:3**

The natural man, or unbeliever, knows nothing about carnality. The desires of the flesh warring against the Spirit, and the Spirit warring against the flesh, which began at rebirth, are what produce carnality and the awareness of it. But Paul said, "Walk in the Spirit, and you shall not fulfill the lust of the flesh" (Galatians 5:16). In other words, carnality will disappear.

Are you quarrelsome and easily upset over small things? Do you think that no one who is a Christian is ever like that? Paul said they are, and he connected these attitudes with carnality. Is there a truth in the Bible that instantly awakens a spirit of malice or resentment in you? If so, that is proof that you are still carnal. If the process of sanctification is continuing in your life, there will be no trace of that kind of spirit remaining.

If the Spirit of God detects anything in you that is wrong, He doesn't ask you to make it right; He only asks you to accept the light of truth, and then He will make it right. A child of the light will confess sin instantly and stand completely open before God. But a child of the darkness will say, "Oh, I can explain that." When the light shines and the Spirit brings conviction of sin, be a child of the light. Confess your wrongdoing, and God will deal with it. If, however, you try to vindicate yourself, you prove yourself to be a child of the darkness.

What is the proof that carnality has gone? Never deceive yourself; when carnality is gone you will know it—it is the most real thing you can imagine. And God will see to it that you have a number of opportunities to prove to yourself the miracle of His grace. The proof is in a very practical test. You will find yourself saying, "If this had happened before, I would have had the spirit of resentment!" And you will never cease to be the most amazed person on earth at what God has done for you on the inside.

Decreasing for His Purpose

"He must increase, but I must decrease." **John 3:30**

If you become a necessity to someone else's life, you are out of God's will. As a servant, your primary responsibility is to be a "friend of the bridegroom" (John 3:29). When you see a person who is close to grasping the claims of Jesus Christ, you know that your influence has been used in the right direction. And when you begin to see that person in the middle of a difficult and painful struggle, don't try to prevent it, but pray that his difficulty will grow even ten times stronger, until no power on earth or in hell could hold him away from Jesus Christ. Over and over again, we try to be amateur providences in someone's life. We are indeed amateurs, coming in and actually preventing God's will and saying, "This person should not have to experience this difficulty." Instead of being friends of the Bridegroom, our sympathy gets in the way. One day that person will say to us, "You are a thief; you stole my desire to follow Jesus, and because of you I lost sight of Him."

Beware of rejoicing with someone over the wrong thing, but always look to rejoice over the right thing. "The friend of the bridegroom . . . rejoices greatly because of the bridegroom's voice. Therefore this joy of mine is fulfilled. He must increase, but I must decrease" (3:29–30). This was spoken with joy, not with sadness—at last they were to see the Bridegroom! And John said this was his joy. It represents a stepping aside, an absolute removal of the servant, never to be thought of again.

Listen intently with your entire being until you hear the Bridegroom's voice in the life of another person. And never give any thought to what devastation, difficulties, or sickness it will bring. Just rejoice with godly excitement that His voice has been heard. You may often have to watch Jesus Christ wreck a life before He saves it (see Matthew 10:34).

Maintaining the Proper Relationship

"*. . . the friend of the bridegroom . . .*" **John 3:29**

Goodness and purity should never be traits that draw attention to themselves, but should simply be magnets that draw people to Jesus Christ. If my holiness is not drawing others to Him, it is not the right kind of holiness; it is only an influence which awakens undue emotions and evil desires in people and diverts them from heading in the right direction. A person who is a beautiful saint can be a hindrance in leading people to the Lord by presenting only what Christ has done for him, instead of presenting Jesus Christ Himself. Others will be left with this thought—"What a fine person that man is!" That is not being a true "friend of the bridegroom"—*I* am increasing all the time; *He* is not.

To maintain this friendship and faithfulness to the Bridegroom, we have to be more careful to have the moral and vital relationship to Him above everything else, including obedience. Sometimes there is nothing to obey and our only task is to maintain a vital connection with Jesus Christ, seeing that nothing interferes with it. Only occasionally is it a matter of obedience. At those times when a crisis arises, we have to find out what God's will is. Yet most of our life is not spent in trying to be consciously obedient, but in maintaining this relationship—being the "friend of the bridegroom." Christian work can actually be a means of diverting a person's focus away from Jesus Christ. Instead of being friends "of the bridegroom," we may become amateur providences of God to someone else, working against Him while we use His weapons.

Spiritual Vision Through Personal Purity

"Blessed are the pure in heart, for they shall see God." **Matthew 5:8**

Purity is not innocence—it is much more than that. Purity is the result of continued spiritual harmony with God. We have to grow in purity. Our life with God may be right and our inner purity unblemished, yet occasionally our outer life may become spotted and stained. God intentionally does not protect us from this possibility, because this is the way we recognize the necessity of maintaining our spiritual vision through personal purity. If the outer level of our spiritual life with God is impaired to the slightest degree, we must put everything else aside until we make it right. Remember that spiritual vision depends on our character—it is *"the pure in heart"* who "see God."

God makes us pure by an act of His sovereign grace, but we still have something that we must carefully watch. It is through our bodily life coming in contact with other people and other points of view that we tend to become tarnished. Not only must our "inner sanctuary" be kept right with God, but also the "outer courts" must be brought into perfect harmony with the purity God gives us through His grace. Our spiritual vision and understanding is immediately blurred when our "outer court" is stained. If we want to maintain personal intimacy with the Lord Jesus Christ, it will mean refusing to do or even think certain things. And some things that are acceptable for others will become unacceptable for us.

A practical help in keeping your personal purity unblemished in your relations with other people is to begin to see them as God does. Say to yourself, "That man or that woman is *perfect in Christ Jesus!* That friend or that relative is *perfect in Christ Jesus!*"

MARCH 27

Spiritual Vision Through Personal Character

"Come up here, and I will show you things which must take place." **Revelation 4:1**

A higher state of mind and spiritual vision can only be achieved through the higher practice of personal character. If you live up to the highest and best that you know in the outer level of your life, God will continually say to you, "Friend, come up even higher." There is also a continuing rule in temptation which calls you to go higher; but when you do, you only encounter other temptations and character traits. Both God and Satan use the strategy of elevation, but Satan uses it in temptation, and the effect is quite different. When the devil elevates you to a certain place, he causes you to fasten your idea of what holiness is far beyond what flesh and blood could ever bear or achieve. Your life becomes a spiritual acrobatic performance high atop a steeple. You cling to it, trying to maintain your balance and daring not to move. But when God elevates you by His grace into heavenly places, you find a vast plateau where you can move about with ease.

Compare this week in your spiritual life with the same week last year to see how God has called you to a higher level. We have all been brought to see from a higher viewpoint. Never allow God to show you a truth which you do not instantly begin to live up to, applying it to your life. Always work through it, staying in its light.

Your growth in grace is not measured by the fact that you haven't turned back, but that you have an insight and understanding into where you are spiritually. Have you heard God say, "Come up higher," not audibly on the outer level, but to the innermost part of your character?

"Shall I hide from Abraham what I am doing . . . ?" (Genesis 18:17). God has to hide from us what He does, until, due to the growth of our personal character, we get to the level where He is then able to reveal it.

Isn't There Some Misunderstanding?

"Let us go to Judea again.' The disciples said to Him, '. . . are You going there again?'" **John 11:7–8**

Just because I don't understand what Jesus Christ says, I have no right to determine that He must be mistaken in what He says. That is a dangerous view, and it is never right to think that my obedience to God's directive will bring dishonor to Jesus. The only thing that will bring dishonor is not obeying Him. To put my view of His honor ahead of what He is plainly guiding me to do is never right, even though it may come from a real desire to prevent Him from being put to an open shame. I know when the instructions have come from God because of their quiet persistence. But when I begin to weigh the *pros* and *cons*, and doubt and debate enter into my mind, I am bringing in an element that is not of God. This will only result in my concluding that His instructions to me were not right. Many of us are faithful to our ideas about Jesus Christ, but how many of us are faithful to Jesus Himself? Faithfulness to Jesus means that I must step out even when and where I can't see anything (see Matthew 14:29). But faithfulness to my own ideas means that I first clear the way mentally. Faith, however, is not intellectual understanding; faith is a deliberate commitment to the Person of Jesus Christ, even when I can't see the way ahead.

Are you debating whether you should take a step of faith in Jesus, or whether you should wait until you can clearly see how to do what He has asked? Simply obey Him with unrestrained joy. When He tells you something and you begin to debate, it is because you have a misunderstanding of what honors Him and what doesn't. Are you faithful to Jesus, or faithful to your ideas about Him? Are you faithful to what He says, or are you trying to compromise His words with thoughts that never came from Him? "Whatever He says to you, *do it*" (John 2:5).

Our Lord's Surprise Visits

"You also be ready." **Luke 12:40**

A Christian worker's greatest need is a readiness to face Jesus Christ at any and every turn. This is not easy, no matter what our experience has been. This battle is not against sin, difficulties, or circumstances, but against being so absorbed in our service to Jesus Christ that we are not ready to face Jesus Himself at every turn. The greatest need is not facing our beliefs or doctrines, or even facing the question of whether or not we are of any use to Him, but the need is to face *Him*.

Jesus rarely comes where we expect Him; He appears where we least expect Him, and always in the most illogical situations. The only way a servant can remain true to God is to be ready for the Lord's surprise visits. This readiness will not be brought about by service, but through intense spiritual reality, expecting Jesus Christ at every turn. This sense of expectation will give our life the attitude of childlike wonder He wants it to have. If we are going to be ready for Jesus Christ, we have to stop being religious. In other words, we must stop using religion as if it were some kind of a lofty lifestyle—we must be spiritually real.

If you are avoiding the call of the religious thinking of today's world, and instead are "looking unto Jesus" (Hebrews 12:2), setting your heart on what He wants, and thinking His thoughts, you will be considered impractical and a daydreamer. But when He suddenly appears in the work of the heat of the day, you will be the only one who is ready. You should trust no one, and even ignore the finest saint on earth if he blocks your sight of Jesus Christ.

Holiness or Hardness Toward God?

"He . . . wondered that there was no intercessor." **Isaiah 59:16**

The reason many of us stop praying and become hard toward God is that we only have an emotional interest in prayer. It sounds good to say that we pray, and we read books on prayer which tell us that prayer is beneficial—that our minds are quieted and our souls are uplifted when we pray. But Isaiah implied in this verse that God is amazed at such thoughts about prayer.

Worship and intercession must go together; one is impossible without the other. Intercession means raising ourselves up to the point of getting the mind of Christ regarding the person for whom we are praying (see Philippians 2:5). Instead of worshiping God, we recite speeches to God about how prayer is supposed to work. Are we worshiping God or disputing Him when we say, "But God, I just don't see how You are going to do this"? This is a sure sign that we are not worshiping. When we lose sight of God, we become hard and dogmatic. We throw our petitions at His throne and dictate to Him what we want Him to do. We don't worship God, nor do we seek to conform our minds to the mind of Christ. And if we are hard toward God, we will become hard toward other people.

Are we worshiping God in a way that will raise us up to where we can take hold of Him, having such intimate contact with Him that we know His mind about the ones for whom we pray? Are we living in a holy relationship with God, or have we become hard and dogmatic?

Do you find yourself thinking that there is no one interceding properly? Then be that person yourself. Be a person who worships God and lives in a holy relationship with Him. Get involved in the real work of intercession, remembering that it truly is work—work that demands all your energy, but work which has no hidden pitfalls. Preaching the gospel has its share of pitfalls, but intercessory prayer has none whatsoever.

Heedfulness or Hypocrisy in Ourselves?

"If anyone sees his brother sinning a sin which does not lead to death, he will ask, and He will give him life for those who commit sin not leading to death." **1 John 5:16**

If we are not heedful and pay no attention to the way the Spirit of God works in us, we will become spiritual hypocrites. We see where other people are failing, and then we take our discernment and turn it into comments of ridicule and criticism, instead of turning it into intercession on their behalf. God reveals this truth about others to us not through the sharpness of our minds but through the direct penetration of His Spirit. If we are not attentive, we will be completely unaware of the source of the discernment God has given us, becoming critical of others and forgetting that God says, "he will ask, and He will give him life for those who commit sin not leading to death." Be careful that you don't become a hypocrite by spending all your time trying to get others right with God before you worship Him yourself.

One of the most subtle and illusive burdens God ever places on us as saints is this burden of discernment concerning others. He gives us discernment so that we may accept the responsibility for those souls before Him and form the mind of Christ about them (see Philippians 2:5). We should intercede in accordance with what God says He will give us, namely, "life for those who commit sin not leading to death." It is not that we are able to bring God into contact with our minds, but that we awaken ourselves to the point where God is able to convey His mind to us regarding the people for whom we intercede.

Can Jesus Christ see the agony of His soul in us? He can't unless we are so closely identified with Him that we have His view concerning the people for whom we pray. May we learn to intercede so wholeheartedly that Jesus Christ will be completely and overwhelmingly satisfied with us as intercessors.

Helpful or Heartless Toward Others?

"It is Christ . . . who also makes intercession for us. . . . the Spirit . . . makes intercession for the saints." **Romans 8:34, 27**

Do we need any more arguments than these to become intercessors—that Christ "always lives to make intercession" (Hebrews 7:25), and that the Holy Spirit "makes intercession for the saints"? Are we living in such a relationship with others that we do the work of intercession as a result of being the children of God who are taught by His Spirit? We should take a look at our current circumstances. Do crises which affect us or others in our home, business, country, or elsewhere, seem to be crushing in on us? Are we being pushed out of the presence of God and left with no time for worship? If so, we must put a stop to such distractions and get into such a living relationship with God that our relationship with others is maintained through the work of intercession, where God works His miracles.

Beware of getting ahead of God by your very desire to do His will. We run ahead of Him in a thousand and one activities, becoming so burdened with people and problems that we don't worship God, and we fail to intercede. If a burden and its resulting pressure come upon us while we are not in an attitude of worship, it will only produce a hardness toward God and despair in our own souls. God continually introduces us to people in whom we have no interest, and unless we are worshiping God the natural tendency is to be heartless toward them. We give them a quick verse of Scripture, like jabbing them with a spear, or leave them with a hurried, uncaring word of counsel before we go. A heartless Christian must be a terrible grief to our Lord.

Are our lives in the proper place so that we may participate in the intercession of our Lord and the Holy Spirit?

APRIL 2

The Glory That's Unsurpassed

"The Lord Jesus . . . has sent me that you may receive your sight." **Acts 9:17**

When Paul received his sight, he also received spiritual insight into the Person of Jesus Christ. His entire life and preaching from that point on were totally consumed with nothing but Jesus Christ—"For I determined not to know anything among you except Jesus Christ and Him crucified" (1 Corinthians 2:2). Paul never again allowed anything to attract and hold the attention of his mind and soul except the face of Jesus Christ.

We must learn to maintain a strong degree of character in our lives, even to the level that has been revealed in our vision of Jesus Christ.

The lasting characteristic of a spiritual man is the ability to understand correctly the meaning of the Lord Jesus Christ in his life, and the ability to explain the purposes of God to others. The overruling passion of his life is Jesus Christ. Whenever you see this quality in a person, you get the feeling that he is truly a man after God's own heart (see Acts 13:22).

Never allow anything to divert you from your insight into Jesus Christ. It is the true test of whether you are spiritual or not. To be unspiritual means that other things have a growing fascination for you.

Since mine eyes have looked on Jesus,
I've lost sight of all beside,
So enchained my spirit's vision,
Gazing on the Crucified.

"If You Had Known!"

"If you had known . . . in this your day, the things that make for your peace! But now they are hidden from your eyes." **Luke 19:42**

Jesus entered Jerusalem triumphantly and the city was stirred to its very foundations, but a strange god was there—the pride of the Pharisees. It was a god that seemed religious and upright, but Jesus compared it to "whitewashed tombs which indeed appear beautiful outwardly, but inside are full of dead men's bones and all uncleanness" (Matthew 23:27).

What is it that blinds you to the peace of God "in this *your* day"? Do you have a strange god—not a disgusting monster but perhaps an unholy nature that controls your life? More than once God has brought me face-to-face with a strange god in my life, and I knew that I should have given it up, but I didn't do it. I got through the crisis "by the skin of my teeth," only to find myself still under the control of that strange god. I am blind to the very things that make for my own peace. It is a shocking thing that we can be in the exact place where the Spirit of God should be having His completely unhindered way with us, and yet we only make matters worse, increasing our blame in God's eyes.

"If you had known . . ." God's words here cut directly to the heart, with the tears of Jesus behind them. These words imply responsibility for our own faults. God holds us accountable for what we refuse to see or are unable to see because of our sin. And "now they are hidden from your eyes" because you have never completely yielded your nature to Him. Oh, the deep, unending sadness for what might have been! God never again opens the doors that have been closed. He opens other doors, but He reminds us that there are doors which we have shut—doors which had no need to be shut. Never be afraid when God brings back your past. Let your memory have its way with you. It is a minister of God bringing its rebuke and sorrow to you. God will turn what might have been into a wonderful lesson of growth for the future.

The Way to Permanent Faith

"Indeed the hour is coming . . . that you will be scattered." **John 16:32**

Jesus was not rebuking the disciples in this passage. Their faith was real, but it was disordered and unfocused, and was not at work in the important realities of life. The disciples were scattered to their own concerns and they had interests apart from Jesus Christ. After we have the perfect relationship with God, through the sanctifying work of the Holy Spirit, our faith must be exercised in the realities of everyday life. We will be scattered, not into service but into the emptiness of our lives where we will see ruin and barrenness, to know what internal death to God's blessings means. Are we prepared for this? It is certainly not of our own choosing, but God engineers our circumstances to take us there. Until we have been through that experience, our faith is sustained only by feelings and by blessings. But once we get there, no matter where God may place us or what inner emptiness we experience, we can praise God that all is well. That is what is meant by faith being exercised in the realities of life.

"You . . . will leave Me alone." Have we been scattered and have we left Jesus alone by not seeing His providential care for us? Do we not see God at work in our circumstances? Dark times are allowed and come to us through the sovereignty of God. Are we prepared to let God do what He wants with us? Are we prepared to be separated from the outward, evident blessings of God? Until Jesus Christ is truly our Lord, we each have goals of our own which we serve. Our faith is real, but it is not yet permanent. And God is never in a hurry. If we are willing to wait, we will see God pointing out that we have been interested only in His blessings, instead of in God Himself. The sense of God's blessings is fundamental.

"Be of good cheer, I have overcome the world" (John 16:33). Unyielding spiritual fortitude is what we need.

APRIL 5

His Agony and Our Access

"Jesus came with them to a place called Gethsemane, and said to the disciples . . . . 'Stay here and watch with Me.'" **Matthew 26:36, 38**

We can never fully comprehend Christ's agony in the Garden of Gethsemane, but at least we don't have to misunderstand it. It is the agony of God and man in one Person, coming face-to-face with sin. We cannot learn about Gethsemane through personal experience. Gethsemane and Calvary represent something totally unique—they are the gateway into life for us.

It was not death on the cross that Jesus agonized over in Gethsemane. In fact, He stated very emphatically that He came with the purpose of dying. His concern here was that He might not get through this struggle as the Son of Man. He was confident of getting through it as the Son of God—Satan could not touch Him there. But Satan's assault was that our Lord would come through for us on His own solely as the Son of Man. If Jesus had done that, He could not have been our Savior (see Hebrews 9:11–15). Read the record of His agony in Gethsemane in light of His earlier wilderness temptation—"the devil . . . departed from Him until an opportune time" (Luke 4:13). In Gethsemane, Satan came back and was overthrown again. Satan's final assault against our Lord as the *Son of Man* was in Gethsemane.

The agony in Gethsemane was the agony of the Son of God in fulfilling His destiny as the Savior of the world. The veil is pulled back here to reveal all that it cost Him to make it possible for us to become sons of God. His agony was the basis for the simplicity of our salvation. The Cross of Christ was a triumph for the *Son of Man.* It was not only a sign that our Lord had triumphed, but that He had triumphed to save the human race. Because of what the Son of Man went through, every human being has been provided with a way of access into the very presence of God.

The Collision of God and Sin

"... who Himself bore our sins in His own body on the tree." **1 Peter 2:24**

The Cross of Christ is the revealed truth of God's judgment on sin. Never associate the idea of martyrdom with the Cross of Christ. It was the supreme triumph, and it shook the very foundations of hell. There is nothing in time or eternity more absolutely certain and irrefutable than what Jesus Christ accomplished on the Cross—He made it possible for the entire human race to be brought back into a right-standing relationship with God. He made redemption the foundation of human life; that is, He made a way for every person to have fellowship with God.

The Cross was not something that *happened* to Jesus—He came to die; the Cross was His purpose in coming. He is "the Lamb slain from the foundation of the world" (Revelation 13:8). The incarnation of Christ would have no meaning without the Cross. Beware of separating "*God was manifested in the flesh*" from "*He made Him . . . to be sin for us*" (1 Timothy 3:16; 2 Corinthians 5:21). The purpose of the incarnation was redemption. God came in the flesh to take sin away, not to accomplish something for Himself. The Cross is the central event in time and eternity, and the answer to all the problems of both.

The Cross is not the cross of a man, but the Cross of God, and it can never be fully comprehended through human experience. The Cross is God exhibiting His nature. It is the gate through which any and every individual can enter into oneness with God. But it is not a gate we pass right through; it is one where we abide in the life that is found there.

The heart of salvation is the Cross of Christ. The reason salvation is so easy to obtain is that it cost God so much. The Cross was the place where God and sinful man merged with a tremendous collision and where the way to life was opened. But all the cost and pain of the collision was absorbed by the heart of God.

Why We Lack Understanding

"He commanded them that they should tell no one the things they had seen, till the Son of Man had risen from the dead." **Mark 9:9**

As the disciples were commanded, you should also say nothing until the Son of Man has risen in you—until the life of the risen Christ so dominates you that you truly understand what He taught while here on earth. When you grow and develop the right condition inwardly, the words Jesus spoke become so clear that you are amazed you did not grasp them before. In fact, you were not able to understand them before because you had not yet developed the proper spiritual condition to deal with them.

Our Lord doesn't hide these things from us, but we are not prepared to receive them until we are in the right condition in our spiritual life. Jesus said, "I still have many things to say to you, but you cannot bear them now" (John 16:12). We must have a oneness with His risen life before we are prepared to bear any particular truth from Him. Do we really know anything about the indwelling of the risen life of Jesus? The evidence that we do is that His Word is becoming understandable to us. God cannot reveal anything to us if we don't have His Spirit. And our own unyielding and headstrong opinions will effectively prevent God from revealing anything to us. But our insensible thinking will end immediately once His resurrection life has its way with us.

"Tell no one." But so many people do tell what they saw on the Mount of Transfiguration—their mountaintop experience. They have seen a vision and they testify to it, but there is no connection between what they say and how they live. Their lives don't add up because the Son of Man has not yet risen in them. How long will it be before His resurrection life is formed and evident in you and in me?

His Resurrection Destiny

"Ought not the Christ to have suffered these things and to enter into His glory?" **Luke 24:26**

Our Lord's Cross is the gateway into His life. His resurrection means that He has the power to convey His life to me. When I was born again, I received the very life of the risen Lord from Jesus Himself.

Christ's resurrection destiny—His foreordained purpose—was to bring "many sons to glory" (Hebrews 2:10). The fulfilling of His destiny gives Him the right to make us sons and daughters of God. We never have exactly the same relationship to God that the Son of God has, but we are brought by the Son into the relation of sonship. When our Lord rose from the dead, He rose to an absolutely new life—a life He had never lived before He was God Incarnate. He rose to a life that had never been before. And what His resurrection means for us is that we are raised to His risen life, not to our old life. One day we will have a body like His glorious body, but we can know here and now the power and effectiveness of His resurrection and can "walk in newness of life" (Romans 6:4). Paul's determined purpose was to "know Him *and the power of His resurrection*" (Philippians 3:10).

Jesus prayed, ". . . as You have given Him authority over all flesh that He should give eternal life to as many as You have given Him" (John 17:2). The term *Holy Spirit* is actually another name for the experience of eternal life working in human beings here and now. The Holy Spirit is the deity of God who continues to apply the power of the atonement by the Cross of Christ to our lives. Thank God for the glorious and majestic truth that His Spirit can work the very nature of Jesus into us, if we will only obey Him.

Have You Seen Jesus?

"After that, He appeared in another form to two of them." **Mark 16:12**

Being saved and seeing Jesus are not the same thing. Many people who have never seen Jesus have received and share in God's grace. But once you have seen Him, you can never be the same. Other things will not have the appeal they did before.

You should always recognize the difference between what you see Jesus to be and what He has done for you. If you see only what He has done for you, your God is not big enough. But if you have had a vision, seeing Jesus as He really is, experiences can come and go, yet you will endure "as seeing Him who is invisible" (Hebrews 11:27). The man who was blind from birth did not know who Jesus was until Christ appeared and revealed Himself to him (see John 9). Jesus appears to those for whom He has done something, but we cannot order or predict when He will come. He may appear suddenly, at any turn. Then you can exclaim, "Now I see Him!" (see John 9:25).

Jesus must appear to you and to your friend individually; no one can see Jesus with your eyes. And division takes place when one has seen Him and the other has not. You cannot bring your friend to the point of seeing; God must do it. Have you seen Jesus? If so, you will want others to see Him too. "And they went and told it to the rest, but they did not believe them either" (Mark 16:13). When you see Him, you must tell, even if they don't believe.

O could I tell, you surely would believe it!
O could I only say what I have seen!
How should I tell or how can you receive it,
How, till He bringeth you where I have been?

Complete and Effective Decision About Sin

"Our old man was crucified with Him, that the body of sin might be done away with, that we should no longer be slaves of sin." **Romans 6:6**

Co-Crucifixion. Have you made the following decision about sin—that it must be completely killed in you? It takes a long time to come to the point of making this complete and effective decision about sin. It is, however, the greatest moment in your life once you decide that sin must die in you—not simply be restrained, suppressed, or counteracted, but crucified—just as Jesus Christ died for the sin of the world. No one can bring anyone else to this decision. We may be mentally and spiritually convinced, but what we need to do is actually make the decision that Paul urged us to do in this passage.

Pull yourself up, take some time alone with God, and make this important decision, saying, "Lord, identify me with Your death until I know that sin is dead in me." Make the moral decision that sin in you must be put to death.

This was not some divine future expectation on the part of Paul, but was a very radical and definite experience in his life. Are you prepared to let the Spirit of God search you until you know what the level and nature of sin is in your life—to see the very things that struggle against God's Spirit in you? If so, will you then agree with God's verdict on the nature of sin—that it should be identified with the death of Jesus? You cannot "reckon yourselves to be dead indeed to sin" (Romans 6:11) unless you have radically dealt with the issue of your will before God.

Have you entered into the glorious privilege of being crucified with Christ, until all that remains in your flesh and blood is His life? "I have been crucified with Christ; it is no longer I who live, but Christ lives in me" (Galatians 2:20).

APRIL 11

Complete and Effective Divinity

"If we have been united together in the likeness of His death, certainly we also shall be in the likeness of His resurrection." **Romans 6:5**

Co-Resurrection. The proof that I have experienced crucifixion with Jesus is that I have a definite likeness to Him. The Spirit of Jesus entering me rearranges my personal life before God. The resurrection of Jesus has given Him the authority to give the life of God to me, and the experiences of my life must now be built on the foundation of His life. I can have the resurrection life of Jesus here and now, and it will exhibit itself through holiness.

The idea all through the apostle Paul's writings is that after the decision to be identified with Jesus in His death has been made, the resurrection life of Jesus penetrates every bit of my human nature. It takes the omnipotence of God—His complete and effective divinity—to live the life of the Son of God in human flesh. The Holy Spirit cannot be accepted as a guest in merely one room of the house—He invades all of it. And once I decide that my "old man" (that is, my heredity of sin) should be identified with the death of Jesus, the Holy Spirit invades me. He takes charge of everything. My part is to walk in the light and to obey all that He reveals to me. Once I have made that important decision about sin, it is easy to "reckon" that I am actually "dead indeed to sin," because I find the life of Jesus in me all the time (Romans 6:11). Just as there is only one kind of humanity, there is only one kind of holiness—the holiness of Jesus. And it is His holiness that has been given to me. God puts the holiness of His Son into me, and I belong to a new spiritual order.

Complete and Effective Dominion

"Death no longer has dominion over Him. . . . the life that He lives, He lives to God. Likewise you also, reckon yourselves to be dead indeed to sin, but alive to God." **Romans 6:9–11**

Co-Eternal Life. Eternal life is the life which Jesus Christ exhibited on the human level. And it is this same life, not simply a copy of it, which is made evident in our mortal flesh when we are born again. Eternal life is not a gift from God; eternal life is the gift *of God*. The energy and the power which was so very evident in Jesus will be exhibited in us by an act of the absolute sovereign grace of God, once we have made that complete and effective decision about sin.

"You shall receive power when the Holy Spirit has come upon you" (Acts 1:8)—not power as a gift from the Holy Spirit; the power *is* the Holy Spirit, not something that He gives us. The life that was in Jesus becomes ours because of His Cross, once we make the decision to be identified with Him. If it is difficult to get right with God, it is because we refuse to make this moral decision about sin. But once we do decide, the full life of God comes in immediately. Jesus came to give us an endless supply of life—"that you may be filled with all the fullness of God" (Ephesians 3:19). Eternal life has nothing to do with time. It is the life which Jesus lived when He was down here, and the only Source of life is the Lord Jesus Christ.

Even the weakest saint can experience the power of the deity of the Son of God, when he is willing to "let go." But any effort to "hang on" to the least bit of our own power will only diminish the life of Jesus in us. We have to keep letting go, and slowly, but surely, the great full life of God will invade us, penetrating every part. Then Jesus will have complete and effective dominion in us, and people will take notice that we have been with Him.

What to Do When Your Burden Is Overwhelming

"Cast your burden on the Lord." **Psalm 55:22**

We must recognize the difference between burdens that are right for us to bear and burdens that are wrong. We should never bear the burdens of sin or doubt, but there are some burdens placed on us by God which He does not intend to lift off. God wants us to roll them back on Him—to literally "cast your burden," which He has given you, "on the Lord." If we set out to serve God and do His work but get out of touch with Him, the sense of responsibility we feel will be overwhelming and defeating. But if we will only roll back on God the burdens He has placed on us, He will take away that immense feeling of responsibility, replacing it with an awareness and understanding of Himself and His presence.

Many servants set out to serve God with great courage and with the right motives. But with no intimate fellowship with Jesus Christ, they are soon defeated. They do not know what to do with their burden, and it produces weariness in their lives. Others will see this and say, "What a sad end to something that had such a great beginning!"

"Cast your burden on the Lord." You have been bearing it all, but you need to deliberately place one end on God's shoulder. ". . . the government will be upon His shoulder" (Isaiah 9:6). Commit to God whatever burden He has placed on you. Don't just cast it aside, but put it over onto Him and place yourself there with it. You will see that your burden is then lightened by the sense of companionship. But you should never try to separate yourself from your burden.

APRIL 14

Inner Invincibility

"Take My yoke upon you and learn from Me."
Matthew 11:29

"Whom the Lord loves He chastens" (Hebrews 12:6). How petty our complaining is! Our Lord begins to bring us to the point where we can have fellowship with Him, only to hear us moan and groan, saying, "Oh Lord, just let me be like other people!" Jesus is asking us to get beside Him and take one end of the yoke, so that we can pull together. That's why Jesus says to us, "My yoke is easy and My burden is light" (Matthew 11:30). Are you closely identified with the Lord Jesus like that? If so, you will thank God when you feel the pressure of His hand upon you.

"To those who have no might He increases strength" (Isaiah 40:29). God comes and takes us out of our emotionalism, and then our complaining turns into a hymn of praise. The only way to know the strength of God is to take the yoke of Jesus upon us and to learn from Him.

"The joy of the Lord is your strength" (Nehemiah 8:10). Where do the saints get their joy? If we did not know some Christians well, we might think from just observing them that they have no burdens at all to bear. But we must lift the veil from our eyes. The fact that the peace, light, and joy of God is in them is proof that a burden is there as well. The burden that God places on us squeezes the grapes in our lives and produces the wine, but most of us see only the wine and not the burden. No power on earth or in hell can conquer the Spirit of God living within the human spirit; it creates an inner invincibility.

If your life is producing only a whine, instead of the wine, then ruthlessly kick it out. It is definitely a crime for a Christian to be weak in God's strength.

The Failure to Pay Close Attention

"The high places were not removed from Israel. Nevertheless the heart of Asa was loyal all his days." **2 Chronicles 15:17**

Asa was not completely obedient in the outward, visible areas of his life. He was obedient in what he considered the most important areas, but he was not entirely right. Beware of ever thinking, "Oh, that thing in my life doesn't matter much." The fact that it doesn't matter much to you may mean that it matters a great deal to God. Nothing should be considered a trivial matter by a child of God. How much longer are we going to prevent God from teaching us even one thing? But He keeps trying to teach us and He never loses patience. You say, "I know I am right with God"—yet the "high places" still remain in your life. There is still an area of disobedience. Do you protest that your heart is right with God, and yet there is something in your life He causes you to doubt? Whenever God causes a doubt about something, stop it immediately, no matter what it may be. Nothing in our lives is a mere insignificant detail to God.

Are there some things regarding your physical or intellectual life to which you have been paying no attention at all? If so, you may think you are all correct in the important areas, but you are careless—you are failing to concentrate or to focus properly. You no more need a day off from spiritual concentration on matters in your life than your heart needs a day off from beating. As you cannot take a day off morally and remain moral, neither can you take a day off spiritually and remain spiritual. God wants you to be entirely His, and it requires paying close attention to keep yourself fit. It also takes a tremendous amount of time. Yet some of us expect to rise above all of our problems, going from one mountaintop experience to another, with only a few minutes' effort.

Can You Come Down from the Mountain?

"While you have the light, believe in the light." **John 12:36**

We all have moments when we feel better than ever before, and we say, "I feel fit for anything; if only I could always be like this!" We are not meant to be. Those moments are moments of insight which we have to live up to even when we do not feel like it. Many of us are no good for the everyday world when we are not on the mountaintop. Yet we must bring our everyday life up to the standard revealed to us on the mountaintop when we were there.

Never allow a feeling that was awakened in you on the mountaintop to evaporate. Don't place yourself on the shelf by thinking, "How great to be in such a wonderful state of mind!" Act immediately—do something, even if your only reason to act is that you would rather not. If, during a prayer meeting, God shows you something to do, don't say, "I'll do it"—just *do it*! Pick yourself up by the back of the neck and shake off your fleshly laziness. Laziness can always be seen in our cravings for a mountaintop experience; all we talk about is our planning for our time on the mountain. We must learn to live in the ordinary "gray" day according to what we saw on the mountain.

Don't give up because you have been blocked and confused once—go after it again. Burn your bridges behind you, and stand committed to God by an act of your own will. Never change your decisions, but be sure to make your decisions in the light of what you saw and learned on the mountain.

All or Nothing?

"When Simon Peter heard that it was the Lord, he put on his outer garment . . . and plunged into the sea." **John 21:7**

Have you ever had a crisis in your life in which you deliberately, earnestly, and recklessly abandoned everything? It is a crisis of the will. You may come to that point many times externally, but it will amount to nothing. The true deep crisis of abandonment, or total surrender, is reached internally, not externally. The giving up of only external things may actually be an indication of your being in total bondage.

Have you deliberately committed your will to Jesus Christ? It is a transaction of the will, not of emotion; any positive emotion that results is simply a superficial blessing arising out of the transaction. If you focus your attention on the emotion, you will never make the transaction. Do not ask God what the transaction is to be, but make the determination to surrender your will regarding whatever you see, whether it is in the shallow or the deep, profound places internally.

If you have heard Jesus Christ's voice on the waves of the sea, you can let your convictions and your consistency take care of themselves by concentrating on maintaining your intimate relationship to Him.

APRIL 18

Readiness

"God called to him . . . . And he said, 'Here I am.'"

Exodus 3:4

When God speaks, many of us are like people in a fog, and we give no answer. Moses' reply to God revealed that he knew where he was and that he was ready. Readiness means having a right relationship to God and having the knowledge of where we are. We are so busy telling God where we would like to go. Yet the man or woman who is ready for God and His work is the one who receives the prize when the summons comes. We wait with the idea that some great opportunity or something sensational will be coming our way, and when it does come we are quick to cry out, "Here I am." Whenever we sense that Jesus Christ is rising up to take authority over some great task, we are there, but we are not ready for some obscure duty.

Readiness for God means that we are prepared to do the smallest thing or the largest thing—it makes no difference. It means we have no choice in what we want to do, but that whatever God's plans may be, we are there and ready. Whenever any duty presents itself, we hear God's voice as our Lord heard His Father's voice, and we are ready for it with the total readiness of our love for Him. Jesus Christ expects to do with us just as His Father did with Him. He can put us wherever He wants, in pleasant duties or in menial ones, because our union with Him is the same as His union with the Father. ". . . that they may be one just as We are one" (John 17:22).

Be ready for the sudden surprise visits of God. A ready person never needs to *get* ready—he *is* ready. Think of the time we waste trying to get ready once God has called! The burning bush is a symbol of everything that surrounds the person who is ready, and it is on fire with the presence of God Himself.

Beware of the Least Likely Temptation

"Joab had defected to Adonijah, though he had not defected to Absalom." **1 Kings 2:28**

Joab withstood the greatest test of his life, remaining absolutely loyal to David by not turning to follow after the fascinating and ambitious Absalom. Yet toward the end of his life he turned to follow after the weak and cowardly Adonijah. Always remain alert to the fact that where one person has turned back is exactly where anyone may be tempted to turn back (see 1 Corinthians 10:11–13). You may have just victoriously gone through a great crisis, but now be alert about the things that may appear to be the least likely to tempt you. Beware of thinking that the areas of your life where you have experienced victory in the past are now the least likely to cause you to stumble and fall.

We are apt to say, "It is not at all likely that having been through the greatest crisis of my life I would now turn back to the things of the world." Do not try to predict where the temptation will come; it is the least likely thing that is the real danger. It is in the aftermath of a great spiritual event that the least likely things begin to have an effect. They may not be forceful and dominant, but they are there. And if you are not careful to be forewarned, they will trip you. You have remained true to God under great and intense trials—now beware of the undercurrent. Do not be abnormally examining your inner self, looking forward with dread, but stay alert; keep your memory sharp before God. Unguarded strength is actually a double weakness, because that is where the least likely temptations will be effective in sapping strength. The Bible characters stumbled over their strong points, never their weak ones.

"Kept by the power of God"—that is the only safety (1 Peter 1:5).

Can a Saint Falsely Accuse God?

"All the promises of God in Him are Yes, and in Him Amen." **2 Corinthians 1:20**

Jesus' parable of the talents recorded in Matthew 25:14–30 was a warning that it is possible for us to misjudge our capacities. This parable has nothing to do with natural gifts and abilities, but relates to the gift of the Holy Spirit as He was first given at Pentecost. We must never measure our spiritual capacity on the basis of our education or our intellect; our capacity in spiritual things is measured on the basis of the promises of God. If we get less than God wants us to have, we will falsely accuse Him as the servant falsely accused his master when he said, "You expect more of me than you gave me the power to do. You demand too much of me, and I cannot stand true to you here where you have placed me." When it is a question of God's Almighty Spirit, never say, "I can't." Never allow the limitation of your own natural ability to enter into the matter. If we have received the Holy Spirit, God expects the work of the Holy Spirit to be exhibited in us.

The servant justified himself, while condemning his lord on every point, as if to say, "Your demand on me is way out of proportion to what you gave to me." Have we been falsely accusing God by daring to worry after He has said, "But seek first the kingdom of God and His righteousness, and all these things shall be added to you"? (Matthew 6:33). Worrying means exactly what this servant implied—"I know your intent is to leave me unprotected and vulnerable." A person who is lazy in the natural realm is always critical, saying, "I haven't had a decent chance," and someone who is lazy in the spiritual realm is critical of God. Lazy people always strike out at others in an independent way.

Never forget that our capacity and capability in spiritual matters is measured by, and based on, the promises of God. Is God able to fulfill His promises? Our answer depends on whether or not we have received the Holy Spirit.

APRIL 21

Don't Hurt the Lord

"Have I been with you so long, and yet you have not known Me, Philip?" **John 14:9**

Our Lord must be repeatedly astounded at us—astounded at how "un-simple" we are. It is our own opinions that make us dense and slow to understand, but when we are simple we are never dense; we have discernment all the time. Philip expected the future revelation of a tremendous mystery, but not in Jesus, the Person he thought he already knew. The mystery of God is not in what is going to be—it is now, though we look for it to be revealed in the future in some overwhelming, momentous event. We have no reluctance to obey Jesus, but it is highly probable that we are hurting Him by what we ask—"Lord, show us the Father" (John 14:8). His response immediately comes back to us as He says, "Can't you see Him? He is always right here or He is nowhere to be found." We look for God to exhibit Himself *to* His children, but God only exhibits Himself *in* His children. And while others see the evidence, the child of God does not. We want to be fully aware of what God is doing in us, but we cannot have complete awareness and expect to remain reasonable or balanced in our expectations of Him. If all we are asking God to give us is experiences, and the awareness of those experiences is blocking our way, we hurt the Lord. The very questions we ask hurt Jesus, because they are not the questions of a child.

"Let not your heart be troubled" (14:1, 27). Am I then hurting Jesus by allowing my heart to be troubled? If I believe in Jesus and His attributes, am I living up to my belief? Am I allowing anything to disturb my heart, or am I allowing any questions to come in which are unsound or unbalanced? I have to get to the point of the absolute and unquestionable relationship that takes everything exactly as it comes from Him. God never guides us at some time in the future, but always here and now. Realize that the Lord is here *now*, and the freedom you receive is immediate.

The Light That Never Fails

"We all, with unveiled face, beholding . . . the glory of the Lord." **2 Corinthians 3:18**

A servant of God must stand so very much alone that he never realizes he is alone. In the early stages of the Christian life, disappointments will come—people who used to be lights will flicker out, and those who used to stand with us will turn away. We have to get so used to it that we will not even realize we are standing alone. Paul said, "No one stood with me, but all forsook me. . . . But the Lord stood with me and strengthened me" (2 Timothy 4:16–17). We must build our faith not on fading lights but on the Light that never fails. When "important" individuals go away we are sad, until we see that they are meant to go, so that only one thing is left for us to do—to look into the face of God for ourselves.

Allow nothing to keep you from looking with strong determination into the face of God regarding yourself and your doctrine. And every time you preach make sure you look God in the face about the message first, then the glory will remain through all of it. A Christian servant is one who perpetually looks into the face of God and then goes forth to talk to others. The ministry of Christ is characterized by an abiding glory of which the servant is totally unaware—"Moses did not know that the skin of his face shone while he talked with Him" (Exodus 34:29).

We are never called on to display our doubts openly or to express the hidden joys and delights of our life with God. The secret of the servant's life is that he stays in tune with God all the time.

Do You Worship the Work?

"We are God's fellow workers." **1 Corinthians 3:9**

Beware of any work for God that causes or allows you to avoid concentrating on Him. A great number of Christian workers worship their work. The only concern of Christian workers should be their concentration on God. This will mean that all the other boundaries of life, whether they are mental, moral, or spiritual limits, are completely free with the freedom God gives His child; that is, a worshiping child, not a wayward one. A worker who lacks this serious controlling emphasis of concentration on God is apt to become overly burdened by his work. He is a slave to his own limits, having no freedom of his body, mind, or spirit. Consequently, he becomes burned out and defeated. There is no freedom and no delight in life at all. His nerves, mind, and heart are so overwhelmed that God's blessing cannot rest on him.

But the opposite case is equally true—once our concentration is on God, all the limits of our life are free and under the control and mastery of God alone. There is no longer any responsibility on you for the work. The only responsibility you have is to stay in living constant touch with God, and to see that you allow nothing to hinder your cooperation with Him. The freedom that comes after sanctification is the freedom of a child, and the things that used to hold your life down are gone. But be careful to remember that you have been freed for only one thing—to be absolutely devoted to your co-Worker.

We have no right to decide where we should be placed, or to have preconceived ideas as to what God is preparing us to do. God engineers everything; and wherever He places us, our one supreme goal should be to pour out our lives in wholehearted devotion to Him in that particular work. "Whatever your hand finds to do, do it with your might" (Ecclesiastes 9:10).

APRIL 24

The Warning Against Desiring Spiritual Success

"Do not rejoice in this, that the spirits are subject to you." **Luke 10:20**

Worldliness is not the trap that most endangers us as Christian workers; nor is it sin. The trap we fall into is extravagantly desiring spiritual success; that is, success measured by, and patterned after, the form set by this religious age in which we now live. Never seek after anything other than the approval of God, and always be willing to go "outside the camp, bearing His reproach" (Hebrews 13:13). In Luke 10:20, Jesus told the disciples not to rejoice in successful service, and yet this seems to be the one thing in which most of us do rejoice. We have a commercialized view—we count how many souls have been saved and sanctified, we thank God, and then we think everything is all right. Yet our work only begins where God's grace has laid the foundation. Our work is not to save souls, but to disciple them. Salvation and sanctification are the work of God's sovereign grace, and our work as His disciples is to disciple others' lives until they are totally yielded to God. One life totally devoted to God is of more value to Him than one hundred lives which have been simply awakened by His Spirit. As workers for God, we must reproduce our own kind spiritually, and those lives will be God's testimony to us as His workers. God brings us up to a standard of life through His grace, and we are responsible for reproducing that same standard in others.

Unless the worker lives a life that "is hidden with Christ in God" (Colossians 3:3), he is apt to become an irritating dictator to others, instead of an active, living disciple. Many of us are dictators, dictating our desires to individuals and to groups. But Jesus never dictates to us in that way. Whenever our Lord talked about discipleship, He always prefaced His words with an "if," never with the forceful or dogmatic statement—"You must." Discipleship carries with it an option.

APRIL 25

"Ready in Season"

"Be ready in season and out of season." **2 Timothy 4:2**

Many of us suffer from the unbalanced tendency to "be ready" only "out of season." The season does not refer to time; it refers to us. This verse says, "Preach the Word! Be ready in season and out of season." In other words, we should "be ready" whether we feel like it or not. If we do only what we feel inclined to do, some of us would never do anything. There are some people who are totally unemployable in the spiritual realm. They are spiritually feeble and weak, and they refuse to do anything unless they are supernaturally inspired. The proof that our relationship is right with God is that we do our best whether we feel inspired or not.

One of the worst traps a Christian worker can fall into is to become obsessed with his own exceptional moments of inspiration. When the Spirit of God gives you a time of inspiration and insight, you tend to say, "Now that I've experienced this moment, I will always be like this for God." No, you will not, and God will make sure of that. Those times are entirely the gift of God. You cannot give them to yourself when you choose. If you say you will only be at your best for God, as during those exceptional times, you actually become an intolerable burden on Him. You will never do anything unless God keeps you consciously aware of His inspiration to you at all times. If you make a god out of your best moments, you will find that God will fade out of your life, never to return until you are obedient in the work He has placed closest to you, and until you have learned not to be obsessed with those exceptional moments He has given you.

The Supreme Climb

"Take now your son . . . and offer him . . . as a burnt offering on one of the mountains of which I shall tell you." **Genesis 22:2**

A person's character determines how he interprets God's will (see Psalm 18:25–26). Abraham interpreted God's command to mean that he had to kill his son, and he could only leave this traditional belief behind through the pain of a tremendous ordeal. God could purify his faith in no other way. If we obey what God says according to our sincere belief, God will break us from those traditional beliefs that misrepresent Him. There are many such beliefs which must be removed—for example, that God removes a child because his mother loves him too much. That is the devil's lie and a travesty on the true nature of God! If the devil can hinder us from taking the supreme climb and getting rid of our wrong traditional beliefs about God, he will do so. But if we will stay true to God, God will take us through an ordeal that will serve to bring us into a better knowledge of Himself.

The great lesson to be learned from Abraham's faith in God is that he was prepared to do anything for God. He was there to obey God, no matter what contrary belief of his might be violated by his obedience. Abraham was not devoted to his own convictions or else he would have slain Isaac and said that the voice of the angel was actually the voice of the devil. That is the attitude of a fanatic. If you will remain true to God, God will lead you directly through every barrier and right into the inner chamber of the knowledge of Himself. But you must always be willing to come to the point of giving up your own convictions and traditional beliefs. Don't ask God to test you. Never declare as Peter did that you are willing to do anything, even "to go . . . both to prison and to death" (Luke 22:33). Abraham did not make any such statement—he simply remained true to God, and God purified his faith.

What Do You Want?

"Do you seek great things for yourself?" **Jeremiah 45:5**

Are you seeking great things for yourself, instead of seeking to be a great person? God wants you to be in a much closer relationship with Himself than simply receiving His gifts—He wants you to get to know Him. Even some large thing we want is only incidental; it comes and it goes. But God never gives us anything incidental. There is nothing easier than getting into the right relationship with God, unless it is not God you seek, but only what He can give you.

If you have only come as far as asking God for things, you have never come to the point of understanding the least bit of what surrender really means. You have become a Christian based on your own terms. You protest, saying, "I asked God for the Holy Spirit, but He didn't give me the rest and the peace I expected." And instantly God puts His finger on the reason—you are not seeking the Lord at all; you are seeking something for yourself. Jesus said, "Ask, and it will be given to you" (Matthew 7:7). Ask God for what you want and do not be concerned about asking for the wrong thing, because as you draw ever closer to Him, you will cease asking for things altogether. "Your Father knows the things you have need of before you ask Him" (Matthew 6:8). Then why should you ask? So that you may get to know Him.

Are you seeking great things for yourself? Have you said, "Oh, Lord, completely fill me with Your Holy Spirit"? If God does not, it is because you are not totally surrendered to Him; there is something you still refuse to do. Are you prepared to ask yourself what it is you want from God and why you want it? God always ignores your present level of completeness in favor of your ultimate future completeness. He is not concerned about making you blessed and happy right now, but He's continually working out His ultimate perfection for you—"that they may be one just as We are one" (John 17:22).

What You Will Get

"I will give your life to you as a prize in all places, wherever you go." **Jeremiah 45:5**

This is the firm and immovable secret of the Lord to those who trust Him—"I will give your life to you." What more does a man want than his life? It is the essential thing. "Your life . . . as a prize" means that wherever you may go, even if it is into hell, you will come out with your life and nothing can harm it. So many of us are caught up in exhibiting things for others to see, not showing off property and possessions, but our blessings. All these things that we so proudly show have to go. But there is something greater that can never go—the life that "is hidden with Christ in God" (Colossians 3:3).

Are you prepared to let God take you into total oneness with Himself, paying no more attention to what you call the great things of life? Are you prepared to surrender totally and let go? The true test of abandonment or surrender is in refusing to say, "Well, what about this?" Beware of your own ideas and speculations. The moment you allow yourself to think, "What about this?" you show that you have not surrendered and that you do not really trust God. But once you do surrender, you will no longer think about what God is going to do. Abandonment means to refuse yourself the luxury of asking any questions. If you totally abandon yourself to God, He immediately says to you, "I will give your life to you as a prize." The reason people are tired of life is that God has not given them anything—they have not been given their life "as a prize." The way to get out of that condition is to abandon yourself to God. And once you do get to the point of total surrender to Him, you will be the most surprised and delighted person on earth. God will have you absolutely, without any limitations, and He will have given you your life. If you are not there, it is either because of disobedience in your life or your refusal to be simple enough.

Gracious Uncertainty

"It has not yet been revealed what we shall be."
1 John 3:2

Our natural inclination is to be so precise—trying always to forecast accurately what will happen next—that we look upon uncertainty as a bad thing. We think that we must reach some predetermined goal, but that is not the nature of the spiritual life. The nature of the spiritual life is that we are certain in our uncertainty. Consequently, we do not put down roots. Our common sense says, "Well, what if I were in that circumstance?" We cannot presume to see ourselves in any circumstance in which we have never been.

Certainty is the mark of the commonsense life—gracious uncertainty is the mark of the spiritual life. To be certain of God means that we are uncertain in all our ways, not knowing what tomorrow may bring. This is generally expressed with a sigh of sadness, but it should be an expression of breathless expectation. We are uncertain of the next step, but we are certain of God. As soon as we abandon ourselves to God and do the task He has placed closest to us, He begins to fill our lives with surprises. When we become simply a promoter or a defender of a particular belief, something within us dies. That is not believing God—it is only believing our belief about Him. Jesus said, "unless you . . . become as little children" (Matthew 18:3). The spiritual life is the life of a child. We are not uncertain of God, just uncertain of what He is going to do next. If our certainty is only in our beliefs, we develop a sense of self-righteousness, become overly critical, and are limited by the view that our beliefs are complete and settled. But when we have the right relationship with God, life is full of spontaneous, joyful uncertainty and expectancy. Jesus said, "Believe also in Me" (John 14:1), not, "Believe certain things about Me." Leave everything to Him and it will be gloriously and graciously uncertain how He will come in—but you can be certain that He will come. Remain faithful to Him.

APRIL 30

Spontaneous Love

"Love suffers long and is kind." **1 Corinthians 13:4**

Love is not premeditated—it is spontaneous; that is, it bursts forth in extraordinary ways. There is nothing of precise certainty in Paul's description of love. We cannot predetermine our thoughts and actions by saying, "Now I will never think any evil thoughts, and I will believe everything that Jesus would have me to believe." No, the characteristic of love is spontaneity. We don't deliberately set the statements of Jesus before us as our standard, but when His Spirit is having His way with us, we live according to His standard without even realizing it. And when we look back, we are amazed at how unconcerned we have been over our emotions, which is the very evidence that real spontaneous love was there. The nature of everything involved in the life of God in us is only discerned when we have been through it and it is in our past.

The fountains from which love flows are in God, not in us. It is absurd to think that the love of God is naturally in our hearts, as a result of our own nature. His love is there only because it "has been poured out in our hearts by the Holy Spirit" (Romans 5:5).

If we try to prove to God how much we love Him, it is a sure sign that we really don't love Him. The evidence of our love for Him is the absolute spontaneity of our love, which flows naturally from His nature within us. And when we look back, we will not be able to determine why we did certain things, but we can know that we did them according to the spontaneous nature of His love in us. The life of God exhibits itself in this spontaneous way because the fountains of His love are in the Holy Spirit.

MAY 1

Faith—Not Emotion

"We walk by faith, not by sight." **2 Corinthians 5:7**

For a while, we are fully aware of God's concern for us. But then, when God begins to use us in His work, we begin to take on a pitiful look and talk only of our trials and difficulties. And all the while God is trying to make us do our work as hidden people who are not in the spotlight. None of us would be hidden spiritually if we could help it. Can we do our work when it seems that God has sealed up heaven? Some of us always want to be brightly illuminated saints with golden halos and with the continual glow of inspiration, and to have other saints of God dealing with us all the time. A self-assured saint is of no value to God. He is abnormal, unfit for daily life, and completely unlike God. We are here, not as immature angels, but as men and women, to do the work of this world. And we are to do it with an infinitely greater power to withstand the struggle because we have been born from above.

If we continually try to bring back those exceptional moments of inspiration, it is a sign that it is not God we want. We are becoming obsessed with the moments when God did come and speak with us, and we are insisting that He do it again. But what God wants us to do is to "walk by faith." How many of us have set ourselves aside as if to say, "I cannot do anything else until God appears to me"? He will never do it. We will have to get up on our own, without any inspiration and without any sudden touch from God. Then comes our surprise and we find ourselves exclaiming, "Why, He was there all the time, and I never knew it!" Never live for those exceptional moments—they are surprises. God will give us His touches of inspiration only when He sees that we are not in danger of being led away by them. We must never consider our moments of inspiration as the standard way of life—our work is our standard.

MAY 2

The Patience to Wait for the Vision

"Though it tarries, wait for it." **Habakkuk 2:3**

Patience is not the same as indifference; patience conveys the idea of someone who is tremendously strong and able to withstand all assaults. Having the vision of God is the source of patience because it gives us God's true and proper inspiration. Moses endured, not because of his devotion to his principles of what was right, nor because of his sense of duty to God, but because he had a vision of God. "He endured as seeing Him who is invisible" (Hebrews 11:27). A person who has the vision of God is not devoted to a cause or to any particular issue—he is devoted to God Himself. You always know when the vision is of God because of the inspiration that comes with it. Things come to you with greatness and add vitality to your life because everything is energized by God. He may give you a time spiritually, with no word from Himself at all, just as His Son experienced during His time of temptation in the wilderness. When God does that, simply endure, and the power to endure will be there because you see God.

"Though it tarries, wait for it." The proof that we have the vision is that we are reaching out for more than we have already grasped. It is a bad thing to be satisfied spiritually. The psalmist said, "What shall I render to the Lord . . . ? I will *take up* the cup of salvation" (Psalm 116:12–13). We are apt to look for satisfaction within ourselves and say, "Now I've got it! Now I am completely sanctified. Now I can endure." Instantly we are on the road to ruin. Our reach must exceed our grasp. Paul said, "Not that I have already attained, or am already perfected; but I press on" (Philippians 3:12). If we have only what we have experienced, we have nothing. But if we have the inspiration of the vision of God, we have more than we can experience. Beware of the danger of spiritual relaxation.

Vital Intercession

". . . praying always with all prayer and supplication in the Spirit." **Ephesians 6:18**

As we continue on in our intercession for others, we may find that our obedience to God in interceding is going to cost those for whom we intercede more than we ever thought. The danger in this is that we begin to intercede in sympathy with those whom God was gradually lifting up to a totally different level in direct answer to our prayers. Whenever we step back from our close identification with God's interest and concern for others and step into having emotional sympathy with them, the vital connection with God is gone. We have then put our sympathy and concern for them in the way, and this is a deliberate rebuke to God.

It is impossible for us to have living and vital intercession unless we are perfectly and completely sure of God. And the greatest destroyer of that confident relationship to God, so necessary for intercession, is our own personal sympathy and preconceived bias. Identification with God is the key to intercession, and whenever we stop being identified with Him it is because of our sympathy with others, not because of sin. It is not likely that sin will interfere with our intercessory relationship with God, but sympathy will. It is sympathy with ourselves or with others that makes us say, "I will not allow that thing to happen." And instantly we are out of that vital connection with God.

Vital intercession leaves you with neither the time nor the inclination to pray for your own "sad and pitiful self." You do not have to struggle to keep thoughts of yourself out, because they are not even there to be kept out of your thinking. You are completely and entirely identified with God's interests and concerns in other lives. God gives us discernment in the lives of others to call us to intercession for them, never so that we may find fault with them.

MAY 4

Vicarious Intercession

". . . having boldness to enter the Holiest by the blood of Jesus." **Hebrews 10:19**

Beware of thinking that intercession means bringing our own personal sympathies and concerns into the presence of God, and then demanding that He do whatever we ask. Our ability to approach God is due entirely to the vicarious, or substitutionary, identification of our Lord with sin. We have "boldness to enter the Holiest *by the blood of Jesus.*"

Spiritual stubbornness is the most effective hindrance to intercession, because it is based on a sympathetic "understanding" of things we see in ourselves and others that we think needs no atonement. We have the idea that there are certain good and virtuous things in each of us that do not need to be based on the atonement by the Cross of Christ. Just the sluggishness and lack of interest produced by this kind of thinking makes us unable to intercede. We do not identify ourselves with God's interests and concerns for others, and we get irritated with Him. Yet we are always ready with our own ideas, and our intercession becomes only the glorification of our own natural sympathies. We have to realize that the identification of Jesus with sin means a radical change of all of our sympathies and interests. Vicarious intercession means that we deliberately substitute God's interests in others for our natural sympathy with them.

Am I stubborn or substituted? Am I spoiled or complete in my relationship to God? Am I irritable or spiritual? Am I determined to have my own way or determined to be identified with Him?

Judgment and the Love of God

"The time has come for judgment to begin at the house of God." **1 Peter 4:17**

The Christian servant must never forget that salvation is God's idea, not man's; therefore, it has an unfathomable depth. Salvation is the great thought of God, not an experience. Experience is simply the door through which salvation comes into the conscious level of our life so that we are aware of what has taken place on a much deeper level. Never preach the experience—preach the great thought of God behind the experience. When we preach, we are not simply proclaiming how people can be saved from hell and be made moral and pure; we are conveying good news about God.

In the teachings of Jesus Christ the element of judgment is always brought out—it is the sign of the love of God. Never sympathize with someone who finds it difficult to get to God; God is not to blame. It is not for us to figure out the reason for the difficulty, but only to present the truth of God so that the Spirit of God will reveal what is wrong. The greatest test of the quality of our preaching is whether or not it brings everyone to judgment. When the truth is preached, the Spirit of God brings each person face-to-face with God Himself.

If Jesus ever commanded us to do something that He was unable to equip us to accomplish, He would be a liar. And if we make our own inability a stumbling block or an excuse not to be obedient, it means that we are telling God that there is something which He has not yet taken into account. Every element of our own self-reliance must be put to death by the power of God. The moment we recognize our complete weakness and our dependence upon Him will be the very moment that the Spirit of God will exhibit His power.

Liberty and the Standards of Jesus

"Stand fast therefore in the liberty by which Christ has made us free." **Galatians 5:1**

A spiritually minded person will never come to you with the demand—"Believe this and that"; a spiritually minded person will demand that you align your life with the standards of Jesus. We are not asked to believe the Bible, but to believe the One whom the Bible reveals (see John 5:39–40). We are called to present liberty for the conscience of others, not to bring them liberty for their thoughts and opinions. And if we ourselves are free with the liberty of Christ, others will be brought into that same liberty—the liberty that comes from realizing the absolute control and authority of Jesus Christ.

Always measure your life solely by the standards of Jesus. Submit yourself to His yoke, and His alone; and always be careful never to place a yoke on others that is not of Jesus Christ. It takes God a long time to get us to stop thinking that unless everyone sees things exactly as we do, they must be wrong. That is never God's view. There is only one true liberty—the liberty of Jesus at work in our conscience enabling us to do what is right.

Don't get impatient with others. Remember how God dealt with you—with patience and with gentleness. But never water down the truth of God. Let it have its way and never apologize for it. Jesus said, "Go . . . and make *disciples*" (Matthew 28:19), not, "Make converts to your own thoughts and opinions."

Building for Eternity

"Which of you, intending to build a tower, does not sit down first and count the cost, whether he has enough to finish it." **Luke 14:28**

Our Lord was not referring here to a cost which we have to count, but to a cost which He has already counted. The cost was those thirty years in Nazareth, those three years of popularity, scandal, and hatred, the unfathomable agony He experienced in Gethsemane, and the assault upon Him at Calvary—the central point upon which all of time and eternity turn. Jesus Christ has counted the cost. In the final analysis, people are not going to laugh at Him and say, "This man began to build and was not able to finish" (Luke 14:30).

The conditions of discipleship given to us by our Lord in verses 26, 27, and 33 mean that the men and women He is going to use in His mighty building enterprises are those in whom He has done everything. "If anyone comes to Me and does not hate his father and mother, wife and children, brothers and sisters, yes, and his own life also, *he cannot be My disciple*" (14:26). This verse teaches us that the only men and women our Lord will use in His building enterprises are those who love Him personally, passionately, and with great devotion—those who have a love for Him that goes far beyond any of the closest relationships on earth. The conditions are strict, but they are glorious.

All that we build is going to be inspected by God. When God inspects us with His searching and refining fire, will He detect that we have built enterprises of our own on the foundation of Jesus? (see 1 Corinthians 3:10–15). We are living in a time of tremendous enterprises, a time when we are trying to work for God, and that is where the trap is. Profoundly speaking, we can never work for God. Jesus, as the Master Builder, takes us over so that He may direct and control us completely for *His* enterprises and *His* building plans; and no one has any right to demand where he will be put to work.

The Faith to Persevere

"Because you have kept My command to persevere . . ." **Revelation 3:10**

Perseverance means more than endurance—more than simply holding on until the end. A saint's life is in the hands of God like a bow and arrow in the hands of an archer. God is aiming at something the saint cannot see, but our Lord continues to stretch and strain, and every once in a while the saint says, "I can't take any more." Yet God pays no attention; He goes on stretching until His purpose is in sight, and then He lets the arrow fly. Entrust yourself to God's hands. Is there something in your life for which you need perseverance right now? Maintain your intimate relationship with Jesus Christ through the perseverance of faith. Proclaim as Job did, "Though He slay me, yet will I trust Him" (Job 13:15).

Faith is not some weak and pitiful emotion, but is strong and vigorous confidence built on the fact that God is holy love. And even though you cannot see Him right now and cannot understand what He is doing, you know *Him*. Disaster occurs in your life when you lack the mental composure that comes from establishing yourself on the eternal truth that God is holy love. Faith is the supreme effort of your life—throwing yourself with abandon and total confidence upon God.

God ventured His all in Jesus Christ to save us, and now He wants us to venture our all with total abandoned confidence in Him. There are areas in our lives where that faith has not worked in us as yet—places still untouched by the life of God. There were none of those places in Jesus Christ's life, and there are to be none in ours. Jesus prayed, "This is eternal life, that they may know You" (John 17:3). The real meaning of eternal life is a life that can face anything it has to face without wavering. If we will take this view, life will become one great romance—a glorious opportunity of seeing wonderful things all the time. God is disciplining us to get us into this central place of power.

Reaching Beyond Our Grasp

"Where there is no revelation [or prophetic vision], the people cast off restraint." **Proverbs 29:18**

There is a difference between holding on to a principle and having a vision. A principle does not come from moral inspiration, but a vision does. People who are totally consumed with idealistic principles rarely *do* anything. A person's own idea of God and His attributes may actually be used to justify and rationalize his deliberate neglect of his duty. Jonah tried to excuse his disobedience by saying to God, "I know that You are a gracious and merciful God, slow to anger and abundant in lovingkindness, One who relents from doing harm" (Jonah 4:2). I too may have the right idea of God and His attributes, but that may be the very reason why I do not do my duty. But wherever there is vision, there is also a life of honesty and integrity, because the vision gives me the moral incentive.

Our own idealistic principles may actually lull us into ruin. Examine yourself spiritually to see if you have vision, or only principles.

Ah, but a man's reach should exceed his grasp,
Or what's a heaven for?

"Where there is no revelation [or prophetic vision] . . ." Once we lose sight of God, we begin to be reckless. We cast off certain restraints from activities we know are wrong. We set prayer aside as well and cease having God's vision in the little things of life. We simply begin to act on our own initiative. If we are eating only out of our own hand, and doing things solely on our own initiative without expecting God to come in, we are on a downward path. We have lost the vision. Is our attitude today an attitude that flows from our vision of God? Are we expecting God to do greater things than He has ever done before? Is there a freshness and a vitality in our spiritual outlook?

Take the Initiative

"Add to your faith virtue." **2 Peter 1:5**

Add means that we have to do something. We are in danger of forgetting that we cannot do what God does, and that God will not do what we can do. We cannot save nor sanctify ourselves—God does that. But God will not give us good habits or character, and He will not force us to walk correctly before Him. We have to do all that ourselves. We must "work *out*" our "own salvation" which God has worked *in* us (Philippians 2:12). *Add* means that we must get into the habit of doing things, and in the initial stages that is difficult. To take the initiative is to make a beginning—to instruct yourself in the way you must go.

Beware of the tendency to ask the way when you know it perfectly well. Take the initiative—stop hesitating—take the first step. Be determined to act immediately in faith on what God says to you when He speaks, and never reconsider or change your initial decisions. If you hesitate when God tells you to do something, you are being careless, spurning the grace in which you stand. Take the initiative yourself, make a decision of your will right now, and make it impossible to go back. Burn your bridges behind you, saying, "I *will* write that letter," or "I *will* pay that debt"; and then do it! Make it irrevocable.

We have to get into the habit of carefully listening to God about everything, forming the habit of finding out what He says and heeding it. If, when a crisis comes, we instinctively turn to God, we will know that the habit has been formed in us. We have to take the initiative where we *are*, not where we have not yet been.

"Love One Another"

"Add to your . . . brotherly kindness love." **2 Peter 1:5, 7**

Love is an indefinite thing to most of us; we don't know what we mean when we talk about love. Love is the loftiest preference of one person for another, and spiritually Jesus demands that this sovereign preference be for Himself (see Luke 14:26). Initially, when "the love of God has been poured out in our hearts by the Holy Spirit" (Romans 5:5), it is easy to put Jesus first. But then we must practice the things mentioned in 2 Peter 1 to see them worked out in our lives.

The first thing God does is forcibly remove any insincerity, pride, and vanity from my life. And the Holy Spirit reveals to me that God loved me not because I was lovable, but because it was His nature to do so. Now He commands me to show the same love to others by saying, "Love one another as I have loved you" (John 15:12). He is saying, "I will bring a number of people around you whom you cannot respect, but you must exhibit My love to them, just as I have exhibited it to you." This kind of love is not a patronizing love for the unlovable—it is His love, and it will not be evidenced in us overnight. Some of us may have tried to force it, but we were soon tired and frustrated.

"The Lord . . . is longsuffering toward us, not willing that any should perish" (2 Peter 3:9). I should look within and remember how wonderfully He has dealt with me. The knowledge that God has loved me beyond all limits will compel me to go into the world to love others in the same way. I may get irritated because I have to live with an unusually difficult person. But just think how disagreeable I have been with God! Am I prepared to be identified so closely with the Lord Jesus that His life and His sweetness will be continually poured out through me? Neither natural love nor God's divine love will remain and grow in me unless it is nurtured. Love is spontaneous, but it has to be maintained through discipline.

MAY 12

The Habit of Having No Habits

"If these things are yours and abound, you will be neither barren nor unfruitful." **2 Peter 1:8**

When we first begin to form a habit, we are fully aware of it. There are times when we are aware of becoming virtuous and godly, but this awareness should only be a stage we quickly pass through as we grow spiritually. If we stop at this stage, we will develop a sense of spiritual pride. The right thing to do with godly habits is to immerse them in the life of the Lord until they become such a spontaneous expression of our lives that we are no longer aware of them. Our spiritual life continually causes us to focus our attention inwardly for the determined purpose of self-examination, because each of us has some qualities we have not yet added to our lives.

Your god may be your little Christian habit—the habit of prayer or Bible reading at certain times of your day. Watch how your Father will upset your schedule if you begin to worship your habit instead of what the habit symbolizes. We say, "I can't do that right now; this is my time alone with God." No, this is your time alone with your habit. There is a quality that is still lacking in you. Identify your shortcoming and then look for opportunities to work into your life that missing quality.

Love means that there are no visible habits—that your habits are so immersed in the Lord that you practice them without realizing it. If you are consciously aware of your own holiness, you place limitations on yourself from doing certain things—things God is not restricting you from at all. This means there is a missing quality that needs to be added to your life. The only supernatural life is the life the Lord Jesus lived, and He was at home with God anywhere. Is there someplace where you are not at home with God? Then allow God to work through whatever that particular circumstance may be until you increase in Him, adding His qualities. Your life will then become the simple life of a child.

The Habit of Keeping a Clear Conscience

"Strive to have a conscience without offense toward God and men." **Acts 24:16**

God's commands to us are actually given to the life of His Son in us. Consequently, to our human nature in which God's Son has been formed (see Galatians 4:19), His commands are difficult. But they become divinely easy once we obey.

Conscience is that ability within me that attaches itself to the highest standard I know, and then continually reminds me of what that standard demands that I do. It is the eye of the soul which looks out either toward God or toward what we regard as the highest standard. This explains why conscience is different in different people. If I am in the habit of continually holding God's standard in front of me, my conscience will always direct me to God's perfect law and indicate what I should do. The question is, will I obey? I have to make an effort to keep my conscience so sensitive that I can live without any offense toward anyone. I should be living in such perfect harmony with God's Son that the spirit of my mind is being renewed through every circumstance of life, and that I may be able to quickly "prove what is that good and acceptable and perfect will of God" (Romans 12:2; also see Ephesians 4:23).

God always instructs us down to the last detail. Is my ear sensitive enough to hear even the softest whisper of the Spirit, so that I know what I should do? "Do not grieve the Holy Spirit of God" (Ephesians 4:30). He does not speak with a voice like thunder—His voice is so gentle that it is easy for us to ignore. And the only thing that keeps our conscience sensitive to Him is the habit of being open to God on the inside. When you begin to debate, stop immediately. Don't ask, "Why can't I do this?" You are on the wrong track. There is no debating possible once your conscience speaks. Whatever it is—drop it, and see that you keep your inner vision clear.

MAY 14

The Habit of Enjoying Adversity

". . . that the life of Jesus also may be manifested in our body." **2 Corinthians 4:10**

We have to develop godly habits to express what God's grace has done in us. It is not just a question of being saved from hell, but of being saved so that "the life of Jesus also may be manifested in our body." And it is adversity that makes us exhibit His life in our mortal flesh. Is my life exhibiting the essence of the sweetness of the Son of God, or just the basic irritation of "myself" that I would have apart from Him? The only thing that will enable me to enjoy adversity is the acute sense of eagerness of allowing the life of the Son of God to evidence itself in me. No matter how difficult something may be, I must say, "Lord, I am delighted to obey You in this." Instantly, the Son of God will move to the forefront of my life, and will manifest in my body that which glorifies Him.

You must not debate. The moment you obey the light of God, His Son shines through you in that very adversity; but if you debate with God, you grieve His Spirit (see Ephesians 4:30). You must keep yourself in the proper condition to allow the life of the Son of God to be manifested in you, and you cannot keep yourself fit if you give way to self-pity. Our circumstances are the means God uses to exhibit just how wonderfully perfect and extraordinarily pure His Son is. Discovering a new way of manifesting the Son of God should make our heart beat with renewed excitement. It is one thing to choose adversity, and quite another to enter into adversity through the orchestrating of our circumstances by God's sovereignty. And if God puts you into adversity, He is adequately sufficient to "supply all your need" (Philippians 4:19).

Keep your soul properly conditioned to manifest the life of the Son of God. Never live on your memories of past experiences, but let the Word of God always be living and active in you.

The Habit of Rising to the Occasion

"*. . . that you may know what is the hope of His calling.*" **Ephesians 1:18**

Remember that you have been saved so that the life of Jesus may be manifested in your body (see 2 Corinthians 4:10). Direct the total energy of your powers so that you may achieve everything your election as a child of God provides; rise every time to whatever occasion may come your way.

You did not do anything to achieve your salvation, but you must do something to exhibit it. You must "work *out* your own salvation" which God has worked *in* you already (Philippians 2:12). Are your speech, your thinking, and your emotions evidence that you are working it "out"? If you are still the same miserable, grouchy person, set on having your own way, then it is a lie to say that God has saved and sanctified you.

God is the Master Designer, and He allows adversities into your life to see if you can jump over them properly—"By my God I can leap over a wall" (Psalm 18:29). God will never shield you from the requirements of being His son or daughter. First Peter 4:12 says, "Beloved, do not think it strange concerning the fiery trial which is to try you, as though some strange thing happened to you." Rise to the occasion—do what the trial demands of you. It does not matter how much it hurts as long as it gives God the opportunity to manifest the life of Jesus in your body.

May God not find complaints in us anymore, but spiritual vitality—a readiness to face anything He brings our way. The only proper goal of life is that we manifest the Son of God; and when this occurs, all of our dictating of our demands to God disappears. Our Lord never dictated demands to His Father, and neither are we to make demands on God. We are here to submit to His will so that He may work through us what He wants. Once we realize this, He will make us broken bread and poured-out wine with which to feed and nourish others.

MAY 16

The Habit of Recognizing God's Provision

". . . you may be partakers of the divine nature . . ." **2 Peter 1:4**

We are made "partakers of the divine nature," receiving and sharing God's own nature through His promises. Then we have to work that divine nature into our human nature by developing godly habits. The first habit to develop is the habit of recognizing God's provision for us. We say, however, "Oh, I can't afford it." One of the worst lies is wrapped up in that statement. We talk as if our heavenly Father has cut us off without a penny! We think it is a sign of true humility to say at the end of the day, "Well, I just barely got by today, but it was a severe struggle." And yet all of Almighty God is ours in the Lord Jesus! And He will reach to the last grain of sand and the remotest star to bless us if we will only obey Him. Does it really matter that our circumstances are difficult? Why shouldn't they be! If we give way to self-pity and indulge in the luxury of misery, we remove God's riches from our lives and hinder others from entering into His provision. No sin is worse than the sin of self-pity, because it removes God from the throne of our lives, replacing Him with our own self-interests. It causes us to open our mouths only to complain, and we simply become spiritual sponges—always absorbing, never giving, and never being satisfied. And there is nothing lovely or generous about our lives.

Before God becomes satisfied with us, He will take everything of our so-called wealth, until we learn that He is our Source; as the psalmist said, "All my springs are in You" (Psalm 87:7). If the majesty, grace, and power of God are not being exhibited in us, God holds us responsible. "God is able to make all grace abound toward you, that you . . . may have an abundance" (2 Corinthians 9:8)—then learn to lavish the grace of God on others, generously giving of yourself. Be marked and identified with God's nature, and His blessing will flow through you all the time.

His Ascension and Our Access

"It came to pass, while He blessed them, that He was parted from them and carried up into heaven." **Luke 24:51**

We have no experiences in our lives that correspond to the events in our Lord's life after the transfiguration. From that moment forward His life was altogether substitutionary. Up to the time of the transfiguration, He had exhibited the normal, perfect life of a man. But from the transfiguration forward—Gethsemane, the Cross, the resurrection—everything is unfamiliar to us. His Cross is the door by which every member of the human race can enter into the life of God; by His resurrection He has the right to give eternal life to anyone, and by His ascension our Lord entered heaven, keeping the door open for humanity.

The transfiguration was completed on the Mount of Ascension. If Jesus had gone to heaven directly from the Mount of Transfiguration, He would have gone alone. He would have been nothing more to us than a glorious Figure. But He turned His back on the glory, and came down from the mountain to identify Himself with fallen humanity.

The ascension is the complete fulfillment of the transfiguration. Our Lord returned to His original glory, but not simply as the Son of God—He returned to His father as the *Son of Man* as well. There is now freedom of access for anyone straight to the very throne of God because of the ascension of the Son of Man. As the Son of Man, Jesus Christ deliberately limited His omnipotence, omnipresence, and omniscience. But now they are His in absolute, full power. As the Son of Man, Jesus Christ now has all the power at the throne of God. From His ascension forward He is the King of kings and Lord of lords.

Living Simply—Yet Focused

"Look at the birds of the air . . . . Consider the lilies of the field." **Matthew 6:26, 28**

"Consider the lilies of the field, how they grow: they neither toil nor spin"—they simply *are*! Think of the sea, the air, the sun, the stars, and the moon—all of these simply *are* as well—yet what a ministry and service they render on our behalf! So often we impair God's designed influence, which He desires to exhibit through us, because of our own conscious efforts to be consistent and useful. Jesus said there is only one way to develop and grow spiritually, and that is through focusing and concentrating on God. In essence, Jesus was saying, "Do not worry about being of use to others; simply believe on Me." In other words, pay attention to the Source, and out of you "will flow rivers of living water" (John 7:38). We cannot discover the source of our natural life through common sense and reasoning, and Jesus is teaching here that growth in our spiritual life comes not from focusing directly on it, but from concentrating on our Father in heaven. Our heavenly Father knows our circumstances, and if we will stay focused on Him, instead of our circumstances, we will grow spiritually—just as "the lilies of the field."

The people who influence us the most are not those who detain us with their continual talk, but those who live their lives like the stars in the sky and "the lilies of the field"—simply and unaffectedly. Those are the lives that mold and shape us.

If you want to be of use to God, maintain the proper relationship with Jesus Christ by staying focused on Him, and He will make use of you every minute you live—yet you will be unaware, on the conscious level of your life, that you are being used of Him.

"Out of the Wreck I Rise"

"Who shall separate us from the love of Christ?" **Romans 8:35**

God does not keep His child immune from trouble; He promises, "I will be with him in trouble" (Psalm 91:15). It doesn't matter how real or intense the adversities may be; nothing can ever separate him from his relationship to God. *"In* all these things we are more than conquerors" (Romans 8:37). Paul was not referring here to imaginary things, but to things that are dangerously real. And he said we are "super-victors" in the midst of them, not because of our own ingenuity, nor because of our courage, but because none of them affects our essential relationship with God in Jesus Christ. I feel sorry for the Christian who doesn't have something in the circumstances of his life that he wishes were not there.

"Shall tribulation . . . ?" Tribulation is never a grand, highly welcomed event; but whatever it may be—whether exhausting, irritating, or simply causing some weakness—it is not able to "separate us from the love of Christ." Never allow tribulations or the "cares of this world" to separate you from remembering that God loves you (Matthew 13:22).

"Shall . . . distress . . . ?" Can God's love continue to hold fast, even when everyone and everything around us seems to be saying that His love is a lie, and that there is no such thing as justice?

"Shall . . . famine . . . ?" Can we not only believe in the love of God but also be "more than conquerors," even while we are being starved?

Either Jesus Christ is a deceiver, having deceived even Paul, or else some extraordinary thing happens to someone who holds on to the love of God when the odds are totally against him. Logic is silenced in the face of each of these things which come against him. Only one thing can account for it—the *love of God in Christ Jesus.* "Out of the wreck I rise" every time.

Taking Possession of Our Own Soul

"By your patience possess your souls." **Luke 21:19**

When a person is born again, there is a period of time when he does not have the same vitality in his thinking or reasoning that he previously had. We must learn to express this new life within us, which comes by forming the mind of Christ (see Philippians 2:5). Luke 21:19 means that we take possession of our souls through patience. But many of us prefer to stay at the entrance to the Christian life, instead of going on to create and build our soul in accordance with the new life God has placed within us. We fail because we are ignorant of the way God has made us, and we blame things on the devil that are actually the result of our own undisciplined natures. Just think what we could be when we are awakened to the truth!

There are certain things in life that we need not pray about—moods, for instance. We will never get rid of moodiness by praying, but we will by kicking it out of our lives. Moods nearly always are rooted in some physical circumstance, not in our true inner self. It is a continual struggle not to listen to the moods which arise as a result of our physical condition, but we must never submit to them for a second. We have to pick ourselves up by the back of the neck and shake ourselves; then we will find that we can do what we believed we were unable to do. The problem that most of us are cursed with is simply that we *won't*. The Christian life is one of spiritual courage and determination lived out in our flesh.

Having God's "Unreasonable" Faith

"Seek first the kingdom of God and His righteousness, and all these things shall be added to you." **Matthew 6:33**

When we look at these words of Jesus, we immediately find them to be the most revolutionary that human ears have ever heard. "Seek *first* the kingdom of God." Even the most spiritually minded of us argue the exact opposite, saying, "But I *must* live; I *must* make a certain amount of money; I *must* be clothed; I *must* be fed." The great concern of our lives is not the kingdom of God but how we are going to take care of ourselves to live. Jesus reversed the order by telling us to get the right relationship with God first, maintaining it as the primary concern of our lives, and never to place our concern on taking care of the other things of life.

"Do not worry about your life" (6:25). Our Lord pointed out that from His standpoint it is absolutely unreasonable for us to be anxious, worrying about how we will live. Jesus did not say that the person who takes no thought for anything in his life is blessed—no, that person is a fool. But Jesus *did* teach that His disciple must make his relationship with God the dominating focus of his life, and to be cautiously carefree about everything else in comparison to that. In essence, Jesus was saying, "Don't make food and drink the controlling factor of your life, but be focused absolutely on God." Some people are careless about what they eat and drink, and they suffer for it; they are careless about what they wear, having no business looking the way they do; they are careless with their earthly matters, and God holds them responsible. Jesus is saying that the greatest concern of life is to place our relationship with God first, and everything else second.

It is one of the most difficult, yet critical, disciplines of the Christian life to allow the Holy Spirit to bring us into absolute harmony with the teaching of Jesus in these verses.

The Explanation for Our Difficulties

". . . that they all may be one, as You, Father, are in Me, and I in You; that they also may be one in Us." **John 17:21**

If you are going through a time of isolation, seemingly all alone, read John 17. It will explain exactly why you are where you are—because Jesus has prayed that you "may be one" with the Father as He is. Are you helping God to answer that prayer, or do you have some other goal for your life? Since you became a disciple, you cannot be as independent as you used to be.

God reveals in John 17 that His purpose is not just to answer our prayers, but that through prayer we might come to discern His mind. Yet there is one prayer which God must answer, and that is the prayer of Jesus—"that they may be one just as We are one" (17:22). Are we as close to Jesus Christ as that?

God is not concerned about our plans; He doesn't ask, "Do you want to go through this loss of a loved one, this difficulty, or this defeat?" No, He allows these things for His own purpose. The things we are going through are either making us sweeter, better, and nobler men and women, or they are making us more critical and fault-finding, and more insistent on our own way. The things that happen either make us evil, or they make us more saintly, depending entirely on our relationship with God and its level of intimacy. If we will pray, regarding our own lives, "Your will be done" (Matthew 26:42), then we will be encouraged and comforted by John 17, knowing that our Father is working according to His own wisdom, accomplishing what is best. When we understand God's purpose, we will not become small-minded and cynical. Jesus prayed nothing less for us than absolute oneness with Himself, just as He was one with the Father. Some of us are far from this oneness; yet God will not leave us alone until we *are* one with Him—because Jesus prayed, "that they *all* may be one."

Our Careful Unbelief

"Do not worry about your life, what you will eat or what you will drink; nor about your body, what you will put on." **Matthew 6:25**

Jesus summed up commonsense carefulness in the life of a disciple as *unbelief*. If we have received the Spirit of God, He will squeeze right through our lives, as if to ask, "Now where do I come into this relationship, this vacation you have planned, or these new books you want to read?" And He always presses the point until we learn to make Him our first consideration. Whenever we put other things first, there is confusion.

"Do not worry about your life." Don't take the pressure of your provision upon yourself. It is not only wrong to worry, it is unbelief; worrying means we do not believe that God can look after the practical details of our lives, and it is never anything but those details that worry us. Have you ever noticed what Jesus said would choke the Word He puts in us? Is it the devil? No—"the cares of this world" (Matthew 13:22). It is always our little worries. We say, "I will not trust when I cannot see"—and that is where unbelief begins. The only cure for unbelief is obedience to the Spirit.

The greatest word of Jesus to His disciples is *abandon*.

The Delight of Despair

"When I saw Him, I fell at His feet as dead." **Revelation 1:17**

It may be that, like the apostle John, you know Jesus Christ intimately. Yet when He suddenly appears to you with totally unfamiliar characteristics, the only thing you can do is fall "at His feet as dead." There are times when God cannot reveal Himself in any other way than in His majesty, and it is the awesomeness of the vision which brings you to the delight of despair. You experience this joy in hopelessness, realizing that if you are ever to be raised up it must be by the hand of God.

"He laid His right hand on me" (1:17). In the midst of the awesomeness, a touch comes, and you know it is the right hand of Jesus Christ. You know it is not the hand of restraint, correction, nor chastisement, but the right hand of the Everlasting Father. Whenever His hand is laid upon you, it gives inexpressible peace and comfort, and the sense that "underneath are the everlasting arms" (Deuteronomy 33:27), full of support, provision, comfort, and strength. And once His touch comes, nothing at all can throw you into fear again. In the midst of all His ascended glory, the Lord Jesus comes to speak to an insignificant disciple, saying, "Do not be afraid" (Revelation 1:17). His tenderness is inexpressibly sweet. Do I know Him like that?

Take a look at some of the things that cause despair. There is despair which has no delight, no limits whatsoever, and no hope of anything brighter. But the delight of despair comes when "I know that in me (that is, in my flesh) nothing good dwells" (Romans 7:18). I delight in knowing that there is something in me which must fall prostrate before God when He reveals Himself to me, and also in knowing that if I am ever to be raised up it must be by the hand of God. God can do nothing for me until I recognize the limits of what is humanly possible, allowing Him to do the impossible.

MAY 25

The Good or the Best?

"If you take the left, then I will go to the right; or, if you go to the right, then I will go to the left." **Genesis 13:9**

As soon as you begin to live the life of faith in God, fascinating and physically gratifying possibilities will open up before you. These things are yours by right, but if you are living the life of faith you will exercise your right to waive your rights, and let God make your choice for you. God sometimes allows you to get into a place of testing where your own welfare would be the appropriate thing to consider, if you were not living the life of faith. But if you are, you will joyfully waive your right and allow God to make your choice for you. This is the discipline God uses to transform the natural into the spiritual through obedience to His voice.

Whenever our *right* becomes the guiding factor of our lives, it dulls our spiritual insight. The greatest enemy of the life of faith in God is not sin, but good choices which are not quite good enough. The good is always the enemy of the best. In this passage, it would seem that the wisest thing in the world for Abram to do would be to choose. It was his right, and the people around him would consider him to be a fool for not choosing.

Many of us do not continue to grow spiritually because we prefer to choose on the basis of our rights, instead of relying on God to make the choice for us. We have to learn to walk according to the standard which has its eyes focused on God. And God says to us, as He did to Abram, *"walk before Me"* (Genesis 17:1).

MAY 26

Thinking of Prayer as Jesus Taught

"Pray without ceasing." **1 Thessalonians 5:17**

Our thinking about prayer, whether right or wrong, is based on our own mental conception of it. The correct concept is to think of prayer as the breath in our lungs and the blood from our hearts. Our blood flows and our breathing continues "without ceasing"; we are not even conscious of it, but it never stops. And we are not always conscious of Jesus keeping us in perfect oneness with God, but if we are obeying Him, He always is. Prayer is not an exercise, it is the life of the saint. Beware of anything that stops the offering up of prayer. "Pray without ceasing"—maintain the childlike habit of offering up prayer in your heart to God all the time.

Jesus never mentioned unanswered prayer. He had the unlimited certainty of knowing that prayer is always answered. Do we have through the Spirit of God that inexpressible certainty that Jesus had about prayer, or do we think of the times when it seemed that God did not answer our prayer? Jesus said, "Everyone who asks receives" (Matthew 7:8). Yet we say, "But . . . , but . . ." God answers prayer in the best way—not just sometimes, but every time. However, the evidence of the answer in the area we want it may not always immediately follow. Do we expect God to answer prayer?

The danger we have is that we want to water down what Jesus said to make it mean something that aligns with our common sense. But if it were only common sense, what He said would not even be worthwhile. The things Jesus taught about prayer are supernatural truths He reveals to us.

The Life to Know Him

"Tarry in the city of Jerusalem until you are endued with power from on high." **Luke 24:49**

The disciples had to tarry, staying in Jerusalem until the day of Pentecost, not only for their own preparation but because they had to wait until the Lord was actually glorified. And as soon as He was glorified, what happened? "Therefore being exalted to the right hand of God, and having received from the Father the promise of the Holy Spirit, He poured out this which you now see and hear" (Acts 2:33). The statement in John 7:39—"for the Holy Spirit was not yet given, because Jesus was not yet glorified"—does not pertain to us. The Holy Spirit *has been* given; the Lord *is* glorified—our waiting is not dependent on the providence of God, but on our own spiritual fitness.

The Holy Spirit's influence and power were at work before Pentecost, but *He* was not here. Once our Lord was glorified in His ascension, the Holy Spirit came into the world, and He has been here ever since. We have to receive the revealed truth that He is here. The attitude of receiving and welcoming the Holy Spirit into our lives is to be the continual attitude of a believer. When we receive the Holy Spirit, we receive reviving life from our ascended Lord.

It is not the baptism of the Holy Spirit that changes people, but the power of the ascended Christ coming into their lives through the Holy Spirit. We all too often separate things that the New Testament never separates. The baptism of the Holy Spirit is not an experience apart from Jesus Christ—it is the evidence of the ascended Christ.

The baptism of the Holy Spirit does not make you think of time or eternity—it is one amazing glorious *now*. "This is eternal life, that they may know You" (John 17:3). Begin to know Him now, and never finish.

MAY 28

Unquestioned Revelation

"In that day you will ask Me nothing." **John 16:23**

When is "that day"? It is when the ascended Lord makes you one with the Father. "In that day" you will be one with the Father just as Jesus is, and He said, "In that day you will ask Me nothing." Until the resurrection life of Jesus is fully exhibited in you, you have questions about many things. Then after a while you find that all your questions are gone—you don't seem to have any left to ask. You have come to the point of total reliance on the resurrection life of Jesus, which brings you into complete oneness with the purpose of God. Are you living that life now? If not, why aren't you?

"In that day" there may be any number of things still hidden to your understanding, but they will not come between your heart and God. "In that day you will ask Me nothing"—you will not need to ask, because you will be certain that God will reveal things in accordance with His will. The faith and peace of John 14:1 has become the real attitude of your heart, and there are no more questions to be asked. If anything is a mystery to you and is coming between you and God, never look for the explanation in your mind, but look for it in your spirit, your true inner nature—that is where the problem is. Once your inner spiritual nature is willing to submit to the life of Jesus, your understanding will be perfectly clear, and you will come to the place where there is no distance between the Father and you, His child, because the Lord has made you one. "In that day you will ask Me nothing."

MAY 29

Untroubled Relationship

"In that day you will ask in My name . . . for the Father Himself loves you." **John 16:26–27**

"In that day you will ask in My name," that is, in My nature. Not—"You will use My name as some magic word," but—"You will be so intimate with Me that you will be one with Me." "That day" is not a day in the next life, but a day meant for here and now. "For the Father Himself loves you"—the Father's love is evidence that our union with Jesus is complete and absolute. Our Lord does not mean that our lives will be free from external difficulties and uncertainties, but that just as He knew the Father's heart and mind, we too can be lifted by Him into heavenly places through the baptism of the Holy Spirit, so that He can reveal the teachings of God to us.

"Whatever you ask the Father in My name . . ." (John 16:23). "That day" is a day of peace and an untroubled relationship between God and His saint. Just as Jesus stood unblemished and pure in the presence of His Father, we too by the mighty power and effectiveness of the baptism of the Holy Spirit can be lifted into that relationship—"that they may be one just as We are one" (John 17:22).

". . . He will give you" (John 16:23). Jesus said that because of His name God will recognize and respond to our prayers. What a great challenge and invitation—to pray in His name! Through the resurrection and ascension power of Jesus, and through the Holy Spirit He has sent, we can be lifted into such a relationship. Once in that wonderful position, having been placed there by Jesus Christ, we can pray to God in Jesus' name—in His nature. This is a gift granted to us through the Holy Spirit, and Jesus said, "Whatever you ask the Father in My name He will give you." The sovereign character of Jesus Christ is tested and proved by His own statements.

"Yes—But . . . !"

"Lord, I will follow You, but . . ." **Luke 9:61**

Suppose God tells you to do something that is an enormous test of your common sense, totally going against it. What will you do? Will you hold back? If you get into the habit of doing something physically, you will do it every time you are tested until you break the habit through sheer determination. And the same is true spiritually. Again and again you will come right up to what Jesus wants, but every time you will turn back at the true point of testing, until you are determined to abandon yourself to God in total surrender. Yet we tend to say, "Yes, but—suppose I do obey God in this matter, what about . . . ?" Or we say, "Yes, I will obey God if what He asks of me doesn't go against my common sense, but don't ask me to take a step in the dark."

Jesus Christ demands the same unrestrained, adventurous spirit in those who have placed their trust in Him that the natural man exhibits. If a person is ever going to do anything worthwhile, there will be times when he must risk everything by his leap in the dark. In the spiritual realm, Jesus Christ demands that you risk everything you hold on to or believe through common sense, and leap by faith into what He says. Once you obey, you will immediately find that what He says is as solidly consistent as common sense.

By the test of common sense, Jesus Christ's statements may seem mad, but when you test them by the trial of faith, your findings will fill your spirit with the awesome fact that they are the very words of God. Trust completely in God, and when He brings you to a new opportunity of adventure, offering it to you, see that you take it. We act like pagans in a crisis—only one out of an entire crowd is daring enough to invest his faith in the character of God.

MAY 31

Put God First

"Jesus did not commit Himself to them . . . for He knew what was in man." **John 2:24–25**

Put Trust in God First. Our Lord never put His trust in any person. Yet He was never suspicious, never bitter, and never lost hope for anyone, because He put His trust in God first. He trusted absolutely in what God's grace could do for others. If I put my trust in human beings first, the end result will be my despair and hopelessness toward everyone. I will become bitter because I have insisted that people be what no person can ever be—absolutely perfect and right. Never trust anything in yourself or in anyone else, except the grace of God.

Put God's Will First. "Behold, I have come to do Your will, O God" (Hebrews 10:9).

A person's obedience is to what he sees to be a need—our Lord's obedience was to the will of His Father. The rallying cry today is, "We must get to work! The heathen are dying without God. We must go and tell them about Him." But we must first make sure that God's "needs" and His will in us personally are being met. Jesus said, "Tarry . . . until you are endued with power from on high" (Luke 24:49). The purpose of our Christian training is to get us into the right relationship to the "needs" of God and His will. Once God's "needs" in us have been met, He will open the way for us to accomplish His will, meeting His "needs" elsewhere.

Put God's Son First. "Whoever receives one little child like this in My name receives Me" (Matthew 18:5).

God came as a baby, giving and entrusting Himself to me. He expects my personal life to be a "Bethlehem." Am I allowing my natural life to be slowly transformed by the indwelling life of the Son of God? God's ultimate purpose is that His Son might be exhibited in me.

JUNE 1

The Staggering Question

He said to me, "Son of man, can these bones live?"
Ezekiel 37:3

Can a sinner be turned into a saint? Can a twisted life be made right? There is only one appropriate answer—"O Lord God, You know" (Ezekiel 37:3). Never forge ahead with your religious common sense and say, "Oh, yes, with just a little more Bible reading, devotional time, and prayer, I see how it can be done."

It is much easier to do something than to trust in God; we see the activity and mistake panic for inspiration. That is why we see so few fellow workers *with* God, yet so many people working *for* God. We would much rather work for God than believe in Him. Do I really believe that God will do in me what I cannot do? The degree of hopelessness I have for others comes from never realizing that God has done anything for me. Is my own personal experience such a wonderful realization of God's power and might that I can never have a sense of hopelessness for anyone else I see? Has any spiritual work been accomplished in me at all? The degree of panic activity in my life is equal to the degree of my lack of personal spiritual experience.

"Behold, O My people, I will open your graves . . ." (Ezekiel 37:12). When God wants to show you what human nature is like separated from Himself, He shows it to you in yourself. If the Spirit of God has ever given you a vision of what you are apart from the grace of God (and He will only do this when His Spirit is at work in you), then you know that in reality there is no criminal half as bad as you yourself could be without His grace. My "grave" has been opened by God and "I know that in me (that is, in my flesh) nothing good dwells" (Romans 7:18). God's Spirit continually reveals to His children what human nature is like apart from His grace.

Are You Obsessed by Something?

"Who is the man that fears the Lord?" **Psalm 25:12**

Are you obsessed by something? You will probably say, "No, by nothing," but all of us are obsessed by something—usually by ourselves, or, if we are Christians, by our own experience of the Christian life. But the psalmist says that we are to be obsessed by God. The abiding awareness of the Christian life is to be God Himself, not just thoughts about Him. The total being of our life inside and out is to be absolutely obsessed by the presence of God. A child's awareness is so absorbed in his mother that although he is not consciously thinking of her, when a problem arises, the abiding relationship is that with the mother. In that same way, we are to "live and move and have our being" in God (Acts 17:28), looking at everything in relation to Him, because our abiding awareness of Him continually pushes itself to the forefront of our lives.

If we are obsessed by God, nothing else can get into our lives—not concerns, nor tribulation, nor worries. And now we understand why our Lord so emphasized the sin of worrying. How can we dare to be so absolutely unbelieving when God totally surrounds us? To be obsessed by God is to have an effective barricade against all the assaults of the enemy.

"He himself shall dwell in prosperity" (Psalm 25:13). God will cause us to "dwell in prosperity," keeping us at ease, even in the midst of tribulation, misunderstanding, and slander, if our "life is hidden with Christ in God" (Colossians 3:3). We rob ourselves of the miraculous, revealed truth of this abiding companionship with God. "God is our refuge" (Psalm 46:1). Nothing can break through His shelter of protection.

"The Secret of the Lord"

"The secret of the LORD *is with those who fear Him."*
Psalm 25:14

What is the sign of a friend? Is it that he tells you his secret sorrows? No, it is that he tells you his secret joys. Many people will confide their secret sorrows to you, but the final mark of intimacy is when they share their secret joys with you. Have we ever let God tell us any of His joys? Or are we continually telling God our secrets, leaving Him no time to talk to us? At the beginning of our Christian life we are full of requests to God. But then we find that God wants to get us into an intimate relationship with Himself—to get us in touch with His purposes. Are we so intimately united to Jesus Christ's idea of prayer—"Your will be done" (Matthew 6:10)—that we catch the secrets of God? What makes God so dear to us is not so much His big blessings to us, but the tiny things, because they show His amazing intimacy with us—He knows every detail of each of our individual lives.

"Him shall He teach in the way He chooses" (Psalm 25:12). At first, we want the awareness of being guided by God. But then as we grow spiritually, we live so fully aware of God that we do not even need to ask what His will is, because the thought of choosing another way will never occur to us. If we are saved and sanctified, God guides us by our everyday choices. And if we are about to choose what He does not want, He will give us a sense of doubt or restraint, which we must heed. Whenever there is doubt, stop at once. Never try to reason it out, saying, "I wonder why I shouldn't do this?" God instructs us in what we choose; that is, He actually guides our common sense. And when we yield to His teachings and guidance, we no longer hinder His Spirit by continually asking, "Now, Lord, what is Your will?"

JUNE 4

The Never-Forsaking God

"He Himself has said, 'I will never leave you nor forsake you.'" **Hebrews 13:5**

What line of thinking do my thoughts take? Do I turn to what God says or to my own fears? Am I simply repeating what God says, or am I learning to truly hear Him and then to respond after I have heard what He says? "For He Himself has said, 'I will never leave you nor forsake you.' So we may boldly say: 'The Lord is my helper; I will not fear. What can man do to me?'" (Hebrews 13:5–6).

"I will never leave you"—not for any reason; not my sin, selfishness, stubbornness, nor waywardness. Have I really let God say to me that He will never leave me? If I have not truly heard this assurance of God, then let me listen again.

"I will never . . . forsake you." Sometimes it is not the difficulty of life but the drudgery of it that makes me think God will forsake me. When there is no major difficulty to overcome, no vision from God, nothing wonderful or beautiful—just the everyday activities of life—do I hear God's assurance even in these?

We have the idea that God is going to do some exceptional thing—that He is preparing and equipping us for some extraordinary work in the future. But as we grow in His grace we find that God is glorifying Himself here and now, at this very moment. If we have God's assurance behind us, the most amazing strength becomes ours, and we learn to sing, glorifying Him even in the ordinary days and ways of life.

JUNE 5

God's Assurance

"He Himself has said . . . . So we may boldly say . . ." **Hebrews 13:5–6**

My assurance is to be built upon God's assurance to me. God says, "I will never leave you," so that then I "may boldly say, 'The Lord is my helper; I will not fear'" (Hebrews 13:5–6). In other words, I will not be obsessed with apprehension. This does not mean that I will not be tempted to fear, but I will remember God's words of assurance. I will be full of courage, like a child who strives to reach the standard his father has set for him. The faith of many people begins to falter when apprehensions enter their thinking, and they forget the meaning of God's assurance—they forget to take a deep spiritual breath. The only way to remove the fear from our lives is to listen to God's assurance to us.

What are you fearing? Whatever it may be, you are not a coward about it—you are determined to face it, yet you still have a feeling of fear. When it seems that there is nothing and no one to help you, say to yourself, "But 'The Lord is my helper' this very moment, even in my present circumstance." Are you learning to listen to God before you speak, or are you saying things and then trying to make God's Word fit what you have said? Take hold of the Father's assurance, and then say with strong courage, "I will not fear." It does not matter what evil or wrong may be in our way, because "He Himself has said, 'I will never leave you.'"

Human frailty is another thing that gets between God's words of assurance and our own words and thoughts. When we realize how feeble we are in facing difficulties, the difficulties become like giants, we become like grasshoppers, and God seems to be nonexistent. But remember God's assurance to us—"*I will never . . . forsake you.*" Have we learned to sing after hearing God's keynote? Are we continually filled with enough courage to say, "The Lord is my helper," or are we yielding to fear?

"Work Out" What God "Works In" You

"Work out your own salvation . . . for it is God who works in you." **Philippians 2:12–13**

Your will agrees with God, but in your flesh there is a nature that renders you powerless to do what you know you ought to do. When the Lord initially comes in contact with our conscience, the first thing our conscience does is awaken our will, and our will always agrees with God. Yet you say, "But I don't know if my will is in agreement with God." Look to Jesus and you will find that your will and your conscience are in agreement with Him every time. What causes you to say "I will not obey" is something less deep and penetrating than your will. It is perversity or stubbornness, and they are never in agreement with God. The most profound thing in a person is his will, not sin.

The will is the essential element in God's creation of human beings—sin is a perverse nature which entered into people. In someone who has been born again, the source of the will is Almighty God. "For it is God who works in you both to will and to do for His good pleasure." With focused attention and great care, you have to "work out" what God "works in" you—not *work* to accomplish or earn "your own salvation," but *work it out* so you will exhibit the evidence of a life based with determined, unshakable faith on the complete and perfect redemption of the Lord. As you do this, you do not bring an opposing will up against God's will—God's will *is* your will. Your natural choices will be in accordance with God's will, and living this life will be as natural as breathing. Stubbornness is an unintelligent barrier, refusing enlightenment and blocking its flow. The only thing to do with this barrier of stubbornness is to blow it up with "dynamite," and the "dynamite" is obedience to the Holy Spirit.

Do I believe that Almighty God is the Source of my will? God not only expects me to do His will, but He is in me to do it.

The Greatest Source of Power

"Whatever you ask in My name, that I will do." **John 14:13**

Am I fulfilling this ministry of intercession deep within the hidden recesses of my life? There is no trap nor any danger at all of being deceived or of showing pride in true intercession. It is a hidden ministry that brings forth fruit through which the Father is glorified. Am I allowing my spiritual life to waste away, or am I focused, bringing everything to one central point—the atonement of my Lord? Is Jesus Christ more and more dominating every interest of my life? If the central point, or the most powerful influence, of my life is the atonement of the Lord, then every aspect of my life will bear fruit for Him.

However, I must take the time to realize what this central point of power is. Am I willing to give one minute out of every hour to concentrate on it? "If you abide in Me"—that is, if you continue to act, and think, and work from that central point—"you will ask what you desire, and it shall be done for you" (John 15:7). Am I abiding? Am I taking the time to abide? What is the greatest source of power in my life? Is it my work, service, and sacrifice for others, or is it my striving to work for God? It should be none of these—what ought to exert the greatest power in my life is the atonement of the Lord. It is not on what we spend the greatest amount of time that molds us the most, but whatever exerts the most power over us. We must make a determination to limit and concentrate our desires and interests on the atonement by the Cross of Christ.

"Whatever you ask in My name, that I will do." The disciple who abides in Jesus *is* the will of God, and what appears to be his free choices are actually God's foreordained decrees. Is this mysterious? Does it appear to contradict sound logic or seem totally absurd? Yes, but what a glorious truth it is to a saint of God.

What's Next to Do?

"If you know these things, blessed are you if you do them." **John 13:17**

Be determined to know more than others. If you yourself do not cut the lines that tie you to the dock, God will have to use a storm to sever them and to send you out to sea. Put everything in your life afloat upon God, going out to sea on the great swelling tide of His purpose, and your eyes will be opened. If you believe in Jesus, you are not to spend all your time in the calm waters just inside the harbor, full of joy, but always tied to the dock. You have to get out past the harbor into the great depths of God, and begin to know things for yourself—begin to have spiritual discernment.

When you know that you should do something and you do it, immediately you know more. Examine where you have become sluggish, where you began losing interest spiritually, and you will find that it goes back to a point where you did not do something you knew you should do. You did not do it because there seemed to be no immediate call to do it. But now you have no insight or discernment, and at a time of crisis you are spiritually distracted instead of spiritually self-controlled. It is a dangerous thing to refuse to continue learning and knowing more.

The counterfeit of obedience is a state of mind in which you create your own opportunities to sacrifice yourself, and your zeal and enthusiasm are mistaken for discernment. It is easier to sacrifice yourself than to fulfill your spiritual destiny, which is stated in Romans 12:1–2. It is much better to fulfill the purpose of God in your life by discerning His will than it is to perform great acts of self-sacrifice. "Behold, to obey is better than sacrifice" (1 Samuel 15:22). Beware of paying attention or going back to what you once were, when God wants you to be something that you have never been. "If anyone wills to do His will, he shall know . . ." (John 7:17).

JUNE 9

Then What's Next to Do?

"Everyone who asks receives." **Luke 11:10**

Ask if you have not received. There is nothing more difficult than asking. We will have yearnings and desires for certain things, and even suffer as a result of their going unfulfilled, but not until we are at the limit of desperation will we *ask*. It is the sense of not being spiritually real that causes us to ask. Have you ever asked out of the depths of your total insufficiency and poverty? "If any of you lacks wisdom, let him ask of God . . ." (James 1:5), but be sure that you do lack wisdom before you ask. You cannot bring yourself to the point of spiritual reality anytime you choose. The best thing to do, once you realize you are not spiritually real, is to ask God for the Holy Spirit, basing your request on the promise of Jesus Christ (see Luke 11:13). The Holy Spirit is the one who makes everything that Jesus did for you real in your life.

"Everyone who asks receives." This does not mean that you will not *get* if you do not ask, but it means that until you come to the point of asking, you will not *receive* from God (see Matthew 5:45). To be able to receive means that you have to come into the relationship of a child of God, and then you comprehend and appreciate mentally, morally, and with spiritual understanding, that these things come from God.

"If any of you lacks wisdom . . ." If you realize that you are lacking, it is because you have come in contact with spiritual reality—do not put the blinders of reason on again. The word *ask* actually means "beg." Some people are poor enough to be interested in their poverty, and some of us are poor enough spiritually to show our interest. Yet we will never receive if we ask with a certain result in mind, because we are asking out of our lust, not out of our poverty. A pauper does not ask out of any reason other than the completely hopeless and painful condition of his poverty. He is not ashamed to beg—blessed are the *paupers* in spirit (see Matthew 5:3).

And After That What's Next to Do?

"Seek, and you will find." **Luke 11:9**

Seek if you have not found. "You ask and do not receive, because you ask amiss" (James 4:3). If you ask for things from life instead of from God, "you ask amiss"; that is, you ask out of your desire for self-fulfillment. The more you fulfill yourself the less you will seek God. "Seek, and you will find." Get to work—narrow your focus and interests to this one thing. Have you ever sought God with your whole heart, or have you simply given Him a feeble cry after some emotionally painful experience? "Seek, [focus,] and you will find."

"Ho! Everyone who thirsts, come to the waters" (Isaiah 55:1). Are you thirsty, or complacent and indifferent—so satisfied with your own experience that you want nothing more of God? Experience is a doorway, not a final goal. Beware of building your faith on experience, or your life will not ring true and will only sound the note of a critical spirit. Remember that you can never give another person what you have found, but you can cause him to have a desire for it.

"Knock, and it will be opened to you" (Luke 11:9). "Draw near to God" (James 4:8). Knock—the door is closed, and your heartbeat races as you knock. "Cleanse your hands" (4:8). Knock a bit louder—you begin to find that you are dirty. "Purify your hearts" (4:8). It is becoming even more personal—you are desperate and serious now—you will do anything. "Lament" (4:9). Have you ever lamented, expressing your sorrow before God for the condition of your inner life? There is no thread of self-pity left, only the heart-rending difficulty and amazement which comes from seeing what kind of person you really are. "Humble yourselves" (4:10). It is a humbling experience to knock at God's door—you have to knock with the crucified thief. "To him who knocks *it will be opened*" (Luke 11:10).

JUNE 11

Getting There

"Come to Me." Matthew 11:28

Where sin and sorrow stops, and the song of the saint starts. Do I really want to get there? I can right now. The questions that truly matter in life are remarkably few, and they are all answered by these words—"Come to Me." Our Lord's words are not, "Do this, or don't do that," but—"Come to me." If I will simply come to Jesus, my real life will be brought into harmony with my real desires. I will actually cease from sin, and will find the song of the Lord beginning in my life.

Have you ever come to Jesus? Look at the stubbornness of your heart. You would rather do anything than this one simple childlike thing—"Come to Me." If you really want to experience ceasing from sin, you must come to Jesus.

Jesus Christ makes Himself the test to determine your genuineness. Look how He used the word *come.* At the most unexpected moments in your life there is this whisper of the Lord—"Come to Me," and you are immediately drawn to Him. Personal contact with Jesus changes everything. Be "foolish" enough to come and commit yourself to what He says. The attitude necessary for you to come to Him is one where your will has made the determination to let go of everything and deliberately commit it all to Him.

". . . and I will give you rest"—that is, "I will sustain you, causing you to stand firm." He is not saying, "I will put you to bed, hold your hand, and sing you to sleep." But, in essence, He is saying, "I will get you out of bed—out of your listlessness and exhaustion, and out of your condition of being half dead while you are still alive. I will penetrate you with the spirit of life, and you will be sustained by the perfection of vital activity." Yet we become so weak and pitiful and talk about "suffering" the will of the Lord! Where is the majestic vitality and the power of the Son of God in that?

Getting There

"They said to Him, 'Rabbi . . . where are You staying?' He said to them, 'Come and see.'" **John 1:38–39**

Where our self-interest sleeps and the real interest is awakened. "They . . . remained with Him that day." That is about all some of us ever do. We stay with Him a short time, only to wake up to our own realities of life. Our self-interest rises up and our abiding with Him is past. Yet there is no circumstance of life in which we cannot abide in Jesus.

"You are Simon. . . . You shall be called Cephas" (John 1:42). God writes our new name only on those places in our lives where He has erased our pride, self-sufficiency, and self-interest. Some of us have our new name written only in certain spots, like spiritual measles. And in those areas of our lives we look all right. When we are in our best spiritual mood, you would think we were the highest quality saints. But don't dare look at us when we are not in that mood. A true disciple is one who has his new name written all over him—self-interest, pride, and self-sufficiency have been completely erased.

Pride is the sin of making "self" our god. And some of us today do this, not like the Pharisee, but like the tax collector (see Luke 18:9–14). For you to say, "Oh, I'm no saint," is acceptable by human standards of pride, but it is unconscious blasphemy against God. You defy God to make you a saint, as if to say, "I am too weak and hopeless and outside the reach of the atonement by the Cross of Christ." Why aren't you a saint? It is either that you do not want to be a saint, or that you do not believe that God can make you into one. You say it would be all right if God saved you and took you straight to heaven. That is exactly what He will do! And not only do we make our home with Him, but Jesus said of His Father and Himself, "We will come to him and make Our home with him" (John 14:23). Put no conditions on your life—let Jesus be everything to you, and He will take you home with Him not only for a day, but for eternity.

Getting There

"Come, follow Me." **Luke 18:22**

Where our individual desire dies and sanctified surrender lives. One of the greatest hindrances in coming to Jesus is the excuse of our own individual temperament. We make our temperament and our natural desires barriers to coming to Jesus. Yet the first thing we realize when we do come to Jesus is that He pays no attention whatsoever to our natural desires. We have the idea that we can dedicate our gifts to God. However, you cannot dedicate what is not yours. There is actually only one thing you can dedicate to God, and that is your right to yourself (see Romans 12:1). If you will give God your right to yourself, He will make a holy experiment out of you—and His experiments always succeed. The one true mark of a saint of God is the inner creativity that flows from being totally surrendered to Jesus Christ. In the life of a saint there is this amazing Well, which is a continual Source of original life. The Spirit of God is a Well of water springing up perpetually fresh. A saint realizes that it is God who engineers his circumstances; consequently there are no complaints, only unrestrained surrender to Jesus. Never try to make your experience a principle for others, but allow God to be as creative and original with others as He is with you.

If you abandon everything to Jesus, and come when He says, "Come," then He will continue to say, "Come," through you. You will go out into the world reproducing the echo of Christ's "Come." That is the result in every soul who has abandoned all and come to Jesus.

Have I come to Him? Will I come *now*?

JUNE 14

Get Moving!

"Abide in Me." **John 15:4**

In the matter of determination. The Spirit of Jesus is put into me by way of the atonement by the Cross of Christ. I then have to build my thinking patiently to bring it into perfect harmony with my Lord. God will not make me think like Jesus—I have to do it myself. I have to bring "every thought into captivity to the obedience of Christ" (2 Corinthians 10:5). "Abide in Me"—in intellectual matters, in money matters, in every one of the matters that make human life what it is. Our lives are not made up of only one neatly confined area.

Am I preventing God from doing things in my circumstances by saying that it will only serve to hinder my fellowship with Him? How irrelevant and disrespectful that is! It does not matter what my circumstances are. I can be as much assured of abiding in Jesus in any one of them as I am in any prayer meeting. It is unnecessary to change and arrange my circumstances myself. Our Lord's inner abiding was pure and unblemished. He was at home with God wherever His body was. He never chose His own circumstances, but was meek, submitting to His Father's plans and directions for Him. Just think of how amazingly relaxed our Lord's life was! But we tend to keep God at a fever pitch in our lives. We have none of the serenity of the life which is "hidden with Christ in God" (Colossians 3:3).

Think of the things that take you out of the position of abiding in Christ. You say, "Yes, Lord, just a minute—I still have this to do. Yes, I will abide as soon as this is finished, or as soon as this week is over. It will be all right, Lord. I will abide then." *Get moving*—begin to abide *now.* In the initial stages it will be a continual effort to abide, but as you continue, it will become so much a part of your life that you will abide in Him without any conscious effort. Make the determination to abide in Jesus wherever you are now or wherever you may be placed in the future.

JUNE 15

Get Moving!

"Also . . . add to your faith . . ." **2 Peter 1:5**

In the matter of drudgery. Peter said in this passage that we have become "partakers of the divine nature" and that we should now be "giving all diligence," concentrating on forming godly habits (2 Peter 1:4–5). We are to "add" to our lives all that character means. No one is born either naturally or supernaturally with character; it must be developed. Nor are we born with habits—we have to form godly habits on the basis of the new life God has placed within us. We are not meant to be seen as God's perfect, bright-shining examples, but to be seen as the everyday essence of ordinary life exhibiting the miracle of His grace. Drudgery is the test of genuine character. The greatest hindrance in our spiritual life is that we will only look for big things to do. Yet, "Jesus . . . took a towel and . . . began to wash the disciples' feet" (John 13:3–5).

We all have those times when there are no flashes of light and no apparent thrill to life, where we experience nothing but the daily routine with its common everyday tasks. The routine of life is actually God's way of saving us between our times of great inspiration which come from Him. Don't always expect God to give you His thrilling moments, but learn to live in those common times of the drudgery of life by the power of God.

It is difficult for us to do the "adding" that Peter mentioned here. We say we do not expect God to take us to heaven on flowery beds of ease, and yet we act as if we do! I must realize that my obedience even in the smallest detail of life has all of the omnipotent power of the grace of God behind it. If I will do my duty, not for duty's sake but because I believe God is engineering my circumstances, then at the very point of my obedience all of the magnificent grace of God is mine through the glorious atonement by the Cross of Christ.

JUNE 16

"Will You Lay Down Your Life?"

"Greater love has no one than this, than to lay down one's life for his friends. . . . I have called you friends." **John 15:13, 15**

Jesus does not ask me to die for Him, but to lay down my life for Him. Peter said to the Lord, "I will lay down my life for Your sake," and he meant it (John 13:37). He had a magnificent sense of the heroic. For us to be incapable of making this same statement Peter made would be a bad thing—our sense of duty is only fully realized through our sense of heroism. Has the Lord ever asked you, "Will you lay down your life for My sake?" (John 13:38). It is much easier to die than to lay down your life day in and day out with the sense of the high calling of God. We are not made for the bright-shining moments of life, but we have to walk in the light of them in our everyday ways. There was only one bright-shining moment in the life of Jesus, and that was on the Mount of Transfiguration. It was there that He emptied Himself of His glory for the second time, and then came down into the demon-possessed valley (see Mark 9:1–29). For thirty-three years Jesus laid down His life to do the will of His Father. "By this we know love, because He laid down His life for us. And we also ought to lay down our lives for the brethren" (1 John 3:16). Yet it is contrary to our human nature to do so.

If I am a friend of Jesus, I must deliberately and carefully lay down my life for Him. It is a difficult thing to do, and thank God that it is. Salvation is easy for us, because it cost God so much. But the exhibiting of salvation in my life is difficult. God saves a person, fills him with the Holy Spirit, and then says, in effect, "Now you work it out in your life, and be faithful to Me, even though the nature of everything around you is to cause you to be unfaithful." And Jesus says to us, "I have called you friends." Remain faithful to your Friend, and remember that His honor is at stake in your bodily life.

Beware of Criticizing Others

"Judge not, that you be not judged." **Matthew 7:1**

Jesus' instructions with regard to judging others is very simply put; He says, *"Don't."* The average Christian is the most piercingly critical individual known. Criticism is one of the ordinary activities of people, but in the spiritual realm nothing is accomplished by it. The effect of criticism is the dividing up of the strengths of the one being criticized. The Holy Spirit is the only one in the proper position to criticize, and He alone is able to show what is wrong without hurting and wounding. It is impossible to enter into fellowship with God when you are in a critical mood. Criticism serves to make you harsh, vindictive, and cruel, and leaves you with the soothing and flattering idea that you are somehow superior to others. Jesus says that as His disciple you should cultivate a temperament that is never critical. This will not happen quickly but must be developed over a span of time. You must constantly beware of anything that causes you to think of yourself as a superior person.

There is no escaping the penetrating search of my life by Jesus. If I see the little speck in your eye, it means that I have a plank of timber in my own (see Matthew 7:3–5). Every wrong thing that I see in you, God finds in me. Every time I judge, I condemn myself (see Romans 2:17–24). Stop having a measuring stick for other people. There is always at least one more fact, which we know nothing about, in every person's situation. The first thing God does is to give us a thorough spiritual cleaning. After that, there is no possibility of pride remaining in us. I have never met a person I could despair of, or lose all hope for, after discerning what lies in me apart from the grace of God.

Keep Recognizing Jesus

"Peter . . . walked on the water to go to Jesus. But when he saw that the wind was boisterous, he was afraid." **Matthew 14:29–30**

The wind really was boisterous and the waves really were high, but Peter didn't see them at first. He didn't consider them at all; he simply recognized his Lord, stepped out in recognition of Him, and "walked on the water." Then he began to take those things around him into account, and instantly, down he went. Why couldn't our Lord have enabled him to walk at the bottom of the waves, as well as on top of them? He could have, yet neither could be done without Peter's continuing recognition of the Lord Jesus.

We step right out with recognition of God in some things, then self-consideration enters our lives and down we go. If you are truly recognizing your Lord, you have no business being concerned about how and where He engineers your circumstances. The things surrounding you *are* real, but when you look at them you are immediately overwhelmed, and even unable to recognize Jesus. Then comes His rebuke, "Why did you doubt?" (Matthew 14:31). Let your actual circumstances be what they may, but keep recognizing Jesus, maintaining complete reliance upon Him.

If you debate for even one second when God has spoken, it is all over for you. Never start to say, "Well, I wonder if He really did speak to me?" Be reckless immediately—totally unrestrained and willing to risk everything—by casting your all upon Him. You do not know when His voice will come to you, but whenever the realization of God comes, even in the faintest way imaginable, be determined to recklessly abandon yourself, surrendering everything to Him. It is only through abandonment of yourself and your circumstances that you will recognize Him. You will only recognize His voice more clearly through recklessness—being willing to risk your all.

The Service of Passionate Devotion

"Do you love Me? . . . Tend My sheep." **John 21:16**

Jesus did not say to make converts to your way of thinking, but He said to look after His sheep, to see that they get nourished in the knowledge of Him. We consider what we do in the way of Christian work as service, yet Jesus Christ calls service to be what we *are* to Him, not what we *do* for Him. Discipleship is based solely on devotion to Jesus Christ, not on following after a particular belief or doctrine. "If anyone comes to Me and does not hate . . . , he cannot be My disciple" (Luke 14:26). In this verse, there is no argument and no pressure from Jesus to follow Him; He is simply saying, in effect, "If you want to be My disciple, you must be devoted solely to Me." A person touched by the Spirit of God suddenly says, "Now I see who Jesus is!"—that is the source of devotion.

Today we have substituted doctrinal belief for personal belief, and that is why so many people are devoted to causes and so few are devoted to Jesus Christ. People do not really want to be devoted to Jesus, but only to the cause He started. Jesus Christ is deeply offensive to the educated minds of today, to those who only want Him to be their Friend, and who are unwilling to accept Him in any other way. Our Lord's primary obedience was to the will of His Father, not to the needs of people—the saving of people was the natural outcome of His obedience to the Father. If I am devoted solely to the cause of humanity, I will soon be exhausted and come to the point where my love will waver and stumble. But if I love Jesus Christ personally and passionately, I can serve humanity, even though people may treat me like a "doormat." The secret of a disciple's life is devotion to Jesus Christ, and the characteristic of that life is its seeming insignificance and its meekness. Yet it is like a grain of wheat that "falls into the ground and dies"—it will spring up and change the entire landscape (John 12:24).

Have You Come to "When" Yet?

"The Lord restored Job's losses when he prayed for his friends." **Job 42:10**

A pitiful, sickly, and self-centered kind of prayer and a determined effort and selfish desire to be right with God are never found in the New Testament. The fact that I am trying to be right with God is actually a sign that I am rebelling against the atonement by the Cross of Christ. I pray, "Lord, I will purify my heart if You will answer my prayer—I will walk rightly before You if You will help me." But I *cannot* make myself right with God; I *cannot* make my life perfect. I can only be right with God if I accept the atonement of the Lord Jesus Christ as an absolute gift. Am I humble enough to accept it? I have to surrender all my rights and demands, and cease from every self-effort. I must leave myself completely alone in His hands, and then I can begin to pour my life out in the priestly work of intercession. There is a great deal of prayer that comes from actual disbelief in the atonement. Jesus is not just beginning to save us—He has already saved us completely. It is an accomplished fact, and it is an insult to Him for us to ask Him to do what He has already done.

If you are not now receiving the "hundredfold" which Jesus promised (see Matthew 19:29), and not getting insight into God's Word, then start praying for your friends—enter into the ministry of the inner life. "The Lord restored Job's losses *when he prayed for his friends*." As a saved soul, the real business of your life is intercessory prayer. Whatever circumstances God may place you in, always pray immediately that His atonement may be recognized and as fully understood in the lives of others as it has been in yours. Pray for your friends *now*, and pray for those with whom you come in contact *now*.

JUNE 21

The Ministry of the Inner Life

"You are . . . a royal priesthood." **1 Peter 2:9**

By what right have we become "a royal priesthood"? It is by the right of the atonement by the Cross of Christ that this has been accomplished. Are we prepared to purposely disregard ourselves and to launch out into the priestly work of prayer? The continual inner-searching we do in an effort to see if we are what we ought to be generates a self-centered, sickly type of Christianity, not the vigorous and simple life of a child of God. Until we get into this right and proper relationship with God, it is simply a case of our "hanging on by the skin of our teeth," although we say, "What a wonderful victory I have!" Yet there is nothing at all in that which indicates the miracle of redemption. Launch out in reckless, unrestrained belief that the redemption is complete. Then don't worry anymore about yourself, but begin to do as Jesus Christ has said, in essence, "Pray for the friend who comes to you at midnight, pray for the saints of God, and pray for all men." Pray with the realization that you are perfect only in Christ Jesus, not on the basis of this argument: "Oh, Lord, I have done my best; please hear me now."

How long is it going to take God to free us from the unhealthy habit of thinking only about ourselves? We must get to the point of being sick to death of ourselves, until there is no longer any surprise at anything God might tell us about ourselves. We cannot reach and understand the depths of our own meagerness. There is only one place where we are right with God, and that is in Christ Jesus. Once we are there, we have to pour out our lives for all we are worth in this ministry of the inner life.

The Unchanging Law of Judgment

"With what judgment you judge, you will be judged; and with the measure you use, it will be measured back to you." **Matthew 7:2**

This statement is not some haphazard theory, but it is an eternal law of God. Whatever judgment you give will be the very way you are judged. There is a difference between retaliation and retribution. Jesus said that the basis of life is retribution—"with the measure you use, it will be measured back to you." If you have been shrewd in finding out the shortcomings of others, remember that will be exactly how you will be measured. The way you pay is the way life will pay you back. This eternal law works from God's throne down to us (see Psalm 18:25–26).

Romans 2:1 applies it in even a more definite way by saying that the one who criticizes another is guilty of the very same thing. God looks not only at the act itself, but also at the possibility of committing it, which He sees by looking at our hearts. To begin with, we do not believe the statements of the Bible. For instance, do we really believe the statement that says we criticize in others the very things we are guilty of ourselves? The reason we see hypocrisy, deceit, and a lack of genuineness in others is that they are all in our own hearts. The greatest characteristic of a saint is humility, as evidenced by being able to say honestly and humbly, "Yes, all those, as well as other evils, would have been exhibited in me if it were not for the grace of God. Therefore, I have no right to judge."

Jesus said, "Judge not, that you be not judged" (Matthew 7:1). He went on to say, in effect, "If you do judge, you will be judged in exactly the same way." Who of us would dare to stand before God and say, "My God, judge me as I have judged others"? We have judged others as sinners—if God should judge us in the same way, we would be condemned to hell. Yet God judges us on the basis of the miraculous atonement by the Cross of Christ.

"Acquainted with Grief"

"He is . . . a Man of sorrows and acquainted with grief." **Isaiah 53:3**

We are not "acquainted with grief" in the same way our Lord was acquainted with it. We endure it and live through it, but we do not become intimate with it. At the beginning of our lives we do not bring ourselves to the point of dealing with the reality of sin. We look at life through the eyes of reason and say that if a person will control his instincts, and educate himself, he can produce a life that will slowly evolve into the life of God. But as we continue on through life, we find the presence of something which we have not yet taken into account, namely, sin—and it upsets all of our thinking and our plans. Sin has made the foundation of our thinking unpredictable, uncontrollable, and irrational.

We have to recognize that sin is a fact of life, not just a shortcoming. Sin is blatant mutiny against God, and either sin or God must die in my life. The New Testament brings us right down to this one issue—if sin rules in me, God's life in me will be killed; if God rules in me, sin in me will be killed. There is nothing more fundamental than that. The culmination of sin was the crucifixion of Jesus Christ, and what was true in the history of God on earth will also be true in your history and in mine—that is, sin will kill the life of God in us. We must mentally bring ourselves to terms with this fact of sin. It is the only explanation why Jesus Christ came to earth, and it is the explanation of the grief and sorrow of life.

Reconciling Yourself to the Fact of Sin

"This is your hour, and the power of darkness." **Luke 22:53**

Not being reconciled to the fact of sin—not recognizing it and refusing to deal with it—produces all the disasters in life. You may talk about the lofty virtues of human nature, but there is something in human nature that will mockingly laugh in the face of every principle you have. If you refuse to agree with the fact that there is wickedness and selfishness, something downright hateful and wrong, in human beings, when it attacks your life, instead of reconciling yourself to it, you will compromise with it and say that it is of no use to battle against it. Have you taken this "hour, and the power of darkness" into account, or do you have a view of yourself which includes no recognition of sin whatsoever? In your human relationships and friendships, have you reconciled yourself to the fact of sin? If not, just around the next corner you will find yourself trapped and you will compromise with it. But if you will reconcile yourself to the fact of sin, you will realize the danger immediately and say, "Yes, I see what this sin would mean." The recognition of sin does not destroy the basis of friendship—it simply establishes a mutual respect for the fact that the basis of sinful life is disastrous. Always beware of any assessment of life which does not recognize the fact that there is sin.

Jesus Christ never trusted human nature, yet He was never cynical nor suspicious, because He had absolute trust in what He could do for human nature. The pure man or woman is the one who is shielded from harm, not the innocent person. The so-called innocent man or woman is never safe. Men and women have no business trying to be innocent; God demands that they be pure and virtuous. Innocence is the characteristic of a child. Any person is deserving of blame if he is unwilling to reconcile himself to the fact of sin.

JUNE 25

Receiving Yourself in the Fires of Sorrow

"What shall I say? 'Father, save Me from this hour'? But for this purpose I came to this hour. 'Father, glorify Your name.'" **John 12:27–28**

As a saint of God, my attitude toward sorrow and difficulty should not be to ask that they be prevented, but to ask that God protect me so that I may remain what He created me to be, in spite of all my fires of sorrow. Our Lord received Himself, accepting His position and realizing His purpose, in the midst of the fire of sorrow. He was saved not *from* the hour, but *out of* the hour.

We say that there ought to be no sorrow, but there *is* sorrow, and we have to accept and receive ourselves in its fires. If we try to evade sorrow, refusing to deal with it, we are foolish. Sorrow is one of the biggest facts in life, and there is no use in saying it should not be. Sin, sorrow, and suffering *are*, and it is not for us to say that God has made a mistake in allowing them.

Sorrow removes a great deal of a person's shallowness, but it does not always make that person better. Suffering either gives me to myself or it destroys me. You cannot find or receive yourself through success, because you lose your head over pride. And you cannot receive yourself through the monotony of your daily life, because you give in to complaining. The only way to find yourself is in the fires of sorrow. Why it should be this way is immaterial. The fact is that it is true in the Scriptures and in human experience. You can always recognize who has been through the fires of sorrow and received himself, and you know that you can go to him in your moment of trouble and find that he has plenty of time for you. But if a person has not been through the fires of sorrow, he is apt to be contemptuous, having no respect or time for you, only turning you away. If you will receive yourself in the fires of sorrow, God will make you nourishment for other people.

Drawing on the Grace of God—Now

"We . . . plead with you not to receive the grace of God in vain." **2 Corinthians 6:1**

The grace you had yesterday will not be sufficient for today. Grace is the overflowing favor of God, and you can always count on it being available to draw upon as needed. "In much patience, in tribulations, in needs, in distresses"—that is where our patience is tested (2 Corinthians 6:4). Are you failing to rely on the grace of God there? Are you saying to yourself, "Oh well, I won't count this time"? It is not a question of praying and asking God to help you—it is taking the grace of God *now*. We tend to make prayer the preparation for our service, yet it is never that in the Bible. Prayer is the practice of drawing on the grace of God. Don't say, "I will endure this until I can get away and pray." Pray *now*—draw on the grace of God in your moment of need. Prayer is the most normal and useful thing; it is not simply a reflex action of your devotion to God. We are very slow to learn to draw on God's grace through prayer.

". . . in stripes, in imprisonments, in tumults, in labors . . ." (6:5)—in all these things, display in your life a drawing on the grace of God, which will show evidence to yourself and to others that you are a miracle of His. Draw on His grace now, not later. The primary word in the spiritual vocabulary is *now*. Let circumstances take you where they will, but keep drawing on the grace of God in whatever condition you may find yourself. One of the greatest proofs that you are drawing on the grace of God is that you can be totally humiliated before others without displaying even the slightest trace of anything but His grace.

". . . having nothing . . ." Never hold anything in reserve. Pour yourself out, giving the best that you have, and always be poor. Never be diplomatic and careful with the treasure God gives you. ". . . and yet possessing all things"—this is poverty triumphant (6:10).

The Overshadowing of God's Personal Deliverance

"'I am with you to deliver you,' says the Lord." **Jeremiah 1:8**

God promised Jeremiah that He would deliver him personally—"your life shall be as a prize to you" (Jeremiah 39:18). That is all God promises His children. Wherever God sends us, He will guard our lives. Our personal property and possessions are to be a matter of indifference to us, and our hold on these things should be very loose. If this is not the case, we will have panic, heartache, and distress. Having the proper outlook is evidence of the deeply rooted belief in the overshadowing of God's personal deliverance.

The Sermon on the Mount indicates that when we are on a mission for Jesus Christ, there is no time to stand up for ourselves. Jesus says, in effect, "Don't worry about whether or not you are being treated justly." Looking for justice is actually a sign that we have been diverted from our devotion to Him. Never look for justice in this world, but never cease to give it. If we look for justice, we will only begin to complain and to indulge ourselves in the discontent of self-pity, as if to say, "Why should I be treated like this?" If we are devoted to Jesus Christ, we have nothing to do with what we encounter, whether it is just or unjust. In essence, Jesus says, "Continue steadily on with what I have told you to do, and I will guard your life. If you try to guard it yourself, you remove yourself from My deliverance." Even the most devout among us become atheistic in this regard—we do not believe Him. We put our common sense on the throne and then attach God's name to it. We *do* lean to our own understanding, instead of trusting God with all our hearts (see Proverbs 3:5–6).

JUNE 28

Held by the Grip of God

"I press on, that I may lay hold of that for which Christ Jesus has also laid hold of me." **Philippians 3:12**

Never choose to be a worker for God, but once God has placed His call on you, woe be to you if you "turn aside to the right hand or to the left" (Deuteronomy 5:32). We are not here to work for God because we have chosen to do so, but because God has "laid hold of" us. And once He has done so, we never have this thought, "Well, I'm really not suited for this." What you are to preach is also determined by God, not by your own natural leanings or desires. Keep your soul steadfastly related to God, and remember that you are called not simply to convey your testimony but also to preach the gospel. Every Christian must testify to the truth of God, but when it comes to the call to preach, there must be the agonizing grip of God's hand on you—your life is in the grip of God for that very purpose. How many of us are held like that?

Never water down the Word of God, but preach it in its undiluted sternness. There must be unflinching faithfulness to the Word of God, but when you come to personal dealings with others, remember who you are—you are not some special being created in heaven, but a sinner saved by grace.

"Brethren, I do not count myself to have apprehended; but *one thing I do* . . . I press toward the goal for the prize of the upward call of God in Christ Jesus" (Philippians 3:13–14).

JUNE 29

The Strictest Discipline

"If your right hand causes you to sin, cut it off and cast it from you; for it is more profitable for you that one of your members perish, than for your whole body to be cast into hell." **Matthew 5:30**

Jesus did not say that everyone must cut off his right hand, but that "if your right hand causes you to sin" in your walk with Him, then it is better to "cut it off." There are many things that are perfectly legitimate, but if you are going to concentrate on God you cannot do them. Your right hand is one of the best things you have, but Jesus says that if it hinders you in following His precepts, then "cut it off." The principle taught here is the strictest discipline or lesson that ever hit humankind.

When God changes you through regeneration, giving you new life through spiritual rebirth, your life initially has the characteristic of being maimed. There are a hundred and one things that you dare not do—things that would be sin for you, and would be recognized as sin by those who really know you. But the unspiritual people around you will say, "What's so wrong with doing that? How absurd you are!" There has never yet been a saint who has not lived a maimed life initially. Yet it is better to enter into life maimed but lovely in God's sight than to appear lovely to man's eyes but lame to God's. At first, Jesus Christ through His Spirit has to restrain you from doing a great many things that may be perfectly right for everyone else but not right for you. Yet, see that you don't use your restrictions to criticize someone else.

The Christian life is a maimed life initially, but in verse 48 Jesus gave us the picture of a perfectly well-rounded life—"You shall be *perfect*, just as your Father in heaven is perfect."

Do It Now!

"Agree with your adversary quickly." **Matthew 5:25**

In this verse, Jesus Christ laid down a very important principle by saying, "Do what you know you must do—*now*. Do it quickly. If you don't, an inevitable process will begin to work 'till you have paid the last penny' (Matthew 5:26) in pain, agony, and distress." God's laws are unchangeable and there is no escape from them. The teachings of Jesus always penetrate right to the heart of our being.

Wanting to make sure that my adversary gives me all my rights is a natural thing. But Jesus says that it is a matter of inescapable and eternal importance to me that I pay my adversary what I owe him. From our Lord's standpoint it doesn't matter whether I am cheated or not, but what does matter is that I don't cheat someone else. Am I insisting on having my own rights, or am I paying what I owe from Jesus Christ's standpoint?

Do it quickly—bring yourself to judgment now. In moral and spiritual matters, you must act immediately. If you don't, the inevitable, relentless process will begin to work. God is determined to have His child as pure, clean, and white as driven snow, and as long as there is disobedience in any point of His teaching, He will allow His Spirit to use whatever process it may take to bring us to obedience. The fact that we insist on proving that we are right is almost always a clear indication that we have some point of disobedience. No wonder the Spirit of God so strongly urges us to stay steadfastly in the light! (see John 3:19–21).

"Agree with your adversary quickly." Have you suddenly reached a certain place in your relationship with someone, only to find that you have anger in your heart? Confess it quickly—make it right before God. Be reconciled to that person—*do it now!*

JULY 1

The Inevitable Penalty

"You will by no means get out of there till you have paid the last penny." **Matthew 5:26**

There is no heaven that has a little corner of hell in it. God is determined to make you pure, holy, and right, and He will not allow you to escape from the scrutiny of the Holy Spirit for even one moment. He urged you to come to judgment immediately when He convicted you, but you did not obey. Then the inevitable process began to work, bringing its inevitable penalty. Now you have been "thrown into prison, [and] . . . you will by no means get out of there till you have paid the last penny" (Matthew 5:25–26). Yet you ask, "Is this a God of mercy and love?" When seen from God's perspective, it is a glorious ministry of love. God is going to bring you out pure, spotless, and undefiled, but He wants you to recognize the nature you were exhibiting—the nature of demanding your right to yourself. The moment you are willing for God to change your nature, His re-creating forces will begin to work. And the moment you realize that God's purpose is to get you into the right relationship with Himself and then with others, He will reach to the very limits of the universe to help you take the right road. Decide to do it right now, saying, "Yes, Lord, I *will* write that letter," or, "I *will* be reconciled to that person now."

These sermons of Jesus Christ are meant for your will and your conscience, not for your head. If you dispute these verses from the Sermon on the Mount with your head, you will dull the appeal to your heart.

If you find yourself asking, "I wonder why I'm not growing spiritually with God?"—then ask yourself if you are paying your debts from God's standpoint. Do *now* what you will have to do someday. Every moral question or call comes with an "ought" behind it—the knowledge of knowing what we ought to do.

The Conditions of Discipleship

"If anyone comes to Me and does not hate his father and mother, wife and children, brothers and sisters, yes, and his own life also . . . . And whoever does not bear his cross and come after Me . . . . So likewise, whoever of you does not forsake all that he has cannot be My disciple." **Luke 14:26–27, 33**

If the closest relationships of a disciple's life conflict with the claims of Jesus Christ, then our Lord requires instant obedience to Himself. Discipleship means personal, passionate devotion to a Person—our Lord Jesus Christ. There is a vast difference between devotion to a person and devotion to principles or to a cause. Our Lord never proclaimed a cause—He proclaimed personal devotion to Himself. To be a disciple is to be a devoted bondservant motivated by love for the Lord Jesus. Many of us who call ourselves Christians are not truly devoted to Jesus Christ. No one on earth has this passionate love for the Lord Jesus unless the Holy Spirit has given it to him. We may admire, respect, and revere Him, but we cannot love Him on our own. The only One who truly loves the Lord Jesus is the Holy Spirit, and it is He who has "poured out in our hearts" the very "love of God" (Romans 5:5). Whenever the Holy Spirit sees an opportunity to glorify Jesus through you, He will take your entire being and set you ablaze with glowing devotion to Jesus Christ.

The Christian life is a life characterized by true and spontaneous creativity. Consequently, a disciple is subject to the same charge that was leveled against Jesus Christ, namely, the charge of inconsistency. But Jesus Christ was always consistent in His relationship to God, and a Christian must be consistent in his relationship to the life of the Son of God in him, not consistent to strict, unyielding doctrines. People pour themselves into their own doctrines, and God has to blast them out of their preconceived ideas before they can become devoted to Jesus Christ.

JULY 3

The Concentration of Personal Sin

"Woe is me, for I am undone! Because I am a man of unclean lips." **Isaiah 6:5**

When I come into the very presence of God, I do not realize that I am a sinner in an indefinite sense, but I suddenly realize and the focus of my attention is directed toward the concentration of sin in a particular area of my life. A person will easily say, "Oh yes, I know I am a sinner," but when he comes into the presence of God he cannot get away with such a broad and indefinite statement. Our conviction is focused on our specific sin, and we realize, as Isaiah did, what we really are. This is always the sign that a person is in the presence of God. There is never any vague sense of sin, but a focusing on the concentration of sin in some specific, personal area of life. God begins by convicting us of the very thing to which His Spirit has directed our mind's attention. If we will surrender, submitting to His conviction of that particular sin, He will lead us down to where He can reveal the vast underlying nature of sin. That is the way God always deals with us when we are consciously aware of His presence.

This experience of our attention being directed to our concentration of personal sin is true in everyone's life, from the greatest of saints to the worst of sinners. When a person first begins climbing the ladder of experience, he might say, "I don't know where I've gone wrong," but the Spirit of God will point out some definite and specific thing to him. The effect of Isaiah's vision of the holiness of the Lord was the directing of his attention to the fact that he was "a man of unclean lips." "He touched my mouth with it, and said: 'Behold, this has touched your lips; your iniquity is taken away, and your sin purged'" (Isaiah 6:7). The cleansing fire had to be applied where the sin had been concentrated.

One of God's Great "Don'ts"

"Do not fret—it only causes harm." **Psalm 37:8**

Fretting means getting ourselves "out of joint" mentally or spiritually. It is one thing to say, "Do not fret," but something very different to have such a nature that you find yourself unable to fret. It's easy to say, "Rest in the Lord, and wait patiently for Him" (Psalm 37:7) until our own little world is turned upside down and we are forced to live in confusion and agony like so many other people. Is it possible to "rest in the Lord" then? If this "Do not" doesn't work there, then it will not work anywhere. This "Do not" must work during our days of difficulty and uncertainty, as well as our peaceful days, or it will never work. And if it will not work in your particular case, it will not work for anyone else. Resting in the Lord is not dependent on your external circumstances at all, but on your relationship with God Himself.

Worrying always results in sin. We tend to think that a little anxiety and worry are simply an indication of how wise we really are, yet it is actually a much better indication of just how wicked we are. Fretting rises from our determination to have our own way. Our Lord never worried and was never anxious, because His purpose was never to accomplish His own plans but to fulfill God's plans. Fretting is wickedness for a child of God.

Have you been propping up that foolish soul of yours with the idea that your circumstances are too much for God to handle? Set all your opinions and speculations aside and "abide under the shadow of the Almighty" (Psalm 91:1). Deliberately tell God that you will not fret about whatever concerns you. All our fretting and worrying is caused by planning without God.

Don't Plan Without God

"Commit your way to the Lord, trust also in Him, and He shall bring it to pass." **Psalm 37:5**

Don't plan without God. God seems to have a delightful way of upsetting the plans we have made, when we have not taken Him into account. We get ourselves into circumstances that were not chosen by God, and suddenly we realize that we have been making our plans without Him—that we have not even considered Him to be a vital, living factor in the planning of our lives. And yet the only thing that will keep us from even the possibility of worrying is to bring God in as the greatest factor in all of our planning.

In spiritual issues it is customary for us to put God first, but we tend to think that it is inappropriate and unnecessary to put Him first in the practical, everyday issues of our lives. If we have the idea that we have to put on our "spiritual face" before we can come near to God, then we will never come near to Him. We must come as we are.

Don't plan with a concern for evil in mind. Does God really mean for us to plan without taking the evil around us into account? "Love . . . thinks no evil" (1 Corinthians 13:4–5). Love is not ignorant of the existence of evil, but it does not take it into account as a factor in planning. When we were apart from God, we did take evil into account, doing all of our planning with it in mind, and we tried to reason out all of our work from its standpoint.

Don't plan with a rainy day in mind. You cannot hoard things for a rainy day if you are truly trusting Christ. Jesus said, "Let not your heart be troubled" (John 14:1). God will not keep your heart from being troubled. It is a command—"*Let not . . .*" To do it, continually pick yourself up, even if you fall a hundred and one times a day, until you get into the habit of putting God first and planning with Him in mind.

JULY 6

Visions Becoming Reality

"The parched ground shall become a pool." **Isaiah 35:7**

We always have a vision of something before it actually becomes real to us. When we realize that the vision is real, but is not yet real in us, Satan comes to us with his temptations, and we are inclined to say that there is no point in even trying to continue. Instead of the vision becoming real to us, we have entered into a valley of humiliation.

> *Life is not as idle ore, / But iron dug from central gloom,*
> *And battered by the shocks of doom / To shape and use.*

God gives us a vision, and then He takes us down to the valley to batter us into the shape of that vision. It is in the valley that so many of us give up and faint. Every God-given vision will become real if we will only have patience. Just think of the enormous amount of free time God has! He is never in a hurry. Yet we are always in such a frantic hurry. While still in the light of the glory of the vision, we go right out to do things, but the vision is not yet real in us. God has to take us into the valley and put us through fires and floods to batter us into shape, until we get to the point where He can trust us with the reality of the vision. Ever since God gave us the vision, He has been at work. He is getting us into the shape of the goal He has for us, and yet over and over again we try to escape from the Sculptor's hand in an effort to batter ourselves into the shape of our own goal.

The vision that God gives is not some unattainable castle in the sky, but a vision of what God wants you to be down here. Allow the Potter to put you on His wheel and whirl you around as He desires. Then as surely as God is God, and you are you, you will turn out as an exact likeness of the vision. But don't lose heart in the process. If you have ever had a vision from God, you may try as you will to be satisfied on a lower level, but God will never allow it.

JULY 7

All Efforts of Worth and Excellence Are Difficult

"Enter by the narrow gate . . . . Because narrow is the gate and difficult is the way which leads to life." **Matthew 7:13–14**

If we are going to live as disciples of Jesus, we have to remember that all efforts of worth and excellence are difficult. The Christian life is gloriously difficult, but its difficulty does not make us faint and cave in—it stirs us up to overcome. Do we appreciate the miraculous salvation of Jesus Christ enough to be our utmost for His highest—our best for His glory?

God saves people by His sovereign grace through the atonement of Jesus, and "it is God who works in you both to will and to do for His good pleasure" (Philippians 2:13). But we have to "work out" that salvation in our everyday, practical living (Philippians 2:12). If we will only start on the basis of His redemption to do what He commands, then we will find that we can do it. If we fail, it is because we have not yet put into practice what God has placed within us. But a crisis will reveal whether or not we have been putting it into practice. If we will obey the Spirit of God and practice in our physical life what God has placed within us by His Spirit, then when a crisis does come we will find that our own nature, as well as the grace of God, will stand by us.

Thank God that He does give us difficult things to do! His salvation is a joyous thing, but it is also something that requires bravery, courage, and holiness. It tests us for all we are worth. Jesus is "bringing many sons to glory" (Hebrews 2:10), and God will not shield us from the requirements of sonship. God's grace produces men and women with a strong family likeness to Jesus Christ, not pampered, spoiled weaklings. It takes a tremendous amount of discipline to live the worthy and excellent life of a disciple of Jesus in the realities of life. And it is always necessary for us to make an effort to live a life of worth and excellence.

JULY 8

Will to Be Faithful

"Choose for yourselves this day whom you will serve."
Joshua 24:15

A person's will is embodied in the actions of the whole person. I cannot *give up* my will—I must exercise it, putting it into action. I must *will* to obey, and I must *will* to receive God's Spirit. When God gives me a vision of truth, there is never a question of what He will do, but only of what I will do. The Lord has been placing in front of each of us some big proposals and plans. The best thing to do is to remember what you did before when you were touched by God. Recall the moment when you were saved, or first recognized Jesus, or realized some truth. It was easy then to yield your allegiance to God. Immediately recall those moments each time the Spirit of God brings some new proposal before you.

"Choose for yourselves this day whom you will serve." Your choice must be a deliberate determination—it is not something into which you will automatically drift. And everything else in your life will be held in temporary suspension until you make a decision. The proposal is between you and God—do not "confer with flesh and blood" about it (Galatians 1:16). With every new proposal, the people around us seem to become more and more isolated, and that is where the tension develops. God allows the opinion of His other saints to matter to you, and yet you become less and less certain that others really understand the step you are taking. You have no business trying to find out where God is leading—the only thing God will explain to you is Himself.

Openly declare to Him, "I will be faithful." But remember that as soon as you choose to be faithful to Jesus Christ, "You are witnesses against yourselves" (Joshua 24:22). Don't consult with other Christians, but simply and freely declare before Him, "I will serve You." *Will* to be faithful—and give other people credit for being faithful too.

Will You Examine Yourself?

"Joshua said to the people, 'You cannot serve the Lord.'" **Joshua 24:19**

Do you have even the slightest reliance on anything or anyone other than God? Is there a remnant of reliance left on any natural quality within you, or on any particular set of circumstances? Are you relying on yourself in any manner whatsoever regarding this new proposal or plan which God has placed before you? Will you examine yourself by asking these probing questions? It really is true to say, "I cannot live a holy life," but you can decide to let Jesus Christ make you holy. "You cannot serve the Lord"—but you can place yourself in the proper position where God's almighty power will flow through you. Is your relationship with God sufficient for you to expect Him to exhibit His wonderful life in you?

"The people said to Joshua, 'No, but we will serve the LORD!'" (24:21). This is not an impulsive action, but a deliberate commitment. We tend to say, "But God could never have called *me* to this. I'm too unworthy. It can't mean *me*." It does mean you, and the more weak and feeble you are, the better. The person who is still relying and trusting in anything within himself is the last person to even come close to saying, "I will serve the Lord."

We say, "Oh, if only I really could believe!" The question is, "*Will* I believe?" No wonder Jesus Christ placed such emphasis on the sin of unbelief. "He did not do many mighty works there because of their unbelief" (Matthew 13:58). If we really believed that God meant what He said, just imagine what we would be like! Do I really dare to let God be to me all that He says He will be?

The Spiritually Lazy Saint

"Let us consider one another in order to stir up love and good works, not forsaking the assembling of ourselves together." **Hebrews 10:24–25**

We are all capable of being spiritually lazy saints. We want to stay off the rough roads of life, and our primary objective is to secure a peaceful retreat from the world. The ideas put forth in these verses from Hebrews 10 are those of stirring up one another and of keeping ourselves together. Both of these require initiative—our willingness to take the first step toward Christ-realization, not the initiative toward self-realization. To live a distant, withdrawn, and secluded life is diametrically opposed to spirituality as Jesus Christ taught it.

The true test of our spirituality occurs when we come up against injustice, degradation, ingratitude, and turmoil, all of which have the tendency to make us spiritually lazy. While being tested, we want to use prayer and Bible reading for the purpose of finding a quiet retreat. We use God only for the sake of getting peace and joy. We seek only our enjoyment of Jesus Christ, not a true realization of Him. This is the first step in the wrong direction. All these things we are seeking are simply effects, and yet we try to make them causes.

"Yes, I think it is right," Peter said, ". . . to stir you up by reminding you" (2 Peter 1:13). It is a most disturbing thing to be hit squarely in the stomach by someone being used of God to stir us up—someone who is full of spiritual activity. Simple active work and spiritual activity are not the same thing. Active work can actually be the counterfeit of spiritual activity. The real danger in spiritual laziness is that we do not want to be stirred up—all we want to hear about is a spiritual retirement from the world. Yet Jesus Christ never encourages the idea of retirement—He says, "Go and tell My brethren . . ." (Matthew 28:10).

JULY 11

The Spiritually Vigorous Saint

"*. . . that I may know Him . . .*" **Philippians 3:10**

A saint is not to take the initiative toward self-realization, but toward knowing Jesus Christ. A spiritually vigorous saint never believes that his circumstances simply happen at random, nor does he ever think of his life as being divided into the secular and the sacred. He sees every situation in which he finds himself as the means of obtaining a greater knowledge of Jesus Christ, and he has an attitude of unrestrained abandon and total surrender about him. The Holy Spirit is determined that we will have the realization of Jesus Christ in every area of our lives, and He will bring us back to the same point over and over again until we do. Self-realization only leads to the glorification of good works, whereas a saint of God glorifies Jesus Christ through his good works. Whatever we may be doing—even eating, drinking, or washing disciples' feet—we have to take the initiative of realizing and recognizing Jesus Christ in it. Every phase of our life has its counterpart in the life of Jesus. Our Lord realized His relationship to the Father even in the most menial task. "Jesus, knowing . . . that He had come from God and was going to God, . . . took a towel . . . and began to wash the disciples' feet" (John 13:3–5).

The aim of a spiritually vigorous saint is "that I may know Him." Do I know Him where I am today? If not, I am failing Him. I am not here for self-realization, but to know Jesus Christ. In Christian work our initiative and motivation are too often simply the result of realizing that there is work to be done and that we must do it. Yet that is never the attitude of a spiritually vigorous saint. His aim is to achieve the realization of Jesus Christ in every set of circumstances.

The Spiritually Self-Seeking Church

". . . till we all come . . . to the measure of the stature of the fullness of Christ." **Ephesians 4:13**

Reconciliation means the restoring of the relationship between the entire human race and God, putting it back to what God designed it to be. This is what Jesus Christ did in redemption. The church ceases to be spiritual when it becomes self-seeking, only interested in the development of its own organization. The reconciliation of the human race according to His plan means realizing Him not only in our lives individually, but also in our lives collectively. Jesus Christ sent apostles and teachers for this very purpose—that the corporate Person of Christ and His church, made up of many members, might be brought into being and made known. We are not here to develop a spiritual life of our own, or to enjoy a quiet spiritual retreat. We are here to have the full realization of Jesus Christ, for the purpose of building His body.

Am I building up the body of Christ, or am I only concerned about my own personal development? The essential thing is my personal relationship with Jesus Christ—"that *I* may know *Him*" (Philippians 3:10). To fulfill God's perfect design for me requires my total surrender—complete abandonment of myself to Him. Whenever I only want things for myself, the relationship is distorted. And I will suffer great humiliation once I come to acknowledge and understand that I have not really been concerned about realizing Jesus Christ Himself, but only concerned with knowing what He has done for me.

My goal is God Himself, not joy nor peace,
Nor even blessing, but Himself, my God.

Am I measuring my life by this standard or by something less?

JULY 13

The Price of the Vision

"In the year that King Uzziah died, I saw the Lord . . ."
Isaiah 6:1

Our soul's personal history with God is often an account of the death of our heroes. Over and over again God has to remove our friends to put Himself in their place, and that is when we falter, fail, and become discouraged. Let me think about this personally—when the person died who represented for me all that God was, did I give up on everything in life? Did I become ill or disheartened? Or did I do as Isaiah did and see the Lord?

My vision of God is dependent upon the condition of my character. My character determines whether or not truth can even be revealed to me. Before I can say, "I saw the Lord," there must be something in my character that conforms to the likeness of God. Until I am born again and really begin to see the kingdom of God, I only see from the perspective of my own biases. What I need is God's surgical procedure—His use of external circumstances to bring about internal purification.

Your priorities must be God first, God second, and God third, until your life is continually face-to-face with God and no one else is taken into account whatsoever. Your prayer will then be, "In all the world there is no one but You, dear God; there is no one but You."

Keep paying the price. Let God see that you are willing to live up to the vision.

JULY 14

Suffering Afflictions and Going the Second Mile

"I tell you not to resist an evil person. But whoever slaps you on your right cheek, turn the other to him also." **Matthew 5:39**

This verse reveals the humiliation of being a Christian. In the natural realm, if a person does not hit back, it is because he is a coward. But in the spiritual realm, it is the very evidence of the Son of God in him if he does not hit back. When you are insulted, you must not only not resent it, but you must make it an opportunity to exhibit the Son of God in your life. And you cannot imitate the nature of Jesus—it is either in you or it is not. A personal insult becomes an opportunity for a saint to reveal the incredible sweetness of the Lord Jesus.

The teaching of the Sermon on the Mount is not, "Do your duty," but is, in effect, "Do what is not your duty." It is not your duty to go the second mile, or to turn the other cheek, but Jesus said that if we are His disciples, we will always do these things. We will not say, "Oh well, I just can't do any more, and I've been so misrepresented and misunderstood." Every time I insist on having my own rights, I hurt the Son of God, while in fact I can prevent Jesus from being hurt if I will take the blow myself. That is the real meaning of filling "up in my flesh what is lacking in the afflictions of Christ" (Colossians 1:24). A disciple realizes that it is his Lord's honor that is at stake in his life, not his own honor.

Never look for righteousness in the other person, but never cease to be righteous yourself. We are always looking for justice, yet the essence of the teaching of the Sermon on the Mount is—Never look for justice, but never cease to give it.

My Life's Spiritual Honor and Duty

"I am a debtor both to Greeks and to barbarians."
Romans 1:14

Paul was overwhelmed with the sense of his indebtedness to Jesus Christ, and he spent his life to express it. The greatest inspiration in Paul's life was his view of Jesus Christ as his spiritual creditor. Do I feel that same sense of indebtedness to Christ regarding every unsaved soul? As a saint, my life's spiritual honor and duty is to fulfill my debt to Christ in relation to these lost souls. Every tiny bit of my life that has value I owe to the redemption of Jesus Christ. Am I doing anything to enable Him to bring His redemption into evident reality in the lives of others? I will only be able to do this as the Spirit of God works into me this sense of indebtedness.

I am not a superior person among other people—I am a bondservant of the Lord Jesus. Paul said, "You are not your own . . . you were bought at a price" (1 Corinthians 6:19–20). Paul sold himself to Jesus Christ and he said, in effect, "I am a debtor to everyone on the face of the earth because of the gospel of Jesus; I am free only that I may be an absolute bondservant of His." That is the characteristic of a Christian's life once this level of spiritual honor and duty becomes real. Quit praying about yourself and spend your life for the sake of others as the bondservant of Jesus. That is the true meaning of being broken bread and poured-out wine in real life.

The Concept of Divine Control

"How much more will your Father who is in heaven give good things to those who ask Him!" **Matthew 7:11**

Jesus is laying down the rules of conduct in this passage for those people who have His Spirit. He urges us to keep our minds filled with the concept of God's control over everything, which means that a disciple must maintain an attitude of perfect trust and an eagerness to ask and to seek.

Fill your mind with the thought that God is there. And once your mind is truly filled with that thought, when you experience difficulties it will be as easy as breathing for you to remember, "My heavenly Father knows all about this!" This will be no effort at all, but will be a natural thing for you when difficulties and uncertainties arise. Before you formed this concept of divine control so powerfully in your mind, you used to go from person to person seeking help, but now you go to God about it. Jesus is laying down the rules of conduct for those people who have His Spirit, and it works on the following principle: God is my Father, He loves me, and I will never think of anything that He will forget, so why should I worry?

Jesus said there are times when God cannot lift the darkness from you, but you should trust Him. At times God will appear like an unkind friend, but He is not; He will appear like an unnatural father, but He is not; He will appear like an unjust judge, but He is not. Keep the thought that the mind of God is behind all things strong and growing. Not even the smallest detail of life happens unless God's will is behind it. Therefore, you can rest in perfect confidence in Him. Prayer is not only asking, but is an attitude of the mind which produces the atmosphere in which asking is perfectly natural. "Ask, and it will be given to you" (Matthew 7:7).

The Miracle of Belief

"My speech and my preaching were not with persuasive words of human wisdom." **1 Corinthians 2:4**

Paul was a scholar and an orator of the highest degree; he was not speaking here out of a deep sense of humility, but was saying that when he preached the gospel, he would veil the power of God if he impressed people with the excellency of his speech. Belief in Jesus is a miracle produced only by the effectiveness of redemption, not by impressive speech, nor by wooing and persuading, but only by the sheer unaided power of God. The creative power of redemption comes through the preaching of the gospel, but never because of the personality of the preacher.

Real and effective fasting by a preacher is not fasting from food, but fasting from eloquence, from impressive diction, and from everything else that might hinder the gospel of God being presented. The preacher is there as the representative of God—"as though God were pleading through us" (2 Corinthians 5:20). He is there to present the gospel of God. If it is only because of my preaching that people desire to be better, they will never get close to Jesus Christ. Anything that flatters me in my preaching of the gospel will result in making me a traitor to Jesus, and I prevent the creative power of His redemption from doing its work.

"And I, if I am lifted up . . . , will draw all peoples to Myself" (John 12:32).

JULY 18

The Mystery of Believing

"He said, 'Who are You, Lord?'" **Acts 9:5**

Through the miracle of redemption, Saul of Tarsus was instantly changed from a strong-willed and forceful Pharisee into a humble and devoted bondservant of the Lord Jesus.

There is nothing miraculous or mysterious about the things we can explain. We control what we are able to explain, consequently it is only natural to seek an explanation for everything. It is not natural to obey, yet it is not necessarily sinful to disobey. There can be no real disobedience, nor any moral virtue in obedience, unless a person recognizes the higher authority of the one giving the orders. If this recognition does not exist, even the one giving the orders may view the other person's disobedience as freedom. If one rules another by saying, "You must do this," and, "You will do that," he breaks the human spirit, making it unfit for God. A person is simply a slave for obeying, unless behind his obedience is the recognition of a holy God.

Many people begin coming to God once they stop being religious, because there is only one master of the human heart—Jesus Christ, not religion. But "Woe is me" if after seeing *Him* I still *will not* obey (Isaiah 6:5, also see verse 1). Jesus will never insist that I obey, but if I don't, I have already begun to sign the death certificate of the Son of God in my soul. When I stand face-to-face with Jesus Christ and say, "I will not obey," He will never insist. But when I do this, I am backing away from the re-creating power of His redemption. It makes no difference to God's grace what an abomination I am, if I will only come to the light. But "Woe is me" if I refuse the light (see John 3:19–21).

The Submission of the Believer

"You call Me Teacher and Lord, and you say well, for so I am." **John 13:13**

Our Lord never insists on having authority over us. He never says, "You *will* submit to me." No, He leaves us perfectly free to choose—so free, in fact, that we can spit in His face or we can put Him to death, as others have done; and yet He will never say a word. But once His life has been created in me through His redemption, I instantly recognize His right to absolute authority over me. It is a complete and effective domination, in which I acknowledge that "You are *worthy*, O Lord" (Revelation 4:11). It is simply the unworthiness within me that refuses to bow down or to submit to one who is worthy. When I meet someone who is more holy than myself, and I don't recognize his worthiness, nor obey his instructions for me, it is a sign of my own unworthiness being revealed. God teaches us by using these people who are a little better than we are; not better intellectually, but more holy. And He continues to do so until we willingly submit. Then the whole attitude of our life is one of obedience to Him.

If our Lord insisted on our obedience, He would simply become a taskmaster and cease to have any real authority. He never insists on obedience, but when we truly see Him we will instantly obey Him. Then He is easily Lord of our life, and we live in adoration of Him from morning till night. The level of my growth in grace is revealed by the way I look at obedience. We should have a much higher view of the word *obedience*, rescuing it from the mire of the world. Obedience is only possible between people who are equals in their relationship to each other; like the relationship between father and son, not that between master and servant. Jesus showed this relationship by saying, "I and My Father are one" (John 10:30). "Though He was a Son, yet He learned obedience by the things which He suffered" (Hebrews 5:8). The Son was obedient as our Redeemer, *because He was the Son,* not in order to become God's Son.

Dependent on God's Presence

"Those who wait on the Lord . . . shall walk and not faint." **Isaiah 40:31**

There is no thrill for us in walking, yet it is the test for all of our steady and enduring qualities. To "walk and not faint" is the highest stretch possible as a measure of strength. The word *walk* is used in the Bible to express the character of a person—"John . . . looking at Jesus *as He walked* . . . said, 'Behold the Lamb of God!'" (John 1:35–36). There is nothing abstract or obscure in the Bible; everything is vivid and real. God does not say, "Be spiritual," but He says, *"Walk before Me"* (Genesis 17:1).

When we are in an unhealthy condition either physically or emotionally, we always look for thrills in life. In our physical life this leads to our efforts to counterfeit the work of the Holy Spirit; in our emotional life it leads to obsessions and to the destruction of our morality; and in our spiritual life, if we insist on pursuing only thrills, on mounting up "with wings like eagles" (Isaiah 40:31), it will result in the destruction of our spirituality.

Having the reality of God's presence is not dependent on our being in a particular circumstance or place, but is only dependent on our determination to keep the Lord before us continually. Our problems arise when we refuse to place our trust in the reality of His presence. The experience the psalmist speaks of—"We will not fear, even though . . ." (Psalm 46:2)—will be ours once we are grounded on the truth of the reality of God's presence, not just a simple awareness of it, but an understanding of the reality of it. Then we will exclaim, "He has been here all the time!" At critical moments in our lives it is necessary to ask God for guidance, but it should be unnecessary to be constantly saying, "Oh, Lord, direct me in this, and in that." Of course He will, and in fact, He is doing it already! If our everyday decisions are not according to His will, He will press through them, bringing restraint to our spirit. Then we must be quiet and wait for the direction of His presence.

The Doorway to the Kingdom

"Blessed are the poor in spirit." **Matthew 5:3**

Beware of thinking of our Lord as only a teacher. If Jesus Christ is only a teacher, then all He can do is frustrate me by setting a standard before me I cannot attain. What is the point of presenting me with such a lofty ideal if I cannot possibly come close to reaching it? I would be happier if I never knew it. What good is there in telling me to be what I can never be—to be "pure in heart" (Matthew 5:8), to do more than my duty, or to be completely devoted to God? I must know Jesus Christ as my Savior before His teaching has any meaning for me other than that of a lofty ideal which only leads to despair. But when I am born again by the Spirit of God, I know that Jesus Christ did not come only to *teach*—He came to *make me what He teaches I should be*. The redemption means that Jesus Christ can place within anyone the same nature that ruled His own life, and all the standards God gives us are based on that nature.

The teaching of the Sermon on the Mount produces a sense of despair in the natural man—exactly what Jesus means for it to do. As long as we have some self-righteous idea that we can carry out our Lord's teaching, God will allow us to continue until we expose our own ignorance by stumbling over some obstacle in our way. Only then are we willing to come to Him as paupers and receive from Him. "Blessed are the poor in spirit." This is the first principle in the kingdom of God. The underlying foundation of Jesus Christ's kingdom is poverty, not possessions; not making decisions for Jesus, but having such a sense of absolute futility that we finally admit, "Lord, I cannot even begin to do it." Then Jesus says, "Blessed are you" (5:11). This is the doorway to the kingdom, and yet it takes us so long to believe that we are actually poor! The knowledge of our own poverty is what brings us to the proper place where Jesus Christ accomplishes His work.

Sanctification

"This is the will of God, your sanctification."
1 Thessalonians 4:3

The Death Side. In sanctification God has to deal with us on the death side as well as on the life side. Sanctification requires our coming to the place of death, but many of us spend so much time there that we become morbid. There is always a tremendous battle before sanctification is realized—something within us pushing with resentment against the demands of Christ. When the Holy Spirit begins to show us what sanctification means, the struggle starts immediately. Jesus said, "If anyone comes to Me and does not hate . . . his own life . . . he cannot be My disciple" (Luke 14:26).

In the process of sanctification, the Spirit of God will strip me down until there is nothing left but myself, and that is the place of death. Am I willing to be myself and nothing more? Am I willing to have no friends, no father, no brother, and no self-interest—simply to be ready for death? That is the condition required for sanctification. No wonder Jesus said, "I did not come to bring peace but a sword" (Matthew 10:34). This is where the battle comes, and where so many of us falter. We refuse to be identified with the death of Jesus Christ on this point. We say, "But this is so strict. Surely He does not require that of me." Our Lord *is* strict, and He *does* require that of us.

Am I willing to reduce myself down to simply "me"? Am I determined enough to strip myself of all that my friends think of me, and all that I think of myself? Am I willing and determined to hand over my simple naked self to God? Once I am, He will immediately sanctify me completely, and my life will be free from being determined and persistent toward anything except God (see 1 Thessalonians 5:23–24).

When I pray, "Lord, show me what sanctification means for me," He will show me. It means being made one with Jesus. Sanctification is not something Jesus puts in me—it is *Himself* in me (see 1 Corinthians 1:30).

Sanctification

"But of Him you are in Christ Jesus, who became for us . . . sanctification." **1 Corinthians 1:30**

The Life Side. The mystery of sanctification is that the perfect qualities of Jesus Christ are imparted as a gift to me, not gradually, but instantly once I enter by faith into the realization that He "became for [me] . . . sanctification." Sanctification means nothing less than the holiness of Jesus becoming mine and being exhibited in my life.

The most wonderful secret of living a holy life does not lie in imitating Jesus, but in letting the perfect qualities of Jesus exhibit themselves in my human flesh. Sanctification is "Christ in you" (Colossians 1:27). It is *His* wonderful life that is imparted to me in sanctification—imparted by faith as a sovereign gift of God's grace. Am I willing for God to make sanctification as real in me as it is in His Word?

Sanctification means the impartation of the holy qualities of Jesus Christ to me. It is the gift of His patience, love, holiness, faith, purity, and godliness that is exhibited in and through every sanctified soul. Sanctification is not drawing from Jesus the power to be holy—it is drawing from Jesus the very holiness that was exhibited in Him, and that He now exhibits in me. Sanctification is an impartation, not an imitation. Imitation is something altogether different. The perfection of everything is in Jesus Christ, and the mystery of sanctification is that all the perfect qualities of Jesus are at my disposal. Consequently, I slowly but surely begin to live a life of inexpressible order, soundness, and holiness—"kept by the power of God" (1 Peter 1:5).

His Nature and Our Motives

"Unless your righteousness exceeds the righteousness of the scribes and Pharisees, you will by no means enter the kingdom of heaven." **Matthew 5:20**

The characteristic of a disciple is not that he does good things, but that he is good in his motives, having been made good by the supernatural grace of God. The only thing that exceeds right-*doing* is right-*being*. Jesus Christ came to place within anyone who would let Him a new heredity that would have a righteousness exceeding that of the scribes and Pharisees. Jesus is saying, "If you are My disciple, you must be right not only in your actions, but also in your motives, your aspirations, and in the deep recesses of the thoughts of your mind." Your motives must be so pure that God Almighty can see nothing to rebuke. Who can stand in the eternal light of God and have nothing for Him to rebuke? Only the Son of God, and Jesus Christ claims that through His redemption He can place within anyone His own nature and make that person as pure and as simple as a child. The purity that God demands is impossible unless I can be remade within, and that is exactly what Jesus has undertaken to do through His redemption.

No one can make himself pure by obeying laws. Jesus Christ does not give us rules and regulations—He gives us His teachings which are truths that can only be interpreted by His nature which He places within us. The great wonder of Jesus Christ's salvation is that He changes our heredity. He does not change human nature—He changes its source, and thereby its motives as well.

Am I Blessed Like This?

"Blessed are . . ." **Matthew 5:3–11**

When we first read the statements of Jesus, they seem wonderfully simple and unstartling, and they sink unnoticed into our subconscious minds. For instance, the Beatitudes initially seem to be merely soothing and beautiful precepts for overly spiritual and seemingly useless people, but of very little practical use in the rigid, fast-paced workdays of the world in which we live. We soon find, however, that the Beatitudes contain the "dynamite" of the Holy Spirit. And they "explode" when the circumstances of our lives cause them to do so. When the Holy Spirit brings to our remembrance one of the Beatitudes, we say, "What a startling statement that is!" Then we must decide whether or not we will accept the tremendous spiritual upheaval that will be produced in our circumstances if we obey His words. That is the way the Spirit of God works. We do not need to be born again to apply the Sermon on the Mount literally. The literal interpretation of the Sermon on the Mount is as easy as child's play. But the interpretation by the Spirit of God as He applies our Lord's statements to our circumstances is the strict and difficult work of a saint.

The teachings of Jesus are all out of proportion when compared to our natural way of looking at things, and they come to us initially with astonishing discomfort. We gradually have to conform our walk and conversation to the precepts of Jesus Christ as the Holy Spirit applies them to our circumstances. The Sermon on the Mount is not a set of rules and regulations—it is a picture of the life we will live when the Holy Spirit is having His unhindered way with us.

JULY 26

The Way to Purity

"Those things which proceed out of the mouth come from the heart . . . . For out of the heart proceed evil thoughts, murders, adulteries, fornications, thefts, false witness, blasphemies. These are the things which defile a man." Matthew 15:18–20

Initially we trust in our ignorance, calling it innocence, and next we trust our innocence, calling it purity. Then when we hear these strong statements from our Lord, we shrink back, saying, "But I never felt any of those awful things in my heart." We resent what He reveals. Either Jesus Christ is the supreme authority on the human heart, or He is not worth paying any attention to. Am I prepared to trust the penetration of His Word into my heart, or would I prefer to trust my own "innocent ignorance"? If I will take an honest look at myself, becoming fully aware of my so-called innocence and putting it to the test, I am very likely to have a rude awakening that what Jesus Christ said is true, and I will be appalled at the possibilities of the evil and the wrong within me. But as long as I remain under the false security of my own "innocence," I am living in a fool's paradise. If I have never been an openly rude and abusive person, the only reason is my own cowardice coupled with the sense of protection I receive from living a civilized life. But when I am open and completely exposed before God, I find that Jesus Christ is right in His diagnosis of me.

The only thing that truly provides protection is the redemption of Jesus Christ. If I will simply hand myself over to Him, I will never have to experience the terrible possibilities that lie within my heart. Purity is something far too deep for me to arrive at naturally. But when the Holy Spirit comes into me, He brings into the center of my personal life the very Spirit that was exhibited in the life of Jesus Christ, namely, the *Holy* Spirit, which is absolute unblemished purity.

JULY 27

The Way to Knowledge

"If anyone wills to do His will, he shall know concerning the doctrine." **John 7:17**

The golden rule to follow to obtain spiritual understanding is not one of intellectual pursuit, but one of obedience. If a person wants scientific knowledge, then intellectual curiosity must be his guide. But if he desires knowledge and insight into the teachings of Jesus Christ, he can only obtain it through obedience. If spiritual things seem dark and hidden to me, then I can be sure that there is a point of disobedience somewhere in my life. Intellectual darkness is the result of ignorance, but spiritual darkness is the result of something that I do not intend to obey.

No one ever receives a word from God without instantly being put to the test regarding it. We disobey and then wonder why we are not growing spiritually. Jesus said, "If you bring your gift to the altar, and there remember that your brother has something against you, leave your gift there before the altar, and go your way. First be reconciled to your brother, and then come and offer your gift" (Matthew 5:23–24). He is saying, in essence, "Don't say another word to me; first be obedient by making things right." The teachings of Jesus hit us where we live. We cannot stand as impostors before Him for even one second. He instructs us down to the very last detail. The Spirit of God uncovers our spirit of self-vindication and makes us sensitive to things that we have never even thought of before.

When Jesus drives something home to you through His Word, don't try to evade it. If you do, you will become a religious impostor. Examine the things you tend simply to shrug your shoulders about, and where you have refused to be obedient, and you will know why you are not growing spiritually. As Jesus said, "*First . . . go.*" Even at the risk of being thought of as fanatical, you must obey what God tells you.

God's Purpose or Mine?

"He made His disciples get into the boat and go before Him to the other side." **Mark 6:45**

We tend to think that if Jesus Christ compels us to do something and we are obedient to Him, He will lead us to great success. We should never have the thought that our dreams of success are God's purpose for us. In fact, His purpose may be exactly the opposite. We have the idea that God is leading us toward a particular end or a desired goal, but He is not. The question of whether or not we arrive at a particular goal is of little importance, and reaching it becomes merely an episode along the way. What we see as only the process of reaching a particular end, God sees as the goal itself.

What is my vision of God's purpose for me? Whatever it may be, His purpose is for me to depend on Him and on His power *now*. If I can stay calm, faithful, and unconfused while in the middle of the turmoil of life, the goal of the purpose of God is being accomplished in me. God is not working toward a particular finish—His purpose is the process itself. What He desires for me is that I see "Him walking on the sea" with no shore, no success, nor goal in sight, but simply having the absolute certainty that everything is all right because I see "Him walking on the sea" (Mark 6:49). It is the process, not the outcome, that is glorifying to God.

God's training is for now, not later. His purpose is for this very minute, not for sometime in the future. We have nothing to do with what will follow our obedience, and we are wrong to concern ourselves with it. What people call preparation, God sees as the goal itself.

God's purpose is to enable me to see that He can walk on the storms of my life right now. If we have a further goal in mind, we are not paying enough attention to the present time. However, if we realize that moment-by-moment obedience is the goal, then each moment as it comes is precious.

Do You See Jesus in Your Clouds?

"Behold, He is coming with clouds . . ." **Revelation 1:7**

In the Bible clouds are always associated with God. Clouds are the sorrows, sufferings, or providential circumstances, within or without our personal lives, which actually seem to contradict the sovereignty of God. Yet it is through these very clouds that the Spirit of God is teaching us how to walk by faith. If there were never any clouds in our lives, we would have no faith. "The clouds are the dust of His feet" (Nahum 1:3). They are a sign that God is there. What a revelation it is to know that sorrow, bereavement, and suffering are actually the clouds that come along with God! God cannot come near us without clouds—He does not come in clear-shining brightness.

It is not true to say that God wants to teach us something in our trials. Through every cloud He brings our way, He wants us to *unlearn* something. His purpose in using the cloud is to simplify our beliefs until our relationship with Him is exactly like that of a child—a relationship simply between God and our own souls, and where other people are but shadows. Until other people become shadows to us, clouds and darkness will be ours every once in a while. Is our relationship with God becoming more simple than it has ever been?

There is a connection between the strange providential circumstances allowed by God and what we know of Him, and we have to learn to interpret the mysteries of life in the light of our knowledge of God. Until we can come face-to-face with the deepest, darkest fact of life without damaging our view of God's character, we do not yet know Him.

"They were fearful as they entered the cloud" (Luke 9:34). Is there anyone except Jesus in your cloud? If so, it will only get darker until you get to the place where there is "no one anymore, but only Jesus" (Mark 9:8; also see verses 2–7).

The Teaching of Disillusionment

"Jesus did not commit Himself to them . . . , for He knew what was in man." **John 2:24–25**

Disillusionment means having no more misconceptions, false impressions, and false judgments in life; it means being free from these deceptions. However, though no longer deceived, our experience of disillusionment may actually leave us cynical and overly critical in our judgment of others. But the disillusionment that comes from God brings us to the point where we see people as they really are, yet without any cynicism or any stinging and bitter criticism. Many of the things in life that inflict the greatest injury, grief, or pain, stem from the fact that we suffer from illusions. We are not true to one another as *facts*, seeing each other as we really are; we are only true to our misconceived *ideas* of one another. According to our thinking, everything is either delightful and good, or it is evil, malicious, and cowardly.

Refusing to be disillusioned is the cause of much of the suffering of human life. And this is how that suffering happens—if we love someone, but do not love God, we demand total perfection and righteousness from that person, and when we do not get it we become cruel and vindictive; yet we are demanding of a human being something which he or she cannot possibly give. There is only one Being who can completely satisfy to the absolute depth of the hurting human heart, and that is the Lord Jesus Christ. Our Lord is so obviously uncompromising with regard to every human relationship because He knows that every relationship that is not based on faithfulness to Himself will end in disaster. Our Lord trusted no one, and never placed His faith in people, yet He was never suspicious or bitter. Our Lord's confidence in God, and in what God's grace could do for anyone, was so perfect that He never despaired, never giving up hope for any person. If our trust is placed in human beings, we will end up despairing of everyone.

Becoming Entirely His

"Let patience have its perfect work, that you may be perfect and complete, lacking nothing." **James 1:4**

Many of us appear to be all right in general, but there are still some areas in which we are careless and lazy; it is not a matter of sin, but the remnants of our carnal life that tend to make us careless. Carelessness is an insult to the Holy Spirit. We should have no carelessness about us either in the way we worship God, or even in the way we eat and drink.

Not only must our relationship to God be right, but the outward expression of that relationship must also be right. Ultimately, God will allow nothing to escape; every detail of our lives is under His scrutiny. God will bring us back in countless ways to the same point over and over again. And He never tires of bringing us back to that one point until we learn the lesson, because His purpose is to produce the finished product. It may be a problem arising from our impulsive nature, but again and again, with the most persistent patience, God has brought us back to that one particular point. Or the problem may be our idle and wandering thinking, or our independent nature and self-interest. Through this process, God is trying to impress upon us the one thing that is not entirely right in our lives.

We have been having a wonderful time in our studies over the revealed truth of God's redemption, and our hearts are perfect toward Him. And His wonderful work in us makes us know that overall we are right with Him. "Let patience have its perfect work." The Holy Spirit speaking through James said, "Now let your patience become a finished product." Beware of becoming careless over the small details of life and saying, "Oh, that will have to do for now." Whatever it may be, God will point it out with persistence until we become entirely His.

Learning About His Ways

"When Jesus finished commanding His twelve disciples . . . He departed from there to teach and to preach in their cities." **Matthew 11:1**

He comes where He commands us to leave. If you stayed home when God told you to go because you were so concerned about your own people there, then you actually robbed them of the teaching of Jesus Christ Himself. When you obeyed and left all the consequences to God, the Lord went into your city to teach, but as long as you were disobedient, you blocked His way. Watch where you begin to debate with Him and put what you call your duty into competition with His commands. If you say, "I know that He told me to go, but my duty is here," it simply means that you do not believe that Jesus means what He says.

He teaches where He instructs us not to teach.

"Master . . . let us make three tabernacles" (Luke 9:33).

Are we playing the part of an amateur providence, trying to play God's role in the lives of others? Are we so noisy in our instruction of other people that God cannot get near them? We must learn to keep our mouths shut and our spirits alert. God wants to instruct us regarding His Son, and He wants to turn our times of prayer into mounts of transfiguration. When we become certain that God is going to work in a particular way, He will never work in that way again.

He works where He sends us to wait.

"Tarry . . . until . . ." (Luke 24:49).

"Wait on the Lord" and He will work (Psalm 37:34). But don't wait sulking spiritually and feeling sorry for yourself, just because you can't see one inch in front of you! Are we detached enough from our own spiritual fits of emotion to "wait patiently for Him"? (37:7). Waiting is not sitting with folded hands doing nothing, but it is learning to do what we are told.

These are some of the facets of His ways that we rarely recognize.

The Teaching of Adversity

"In the world you will have tribulation; but be of good cheer, I have overcome the world." **John 16:33**

The typical view of the Christian life is that it means being delivered from all adversity. But it actually means being delivered *in* adversity, which is something very different. "He who dwells in the secret place of the Most High shall abide under the shadow of the Almighty. No evil shall befall you, nor shall any plague come near your dwelling" (Psalm 91:1, 10)—the place where you are at one with God.

If you are a child of God, you will certainly encounter adversities, but Jesus says you should not be surprised when they come. "In the world you will have tribulation; but be of good cheer, I have overcome the world." He is saying, "There is nothing for you to fear." The same people who refused to talk about their adversities before they were saved often complain and worry after being born again because they have the wrong idea of what it means to live the life of a saint.

God does not give us overcoming life—He gives us life as we overcome. The strain of life is what builds our strength. If there is no strain, there will be no strength. Are you asking God to give you life, liberty, and joy? He cannot, unless you are willing to accept the strain. And once you face the strain, you will immediately get the strength. Overcome your own timidity and take the first step. Then God will give you nourishment—"To him who overcomes I will give to eat from the tree of life" (Revelation 2:7). If you completely give of yourself physically, you become exhausted. But when you give of yourself spiritually, you get more strength. God never gives us strength for tomorrow, or for the next hour, but only for the strain of the moment. Our temptation is to face adversities from the standpoint of our own common sense. But a saint can "be of good cheer" even when seemingly defeated by adversities, because victory is absurdly impossible to everyone, except God.

The Compelling Purpose of God

"He . . . said to them, 'Behold, we are going up to Jerusalem.'" **Luke 18:31**

Jerusalem, in the life of our Lord, represents the place where He reached the culmination of His Father's will. Jesus said, "I do not seek My own will but the will of the Father who sent Me" (John 5:30). Seeking to do "the will of the Father" was the one dominating concern throughout our Lord's life. And whatever He encountered along the way, whether joy or sorrow, success or failure, He was never deterred from that purpose. "He steadfastly set His face to go to Jerusalem" (Luke 9:51).

The greatest thing for us to remember is that we go up to Jerusalem to fulfill God's purpose, not our own. In the natural life our ambitions are our own, but in the Christian life we have no goals of our own. We talk so much today about our decisions for Christ, our determination to be Christians, and our decisions for this and that, but in the New Testament the only aspect that is brought out is the compelling purpose of God. "You did not choose Me, but I chose you" (John 15:16).

We are not taken into a conscious agreement with God's purpose—we are taken into God's purpose with no awareness of it at all. We have no idea what God's goal may be; as we continue, His purpose becomes even more and more vague. God's aim appears to have missed the mark, because we are too nearsighted to see the target at which He is aiming. At the beginning of the Christian life, we have our own ideas as to what God's purpose is. We say, "God means for me to go over there," and, "God has called me to do this special work." We do what we think is right, and yet the compelling purpose of God remains upon us. The work we do is of no account when compared with the compelling purpose of God. It is simply the scaffolding surrounding His work and His plan. "He took the twelve aside . . ." (Luke 18:31). God takes us aside all the time. We have not yet understood all there is to know of the compelling purpose of God.

AUGUST 4

The Brave Friendship of God

"He took the twelve aside." **Luke 18:31**

Oh, the bravery of God in trusting us! Do you say, "But He has been unwise to choose me, because there is nothing good in me and I have no value"? That is exactly why He chose you. As long as you think that you are of value to Him He cannot choose you, because you have purposes of your own to serve. But if you will allow Him to take you to the end of your own self-sufficiency, then He can choose you to go with Him "to Jerusalem" (Luke 18:31). And that will mean the fulfillment of purposes which He does not discuss with you.

We tend to say that because a person has natural ability, he will make a good Christian. It is not a matter of our equipment, but a matter of our poverty; not of what we bring with us, but of what God puts into us; not a matter of natural virtues, of strength of character, of knowledge, or of experience—all of that is of no avail in this concern. The only thing of value is being taken into the compelling purpose of God and being made His friends (see 1 Corinthians 1:26–31). God's friendship is with people who know their poverty. He can accomplish nothing with the person who thinks that he is of use to God. As Christians we are not here for our own purpose at all—we are here for the purpose of God, and the two are not the same. We do not know what God's compelling purpose is, but whatever happens, we must maintain our relationship with Him. We must never allow anything to damage our relationship with God, but if something does damage it, we must take the time to make it right again. The most important aspect of Christianity is not the work we do, but the relationship we maintain and the surrounding influence and qualities produced by that relationship. That is all God asks us to give our attention to, and it is the one thing that is continually under attack.

The Bewildering Call of God

"And all things that are written by the prophets concerning the Son of Man will be accomplished.' . . . But they understood none of these things." **Luke 18:31, 34**

God called Jesus Christ to what seemed absolute disaster. And Jesus Christ called His disciples to see Him put to death, leading every one of them to the place where their hearts were broken. His life was an absolute failure from every standpoint except God's. But what seemed to be failure from man's standpoint was a triumph from God's standpoint, because God's purpose is never the same as man's purpose.

This bewildering call of God comes into our lives as well. The call of God can never be understood absolutely or explained externally; it is a call that can only be perceived and understood internally by our true inner nature. The call of God is like the call of the sea—no one hears it except the person who has the nature of the sea in him. What God calls us to cannot be definitely stated, because His call is simply to be His friend to accomplish His own purposes. Our real test is in truly believing that God knows what He desires. The things that happen do not happen by chance—they happen entirely by the decree of God. God is sovereignly working out His own purposes.

If we are in fellowship and oneness with God and recognize that He is taking us into His purposes, then we will no longer strive to find out what His purposes are. As we grow in the Christian life, it becomes simpler to us, because we are less inclined to say, "I wonder why God allowed this or that?" And we begin to see that the compelling purpose of God lies behind everything in life, and that God is divinely shaping us into oneness with that purpose. A Christian is someone who trusts in the knowledge and the wisdom of God, not in his own abilities. If we have a purpose of our own, it destroys the simplicity and the calm, relaxed pace which should be characteristic of the children of God.

AUGUST 6

The Cross in Prayer

"In that day you will ask in My name." **John 16:26**

We too often think of the Cross of Christ as something we have to get through, yet we get *through* for the purpose of getting *into* it. The Cross represents only one thing for us—complete, entire, absolute identification with the Lord Jesus Christ—and there is nothing in which this identification is more real to us than in prayer.

"Your Father knows the things you have need of before you ask Him" (Matthew 6:8). Then why should we ask? The point of prayer is not to get answers from God, but to have perfect and complete oneness with Him. If we pray only because we want answers, we will become irritated and angry with God. We receive an answer every time we pray, but it does not always come in the way we expect, and our spiritual irritation shows our refusal to identify ourselves truly with our Lord in prayer. We are not here to prove that God answers prayer, but to be living trophies of God's grace.

"I do not say to you that I shall pray the Father for you; for the Father Himself loves you" (John 16:26–27). Have you reached such a level of intimacy with God that the only thing that can account for your prayer life is that it has become one with the prayer life of Jesus Christ? Has our Lord exchanged your life with His vital life? If so, then "in that day" you will be so closely identified with Jesus that there will be no distinction.

When prayer seems to be unanswered, beware of trying to place the blame on someone else. That is always a trap of Satan. When you seem to have no answer, there is always a reason—God uses these times to give you deep personal instruction, and it is not for anyone else but you.

Prayer in the Father's House

"They found Him in the temple . . . . And He said to them, '. . . Did you not know that I must be about My Father's business?'" **Luke 2:46, 49**

Our Lord's childhood was not immaturity waiting to grow into manhood—His childhood is an eternal fact. Am I a holy, innocent child of God as a result of my identification with my Lord and Savior? Do I look at my life as being in my Father's house? Is the Son of God living in His Father's house within me?

The only abiding reality is God Himself, and His order comes to me moment by moment. Am I continually in touch with the reality of God, or do I pray only when things have gone wrong—when there is some disturbance in my life? I must learn to identify myself closely with my Lord in ways of holy fellowship and oneness that some of us have not yet even begun to learn. "I must be about My Father's business"—and I must learn to live every moment of my life in my Father's house.

Think about your own circumstances. Are you so closely identified with the Lord's life that you are simply a child of God, continually talking to Him and realizing that everything comes from His hands? Is the eternal Child in you living in His Father's house? Is the grace of His ministering life being worked out through you in your home, your business, and in your circle of friends? Have you been wondering why you are going through certain circumstances? In fact, it is not that *you* have to go through them. It is because of your relationship with the Son of God who comes, through the providential will of His Father, into your life. You must allow *Him* to have His way with you, staying in perfect oneness with Him.

The life of your Lord is to become your vital, simple life, and the way He worked and lived among people while here on earth must be the way He works and lives in you.

AUGUST 8

Prayer in the Father's Honor

"That Holy One who is to be born will be called the Son of God." **Luke 1:35**

If the Son of God has been born into my human flesh, then am I allowing His holy innocence, simplicity, and oneness with the Father the opportunity to exhibit itself in me? What was true of the Virgin Mary in the history of the Son of God's birth on earth is true of every saint. God's Son is born into me through the direct act of God; then I as His child must exercise the right of a child—the right of always being face-to-face with my Father through prayer. Do I find myself continually saying in amazement to the commonsense part of my life, "Why did you want me to turn here or to go over there? 'Did you not know that I must be about My Father's business?'" (Luke 2:49). Whatever our circumstances may be, that holy, innocent, and eternal Child must be in contact with His Father.

Am I simple enough to identify myself with my Lord in this way? Is He having His wonderful way with me? Is God's will being fulfilled in that His Son has been formed in me (see Galatians 4:19), or have I carefully pushed Him to one side? Oh, the noisy outcry of today! Why does everyone seem to be crying out so loudly? People today are crying out for the Son of God to be put to death. There is no room here for God's Son right now—no room for quiet, holy fellowship and oneness with the Father.

Is the Son of God praying in me, bringing honor to the Father, or am I dictating my demands to Him? Is He ministering in me as He did in the time of His manhood here on earth? Is God's Son in me going through His passion, suffering so that His own purposes might be fulfilled? The more a person knows of the inner life of God's most mature saints, the more he sees what God's purpose really is: to "fill up in my flesh what is lacking in the afflictions of Christ" (Colossians 1:24). And when we think of what it takes to "fill up," there is always something yet to be done.

AUGUST 9

Prayer in the Father's Hearing

"Jesus lifted up His eyes and said, 'Father, I thank You that You have heard Me.'" **John 11:41**

When the Son of God prays, He is mindful and consciously aware of only His Father. God always hears the prayers of His Son, and if the Son of God has been formed in me (see Galatians 4:19) the Father will always hear my prayers. But I must see to it that the Son of God is exhibited in my human flesh. "Your body is the temple of the Holy Spirit" (1 Corinthians 6:19), that is, your body is the Bethlehem of God's Son. Is the Son of God being given His opportunity to work in me? Is the direct simplicity of His life being worked out in me exactly as it was worked out in His life while here on earth? When I come into contact with the everyday occurrences of life as an ordinary human being, is the prayer of God's eternal Son to His Father being prayed in me? Jesus says, "In that day you will ask in My name . . ." (John 16:26). What day does He mean? He is referring to the day when the Holy Spirit has come to me and made me one with my Lord.

Is the Lord Jesus Christ being abundantly satisfied by your life, or are you exhibiting a walk of spiritual pride before Him? Never let your common sense become so prominent and forceful that it pushes the Son of God to one side. Common sense is a gift that God gave to our human nature—but common sense is not the gift of His Son. Supernatural sense is the gift of His Son, and we should never put our common sense on the throne. The Son always recognizes and identifies with the Father, but common sense has never yet done so and never will. Our ordinary abilities will never worship God unless they are transformed by the indwelling Son of God. We must make sure that our human flesh is kept in perfect submission to Him, allowing Him to work through it moment by moment. Are we living at such a level of human dependence upon Jesus Christ that His life is being exhibited moment by moment in us?

The Holy Suffering of the Saint

"Let those who suffer according to the will of God commit their souls to Him in doing good." **1 Peter 4:19**

Choosing to suffer means that there must be something wrong with you, but choosing God's will—even if it means you will suffer—is something very different. No normal, healthy saint ever chooses suffering; he simply chooses God's will, just as Jesus did, whether it means suffering or not. And no saint should ever dare to interfere with the lesson of suffering being taught in another saint's life.

The saint who satisfies the heart of Jesus will make other saints strong and mature for God. But the people used to strengthen us are never those who sympathize with us; in fact, we are hindered by those who give us their sympathy, because sympathy only serves to weaken us. No one better understands a saint than the saint who is as close and as intimate with Jesus as possible. If we accept the sympathy of another saint, our spontaneous feeling is, "God is dealing too harshly with me and making my life too difficult." That is why Jesus said that self-pity was of the devil (see Matthew 16:21–23). We must be merciful to God's reputation. It is easy for us to tarnish God's character because He never argues back; He never tries to defend or vindicate Himself. Beware of thinking that Jesus needed sympathy during His life on earth. He refused the sympathy of people because in His great wisdom He knew that no one on earth understood His purpose (see 16:23). He accepted only the sympathy of His Father and the angels (see Luke 15:10).

Look at God's incredible waste of His saints, according to the world's judgment. God seems to plant His saints in the most useless places. And then we say, "God intends for me to be here because I am so useful to Him." Yet Jesus never measured His life by how or where He was of the greatest use. God places His saints where they will bring the most glory to Him, and we are totally incapable of judging where that may be.

This Experience Must Come

"Elijah went up by a whirlwind into heaven. And Elisha . . . saw him no more." **2 Kings 2:11–12**

It is not wrong for you to depend on your "Elijah" for as long as God gives him to you. But remember that the time will come when he must leave and will no longer be your guide and your leader, because God does not intend for him to stay. Even the thought of that causes you to say, "I cannot continue without my 'Elijah.'" Yet God says you must continue.

Alone at Your "Jordan" (2 Kings 2:14). The Jordan River represents the type of separation where you have no fellowship with anyone else, and where no one else can take your responsibility from you. You now have to put to the test what you learned when you were with your "Elijah." You have been to the Jordan over and over again with Elijah, but now you are facing it alone. There is no use in saying that you cannot go—the experience is here, and you must go. If you truly want to know whether or not God is the God your faith believes Him to be, then go through your "Jordan" alone.

Alone at Your "Jericho" (2:15). Jericho represents the place where you have seen your "Elijah" do great things. Yet when you come alone to your "Jericho," you have a strong reluctance to take the initiative and trust in God, wanting, instead, for someone else to take it for you. But if you remain true to what you learned while with your "Elijah," you will receive a sign, as Elisha did, that God is with you.

Alone at Your "Bethel" (2:23). At your "Bethel" you will find yourself at your wits' end but at the beginning of God's wisdom. When you come to your wits' end and feel inclined to panic—don't! Stand true to God and He will bring out His truth in a way that will make your life an expression of worship. Put into practice what you learned while with your "Elijah"—use his mantle and pray (see 2:13–14). Make a determination to trust in God, and do not even look for Elijah anymore.

AUGUST 12

The Theology of Resting in God

"Why are you fearful, O you of little faith?" **Matthew 8:26**

When we are afraid, the least we can do is pray to God. But our Lord has a right to expect that those who name His name have an underlying confidence in Him. God expects His children to be so confident in Him that in any crisis they are the ones who are reliable. Yet our trust is only in God up to a certain point, then we turn back to the elementary panic-stricken prayers of those people who do not even know God. We come to our wits' end, showing that we don't have even the slightest amount of confidence in Him or in His sovereign control of the world. To us He seems to be asleep, and we can see nothing but giant, breaking waves on the sea ahead of us.

"O you of little faith!" What a stinging pain must have shot through the disciples as they surely thought to themselves, "We missed the mark again!" And what a sharp pain will go through us when we suddenly realize that we could have produced complete and utter joy in the heart of Jesus by remaining absolutely confident in Him, in spite of what we were facing.

There are times when there is no storm or crisis in our lives, and we do all that is humanly possible. But it is when a crisis arises that we instantly reveal upon whom we rely. If we have been learning to worship God and to place our trust in Him, the crisis will reveal that we can go to the point of breaking, yet without breaking our confidence in Him.

We have been talking quite a lot about sanctification, but what will be the result in our lives? It will be expressed in our lives as a peaceful resting in God, which means a total oneness with Him. And this oneness will make us not only blameless in His sight, but also a profound joy to Him.

"Do Not Quench the Spirit"

"Do not quench the Spirit." **1 Thessalonians 5:19**

The voice of the Spirit of God is as gentle as a summer breeze—so gentle that unless you are living in complete fellowship and oneness with God, you will never hear it. The sense of warning and restraint that the Spirit gives comes to us in the most amazingly gentle ways. And if you are not sensitive enough to detect His voice, you will quench it, and your spiritual life will be impaired. This sense of restraint will always come as a "still small voice" (1 Kings 19:12), so faint that no one except a saint of God will notice it.

Beware if in sharing your personal testimony you continually have to look back, saying, "Once, a number of years ago, I was saved." If you have put your "hand to the plow" and are walking in the light, there is no "looking back"—the past is instilled into the present wonder of fellowship and oneness with God (Luke 9:62; also see 1 John 1:6–7). If you get out of the light, you become a sentimental Christian, and live only on your memories, and your testimony will have a hard metallic ring to it. Beware of trying to cover up your present refusal to "walk in the light" by recalling your past experiences when you did "walk in the light" (1 John 1:7). Whenever the Spirit gives you that sense of restraint, call a halt and make things right, or else you will go on quenching and grieving Him without even knowing it.

Suppose God brings you to a crisis and you almost endure it, but not completely. He will engineer the crisis again, but this time some of the intensity will be lost. You will have less discernment and more humiliation at having disobeyed. If you continue to grieve His Spirit, there will come a time when that crisis cannot be repeated, because you have totally quenched Him. But if you will go on through the crisis, your life will become a hymn of praise to God. Never become attached to anything that continues to hurt God. For you to be free of it, God must be allowed to hurt whatever it may be.

AUGUST 14

The Discipline of the Lord

"My son, do not despise the chastening of the Lord, nor be discouraged when you are rebuked by Him." **Hebrews 12:5**

It is very easy to grieve the Spirit of God; we do it by despising the discipline of the Lord, or by becoming discouraged when He rebukes us. If our experience of being set apart from sin and being made holy through the process of sanctification is still very shallow, we tend to mistake the reality of God for something else. And when the Spirit of God gives us a sense of warning or restraint, we are apt to say mistakenly, "Oh, that must be from the devil."

"Do not quench the Spirit" (1 Thessalonians 5:19), and do not despise Him when He says to you, in effect, "Don't be blind on this point anymore—you are not as far along spiritually as you thought you were. Until now I have not been able to reveal this to you, but I'm revealing it to you right now." When the Lord disciplines you like that, let Him have His way with you. Allow Him to put you into a right-standing relationship before God.

". . . nor be discouraged when you are rebuked by Him." We begin to pout, become irritated with God, and then say, "Oh well, I can't help it. I prayed and things didn't turn out right anyway. So I'm simply going to give up on everything." Just think what would happen if we acted like this in any other area of our lives!

Am I fully prepared to allow God to grip me by His power and do a work in me that is truly worthy of Himself? Sanctification is not my idea of what I want God to do for me—sanctification is God's idea of what He wants to do for me. But He has to get me into the state of mind and spirit where I will allow Him to sanctify me completely, whatever the cost (see 1 Thessalonians 5:23–24).

The Evidence of the New Birth

"You must be born again." **John 3:7**

The answer to Nicodemus' question, "How can a man be born when he is old?" is: Only when he is willing to die to everything in his life, including his rights, his virtues, and his religion, and becomes willing to receive into himself a new life that he has never before experienced (John 3:4). This new life exhibits itself in our conscious repentance and through our unconscious holiness.

"But as many as received Him . . ." (John 1:12). Is my knowledge of Jesus the result of my own internal spiritual perception, or is it only what I have learned through listening to others? Is there something in my life that unites me with the Lord Jesus as my personal Savior? My spiritual history must have as its underlying foundation a personal knowledge of Jesus Christ. To be born again means that I see Jesus.

"Unless one is born again, he cannot see the kingdom of God" (John 3:3). Am I seeking only for the evidence of God's kingdom, or am I actually recognizing His absolute sovereign control? The new birth gives me a new power of vision by which I begin to discern God's control. His sovereignty was there all the time, but with God being true to His nature, I could not see it until I received His very nature myself.

"*Whoever has been born of God does not sin*" (1 John 3:9). Am I seeking to stop sinning or have I actually stopped? To be born of God means that I have His supernatural power to stop sinning. The Bible never asks, "Should a Christian sin?" The Bible emphatically states that *a Christian must not sin*. The work of the new birth is being effective in us when we do not commit sin. It is not merely that we have the power not to sin, but that we have actually stopped sinning. Yet 1 John 3:9 does not mean that we *cannot* sin—it simply means that if we will obey the life of God in us, that we *do not have to sin*.

Does He Know Me . . . ?

"He calls his own . . . by name." **John 10:3**

When I have sadly misunderstood Him? (see John 20:11–18). It is possible to know all about doctrine and still not know Jesus. A person's soul is in grave danger when the knowledge of doctrine surpasses Jesus, avoiding intimate touch with Him. Why was Mary weeping? Doctrine meant no more to her than the grass under her feet. In fact, any Pharisee could have made a fool of Mary doctrinally, but one thing they could never ridicule was the fact that Jesus had cast seven demons out of her (see Luke 8:2); yet His blessings were nothing to her in comparison with knowing Jesus Himself. "She turned around and saw Jesus standing there, and did not know that it was Jesus . . . . Jesus said to her, 'Mary!'" (John 20:14, 16). Once He called Mary by her name, she immediately knew that she had a personal history with the One who spoke. "She turned and said to Him, 'Rabboni!'" (20:16).

When I have stubbornly doubted? (see John 20:24–29). Have I been doubting something about Jesus—maybe an experience to which others testify, but which I have not yet experienced? The other disciples said to Thomas, "We have seen the Lord" (20:25). But Thomas doubted, saying, "Unless I see . . . I will not believe" (20:25). Thomas needed the personal touch of Jesus. When His touches will come we never know, but when they do come they are indescribably precious. "Thomas . . . said to Him, 'My Lord and my God!'" (20:28).

When I have selfishly denied Him? (see John 21:15–17). Peter denied Jesus Christ with oaths and curses (see Matthew 26:69–75), and yet after His resurrection Jesus appeared to Peter alone. Jesus restored Peter in private, and then He restored him publicly before the others. And Peter said to Him, "Lord . . . You know that I love You" (John 21:17).

Do I have a personal history with Jesus Christ? The one true sign of discipleship is intimate oneness with Him—a knowledge of Jesus that nothing can shake.

Are You Discouraged or Devoted?

"Jesus . . . said to him, 'You still lack one thing. Sell all that you have . . . and come, follow Me.' But when he heard this, he became very sorrowful, for he was very rich." **Luke 18:22–23**

Have you ever heard the Master say something very difficult to you? If you haven't, I question whether you have ever heard Him say anything at all. Jesus says a tremendous amount to us that we listen to, but do not actually hear. And once we do hear Him, His words are harsh and unyielding.

Jesus did not show the least concern that this rich young ruler should do what He told him, nor did Jesus make any attempt to keep this man with Him. He simply said to him, "Sell all that you have . . . and come, follow Me." Our Lord never pleaded with him; He never tried to lure him—He simply spoke the strictest words that human ears have ever heard, and then left him alone.

Have I ever heard Jesus say something difficult and unyielding to me? Has He said something personally to me to which I have deliberately listened—not something I can explain for the sake of others, but something I have heard Him say directly to me? This man understood what Jesus said. He heard it clearly, realizing the full impact of its meaning, and it broke his heart. He did not go away as a defiant person, but as one who was sorrowful and discouraged. He had come to Jesus on fire with zeal and determination, but the words of Jesus simply froze him. Instead of producing enthusiastic devotion to Jesus, they produced heartbreaking discouragement. And Jesus did not go after him, but let him go. Our Lord knows perfectly well that once His word is truly heard, it will bear fruit sooner or later. What is so terrible is that some of us prevent His words from bearing fruit in our present life. I wonder what we will say when we finally make up our minds to be devoted to Him on that particular point? One thing is certain—He will never throw our past failures back in our faces.

AUGUST 18

Have You Ever Been Speechless with Sorrow?

"When he heard this, he became very sorrowful, for he was very rich." **Luke 18:23**

The rich young ruler went away from Jesus speechless with sorrow, having nothing to say in response to Jesus' words. He had no doubt about what Jesus had said or what it meant, and it produced in him a sorrow with no words with which to respond. Have you ever been there? Has God's Word ever come to you, pointing out an area of your life, requiring you to yield it to Him? Maybe He has pointed out certain personal qualities, desires, and interests, or possibly relationships of your heart and mind. If so, then you have often been speechless with sorrow. The Lord will not go after you, and He will not plead with you. But every time He meets you at the place where He has pointed, He will simply repeat His words, saying, "If you really mean what you say, these are the conditions."

"Sell all that you have" (Luke 18:22). In other words, rid yourself before God of everything that might be considered a possession until you are a mere conscious human being standing before Him, and then give God that. That is where the battle is truly fought—in the realm of your will before God. Are you more devoted to your idea of what Jesus wants than to Jesus Himself? If so, you are likely to hear one of His harsh and unyielding statements that will produce sorrow in you. What Jesus says *is* difficult—it is only easy when it is heard by those who have His nature in them. Beware of allowing anything to soften the hard words of Jesus Christ.

I can be so rich in my own poverty, or in the awareness of the fact that I am nobody, that I will never be a disciple of Jesus. Or I can be so rich in the awareness that I am somebody that I will never be a disciple. Am I willing to be destitute and poor even in my sense of awareness of my destitution and poverty? If not, that is why I become discouraged. Discouragement is disillusioned self-love, and self-love may be love for my devotion to Jesus—not love for Jesus Himself.

AUGUST 19

Self-Awareness

"Come to Me." **Matthew 11:28**

God intends for us to live a well-rounded life in Christ Jesus, but there are times when that life is attacked from the outside. Then we tend to fall back into self-examination, a habit that we thought was gone. Self-awareness is the first thing that will upset the completeness of our life in God, and self-awareness continually produces a sense of struggling and turmoil in our lives. Self-awareness is not sin, and it can be produced by nervous emotions or by suddenly being dropped into a totally new set of circumstances. Yet it is never God's will that we should be anything less than absolutely complete in Him. Anything that disturbs our rest in Him must be rectified at once, and it is not rectified by being ignored but only by coming to Jesus Christ. If we will come to Him, asking Him to produce Christ-awareness in us, He will always do it, until we fully learn to abide in Him.

Never allow anything that divides or destroys the oneness of your life with Christ to remain in your life without facing it. Beware of allowing the influence of your friends or your circumstances to divide your life. This only serves to sap your strength and slow your spiritual growth. Beware of anything that can split your oneness with Him, causing you to see yourself as separate from Him. Nothing is as important as staying right spiritually. And the only solution is a very simple one— "Come to Me." The intellectual, moral, and spiritual depth of our reality as a person is tested and measured by these words. Yet in every detail of our lives where we are found not to be real, we would rather dispute the findings than come to Jesus.

AUGUST 20

Christ-Awareness

"And I will give you rest." **Matthew 11:28**

Whenever anything begins to disintegrate your life with Jesus Christ, turn to Him at once, asking Him to reestablish your rest. Never allow anything to remain in your life that is causing the unrest. Think of every detail of your life that is causing the disintegration as something to fight against, not as something you should allow to remain. Ask the Lord to put awareness of Himself in you, and your self-awareness will disappear. Then He will be your all in all. Beware of allowing your self-awareness to continue, because slowly but surely it will awaken self-pity, and self-pity is satanic. Don't allow yourself to say, "Well, they have just misunderstood me, and this is something over which they should be apologizing to me; I'm sure I must have this cleared up with them already." Learn to leave others alone regarding this. Simply ask the Lord to give you Christ-awareness, and He will steady you until your completeness in Him is absolute.

A complete life is the life of a child. When I am fully conscious of my awareness of Christ, there is something wrong. It is the sick person who really knows what health is. A child of God is not aware of the will of God because he *is* the will of God. When we have deviated even slightly from the will of God, we begin to ask, "Lord, what is your will?" A child of God never prays to be made aware of the fact that God answers prayer, because he is so restfully certain that God always answers prayer.

If we try to overcome our self-awareness through any of our own commonsense methods, we will only serve to strengthen our self-awareness tremendously. Jesus says, "Come to Me . . . and I will give you rest," that is, Christ-awareness will take the place of self-awareness. Wherever Jesus comes He establishes rest—the rest of the completion of activity in our lives that is never aware of itself.

AUGUST 21

The Ministry of the Unnoticed

"Blessed are the poor in spirit." **Matthew 5:3**

The New Testament notices things that do not seem worthy of notice by our standards. "Blessed are the poor in spirit." This literally means, "Blessed are the paupers." Paupers are remarkably commonplace! The preaching of today tends to point out a person's strength of will or the beauty of his character—things that are easily noticed. The statement we so often hear, "Make a decision for Jesus Christ," places the emphasis on something our Lord never trusted. He never asks us to decide for Him, but to yield to Him—something very different. At the foundation of Jesus Christ's kingdom is the genuine loveliness of those who are commonplace. I am truly blessed in my poverty. If I have no strength of will and a nature without worth or excellence, then Jesus says to me, "Blessed are you, because it is through your poverty that you can enter My kingdom." I cannot enter His kingdom by virtue of my goodness—I can only enter it as an absolute pauper.

The true character of the loveliness that speaks for God is always unnoticed by the one possessing that quality. Conscious influence is prideful and unchristian. If I wonder if I am being of any use to God, I instantly lose the beauty and the freshness of the touch of the Lord. "He who believes in Me . . . out of his heart will flow rivers of living water" (John 7:38). And if I examine the outflow, I lose the touch of the Lord.

Who are the people who have influenced us most? Certainly not the ones who thought they did, but those who did not have even the slightest idea that they were influencing us. In the Christian life, godly influence is never conscious of itself. If we are conscious of our influence, it ceases to have the genuine loveliness which is characteristic of the touch of Jesus. We always know when Jesus is at work because He produces in the commonplace something that is inspiring.

AUGUST 22

"I Indeed . . . But He"

"I indeed baptize you with water . . . but He . . . will baptize you with the Holy Spirit and fire." **Matthew 3:11**

Have I ever come to the point in my life where I can say, "I indeed . . . but He . . ."? Until that moment comes, I will never know what the baptism of the Holy Spirit means. *I indeed* am at the end, and I cannot do anything more—*but He* begins right there—He does the things that no one else can ever do. Am I prepared for His coming? Jesus cannot come and do His work in me as long as there is anything blocking the way, whether it is something good or bad. When He comes to me, am I prepared for Him to drag every wrong thing I have ever done into the light? That is exactly where He comes. Wherever I know I am unclean is where He will put His feet and stand, and wherever I think I am clean is where He will remove His feet and walk away.

Repentance does not cause a sense of sin—it causes a sense of inexpressible unworthiness. When I repent, I realize that I am absolutely helpless, and I know that through and through I am not worthy even to carry His sandals. Have I repented like that, or do I have a lingering thought of possibly trying to defend my actions? The reason God cannot come into my life is that I am not at the point of complete repentance.

"He will baptize you with the Holy Spirit and fire." John is not speaking here of the baptism of the Holy Spirit as an experience, but as a work performed by Jesus Christ. "*He* will baptize you." The only experience that those who are baptized with the Holy Spirit are ever conscious of is the experience of sensing their absolute unworthiness.

"I indeed" was this in the past, *"but He"* came and something miraculous happened. Get to the end of yourself where you can do nothing, but where He does everything.

Prayer—Battle in "The Secret Place"

"When you pray, go into your room, and when you have shut your door, pray to your Father who is in the secret place; and your Father who sees in secret will reward you openly." **Matthew 6:6**

Jesus did not say, "Dream about your Father who is in the secret place," but He said, "*Pray* to your Father who is in the secret place." Prayer is an effort of the will. After we have entered our secret place and shut the door, the most difficult thing to do is to pray. We cannot seem to get our minds into good working order, and the first thing we have to fight is wandering thoughts. The great battle in private prayer is overcoming this problem of our idle and wandering thinking. We have to learn to discipline our minds and concentrate on willful, deliberate prayer.

We must have a specially selected place for prayer, but once we get there this plague of wandering thoughts begins, as we begin to think to ourselves, "This needs to be done, and I have to do that today." Jesus says to "shut your door." Having a secret stillness before God means deliberately shutting the door on our emotions and remembering Him. God is in secret, and He sees us from "the secret place"—He does not see us as other people do, or as we see ourselves. When we truly live in "the secret place," it becomes impossible for us to doubt God. We become more sure of Him than of anyone or anything else. Enter into "the secret place," and you will find that God was right in the middle of your everyday circumstances all the time. Get into the habit of dealing with God about everything. Unless you learn to open the door of your life completely and let God in from your first waking moment of each new day, you will be working on the wrong level throughout the day. But if you will swing the door of your life fully open and "pray to your Father who is in the secret place," every public thing in your life will be marked with the lasting imprint of the presence of God.

AUGUST 24

The Spiritual Search

"What man is there among you who, if his son asks for bread, will give him a stone?" **Matthew 7:9**

The illustration of prayer that our Lord used here is one of a good child who is asking for something good. We talk about prayer as if God hears us regardless of what our relationship is to Him (see Matthew 5:45). Never say that it is not God's will to give you what you ask. Don't faint and give up, but find out the reason you have not received; increase the intensity of your search and examine the evidence. Is your relationship right with your spouse, your children, and your fellow students? Are you a "good child" in those relationships? Do you have to say to the Lord, "I have been irritable and cross, but I still want spiritual blessings"? You cannot receive and will have to do without them until you have the attitude of a "good child."

We mistake defiance for devotion, arguing with God instead of surrendering. We refuse to look at the evidence that clearly indicates where we are wrong. Have I been asking God to give me money for something I want, while refusing to pay someone what I owe him? Have I been asking God for liberty while I am withholding it from someone who belongs to me? Have I refused to forgive someone, and have I been unkind to that person? Have I been living as God's child among my relatives and friends? (See Matthew 7:12.)

I am a child of God only by being born again, and as His child I am good only as I "walk in the light" (1 John 1:7). For most of us, prayer simply becomes some trivial religious expression, a matter of mystical and emotional fellowship with God. We are all good at producing spiritual fog that blinds our sight. But if we will search out and examine the evidence, we will see very clearly what is wrong—a friendship, an unpaid debt, or an improper attitude. There is no use praying unless we are living as children of God. Then Jesus says, regarding His children, "Everyone who asks receives" (Matthew 7:8).

AUGUST 25

Sacrifice and Friendship

"I have called you friends." **John 15:15**

We will never know the joy of self-sacrifice until we surrender in every detail of our lives. Yet self-surrender is the most difficult thing for us to do. We make it conditional by saying, "I'll surrender if . . . !" Or we approach it by saying, "I suppose I have to devote my life to God." We will never find the joy of self-sacrifice in either of these ways.

But as soon as we do totally surrender, abandoning ourselves to Jesus, the Holy Spirit gives us a taste of His joy. The ultimate goal of self-sacrifice is to lay down our lives for our Friend (see John 15:13–14). When the Holy Spirit comes into our lives, our greatest desire is to lay down our lives for Jesus. Yet the thought of self-sacrifice never even crosses our minds, because sacrifice is the Holy Spirit's ultimate expression of love.

Our Lord is our example of a life of self-sacrifice, and He perfectly exemplified Psalm 40:8, "I delight to do Your will, O my God." He endured tremendous personal sacrifice, yet with overflowing joy. Have I ever yielded myself in absolute submission to Jesus Christ? If He is not the One to whom I am looking for direction and guidance, then there is no benefit in my sacrifice. But when my sacrifice is made with my eyes focused on Him, slowly but surely His molding influence becomes evident in my life (see Hebrews 12:1–2).

Beware of letting your natural desires hinder your walk in love before God. One of the cruelest ways to kill natural love is through the rejection that results from having built the love on natural desires. But the one true desire of a saint is the Lord Jesus. Love for God is not something sentimental or emotional—for a saint to love as God loves is the most practical thing imaginable.

"I have called you friends." Our friendship with Jesus is based on the new life He created in us, which has no resemblance or attraction to our old life but only to the life of God. It is a life that is completely humble, pure, and devoted to God.

Are You Ever Troubled?

"Peace I leave with you, My peace I give to you." **John 14:27**

There are times in our lives when our peace is based simply on our own ignorance. But when we are awakened to the realities of life, true inner peace is impossible unless it is received from Jesus. When our Lord speaks peace, He creates peace, because the words that He speaks are always "spirit, and they are life" (John 6:63). Have I ever received what Jesus speaks? *"My peace I give to you"*—a peace that comes from looking into His face and fully understanding and receiving His quiet contentment.

Are you severely troubled right now? Are you afraid and confused by the waves and the turbulence God sovereignly allows to enter your life? Have you left no stone of your faith unturned, yet still not found any well of peace, joy, or comfort? Does your life seem completely barren to you? Then look up and receive the quiet contentment of the Lord Jesus. Reflecting His peace is proof that you are right with God, because you are exhibiting the freedom to turn your mind to Him. If you are not right with God, you can never turn your mind anywhere but on yourself. Allowing anything to hide the face of Jesus Christ from you either causes you to become troubled or gives you a false sense of security.

With regard to the problem that is pressing in on you right now, are you "looking unto Jesus" (Hebrews 12:2) and receiving peace from Him? If so, He will be a gracious blessing of peace exhibited in and through you. But if you only try to worry your way out of the problem, you destroy His effectiveness in you, and you deserve whatever you get. We become troubled because we have not been taking Him into account. When a person confers with Jesus Christ, the confusion stops, because there is no confusion in Him. Lay everything out before Him, and when you are faced with difficulty, bereavement, and sorrow, listen to Him say, "Let not your heart be troubled" (John 14:27).

Living Your Theology

"Walk while you have the light, lest darkness overtake you." **John 12:35**

Beware of not acting upon what you see in your moments on the mountaintop with God. If you do not obey the light, it will turn into darkness. "If therefore the light that is in you is darkness, how great is that darkness!" (Matthew 6:23). The moment you forsake the matter of sanctification or neglect anything else on which God has given you His light, your spiritual life begins to disintegrate within you. Continually bring the truth out into your real life, working it out into every area, or else even the light that you possess will itself prove to be a curse.

The most difficult person to deal with is the one who has the prideful self-satisfaction of a past experience, but is not working that experience out in his everyday life. If you *say* you are sanctified, *show it*. The experience must be so genuine that it shows in your life. Beware of any belief that makes you self-indulgent or self-gratifying; that belief came from the pit of hell itself, regardless of how beautiful it may sound.

Your theology must work itself out, exhibiting itself in your most common everyday relationships. Our Lord said, "Unless your righteousness *exceeds* the righteousness of the scribes and Pharisees, you will by no means enter the kingdom of heaven" (Matthew 5:20). In other words, you must be more moral than the most moral person you know. You may know all about the doctrine of sanctification, but are you working it out in the everyday issues of your life? Every detail of your life, whether physical, moral, or spiritual, is to be judged and measured by the standard of the atonement by the Cross of Christ.

The Purpose of Prayer

"One of His disciples said to Him, 'Lord, teach us to pray.'" **Luke 11:1**

Prayer is not a normal part of the life of the natural man. We hear it said that a person's life will suffer if he doesn't pray, but I question that. What will suffer is the life of the Son of God in him, which is nourished not by food, but by prayer. When a person is born again from above, the life of the Son of God is born in him, and he can either starve or nourish that life. Prayer is the way that the life of God in us is nourished. Our common ideas regarding prayer are not found in the New Testament. We look upon prayer simply as a means of getting things for ourselves, but the biblical purpose of prayer is that we may get to know God Himself.

"Ask, and you will receive" (John 16:24). We complain before God, and sometimes we are apologetic or indifferent to Him, but we actually *ask* Him for very few things. Yet a child exhibits a magnificent boldness to ask! Our Lord said, "unless you . . . become as little children" (Matthew 18:3). Ask and God will do. Give Jesus Christ the opportunity and the room to work. The problem is that no one will ever do this until he is at his wits' end. When a person is at his wits' end, it no longer seems to be a cowardly thing to pray; in fact, it is the only way he can get in touch with the truth and the reality of God Himself. Be yourself before God and present Him with your problems—the very things that have brought you to your wits' end. But as long as you think you are self-sufficient, you do not need to ask God for anything.

To say that "prayer changes things" is not as close to the truth as saying, "Prayer changes *me* and then I change things." God has established things so that prayer, on the basis of redemption, changes the way a person looks at things. Prayer is not a matter of changing things externally, but one of working miracles in a person's inner nature.

The Unsurpassed Intimacy of Tested Faith

"Jesus said to her, 'Did I not say to you that if you would believe you would see the glory of God?'" **John 11:40**

Every time you venture out in your life of faith, you will find something in your circumstances that, from a commonsense standpoint, will flatly contradict your faith. But common sense is not faith, and faith is not common sense. In fact, they are as different as the natural life and the spiritual. Can you trust Jesus Christ where your common sense cannot trust Him? Can you venture out with courage on the words of Jesus Christ, while the realities of your commonsense life continue to shout, "It's all a lie"? When you are on the mountaintop, it's easy to say, "Oh yes, I believe God can do it," but you have to come down from the mountain to the demon-possessed valley and face the realities that scoff at your Mount-of-Transfiguration belief (see Luke 9:28–42). Every time my theology becomes clear to my own mind, I encounter something that contradicts it. As soon as I say, "I believe 'God shall supply all [my] need,'" the testing of my faith begins (Philippians 4:19). When my strength runs dry and my vision is blinded, will I endure this trial of my faith victoriously or will I turn back in defeat?

Faith must be tested, because it can only become your intimate possession through conflict. What is challenging your faith right now? The test will either prove your faith right, or it will kill it. Jesus said, "Blessed is he who is not offended because of Me" (Matthew 11:6). The ultimate thing is confidence in Jesus. "We have become partakers of Christ if we hold the beginning of our confidence steadfast to the end" (Hebrews 3:14). Believe steadfastly on Him and everything that challenges you will strengthen your faith. There is continual testing in the life of faith up to the point of our physical death, which is the last great test. Faith is absolute trust in God—trust that could never imagine that He would forsake us (see Hebrews 13:5–6).

Usefulness or Relationship?

"Do not rejoice in this, that the spirits are subject to you, but rather rejoice because your names are written in heaven." **Luke 10:20**

Jesus Christ is saying here, "Don't rejoice in your successful service for Me, but rejoice because of your right relationship with Me." The trap you may fall into in Christian work is to rejoice in successful service—rejoicing in the fact that God has used you. Yet you never can measure what God will do through you if you have a right-standing relationship with Jesus Christ. If you keep your relationship right with Him, then regardless of your circumstances or whoever you encounter each day, He will continue to pour "rivers of living water" through you (John 7:38). And it is actually by His mercy that He does not let you know it. Once you have the right relationship with God through salvation and sanctification, remember that whatever your circumstances may be, you have been placed in them by God. And God uses the reaction of your life to your circumstances to fulfill His purpose, as long as you continue to "walk in the light as He is in the light" (1 John 1:7).

Our tendency today is to put the emphasis on service. Beware of the people who make their request for help on the basis of someone's usefulness. If you make usefulness the test, then Jesus Christ was the greatest failure who ever lived. For the saint, direction and guidance come from God Himself, not some measure of that saint's usefulness. It is the work that God does through us that counts, not what we do for Him. All that our Lord gives His attention to in a person's life is that person's relationship with God—something of great value to His Father. Jesus is "bringing many *sons* to glory" (Hebrews 2:10).

"My Joy . . . Your Joy"

"These things I have spoken to you, that My joy may remain in you, and that your joy may be full." **John 15:11**

What was the joy that Jesus had? Joy should not be confused with happiness. In fact, it is an insult to Jesus Christ to use the word *happiness* in connection with Him. The joy of Jesus was His absolute self-surrender and self-sacrifice to His Father—the joy of doing that which the Father sent Him to do—"who for the joy that was set before Him endured the cross" (Hebrews 12:2). "I delight to do Your will, O my God" (Psalm 40:8). Jesus prayed that our joy might continue fulfilling itself until it becomes the same joy as His. Have I allowed Jesus Christ to introduce His joy to me?

Living a full and overflowing life does not rest in bodily health, in circumstances, nor even in seeing God's work succeed, but in the perfect understanding of God, and in the same fellowship and oneness with Him that Jesus Himself enjoyed. But the first thing that will hinder this joy is the subtle irritability caused by giving too much thought to our circumstances. Jesus said, "The cares of this world, . . . choke the word, and it becomes unfruitful" (Mark 4:19). And before we even realize what has happened, we are caught up in our cares. All that God has done for us is merely the threshold—He wants us to come to the place where we will be His witnesses and proclaim who Jesus is.

Have the right relationship with God, finding your joy there, and out of you "will flow rivers of living water" (John 7:38). Be a fountain through which Jesus can pour His "living water." Stop being hypocritical and proud, aware only of yourself, and live "your life . . . hidden with Christ in God" (Colossians 3:3). A person who has the right relationship with God lives a life as natural as breathing wherever he goes. The lives that have been the greatest blessing to you are the lives of those people who themselves were unaware of having been a blessing.

SEPTEMBER 1

Destined to Be Holy

"It is written, 'Be holy, for I am holy.'" **1 Peter 1:16**

We must continually remind ourselves of the purpose of life. We are not destined to happiness, nor to health, but to holiness. Today we have far too many desires and interests, and our lives are being consumed and wasted by them. Many of them may be right, noble, and good, and may later be fulfilled, but in the meantime God must cause their importance to us to decrease. The only thing that truly matters is whether a person will accept the God who will make him holy. At all costs, a person must have the right relationship with God.

Do I believe I need to be holy? Do I believe that God can come into me and make me holy? If through your preaching you convince me that I am unholy, I then resent your preaching. The preaching of the gospel awakens an intense resentment because it is designed to reveal my unholiness, but it also awakens an intense yearning and desire within me. God has only one intended destiny for mankind—holiness. His only goal is to produce saints. God is not some eternal blessing-machine for people to use, and He did not come to save us out of pity—He came to save us because He created us to be holy. Atonement through the Cross of Christ means that God can put me back into perfect oneness with Himself through the death of Jesus Christ, without a trace of anything coming between us any longer.

Never tolerate, because of sympathy for yourself or for others, any practice that is not in keeping with a holy God. Holiness means absolute purity of your walk before God, the words coming from your mouth, and every thought in your mind—placing every detail of your life under the scrutiny of God Himself. Holiness is not simply what God gives me, but what God has given me that is being exhibited in my life.

A Life of Pure and Holy Sacrifice

"He who believes in Me . . . out of his heart will flow . . ." **John 7:38**

Jesus did not say, "He who believes in Me will realize all the blessings of the fullness of God," but, in essence, "He who believes in Me will have everything he receives escape out of him." Our Lord's teaching was always *anti*-self-realization. His purpose is not the development of a person—His purpose is to make a person exactly like Himself, and the Son of God is characterized by self-expenditure. If we believe in Jesus, it is not what we gain but what He pours through us that really counts. God's purpose is not simply to make us beautiful, plump grapes, but to make us grapes so that He may squeeze the sweetness out of us. Our spiritual life cannot be measured by success as the world measures it, but only by what God pours through us—and we cannot measure that at all.

When Mary of Bethany "broke the flask . . . of very costly oil . . . and poured it on [Jesus'] head," it was an act for which no one else saw any special occasion; in fact, "there were some who . . . said, 'Why was this fragrant oil wasted?'" (Mark 14:3–4). But Jesus commended Mary for her extravagant act of devotion, and said, "Wherever this gospel is preached . . . what this woman has done will also be told as a memorial to her" (Mark 14:9). Our Lord is filled with overflowing joy whenever He sees any of us doing what Mary did—not being bound by a particular set of rules, but being totally surrendered to Him. God poured out the life of His Son "that the world through Him might be saved" (John 3:17). Are we prepared to pour out our lives for Him?

"He who believes in Me . . . out of his heart will flow rivers of living water"—and hundreds of other lives will be continually refreshed. Now is the time for us to break "the flask" of our lives, to stop seeking our own satisfaction, and to pour out our lives before Him. Our Lord is asking who of us will do it for Him?

Pouring Out the Water of Satisfaction

"He would not drink it, but poured it out to the Lord." **2 Samuel 23:16**

What has been like "water from the well of Bethlehem" to you recently—love, friendship, or maybe some spiritual blessing (2 Samuel 23:16)? Have you taken whatever it may be, even at the risk of damaging your own soul, simply to satisfy yourself? If you have, then you cannot pour it out "to the Lord." You can never set apart for God something that you desire for yourself to achieve your own satisfaction. If you try to satisfy yourself with a blessing from God, it will corrupt you. You must sacrifice it, pouring it out to God—something that your common sense says is an absurd waste.

How can I pour out "to the Lord" natural love and spiritual blessings? There is only one way—I must make a determination in my mind to do so. There are certain things other people do that could never be received by someone who does not know God, because it is humanly impossible to repay them. As soon as I realize that something is too wonderful for me, that I am not worthy to receive it, and that it is not meant for a human being at all, I must pour it out "to the Lord." Then these very things that have come to me will be poured out as "rivers of living water" all around me (John 7:38). And until I pour these things out to God, they actually endanger those I love, as well as myself, because they will be turned into lust. Yes, we can be lustful in things that are not sordid and vile. Even love must be transformed by being poured out "to the Lord."

If you have become bitter and sour, it is because when God gave you a blessing you hoarded it. Yet if you had poured it out to Him, you would have been the sweetest person on earth. If you are always keeping blessings to yourself and never learning to pour out anything "to the Lord," other people will never have their vision of God expanded through you.

His!

"They were Yours, You gave them to Me." **John 17:6**

A missionary is someone in whom the Holy Spirit has brought about this realization: "You are not your own" (1 Corinthians 6:19). To say, "I am not my own," is to have reached a high point in my spiritual stature. The true nature of that life in actual everyday confusion is evidenced by the deliberate giving up of myself to another Person through a sovereign decision, and that Person is Jesus Christ. The Holy Spirit interprets and explains the nature of Jesus to me to make me one with my Lord, not that I might simply become a trophy for His showcase. Our Lord never sent any of His disciples out on the basis of what He had done for them. It was not until after the resurrection, when the disciples had perceived through the power of the Holy Spirit who Jesus really was, that He said, "Go" (Matthew 28:19; also see Luke 24:49 and Acts 1:8).

"If anyone comes to Me and does not hate his father and mother, wife and children, brothers and sisters, yes, and his own life also, he cannot be My disciple" (Luke 14:26). He was not saying that this person cannot be good and upright, but that he cannot be someone over whom Jesus can write the word *Mine.* Any one of the relationships our Lord mentions in this verse can compete with our relationship with Him. I may prefer to belong to my mother, or to my wife, or to myself, but if that is the case, then, Jesus said, "[You] cannot be My disciple." This does not mean that I will not be saved, but it does mean that I cannot be entirely *His.*

Our Lord makes His disciple His very own possession, becoming responsible for him. "You shall be witnesses to Me" (Acts 1:8). The desire that comes into a disciple is not one of *doing* anything for Jesus, but of *being* a perfect delight to Him. The missionary's secret is truly being able to say, "I am His, and He is accomplishing His work and His purposes through me."

Be entirely His!

Watching with Jesus

"Stay here and watch with Me." **Matthew 26:38**

"Watch with Me." Jesus was saying, in effect, "Watch with no private point of view at all, but watch solely and entirely with Me." In the early stages of our Christian life, we do not watch *with* Jesus, we watch *for* Him. We do not watch with Him through the revealed truth of the Bible even in the circumstances of our own lives. Our Lord is trying to introduce us to identification with Himself through a particular "Gethsemane" experience of our own. But we refuse to go, saying, "No, Lord, I can't see the meaning of this, and besides, it's very painful." And how can we possibly watch with Someone who is so incomprehensible? How are we going to understand Jesus sufficiently to watch with Him in His Gethsemane, when we don't even know why He is suffering? We don't know how to watch with Him—we are only used to the idea of Jesus watching with us.

The disciples loved Jesus Christ to the limit of their natural capacity, but they did not fully understand His purpose. In the Garden of Gethsemane they slept as a result of their own sorrow, and at the end of three years of the closest and most intimate relationship of their lives they "all . . . forsook Him and fled" (Matthew 26:56).

"They were all filled with the Holy Spirit" (Acts 2:4). "They" refers to the same people, but something wonderful has happened between these two events—our Lord's death, resurrection, and ascension—and the disciples have now been invaded and "filled with the Holy Spirit." Our Lord had said, "You shall receive power when the Holy Spirit has come upon you" (Acts 1:8). This meant that they learned to watch *with* Him the rest of their lives.

SEPTEMBER 6

The Far-Reaching Rivers of Life

"He who believes in Me . . . out of his heart will flow rivers of living water." **John 7:38**

A river reaches places which its source never knows. And Jesus said that, if we have received His fullness, "rivers of living water" will flow out of us, reaching in blessing even "to the end of the earth" (Acts 1:8) regardless of how small the visible effects of our lives may appear to be. We have nothing to do with the outflow—"This is the work of God, that you *believe* . . ." (John 6:29). God rarely allows a person to see how great a blessing he is to others.

A river is victoriously persistent, overcoming all barriers. For a while it goes steadily on its course, but then comes to an obstacle. And for a while it is blocked, yet it soon makes a pathway around the obstacle. Or a river will drop out of sight for miles, only later to emerge again even broader and greater than ever. Do you see God using the lives of others, but an obstacle has come into your life and you do not seem to be of any use to God? Then keep paying attention to the Source, and God will either take you around the obstacle or remove it. The river of the Spirit of God overcomes all obstacles. Never focus your eyes on the obstacle or the difficulty. The obstacle will be a matter of total indifference to the river that will flow steadily through you if you will simply remember to stay focused on the Source. Never allow anything to come between you and Jesus Christ—not emotion nor experience—nothing must keep you from the one great sovereign Source.

Think of the healing and far-reaching rivers developing and nourishing themselves in our souls! God has been opening up wonderful truths to our minds, and every point He has opened up is another indication of the wider power of the river that He will flow through us. If you believe in Jesus, you will find that God has developed and nourished in you mighty, rushing rivers of blessing for others.

Fountains of Blessings

"The water that I shall give him will become in him a fountain of water springing up into everlasting life." **John 4:14**

The picture our Lord described here is not that of a simple stream of water, but an overflowing fountain. Continue to "be filled" (Ephesians 5:18) and the sweetness of your vital relationship to Jesus will flow as generously out of you as it has been given to you. If you find that His life is not springing up as it should, you are to blame—something is obstructing the flow. Was Jesus saying to stay focused on the Source so that you may be blessed personally? No, you are to focus on the Source so that out of you "will flow rivers of living water"—irrepressible life (John 7:38).

We are to be fountains through which Jesus can flow as "rivers of living water" in blessing to everyone. Yet some of us are like the Dead Sea, always receiving but never giving, because our relationship is not right with the Lord Jesus. As surely as we receive blessings from Him, He will pour out blessings through us. But whenever the blessings are not being poured out in the same measure they are received, there is a defect in our relationship with Him. Is there anything between you and Jesus Christ? Is there anything hindering your faith in Him? If not, then Jesus says that out of you "will flow rivers of living water." It is not a blessing that you pass on, or an experience that you share with others, but a river that continually flows through you. Stay at the Source, closely guarding your faith in Jesus Christ and your relationship to Him, and there will be a steady flow into the lives of others with no dryness or deadness whatsoever.

Is it excessive to say that rivers will flow out of one individual believer? Do you look at yourself and say, "But I don't see the rivers"? Through the history of God's work you will usually find that He has started with the obscure, the unknown, the ignored, but with those who have been steadfastly true to Jesus Christ.

Do It Yourself

". . . casting down arguments and every high thing that exalts itself against the knowledge of God." **2 Corinthians 10:5**

Determinedly Demolish Some Things. Deliverance from sin is not the same as deliverance from human nature. There are things in human nature, such as prejudices, that the saint can only destroy through sheer neglect. But there are other things that have to be destroyed through violence, that is, through God's divine strength imparted by His Spirit. There are some things over which we are not to fight, but only to "stand still, and see the salvation of the Lord" (Exodus 14:13). But every theory or thought that raises itself up as a fortified barrier "against the knowledge of God" is to be determinedly demolished by drawing on God's power, not through human effort or by compromise (see 2 Corinthians 10:4).

It is only when God has transformed our nature and we have entered into the experience of sanctification that the fight begins. The warfare is not against sin; we can never fight against sin—Jesus Christ conquered that in His redemption of us. The conflict is waged over turning our natural life into a spiritual life. This is never done easily, nor does God intend that it be so. It is accomplished only through a series of moral choices. God does not make us holy in the sense that He makes our character holy. He makes us holy in the sense that He has made us innocent before Him. And then we have to turn that innocence into holy character through the moral choices we make. These choices are continually opposed and hostile to the things of our natural life which have become so deeply entrenched—the very things that raise themselves up as fortified barriers "against the knowledge of God." We can either turn back, making ourselves of no value to the kingdom of God, or we can determinedly demolish these things, allowing Jesus to bring another son to glory (see Hebrews 2:10).

Do It Yourself

". . . bringing every thought into captivity to the obedience of Christ." **2 Corinthians 10:5**

Determinedly Discipline Other Things. This is another difficult aspect of the strenuous nature of sainthood. Paul said, according to the Moffatt translation of this verse, "I take every project prisoner to make it obey Christ." So much Christian work today has never been disciplined, but has simply come into being by impulse! In our Lord's life every project was disciplined to the will of His Father. There was never the slightest tendency to follow the impulse of His own will as distinct from His Father's will—"the Son can do nothing of Himself" (John 5:19). Then compare this with what we do—we take "every thought" or project that comes to us by impulse and jump into action immediately, instead of imprisoning and disciplining ourselves to obey Christ.

Practical work for Christians is greatly overemphasized today, and the saints who are "bringing every thought [and project] into captivity" are criticized and told that they are not determined, and that they lack zeal for God or zeal for the souls of others. But true determination and zeal are found in obeying God, not in the inclination to serve Him that arises from our own undisciplined human nature. It is inconceivable, but true nevertheless, that saints are not "bringing every thought [and project] into captivity," but are simply doing work for God that has been instigated by their own human nature, and has not been made spiritual through determined discipline.

We have a tendency to forget that a person is not only committed to Jesus Christ for salvation, but is also committed, responsible, and accountable to Jesus Christ's view of God, the world, and of sin and the devil. This means that each person must recognize the responsibility to "be transformed by the renewing of [his] mind" (Romans 12:2).

Missionary Weapons

"When you were under the fig tree, I saw you." **John 1:48**

Worshiping in Everyday Occasions. We presume that we would be ready for battle if confronted with a great crisis, but it is not the crisis that builds something within us—it simply reveals what we are made of already. Do you find yourself saying, "If God calls me to battle, of course I will rise to the occasion"? Yet you won't rise to the occasion unless you have done so on God's training ground. If you are not doing the task that is closest to you now, which God has engineered into your life, when the crisis comes, instead of being fit for battle, you will be revealed as being unfit. Crises always reveal a person's true character.

A private relationship of worshiping God is the greatest essential element of spiritual fitness. The time will come, as Nathanael experienced in this passage, that a private "fig-tree" life will no longer be possible. Everything will be out in the open, and you will find yourself to be of no value there if you have not been worshiping in everyday occasions in your own home. If your worship is right in your private relationship with God, then when He sets you free, you will be ready. It is in the unseen life, which only God saw, that you have become perfectly fit. And when the strain of the crisis comes, you can be relied upon by God.

Are you saying, "But I can't be expected to live a sanctified life in my present circumstances; I have no time for prayer or Bible study right now; besides, my opportunity for battle hasn't come yet, but when it does, of course I will be ready"? No, you will not. If you have not been worshiping in everyday occasions, when you get involved in God's work, you will not only be useless yourself but also a hindrance to those around you.

God's training ground, where the missionary weapons are found, is the hidden, personal, worshiping life of the saint.

Missionary Weapons

"If I then, your Lord and Teacher, have washed your feet, you also ought to wash one another's feet." **John 13:14**

Ministering in Everyday Opportunities. Ministering in everyday opportunities that surround us does not mean that we select our own surroundings—it means being God's very special choice to be available for use in any of the seemingly random surroundings which He has engineered for us. The very character we exhibit in our present surroundings is an indication of what we will be like in other surroundings.

The things Jesus did were the most menial of everyday tasks, and this is an indication that it takes all of God's power in me to accomplish even the most common tasks in His way. Can I use a towel as He did? Towels, dishes, sandals, and all the other ordinary things in our lives reveal what we are made of more quickly than anything else. It takes God Almighty Incarnate in us to do the most menial duty as it ought to be done.

Jesus said, "I have given you an example, that you should do as I have done to you" (John 13:15). Notice the kind of people that God brings around you, and you will be humiliated once you realize that this is actually His way of revealing to you the kind of person you have been to Him. Now He says we should exhibit to those around us exactly what He has exhibited to us.

Do you find yourself responding by saying, "Oh, I will do all that once I'm out on the mission field"? Talking in this way is like trying to produce the weapons of war while in the trenches of the battlefield—you will be killed while trying to do it.

We have to go the "second mile" with God (see Matthew 5:41). Yet some of us become worn out in the first ten steps. Then we say, "Well, I'll just wait until I get closer to the next big crisis in my life." But if we do not steadily minister in everyday opportunities, we will do nothing when the crisis comes.

Going Through Spiritual Confusion

"Jesus answered and said, 'You do not know what you ask.'" **Matthew 20:22**

There are times in your spiritual life when there is confusion, and the way out of it is not simply to say that you should not be confused. It is not a matter of right and wrong, but a matter of God taking you through a way that you temporarily do not understand. And it is only by going through the spiritual confusion that you will come to the understanding of what God wants for you.

The Shrouding of His Friendship (see Luke 11:5–8). Jesus gave the illustration here of a man who appears not to care for his friend. He was saying, in effect, that is how the heavenly Father will appear to you at times. You will think that He is an unkind friend, but remember—He is not. The time will come when everything will be explained. There seems to be a cloud on the friendship of the heart, and often even love itself has to wait in pain and tears for the blessing of fuller fellowship and oneness. When God appears to be completely shrouded, will you hang on with confidence in Him?

The Shadow on His Fatherhood (see Luke 11:11–13). Jesus said that there are times when your Father will appear as if He were an unnatural father—as if He were callous and indifferent—but remember, He is not. "Everyone who asks receives" (Luke 11:10). If all you see is a shadow on the face of the Father right now, hang on to the fact that He will ultimately give you clear understanding and will fully justify Himself in everything that He has allowed into your life.

The Strangeness of His Faithfulness (see Luke 18:1–8). "When the Son of Man comes, will He really find faith on the earth?" (Luke 18:8). Will He find the kind of faith that counts on Him in spite of the confusion? Stand firm in faith, believing that what Jesus said is true, although in the meantime you do not understand what God is doing. He has bigger issues at stake than the particular things you are asking of Him right now.

After Surrender—Then What?

"I have finished the work which You have given Me to do." **John 17:4**

True surrender is not simply surrender of our external life but surrender of our will—and once that is done, surrender is complete. The greatest crisis we ever face is the surrender of our will. Yet God never forces a person's will into surrender, and He never begs. He patiently waits until that person willingly yields to Him. And once that battle has been fought, it never needs to be fought again.

Surrender for Deliverance. "Come to Me . . . and I will give you rest" (Matthew 11:28). It is only after we have begun to experience what salvation really means that we surrender our will to Jesus for rest. Whatever is causing us a sense of uncertainty is actually a call to our will—"Come to Me." And it is a voluntary coming.

Surrender for Devotion. "If anyone desires to come after Me, let him deny himself" (Matthew 16:24). The surrender here is of my *self* to Jesus, with His rest at the heart of my being. He says, "If you want to be My disciple, you must give up your right to yourself to Me." And once this is done, the remainder of your life will exhibit nothing but the evidence of this surrender, and you never need to be concerned again with what the future may hold for you. Whatever your circumstances may be, Jesus is totally sufficient (see 2 Corinthians 12:9 and Philippians 4:19).

Surrender for Death. ". . . another will gird you" (John 21:18; also see verse 19). Have you learned what it means to be girded for death? Beware of some surrender that you make to God in an ecstatic moment in your life, because you are apt to take it back again. True surrender is a matter of being "united together [with Jesus] in the likeness of His death" (Romans 6:5) until nothing ever appeals to you that did not appeal to Him.

And after you surrender—then what? Your entire life should be characterized by an eagerness to maintain unbroken fellowship and oneness with God.

Arguments or Obedience?

"*. . . the simplicity that is in Christ.*" **2 Corinthians 11:3**

Simplicity is the secret to seeing things clearly. A saint does not *think* clearly until a long time passes, but a saint ought to *see* clearly without any difficulty. You cannot think through spiritual confusion to make things clear; to make things clear, you must obey. In intellectual matters you can think things out, but in spiritual matters you will only think yourself into further wandering thoughts and more confusion. If there is something in your life upon which God has put His pressure, then obey Him in that matter. Bring all your "arguments and . . . every thought into captivity to the obedience of Christ" regarding the matter, and everything will become as clear as daylight to you (2 Corinthians 10:5). Your reasoning capacity will come later, but reasoning is not how we see. We see like children, and when we try to be wise we see nothing (see Matthew 11:25).

Even the very smallest thing that we allow in our lives that is not under the control of the Holy Spirit is completely sufficient to account for spiritual confusion, and spending all of our time thinking about it will still never make it clear. Spiritual confusion can only be conquered through obedience. As soon as we obey, we have discernment. This is humiliating, because when we are confused we know that the reason lies in the state of our mind. But when our natural power of sight is devoted and submitted in obedience to the Holy Spirit, it becomes the very power by which we perceive God's will, and our entire life is kept in simplicity.

What to Renounce

"We have renounced the hidden things of shame." **2 Corinthians 4:2**

Have you "renounced the hidden things of shame" in your life—the things that your sense of honor or pride will not allow to come into the light? You can easily hide them. Is there a thought in your heart about anyone that you would not like to be brought into the light? Then renounce it as soon as it comes to mind—renounce everything in its entirety until there is no hidden dishonesty or craftiness about you at all. Envy, jealousy, and strife don't necessarily arise from your old nature of sin, but from the flesh which was used for these kinds of things in the past (see Romans 6:19 and 1 Peter 4:1–3). You must maintain continual watchfulness so that nothing arises in your life that would cause you shame.

". . . not walking in craftiness" (2 Corinthians 4:2). This means not resorting to something simply to make your own point. This is a terrible trap. You know that God will allow you to work in only one way—the way of truth. Then be careful never to catch people through the other way—the way of deceit. If you act deceitfully, God's blight and ruin will be upon you. What may be craftiness for you, may not be for others—God has called you to a higher standard. Never dull your sense of being your utmost for His highest—your best for His glory. For you, doing certain things would mean craftiness coming into your life for a purpose other than what is the highest and best, and it would dull the motivation that God has given you. Many people have turned back because they are afraid to look at things from God's perspective. The greatest spiritual crisis comes when a person has to move a little farther on in his faith than the beliefs he has already accepted.

Praying to God in Secret

"When you pray, go into your room, and when you have shut your door, pray to your Father who is in the secret place." **Matthew 6:6**

The primary thought in the area of religion is—keep your eyes on God, not on people. Your motivation should not be the desire to be known as a praying person. Find an inner room in which to pray where no one even knows you are praying, shut the door, and talk to God in secret. Have no motivation other than to know your Father in heaven. It is impossible to carry on your life as a disciple without definite times of secret prayer.

"When you pray, do not use vain repetitions . . ." (Matthew 6:7). God does not hear us because we pray earnestly—He hears us solely on the basis of redemption. God is never impressed by our earnestness. Prayer is not simply getting things from God—that is only the most elementary kind of prayer. Prayer is coming into perfect fellowship and oneness with God. If the Son of God has been formed in us through regeneration (see Galatians 4:19), then He will continue to press on beyond our common sense and will change our attitude about the things for which we pray.

"Everyone who *asks* receives" (Matthew 7:8). We pray religious nonsense without even involving our will, and then we say that God did not answer—but in reality we have never *asked* for anything. Jesus said, "You will ask what you *desire*" (John 15:7). Asking means that our will must be involved. Whenever Jesus talked about prayer, He spoke with wonderful childlike simplicity. Then we respond with our critical attitude, saying, "Yes, but even Jesus said that we must *ask*." But remember that we have to ask things of God that are in keeping with the God whom Jesus Christ revealed.

Is There Good in Temptation?

"No temptation has overtaken you except such as is common to man." **1 Corinthians 10:13**

The word *temptation* has come to mean something bad to us today, but we tend to use the word in the wrong way. Temptation itself is not sin; it is something we are bound to face simply by virtue of being human. Not to be tempted would mean that we were already so shameful that we would be beneath contempt. Yet many of us suffer from temptations we should never have to suffer, simply because we have refused to allow God to lift us to a higher level where we would face temptations of another kind.

A person's inner nature, what he possesses in the inner, spiritual part of his being, determines what he is tempted by on the outside. The temptation fits the true nature of the person being tempted and reveals the possibilities of his nature. Every person actually determines or sets the level of his own temptation, because temptation will come to him in accordance with the level of his controlling, inner nature.

Temptation comes to me, suggesting a possible shortcut to the realization of my highest goal—it does not direct me toward what I understand to be evil, but toward what I understand to be good. Temptation is something that confuses me for a while, and I don't know whether something is right or wrong. When I yield to it, I have made lust a god, and the temptation itself becomes the proof that it was only my own fear that prevented me from falling into the sin earlier.

Temptation is not something we can escape; in fact, it is essential to the well-rounded life of a person. Beware of thinking that you are tempted as no one else—what you go through is the common inheritance of the human race, not something that no one has ever before endured. God does not save us from temptations—He sustains us in the midst of them (see Hebrews 2:18 and 4:15–16).

His Temptation and Ours

"We do not have a High Priest who cannot sympathize with our weaknesses, but was in all points tempted as we are, yet without sin." **Hebrews 4:15**

Until we are born again, the only kind of temptation we understand is the kind mentioned in James 1:14, "Each one is tempted when he is drawn away by his own desires and enticed." But through regeneration we are lifted into another realm where there are other temptations to face, namely, the kind of temptations our Lord faced. The temptations of Jesus had no appeal to us as unbelievers because they were not at home in our human nature. Our Lord's temptations and ours are in different realms until we are born again and become His brothers. The temptations of Jesus are not those of a mere man, but the temptations of God as Man. Through regeneration, the Son of God is formed in us (see Galatians 4:19), and in our physical life He has the same setting that He had on earth. Satan does not tempt us just to make us do wrong things—he tempts us to make us lose what God has put into us through regeneration, namely, the possibility of being of value to God. He does not come to us on the premise of tempting us to sin, but on the premise of shifting our point of view, and only the Spirit of God can detect this as a temptation of the devil.

Temptation means a test of the possessions held within the inner, spiritual part of our being by a power outside us and foreign to us. This makes the temptation of our Lord explainable. After Jesus' baptism, having accepted His mission of being the One "who takes away the sin of the world" (John 1:29) He "was led up by the Spirit into the wilderness" (Matthew 4:1) and into the testing devices of the devil. Yet He did not become weary or exhausted. He went through the temptation "without sin," and He retained all the possessions of His spiritual nature completely intact.

SEPTEMBER 19

Are You Going On with Jesus?

"You are those who have continued with Me in My trials." **Luke 22:28**

It is true that Jesus Christ is with us through our temptations, but are we going on with Him through His temptations? Many of us turn back from going on with Jesus from the very moment we have an experience of what He can do. Watch when God changes your circumstances to see whether you are going on with Jesus, or siding with the world, the flesh, and the devil. We wear His name, but are we going on with Him? "From that time many of His disciples went back and walked with Him no more" (John 6:66).

The temptations of Jesus continued throughout His earthly life, and they will continue throughout the life of the Son of God in us. Are we going on with Jesus in the life we are living right now?

We have the idea that we ought to shield ourselves from some of the things God brings around us. May it never be! It is God who engineers our circumstances, and whatever they may be we must see that we face them while continually abiding with Him in His temptations. They are *His* temptations, not temptations to us, but temptations to the life of the Son of God in us. Jesus Christ's honor is at stake in our bodily lives. Are we remaining faithful to the Son of God in everything that attacks His life in us?

Are you going on with Jesus? The way goes through Gethsemane, through the city gate, and on "outside the camp" (Hebrews 13:13). The way is lonely and goes on until there is no longer even a trace of a footprint to follow—but only the voice saying, "*Follow Me*" (Matthew 4:19).

The Divine Commandment of Life

"Be perfect, just as your Father in heaven is perfect." **Matthew 5:48**

Our Lord's exhortation to us in Matthew 5:38–48 is to be generous in our behavior toward everyone. Beware of living according to your natural affections in your spiritual life. Everyone has natural affections—some people we like and others we don't like. Yet we must never let those likes and dislikes rule our Christian life. "If we walk in the light as He is in the light, we have fellowship with one another" (1 John 1:7), even those toward whom we have no affection.

The example our Lord gave us here is not that of a good person, or even of a good Christian, but of God Himself. "Be perfect, just as your Father in heaven is perfect." In other words, simply show to the other person what God has shown to you. And God will give you plenty of real life opportunities to prove whether or not you are "perfect, just as your Father in heaven is perfect." Being a disciple means deliberately identifying yourself with God's interests in other people. Jesus says, "A new commandment I give to you, that you love one another; as I have loved you, that you also love one another. By this all will know that you are My disciples, if you have love for one another" (John 13:34–35).

The true expression of Christian character is not in good-doing, but in God-likeness. If the Spirit of God has transformed you within, you will exhibit divine characteristics in your life, not just good human characteristics. God's life in us expresses itself as *God's* life, not as human life trying to be godly. The secret of a Christian's life is that the supernatural becomes natural in him as a result of the grace of God, and the experience of this becomes evident in the practical, everyday details of life, not in times of intimate fellowship with God. And when we come in contact with things that create confusion and a flurry of activity, we find to our own amazement that we have the power to stay wonderfully poised even in the center of it all.

The Missionary's Predestined Purpose

"Now the Lord says, who formed Me from the womb to be His Servant . . ." **Isaiah 49:5**

The first thing that happens after we recognize our election by God in Christ Jesus is the destruction of our preconceived ideas, our narrow-minded thinking, and all of our other allegiances—we are turned solely into servants of God's own purpose. The entire human race was created to glorify God and to enjoy Him forever. Sin has diverted the human race onto another course, but it has not altered God's purpose to the slightest degree. And when we are born again we are brought into the realization of God's great purpose for the human race, namely, that He created us for Himself. This realization of our election by God is the most joyful on earth, and we must learn to rely on this tremendous creative purpose of God. The first thing God will do is force the interests of the whole world through the channel of our hearts. The love of God, and even His very nature, is introduced into us. And we see the nature of Almighty God purely focused in John 3:16—*"For God so loved the world . . ."*

We must continually keep our soul open to the fact of God's creative purpose, and never confuse or cloud it with our own intentions. If we do, God will have to force our intentions aside no matter how much it may hurt. A missionary is created for the purpose of being God's servant, one in whom God is glorified. Once we realize that it is through the salvation of Jesus Christ that we are made perfectly fit for the purpose of God, we will understand why Jesus Christ is so strict and relentless in His demands. He demands absolute righteousness from His servants, because He has put into them the very nature of God.

Beware lest you forget God's purpose for your life.

The Missionary's Master and Teacher

"You call Me Teacher and Lord, and you say well, for so I am . . . . I say to you, a servant is not greater than his master." **John 13:13, 16**

To have a master and teacher is not the same thing as being mastered and taught. Having a master and teacher means that there is someone who knows me better than I know myself, who is closer than a friend, and who understands the remotest depths of my heart and is able to satisfy them fully. It means having someone who has made me secure in the knowledge that he has met and solved all the doubts, uncertainties, and problems in my mind. To have a master and teacher is this and nothing less—"for One is your Teacher, the Christ" (Matthew 23:8).

Our Lord never takes measures to make me do what He wants. Sometimes I wish God would master and control me to make me do what He wants, but He will not. And at other times I wish He would leave me alone, and He does not.

"You call Me Teacher and Lord"—but *is* He? *Teacher*, *Master*, and *Lord* have little place in our vocabulary. We prefer the words *Savior*, *Sanctifier*, and *Healer*. The only word that truly describes the experience of being mastered is *love*, and we know little about love as God reveals it in His Word. The way we use the word *obey* is proof of this. In the Bible, obedience is based on a relationship between equals; for example, that of a son with his father. Our Lord was not simply God's servant—He was His Son. "*Though He was a Son*, yet He learned obedience . . ." (Hebrews 5:8). If we are consciously aware that we are being mastered, that idea itself is proof that we have no master. If that is our attitude toward Jesus, we are far away from having the relationship He wants with us. He wants us in a relationship where He is so easily our Master and Teacher that we have no conscious awareness of it—a relationship where all we know is that we are His to obey.

SEPTEMBER 23

The Missionary's Goal

"He . . . said to them, 'Behold, we are going up to Jerusalem.'" **Luke 18:31**

In our natural life our ambitions change as we grow, but in the Christian life the goal is given at the very beginning, and the beginning and the end are exactly the same, namely, our Lord Himself. We start with Christ and we end with Him—"till we all come . . . to the measure of the stature of the fullness of Christ" (Ephesians 4:13), not simply to our own idea of what the Christian life should be. The goal of the missionary is to do God's will, not to be useful or to win the lost. A missionary *is* useful and he *does* win the lost, but that is not his goal. His goal is to do the will of his Lord.

In our Lord's life, Jerusalem was the place where He reached the culmination of His Father's will upon the cross, and unless we go there with Jesus we will have no friendship or fellowship with Him. Nothing ever diverted our Lord on His way to Jerusalem. He never hurried through certain villages where He was persecuted, or lingered in others where He was blessed. Neither gratitude nor ingratitude turned our Lord even the slightest degree away from His purpose to go "up to Jerusalem."

"A disciple is not above his teacher, nor a servant above his master" (Matthew 10:24). In other words, the same things that happened to our Lord will happen to us on our way to our "Jerusalem." There will be works of God exhibited through us, people will get blessed, and one or two will show gratitude while the rest will show total ingratitude, but nothing must divert us from going "up to [our] Jerusalem."

"There they crucified Him" (Luke 23:33). That is what happened when our Lord reached Jerusalem, and that event is the doorway to our salvation. The saints, however, do not end in crucifixion; by the Lord's grace they end in glory. In the meantime our watchword should be summed up by each of us saying, "I too go 'up to Jerusalem.'"

The "Go" of Preparation

"If you bring your gift to the altar, and there remember that your brother has something against you, leave your gift there before the altar, and go your way. First be reconciled to your brother, and then come and offer your gift." **Matthew 5:23–24**

It is easy for us to imagine that we will suddenly come to a point in our lives where we are fully prepared, but preparation is not suddenly accomplished. In fact, it is a process that must be steadily maintained. It is dangerous to become settled and complacent in our present level of experience. The Christian life requires preparation *and* more preparation.

The sense of sacrifice in the Christian life is readily appealing to a new Christian. From a human standpoint, the one thing that attracts us to Jesus Christ is our sense of the heroic, and a close examination of us by our Lord's words suddenly puts this tide of enthusiasm to the test. "*Go* your way. First be reconciled to your brother." The "go" of preparation is to allow the Word of God to examine you closely. Your sense of heroic sacrifice is not good enough. The thing the Holy Spirit will detect in you is your nature that can never work in His service. And no one but God can detect that nature in you. Do you have anything to hide from God? If you do, then let God search you with His light. If there is sin in your life, don't just *admit* it—*confess* it. Are you willing to obey your Lord and Master, whatever the humiliation to your right to yourself may be?

Never disregard a conviction that the Holy Spirit brings to you. If it is important enough for the Spirit of God to bring it to your mind, it is the very thing He is detecting in you. You were looking for some big thing to give up, while God is telling you of some tiny thing that must go. But behind that tiny thing lies the stronghold of obstinacy, and you say, "I will not give up my right to myself"—the very thing that God intends you to give up if you are to be a disciple of Jesus Christ.

The "Go" of Relationship

"Whoever compels you to go one mile, go with him two." **Matthew 5:41**

Our Lord's teaching can be summed up in this: the relationship that He demands for us is an impossible one unless He has done a supernatural work in us. Jesus Christ demands that His disciple does not allow even the slightest trace of resentment in his heart when faced with tyranny and injustice. No amount of enthusiasm will ever stand up to the strain that Jesus Christ will put upon His servant. Only one thing will bear the strain, and that is a personal relationship with Jesus Christ Himself—a relationship that has been examined, purified, and tested until only one purpose remains and I can truly say, "I am here for God to send me where He will." Everything else may become blurred, but this relationship with Jesus Christ must never be.

The Sermon on the Mount is not some unattainable goal; it is a statement of what will happen in me when Jesus Christ has changed my nature by putting His own nature in me. Jesus Christ is the only One who can fulfill the Sermon on the Mount.

If we are to be disciples of Jesus, we must be made disciples supernaturally. And as long as we consciously maintain the determined purpose to be His disciples, we can be sure that we are not disciples. Jesus says, "You did not choose Me, but *I chose you*" (John 15:16). That is the way the grace of God begins. It is a constraint we can never escape; we can disobey it, but we can never start it or produce it ourselves. We are drawn to God by a work of His supernatural grace, and we can never trace back to find where the work began. Our Lord's making of a disciple is supernatural. He does not build on any natural capacity of ours at all. God does not ask us to do the things that are naturally easy for us—He only asks us to do the things that we are perfectly fit to do through His grace, and that is where the cross we must bear will always come.

SEPTEMBER 26

The "Go" of Reconciliation

"If you . . . remember that your brother has something against you . . ." **Matthew 5:23**

This verse says, "If you bring your gift to the altar, and there remember that your brother has something against you . . ." It is not saying, "If you search and find something because of your unbalanced sensitivity," but, "If you . . . remember." In other words, if something is brought to your conscious mind by the Spirit of God—"First be reconciled to your brother, and then come and offer your gift" (Matthew 5:24). Never object to the intense sensitivity of the Spirit of God in you when He is instructing you down to the smallest detail.

"First be reconciled to your brother . . ." Our Lord's directive is simple—"First be reconciled." He says, in effect, "Go back the way you came—the way indicated to you by the conviction given to you at the altar; have an attitude in your mind and soul toward the person who has something against you that makes reconciliation as natural as breathing." Jesus does not mention the other person—He says for *you* to go. It is not a matter of your rights. The true mark of the saint is that he can waive his own rights and obey the Lord Jesus.

". . . and then come and offer your gift." The process of reconciliation is clearly marked. First we have the heroic spirit of self-sacrifice, then the sudden restraint by the sensitivity of the Holy Spirit, and then we are stopped at the point of our conviction. This is followed by obedience to the Word of God, which builds an attitude or state of mind that places no blame on the one with whom you have been in the wrong. And finally there is the glad, simple, unhindered offering of your gift to God.

The "Go" of Renunciation

"Someone said to Him, 'Lord, I will follow You wherever You go.'" **Luke 9:57**

Our Lord's attitude toward this man was one of severe discouragement, "for He knew what was in man" (John 2:25). We would have said, "I can't imagine why He lost the opportunity of winning that man! Imagine being so cold to him and turning him away so discouraged!" Never apologize for your Lord. The words of the Lord hurt and offend until there is nothing left to be hurt or offended. Jesus Christ had no tenderness whatsoever toward anything that was ultimately going to ruin a person in his service to God. Our Lord's answers were not based on some whim or impulsive thought, but on the knowledge of "what was in man." If the Spirit of God brings to your mind a word of the Lord that hurts you, you can be sure that there is something in you that He wants to hurt to the point of its death.

Luke 9:58. These words destroy the argument of serving Jesus Christ because it is a pleasant thing to do. And the strictness of the rejection that He demands of me allows for nothing to remain in my life but my Lord, myself, and a sense of desperate hope. He says that I must let everyone else come or go, and that I must be guided solely by my relationship to Him. And He says, "The Son of Man has nowhere to lay His head."

Luke 9:59. This man did not want to disappoint Jesus, nor did he want to show a lack of respect for his father. We put our sense of loyalty to our relatives ahead of our loyalty to Jesus Christ, forcing Him to take last place. When your loyalties conflict, always obey Jesus Christ whatever the cost.

Luke 9:61. The person who says, "Lord, I will follow You, but . . ." is the person who is intensely ready to go, but never goes. This man had reservations about going. The exacting call of Jesus has no room for good-byes; good-byes, as we often use them, are pagan, not Christian, because they divert us from the call. Once the call of God comes to you, start going and never stop.

The "Go" of Unconditional Identification

"Jesus . . . said to him, 'One thing you lack: Go your way, sell whatever you have and give to the poor . . . and come, take up the cross, and follow Me.'" **Mark 10:21**

The rich young ruler had the controlling passion to be perfect. When he saw Jesus Christ, he wanted to be like Him. Our Lord never places anyone's personal holiness above everything else when He calls a disciple. Jesus' primary consideration is my absolute annihilation of my right to myself and my identification with Him, which means having a relationship with Him in which there are no other relationships. Luke 14:26 has nothing to do with salvation or sanctification, but deals solely with unconditional identification with Jesus Christ. Very few of us truly know what is meant by the absolute "go" of unconditional identification with, and abandonment and surrender to, Jesus.

"Then Jesus, looking at him, loved him" (Mark 10:21). This look of Jesus will require breaking your heart away forever from allegiance to any other person or thing. Has Jesus ever looked in this way at you? This look of Jesus transforms, penetrates, and captivates. Where you are soft and pliable with God is where the Lord has looked at you. If you are hard and vindictive, insistent on having your own way, and always certain that the other person is more likely to be in the wrong than you are, then there are whole areas of your nature that have never been transformed by His gaze.

"One thing you lack . . ." From Jesus Christ's perspective, oneness with Him, with nothing between, is the only good thing.

". . . sell whatever you have . . ." I must humble myself until I am merely a living person. I must essentially renounce possessions of all kinds, not for salvation (for only one thing saves a person and that is absolute reliance in faith upon Jesus Christ), but to follow Jesus. ". . . and come . . . and follow Me." And the road is the way He went.

The Awareness of the Call

"For necessity is laid upon me; yes, woe is me if I do not preach the gospel!" **1 Corinthians 9:16**

We are inclined to forget the deeply spiritual and supernatural touch of God. If you are able to tell exactly where you were when you received the call of God and can explain all about it, I question whether you have truly been called. The call of God does not come like that; it is much more supernatural. The realization of the call in a person's life may come like a clap of thunder or it may dawn gradually. But however quickly or slowly this awareness comes, it is always accompanied with an undercurrent of the supernatural—something that is inexpressible and produces a "glow." At any moment the sudden awareness of this incalculable, supernatural, surprising call that has taken hold of your life may break through—"I chose you" (John 15:16). The call of God has nothing to do with salvation and sanctification. You are not called to preach the gospel because you are sanctified; the call to preach the gospel is infinitely different. Paul describes it as a compulsion that was placed upon him.

If you have ignored, and thereby removed, the great supernatural call of God in your life, take a review of your circumstances. See where you have put your own ideas of service or your particular abilities ahead of the call of God. Paul said, "Woe is me if I do not preach the gospel!" He had become aware of the call of God, and his compulsion to "preach the gospel" was so strong that nothing else was any longer even a competitor for his strength.

If a man or woman is called of God, it doesn't matter how difficult the circumstances may be. God orchestrates every force at work for His purpose in the end. If you will agree with God's purpose, He will bring not only your conscious level but also all the deeper levels of your life, which you yourself cannot reach, into perfect harmony.

The Assigning of the Call

"I now rejoice in my sufferings for you, and fill up in my flesh what is lacking in the afflictions of Christ, for the sake of His body, which is the church." **Colossians 1:24**

We take our own spiritual consecration and try to make it into a call of God, but when we get right with Him He brushes all this aside. Then He gives us a tremendous, riveting pain to fasten our attention on something that we never even dreamed could be His call for us. And for one radiant, flashing moment we see His purpose, and we say, "Here am I! Send me" (Isaiah 6:8).

This call has nothing to do with personal sanctification, but with being made broken bread and poured-out wine. Yet God can never make us into wine if we object to the fingers He chooses to use to crush us. We say, "If God would only use His own fingers, and make me broken bread and poured-out wine in a special way, then I wouldn't object!" But when He uses someone we dislike, or some set of circumstances to which we said we would never submit, to crush us, then we object. Yet we must never try to choose the place of our own martyrdom. If we are ever going to be made into wine, we will have to be crushed—you cannot drink grapes. Grapes become wine only when they have been squeezed.

I wonder what finger and thumb God has been using to squeeze you? Have you been as hard as a marble and escaped? If you are not ripe yet, and if God *had* squeezed you anyway, the wine produced would have been remarkably bitter. To be a holy person means that the elements of our natural life experience the very presence of God as they are providentially broken in His service. We have to be placed into God and brought into agreement with Him before we can be broken bread in His hands. Stay right with God and let Him do as He likes, and you will find that He is producing the kind of bread and wine that will benefit His other children.

The Place of Exaltation

"Jesus took . . . them up on a high mountain apart by themselves." **Mark 9:2**

We have all experienced times of exaltation on the mountain, when we have seen things from God's perspective and have wanted to stay there. But God will never allow us to stay there. The true test of our spiritual life is in exhibiting the power to descend from the mountain. If we only have the power to go up, something is wrong. It is a wonderful thing to be on the mountain with God, but a person only gets there so that he may later go down and lift up the demon-possessed people in the valley (see Mark 9:14–18). We are not made for the mountains, for sunrises, or for the other beautiful attractions in life—those are simply intended to be moments of inspiration. We are made for the valley and the ordinary things of life, and that is where we have to prove our stamina and strength. Yet our spiritual selfishness always wants repeated moments on the mountain. We feel that we could talk and live like perfect angels, if we could only stay on the mountaintop. Those times of exaltation are exceptional and they have their meaning in our life with God, but we must beware to prevent our spiritual selfishness from wanting to make them the only time.

We are inclined to think that everything that happens is to be turned into useful teaching. In actual fact, it is to be turned into something even better than teaching, namely, character. The mountaintop is not meant to *teach* us anything, it is meant to *make* us something. There is a terrible trap in always asking, "What's the use of this experience?" We can never measure spiritual matters in that way. The moments on the mountaintop are rare moments, and they are meant for something in God's purpose.

OCTOBER 2

The Place of Humiliation

"If You can do anything, have compassion on us and help us." **Mark 9:22**

After every time of exaltation, we are brought down with a sudden rush into things as they really are, where it is neither beautiful, poetic, nor thrilling. The height of the mountaintop is measured by the dismal drudgery of the valley, but it is in the valley that we have to live for the glory of God. We *see* His glory on the mountain, but we never *live* for His glory there. It is in the place of humiliation that we find our true worth to God—that is where our faithfulness is revealed. Most of us can do things if we are always at some heroic level of intensity, simply because of the natural selfishness of our own hearts. But God wants us to be at the drab everyday level, where we live in the valley according to our personal relationship with Him. Peter thought it would be a wonderful thing for them to remain on the mountain, but Jesus Christ took the disciples down from the mountain and into the valley, where the true meaning of the vision was explained (see Mark 9:5–6, 14–23).

"If you can do anything . . ." It takes the valley of humiliation to remove the skepticism from us. Look back at your own experience and you will find that until you learned who Jesus really was, you were a skillful skeptic about His power. When you were on the mountaintop you could believe anything, but what about when you were faced with the facts of the valley? You may be able to give a testimony regarding your sanctification, but what about the thing that is a humiliation to you right now? The last time you were on the mountain with God, you saw that all the power in heaven and on earth belonged to Jesus—will you be skeptical now, simply because you are in the valley of humiliation?

OCTOBER 3

The Place of Ministry

"He said to them, 'This kind [of unclean spirit] can come out by nothing but prayer and fasting.'" **Mark 9:29**

His disciples asked Him privately, 'Why could we not cast it out?' (9:28). The answer lies in a personal relationship with Jesus Christ. "This kind can come out by nothing but" concentrating on Him, and then doubling and redoubling that concentration on Him. We can remain powerless forever, as the disciples were in this situation, by trying to do God's work without concentrating on His power, and by following instead the ideas that we draw from our own nature. We actually slander and dishonor God by our very eagerness to serve Him without knowing Him.

When you are brought face to face with a difficult situation and nothing happens externally, you can still know that freedom and release will be given because of your continued concentration on Jesus Christ. Your duty in service and ministry is to see that there is nothing between Jesus and yourself. Is there anything between you and Jesus even now? If there is, you must get through it, not by ignoring it as an irritation, or by going up and over it, but by facing it and getting through it into the presence of Jesus Christ. Then that very problem itself, and all that you have been through in connection with it, will glorify Jesus Christ in a way that you will never know until you see Him face to face.

We must be able to "mount up with wings like eagles" (Isaiah 40:31), but we must also know how to come down. The power of the saint lies in the coming down and in the living that is done in the valley. Paul said, "I can do all things through Christ who strengthens me" (Philippians 4:13) and what he was referring to were mostly humiliating things. And yet it is in our power to refuse to be humiliated and to say, "No, thank you, I much prefer to be on the mountaintop with God." Can I face things as they actually are in the light of the reality of Jesus Christ, or do things as they really are destroy my faith in Him, and put me into a panic?

OCTOBER 4

The Vision and the Reality

"To those who are . . . called to be saints . . ."
1 Corinthians 1:2

Thank God for being able to see all that you have not yet been. You have had the vision, but you are not yet to the reality of it by any means. It is when we are in the valley, where we prove whether we will be the choice ones, that most of us turn back. We are not quite prepared for the bumps and bruises that must come if we are going to be turned into the shape of the vision. We have seen what we are not, and what God wants us to be, but are we willing to be battered into the shape of the vision to be used by God? The beatings will always come in the most common, everyday ways and through common, everyday people.

There are times when we do know what God's purpose is; whether we will let the vision be turned into actual character depends on us, not on God. If we prefer to relax on the mountaintop and live in the memory of the vision, then we will be of no real use in the ordinary things of which human life is made. We have to learn to live in reliance upon what we saw in the vision, not simply live in ecstatic delight and conscious reflection upon God. This means living the realities of our lives in the light of the vision until the truth of the vision is actually realized in us. Every bit of our training is in that direction. Learn to thank God for making His demands known.

Our little "I am" always sulks and pouts when God says *do*. Let your little "I am" be shriveled up in God's wrath and indignation—"I AM WHO I AM . . . has sent me to you" (Exodus 3:14). He must dominate. Isn't it piercing to realize that God not only knows where we live, but also knows the gutters into which we crawl! He will hunt us down as fast as a flash of lightning. No human being knows human beings as God does.

OCTOBER 5

The Nature of Degeneration

"Just as through one man sin entered the world, and death through sin, and thus death spread to all men, because all sinned." **Romans 5:12**

The Bible does not say that God punished the human race for one man's sin, but that the nature of sin, namely, my claim to my right to myself, entered into the human race through one man. But it also says that another Man took upon Himself the sin of the human race and put it away—an infinitely more profound revelation (see Hebrews 9:26). The nature of sin is not immorality and wrongdoing, but the nature of self-realization which leads us to say, "I am my own god." This nature may exhibit itself in proper morality or in improper immorality, but it always has a common basis—my claim to my right to myself. When our Lord faced either people with all the forces of evil in them, or people who were clean-living, moral, and upright, He paid no attention to the moral degradation of one, nor any attention to the moral attainment of the other. He looked at something we do not see, namely, the nature of man (see John 2:25).

Sin is something I am born with and cannot touch—only God touches sin through redemption. It is through the Cross of Christ that God redeemed the entire human race from the possibility of damnation through the heredity of sin. God nowhere holds a person responsible for having the heredity of sin, and does not condemn anyone because of it. Condemnation comes when I realize that Jesus Christ came to deliver me from this heredity of sin, and yet I refuse to let Him do so. From that moment I begin to get the seal of damnation. "This is the condemnation [and the critical moment], that the light has come into the world, and men loved darkness rather than light" (John 3:19).

The Nature of Regeneration

"When it pleased God . . . to reveal His Son in me . . ." **Galatians 1:15–16**

If Jesus Christ is going to regenerate me, what is the problem He faces? It is simply this—I have a heredity in which I had no say or decision; I am not holy, nor am I likely to be; and if all Jesus Christ can do is tell me that I must be holy, His teaching only causes me to despair. But if Jesus Christ is truly a regenerator, someone who can put His own heredity of holiness into me, then I can begin to see what He means when He says that I have to be holy. Redemption means that Jesus Christ can put into anyone the hereditary nature that was in Himself, and all the standards He gives us are based on that nature—*His teaching is meant to be applied to the life which He puts within us.* The proper action on my part is simply to agree with God's verdict on sin as judged on the Cross of Christ.

The New Testament teaching about regeneration is that when a person is hit by his own sense of need, God will put the Holy Spirit into his spirit, and his personal spirit will be energized by the Spirit of the Son of God—"until Christ is formed in you" (Galatians 4:19). The moral miracle of redemption is that God can put a new nature into me through which I can live a totally new life. When I finally reach the edge of my need and know my own limitations, then Jesus says, "Blessed are you" (Matthew 5:11). But I must get to that point. God cannot put into me, the responsible moral person that I am, the nature that was in Jesus Christ unless I am aware of my need for it.

Just as the nature of sin entered into the human race through one man, the Holy Spirit entered into the human race through another Man (see Romans 5:12–19). And redemption means that I can be delivered from the heredity of sin, and that through Jesus Christ I can receive a pure and spotless heredity, namely, the Holy Spirit.

The Nature of Reconciliation

"He made Him who knew no sin to be sin for us, that we might become the righteousness of God in Him." **2 Corinthians 5:21**

Sin is a fundamental relationship—it is not wrong *doing*, but wrong *being*—it is deliberate and determined independence from God. The Christian faith bases everything on the extreme, self-confident nature of sin. Other faiths deal with *sins*—the Bible alone deals with *sin*. The first thing Jesus Christ confronted in people was the heredity of sin, and it is because we have ignored this in our presentation of the gospel that the message of the gospel has lost its sting and its explosive power.

The revealed truth of the Bible is not that Jesus Christ took on Himself our fleshly sins, but that He took on Himself the heredity of sin that no man can even touch. God made His own Son "to be sin" that He might make the sinner into a saint. It is revealed throughout the Bible that our Lord took on Himself the sin of the world through *identification with us*, not through *sympathy for us*. He deliberately took on His own shoulders, and endured in His own body, the complete, cumulative sin of the human race. "He made Him who knew no sin *to be sin for us*" and by so doing He placed salvation for the entire human race solely on the basis of redemption. Jesus Christ reconciled the human race, putting it back to where God designed it to be. And now anyone can experience that reconciliation, being brought into oneness with God, on the basis of what our Lord has done on the cross.

A man cannot redeem himself—redemption is the work of God, and is absolutely finished and complete. And its application to individual people is a matter of their own individual action or response to it. A distinction must always be made between the revealed truth of redemption and the actual conscious experience of salvation in a person's life.

OCTOBER 8

Coming to Jesus

"Come to Me." **Matthew 11:28**

Isn't it humiliating to be told that we must come to Jesus! Think of the things about which we will not come to Jesus Christ. If you want to know how real you are, test yourself by these words—"Come to Me." In every dimension in which you are not real, you will argue or evade the issue altogether rather than come; you will go through sorrow rather than come; and you will do anything rather than come the last lap of the race of seemingly unspeakable foolishness and say, "Just as I am, I come." As long as you have even the least bit of spiritual disrespect, it will always reveal itself in the fact that you are expecting God to tell you to do something very big, and yet all He is telling you to do is to "Come."

"Come to Me." When you hear those words, you will know that something must happen in you before you can come. The Holy Spirit will show you what you have to do, and it will involve anything that will uproot whatever is preventing you from getting through to Jesus. And you will never get any further until you are willing to do that very thing. The Holy Spirit will search out that one immovable stronghold within you, but He cannot budge it unless you are willing to let Him do so.

How often have you come to God with your requests and gone away thinking, "I've really received what I wanted this time!" And yet you go away with nothing, while all the time God has stood with His hands outstretched not only to take you but also for you to take Him. Just think of the invincible, unconquerable, and untiring patience of Jesus, who lovingly says, "*Come to Me.*"

OCTOBER 9

Building on the Atonement

"Present . . . your members as instruments of righteousness to God." **Romans 6:13**

I cannot save and sanctify myself; I cannot make atonement for sin; I cannot redeem the world; I cannot right what is wrong, purify what is impure, or make holy what is unholy. That is all the sovereign work of God. Do I have faith in what Jesus Christ has done? He has made the perfect atonement for sin. Am I in the habit of constantly realizing it? The greatest need we have is not to *do* things, but to *believe* things. The redemption of Christ is not an experience, it is the great act of God which He has performed through Christ, and I have to build my faith on it. If I construct my faith on my own experience, I produce the most unscriptural kind of life—an isolated life, with my eyes focused solely on my own holiness. Beware of that human holiness that is not based on the atonement of the Lord. It has no value for anything except a life of isolation—it is useless to God and a nuisance to man. Measure every kind of experience you have by our Lord Himself. We cannot do anything pleasing to God unless we deliberately build on the foundation of the atonement by the Cross of Christ.

The atonement of Jesus must be exhibited in practical, unassuming ways in my life. Every time I obey, the absolute deity of God is on my side, so that the grace of God and my natural obedience are in perfect agreement. Obedience means that I have completely placed my trust in the atonement, and my obedience is immediately met by the delight of the supernatural grace of God.

Beware of the human holiness that denies the reality of the natural life—it is a fraud. Continually bring yourself to the trial or test of the atonement and ask, "Where is the discernment of the atonement in this, and in that?"

How Will I Know?

"Jesus answered and said, 'I thank You, Father . . . that You have hidden these things from the wise and prudent and have revealed them to babes.'" **Matthew 11:25**

We do not grow into a spiritual relationship step by step—we either have a relationship or we do not. God does not continue to cleanse us more and more from sin—"But if we walk in the light," we *are* cleansed "from all sin" (1 John 1:7). It is a matter of obedience, and once we obey, the relationship is instantly perfected. But if we turn away from obedience for even one second, darkness and death are immediately at work again.

All of God's revealed truths are sealed until they are opened to us through obedience. You will never open them through philosophy or thinking. But once you obey, a flash of light comes immediately. Let God's truth work into you by immersing yourself in it, not by worrying into it. The only way you can get to know the truth of God is to stop trying to find out and by being born again. If you obey God in the first thing He shows you, then He instantly opens up the next truth to you. You could read volumes on the work of the Holy Spirit, when five minutes of total, uncompromising obedience would make things as clear as sunlight. Don't say, "I suppose I will understand these things someday!" You can understand them now. And it is not study that brings understanding to you, but obedience. Even the smallest bit of obedience opens heaven, and the deepest truths of God immediately become yours. Yet God will never reveal more truth about Himself to you, until you have obeyed what you know already. Beware of becoming one of the "wise and prudent." "If anyone wills to do His will, he shall know" (John 7:17).

OCTOBER 11

God's Silence—Then What?

"When He heard that he was sick, He stayed two more days in the place where He was." **John 11:6**

Has God trusted you with His silence—a silence that has great meaning? God's silences are actually His answers. Just think of those days of absolute silence in the home at Bethany! Is there anything comparable to those days in your life? Can God trust you like that, or are you still asking Him for a visible answer? God will give you the very blessings you ask if you refuse to go any further without them, but His silence is the sign that He is bringing you into an even more wonderful understanding of Himself. Are you mourning before God because you have not had an audible response? When you cannot hear God, you will find that He has trusted you in the most intimate way possible—with absolute silence, not a silence of despair, but one of pleasure, because He saw that you could withstand an even bigger revelation. If God has given you a silence, then praise Him—He is bringing you into the mainstream of His purposes. The actual evidence of the answer in time is simply a matter of God's sovereignty. Time is nothing to God. For a while you may have said, "I asked God to give me bread, but He gave me a stone instead" (see Matthew 7:9). He did not give you a stone, and today you find that He gave you the "bread of life" (John 6:35).

A wonderful thing about God's silence is that His stillness is contagious—it gets into you, causing you to become perfectly confident so that you can honestly say, "I know that God has heard me." His silence is the very proof that He has. As long as you have the idea that God will always bless you in answer to prayer, He will do it, but He will never give you the grace of His silence. If Jesus Christ is bringing you into the understanding that prayer is for the glorifying of His Father, then He will give you the first sign of His intimacy—silence.

Getting into God's Stride

"Enoch walked with God." **Genesis 5:24**

The true test of a person's spiritual life and character is not what he does in the extraordinary moments of life, but what he does during the ordinary times when there is nothing tremendous or exciting happening. A person's worth is revealed in his attitude toward the ordinary things of life when he is not under the spotlight (see John 1:35–37 and 3:30). It is painful work to get in step with God and to keep pace with Him—it means getting your second wind spiritually. In learning to walk with God, there is always the difficulty of getting into His stride, but once we have done so, the only characteristic that exhibits itself is the very life of God Himself. The individual person is merged into a personal oneness with God, and God's stride and His power alone are exhibited.

It is difficult to get into stride with God, because as soon as we start walking with Him we find that His pace has surpassed us before we have even taken three steps. He has different ways of doing things, and we have to be trained and disciplined in His ways. It was said of Jesus—"He will not fail nor be discouraged" (Isaiah 42:4) because He never worked from His own individual standpoint, but always worked from the standpoint of His Father. And we must learn to do the same. Spiritual truth is learned through the atmosphere that surrounds us, not through intellectual reasoning. It is God's Spirit that changes the atmosphere of our way of looking at things, and then things begin to be possible which before were impossible. Getting into God's stride means nothing less than oneness with Him. It takes a long time to get there, but keep at it. Don't give up because the pain is intense right now—get on with it, and before long you will find that you have a new vision and a new purpose.

Individual Discouragement and Personal Growth

"When Moses was grown . . . he went out to his brethren and looked at their burdens." **Exodus 2:11**

Moses saw the oppression of his people and felt certain that he was the one to deliver them, and in the righteous indignation of his own spirit he started to right their wrongs. After he launched his first strike for God and for what was right, God allowed Moses to be driven into empty discouragement, sending him into the desert to feed sheep for forty years. At the end of that time, God appeared to Moses and said to him, "'Bring My people . . . out of Egypt.' But Moses said to God, 'Who am I that I should go . . . ?'" (Exodus 3:10–11). In the beginning Moses had realized that he was the one to deliver the people, but he had to be trained and disciplined by God first. He was right in his individual perspective, but he was not the person for the work until he had learned true fellowship and oneness with God.

We may have the vision of God and a very clear understanding of what God wants, and yet when we start to do it, there comes to us something equivalent to Moses' forty years in the wilderness. It's as if God had ignored the entire thing, and when we are thoroughly discouraged, God comes back and revives His call to us. And then we begin to tremble and say, "Who am I that I should go . . . ?" We must learn that God's great stride is summed up in these words—"I AM WHO I AM . . . has sent me to you" (Exodus 3:14). We must also learn that our individual effort for God shows nothing but disrespect for Him—our individuality is to be rendered radiant through a personal relationship with God, so that He may be "well pleased" (Matthew 3:17). We are focused on the right individual perspective of things; we have the vision and can say, "I know this is what God wants me to do." But we have not yet learned to get into God's stride. If you are going through a time of discouragement, there is a time of great personal growth ahead.

The Key to the Missionary's Work

"Jesus came and spoke to them, saying, 'All authority has been given to Me in heaven and on earth. Go therefore and make disciples of all the nations.'" **Matthew 28:18–19**

The key to the missionary's work is the authority of Jesus Christ, not the needs of the lost. We are inclined to look on our Lord as one who assists us in our endeavors for God. Yet our Lord places Himself as the absolute sovereign and supreme Lord over His disciples. He does not say that the lost will never be saved if we don't go—He simply says, "Go therefore and make disciples of all the nations." He says, "Go on the basis of the revealed truth of My sovereignty, teaching and preaching out of your living experience of Me."

"Then the eleven disciples went . . . to the mountain which Jesus had appointed for them" (Matthew 28:16). If I want to know the universal sovereignty of Christ, I must know Him myself. I must take time to worship the One whose name I bear. Jesus says, "Come to Me"—that is the place to meet Jesus—"all you who labor and are heavy laden" (Matthew 11:28)—and how many missionaries are! We completely dismiss these wonderful words of the universal Sovereign of the world, but they are the words of Jesus to His disciples meant for here and now.

"Go therefore . . ." To "go" simply means to live. Acts 1:8 is the description of *how* to go. Jesus did not say in this verse, "Go into Jerusalem, Judea, and Samaria," but, "You shall *be witnesses* to Me in [all these places]." He takes upon Himself the work of sending us.

"If you abide in Me, and My words abide in you . . ." (John 15:7)—that is the way to keep *going.* Where we are placed is then a matter of indifference to us, because God sovereignly engineers our *goings.*

"None of these things move me; nor do I count my life dear to myself, so that I may finish my race with joy, and the ministry which I received from the Lord Jesus" (Acts 20:24). That is how to keep going until we are gone from this life.

OCTOBER 15

The Key to the Missionary's Message

"He Himself is the propitiation for our sins, and not for ours only but also for the whole world." **1 John 2:2**

The key to the missionary's message is the propitiation of Christ Jesus—His sacrifice for us that completely satisfied the wrath of God. Look at any other aspect of Christ's work, whether it is healing, saving, or sanctifying, and you will see that there is nothing limitless about those. But—"The Lamb of God who takes away the sin of the world!"—that is limitless (John 1:29). The missionary's message is the limitless importance of Jesus Christ as the propitiation for our sins, and a missionary is someone who is immersed in the truth of that revelation.

The real key to the missionary's message is the "remissionary" aspect of Christ's life, not His kindness, His goodness, or even His revealing of the fatherhood of God to us. "Repentance and *remission* of sins should be preached . . . to all nations" (Luke 24:47). The greatest message of limitless importance is that "He Himself is the propitiation for our sins." The missionary's message is not nationalistic, favoring nations or individuals; it is "for the whole world." When the Holy Spirit comes into me, He does not consider my partialities or preferences; He simply brings me into oneness with the Lord Jesus.

A missionary is someone who is bound by marriage to the stated mission and purpose of his Lord and Master. He is not to proclaim his own point of view, but is only to proclaim "the Lamb of God." It is easier to belong to a faction that simply tells what Jesus Christ has done for me, and easier to become a devotee of divine healing, or of a special type of sanctification, or of the baptism of the Holy Spirit. But Paul did not say, "Woe is me if I do not preach what Christ has done for me," but, "Woe is me if I do not preach the gospel!" (1 Corinthians 9:16). And this is the gospel—"the Lamb of God who takes away the sin of the world!"

The Key to the Master's Orders

"Pray the Lord of the harvest to send out laborers into His harvest." **Matthew 9:38**

The key to the missionary's difficult task is in the hand of God, and that key is prayer, not work—that is, not work as the word is commonly used today, which often results in the shifting of our focus away from God. The key to the missionary's difficult task is also not the key of common sense, nor is it the key of medicine, civilization, education, or even evangelization. The key is in following the Master's orders—the key is prayer. "Pray the Lord of the harvest . . ." In the natural realm, prayer is not practical but absurd. We have to realize that prayer is foolish from the commonsense point of view.

From Jesus Christ's perspective, there are no nations, but only *the world*. How many of us pray without regard to the persons, but with regard to only one Person—Jesus Christ? He owns the harvest that is produced through distress and through conviction of sin. This is the harvest for which we have to pray that laborers be sent out to reap. We stay busy at work, while people all around us are ripe and ready to be harvested; we do not reap even one of them, but simply waste our Lord's time in over-energized activities and programs. Suppose a crisis were to come into your father's or your brother's life—are you there as a laborer to reap the harvest for Jesus Christ? Is your response, "Oh, but I have a special work to do!" No Christian has a special work to do. A Christian is called to be Jesus Christ's own, "a servant [who] is not greater than his master" (John 13:16), and someone who does not dictate to Jesus Christ what he intends to do. Our Lord calls us to no special work—He calls us to Himself. "Pray the Lord of the harvest," and He will engineer your circumstances to send you out as His laborer.

OCTOBER 17

The Key of the Greater Work

"I say to you, he who believes in Me, . . . greater works than these he will do, because I go to My Father." **John 14:12**

Prayer does not equip us for greater works—prayer *is* the greater work. Yet we think of prayer as some commonsense exercise of our higher powers that simply prepares us for God's work. In the teachings of Jesus Christ, prayer is the working of the miracle of redemption in me, which produces the miracle of redemption in others, through the power of God. The way fruit remains firm is through prayer, but remember that it is prayer based on the agony of Christ in redemption, not on my own agony. We must go to God as His child, because only a child gets his prayers answered; a "wise" man does not (see Matthew 11:25).

Prayer is *the* battle, and it makes no difference where you are. However God may engineer your circumstances, your duty is to pray. Never allow yourself this thought, "I am of no use where I am," because you certainly cannot be used where you have not yet been placed. Wherever God has placed you and whatever your circumstances, you should pray, continually offering up prayers to Him. And He promises, "Whatever you ask in My name, that I will do" (John 14:13). Yet we refuse to pray unless it thrills or excites us, which is the most intense form of spiritual selfishness. We must learn to work according to God's direction, and He says to *pray.* "Pray the Lord of the harvest to send out laborers into His harvest" (Matthew 9:38).

There is nothing thrilling about a laboring person's work, but it is the laboring person who makes the ideas of the genius possible. And it is the laboring saint who makes the ideas of his Master possible. When you labor at prayer, from God's perspective there are always results. What an astonishment it will be to see, once the veil is finally lifted, all the souls that have been reaped by you, simply because you have been in the habit of taking your orders from Jesus Christ.

OCTOBER 18

The Key to the Missionary's Devotion

"They went forth for His name's sake." **3 John 7**

Our Lord told us how our love for Him is to exhibit itself when He asked, "Do you love Me?" (John 21:17). And then He said, "Feed My sheep." In effect, He said, "Identify *yourself* with *My* interests in other people," not, "Identify *Me* with *your* interests in other people." First Corinthians 13:4–8 shows us the characteristics of this love—it is actually the love *of God* expressing itself. The true test of my love for Jesus is a very practical one, and all the rest is sentimental talk.

Faithfulness to Jesus Christ is the supernatural work of redemption that has been performed in me by the Holy Spirit—"the love of God has been poured out in our hearts by the Holy Spirit" (Romans 5:5). And it is that love in me that effectively works through me and comes in contact with everyone I meet. I remain faithful to His name, even though the commonsense view of my life may seemingly deny that, and may appear to be declaring that He has no more power than the morning mist.

The key to the missionary's devotion is that he is attached to nothing and to no one except our Lord Himself. It does not mean simply being detached from the external things surrounding us. Our Lord was amazingly in touch with the ordinary things of life, but He had an inner detachment except toward God. External detachment is often an actual indication of a secret, growing, inner attachment to the things we stay away from externally.

The duty of a faithful missionary is to concentrate on keeping his soul completely and continually open to the nature of the Lord Jesus Christ. The men and women our Lord sends out on His endeavors are ordinary human people, but people who are controlled by their devotion to Him, which has been brought about through the work of the Holy Spirit.

The Unheeded Secret

"Jesus answered, 'My kingdom is not of this world.'" **John 18:36**

The great enemy of the Lord Jesus Christ today is the idea of practical work that has no basis in the New Testament but comes from the systems of the world. This work insists upon endless energy and activities, but no private life with God. The emphasis is put on the wrong thing. Jesus said, "The kingdom of God does not come with observation . . . . For indeed, the kingdom of God is within you" (Luke 17:20–21). It is a hidden, obscure thing. An active Christian worker too often lives to be seen by others, while it is the innermost, personal area that reveals the power of a person's life.

We must get rid of the plague of the spirit of this religious age in which we live. In our Lord's life there was none of the pressure and the rushing of tremendous activity that we regard so highly today, and a disciple is to be like His Master. The central point of the kingdom of Jesus Christ is a personal relationship with Him, not public usefulness to others.

It is not the practical activities that are the strength of this Bible Training College—its entire strength lies in the fact that here you are immersed in the truths of God to soak in them before Him. You have no idea of where or how God is going to engineer your future circumstances, and no knowledge of what stress and strain is going to be placed on you either at home or abroad. And if you waste your time in overactivity, instead of being immersed in the great fundamental truths of God's redemption, then you will snap when the stress and strain do come. But if this time of soaking before God is being spent in getting rooted and grounded in Him, which may appear to be impractical, then you will remain true to Him whatever happens.

Is God's Will My Will?

"This is the will of God, your sanctification."
1 Thessalonians 4:3

Sanctification is not a question of whether God is willing to sanctify me—is it *my* will? Am I willing to let God do in me everything that has been made possible through the atonement of the Cross of Christ? Am I willing to let Jesus become sanctification to me, and to let His life be exhibited in my human flesh? (See 1 Corinthians 1:30.) Beware of saying, "Oh, I am longing to be sanctified." No, you are not. Recognize your need, but stop longing and make it a matter of action. Receive Jesus Christ to become sanctification for you by absolute, unquestioning faith, and the great miracle of the atonement of Jesus will become real in you.

All that Jesus made possible becomes mine through the free and loving gift of God on the basis of what Christ accomplished on the cross. And my attitude as a saved and sanctified soul is that of profound, humble holiness (there is no such thing as proud holiness). It is a holiness based on agonizing repentance, a sense of inexpressible shame and degradation, and also on the amazing realization that the love of God demonstrated itself to me while I cared nothing about Him (see Romans 5:8). He completed everything for my salvation and sanctification. No wonder Paul said that nothing "shall be able to separate us from the love of God which is in Christ Jesus our Lord" (Romans 8:39).

Sanctification makes me one with Jesus Christ, and in Him one with God, and it is accomplished only through the magnificent atonement of Christ. Never confuse the effect with the cause. The effect in me is obedience, service, and prayer, and is the outcome of inexpressible thanks and adoration for the miraculous sanctification that has been brought about in me because of the atonement through the Cross of Christ.

OCTOBER 21

Impulsiveness or Discipleship?

"But you, beloved, building yourselves up on your most holy faith . . ." **Jude 20**

There was nothing of the nature of impulsive or thoughtless action about our Lord, but only a calm strength that never got into a panic. Most of us develop our Christianity along the lines of our own nature, not along the lines of God's nature. Impulsiveness is a trait of the natural life, and our Lord always ignores it, because it hinders the development of the life of a disciple. Watch how the Spirit of God gives a sense of restraint to impulsiveness, suddenly bringing us a feeling of self-conscious foolishness, which makes us instantly want to vindicate ourselves. Impulsiveness is all right in a child, but is disastrous in a man or woman—an impulsive adult is always a spoiled person. Impulsiveness needs to be trained into intuition through discipline.

Discipleship is built entirely on the supernatural grace of God. Walking on water is easy to someone with impulsive boldness, but walking on dry land as a disciple of Jesus Christ is something altogether different. Peter walked on the water to go to Jesus, but he "followed Him at a distance" on dry land (Mark 14:54). We do not need the grace of God to withstand crises—human nature and pride are sufficient for us to face the stress and strain magnificently. But it does require the supernatural grace of God to live twenty-four hours of every day as a saint, going through drudgery, and living an ordinary, unnoticed, and ignored existence as a disciple of Jesus. It is ingrained in us that we have to do exceptional things for God—but we do not. We have to be exceptional in the ordinary things of life, and holy on the ordinary streets, among ordinary people—and this is not learned in five minutes.

The Witness of the Spirit

"The Spirit Himself bears witness with our spirit."
Romans 8:16

We are in danger of getting into a bargaining spirit with God when we come to Him—we want the witness of the Spirit before we have done what God tells us to do.

Why doesn't God reveal Himself to you? He cannot. It is not that He will not, but He cannot, because you are in the way as long as you won't abandon yourself to Him in total surrender. Yet once you do, immediately God witnesses to Himself—He cannot witness to you, but He instantly witnesses to His own nature in you. If you received the witness of the Spirit before the reality and truth that comes from obedience, it would simply result in sentimental emotion. But when you act on the basis of redemption, and stop the disrespectfulness of debating with God, He immediately gives His witness. As soon as you abandon your own reasoning and arguing, God witnesses to what He has done, and you are amazed at your total disrespect in having kept Him waiting. If you are debating as to whether or not God can deliver from sin, then either let Him do it or tell Him that He cannot. Do not quote this or that person to Him. Simply obey Matthew 11:28, "Come to Me, all you who labor and are heavy laden." *Come*, if you are weary, and *ask*, if you know you are evil (see Luke 11:9–13).

The Spirit of God witnesses to the redemption of our Lord, and to nothing else. He cannot witness to our reason. We are inclined to mistake the simplicity that comes from our natural commonsense decisions for the witness of the Spirit, but the Spirit witnesses only to His own nature, and to the work of redemption, never to our reason. If we are trying to make Him witness to our reason, it is no wonder that we are in darkness and uncertainty. Throw it all overboard, trust in Him, and He will give you the witness of the Spirit.

Nothing of the Old Life!

"If anyone is in Christ, he is a new creation; old things have passed away; behold, all things have become new." **2 Corinthians 5:17**

Our Lord never tolerates our prejudices—He is directly opposed to them and puts them to death. We tend to think that God has some special interest in our particular prejudices, and are very sure that He will never deal with us as He has to deal with others. We even say to ourselves, "God has to deal with other people in a very strict way, but of course He knows that my prejudices are all right." But we must learn that God accepts nothing of the old life! Instead of being on the side of our prejudices, He is deliberately removing them from us. It is part of our moral education to see our prejudices put to death by His providence, and to watch how He does it. God pays no respect to anything we bring to Him. There is only one thing God wants of us, and that is our unconditional surrender.

When we are born again, the Holy Spirit begins to work His new creation in us, and there will come a time when there is nothing remaining of the old life. Our old gloomy outlook disappears, as does our old attitude toward things, and "all things are of God" (2 Corinthians 5:18). How are we going to get a life that has no lust, no self-interest, and is not sensitive to the ridicule of others? How will we have the type of love that "is kind . . . is not provoked, [and] thinks no evil"? (1 Corinthians 13:4–5). The only way is by allowing nothing of the old life to remain, and by having only simple, perfect trust in God—such a trust that we no longer want God's blessings, but only want God Himself. Have we come to the point where God can withdraw His blessings from us without our trust in Him being affected? Once we truly see God at work, we will never be concerned again about the things that happen, because we are actually trusting in our Father in heaven, whom the world cannot see.

OCTOBER 24

The Proper Perspective

"Thanks be to God who always leads us in triumph in Christ." **2 Corinthians 2:14**

The proper perspective of a servant of God must not simply be as near to the highest as he can get, but it must be *the* highest. Be careful that you vigorously maintain God's perspective, and remember that it must be done every day, little by little. Don't think on a finite level. No outside power can touch the proper perspective.

The proper perspective to maintain is that we are here for only one purpose—to be captives marching in the procession of Christ's triumphs. We are not on display in God's showcase—we are here to exhibit only one thing—the "captivity [of our lives] to the obedience of Christ" (2 Corinthians 10:5). How small all the other perspectives are! For example, the ones that say, "I am standing all alone, battling for Jesus," or, "I have to maintain the cause of Christ and hold down this fort for Him." But Paul said, in essence, "I am in the procession of a conqueror, and it doesn't matter what the difficulties are, for I am always led in triumph." Is this idea being worked out practically in us? Paul's secret joy was that God took him as a blatant rebel against Jesus Christ, and made him a captive—and that became his purpose. It was Paul's joy to be a captive of the Lord, and he had no other interest in heaven or on earth. It is a shameful thing for a Christian to talk about getting the victory. We should belong so completely to the Victor that it is always His victory, and "we are more than conquerors through Him" (Romans 8:37).

"We are to God the fragrance of Christ" (2 Corinthians 2:15). We are encompassed with the sweet aroma of Jesus, and wherever we go we are a wonderful refreshment to God.

Submitting to God's Purpose

"I have become all things to all men, that I might by all means save some." **1 Corinthians 9:22**

A Christian worker has to learn how to be God's man or woman of great worth and excellence in the midst of a multitude of meager and worthless things. Never protest by saying, "If only I were somewhere else!" All of God's people are ordinary people who have been made extraordinary by the purpose He has given them. Unless we have the right purpose intellectually in our minds and lovingly in our hearts, we will very quickly be diverted from being useful to God. We are not workers for God by choice. Many people deliberately choose to be workers, but they have no purpose of God's almighty grace or His mighty Word in them. Paul's whole heart, mind, and soul were consumed with the great purpose of what Jesus Christ came to do, and he never lost sight of that one thing. We must continually confront ourselves with one central fact—"Jesus Christ and Him crucified" (1 Corinthians 2:2).

"I chose you" (John 15:16). Keep these words as a wonderful reminder in your theology. It is not that you have gotten God, but that He has gotten you. God is at work bending, breaking, molding, and doing exactly as He chooses. And why is He doing it? He is doing it for only one purpose—that He may be able to say, "This is My man, and this is My woman." We have to be in God's hand so that He can place others on the Rock, Jesus Christ, just as He has placed us.

Never choose to be a worker, but once God has placed His call upon you, woe be to you if you "turn aside . . . to the right or the left" (Deuteronomy 28:14). He will do with you what He never did before His call came to you, and He will do with you what He is not doing with other people. Let Him have His way.

What Is a Missionary?

"Jesus said to them again, '. . . As the Father has sent Me, I also send you.'" **John 20:21**

A missionary is someone sent by Jesus Christ just as He was sent by God. The great controlling factor is not the needs of people, but the command of Jesus. The source of our inspiration in our service for God is behind us, not ahead of us. The tendency today is to put the inspiration out in front—to sweep everything together in front of us and make it conform to our definition of success. But in the New Testament the inspiration is put behind us, and is the Lord Jesus Himself. The goal is to be true to Him—to carry out *His* plans.

Personal attachment to the Lord Jesus and to His perspective is the one thing that must not be overlooked. In missionary work the great danger is that God's call will be replaced by the needs of the people, to the point that human sympathy for those needs will absolutely overwhelm the meaning of being sent by Jesus. The needs are so enormous, and the conditions so difficult, that every power of the mind falters and fails. We tend to forget that the one great reason underneath all missionary work is not primarily the elevation of the people, their education, nor their needs, but is first and foremost the command of Jesus Christ—"Go therefore and make disciples of all the nations" (Matthew 28:19).

When looking back on the lives of men and women of God, the tendency is to say, "What wonderfully keen and intelligent wisdom they had, and how perfectly they understood all that God wanted!" But the keen and intelligent mind behind them was the mind of God, not human wisdom at all. We give credit to human wisdom when we should give credit to the divine guidance of God being exhibited through childlike people who were "foolish" enough to trust God's wisdom and His supernatural equipment.

The Method of Missions

"Go therefore and make disciples of all the nations." **Matthew 28:19**

Jesus Christ did not say, "Go and save souls" (the salvation of souls is the supernatural work of God), but He said, "Go . . . make disciples of all the nations." Yet you cannot make disciples unless you are a disciple yourself. When the disciples returned from their first mission, they were filled with joy because even the demons were subject to them. But Jesus said, in effect, "Don't rejoice in successful service—the great secret of joy is that you have the right relationship with Me" (see Luke 10:17–20). The missionary's great essential is remaining true to the call of God, and realizing that his one and only purpose is to disciple men and women to Jesus. Remember that there is a passion for souls that does not come from God, but from our desire to make converts to our point of view.

The challenge to the missionary does not come from the fact that people are difficult to bring to salvation, that backsliders are difficult to reclaim, or that there is a barrier of callous indifference. No, the challenge comes from the perspective of the missionary's own personal relationship with Jesus Christ—"Do you believe that I am able to do this?" (Matthew 9:28). Our Lord unwaveringly asks us that question, and it confronts us in every individual situation we encounter. The one great challenge to us is—do I know my risen Lord? Do I know the power of His indwelling Spirit? Am I wise enough in God's sight, but foolish enough according to the wisdom of the world, to trust in what Jesus Christ has said? Or am I abandoning the great supernatural position of limitless confidence in Christ Jesus, which is really God's only call for a missionary? If I follow any other method, I depart altogether from the methods prescribed by our Lord—"All authority has been given to Me . . . . *Go therefore . . .*" (Matthew 28:18–19).

Justification by Faith

"If when we were enemies we were reconciled to God through the death of His Son, much more, having been reconciled, we shall be saved by His life." **Romans 5:10**

I am not saved by believing—I simply realize I am saved by believing. And it is not repentance that saves me—repentance is only the sign that I realize what God has done through Christ Jesus. The danger here is putting the emphasis on the effect, instead of on the cause. Is it my obedience, consecration, and dedication that make me right with God? It is never that! I am made right with God because, prior to all of that, Christ died. When I turn to God and by belief accept what God reveals, the miraculous atonement by the Cross of Christ instantly places me into a right relationship with God. And as a result of the supernatural miracle of God's grace I stand justified, not because I am sorry for my sin, or because I have repented, but because of what Jesus has done. The Spirit of God brings justification with a shattering, radiant light, and I know that I am saved, even though I don't know how it was accomplished.

The salvation that comes from God is not based on human logic, but on the sacrificial death of Jesus. We can be born again solely because of the atonement of our Lord. Sinful men and women can be changed into new creations, not through their repentance or their belief, but through the wonderful work of God in Christ Jesus which preceded all of our experience (see 2 Corinthians 5:17–19). The unconquerable safety of justification and sanctification is God Himself. We do not have to accomplish these things ourselves—they have been accomplished through the atonement of the Cross of Christ. The supernatural becomes natural to us through the miracle of God, and there is the realization of what Jesus Christ has already done—*"It is finished!"* (John 19:30).

OCTOBER 29

Substitution

"He made Him who knew no sin to be sin for us, that we might become the righteousness of God in Him." **2 Corinthians 5:21**

The modern view of the death of Jesus is that He died for our sins out of sympathy for us. Yet the New Testament view is that He took our sin on Himself not because of sympathy, but because of His identification with us. He was "*made . . . to be sin*." Our sins are removed because of the death of Jesus, and the only explanation for His death is His obedience to His Father, not His sympathy for us. We are acceptable to God not because we have obeyed, nor because we have promised to give up things, but because of the death of Christ, and for no other reason. We say that Jesus Christ came to reveal the fatherhood and the lovingkindness of God, but the New Testament says that He came to take "away the sin of the world!" (John 1:29). And the revealing of the fatherhood of God is only to those to whom Jesus has been introduced as Savior. In speaking to the world, Jesus Christ never referred to Himself as One who revealed the Father, but He spoke instead of being a stumbling block (see John 15:22–24). John 14:9, where Jesus said, "He who has seen Me has seen the Father," was spoken to His disciples.

That Christ died for me, and therefore I am completely free from penalty, is never taught in the New Testament. What *is* taught in the New Testament is that "He died for all" (2 Corinthians 5:15)—not, "He died my death"—and that through identification with His death I can be freed from sin, and have His very righteousness imparted as a gift to me. The substitution which is taught in the New Testament is twofold—"For He made Him who knew no sin to be sin for us, *that we might become the righteousness of God in Him*." The teaching is not Christ *for* me unless I am determined to have Christ formed *in* me (see Galatians 4:19).

OCTOBER 30

Faith

"Without faith it is impossible to please Him."
Hebrews 11:6

Faith in active opposition to common sense is mistaken enthusiasm and narrow-mindedness, and common sense in opposition to faith demonstrates a mistaken reliance on reason as the basis for truth. The life of faith brings the two of these into the proper relationship. Common sense and faith are as different from each other as the natural life is from the spiritual, and as impulsiveness is from inspiration. Nothing that Jesus Christ ever said is common sense, but is revelation sense, and is complete, whereas common sense falls short. Yet faith must be tested and tried before it becomes real in your life. "We know that all things work together for good" (Romans 8:28) so that no matter what happens, the transforming power of God's providence transforms perfect faith into reality. Faith always works in a personal way, because the purpose of God is to see that perfect faith is made real in His children.

For every detail of common sense in life, there is a truth God has revealed by which we can prove in our practical experience what we believe God to be. Faith is a tremendously active principle that always puts Jesus Christ first. The life of faith says, "Lord, You have said it, it appears to be irrational, but I'm going to step out boldly, trusting in Your Word" (for example, see Matthew 6:33). Turning intellectual faith into our personal possession is *always* a fight, not just sometimes. God brings us into particular circumstances to educate our faith, because the nature of faith is to make the object of our faith very real to us. Until we know Jesus, God is merely a concept, and we can't have faith in Him. But once we hear Jesus say, "He who has seen Me has seen the Father" (John 14:9) we immediately have something that is real, and our faith is limitless. Faith is the entire person in the right relationship with God through the power of the Spirit of Jesus Christ.

OCTOBER 31

The Trial of Faith

"If you have faith as a mustard seed . . . nothing will be impossible for you." **Matthew 17:20**

We have the idea that God rewards us for our faith, and it may be so in the initial stages. But we do not earn anything through faith—faith brings us into the right relationship with God and gives Him His opportunity to work. Yet God frequently has to knock the bottom out of your experience as His saint to get you in direct contact with Himself. God wants you to understand that it is a life of *faith*, not a life of emotional enjoyment of His blessings. The beginning of your life of faith was very narrow and intense, centered on a small amount of experience that had as much emotion as faith in it, and it was full of light and sweetness. Then God withdrew His conscious blessings to teach you to "walk by faith" (2 Corinthians 5:7). And you are worth much more to Him now than you were in your days of conscious delight with your thrilling testimony.

Faith by its very nature must be tested and tried. And the real trial of faith is not that we find it difficult to trust God, but that God's character must be proven as trustworthy in our own minds. Faith being worked out into reality must experience times of unbroken isolation. Never confuse the trial of faith with the ordinary discipline of life, because a great deal of what we call the trial of faith is the inevitable result of being alive. Faith, as the Bible teaches it, is faith in God coming against everything that contradicts Him—a faith that says, "I will remain true to God's character whatever He may do." The highest and the greatest expression of faith in the whole Bible is—"Though He slay me, yet will I trust Him" (Job 13:15).

"You Are Not Your Own"

"Do you not know that . . . you are not your own?" **1 Corinthians 6:19**

There is no such thing as a private life, or a place to hide in this world, for a man or woman who is intimately aware of and shares in the sufferings of Jesus Christ. God divides the private life of His saints and makes it a highway for the world on one hand and for Himself on the other. No human being can stand that unless he is identified with Jesus Christ. We are not sanctified for ourselves. We are called into intimacy with the gospel, and things happen that appear to have nothing to do with us. But God is getting us into fellowship with Himself. Let Him have His way. If you refuse, you will be of no value to God in His redemptive work in the world, but will be a hindrance and a stumbling block.

The first thing God does is get us grounded on strong reality and truth. He does this until our cares for ourselves individually have been brought into submission to His way for the purpose of His redemption. Why shouldn't we experience heartbreak? Through those doorways God is opening up ways of fellowship with His Son. Most of us collapse at the first grip of pain. We sit down at the door of God's purpose and enter a slow death through self-pity. And all the so-called Christian sympathy of others helps us to our deathbed. But God will not. He comes with the grip of the pierced hand of His Son, as if to say, "Enter into fellowship with Me; arise and shine." If God can accomplish His purposes in this world through a broken heart, then why not thank Him for breaking yours?

NOVEMBER 2

Obedience or Independence?

"If you love Me, keep My commandments."
John 14:15

Our Lord never insists on our obedience. He stresses very definitely what we *ought* to do, but He never *forces* us to do it. We have to obey Him out of a oneness of spirit with Him. That is why whenever our Lord talked about discipleship, He prefaced it with an "If," meaning, "You do not need to do this unless you desire to do so." "*If* anyone desires to come after Me, let him deny himself" (Luke 9:23). In other words, "To be My disciple, let him give up his right to himself to Me." Our Lord is not talking about our eternal position, but about our being of value to Him in this life here and now. That is why He sounds so stern (see Luke 14:26). Never try to make sense from these words by separating them from the One who spoke them.

The Lord does not give me rules, but He makes His standard very clear. If my relationship to Him is that of love, I will do what He says without hesitation. If I hesitate, it is because I love someone I have placed in competition with Him, namely, myself. Jesus Christ will not force me to obey Him, but I must. And as soon as I obey Him, I fulfill my spiritual destiny. My personal life may be crowded with small, petty happenings, altogether insignificant. But if I obey Jesus Christ in the seemingly random circumstances of life, they become pinholes through which I see the face of God. Then, when I stand face-to-face with God, I will discover that through my obedience thousands were blessed. When God's redemption brings a human soul to the point of obedience, it always produces. If I obey Jesus Christ, the redemption of God will flow through me to the lives of others, because behind the deed of obedience is the reality of Almighty God.

A Bondservant of Jesus

"I have been crucified with Christ; it is no longer I who live, but Christ lives in me." **Galatians 2:20**

These words mean the breaking and collapse of my independence brought about by my own hands, and the surrendering of my life to the supremacy of the Lord Jesus. No one can do this for me, I must do it myself. God may bring me up to this point three hundred and sixty-five times a year, but He cannot push me through it. It means breaking the hard outer layer of my individual independence from God, and the liberating of myself and my nature into oneness with Him; not following my own ideas, but choosing absolute loyalty to Jesus. Once I am at that point, there is no possibility of misunderstanding. Very few of us know anything about loyalty to Christ or understand what He meant when He said, ". . . *for My sake*" (Matthew 5:11). That is what makes a strong saint.

Has that breaking of my independence come? All the rest is religious fraud. The one point to decide is—will I give up? Will I surrender to Jesus Christ, placing no conditions whatsoever as to how the brokenness will come? I must be broken from my own understanding of myself. When I reach that point, immediately the reality of the supernatural identification with Jesus Christ takes place. And the witness of the Spirit of God is unmistakable—"I have been crucified with Christ."

The passion of Christianity comes from deliberately signing away my own rights and becoming a bondservant of Jesus Christ. Until I do that, I will not begin to be a saint.

One student a year who hears God's call would be sufficient for God to have called the Bible Training College into existence. This college has no value as an organization, not even academically. Its sole value for existence is for God to help Himself to lives. Will we allow Him to help Himself to us, or are we more concerned with our own ideas of what we are going to be?

NOVEMBER 4

The Authority of Truth

"Draw near to God and He will draw near to you."
James 4:8

It is essential that you give people the opportunity to act on the truth of God. The responsibility must be left with the individual—you cannot act for him. It must be his own deliberate act, but the evangelical message should always lead him to action. Refusing to act leaves a person paralyzed, exactly where he was previously. But once he acts, he is never the same. It is the apparent folly of the truth that stands in the way of hundreds who have been convicted by the Spirit of God. Once I press myself into action, I immediately begin to live. Anything less is merely existing. The moments I truly live are the moments when I act with my entire will.

When a truth of God is brought home to your soul, never allow it to pass without acting on it internally in your will, not necessarily externally in your physical life. Record it with ink and with blood—work it into your life. The weakest saint who transacts business with Jesus Christ is liberated the second he acts and God's almighty power is available on his behalf. We come up to the truth of God, confess we are wrong, but go back again. Then we approach it again and turn back, until we finally learn we have no business going back. When we are confronted with such a word of truth from our redeeming Lord, we must move directly to transact business with Him. "Come to Me" (Matthew 11:28). His word *come* means "to act." Yet the last thing we want to do is come. But everyone who does come knows that, at that very moment, the supernatural power of the life of God invades him. The dominating power of the world, the flesh, and the devil is now paralyzed; not by your act, but because your act has joined you to God and tapped you in to His redemptive power.

Partakers of His Sufferings

"But rejoice to the extent that you partake of Christ's sufferings." **1 Peter 4:13**

If you are going to be used by God, He will take you through a number of experiences that are not meant for you personally at all. They are designed to make you useful in His hands, and to enable you to understand what takes place in the lives of others. Because of this process, you will never be surprised by what comes your way. You say, "Oh, I can't deal with that person." Why can't you? God gave you sufficient opportunities to learn from Him about that problem; but you turned away, not heeding the lesson, because it seemed foolish to spend your time that way.

The sufferings of Christ were not those of ordinary people. He suffered "according to the will of God" (1 Peter 4:19), having a different point of view of suffering from ours. It is only through our relationship with Jesus Christ that we can understand what God is after in His dealings with us. When it comes to suffering, it is part of our Christian culture to want to know God's purpose beforehand. In the history of the Christian church, the tendency has been to avoid being identified with the sufferings of Jesus Christ. People have sought to carry out God's orders through a shortcut of their own. God's way is always the way of suffering—the way of the "long road home."

Are we partakers of Christ's sufferings? Are we prepared for God to stamp out our personal ambitions? Are we prepared for God to destroy our individual decisions by supernaturally transforming them? It will mean not knowing why God is taking us that way, because knowing would make us spiritually proud. We never realize at the time what God is putting us through—we go through it more or less without understanding. Then suddenly we come to a place of enlightenment, and realize—"God has strengthened me and I didn't even know it!"

NOVEMBER 6

Intimate Theology

"Do you believe this?" **John 11:26**

Martha believed in the power available to Jesus Christ; she believed that if He had been there He could have healed her brother; she also believed that Jesus had a special intimacy with God, and that whatever He asked of God, God would do. But—she needed a closer personal intimacy with Jesus. Martha's theology had its fulfillment in the future. But Jesus continued to attract and draw her in until her belief became an intimate possession. It then slowly emerged into a personal inheritance—"Yes, Lord, I believe that You are the Christ . . ." (John 11:27).

Is the Lord dealing with you in the same way? Is Jesus teaching you to have a personal intimacy with Himself? Allow Him to drive His question home to you—"Do you believe *this*?" Are you facing an area of doubt in your life? Have you come, like Martha, to a crossroads of overwhelming circumstances where your theology is about to become a very personal belief? This happens only when a personal problem brings the awareness of our personal need.

To believe is to commit. In the area of intellectual learning I commit myself mentally, and reject anything not related to that belief. In the realm of personal belief I commit myself morally to my convictions and refuse to compromise. But in intimate personal belief I commit myself spiritually to Jesus Christ and make a determination to be dominated by Him alone.

Then, when I stand face-to-face with Jesus Christ and He says to me, "Do you believe this?" I find that faith is as natural as breathing. And I am staggered when I think how foolish I have been in not trusting Him earlier.

The Undetected Sacredness of Circumstances

"We know that all things work together for good to those who love God." **Romans 8:28**

The circumstances of a saint's life are ordained of God. In the life of a saint there is no such thing as chance. God by His providence brings you into circumstances that you can't understand at all, but the Spirit of God understands. God brings you to places, among people, and into certain conditions to accomplish a definite purpose through the intercession of the Spirit in you. Never put yourself in front of your circumstances and say, "I'm going to be my own providence here; I will watch this closely, or protect myself from that." All your circumstances are in the hand of God, and therefore you don't ever have to think they are unnatural or unique. Your part in intercessory prayer is not to agonize over how to intercede, but to use the everyday circumstances and people God puts around you by His providence to bring them before His throne, and to allow the Spirit in you the opportunity to intercede for them. In this way God is going to touch the whole world with His saints.

Am I making the Holy Spirit's work difficult by being vague and unsure, or by trying to do His work for Him? I must do the human side of intercession—utilizing the circumstances in which I find myself and the people who surround me. I must keep my conscious life as a sacred place for the Holy Spirit. Then as I lift different ones to God through prayer, the Holy Spirit intercedes for them.

Your intercessions can never be mine, and my intercessions can never be yours, "but the Spirit Himself makes intercession" in each of our lives (Romans 8:26). And without that intercession, the lives of others would be left in poverty and in ruin.

The Unrivaled Power of Prayer

"We do not know what we should pray for as we ought, but the Spirit Himself makes intercession for us with groanings which cannot be uttered." **Romans 8:26**

We realize that we are energized by the Holy Spirit for prayer; and we know what it is to pray in accordance with the Spirit; but we don't often realize that the Holy Spirit Himself prays prayers in us which we cannot utter ourselves. When we are born again of God and are indwelt by the Spirit of God, He expresses for us the unutterable.

"He," the Holy Spirit in you, "makes intercession for the saints according to the will of God" (Romans 8:27). And God searches your heart, not to know what your conscious prayers are, but to find out what the prayer of the Holy Spirit is.

The Spirit of God uses the nature of the believer as a temple in which to offer His prayers of intercession. "Your body is the temple of the Holy Spirit" (1 Corinthians 6:19). When Jesus Christ cleansed the temple, "He would not allow anyone to carry wares through the temple" (Mark 11:16). The Spirit of God will not allow you to use your body for your own convenience. Jesus ruthlessly cast out everyone who bought and sold in the temple, and said, "My house shall be called a house of prayer . . . . But you have made it a 'den of thieves'" (Mark 11:17).

Have we come to realize that our "body is the temple of the Holy Spirit"? If so, we must be careful to keep it undefiled for Him. We have to remember that our conscious life, even though only a small part of our total person, is to be regarded by us as a "temple of the Holy Spirit." He will be responsible for the unconscious part which we don't know, but we must pay careful attention to and guard the conscious part for which we are responsible.

Sacred Service

"I now rejoice in my sufferings for you, and fill up in my flesh what is lacking in the afflictions of Christ." **Colossians 1:24**

The Christian worker has to be a sacred "go-between." He must be so closely identified with his Lord and the reality of His redemption that Christ can continually bring His creating life through him. I am not referring to the strength of one individual's personality being superimposed on another, but the real presence of Christ coming through every aspect of the worker's life. When we preach the historical facts of the life and death of our Lord as they are conveyed in the New Testament, our words are made sacred. God uses these words, on the basis of His redemption, to create something in those who listen which otherwise could never have been created. If we simply preach the effects of redemption in the human life instead of the revealed, divine truth regarding Jesus Himself, the result is not new birth in those who listen. The result is a refined religious lifestyle, and the Spirit of God cannot witness to it because such preaching is in a realm other than His. We must make sure that we are living in such harmony with God that as we proclaim His truth He can create in others those things which He alone can do.

When we say, "What a wonderful personality, what a fascinating person, and what wonderful insight!" then what opportunity does the gospel of God have through all of that? It cannot get through, because the attraction is to the messenger and not the message. If a person attracts through his personality, that becomes his appeal. If, however, he is identified with the Lord Himself, then the appeal becomes what Jesus Christ can do. The danger is to glory in men, yet Jesus says we are to lift up only *Him* (see John 12:32).

Fellowship in the Gospel

". . . fellow laborer in the gospel of Christ."
1 Thessalonians 3:2

After sanctification, it is difficult to state what your purpose in life is, because God has moved you into His purpose through the Holy Spirit. He is using you now for His purposes throughout the world as He used His Son for the purpose of our salvation. If you seek great things for yourself, thinking, "God has called me for this and for that," you barricade God from using you. As long as you maintain your own personal interests and ambitions, you cannot be completely aligned or identified with God's interests. This can only be accomplished by giving up all of your personal plans once and for all, and by allowing God to take you directly into His purpose for the world. Your understanding of your ways must also be surrendered, because they are now the ways of the Lord.

I must learn that the purpose of my life belongs to God, not me. God is using me from His great personal perspective, and all He asks of me is that I trust Him. I should never say, "Lord, this causes me such heartache." To talk that way makes me a stumbling block. When I stop telling God what I want, He can freely work His will in me without any hindrance. He can crush me, exalt me, or do anything else He chooses. He simply asks me to have absolute faith in Him and His goodness. Self-pity is of the devil, and if I wallow in it I cannot be used by God for His purpose in the world. Doing this creates for me my own cozy "world within the world," and God will not be allowed to move me from it because of my fear of being "frostbitten."

The Supreme Climb

"He said, 'Take now your son . . .'" **Genesis 22:2**

God's command is, "Take *now*," not later. It is incredible how we debate! We know something is right, but we try to find excuses for not doing it immediately. If we are to climb to the height God reveals, it can never be done later—it must be done now. And the sacrifice must be worked through our will before we actually perform it.

"So Abraham rose early in the morning . . . and went to the place of which God had told him" (Genesis 22:3). Oh, the wonderful simplicity of Abraham! When God spoke, he did not "confer with flesh and blood" (Galatians 1:16). Beware when you want to "confer with flesh and blood" or even your own thoughts, insights, or understandings—anything that is not based on your personal relationship with God. These are all things that compete with and hinder obedience to God.

Abraham did not choose what the sacrifice would be. Always guard against self-chosen service for God. Self-sacrifice may be a disease that impairs your service. If God has made your cup sweet, drink it with grace; or even if He has made it bitter, drink it in communion with Him. If the providential will of God means a hard and difficult time for you, go through it. But never decide the place of your own martyrdom, as if to say, "I will only go to there, but no farther." God chose the test for Abraham, and Abraham neither delayed nor protested, but steadily obeyed. If you are not living in touch with God, it is easy to blame Him or pass judgment on Him. You must go through the trial before you have any right to pronounce a verdict, because by going through the trial you learn to know God better. God is working in us to reach His highest goals until His purpose and our purpose become one.

NOVEMBER 12

The Changed Life

"If anyone is in Christ, he is a new creation; old things have passed away; behold, all things have become new." **2 Corinthians 5:17**

What understanding do you have of the salvation of your soul? The work of salvation means that in your real life things are dramatically changed. You no longer look at things in the same way. Your desires are new and the old things have lost their power to attract you. One of the tests for determining if the work of salvation in your life is genuine is—has God changed the things that really matter to you? If you still yearn for the old things, it is absurd to talk about being born from above—you are deceiving yourself. If you are born again, the Spirit of God makes the change very evident in your real life and thought. And when a crisis comes, you are the most amazed person on earth at the wonderful difference there is in you. There is no possibility of imagining that *you* did it. It is this complete and amazing change that is the very evidence that you are saved.

What difference has my salvation and sanctification made? For instance, can I stand in the light of 1 Corinthians 13, or do I squirm and evade the issue? True salvation, worked out in me by the Holy Spirit, frees me completely. And as long as I "walk in the light as He is in the light" (1 John 1:7), God sees nothing to rebuke because His life is working itself into every detailed part of my being, not on the conscious level, but even deeper than my consciousness.

NOVEMBER 13

Faith or Experience?

". . . the Son of God, who loved me and gave Himself for me." **Galatians 2:20**

We should battle through our moods, feelings, and emotions into absolute devotion to the Lord Jesus. We must break out of our own little world of experience into abandoned devotion to Him. Think who the New Testament says Jesus Christ is, and then think of the despicable meagerness of the miserable faith we exhibit by saying, "I haven't had this experience or that experience"! Think what faith in Jesus Christ claims and provides—He can present us faultless before the throne of God, inexpressibly pure, absolutely righteous, and profoundly justified. Stand in absolute adoring faith "in Christ Jesus, who became for us wisdom from God—and righteousness and sanctification and redemption" (1 Corinthians 1:30). How dare we talk of making a sacrifice for the Son of God! We are saved from hell and total destruction, and then we talk about making sacrifices!

We must continually focus and firmly place our faith in Jesus Christ—not a "prayer meeting" Jesus Christ, or a "book" Jesus Christ, but the New Testament Jesus Christ, who is God Incarnate, and who ought to strike us dead at His feet. Our faith must be in the One from whom our salvation springs. Jesus Christ wants our absolute, unrestrained devotion to Himself. We can never *experience* Jesus Christ, or selfishly bind Him in the confines of our own hearts. Our faith must be built on strong determined confidence in Him.

It is because of our trusting in experience that we see the steadfast impatience of the Holy Spirit against unbelief. All of our fears are sinful, and we create our own fears by refusing to nourish ourselves in our faith. How can anyone who is identified with Jesus Christ suffer from doubt or fear! Our lives should be an absolute hymn of praise resulting from perfect, irrepressible, triumphant belief.

Discovering Divine Design

"As for me, being on the way, the LORD led me . . ."
Genesis 24:27

We should be so one with God that we don't need to ask continually for guidance. Sanctification means that we are made the children of God. A child's life is normally obedient, until he chooses disobedience. But as soon as he chooses to disobey, an inherent inner conflict is produced. On the spiritual level, inner conflict is the warning of the Spirit of God. When He warns us in this way, we must stop at once and be renewed in the spirit of our mind to discern God's will (see Romans 12:2). If we are born again by the Spirit of God, our devotion to Him is hindered, or even stopped, by continually asking Him to guide us here and there. "The Lord led me . . ." and on looking back we see the presence of an amazing design. If we are born of God we will see His guiding hand and give Him the credit.

We can all see God in exceptional things, but it requires the growth of spiritual discipline to see God in every detail. Never believe that the so-called random events of life are anything less than God's appointed order. Be ready to discover His divine designs anywhere and everywhere.

Beware of being obsessed with consistency to your own convictions instead of being devoted to God. If you are a saint and say, "I will never do this or that," in all probability this will be exactly what God will require of you. There was never a more inconsistent being on this earth than our Lord, but He was never inconsistent with His Father. The important consistency in a saint is not to a principle but to the divine life. It is the divine life that continually makes more and more discoveries about the divine mind. It is easier to be an excessive fanatic than it is to be consistently faithful, because God causes an amazing humbling of our religious conceit when we are faithful to Him.

"What Is That to You?"

"Peter . . . said to Jesus, 'But Lord, what about this man?' Jesus said to him, '. . . what is that to you? You follow Me.'" **John 21:21–22**

One of the hardest lessons to learn comes from our stubborn refusal to refrain from interfering in other people's lives. It takes a long time to realize the danger of being an amateur providence, that is, interfering with God's plan for others. You see someone suffering and say, "He will not suffer, and I will make sure that he doesn't." You put your hand right in front of God's permissive will to stop it, and then God says, "What is that to you?" Is there stagnation in your spiritual life? Don't allow it to continue, but get into God's presence and find out the reason for it. You will possibly find it is because you have been interfering in the life of another—proposing things you had no right to propose, or advising when you had no right to advise. When you do have to give advice to another person, God will advise through you with the direct understanding of His Spirit. Your part is to maintain the right relationship with God so that His discernment can come through you continually for the purpose of blessing someone else.

Most of us live only within the level of consciousness—consciously serving and consciously devoted to God. This shows immaturity and the fact that we're not yet living the real Christian life. Maturity is produced in the life of a child of God on the unconscious level, until we become so totally surrendered to God that we are not even aware of being used by Him. When we are consciously aware of being used as broken bread and poured-out wine, we have yet another level to reach—a level where all awareness of ourselves and of what God is doing through us is completely eliminated. A saint is never consciously a saint—a saint is consciously dependent on God.

NOVEMBER 16

Still Human!

"Whatever you do, do all to the glory of God."
1 Corinthians 10:31

In the Scriptures, the great miracle of the incarnation slips into the ordinary life of a child; the great miracle of the transfiguration fades into the demon-possessed valley below; the glory of the resurrection descends into a breakfast on the seashore. This is not an anticlimax, but a great revelation of God.

We have a tendency to look for wonder in our experience, and we mistake heroic actions for real heroes. It's one thing to go through a crisis grandly, yet quite another to go through every day glorifying God when there is no witness, no limelight, and no one paying even the remotest attention to us. If we are not looking for halos, we at least want something that will make people say, "What a wonderful man of prayer he is!" or, "What a great woman of devotion she is!" If you are properly devoted to the Lord Jesus, you have reached the lofty height where no one would ever notice you personally. All that is noticed is the power of God coming through you all the time.

We want to be able to say, "Oh, I have had a wonderful call from God!" But to do even the most humbling tasks to the glory of God takes the Almighty God Incarnate working in us. To be utterly unnoticeable requires God's Spirit in us making us absolutely humanly His. The true test of a saint's life is not successfulness but faithfulness on the human level of life. We tend to set up success in Christian work as our purpose, but our purpose should be to display the glory of God in human life, to live a life "hidden with Christ in God" in our everyday human conditions (Colossians 3:3). Our human relationships are the very conditions in which the ideal life of God should be exhibited.

The Eternal Goal

"By Myself I have sworn, says the Lord, because you have done this thing . . . I will bless you." **Genesis 22:16–17**

Abraham, at this point, has reached the place where he is in touch with the very nature of God. He now understands the reality of God.

My goal is God Himself . . . / At any cost, dear Lord, by any road.

"At any cost . . . by any road" means submitting to God's way of bringing us to the goal.

There is no possibility of questioning God when He speaks, if He speaks to His own nature in me. Prompt obedience is the only result. When Jesus says, "Come," I simply come; when He says, "Let go," I let go; when He says, "Trust God in this matter," I trust. This work of obedience is the evidence that the nature of God is in me.

God's revelation of Himself to me is influenced by my character, not by God's character.

'Tis because I am ordinary, / Thy ways so often look ordinary to me.

It is through the discipline of obedience that I get to the place where Abraham was and I see who God is. God will never be real to me until I come face-to-face with Him in Jesus Christ. Then I will know and can boldly proclaim, "In all the world, my God, there is none but Thee, there is none but Thee."

The promises of God are of no value to us until, through obedience, we come to understand the nature of God. We may read some things in the Bible every day for a year and they may mean nothing to us. Then, because we have been obedient to God in some small detail, we suddenly see what God means and His nature is instantly opened up to us. "All the promises of God in Him are Yes, and in Him Amen" (2 Corinthians 1:20). Our "Yes" must be born of obedience; when by obedience we ratify a promise of God by saying, "Amen," or, "So be it." That promise becomes ours.

Winning into Freedom

"If the Son makes you free, you shall be free indeed." **John 8:36**

If there is even a trace of individual self-satisfaction left in us, it always says, "I can't surrender," or "I can't be free." But the spiritual part of our being never says "I can't"; it simply soaks up everything around it. Our spirit hungers for more and more. It is the way we are built. We are designed with a great capacity for God, but sin, our own individuality, and wrong thinking keep us from getting to Him. God delivers us from sin—we have to deliver ourselves from our individuality. This means offering our natural life to God and sacrificing it to Him, so He may transform it into spiritual life through our obedience.

God pays no attention to our natural individuality in the development of our spiritual life. His plan runs right through our natural life. We must see to it that we aid and assist God, and not stand against Him by saying, "I can't do that." God will not discipline us; we must discipline ourselves. God will not bring our "arguments . . . and every thought into captivity to the obedience of Christ" (2 Corinthians 10:5)—we have to do it. Don't say, "Oh, Lord, I suffer from wandering thoughts." *Don't* suffer from wandering thoughts. Stop listening to the tyranny of your individual natural life and win freedom into the spiritual life.

"If the Son makes you free . . ." Do not substitute *Savior* for *Son* in this passage. The *Savior* has set us free from sin, but this is the freedom that comes from being set free from myself *by the Son*. It is what Paul meant in Galatians 2:20 when he said, "I have been crucified with Christ." His individuality had been broken and his spirit had been united with his Lord; not just merged into Him, but made one with Him. "You shall be free indeed"—free to the very core of your being; free from the inside to the outside. We tend to rely on our own energy, instead of being energized by the power that comes from identification with Jesus.

NOVEMBER 19

"When He Has Come"

"When He has come, He will convict the world of sin."
John 16:8

Very few of us know anything about conviction of sin. We know the experience of being disturbed because we have done wrong things. But conviction of sin by the Holy Spirit blots out every relationship on earth and makes us aware of only one—"Against You, You only, have I sinned" (Psalm 51:4). When a person is convicted of sin in this way, he knows with every bit of his conscience that God would not dare to forgive him. If God did forgive him, then this person would have a stronger sense of justice than God. God does forgive, but it cost the breaking of His heart with grief in the death of Christ to enable Him to do so. The great miracle of the grace of God is that He forgives sin, and it is the death of Jesus Christ alone that enables the divine nature to forgive and to remain true to itself in doing so. It is shallow nonsense to say that God forgives us because He is love. Once we have been convicted of sin, we will never say this again. The love of God means Calvary—nothing less! The love of God is spelled out on the Cross and nowhere else. The only basis for which God can forgive me is the Cross of Christ. It is there that His conscience is satisfied.

Forgiveness doesn't merely mean that I am saved from hell and have been made ready for heaven (no one would accept forgiveness on that level). Forgiveness means that I am forgiven into a newly created relationship which identifies me with God in Christ. The miracle of redemption is that God turns me, the unholy one, into the standard of Himself, the Holy One. He does this by putting into me a new nature, the nature of Jesus Christ.

NOVEMBER 20

The Forgiveness of God

"In Him we have . . . the forgiveness of sins." **Ephesians 1:7**

Beware of the pleasant view of the fatherhood of God: God is so kind and loving that of course He will forgive us. That thought, based solely on emotion, cannot be found anywhere in the New Testament. The only basis on which God can forgive us is the tremendous tragedy of the Cross of Christ. To base our forgiveness on any other ground is unconscious blasphemy. The only ground on which God can forgive our sin and reinstate us to His favor is through the Cross of Christ. There is no other way! Forgiveness, which is so easy for us to accept, cost the agony at Calvary. We should never take the forgiveness of sin, the gift of the Holy Spirit, and our sanctification in simple faith, and then forget the enormous cost to God that made all of this ours.

Forgiveness is the divine miracle of grace. The cost to God was the Cross of Christ. To forgive sin, while remaining a holy God, this price had to be paid. Never accept a view of the fatherhood of God if it blots out the atonement. The revealed truth of God is that without the atonement He cannot forgive—He would contradict His nature if He did. The only way we can be forgiven is by being brought back to God through the atonement of the Cross. God's forgiveness is possible only in the supernatural realm.

Compared with the miracle of the forgiveness of sin, the experience of sanctification is small. Sanctification is simply the wonderful expression or evidence of the forgiveness of sins in a human life. But the thing that awakens the deepest fountain of gratitude in a human being is that God has forgiven his sin. Paul never got away from this. Once you realize all that it cost God to forgive you, you will be held as in a vise, constrained by the love of God.

"It Is Finished!"

"I have finished the work which You have given Me to do." **John 17:4**

The death of Jesus Christ is the fulfillment in history of the very mind and intent of God. There is no place for seeing Jesus Christ as a martyr. His death was not something that happened *to* Him—something that might have been prevented. His death was the very reason He came.

Never build your case for forgiveness on the idea that God is our Father and He will forgive us because He loves us. That contradicts the revealed truth of God in Jesus Christ. It makes the Cross unnecessary, and the redemption "much ado about nothing." God forgives sin only because of the death of Christ. God could forgive people in no other way than by the death of His Son, and Jesus is exalted as Savior because of His death. "We see Jesus . . . *for the suffering of death* crowned with glory and honor" (Hebrews 2:9). The greatest note of triumph ever sounded in the ears of a startled universe was that sounded on the Cross of Christ—"*It is finished!*" (John 19:30). That is the final word in the redemption of humankind.

Anything that lessens or completely obliterates the holiness of God, through a false view of His love, contradicts the truth of God as revealed by Jesus Christ. Never allow yourself to believe that Jesus Christ stands with us, and against God, out of pity and compassion, or that He became a curse for us out of sympathy for us. Jesus Christ became a curse for us by divine decree. Our part in realizing the tremendous meaning of His curse is the conviction of sin. Conviction is given to us as a gift of shame and repentance; it is the great mercy of God. Jesus Christ hates the sin in people, and Calvary is the measure of His hatred.

NOVEMBER 22

Shallow and Profound

"Whether you eat or drink, or whatever you do, do all to the glory of God." **1 Corinthians 10:31**

Beware of allowing yourself to think that the shallow aspects of life are not ordained by God; they are ordained by Him equally as much as the profound. We sometimes refuse to be shallow, not out of our deep devotion to God but because we wish to impress other people with the fact that we are not shallow. This is a sure sign of spiritual pride. We must be careful, for this is how contempt for others is produced in our lives. And it causes us to be a walking rebuke to other people because they are more shallow than we are. Beware of posing as a profound person—God became a baby.

To be shallow is not a sign of being sinful, nor is shallowness an indication that there is no depth to your life at all—the ocean has a shore. Even the shallow things of life, such as eating and drinking, walking and talking, are ordained by God. These are all things our Lord did. He did them as the Son of God, and He said, "A disciple is not above his teacher" (Matthew 10:24).

We are safeguarded by the shallow things of life. We have to live the surface, commonsense life in a commonsense way. Then when God gives us the deeper things, they are obviously separated from the shallow concerns. Never show the depth of your life to anyone but God. We are so nauseatingly serious, so desperately interested in our own character and reputation, we refuse to behave like Christians in the shallow concerns of life.

Make a determination to take no one seriously except God. You may find that the first person you must be the most critical with, as being the greatest fraud you have ever known, is yourself.

The Distraction of Contempt

"Have mercy on us, O LORD, have mercy on us! For we are exceedingly filled with contempt." **Psalm 123:3**

What we must beware of is not damage to our belief in God but damage to our Christian disposition or state of mind. "Take heed to your spirit, that you do not deal treacherously" (Malachi 2:16). Our state of mind is powerful in its effects. It can be the enemy that penetrates right into our soul and distracts our mind from God. There are certain attitudes we should never dare to indulge. If we do, we will find they have distracted us from faith in God. Until we get back into a quiet mood before Him, our faith is of no value, and our confidence in the flesh and in human ingenuity is what rules our lives.

Beware of "the cares of this world" (Mark 4:19). They are the very things that produce the wrong attitudes in our soul. It is incredible what enormous power there is in simple things to distract our attention away from God. Refuse to be swamped by "the cares of this world."

Another thing that distracts us is our passion for vindication. St. Augustine prayed, "O Lord, deliver me from this lust of always vindicating myself." Such a need for constant vindication destroys our soul's faith in God. Don't say, "I must explain myself," or, "I must get people to understand." Our Lord never explained anything—He left the misunderstandings or misconceptions of others to correct themselves.

When we discern that other people are not growing spiritually and allow that discernment to turn to criticism, we block our fellowship with God. God never gives us discernment so that we may criticize, but that we may intercede.

NOVEMBER 24

Direction of Focus

"Behold, as the eyes of servants look to the hand of their masters . . . , so our eyes look to the LORD our God." **Psalm 123:2**

This verse is a description of total reliance on God. Just as the eyes of a servant are riveted on his master, our eyes should be directed to and focused on God. This is how knowledge of His countenance is gained and how God reveals Himself to us (see Isaiah 53:1). Our spiritual strength begins to be drained when we stop lifting our eyes to Him. Our stamina is sapped, not so much through external troubles surrounding us but through problems in our thinking. We wrongfully think, "I suppose I've been stretching myself a little too much, standing too tall and trying to look like God instead of being an ordinary humble person." We have to realize that no effort can be too high.

For example, you came to a crisis in your life, took a stand for God, and even had the witness of the Spirit as a confirmation that what you did was right. But now, maybe weeks or years have gone by, and you are slowly coming to the conclusion—"Well, maybe what I did showed too much pride or was superficial. Was I taking a stand a bit too high for me?" Your "rational" friends come and say, "Don't be silly. We knew when you first talked about this spiritual awakening that it was a passing impulse, that you couldn't hold up under the strain. And anyway, God doesn't expect you to endure." You respond by saying, "Well, I suppose I was expecting too much." That sounds humble to say, but it means that your reliance on God is gone, and you are now relying on worldly opinion. The danger comes when, no longer relying on God, you neglect to focus your eyes on Him. Only when God brings you to a sudden stop will you realize that you have been the loser. Whenever there is a spiritual drain in your life, correct it immediately. Realize that something has been coming between you and God, and change or remove it at once.

NOVEMBER 25

The Secret of Spiritual Consistency

"God forbid that I should boast except in the cross of our Lord Jesus Christ." **Galatians 6:14**

When a person is newly born again, he seems inconsistent due to his unrelated emotions and the state of the external things or circumstances in his life. The apostle Paul had a strong and steady underlying consistency in his life. Consequently, he could let his external life change without internal distress because he was rooted and grounded in God. Most of us are not consistent spiritually because we are more concerned about being consistent externally. In the external expression of things, Paul lived in the basement, while his critics lived on the upper level. And these two levels do not begin to touch each other. But Paul's consistency was down deep in the fundamentals. The great basis of his consistency was the agony of God in the redemption of the world, namely, the Cross of Christ.

State your beliefs to yourself again. Get back to the foundation of the Cross of Christ, doing away with any belief not based on it. In secular history the Cross is an infinitesimally small thing, but from the biblical perspective it is of more importance than all the empires of the world. If we get away from dwelling on the tragedy of God on the Cross in our preaching, our preaching produces nothing. It will not transmit the energy of God to man; it may be interesting, but it will have no power. However, when we preach the Cross, the energy of God is released. "It pleased God through the foolishness of the message preached to save those who believe. . . . we preach Christ crucified" (1 Corinthians 1:21, 23).

NOVEMBER 26

The Focal Point of Spiritual Power

". . . except in the cross of our Lord Jesus Christ." **Galatians 6:14**

If you want to know the power of God (that is, the resurrection life of Jesus) in your human flesh, you must dwell on the tragedy of God. Break away from your personal concern over your own spiritual condition, and with a completely open spirit consider the tragedy of God. Instantly the power of God will be in you. "Look to *Me*" (Isaiah 45:22). Pay attention to the external Source and the internal power will be there. We lose power because we don't focus on the right thing. The effect of the Cross is salvation, sanctification, healing, etc., but we are not to preach any of these. We are to preach "Jesus Christ and Him crucified" (1 Corinthians 2:2). The proclaiming of Jesus will do its own work. Concentrate on God's focal point in your preaching, and even if your listeners seem to pay it no attention, they will never be the same again. If I share my own words, they are of no more importance than your words are to me. But if we share the truth of God with one another, we will encounter it again and again. We have to focus on the great point of spiritual power—the Cross. If we stay in contact with that center of power, its energy is released in our lives. In holiness movements and spiritual experience meetings, the focus tends to be put not on the Cross of Christ but on the effects of the Cross.

The feebleness of the church is being criticized today, and the criticism is justified. One reason for the feebleness is that there has not been this focus on the true center of spiritual power. We have not dwelt enough on the tragedy of Calvary or on the meaning of redemption.

The Consecration of Spiritual Power

". . . by whom the world has been crucified to me, and I to the world." **Galatians 6:14**

If I dwell on the Cross of Christ, I do not simply become inwardly devout and solely interested in my own holiness—I become strongly focused on Jesus Christ's interests. Our Lord was not a recluse nor a fanatical holy man practicing self-denial. He did not physically cut Himself off from society, but He was inwardly disconnected all the time. He was not aloof, but He lived in another world. In fact, He was so much in the common everyday world that the religious people of His day accused Him of being a glutton and a drunkard. Yet our Lord never allowed anything to interfere with His consecration of spiritual power.

It is not genuine consecration to think that we can refuse to be used of God now in order to store up our spiritual power for later use. That is a hopeless mistake. The Spirit of God has set a great many people free from their sin, yet they are experiencing no fullness in their lives—no true sense of freedom. The kind of religious life we see around the world today is entirely different from the vigorous holiness of the life of Jesus Christ. "I do not pray that You should take them out of the world, but that You should keep them from the evil one" (John 17:15). We are to be *in* the world but not *of* it—to be separated internally, not externally (see John 17:16).

We must never allow anything to interfere with the consecration of our spiritual power. Consecration (being dedicated to God's service) is our part; sanctification (being set apart from sin and being made holy) is God's part. We must make a deliberate determination to be interested only in what God is interested. The way to make that determination, when faced with a perplexing problem, is to ask yourself, "Is this the kind of thing in which Jesus Christ is interested, or is it something in which the spirit that is diametrically opposed to Jesus is interested?"

The Riches of the Destitute

"*. . . being justified freely by His grace.*" **Romans 3:24**

The gospel of the grace of God awakens an intense longing in human souls and an equally intense resentment, because the truth that it reveals is not palatable or easy to swallow. There is a certain pride in people that causes them to give and give, but to come and accept a gift is another thing. I will give my life to martyrdom; I will dedicate my life to service—I will do anything. But do not humiliate me to the level of the most hell-deserving sinner and tell me that all I have to do is accept the gift of salvation through Jesus Christ.

We have to realize that we cannot earn or win anything from God through our own efforts. We must either receive it as a gift or do without it. The greatest spiritual blessing we receive is when we come to the knowledge that we are destitute. Until we get there, our Lord is powerless. He can do nothing for us as long as we think we are sufficient in and of ourselves. We must enter into His kingdom through the door of destitution. As long as we are "rich," particularly in the area of pride or independence, God can do nothing for us. It is only when we get hungry spiritually that we receive the Holy Spirit. The gift of the essential nature of God is placed and made effective in us by the Holy Spirit. He imparts to us the quickening life of Jesus, making us truly alive. He takes that which was "beyond" us and places it "within" us. And immediately, once "the beyond" has come "within," it rises up to "the above," and we are lifted into the kingdom where Jesus lives and reigns (see John 3:5).

The Supremacy of Jesus Christ

"He will glorify Me." **John 16:14**

The holiness movements of today have none of the rugged reality of the New Testament about them. There is nothing about them that needs the death of Jesus Christ. All that is required is a pious atmosphere, prayer, and devotion. This type of experience is not supernatural nor miraculous. It did not cost the sufferings of God, nor is it stained with "the blood of the Lamb" (Revelation 12:11). It is not marked or sealed by the Holy Spirit as being genuine, and it has no visual sign that causes people to exclaim with awe and wonder, "That is the work of God Almighty!" Yet the New Testament is about the work of God and nothing else.

The New Testament example of the Christian experience is that of a personal, passionate devotion to the Person of Jesus Christ. Every other kind of so-called Christian experience is detached from the Person of Jesus. There is no regeneration—no being born again into the kingdom in which Christ lives and reigns supreme. There is only the idea that He is our pattern. In the New Testament Jesus Christ is the Savior long before He is the pattern. Today He is being portrayed as the figurehead of a religion—a mere example. He is that, but He is infinitely more. He is salvation itself; He *is* the gospel of God!

Jesus said, "When He, the Spirit of truth, has come, . . . He will glorify Me" (John 16:13–14). When I commit myself to the revealed truth of the New Testament, I receive from God the gift of the Holy Spirit, who then begins interpreting to me what Jesus did. The Spirit of God does in me internally all that Jesus Christ did for me externally.

"By the Grace of God I Am What I Am"

"By the grace of God I am what I am, and His grace toward me was not in vain." **1 Corinthians 15:10**

The way we continually talk about our own inabilities is an insult to our Creator. To complain over our incompetence is to accuse God falsely of having overlooked us. Get into the habit of examining from God's perspective those things that sound so humble to men. You will be amazed at how unbelievably inappropriate and disrespectful they are to Him. We say things such as, "Oh, I shouldn't claim to be sanctified; I'm not a saint." But to say that before God means, "No, Lord, it is impossible for You to save and sanctify me; there are opportunities I have not had and so many imperfections in my brain and body; no, Lord, it isn't possible." That may sound wonderfully humble to others, but before God it is an attitude of defiance.

Conversely, the things that sound humble before God may sound exactly the opposite to people. To say, "Thank God, I know I am saved and sanctified," is in God's eyes the purest expression of humility. It means you have so completely surrendered yourself to God that you know He is true. Never worry about whether what you say sounds humble before others or not. But always be humble before God, and allow Him to be your all in all.

There is only one relationship that really matters, and that is your personal relationship to your personal Redeemer and Lord. If you maintain that at all costs, letting everything else go, God will fulfill His purpose through your life. One individual life may be of priceless value to God's purposes, and yours may be that life.

The Law and the Gospel

"Whoever shall keep the whole law, and yet stumble in one point, he is guilty of all." **James 2:10**

The moral law does not consider our weaknesses as human beings; in fact, it does not take into account our heredity or infirmities. It simply demands that we be absolutely moral. The moral law never changes, either for the highest of society or for the weakest in the world. It is enduring and eternally the same. The moral law, ordained by God, does not make itself weak to the weak by excusing our shortcomings. It remains absolute for all time and eternity. If we are not aware of this, it is because we are less than alive. Once we do realize it, our life immediately becomes a fatal tragedy. "I was alive once without the law, but when the commandment came, sin revived and I died" (Romans 7:9). The moment we realize this, the Spirit of God convicts us of sin. Until a person gets there and sees that there is no hope, the Cross of Christ remains absurd to him. Conviction of sin always brings a fearful, confining sense of the law. It makes a person hopeless—"*sold under sin*" (Romans 7:14). I, a guilty sinner, can never work to get right with God—it is impossible. There is only one way by which I can get right with God, and that is through the death of Jesus Christ. I must get rid of the underlying idea that I can ever be right with God because of my obedience. Who of us could ever obey God to absolute perfection!

We only begin to realize the power of the moral law once we see that it comes with a condition and a promise. But God never coerces us. Sometimes we wish He would make us be obedient, and at other times we wish He would leave us alone. Whenever God's will is in complete control, He removes all pressure. And when we deliberately choose to obey Him, He will reach to the remotest star and to the ends of the earth to assist us with all of His almighty power.

Christian Perfection

"Not that I have already attained, or am already perfect . . ." **Philippians 3:12**

It is a trap to presume that God wants to make us perfect specimens of what He can do—God's purpose is to make us one with Himself. The emphasis of holiness movements tends to be that God is producing specimens of holiness to put in His museum. If you accept this concept of personal holiness, your life's determined purpose will not be for God, but for what you call the evidence of God in your life. How can we say, "It could never be God's will for me to be sick"? If it was God's will to bruise His own Son (Isaiah 53:10), why shouldn't He bruise you? What shines forth and reveals God in your life is not your relative consistency to an idea of what a saint should be, but your genuine, living relationship with Jesus Christ, and your unrestrained devotion to Him whether you are well or sick.

Christian perfection is not, and never can be, human perfection. Christian perfection is the perfection of a relationship with God that shows itself to be true even amid the seemingly unimportant aspects of human life. When you obey the call of Jesus Christ, the first thing that hits you is the pointlessness of the things you have to do. The next thought that strikes you is that other people seem to be living perfectly consistent lives. Such lives may leave you with the idea that God is unnecessary—that through your own human effort and devotion you can attain God's standard for your life. In a fallen world this can never be done. I am called to live in such a perfect relationship with God that my life produces a yearning for God in the lives of others, not admiration for myself. Thoughts about myself hinder my usefulness to God. God's purpose is not to perfect me to make me a trophy in His showcase; He is getting me to the place where He can use me. Let Him do what He wants.

"Not by Might nor by Power"

"My speech and my preaching were not with persuasive words of human wisdom, but in demonstration of the Spirit and of power." **1 Corinthians 2:4**

If in preaching the gospel you substitute your knowledge of the way of salvation for confidence in the power of the gospel, you hinder people from getting to reality. Take care to see while you proclaim your knowledge of the way of salvation, that you yourself are rooted and grounded by faith in God. Never rely on the clearness of your presentation, but as you give your explanation make sure that you are relying on the Holy Spirit. Rely on the certainty of God's redemptive power, and He will create His own life in people.

Once you are rooted in reality, nothing can shake you. If your faith is in experiences, anything that happens is likely to upset that faith. But nothing can ever change God or the reality of redemption. Base your faith on that, and you are as eternally secure as God Himself. Once you have a personal relationship with Jesus Christ, you will never be moved again. That is the meaning of sanctification. God disapproves of our human efforts to cling to the concept that sanctification is merely an experience, while forgetting that even our sanctification must also be sanctified (see John 17:19). I must deliberately give my sanctified life to God for His service, so that He can use me as His hands and His feet.

The Law of Opposition

"To him who overcomes . . ." **Revelation 2:7**

Life without war is impossible in the natural or the supernatural realm. It is a fact that there is a continuing struggle in the physical, mental, moral, and spiritual areas of life.

Health is the balance between the physical parts of my body and all the things and forces surrounding me. To maintain good health I must have sufficient internal strength to fight off the things that are external. Everything outside my physical life is designed to cause my death. The very elements that sustain me while I am alive work to decay and disintegrate my body once it is dead. If I have enough inner strength to fight, I help to produce the balance needed for health. The same is true of the mental life. If I want to maintain a strong and active mental life, I have to fight. This struggle produces the mental balance called thought.

Morally it is the same. Anything that does not strengthen me morally is the enemy of virtue within me. Whether I overcome, thereby producing virtue, depends on the level of moral excellence in my life. But we must fight to be moral. Morality does not happen by accident; moral virtue is acquired.

And spiritually it is also the same. Jesus said, "In the world you will have tribulation . . ." (John 16:33). This means that anything which is not spiritual leads to my downfall. Jesus went on to say, ". . . but be of good cheer, I have overcome the world." I must learn to fight against and overcome the things that come against me, and in that way produce the balance of holiness. Then it becomes a delight to meet opposition.

Holiness is the balance between my nature and the law of God as expressed in Jesus Christ.

DECEMBER 5

"The Temple of the Holy Spirit"

"Only in regard to the throne will I be greater than you." **Genesis 41:40**

I am accountable to God for the way I control my body under His authority. Paul said he did not "set aside the grace of God"—make it ineffective (Galatians 2:21). The grace of God is absolute and limitless, and the work of salvation through Jesus is complete and finished forever. I am not being saved—I am saved. Salvation is as eternal as God's throne, but I must put to work or use what God has placed within me. To "work out [my] own salvation" (Philippians 2:12) means that I am responsible for using what He has given me. It also means that I must exhibit in my own body the life of the Lord Jesus, not mysteriously or secretly, but openly and boldly. "I discipline my body and bring it into subjection" (1 Corinthians 9:27). Every Christian can have his body under absolute control for God. God has given us the responsibility to rule over all "the temple of the Holy Spirit," including our thoughts and desires (1 Corinthians 6:19). We are responsible for these, and we must never give way to improper ones. But most of us are much more severe in our judgment of others than we are in judging ourselves. We make excuses for things in ourselves, while we condemn things in the lives of others simply because we are not naturally inclined to do them.

Paul said, "I beseech you . . . that you present your bodies a living sacrifice" (Romans 12:1). What I must decide is whether or not I will agree with my Lord and Master that my body will indeed be His temple. Once I agree, all the rules, regulations, and requirements of the law concerning the body are summed up for me in this revealed truth—my body is "the temple of the Holy Spirit."

"My Rainbow in the Cloud"

"I set My rainbow in the cloud, and it shall be for the sign of the covenant between Me and the earth." **Genesis 9:13**

It is the will of God that human beings should get into a right-standing relationship with Him, and His covenants are designed for this purpose. Why doesn't God save me? He has accomplished and provided for my salvation, but I have not yet entered into a relationship with Him. Why doesn't God do everything we ask? He has done it. The point is—will I step into that covenant relationship? All the great blessings of God are finished and complete, but they are not mine until I enter into a relationship with Him on the basis of His covenant.

Waiting for God to act is fleshly unbelief. It means that I have no faith in Him. I wait for Him to do something in me so I may trust in that. But God won't do it, because that is not the basis of the God-and-man relationship. Man must go beyond the physical body and feelings in his covenant with God, just as God goes beyond Himself in reaching out with His covenant to man. It is a question of faith in God—a very rare thing. We only have faith in our feelings. I don't believe God until He puts something tangible in my hand, so that I know I have it. Then I say, "Now I believe." There is no faith exhibited in that. God says, "*Look to Me*, and be saved" (Isaiah 45:22).

When I have really transacted business with God on the basis of His covenant, letting everything else go, there is no sense of personal achievement—no human ingredient in it at all. Instead, there is a complete overwhelming sense of being brought into union with God, and my life is transformed and radiates peace and joy.

Repentance

"Godly sorrow produces repentance leading to salvation." **2 Corinthians 7:10**

Conviction of sin is best described in the words:

My sins, my sins, my Savior, / How sad on Thee they fall.

Conviction of sin is one of the most uncommon things that ever happens to a person. It is the beginning of an understanding of God. Jesus Christ said that when the Holy Spirit came He would convict people of sin (see John 16:8). And when the Holy Spirit stirs a person's conscience and brings him into the presence of God, it is not that person's relationship with others that bothers him but his relationship with God—"Against You, You only, have I sinned, and done this evil in your sight" (Psalm 51:4). The wonders of conviction of sin, forgiveness, and holiness are so interwoven that it is only the forgiven person who is truly holy. He proves he is forgiven by being the opposite of what he was previously, by the grace of God. Repentance always brings a person to the point of saying, "I have sinned." The surest sign that God is at work in his life is when he says that and means it. Anything less is simply sorrow for having made foolish mistakes—a reflex action caused by self-disgust.

The entrance into the kingdom of God is through the sharp, sudden pains of repentance colliding with man's respectable "goodness." Then the Holy Spirit, who produces these struggles, begins the formation of the Son of God in the person's life (see Galatians 4:19). This new life will reveal itself in conscious repentance followed by unconscious holiness, never the other way around. The foundation of Christianity is repentance. Strictly speaking, a person cannot repent when he chooses—repentance is a gift of God. The old Puritans used to pray for "the gift of tears." If you ever cease to understand the value of repentance, you allow yourself to remain in sin. Examine yourself to see if you have forgotten how to be truly repentant.

The Impartial Power of God

"By one offering He has perfected forever those who are being sanctified." **Hebrews 10:14**

We trample the blood of the Son of God underfoot if we think we are forgiven because we are sorry for our sins. The only reason for the forgiveness of our sins by God, and the infinite depth of His promise to forget them, is the death of Jesus Christ. Our repentance is merely the result of our personal realization of the atonement by the Cross of Christ, which He has provided for us. "Christ Jesus . . . became for us wisdom from God—and righteousness and sanctification and redemption" (1 Corinthians 1:30). Once we realize that Christ has become all this for us, the limitless joy of God begins in us. And wherever the joy of God is not present, the death sentence is still in effect.

No matter who or what we are, God restores us to right standing with Himself only by means of the death of Jesus Christ. God does this, not because Jesus pleads with Him to do so but because He died. It cannot be earned, just accepted. All the pleading for salvation which deliberately ignores the Cross of Christ is useless. It is knocking at a door other than the one which Jesus has already opened. We protest by saying, "But I don't want to come that way. It is too humiliating to be received as a sinner." God's response, through Peter, is, "There is no other name . . . by which we must be saved" (Acts 4:12). What at first appears to be heartlessness on God's part is actually the true expression of His heart. There is unlimited entrance His way. "In Him we have redemption through His blood" (Ephesians 1:7). To identify with the death of Jesus Christ means that we must die to everything that was never a part of Him.

God is just in saving bad people only as He makes them good. Our Lord does not pretend we are all right when we are all wrong. The atonement by the Cross of Christ is the propitiation God uses to make unholy people holy.

The Opposition of the Natural

"Those who are Christ's have crucified the flesh with its passions and desires." **Galatians 5:24**

The natural life itself is not sinful. But we must abandon sin, having nothing to do with it in any way whatsoever. Sin belongs to hell and to the devil. I, as a child of God, belong to heaven and to God. It is not a question of giving up sin, but of giving up my right to myself, my natural independence, and my self-will. This is where the battle has to be fought. The things that are right, noble, and good from the natural standpoint are the very things that keep us from being God's best. Once we come to understand that natural moral excellence opposes or counteracts surrender to God, we bring our soul into the center of its greatest battle. Very few of us would debate over what is filthy, evil, and wrong, but we do debate over what is good. It is the good that opposes the best. The higher up the scale of moral excellence a person goes, the more intense the opposition to Jesus Christ. "Those who are Christ's have crucified the flesh." The cost to your natural life is not just one or two things, but everything. Jesus said, "If anyone desires to come after Me, let him deny *himself*" (Matthew 16:24). That is, he must deny his right to himself, and he must realize who Jesus Christ is before he will bring himself to do it. Beware of refusing to go to the funeral of your own independence.

The natural life is not spiritual, and it can be made spiritual only through sacrifice. If we do not purposely sacrifice the natural, the supernatural can never become natural to us. There is no high or easy road. Each of us has the means to accomplish it entirely in his own hands. It is not a question of praying, but of sacrificing, and thereby performing His will.

The Offering of the Natural

"It is written that Abraham had two sons: the one by a bondwoman, the other by a freewoman." **Galatians 4:22**

Paul was not dealing with sin in this chapter of Galatians, but with the relation of the natural to the spiritual. The natural can be turned into the spiritual only through sacrifice. Without this a person will lead a divided life. Why did God demand that the natural must be sacrificed? God did not demand it. It is not God's perfect will, but His permissive will. God's perfect will was for the natural to be changed into the spiritual through obedience. Sin is what made it necessary for the natural to be sacrificed.

Abraham had to offer up Ishmael before he offered up Isaac (see Genesis 21:8–14). Some of us are trying to offer up spiritual sacrifices to God before we have sacrificed the natural. The only way we can offer a spiritual sacrifice to God is to "present [our] bodies a living sacrifice" (Romans 12:1). Sanctification means more than being freed from sin. It means the deliberate commitment of myself to the God of my salvation, and being willing to pay whatever it may cost.

If we do not sacrifice the natural to the spiritual, the natural life will resist and defy the life of the Son of God in us and will produce continual turmoil. This is always the result of an undisciplined spiritual nature. We go wrong because we stubbornly refuse to discipline ourselves physically, morally, or mentally. We excuse ourselves by saying, "Well, I wasn't taught to be disciplined when I was a child." Then discipline yourself now! If you don't, you will ruin your entire personal life for God.

God is not actively involved with our natural life as long as we continue to pamper and gratify it. But once we are willing to put it out in the desert and are determined to keep it under control, God will be with it. He will then provide wells and oases and fulfill all His promises for the natural (see Genesis 21:15–19).

Individuality

"Jesus said to His disciples, 'If anyone desires to come after Me, let him deny himself.'" **Matthew 16:24**

Individuality is the hard outer layer surrounding the inner spiritual life. Individuality shoves others aside, separating and isolating people. We see it as the primary characteristic of a child, and rightly so. When we confuse individuality with the spiritual life, we remain isolated. This shell of individuality is God's created natural covering designed to protect the spiritual life. But our individuality must be yielded to God so that our spiritual life may be brought forth into fellowship with Him. Individuality counterfeits spirituality, just as lust counterfeits love. God designed human nature for Himself, but individuality corrupts that human nature for its own purposes.

The characteristics of individuality are independence and self-will. We hinder our spiritual growth more than any other way by continually asserting our individuality. If you say, "I can't believe," it is because your individuality is blocking the way; individuality can never believe. But our spirit cannot help believing. Watch yourself closely when the Spirit of God is at work in you. He pushes you to the limits of your individuality where a choice must be made. The choice is either to say, "I will not surrender," or to surrender, breaking the hard shell of individuality, which allows the spiritual life to emerge. The Holy Spirit narrows it down every time to one thing (see Matthew 5:23–24). It is your individuality that refuses to "be reconciled to your brother" (5:24). God wants to bring you into union with Himself, but unless you are willing to give up your right to yourself, He cannot. "Let him deny himself"—deny his independent right to himself. Then the real life—the spiritual life—is allowed the opportunity to grow.

Personality

". . . that they may be one just as We are one." **John 17:22**

Personality is the unique, limitless part of our life that makes us distinct from everyone else. It is too vast for us even to comprehend. An island in the sea may be just the top of a large mountain, and our personality is like that island. We don't know the great depths of our being, therefore we cannot measure ourselves. We start out thinking we can, but soon realize that there is really only one Being who fully understands us, and that is our Creator.

Personality is the characteristic mark of the inner, spiritual man, just as individuality is the characteristic of the outer, natural man. Our Lord can never be described in terms of individuality and independence, but only in terms of His total Person—"I and My Father are one" (John 10:30). Personality merges, and you only reach your true identity once you are merged with another person. When love or the Spirit of God come upon a person, he is transformed. He will then no longer insist on maintaining his individuality. Our Lord never referred to a person's individuality or his isolated position, but spoke in terms of the total person—"that they may be one just as We are one." Once your rights to yourself are surrendered to God, your true personal nature begins responding to God immediately. Jesus Christ brings freedom to your total person, and even your individuality is transformed. The transformation is brought about by love—personal devotion to Jesus. Love is the overflowing result of one person in true fellowship with another.

Intercessory Prayer

"Men always ought to pray and not lose heart." **Luke 18:1**

You cannot truly intercede through prayer if you do not believe in the reality of redemption. Instead, you will simply be turning intercession into useless sympathy for others, which will serve only to increase the contentment they have for remaining out of touch with God. True intercession involves bringing the person, or the circumstance that seems to be crashing in on you, before God, until you are changed by His attitude toward that person or circumstance. Intercession means to "fill up . . . [with] what is lacking in the afflictions of Christ" (Colossians 1:24), and this is precisely why there are so few intercessors. People describe intercession by saying, "It is putting yourself in someone else's place." That is not true! Intercession is putting yourself in God's place; it is having His mind and His perspective.

As an intercessor, be careful not to seek too much information from God regarding the situation you are praying about, because you may be overwhelmed. If you know too much, more than God has ordained for you to know, you can't pray; the circumstances of the people become so overpowering that you are no longer able to get to the underlying truth.

Our work is to be in such close contact with God that we may have His mind about everything, but we shirk that responsibility by substituting doing for interceding. And yet intercession is the only thing that has no drawbacks, because it keeps our relationship completely open with God.

What we must avoid in intercession is praying for someone to be simply "patched up." We must pray that person completely through into contact with the very life of God. Think of the number of people God has brought across our path, only to see us drop them! When we pray on the basis of redemption, God creates something He can create in no other way than through intercessory prayer.

The Great Life

"Peace I leave with you, My peace I give to you; not as the world gives do I give to you. Let not your heart be troubled." **John 14:27**

Whenever we experience something difficult in our personal life, we are tempted to blame God. But we are the ones in the wrong, not God. Blaming God is evidence that we are refusing to let go of some disobedience somewhere in our lives. But as soon as we let go, everything becomes as clear as daylight to us. As long as we try to serve two masters, ourselves and God, there will be difficulties combined with doubt and confusion. Our attitude must be one of complete reliance on God. Once we get to that point, there is nothing easier than living the life of a saint. We encounter difficulties when we try to usurp the authority of the Holy Spirit for our own purposes.

God's mark of approval, whenever you obey Him, is peace. He sends an immeasurable, deep peace; not a natural peace, "as the world gives," but the peace of Jesus. Whenever peace does not come, wait until it does, or seek to find out why it is not coming. If you are acting on your own impulse, or out of a sense of the heroic, to be seen by others, the peace of Jesus will not exhibit itself. This shows no unity with God or confidence in Him. The spirit of simplicity, clarity, and unity is born through the Holy Spirit, not through your decisions. God counters our self-willed decisions with an appeal for simplicity and unity.

My questions arise whenever I cease to obey. When I do obey God, problems come, not between me and God, but as a means to keep my mind examining with amazement the revealed truth of God. But any problem that comes between God and myself is the result of disobedience. Any problem that comes while I obey God (and there will be many) increases my overjoyed delight, because I know that my Father knows and cares, and I can watch and anticipate how He will unravel my problems.

"Approved to God"

"Be diligent to present yourself approved to God, a worker who does not need to be ashamed, rightly dividing the word of truth." 2 Timothy 2:15

If you cannot express yourself well on each of your beliefs, work and study until you can. If you don't, other people may miss out on the blessings that come from knowing the truth. Strive to reexpress a truth of God to yourself clearly and understandably, and God will use that same explanation when you share it with someone else. But you must be willing to go through God's winepress where the grapes are crushed. You must struggle, experiment, and rehearse your words to express God's truth clearly. Then the time will come when that very expression will become God's wine of strength to someone else. But if you are not diligent and say, "I'm not going to study and struggle to express this truth in my own words; I'll just borrow my words from someone else," then the words will be of no value to you or to others. Try to state to yourself what you believe to be the absolute truth of God, and you will be allowing God the opportunity to pass it on through you to someone else.

Always make it a practice to stir your own mind thoroughly to think through what you have easily believed. Your position is not really yours until you make it yours through suffering and study. The author or speaker from whom you learn the most is not the one who teaches you something you didn't know before, but the one who helps you take a truth with which you have quietly struggled, give it expression, and speak it clearly and boldly.

DECEMBER 16

Wrestling Before God

"Take up the whole armor of God . . . praying always." **Ephesians 6:13, 18**

You must learn to wrestle *against* the things that hinder your communication with God, and wrestle in prayer *for* other people; but to wrestle *with* God in prayer is unscriptural. If you ever do wrestle with God, you will be crippled for the rest of your life. If you grab hold of God and wrestle with Him, as Jacob did, simply because He is working in a way that doesn't meet with your approval, you force Him to put you out of joint (see Genesis 32:24–25). Don't become a cripple by wrestling with the ways of God, but be someone who wrestles before God with the things of this world, because "we are more than conquerors through Him" (Romans 8:37). Wrestling before God makes an impact in His kingdom. If you ask me to pray for you, and I am not complete in Christ, my prayer accomplishes nothing. But if I am complete in Christ, my prayer brings victory all the time. Prayer is effective only when there is completeness—"take up the whole armor of God."

Always make a distinction between God's perfect will and His permissive will, which He uses to accomplish His divine purpose for our lives. God's perfect will is unchangeable. It is with His permissive will, or the various things that He allows into our lives, that we must wrestle before Him. It is our reaction to these things allowed by His permissive will that enables us to come to the point of seeing His perfect will for us. "We know that all things work together for good to those who love God" (Romans 8:28)—to those who remain true to God's perfect will—His calling in Christ Jesus. God's permissive will is the testing He uses to reveal His true sons and daughters. We should not be spineless and automatically say, "Yes, it is the Lord's will." We don't have to fight or wrestle *with God*, but we must wrestle before God *with things*. Beware of lazily giving up. Instead, put up a glorious fight and you will find yourself empowered with His strength.

Redemption—Creating the Need It Satisfies

"The natural man does not receive the things of the Spirit of God, for they are foolishness to him." **1 Corinthians 2:14**

The gospel of God creates the sense of need for the gospel. Is the gospel hidden to those who are servants already? No, Paul said, "But even if our gospel is veiled, it is veiled to those who are perishing, whose minds the god of this age has blinded, who do not believe" (2 Corinthians 4:3–4). The majority of people think of themselves as being completely moral, and have no sense of need for the gospel. It is God who creates this sense of need in a human being, but that person remains totally unaware of his need until God makes Himself evident. Jesus said, "Ask, and it will be given to you" (Matthew 7:7). But God cannot give until a man asks. It is not that He wants to withhold something from us, but that is the plan He has established for the way of redemption. Through our asking, God puts His process in motion, creating something in us that was nonexistent until we asked. The inner reality of redemption is that it creates all the time. And as redemption creates the life of God in us, it also creates the things which belong to that life. The only thing that can possibly satisfy the need is what created the need. This is the meaning of redemption—it creates and it satisfies.

Jesus said, "And I, if I am lifted up from the earth, will draw all peoples to Myself" (John 12:32). When we preach our own experiences, people may be interested, but it awakens no real sense of need. But once Jesus Christ is "lifted up," the Spirit of God creates an awareness of the need for Him. The creative power of the redemption of God works in the souls of men only through the preaching of the gospel. It is never the sharing of personal experiences that saves people, but the truth of redemption. "The words that *I* speak to you are spirit, and they are life" (John 6:63).

DECEMBER 18

Test of Faithfulness

"We know that all things work together for good to those who love God." **Romans 8:28**

It is only a faithful person who truly believes that God sovereignly controls his circumstances. We take our circumstances for granted, saying God is in control, but not really believing it. We act as if the things that happen were completely controlled by people. To be faithful in every circumstance means that we have only one loyalty, or object of our faith—the Lord Jesus Christ. God may cause our circumstances to suddenly fall apart, which may bring the realization of our unfaithfulness to Him for not recognizing that He had ordained the situation. We never saw what He was trying to accomplish, and that exact event will never be repeated in our life. This is where the test of our faithfulness comes. If we will just learn to worship God even during the difficult circumstances, He will change them for the better very quickly if He so chooses.

Being faithful to Jesus Christ is the most difficult thing we try to do today. We will be faithful to our work, to serving others, or to anything else; just don't ask us to be faithful to Jesus Christ. Many Christians become very impatient when we talk about faithfulness to Jesus. Our Lord is dethroned more deliberately by Christian workers than by the world. We treat God as if He were a machine designed only to bless us, and we think of Jesus as just another one of the workers.

The goal of faithfulness is not that we will do work for God, but that He will be free to do His work through us. God calls us to His service and places tremendous responsibilities on us. He expects no complaining on our part and offers no explanation on His part. God wants to use us as He used His own Son.

DECEMBER 19

The Focus of Our Message

"I did not come to bring peace but a sword."
Matthew 10:34

Never be sympathetic with a person whose situation causes you to conclude that God is dealing harshly with him. God can be more tender than we can conceive, and every once in a while He gives us the opportunity to deal firmly with someone so that He may be viewed as the tender One. If a person cannot go to God, it is because he has something secret which he does not intend to give up—he may admit his sin, but would no more give up that thing than he could fly under his own power. It is impossible to deal sympathetically with people like that. We must reach down deep in their lives to the root of the problem, which will cause hostility and resentment toward the message. People want the blessing of God, but they can't stand something that pierces right through to the heart of the matter.

If you are sensitive to God's way, your message as His servant will be merciless and insistent, cutting to the very root. Otherwise, there will be no healing. We must drive the message home so forcefully that a person cannot possibly hide, but must apply its truth. Deal with people where they are, until they begin to realize their true need. Then hold high the standard of Jesus for their lives. Their response may be, "We can never be that." Then drive it home with, "Jesus Christ says you must." "But how can we be?" "You can't, unless you have a new Spirit" (see Luke 11:13).

There must be a sense of need created before your message is of any use. Thousands of people in this world profess to be happy without God. But if we could be truly happy and moral without Jesus, then why did He come? He came because that kind of happiness and peace is only superficial. Jesus Christ came to "bring . . . a sword" through every kind of peace that is not based on a personal relationship with Himself.

The Right Kind of Help

"And I, if I am lifted up . . . will draw all peoples to Myself." **John 12:32**

Very few of us have any understanding of the reason why Jesus Christ died. If sympathy is all that human beings need, then the Cross of Christ is an absurdity and there is absolutely no need for it. What the world needs is not "a little bit of love," but major surgery.

When you find yourself face-to-face with a person who is spiritually lost, remind yourself of Jesus Christ on the cross. If that person can get to God in any other way, then the Cross of Christ is unnecessary. If you think you are helping lost people with your sympathy and understanding, you are a traitor to Jesus Christ. You must have a right-standing relationship with Him yourself, and pour your life out in helping others in His way—not in a human way that ignores God. The theme of the world's religion today is to serve in a pleasant, nonconfrontational manner.

But our only priority must be to present Jesus Christ crucified—to lift Him up all the time (see 1 Corinthians 2:2). Every belief that is not firmly rooted in the Cross of Christ will lead people astray. If the worker himself believes in Jesus Christ and is trusting in the reality of redemption, his words will be compelling to others. What is extremely important is for the worker's simple relationship with Jesus Christ to be strong and growing. His usefulness to God depends on that, and that alone.

The calling of a New Testament worker is to expose sin and to reveal Jesus Christ as Savior. Consequently, he cannot always be charming and friendly, but must be willing to be stern to accomplish major surgery. We are sent by God to lift up Jesus Christ, not to give wonderfully beautiful speeches. We must be willing to examine others as deeply as God has examined us. We must also be sharply intent on sensing those Scripture passages that will drive the truth home, and then not be afraid to apply them.

Experience or God's Revealed Truth?

"We have received . . . the Spirit who is from God, that we might know the things that have been freely given to us by God." **1 Corinthians 2:12**

My experience is not what makes redemption real—redemption *is* reality. Redemption has no real meaning for me until it is worked out through my conscious life. When I am born again, the Spirit of God takes me beyond myself and my experiences, and identifies me with Jesus Christ. If I am left only with my personal experiences, I am left with something not produced by redemption. But experiences produced by redemption prove themselves by leading me beyond myself, to the point of no longer paying any attention to experiences as the basis of reality. Instead, I see that only the reality itself produced the experiences. My experiences are not worth anything unless they keep me at the Source of truth—Jesus Christ.

If you try to hold back the Holy Spirit within you, with the desire of producing more inner spiritual experiences, you will find that He will break the hold and take you again to the historic Christ. Never support an experience which does not have God as its Source and faith in God as its result. If you do, your experience is anti-Christian, no matter what visions or insights you may have had. Is Jesus Christ Lord of your experiences, or do you place your experiences above Him? Is any experience dearer to you than your Lord? You must allow Him to be Lord over you, and pay no attention to any experience over which He is not Lord. Then there will come a time when God will make you impatient with your own experience, and you can truthfully say, "I do not care what I experience—I am sure of Him!"

Be relentless and hard on yourself if you are in the habit of talking about the experiences you have had. Faith based on experience is not faith; faith based on God's revealed truth is the only faith there is.

DECEMBER 22

The Drawing of the Father

"No one can come to Me unless the Father who sent Me draws him." **John 6:44**

When God begins to draw me to Himself, the problem of my will comes in immediately. Will I react positively to the truth that God has revealed? Will I come to Him? To discuss or deliberate over spiritual matters when God calls is inappropriate and disrespectful to Him. When God speaks, never discuss it with anyone as if to decide what your response may be (see Galatians 1:15–16). Belief is not the result of an intellectual act, but the result of an act of my will whereby I deliberately commit myself. But will I commit, placing myself completely and absolutely on God, and be willing to act solely on what He says? If I will, I will find that I am grounded on reality as certain as God's throne.

In preaching the gospel, always focus on the matter of the will. Belief must come from the *will* to believe. There must be a surrender of the will, not a surrender to a persuasive or powerful argument. I must deliberately step out, placing my faith in God and in His truth. And I must place no confidence in my own works, but only in God. Trusting in my own mental understanding becomes a hindrance to complete trust in God. I must be willing to ignore and leave my feelings behind. I must *will* to believe. But this can never be accomplished without my forceful, determined effort to separate myself from my old ways of looking at things. I must surrender myself completely to God.

Everyone has been created with the ability to reach out beyond his own grasp. But it is God who draws me, and my relationship to Him in the first place is an inner, personal one, not an intellectual one. I come into the relationship through the miracle of God and through my own will to believe. Then I begin to get an intelligent appreciation and understanding of the wonder of the transformation in my life.

Sharing in the Atonement

"God forbid that I should boast except in the cross of our Lord Jesus Christ." **Galatians 6:14**

The gospel of Jesus Christ always forces a decision of our will. Have I accepted God's verdict on sin as judged on the Cross of Christ? Do I have even the slightest interest in the death of Jesus? Do I want to be identified with His death—to be completely dead to all interest in sin, worldliness, and self? Do I long to be so closely identified with Jesus that I am of no value for anything except Him and His purposes? The great privilege of discipleship is that I can commit myself under the banner of His Cross, and that means death to sin. You must get alone with Jesus and either decide to tell Him that you do not want sin to die out in you, or that at any cost you want to be identified with His death. When you act in confident faith in what our Lord did on the cross, a supernatural identification with His death takes place immediately. And you will come to know through a higher knowledge that your old life was "crucified with Him" (Romans 6:6). The proof that your old life is dead, having been "crucified with Christ" (Galatians 2:20), is the amazing ease with which the life of God in you now enables you to obey the voice of Jesus Christ.

Every once in a while our Lord gives us a glimpse of what we would be like if it were not for Him. This is a confirmation of what He said—"without Me you can do nothing" (John 15:5). That is why the underlying foundation of Christianity is personal, passionate devotion to the Lord Jesus. We mistake the joy of our first introduction into God's kingdom as His purpose for getting us there. Yet God's purpose in getting us into His kingdom is that we may realize all that identification with Jesus Christ means.

DECEMBER 24

The Hidden Life

"Your life is hidden with Christ in God." **Colossians 3:3**

The Spirit of God testifies to and confirms the simple, but almighty, security of the life that "is hidden with Christ in God." Paul continually brought this out in his New Testament letters. We talk as if living a sanctified life were the most uncertain and insecure thing we could do. Yet it is the most secure thing possible, because it has Almighty God in and behind it. The most dangerous and unsure thing is to try to live without God. For one who is born again, it is easier to live in a right-standing relationship with God than it is to go wrong, provided we heed God's warnings and "walk in the light" (1 John 1:7).

When we think of being delivered from sin, being "filled with the Spirit" (Ephesians 5:18), and "walk[ing] in the light," we picture the peak of a great mountain. We see it as very high and wonderful, but we say, "Oh, I could never live up there!" However, when we do get there through God's grace, we find it is not a mountain peak at all, but a plateau with plenty of room to live and to grow. "You enlarged my path under me, so my feet did not slip" (Psalm 18:36).

When you really see Jesus, I defy you to doubt Him. If you see Him when He says, "Let not your heart be troubled" (John 14:27), I defy you to worry. It is virtually impossible to doubt when He is there. Every time you are in personal contact with Jesus, His words are real to you. "My peace I give to you" (John 14:27)—a peace which brings an unconstrained confidence and covers you completely, from the top of your head to the soles of your feet. "Your life is hidden with Christ in God," and the peace of Jesus Christ that cannot be disturbed has been imparted to you.

His Birth and Our New Birth

"'Behold, the virgin shall be with child, and bear a Son, and they shall call His name Immanuel,' which is translated, 'God with us.'" **Matthew 1:23**

His Birth in History. ". . . that Holy One who is to be born will be called the Son of God" (Luke 1:35). Jesus Christ was born *into* this world, not *from* it. He did not emerge out of history; He came into history from the outside. Jesus Christ is not the best human being the human race can boast of—He is a Being for whom the human race can take no credit at all. He is not man becoming God, but God Incarnate—God coming into human flesh from outside it. His life is the highest and the holiest entering through the most humble of doors. Our Lord's birth was an advent—the appearance of God in human form.

His Birth in Me. "My little children, for whom I labor in birth again until Christ is formed in you" (Galatians 4:19). Just as our Lord came into human history from outside it, He must also come into me from outside. Have I allowed my personal human life to become a "Bethlehem" for the Son of God? I cannot enter the realm of the kingdom of God unless I am born again from above by a birth totally unlike physical birth. "You must be born again" (John 3:7). This is not a command, but a fact based on the authority of God. The evidence of the new birth is that I yield myself so completely to God that "Christ is formed" in me. And once "Christ is formed" in me, His nature immediately begins to work through me.

God Evident in the Flesh. This is what is made so profoundly possible for you and for me through the redemption of man by Jesus Christ.

"Walk in the Light"

"If we walk in the light as He is in the light . . . the blood of Jesus Christ His Son cleanses us from all sin." **1 John 1:7**

To mistake freedom from sin only on the conscious level of our lives for complete deliverance from sin by the atonement through the Cross of Christ is a great error. No one fully knows what sin is until he is born again. Sin is what Jesus Christ faced at Calvary. The evidence that I have been delivered from sin is that I know the real nature of sin in me. For a person to really know what sin is requires the full work and deep touch of the atonement of Jesus Christ, that is, the imparting of His absolute perfection.

The Holy Spirit applies or administers the work of the atonement to us in the deep unconscious realm as well as in the conscious realm. And it is not until we truly perceive the unrivaled power of the Spirit in us that we understand the meaning of 1 John 1:7, which says, "*The blood of Jesus Christ His Son cleanses us from all sin*." This verse does not refer only to conscious sin, but also to the tremendously profound understanding of sin which only the Holy Spirit in me can accomplish.

I must "walk in the light as He is in the light"—not in the light of my own conscience, but in God's light. If I will walk there, with nothing held back or hidden, then this amazing truth is revealed to me: "the blood of Jesus Christ His Son cleanses [me] from all sin" so that God Almighty can see nothing to rebuke in me. On the conscious level it produces a keen, sorrowful knowledge of what sin really is. The love of God working in me causes me to hate, with the Holy Spirit's hatred for sin, anything that is not in keeping with God's holiness. To "walk in the light" means that everything that is of the darkness actually drives me closer to the center of the light.

Where the Battle Is Won or Lost

"'If you will return, O Israel,' says the Lord . . ."
Jeremiah 4:1

Our battles are first won or lost in the secret places of our will in God's presence, never in full view of the world. The Spirit of God seizes me and I am compelled to get alone with God and fight the battle before Him. Until I do this, I will lose every time. The battle may take one minute or one year, but that will depend on me, not God. However long it takes, I must wrestle with it alone before God, and I must resolve to go through the hell of renunciation or rejection before Him. Nothing has any power over someone who has fought the battle before God and won there.

I should never say, "I will wait until I get into difficult circumstances and then I'll put God to the test." Trying to do that will not work. I must first get the issue settled between God and myself in the secret places of my soul, where no one else can interfere. Then I can go ahead, knowing with certainty that the battle is won. Lose it there, and calamity, disaster, and defeat before the world are as sure as the laws of God. The reason the battle is lost is that I fight it first in the external world. Get alone with God, do battle before Him, and settle the matter once and for all.

In dealing with other people, our stance should always be to drive them toward making a decision of their will. That is how surrendering to God begins. Not often, but every once in a while, God brings us to a major turning point—a great crossroads in our life. From that point we either go toward a more and more slow, lazy, and useless Christian life, or we become more and more on fire, giving our utmost for *His* highest—our best for *His* glory.

DECEMBER 28

Continuous Conversion

"Unless you are converted and become as little children, you will by no means enter the kingdom of heaven." **Matthew 18:3**

These words of our Lord refer to our initial conversion, but we should continue to turn to God as children, being continuously converted every day of our lives. If we trust in our own abilities, instead of God's, we produce consequences for which God will hold us responsible. When God through His sovereignty brings us into new situations, we should immediately make sure that our natural life submits to the spiritual, obeying the orders of the Spirit of God. Just because we have responded properly in the past is no guarantee that we will do so again. The response of the natural to the spiritual should be continuous conversion, but this is where we so often refuse to be obedient. No matter what our situation is, the Spirit of God remains unchanged and His salvation unaltered. But we must "put on the new man" (Ephesians 4:24). God holds us accountable every time we refuse to convert ourselves, and He sees our refusal as willful disobedience. Our natural life must not rule—God must rule in us.

To refuse to be continuously converted puts a stumbling block in the growth of our spiritual life. There are areas of self-will in our lives where our pride pours contempt on the throne of God and says, "I won't submit." We deify our independence and self-will and call them by the wrong name. What God sees as stubborn weakness, we call strength. There are whole areas of our lives that have not yet been brought into submission, and this can only be done by this continuous conversion. Slowly but surely we can claim the whole territory for the Spirit of God.

DECEMBER 29

Deserter or Disciple?

"From that time many of His disciples went back and walked with Him no more." **John 6:66**

When God, by His Spirit through His Word, gives you a clear vision of His will, you must "walk in the light" of that vision (1 John 1:7). Even though your mind and soul may be thrilled by it, if you don't "walk in the light" of it you will sink to a level of bondage never envisioned by our Lord. Mentally disobeying the "heavenly vision" (Acts 26:19) will make you a slave to ideas and views that are completely foreign to Jesus Christ. Don't look at someone else and say, "Well, if he can have those views and prosper, why can't I?" You have to "walk in the light" of the vision that has been given to *you*. Don't compare yourself with others or judge them—that is between God and them. When you find that one of your favorite and strongly held views clashes with the "heavenly vision," do not begin to debate it. If you do, a sense of property and personal right will emerge in you—things on which Jesus placed no value. He was against these things as being the root of everything foreign to Himself—"for one's life does not consist in the abundance of the things he possesses" (Luke 12:15). If we don't see and understand this, it is because we are ignoring the underlying principles of our Lord's teaching.

Our tendency is to lie back and bask in the memory of the wonderful experience we had when God revealed His will to us. But if a New Testament standard is revealed to us by the light of God, and we don't try to measure up, or even feel inclined to do so, then we begin to backslide. It means your conscience does not respond to the truth. You can never be the same after the unveiling of a truth. That moment marks you as one who either continues on with even more devotion as a disciple of Jesus Christ, or as one who turns to go back as a deserter.

"And Every Virtue We Possess"

"All my springs are in you." **Psalm 87:7**

Our Lord never "patches up" our natural virtues, that is, our natural traits, qualities, or characteristics. He completely remakes a person on the inside—"put on the new man" (Ephesians 4:24). In other words, see that your natural human life is putting on all that is in keeping with the new life. The life God places within us develops its own new virtues, not the virtues of the seed of Adam, but of Jesus Christ. Once God has begun the process of sanctification in your life, watch and see how God causes your confidence in your own natural virtues and power to wither away. He will continue until you learn to draw your life from the reservoir of the resurrection life of Jesus. Thank God if you are going through this drying-up experience!

The sign that God is at work in us is that He is destroying our confidence in the natural virtues, because they are not promises of what we are going to be, but only a wasted reminder of what God created man to be. We want to cling to our natural virtues, while all the time God is trying to get us in contact with the life of Jesus Christ—a life that can never be described in terms of natural virtues. It is the saddest thing to see people who are trying to serve God depending on that which the grace of God never gave them. They are depending solely on what they have by virtue of heredity. God does not take our natural virtues and transform them, because our natural virtues could never even come close to what Jesus Christ wants. No natural love, no natural patience, no natural purity can ever come up to His demands. But as we bring every part of our natural bodily life into harmony with the new life God has placed within us, He will exhibit in us the virtues that were characteristic of the Lord Jesus.

And every virtue we possess
Is His alone.

Yesterday

"You shall not go out with haste, . . . for the Lord will go before you, and the God of Israel will be your rear guard." **Isaiah 52:12**

Security from Yesterday. "God requires an account of what is past" (Ecclesiastes 3:15). At the end of the year we turn with eagerness to all that God has for the future, and yet anxiety is apt to arise when we remember our yesterdays. Our present enjoyment of God's grace tends to be lessened by the memory of yesterday's sins and blunders. But God is the God of our yesterdays, and He allows the memory of them to turn the past into a ministry of spiritual growth for our future. God reminds us of the past to protect us from a very shallow security in the present.

Security for Tomorrow. "The Lord will go before you." This is a gracious revelation—that God will send His forces out where we have failed to do so. He will keep watch so that we will not be tripped up again by the same failures, as would undoubtedly happen if He were not our "rear guard." And God's hand reaches back to the past, settling all the claims against our conscience.

Security for Today. "You shall not go out with haste." As we go forth into the coming year, let it not be in the haste of impetuous, forgetful delight, nor with the quickness of impulsive thoughtlessness. But let us go out with the patient power of knowing that the God of Israel will go before us. Our yesterdays hold broken and irreversible things for us. It is true that we have lost opportunities that will never return, but God can transform this destructive anxiety into a constructive thoughtfulness for the future. Let the past rest, but let it rest in the sweet embrace of Christ.

Leave the broken, irreversible past in His hands, and step out into the invincible future with Him.

Indexes

SCRIPTURE INDEX

PSALMS

PROVERBS

ECCLESIASTES

ISAIAH

MARK

LUKE

JOHN

1 CORINTHIANS

2 CORINTHIANS

3 JOHN

JUDE

REVELATION

SUBJECT INDEX

C

D

G

H

I

K

L

P

Q

R

S

T

U

V

W

X, Y, Z

Help us get the word out!

Our Daily Bread Publishing exists to feed the soul with the Word of God.

If you appreciated this book, please let others know.

- Pick up another copy to give as a gift.
- Share a link to the book or mention it on social media.
- Write a review on your blog, on a bookseller's website, or at our own site (odb.org/store).
- Recommend this book for your church, book club, or small group.

Connect with us:

@ourdailybread

@ourdailybread

@ourdailybread

Our Daily Bread Publishing
PO Box 3566
Grand Rapids, Michigan 49501 USA

books@odb.org

Praise for #1 *New York Times* bestselling author Robyn Carr

"This novel of sisters and secrets has a pleasant setting, a leisurely pace, and a sweet story line for Krista that will please fans of Carr's Virgin River series. Themes of responsibility, forgiveness, and the agony and ecstasy of female relatives will appeal to readers of Debbie Macomber and Susan Wiggs."

—*Booklist* on *The Summer That Made Us*

"The summer flies by as old wounds are healed, new alliances are formed, and lives are changed forever.... With strong relationship dynamics, juicy secrets, and a heartwarming ending, it's a blissful beach read."

—*Kirkus Reviews* on *The Summer That Made Us*

"Carr addresses serious problems...realistically and sympathetically while seamlessly weaving them into the fabric of her engrossing story."

—*Booklist*, starred review, on *Any Day Now*

"A satisfying reinvention story that handles painful issues with a light and uplifting touch."

—*Kirkus Reviews* on *The Life She Wants*

"Insightfully realized central figures, a strong supporting cast, family issues, and uncommon emotional complexity make this uplifting story a heart-grabber that won't let readers go until the very end.... A rewarding (happy) story that will appeal across the board and might require a hanky or two."

—*Library Journal*, starred review, on *What We Find*

"Robyn Carr has done it again... *What We Find* is complex, inspirational, and well-written. A romance that truly inspires readers as life hits them the hardest."

—*San Francisco Review Journal* on *What We Find*

"Carr's new novel demonstrates that classic women's fiction, illuminating the power of women's friendships, is still alive and well."

—*Booklist* on *Four Friends*

Also available from ROBYN CARR and MIRA Books

Sullivan's Crossing

THE BEST OF US
THE FAMILY GATHERING
ANY DAY NOW
WHAT WE FIND

Thunder Point

WILDEST DREAMS
A NEW HOPE
ONE WISH
THE HOMECOMING
THE PROMISE
THE CHANCE
THE HERO
THE NEWCOMER
THE WANDERER

Virgin River

MY KIND OF CHRISTMAS
SUNRISE POINT
REDWOOD BEND
HIDDEN SUMMIT
BRING ME HOME FOR CHRISTMAS
HARVEST MOON
WILD MAN CREEK
PROMISE CANYON
MOONLIGHT ROAD
ANGEL'S PEAK
FORBIDDEN FALLS
PARADISE VALLEY
TEMPTATION RIDGE
SECOND CHANCE PASS
A VIRGIN RIVER CHRISTMAS
WHISPERING ROCK
SHELTER MOUNTAIN
VIRGIN RIVER

Grace Valley

DEEP IN THE VALLEY
JUST OVER THE MOUNTAIN
DOWN BY THE RIVER

Stand-Alone Novels

THE SUMMER THAT MADE US
THE LIFE SHE WANTS
FOUR FRIENDS
A SUMMER IN SONOMA
NEVER TOO LATE
SWEPT AWAY (formerly titled RUNAWAY MISTRESS)
BLUE SKIES
THE WEDDING PARTY
THE HOUSE ON OLIVE STREET

Look for Robyn Carr's next novel
THE VIEW FROM ALAMEDA ISLAND,
available soon from MIRA Books.

ROBYN CARR

The Life She Wants

Recycling programs for this product may not exist in your area.

ISBN-13: 978-0-7783-0849-2

The Life She Wants

For questions and comments about the quality of this book, please contact us at CustomerService@Harlequin.com.

www.Harlequin.com

Printed in U.S.A.

This is for Therese Plummer, beloved narrator,
gifted actress and the voice of my heart.

The Life She Wants

Prologue

When the truth became brutally evident she wondered how it had escaped her for so long.

Emma Shay Compton knew that her marriage to Richard looked like a fairy tale to many and though she had loved Richard, she had always felt something was lacking. She couldn't put her finger on it, it was so vague. Richard was good to her, generous, though he was an extremely busy man, and soon after their wedding he became remote. Distant. She told herself mega-rich brokers don't sit around the house coddling their young wives; they work sixteen-hour days. They're never far from their phones. They seem to command multitudes. And if a person, even his wife, wanted to get on his calendar, she had to plan ahead. So, whenever she felt that something was wrong with her marriage, she'd blame herself.

When Richard's lawyers began to meet with him to discuss problems with the SEC, she barely noticed. When she asked him about media reports that his company was being investigated for securities fraud, he calmly said, "Slow news day."

Then he lectured her. "Pay attention to the financial pages—it happens every day. Several multibillion-dollar banking and investment corporations are currently being investigated. The SEC has to justify its existence somehow. I resent the time suck, but it won't last long."

She didn't worry about it, though she did pay attention as he suggested. Of course he was right—there were many investigations, steep fines, reorganizations, buyouts, companies shutting down. The banking and investment world was under very close scrutiny.

Then he said they had to appear in court, he and his legal team. He wanted her by his side and asked if she could get it on her schedule and she laughed. "I'm not the one with a full schedule, Richard."

He smiled his perfect, confident, calm smile. He touched her cheek. "You won't have to do or say anything."

The morning they were to appear in court he had noticed the suit she laid over the chair and said, "Perfect." Then he went into his bathroom. Sitting at her dressing table, she was smoothing lotion on her legs. She heard the water running in his sink. And then she heard, "Son of a bitch!"

He'd cut himself shaving and swore—not unusual for him. But she met her own eyes in the mirror. Suddenly she knew. She'd been living a lie and everything said about him was true.

Her husband was a cold, calculating liar and thief. And she couldn't pretend anymore.

One

It's the little things that will break you. Emma Shay had been thinking about that a lot lately. She stood strong while everything was taken from her, while she was virtually imprisoned at a little motel near the Jersey shore, while her husband was buried, while the media spun a sordid tale of deceit and thievery that implied she'd been aware, if not complicit, in her late husband's crimes. Stood. Strong. But, when the heel broke on her best sling-back pumps and she tumbled down the courthouse steps, she collapsed in tears. The photo was printed everywhere, even *People* magazine. When she was asked to please stop coming to her yoga studio, she thought she would die of shame and cried herself to sleep. No one had ever explained to her that the last straw weighed almost nothing.

Everything in her Manhattan apartment and vacation home had been auctioned off. She packed up some practical items to take with her and donated some of her casual clothing to women's shelters. Of course anything of value—the art, crystal, china, silver and jewelry had been seized quickly, even items she could prove had nothing to do with Richard's business, including wedding gifts from friends. They took her designer clothing. Her Vera Wang wedding gown was gone. She was allowed to keep a couple sets of good sheets, towels, one set of kitchenware, some glasses, a few place mats, napkins and so on. She had a box of photos, most from before Richard. She stuffed it all in her Prius. The Jag was gone, of course.

She had been offered a financial settlement, since they couldn't establish that she had anything to do with Richard's Ponzi scheme; couldn't prove it since she was innocent. She hadn't testified against him—not out of loyalty or because it was her legal prerogative, but rather because she had nothing to say, nothing upon which to leverage some kind of deal. She hadn't been in court every day out of support for Richard but because it was the best way for her to learn about the crimes he was accused of. She had come into the marriage with nine thousand dollars in savings; she left as a widow, keeping nine thousand in a checking account. It would be her emergency fund. She started a trip across the country, leaving New York behind and heading for Sonoma County, where she grew up.

She'd given it all a great deal of thought. She'd been thinking about it for months before Richard's death. She could've kept the entire settlement and retired to the Caribbean. Or maybe Europe. She'd been fond of Switzerland. She could change her name, color her hair, lie about her past… But eventually people would figure her out and then what? Run again?

Instead, she surrendered the settlement, gave up everything she could have kept. She didn't want Richard's ill-gotten gains. Even though she hadn't swindled anyone, she couldn't, in good conscience, touch any of it.

There were people she knew back in the Santa Rosa area, a few she'd stayed in touch with. The area was familiar to her. There wasn't much family anymore—her stepmother, Rosemary, had moved to Palm Springs with her third husband. As far as she knew, Emma's stepsister, Anna, and half sister, Lauren, still lived in the house they'd all grown up in. They'd all washed their hands of Emma when Richard was indicted. In fact, the last time she'd talked to her stepmother was right before Richard's death, when all the walls were tumbling down. Emma was literally in hiding from the angry victims of Richard's fraud—victims who believed Emma had gotten away with some of their money. Rosemary had said, "Well, your greed has certainly cost you this time."

"Rosemary, I didn't do anything," Emma reminded her.

And then Rosemary said what everyone thought. "So you *say*."

Well, Rosemary had always thought the worst of her. But Emma hoped the people she knew in Sonoma County wouldn't. She'd grown up there, gone to Catholic school and public high school there. And she thought it was extremely unlikely any clients, now victims, of Richard's New York-based investment company hailed from the little towns in Sonoma County.

Her closest friend, possibly her only friend at this point, Lyle Dressler, found her a little furnished bungalow in Sebastopol. Lyle and his partner lived in the town, so she had some moral support there.

Emma was thirty-four and had married Richard Compton nine years ago. He was a sharp, handsome, successful forty-five when they married. At twenty-five she'd been completely under his spell. He might have been twenty years older than her, but forty-five was hardly considered old. He was fit, handsome, brilliant, rich and powerful. In fact, he was considered one of the most desired bachelors in New York City.

Rosemary and Emma's sisters had certainly liked him *then*. They were eager to travel to New York to attend any social event Richard would grudgingly include them in. But they hadn't offered one ounce of support to Emma during the takedown.

The few years of marriage before the investigation and indictment hadn't been heaven on earth, but they weren't bad. Her complaints seemed to be standard among people she knew—he was busy, preoccupied, they didn't spend enough time together even when they were traveling. The first friends she'd made through work in New York had gradually drifted away once she settled into her multimillion-dollar marriage. She'd never quite fit in with the elite crowd, so she'd been a little lonely. It seemed like she was always around people, doing her part with committee work, exercising, decorating, entertaining, feeling that she must be indispensable to Richard. However, he was all she really had. It was a dark and terrible day when she realized he was a complete stranger.

Before her fifth anniversary, the investigation had begun. Before the seventh, indictments had been handed down and assets frozen. She spent her eighth anniversary in court. Richard's defense attorneys had managed many a delay but eventually there was a trial—a circus of a trial—and she appeared to be the trusting, good wife, head held high. Richard's mother and sister had not come to the trial and refused interviews. She'd always assumed they didn't think she was good enough for Richard, but after the trial she changed her opinion. They must have known all about him. He was dark and empty inside.

He never talked to her about it, at least not until the ugly, bitter end. When she asked about the investigation he just said they were out to get him, that business was tough but he was tougher, that they'd never prove anything. At the end there had been a few brief, nasty but revealing discourses. *How could you? How could I not? How could you justify the greed? My greed? How about their greed? Do they have to justify it? They wanted me to do anything to make them money! They wanted me to spin straw into gold even if I had to lie, cheat and steal! Each one of them just wanted their payday before it all broke!*

The feds proved everything with ease. Employees cut deals and testified against him. Truckloads of documentation proved securities fraud, theft, mail fraud, wire fraud, money laundering… The list was long. When the end was near, when he'd attempted a getaway and been unceremoniously returned by US Marshals, when his offshore accounts had been located and identified, when he faced a long jail sentence with no nest egg left hidden away, Richard shot himself.

Of course no one believed Emma had no idea. Apparently people thought he came home from the office and bared his soul over a drink. He had not.

The Richard she knew was obviously a con man, a chameleon. He could be so charming, so devoted. But he always had a plan and always wanted something more. *Why wouldn't I marry you? You were an outstanding invest-*

ment. Perfect for the role! It's a well-known fact—people trust married men more than single men. He was a narcissist, a manipulator, a liar and cheat. He was so damn good at it, a person could feel almost honored to be manipulated and lied to by him. He had the looks of Richard Gere, the brilliance of Steve Jobs, the ethics of Bernie Madoff. Thank God he wasn't as successful as Bernie. Richard had only managed to steal about a hundred million.

What *did* she know? She knew he was private; he didn't talk about work, which she thought was normal behavior for a powerful man. He was an amazing communicator socially and in business, but once he stopped courting her, he stopped telling her stories about his family, his youth, college, about his early years on Wall Street. She knew he didn't have many old friends, just a lot of business contacts. She never met college pals or colleagues from his early professional days. He did routinely ask her about her day, however. He'd ask her about her schedule, her projects, what she did, who she talked to, what was happening in her world. When he was home, that is—he was often working late or traveling. The thing that set Richard apart from other, mediocre con men—he knew how to *listen*. People, herself included, thought they'd learned something about him when he hadn't said a word about himself. But he listened to them. Raptly. They were thrilled by this attention.

One nine-year marriage, a few years of which had been weirdly adequate, five years of which had been a nightmare. Now she wondered when the nightmare would end.

Emma drove directly to Lyle's flower shop, Hello, Gorgeous, named for Barbra Streisand, of course. Lyle had been wonderful to her through this whole ordeal. He hadn't been able to be in New York with her very often. Not only was it a great, costly distance but there was also the small complication that his partner, Ethan, had never been particularly fond of Emma, though he didn't really know her. Lyle had made a couple of trips, however, and called almost daily during the rough patches. She understood about Ethan. But Lyle and Emma had been friends long before Ethan came into his life. For reasons unknown, Ethan had never warmed to her. Emma suspected good old-fashioned jealousy, as if Emma might bring out Lyle's straight side or something. So Emma and Ethan had always had a rather cool regard for each other. But since Richard's debacle, Ethan's regard had gone from cool to frigid.

But—and this was an important but—if Ethan went on about his dislike and disapproval of Emma too much, he was going to lose Lyle, and he might be bitchy but he wasn't stupid.

Emma stood outside the shop and took a deep breath before walking through the door. And of course, who should be behind the counter but Ethan. "Well, Emma, I see you made it," he said as though it took effort to be kind.

"Yes, thank you," she answered carefully.

"Rough journey?" Ethan surprised her by asking.

"In every way," she said.

"Well, there you are," Lyle said as he came from the back and rushed over to embrace her. "Would you like a cup of coffee or something before we head over to Penny's house?"

She shook her head. "I parked down the block in the only available space. I'd like to get going—I have a lot to do."

"Sure," he said. He turned to Ethan. "I'm going to give Em a hand, visit with Penny a little. I'll probably grab something to eat with them. I won't be late."

Ethan lifted his chin and sniffed, but his reply was perfectly appropriate. "I think I'll drop in on Nora and Ed. Sounds like a good night to get a little uncle time."

"Excellent. Give them my love."

Then, hand on her elbow, Lyle escorted her out of the shop. "I'm parked right here. I'll drive you down to your car," he said.

"Oh, please, no," she said, laughing. "My butt hurts so bad, I hate to even get back in the car. I'm going to walk—it's only a block. And I have a cooler with some drinks for us. Listen, I don't want to..." She tilted her head toward the store. "I don't want to cause any friction. If you'll just get me to the house and introduce me to your friend, I can manage from there."

"No worries, Emma. I explained to Ethan days ago that I was going to lend a hand when you got here." He chuckled. "He was very adult about it. It's time for him to pay his sister a visit anyway. They live a mile away and Ethan doesn't visit as often as he should. I think I visit more than he does—we have a gorgeous niece. He can go over there and complain about me and my stubborn ways. Besides, I want to make sure you're all right."

She smiled at him with gratitude. "I might never be all right again," she said. "All I want right now is a little quiet and anonymity."

"Have you heard from Rosemary?" he asked.

"I did her the courtesy of emailing her that I'd be moving to a small bungalow in Sebastopol and told her I could be reached through you. I don't even trust her enough to give her my new cell number—I bet she'd sell it to the press. I take it you haven't heard from her?" He shook his head and this came as no surprise. Rosemary had been in touch when she thought Richard was rich and powerful; after his fall from grace, she behaved as if she didn't know him. "We haven't made amends. She wasn't exactly supportive."

"Your sisters should be helping you now," he said.

They had never done anything to help her. "We've never been that kind of family," she said. Indeed, they weren't family at all.

"I can relate," Lyle said.

Emma knew Lyle had always had a hard time with his father, but at least his mother adored him. She gave his upper arm a squeeze. "Well, you've saved my life here. I'd be lost without this little place you found."

"It found me. Penny is elderly, but don't use that word around her. She's what we'd call spry. Almost eighty and still walking three miles a day, gardening and playing the occasional game of tennis. But the problem with living forever, the money thins out eventually."

"And she knows everything?" Emma asked.

He nodded. "As you wished. She said, 'We've all hooked up with the wrong person here and there, poor girl.' This little bungalow is a sort of guesthouse, a casita, though her house, the main house, isn't that much bigger. Prepare yourself, it's all quite small. She doesn't need a keeper. No care involved. But a little bit of rent will probably help you both." He shook his head. "I don't know that you've ever lived in anything this simple, Em. It's old, musty, small and tacky."

"You have no idea how much I'm looking forward to it."

The guesthouse was actually a remodeled freestanding garage with a wall and large picture window where the doors once were. The window looked out onto a pleasant tree-lined street. It was a tiny, two-room bungalow with a small bathroom and galley kitchen. A patio separated the guesthouse from Penelope Pennington's two-bedroom house. "And of course you're welcome to use the patio at any time," Penny assured her. "And if you ever have any serious cooking to do, feel free to borrow my kitchen."

It was an attractive little arrangement. Penny had the driveway removed years before and now there was a carport and storage unit. In front of both little houses and on either side of the driveway and carport were two small patches of grass, shrubs, trees and flowers. From the patio one could reach Emma's little abode on the right or Penny's on the left. A tall, white fence with a gate bordered the property.

It took less than half an hour to unload Emma's small car. There wasn't much furniture in the bungalow—a bed and bureau, a small table and two chairs, a couple of lamps, a small sofa and two armchairs. She had her own bedding and kitchenware. She found the guesthouse quaint and cozy. Her boxes and suitcases had yet to be unpacked, but she didn't care. Lyle went off to a nearby market to get dinner, bringing Penny and Emma a huge Greek salad, some hummus, flatbread and a bottle of wine. They had their dinner at Penny's, sitting around her little dining table, and Emma loved her at once.

Then at last it was just Emma and Lyle, sitting in her cozy living room with a final glass of wine. She sat in a musty old overstuffed chair upholstered with a floral pattern, her feet up on an ottoman that didn't quite match. Lyle relaxed on the sofa, his feet up on the coffee table.

"This place really needs a fluff and buff," he said.

"I love it," she said. "I think this will be my reading chair."

"How can you read with the flowers in that gaudy print screaming at you?"

She laughed at him.

"Have you given any thought to what kind of job you're going to get?" he asked.

"Well," she said, taking a thoughtful sip. "I was considering being a life coach. What do you think?"

"You can certainly provide plenty of experience with what *not* to do," he said.

"I can honestly say I haven't felt this relaxed in years," she said.

Lyle was quiet for a moment. "Emmie, I don't know what it's going to be like for you around here. It's a quiet town, but not without its resident gossips and petty meanness. Know what I mean?"

"I grew up around here, remember?" she said. "No matter where I go, it's going to follow me. But I was never indicted for any crime. And believe me, they looked hard and long."

"I just want you to be ready. In case."

"In case people are nasty to me or snigger when I walk by? That's why I came here rather than trying to find some new place where I could be a stranger with a new identity—everyone figures it out eventually. Lies don't last—Richard was proof of that. Let's just get it over with. I was married to the late Richard Compton, the infamous broker and thief. There's no way to undo it. And I didn't have to think about it long—the stress of trying to keep it secret is something I'm just not up to. I could change my name, color my hair, even get a nose job if I had any money, but eventually everyone is going to know it's me. It's hopeless, Lyle—Google me and see for yourself."

"Under Emma Shay?"

"And Emma Shay Compton, Emma Compton, Emma Catherine Shay."

"Dear God," he groaned. "I hope it dwindles away quickly," he said.

"It's all on the record. Anyone who's curious is welcome to read all about it. There are even a couple of books, though they're not very accurate."

"How'd he do it, Em?"

She knew exactly what he was talking about. Richard's suicide. She took a breath. She was surprised he hadn't just looked it up—it was splattered, like Richard's brains, across all the papers and internet news sites.

"After he'd attempted to run via a colleague's private jet with a fake passport, he was returned to jail and held without bond. The lawyers managed to negotiate house arrest with an ankle bracelet. After the guilty verdict was returned he tried to negotiate sentencing by giving up offshore account numbers, hoping to reduce his sentence. But no matter what, he was going to jail for a long time. He opened the hidden safe behind the bookcase in his home office, pulled out his loaded Glock and shot himself. In the head."

Lyle shook his head. "He didn't want to go to prison…"

"I'm sure it was more than that," she said. "Oh, there was no doubt prison would be horrendous, but that's not why he did it. There was no material wealth left. There were no more offshore or Swiss accounts. It was really over. He was going to go to prison for fifty years and even if he was paroled early or could escape, there was nothing to allow him to retire quietly in Aruba, or some other remote island. With his stash." She sighed. "It was the most important thing to him. The wealth."

"I'm surprised the police didn't know about the safe or the gun," he said. "Didn't you say they searched the apartment?"

She shrugged. "I don't know if they ever saw it—they weren't looking for it. They confiscated his computers and lots of files from home and his office, all his electronics, but their warrant wasn't for things like guns or drugs. I didn't know about the gun."

"Did he do anything at all to try to protect you?" Lyle asked.

She just shook her head.

"And after he was buried?"

"It was a couple of weeks yet until everything was gone and the paperwork on the auction and the sale of the apartment was final. I closed his office door and slept on a cot in the kitchen. It was the safest place for me. Marshals were watching the apartment and there was a doorman." She made a face. "It was so horrible."

"I'm only going to say this one more time, Emmie, then we're moving on. I'm just so, so sorry."

"Thank you," she said softly. "Listen, you go home. And tell Ethan that I appreciate how decent he's been and assure him I'm not going to be pestering the two of you. I found I do very well on my own. It's lovely to be near you, but you don't have to worry that this out-of-place girlfriend is going to be the needy type and make you feel invaded. I'm not going to be your third wheel."

"We have some very nice friends, a lot of them gay men, and there are more than enough third wheels in our crowd. Don't worry about it. Call us whenever you feel like it."

"You've been wonderful. You've always been a better friend to me than I've been to you," she said.

"Not true. There've been very kind gestures here and there…"

"Shhhh," she warned. Before the trouble began, she had a household budget that was ridiculously large and she economized, leaving her a nice balance. It was her money and she used some to help fund the start-up of Hello, Gorgeous. Best if no one ever knew. Lyle had been interviewed about their relationship, possibly even investigated, but had never been any kind of suspect. In fact, they didn't speak of it. Emma was fairly sure Ethan didn't even know the details.

"Suffice it to say, I'm glad you're here," Lyle said. "I've missed you. And now there are a couple of things I should tell you. People have asked about you, which of course they would. But a couple of old friends have asked a few times recently. Asked what you would do now. Riley came into the shop and asked if you were all right. She knows we've always been in touch, just as you know I keep up with her, but where you two are concerned I made it a policy to never carry tales between you. She wanted to know if there was anything you needed."

"Guilty conscience," Emma said.

"Easy, Emma. She might be one of the few people who can actually understand what you're going through," he said. "I know you're not sympathetic, but she had to rebuild her life after you left. And Jock called. Divorced and living in Santa Rosa. He wanted to know if there was any chance you'd be coming back this way when it was all over. He said to tell you that if you need anything…"

"Seriously?" she asked.

"Very sincerely. I'm not his biggest fan, but he did offer support."

She said nothing. Of course she knew they were both here, Riley and Jock. Back when they were all so young, her best friend and her boyfriend. She'd returned for brief visits a few times after leaving so long ago and had not spoken to them, but she always knew they were still around. When she decided to come back here for good she knew it was possible she'd run into one or both of them eventually.

"Might be time to move on from that haunt, Emma," Lyle said.

"I have moved on," she answered. "I've moved on from a lot of things. And I'm not going back one step."

Two

When Emma Catherine Shay was nine years old, a fourth grader at St. Pascal's elementary school in Santa Rosa, a couple of new kids came to school. Riley and Adam Kerrigan. Riley was in Emma's class and the teacher asked her to be responsible for helping Riley get acquainted and adjusted.

Emma, known for being friendly and a child who wished to please, was annoyed. First of all, she already had two best friends—Susanna and Paula—and Riley's hanging around was interfering with her routine. Second, Riley apparently couldn't talk. She followed along or sat at the lunch table all quiet and nervous. When she did speak, she could barely be heard. Third, and Emma knew this was wrong, but the girl was a rag doll. She wore old clothes that didn't even fit her right.

Riley's older brother, Adam, so somber and quiet, waited after school to walk home together so at least Emma didn't have that chore. And all of it—spending time with Riley—was monotonous. But, so Sister Judith would be proud of her, Emma did the best she could with the odd little creature with the unhappy personality. At the end of the second day Riley surprised Emma when she spoke softly. "I know where to go and what to do now. You can go be with your friends."

Emma felt like a turd. "We'll just *all* hang out together," she said, hating her overzealous conscience.

Then, over the next few days, Emma learned that Riley, Adam and their mother came to Santa Rosa to live with Riley's grandparents in their tiny house because Riley's dad had gotten very sick and died. So now Riley wasn't just shy and poor, she was also bereaved. Emma was stuck with her.

But Emma couldn't deny that she was completely sympathetic—she'd lost her own mother, though she had been too young to remember her. Her father had remarried when she was just a toddler, probably largely to have help with his child. He had married Rosemary, an efficient and hardworking widow with a three-year-old daughter, Anna. Three years later they had a baby together, another girl. Baby Lauren. The only mother she had ever known was her stepmother, and of the three children, Rosemary liked Emma least. Emma understood by the time she was ten that it had been a marriage of convenience.

Emma was plotting her escape from Riley when a few things shifted as Riley got more comfortable with her new surroundings. First off, she was hilarious and once they got laughing, they could hardly stop. When she wasn't feeling scared and lonely, Riley's voice was strong and confident. She was very good in school and rose to the head of the class quickly. She could help Emma and not the other way around. And Riley's mother, June, turned out to be the most wonderful, loving, fun and positive woman in the entire world, embracing Emma and making her feel so cherished. Riley's grandparents acted like it was their lucky day the Kerrigans moved in even though they were stuffed into the little house. They were crowded and money was tight but there was more laughter there than there had ever been in Emma's house. Riley and Adam wore hand-me-down clothes, their grandparents were elderly, and June Kerrigan cleaned houses and waitressed to make ends meet, but Emma was always welcome, made to feel like a member of the family.

Emma's home life wasn't nearly so happy. Rosemary wasn't abusive in any obvious way but she was emotionally flat where Emma was concerned.

Rosemary complained about how hard she had to work at the DMV, how much stress she had in her life, how messy and lazy Emma's father was, her weight, her friends and a variety of issues. Aside from Anna and Lauren, there didn't seem to be much she enjoyed. Although Rosemary always referred to Emma and Lauren as her daughters, there was little doubt that Anna was her favorite. It wasn't long before Emma was happier at Riley's house than at her own. And hardly surprisingly, Rosemary didn't mind her absence at home much.

We were going to be each other's maid of honor. We were going to have children at the same time so they could be best friends, too.

From the day Sister Judith forced them together until high school graduation, Emma and Riley were inseparable. Riley's grandpa called them conjoined twins. They stuck together through thick and thin, through the sudden death of Emma's father when she was sixteen, Rosemary's third marriage to Vince Kingston, and every issue that plagued teenagedom. Their friendship was cast in iron and they had very few tiffs. Until they fell out over a boy. One Jock Curry. Yes, it was his given name. He was named for a grandfather.

They'd both crushed on him in high school. They thought he was smart, sexy, athletic, funny. Every girl wanted him and he apparently wanted every girl, but once he settled on Emma during their senior year, that was it for him. He said his roaming days were over. Of course, he was all of seventeen at the time. He tried to talk Emma into going to the same community college he'd chosen or at least staying close to home, but she had a scholarship and was going to Seattle Pacific University, known for its interior-design program. Of the two girls, she was the least likely to get a scholarship, but even with one, Riley's family couldn't afford any part of the expense of living away from home or attending an out-of-state university. Emma could manage with working part-time, taking out loans, and Rosemary was able to send a little money—fifty here, fifty there. And she had big dreams; she was going to design the interiors of five-star hotels and luxurious mansions!

Riley enrolled in the same community college as Jock, lived at home and began cleaning houses just like her mom always had.

Jock had no specific plans except to get the minimum education, work part time, play a little baseball and enjoy himself.

Emma didn't suspect anything was going on in her absence until right before Christmas break. Riley was acting strangely. Jock and Riley were hanging out together a lot, but shouldn't that be expected? Her guy and her best friend, going to school together and everything? She trusted them, after all. Then she had this nagging feeling it wasn't all right, that it was a betrayal. Riley was different toward her; Jock was a little too much himself—jovial and confident and relaxed. He'd gone from ragging on her about taking more time to talk to him on the phone to not noticing how long it had been since they'd had one of those long, whispery, late-night conversations.

She suspected her best friend was too close to her boyfriend. When Emma confronted her, Riley burst into tears, admitted it, swore it wasn't entirely her fault, that Jock had taken advantage of the fact that she'd always liked him a lot, that she had been so lonely without her best friend.

Jock had said, "Hey, grow up. It didn't really mean anything. Besides, what did you expect? You didn't have time for either one of us."

Emma never really did understand how something like that *just happens*, especially when both Riley and Jock insisted they hadn't meant it to, that it was all a terrible mistake. Then they both turned it back on her, as if it was her fault for going away to school. All she knew was that she was devastated and had lost the two most important people in her life. She could never trust either one of them again and the feeling was so painful it doubled her over. She went back to Seattle after Christmas break completely decimated by the hurt. She tried to date and that didn't go well. Riley wrote her a couple of letters, left her a few messages, but Emma was too hurt to respond. And she didn't go back to Santa Rosa until summer break. Even then, she hadn't wanted to—there was nothing there for her anymore. Her father was dead, her stepmother was a cold fish who clearly hated her, her stepmother's new husband was an old lecher, her sisters didn't care about her…

She didn't stay in Santa Rosa long. She learned what no one wanted to tell her. Oh, but Emma's stepsister Anna couldn't *wait* to tell her—Riley was pregnant. While Emma was at school, those two had been knocking boots like mad and now they were having a baby. Emma bid a tearful goodbye to Lyle, cleared everything out of her father's house, the house she grew up in, and headed back to Seattle as fast as she could. She got herself a job, joined a sorority, visited Santa Rosa very rarely and very briefly. When she did go, she stayed with Lyle.

Even Seattle wasn't far enough away. Upon her graduation, she secured a job in New York and moved to the other coast. Within three years she was a buyer for one of the largest independent department stores in the US and traveled all over the world for her household wares. She was a specialist in interiors and had fantasies about starting her own design firm.

But then she met Richard…

If there was one thing Emma had learned from the experience it was that she could hold a grudge. The fact that Riley's relationship with Jock hadn't lasted, proving that he wasn't exactly a good catch, didn't lessen her feelings of being betrayed. The undeniable truth that she'd dodged a bullet when her relationship with Jock fell apart didn't give her much comfort. The further fact that she'd gone on to marry a handsome, rich, successful man also hadn't induced her to forgive and forget.

But then what she went through with Richard—his fraud, deceit, demise—taught her something else. There were bigger things to worry about than a fifteen-year-old feud with a childhood friend.

There was no going back, Emma reminded herself. She was moving forward.

* * *

Emma hadn't worked outside her home and marriage for nine years but boy, had she worked in it. She visited several employment agencies with her résumé, her degree, even details of her experience volunteering at the Metropolitan Museum of Art, working on gigantic fund-raisers, massive decorating projects and entertaining on an enormous scale, but that simply wouldn't do it after the interview. She felt it was in her best interest to be honest, then immediately doubted her wisdom in that. If they didn't want to take her on as a client because they feared trusting her, then they didn't want her because of the potential negative press attention it might draw to them. Clients might leave businesses that employed her because of her notoriety. Of course, they didn't say that. They said they were sorry, there didn't seem to be anything available, but if she'd leave a number…

She had to throw her net wider. She had a list of businesses to apply to that ranged from galleries and stores to convention centers, wineries and even political parties. She stopped explaining that her late husband had been *the* Richard Compton and instead said that after a bad marriage, she was reentering the workforce. After two weeks with zero success, she went to several smaller employment agencies, not the ones that specialized in decorating, customer service, event planning and those things that were ideal for her. After all, she could always type and file. She could operate a computer. She thought the reception she received was positive…until they looked into her background, which was a simple matter nowadays with a computer search. Even though she wasn't up-front about her history, they obviously

Googled her and she was politely informed there was nothing available that might suit her.

After four weeks, she was inconsolable.

"Isn't this some kind of discrimination?" she asked Lyle.

"It definitely is," Lyle said. "But I'm not sure what kind."

Just when she thought things couldn't possibly get bleaker, she took a job in a fast food restaurant. She thought of it as a placeholder until she found a real job. Her boss was nineteen years old. She did everything she was told to do, putting great effort into it. They'd given her an evening shift because she was mature and the restaurant was overrun with high school and college kids. But she had trouble keeping up. She took home a paycheck for five days of shift work at about five hours a day in the amount of $91.75—they deducted FICA, Social Security, state and federal taxes, uniform costs. Her net pay was $3.67 per hour. Her feet and back were killing her.

She wondered if she'd have to succumb to a disguise and create a new identity.

Emma answered her cell phone knowing it would be Lyle, but praying it would be someone with an offer of a better job. It was Lyle.

"Do you know a man by the name of Aaron Justice?"

She laughed. "Unforgettable. A friend of my father's. An attorney. He must be a hundred years old by now."

"More like seventy-five. Apparently one of your sisters said you could be reached through me and he'd love to hear from you. He said maybe you could meet for a coffee or something. He's been concerned about you. He would like to see you, to assure himself you're okay."

"Now, isn't that sweet," she said. "It's not a trap, is it? He's not representing someone Richard screwed, is he?"

"Does that actually happen?" Lyle asked.

"It hasn't happened yet, but I'm ready for it."

"I have his number," Lyle said. "Call him, ask him what he wants before you make a date to see him. But really, he's just a little old man."

"Oh, you have no idea," she said with a laugh. "Aaron is only a little old man on the outside. I think in his day he was a very prominent attorney."

It took her a few minutes to work up her courage because it would simply break her heart if Aaron Justice were foe, not friend. Her father, a CPA with a small but busy business, was close to Aaron, and Emma had known him all her life. Not only had they seen him and his family socially, Aaron was the lawyer who took care of John Shay's will and a few other legal matters, too.

"I want only to see you, my dear girl," Aaron said. "I've followed your ordeal in the news and have been concerned. Come and have a cup of coffee with me."

The very next afternoon that she didn't have to work they met in a coffee shop in Santa Rosa, and when she saw him, it brought her to tears. He seemed to have gotten smaller, but his embrace was still strong and she might have held on too tight. He was a very dapper, classy gentleman and of course just seeing him again after eighteen years made her miss her father.

They sat in a small booth, ordered coffee and held hands across the table as they caught up on the more personal news. His wife had passed away a few years earlier, his grandsons were teenagers and he'd taken them on a few exciting trips. He was relieved to see her looking so well, as beautiful as ever and he was glad she was back. Finally, after about twenty minutes, he asked her if she could talk about it.

She tried to give him the bullet points; how shocked she was by the facts, stunned to learn she was married to a stranger, how the walls came tumbling down and Richard bailed out. "Once they were satisfied that I had nothing to do with the scheme, I was offered a settlement. My conscience wouldn't let me take it, of course."

"Your father would have been proud of that," Aaron said.

"If my father had witnessed that horrific takedown, he would have been mortified."

"He was a staunch and conservative man," Aaron said. "It sounds as if he would have approved of the way you chose to handle it. I hope your father's trust helped out a bit."

She laughed. "What trust, Aaron? Rosemary said there wasn't much."

"I seem to remember it being a tidy sum for his family."

"Eighteen years ago, maybe," Emma said.

He frowned. "I realize you were only a girl and John hadn't wanted the balances to be reported to anyone—it might've filled the three of you girls with fanciful notions, sent you out car shopping or something. But it was divided—your share and those of your sisters could only be used for health and welfare. Rosemary would have needed it to sustain the family, and there was tuition to pay, of course…"

Emma was shaking her head. "I borrowed and had a partial scholarship. She might've used it for education for Lauren and Anna."

"Didn't Rosemary give you money for college?"

"She sent me spending money from time to time. Maybe she was afraid to touch the money, saving it for her old age. She ended up marrying a real jerk. They moved to Palm Springs."

"Rosemary changed lawyers immediately," Aaron said. "I have no idea what's happened in the last eighteen years, but you were due to inherit from your father's estate—half at the age of thirty and half at thirty-five. It was important to John that you learn to make your own way and earn a living before you came into any money or you'd have blown it on shoes or something."

She smiled. "That sounds like him," she said. "He was so cautious."

"It was an irrevocable trust, Emma. As trustee, Rosemary could only use your portion on your needs, not on Anna's or Lauren's. Have you ever had an accounting done?" Aaron asked.

"Of what?"

"Of your father's estate. The terms of his will."

"Aaron, I was married to one of the richest men in New York. Why would I worry about my father's will? He had a small office in a small town and lectured me if I threw a pen out before it was writing in invisible ink! I wouldn't call him a tightwad, but he didn't let go of a dime before he'd squeezed all the juice out of it."

Aaron laughed. "It's true. And he married a woman who liked nice things..."

"Well, she didn't waste any money on me. After my first year of college I admitted defeat with Rosemary and hardly ever came home to visit. And you know what happened when I struck out on my own. I fell in love with and married a thief."

"May I make a suggestion? You should ask for an accounting of your father's estate. There's still the house. It's a substantial house."

"She said the mortgage alone was killing her," Emma pointed out.

"Emma, the house was insured against your father's death. There was no mortgage. I still have a small practice, mostly just for old clients and friends. If I were your attorney, I could look into this."

She started to laugh. "Oh, Aaron, you are so sweet. I can't afford an attorney! I'm working at a fast food restaurant! Besides, if there turned out to be something left of his estate after all these years, would I have to fight for it? Because I can't even consider going to court. Not ever again."

"Here's what would happen. I would see her lawyer or accountant, petition for an accounting of the proceeds of the estate on your behalf, and if there turned out to be something left for you, you'd have to sue. It usually doesn't go that far unless there are millions at stake. If it's a small amount, the trustee is usually happy to settle to save money. And if there is anything, I won't charge a fee of any kind until you can afford it. It wouldn't be a contingency or percentage, just my usual fee. Which," he said, laughing at himself, "is a steal."

"Well, I won't be suing anyone, that's for sure. I won't even ask for anything from her—she hates me and at this point the feeling is mutual. I'm starting over. But you are kind and I appreciate your generosity."

"Let's find out, Emma. There was once some money involved. And your father's house. That was a rich house, wasn't it? Everyone envied it."

"He built it with my mother," she said. "He never said but I think they hoped to have a few children." She shook her head. "Even the idea of money makes me sick. I live in two rooms. I pinch my pennies in a way that would make John Shay so proud. And I can't bear the idea of owing you money for services that you're really doing as a favor."

"If it turns out there's nothing there or if you choose not to pursue the recovery of it, my fee will be zero."

Her eyes got a little round. "Why, Aaron, I think you wouldn't mind catching Rosemary with her hand in the cookie jar!"

"You found me out," he said. "John was such a gentle man. She seemed to suck the life out of him."

"I think he married Rosemary to have help with me," she said. "It must have been so hard for him. And everyone who knew my mother loved her. I don't think people even like Rosemary. She's a hard woman."

He was quiet for a moment. "John was a good friend. He was careful with his will. It would take months to get an answer, Emma. Months before you have to decide how to proceed. For your peace of mind, I'd be happy to look into this for you."

She shrugged. "Why not? What can it hurt? I won't get my hopes up. If Rosemary was involved, I'm sure she's had a real party spending it. She quit working the week my dad died."

"Then I have something important to do and it makes me so happy to do it for you." He squeezed her hand. "I'm glad you came home, Emma."

Lyle was finishing up for the day, standing at the counter while he looked at the orders for Saturday delivery. In August sales started picking up again after summer. In summer there weren't any floral holidays and people had their own blooms. Summer in Sonoma County was pure heaven.

The door to the shop opened and he smiled to see Riley Kerrigan come in. Took her long enough, he thought. He hadn't seen her in at least a couple of months. She looked fantastic, as usual. You'd never guess by looking at her that she owned a domestic and industrial cleaning service. She looked more like a bank executive or high-powered attorney. After all her years of secondhand clothes followed by scrimping to get by and build her business, Riley was making up for lost time in the wardrobe category.

"Hi," she said. "I thought I might catch you before you left for the day. How's it going?"

"It's all good. How's everything at Happy Housekeeping?" he asked, knowing full well that was not the name of her business.

"Happy, happy, happy. So. Is she back?"

He nodded. "Over a month now," he said. "Tell me something—did it take willpower to wait this long to ask?"

"I didn't expect her to call, if that's what you're getting at. How is she?" Riley asked.

"Doing very well, in spite of everything."

Riley's smile was very small. "Emma has a way of bouncing back."

"If she can bounce back from this, she's a superhero. She stayed in that apartment alone, slept on a cot, even though her husband's blood was all over his study. Because no one offered her a guest room, not even the legal team who were so well paid. And she wasn't safe in a hotel—too many victims of Richard's fraud threatened her. I offered to go out there but she wouldn't have it—she didn't want me in jeopardy. She made the drive to California by herself—she said she needed the time alone and away. Her husband has been dead a few months. It took her a month here to find a bad job. She says she's holding up very well. I'm amazed she's even standing."

"I'm sorry she's going through this, but she wouldn't want my sympathy or my help. If you think of anything I can do without, you know, getting involved, let me know."

"Sure," he said. "She says she's over it, by the way. Your feud."

"Me, too," Riley said. "But still…"

"She said that, too."

Riley smiled at her dear friend. They'd been the three musketeers in high school—Emma, Lyle and Riley. She gave a quiet laugh and shook her head. "Can I buy the man in the middle a drink?" she asked.

"By all means," Lyle said. "I think she's forgiven you by now."

"Good to know. I still hate her, but I'm not mad at her anymore."

"Oh, great." He started turning off lights. "Let's go drink."

Riley stopped by the grocery after a glass of wine with Lyle. They'd been friends for a long time. Usually threesomes don't work very well, but in this case, Lyle being a guy and all, there was no issue. At least not until Emma and Riley had their epic breakup. Then Lyle was stuck in the middle, trying not to take sides. He'd managed to remain loyal to both women for sixteen years.

She was lost in thought, her hand absently palming a honeydew melon.

"I'm not sure if you're going to bowl with that or put it in your cart," a male voice said.

She looked up and smiled. She'd seen this guy before. Starbucks, maybe. "Sorry," she said, taking the melon, though she didn't really want it.

"They look good today, don't they?" he asked. "Hey, do you know where I can find roasted peppers? Fire roasted," he said, consulting a list.

She shook herself for a second, coming back to grocery land and leaving thoughts of poor Lyle and their triangle far behind. "Um, over there with the olives are some prepared in the jar. That's all I know about."

"Artichoke hearts?"

"Same place in the jar, or some in the frozen section."

"Parmesan?"

She smiled at him. He was very good-looking. "You're making artichoke dip, aren't you? Let me see that," she said. She glanced over the recipe. "There aren't any roasted peppers in this recipe."

"I know—it's for something else. I'm just picking them up for a…a neighbor."

"Thank goodness. Okay, be sure the artichokes are packed in water, add a half cup of mozzarella, a sprinkle of chili powder and a cup of chopped spinach and some lucky woman will propose."

"Dynamite. Thank you," he said, turning to go. Then he turned back and said, "Chili powder?"

"With the spices. Not too much, now." She blessed him with a sweet smile. Then she resumed her vegetable shopping. *Hmm*, she thought. *A straight guy in the grocery store. If he were gay, he'd know how to make artichoke dip.*

Her thoughts fled instantly back to Emma and Lyle. Well, they were going to have to share Lyle. He was the best friend she had.

Three

Emma faced an entirely new set of priorities. She was able to pick up extra hours at Burger Purgatory and in her spare time she looked for a better or second job. They kept her hours just under full-time to save costs on benefits, but she had to buy health insurance anyway—it was now the law. Terrified to touch that emergency money she had stowed away, she was stretching her money as far as it would go—rent for Penny took the top position because she was certain the elderly darling needed it. Plus, she needed a place to live while she starved to death. Utilities for her little bungalow was second and she conserved dramatically, even shortening the length of her hot showers, which was a huge sacrifice as she now smelled like French fries all the time. Car insurance and gas came next and only then did she buy food. She did manage to eat at the burger joint sometimes, though that was problematic. First of all, it wasn't part of the deal, but she noticed that all employees partook. There seemed to be an unwritten policy—they'll never miss a few fries, but let's not be obvious about it. And *never* in front of customers. Also, it was not healthy! It was calorie intense, carb heavy and salted to the max. After a few weeks, her pants felt uncomfortably tight and her ankles seemed chronically swollen.

September arrived and with the start of school, the teenage employees vacated the day hours, so at least she worked that shift. She was sure there had to be a better job for her somewhere and equally sure it wouldn't be easy to find it. Emma never thought of herself as having it easy while growing up—she held part-time jobs during high school and college, went to college on loans and scholarships, but she was given an old car to use to get to school and work. Still, she'd had it a lot easier than Riley had.

Her first couple of years in New York had been a real eye-opener—urban living was incredibly expensive. But she was a beautiful, single young woman in a city full of them and in no time she had roommates. She took the subway, learned all the cheap haunts for entertainment and had dates—quite a few of them. The thing about New York City—she never felt alone.

And here, in her two rooms in Sebastopol there was an interesting transformation—the girl who had wanted to design and decorate the interiors of mansions and five-star hotels found living simply to be a welcome pleasure. There was no flab in her life, no unnecessary junk to carry.

She had one dinner with Lyle and Ethan and it had been passably friendly on Ethan's part. She visited with Penny when Penny was enjoying the patio, but fall was approaching, the weather was getting cooler, so Penny wasn't outside as much. Penny's car was often gone; she was a very active senior and had many friends.

Emma walked through Sebastopol on her days off,

anonymous and reluctant to look for work there for fear she'd alert them that the notorious widow was among them. She answered every ad for work in Sonoma County that paid more than minimum wage.

Sebastopol was lovely; old buildings and storefronts were brightly painted, many with their wares and fresh fruits and vegetables on sidewalk display. Ethan liked to put out big pots of fresh blooms, and Emma stopped there often, complimenting him lavishly, fully intending to win him over to her side. She loved buying two apples, two tomatoes and one banana at a time. She even occasionally splurged on a small bunch of flowers and when she did, she noticed Ethan gave her a discount and Lyle smiled slyly.

And, after eight weeks, when the leaves were just beginning to turn, she went home from Burger Brain-Bleed, hungry and swollen, smelling like grease and body odor, and lay down on her bed and cried. If this was what her life was going to look like from now on, she wasn't sure she had the stamina for it. And she was damned afraid if she started dipping into her precious nine thousand dollars, she could end up homeless.

Spoiled, the devil on her shoulder chided her. *You said walking away from the money was the least of your concerns, but did you really mean it? Because here you are, working for a living like the rest of the world and you can't take it!*

She was immediately ashamed. So she got in the shower to cry, trying to hide from her conscience. Then she got out and dried her hair and heard that voice again. *If you think it's hard busting your ass for minimum wage, think about how you'd feel when you learn your life savings is gone. That it was spent on a second home in Aruba and a private jet.*

"I can't do this," she said aloud. "Please, it wasn't my fault. Please."

The next afternoon, while she was wiping down tables in the burger joint, she saw a familiar face. Actually, she saw the familiar back of a head. She knew it was him; she'd know that thick, willful brown hair anywhere. Adam Kerrigan, Riley's brother. He was with a teenage girl who had to be Maddie, Riley's daughter. She took a couple of steps, smile on her face, then stopped herself suddenly. What if he hated her? Adam had kept in touch for a while after Emma's falling out with Riley, but when she married Richard she didn't hear from him anymore.

But why should he hate her? Because of what Richard had done? Would he, like so many others, assume she knew what was going on? Or that she had some stash just waiting for the heat to fade? *Let's just find out*, she thought. *Let's find out right now.*

"Adam?" she asked.

He looked up, his mouth full of burger. His eyes were round and surprised. He chewed and swallowed quickly and the girl covered her mouth as she laughed at him. He wiped his lips with a napkin. "Emmie Cat?" he asked in disbelief, falling back on an old pet name he'd given her when they were kids. It was short for Emma Catherine.

The nickname reassured her and made her smile. "It's me. How are you?" He started to get up. "No, no," she said with a laugh. "Don't get up." And she slid onto the plastic bench at the table across the aisle from him, hanging on to her cleaning rag.

"You work here?" he asked.

"I do," she said. "And believe me, I do work. No wonder this place runs on teenagers. They're the only ones with the energy to keep up. How are you?"

"I'm well, thanks. Emma, this is Maddie. Maddie, meet Emma Shay. We went to school together."

"Although he's much older," Emma teased. He was, in fact, three years older.

"How long have you been back?" he asked. And he asked with a distinct absence of hostility.

"A couple of months. Remember Lyle? He found me a little place I could rent and it seemed like the logical thing to do."

"Of course I remember Lyle. I see him all the time. How is it? Being back after all this time?"

She shrugged. "Tough," she said. "But tell me all about you. I confess, I haven't been in touch so I have no idea—"

"Excuse me," Maddie said. "I'm going to take a quick run to the ladies' room while you two visit." She grinned impishly. "I'll try to stretch it out." And with that, she slid out of the booth and left them alone but for the half dozen customers at the counter.

Emma smiled. "She's so beautiful, Adam. And so sweet."

"She is," he agreed.

"And how about you? Did you marry?"

She thought his expression was sweet and maybe a little sad. "I came close a couple of times, but it wasn't in the cards. Uncle duty keeps me busy enough."

"Isn't Jock around?"

"Sure, he's around now and then. He was briefly married when Maddie was very young and…well, no one knows better than you how hard it can be if the chemistry isn't right with the stepmother…"

Only too well, she thought. And suddenly she fought tears. Not because she was faced with the child of her best friend and boyfriend. *Ex*-friend and *ex*-boyfriend. Conceived while she was away at college. "Wow," she said, her eyes having gone a little liquid. He would probably think she wept from some long-ago broken heart, but that had nothing to do with it.

Adam surprised her by reaching out, putting a big hand on her shoulder. "You shouldn't have stayed so out of touch, Emmie Cat. Fifteen years is too long for old friends."

"Uncle Adam," she said uncomfortably, looking down and giving her eyes a wipe.

"Well, it turns out it really does take a village," he said with a laugh. "Riley, me, my mom, Jock—it was a community effort. Worked out pretty well," he added. "Maddie is an awesome kid."

"I bet you're an awesome uncle."

"I do my best. I teach high school so I'm kind of an expert on her species. And Jock works at an electronics store so we have all the phones and toys and laptops we need."

"The same store he worked at way back when?" she asked.

"Same one, but he's a manager now."

"And you're still teaching?" Emma asked. "I guess you chose the right profession if you're still at it."

"I think that's a yes. Listen, I'm sorry about everything you went through. Condolences, Emmie."

"Thank you."

"There were a hundred times I thought about getting in touch, not knowing how you were holding up. When I did finally get to it, your number had changed so I just checked with Lyle now and then. Everyone knows you had nothing to do with anything…illegal."

"Thank you, again."

"We were just talking about you a few weeks ago, wondering if you had made it back home. We were remembering the old days."

"We?" she asked before she could stop herself.

"Me. Mom. Riley. This is a coincidence, running into you here, like this."

A tall, skinny kid came over to the table. "Taking a break, Ms. Shay?" he asked.

"Just answering a couple of questions for a customer, Justin."

"Can I help?" Justin asked, turning to Adam.

"I don't believe so," Adam said authoritatively. "I'll just take a moment of Emma's time. If you'll excuse us."

Justin looked taken aback, but then he turned and left them.

"He's a despot," she quietly informed Adam. "But jobs are in short supply, it seems."

"Could you use a letter of recommendation?" he asked.

She stood. "I could use a do-over," she said. "But thanks for asking. Do you teach around here?"

He shook his head. "Napa. High school science. I'm playing a little hooky with Maddie today. We were at the DMV so she could take her test for her learner's permit. Riley wanted to do it but the truth is, Riley and Maddie don't do well in the car together so Maddie prefers driving with me or with Jock, and he's working this afternoon. Of course Maddie couldn't wait. When do you get off work?"

"Not until nine, why?"

"We should have a cup of coffee or glass of wine, talk about how you'd like me to word that letter of recommendation."

Maddie was back, sliding into their booth.

"Oh...ah... Listen, you don't know what you're suggesting..."

"I don't? Why not? We're still friends, right?"

"It's not that... Well, it's partly that since, you know..." She took a breath. She wasn't going to say in front of this sweet fifteen-year-old, *That's my boyfriend's baby and probably the major reason I went off the rails in the first place.* She leaned closer to Adam. "Take a whiff of this place. This is what I smell like after work."

He threw back his head with a hearty laugh. "See you later," he said.

She meandered back behind the counter, kind of dazed. Half of her wanted to run and hide—being around Adam would only serve to remind her of the past and all she'd lost. But the other half was elated. Could she and Adam be friends? They'd talked a few times after Maddie was born, but their conversations had been so superficial, both of them afraid to let the standoff she had with Riley taint the relationship she had with Adam, who she had always so admired. Truth was, she'd always wondered if Adam had kept in touch out of guilt over what his sister had done.

She'd done all right in the friends department during college and her first years as a single woman in New

York, but she'd always kept people at a safe distance, afraid to trust again.

That was perhaps the deepest wound of all.

Emma's earliest memory of Adam was him standing by the fence outside the school playground to make sure Riley got home all right. Even before she realized she liked Riley, she wished she had a big brother like Adam. When she left Burger or Bust that night, he was across the parking lot, leaning against the hood of his SUV, arms crossed over his chest. Waiting. He looked like an older version of that twelve-year-old boy. Except he looked a lot happier now, like maybe the chip on his shoulder was gone.

Yeah, that's what it had been—that serious, stubborn, perhaps fearful boy in his scuffed shoes and torn jacket, left to take care of the family after his father had died. Emma had worried about this faux date all afternoon until she saw him and then realized she was always thinking about herself, her troubles. She was always afraid of being found out, exposed, blamed. But Adam had been only a kid when he lost a parent, but a kid old enough to understand and remember his loss. And he'd been so brave, always looking out for his mother and sister. He was right there at St. Pascal's until high school, but even when he was older and went to a different school, he was so often on hand to watch over Riley. And Emma, as well.

"I can't believe you're really here," she said. "You have a date with someone who smells like burgers and fries."

"I think we'll get through it. How do you feel about a glass of wine or a drink?"

"I'd love a glass of wine."

"Great. Where do you hang your hat these days?"

"A little spot in Sebastopol. Not too far from Lyle's."

"Perfect. I know just the place, right on the way to your place. Follow me?"

"I'm parked right over there. The Prius."

"Let's do it," he said.

She followed him along some of the back roads toward her little town, but he turned down an alley and she got a little confused. Concerned. But then he parked behind what she thought, by the twinkle lights strung between the boughs of trees, must be the patio of a restaurant. The Cellar, the sign on the back gate said. He got out of his car, she got out of hers and he opened the gate to a patio. There were a half dozen tables; a couple of women sat at one, wine and fruit before them, but it was otherwise deserted. "They're going to close soon, but we're friends. I'll get us some wine, something to snack on and they'll say good-night before they leave."

"Huh?"

Adam chuckled. "Would you like to see a wine list?"

"No," she said. "I usually just have a sauvignon blanc."

A woman wearing an apron came out of the back door. "Just in time, as usual," she said. "How are you, Adam?"

Adam leaned toward her to kiss her cheek. "Excellent. Kate, meet my friend, Emma."

"Nice to meet you. What can I get you?"

"Get us a bottle of Napa Cellars sauvignon blanc, a half wheel of Brie with some crackers and fruit, two waters. And thanks."

"Just give me two minutes," she said.

He held out a chair for Emma. "What kind of place is this?" she asked.

"Just a small wine bar. I've known the owners for a long time. For friends and relatives, they say good-night when they lock up, we take the bottle if there's anything left, leave the glasses on the table and slide the dishes and leftover food right through that little serving slot so the birds don't invade. They'll close in about..." He looked at his watch. "I'm sure they're cleaning up now and will be out of here in fifteen minutes."

Sure enough, Kate was back instantly with the wine, glasses, a tray of food. Right behind her a young man followed with a bucket of ice on a stand, placing it beside the table. Kate opened the wine and Adam indicated that Emma should taste. And she presented a bill. Adam signed off on everything and thanked her. Before Kate escaped into the bar the women bid her good-night and went out the back gate.

"Why couldn't I have found a job in a place like this instead of Burger Buster?" Emma said.

"This particular place is run by a family and I think you have to marry in, but it's perfect, isn't it?"

"I think I have to broaden my search, now that I have restaurant experience, if you use the term loosely."

"Listen, I want to hear all about it—your return, your job-hunting, anything you feel like talking about, but we have to get one thing out of the way first. Maddie. She doesn't know that you were Jock's girlfriend or that you and Riley were best friends and...that whole complicated mess. She's innocent of that."

Emma considered this for a second. "Jock and Riley never told her the details?"

"Emmie, I don't think *I* even know all the details,

when you put it that way. I didn't have any trouble guessing. Riley and Jock never married. They weren't even together when Maddie was born."

Her mouth fell open. All these years she had this mental image of Riley and Jock, young and in love. Of course she knew they hadn't stayed together, that he'd gone on to marry and divorce another woman, but she thought that for at least a while they were a couple. "You're kidding!"

He shook his head.

"Doesn't that just figure?"

"What are you saying?" he asked her.

"Well, my half sister and stepsister, Drizella and Anastasia, couldn't wait to bring me the news that my best friend was pregnant and planning to marry my boyfriend, but they never mentioned the happy couple didn't stay together. I found out later, of course, but not while I was hurting over it. Because, hey, that might've made me actually feel less…" She stopped herself. "In fact, those few times we talked, you didn't mention they weren't a couple."

"I tried not to mention Riley and Jock at all," he said. "They were on and off for a little while. Maybe that's not accurate, either—they weren't together. They tried to create an amicable relationship for Maddie's sake, but they never even lived together. In fact, I think I'd need a chart and a graph to understand where Maddie came from because Riley and Jock were like oil and water. But I don't want Maddie to think badly of either of them. Well, let me be honest, I wouldn't be devastated to learn she thinks a little badly of Jock. He pissed me off. He got my sister pregnant and didn't exactly step up to the plate. He was pretty useless back then, but he was just a kid. And he is her father. I'd rather we all get along. And I don't want Maddie blindsided by a lot of nasty gossip."

"I won't be saying anything, Adam. I'd prefer to forget it ever happened," Emma said. "At the time, it was awful."

"I think it's safe to say a lot of people were hurt."

"You're in luck. If anyone remembers me they will have much juicier stuff than my best friend and boyfriend getting together while I was away at school sixteen years ago. All the same, Riley and Jock should explain it to her before anyone else does."

"Of course. The minute she's capable of understanding at least a little bit. I'm kind of an expert on teenagers. Girls Maddie's age are filled with a kind of tragic drama and fatalism that can easily cast them in a dark place. I've watched it. We've had our challenges as a family and it hasn't always been easy, but one thing we did manage. We managed to make sure Maddie never felt like a mistake. She always felt loved and wanted. I think."

"It never came up?" Emma asked. "Didn't anyone ask how Riley ended up having Jock's baby when he was supposed to be my boyfriend?"

"I only recall once or twice. Riley said you and Jock had broken up when you went away to school, which was at least partially true. It's been a long time—I just want to be sure Maddie always feels secure."

How lucky, Emma thought. Since she was just a kid she had known two things about the Kerrigan family. They had very obvious struggles; life for them had never been easy. But they had enough familial loyalty and love to glue them together. Emma had always envied that because she'd never had it.

Emma's problems began long before she lost her boyfriend to her best friend.

Emma was a bit too young to understand her placement in the family when her father married Rosemary Caliban, but it didn't take her long to instinctively know she was only loved by her father, and her father was a lonely, unhappy, broken man.

His wife gone, John Shay married someone who appeared, on the surface, to be a good match. A woman who was willing to help raise Emma. But Rosemary was a stern woman with a mean side and a streak of jealousy a mile wide. She brought a daughter to the marriage, produced a second and clearly preferred both of them to Emma. Once Emma was an adult and could look back on it she supposed it didn't help that people often remarked on how pretty she was. And her daddy couldn't stop himself from commenting on how much she resembled her late mother, with her chestnut hair and large dark eyes. Rosemary undoubtedly despised hearing that, and who wouldn't?

Emma remembered Rosemary doing subtle things to show her favoritism. She'd fold Anna's and Lauren's clothes and toss Emma's on the bed, took her two girls shopping and to lunch while Emma was with Riley, never inviting her. Emma even suspected the gifts she got at Christmas were of lesser value and almost never fit. Rosemary would help her daughters with the kitchen cleanup when it was their turn but Emma was left on her own. When John Shay stepped in to help Emma, she knew he had noticed and that made her feel worse, not better. When her father died it was the Kerrigan family that comforted her more than her own. It was obvious Rosemary didn't miss John much.

It wasn't long before a man moved in—her new stepfather, Vince Kingston. Vince wasn't gentle and sweet like her father had been. He was a crass idiot who made crude and suggestive remarks to his new stepdaughters, but Rosemary just ignored him. Emma gave him a wide berth, as did Anna and Lauren. Emma wasn't quite sure where she belonged. Or if she belonged anywhere at all.

That was always an issue with her, that she had no real family. This seemed especially important during her high school years, and when her father died…it seemed hopeless. She felt so self-conscious, as if everyone at school knew she was basically an orphan. And who was there for her through the confusion and sadness? Riley, Adam, their mother, June, and Riley's grandparents. They were the family she always longed for.

It was like Adam was always watching over them all.

On her second glass of wine, fortified with a little cheese and fruit, she asked him about his grandparents. She knew they had passed away, but hadn't heard until they'd been gone awhile.

"Well, Grandpa died when I was twenty-two. He wasn't sick long. Cancer took him quickly. Gram just went along, died in her sleep a year later. I was twenty-three and had just finished my teaching degree. My grandparents left the house to Mom, of course. It took me five more years to move out, get my own place. Riley and Maddie took a little longer and for the life of me I'm not sure why they even bothered—they're at Mom's all the time." He laughed. "But then, so am I. I check on her a lot. I do the guy chores around the house and try to take her out to dinner regularly. I hate her always cooking for all of us, even though she loves to cook. She volunteers with a bunch of church ladies, taking meals to the elderly and infirm."

Emma looked down. "I missed your family. Your mother most of all. I think she was more family to me than Rosemary ever was."

"And she misses you. You know, it wouldn't look like you're giving in to stop by the house and say hello. There's no commitment involved. It might be time to rethink this feud."

She laughed uncomfortably. "You don't understand. I'm not angry anymore. It's just… We can't be friends again, Adam."

"Who? Me and you?"

"Oh, I like the idea of being your friend," she said with a little laugh. "Especially since you know these nifty little hideaways where you can have wine under the stars. But I can't have you trying to work things out between me and Riley. We're done."

He gave her a steady, half-amused look. "Really, Emmie Cat? After all you've gone through in the past few years, you're worried about friendship with Riley?"

"We wouldn't trust each other anyway…"

He laughed. "It's been over fifteen years. You don't have to trust her. Who cares if you trust her? You don't even have to like her. But when you think about things, you'll figure out she was never your enemy."

"She wasn't exactly my friend!"

"If she'd been a better friend, maybe you could've married Jock. I'm sure that would've been great."

"Compared to who I did marry? Might've been, yeah! At least it wouldn't have been Richard. But determined to have a better life than the one I left behind, I—" She paused for a moment. "All right, all right," she said. "Don't think I haven't looked at it from that angle. But please, don't get ideas about reuniting us."

He put up his hands, palms toward her. "Heaven help me." He took a sip of his wine. "The truth? I wish the two of you could make amends. You were always stronger together than apart. I refuse to believe you still mourn the loss of Jock. It just seems that now, after everything, staying mad at my sister wouldn't be very high on your list of priorities."

After what she'd been through with Richard, there was a part of her that wished she'd married Jock, let *him* ruin her life, that she'd never left California, never met Richard. She shook her head. "That's certainly true—my priorities are completely different now. And I don't really think of our situation as a feud. I'm sure if we ran into each other we'd be perfectly cordial. Even friendly. But the days of slumber parties are over. I have to get on my feet. I didn't think I'd start off with a great job, but I thought I'd get a decent job, even after not working for nine years. I have a degree. With my experience, I could make a damn good concierge or event planner. Turns out that even though I didn't do anything wrong, I also have a shady past by association. Even though I wasn't arrested, people don't trust me. They're afraid I was his partner in crime. After all, he had several employees who rolled over on him, took deals to testify. People suspect me, think I didn't testify because I was protecting him. I didn't testify because I had nothing relevant to say. Let that be a lesson to you, Adam.

Don't hang around with felons. Sitting in the courtroom while they're being tried might help them, but it won't do much for you."

"Why'd you come back, Emmie?" he asked. "I thought you'd disappear and we'd never see you again."

"I had nowhere to go," she said. "Oh, I thought about going somewhere I could be unknown but you know what? Someone's going to figure me out eventually and then it'll only be worse. I will have added deception to suspicion. Besides, my credentials are in my name! And I couldn't stay back there. I was a leper. Not only couldn't I even get a job with McBurger back east, there were also hostile people who wanted revenge on me just for being associated with Richard. I was in hiding for months. Around here I've found some resistance, but I did manage to get a job. A small job, but a job. Maybe when people see I'm a hard worker, it'll ease up. I'm a little afraid to think about how long that might take." She took a sip of her wine. "I have to admit, I didn't think it would be this hard. Have you ever tried to make it on minimum wage?"

He just gave her a wan smile. Of course he had. When they'd moved to town, June had worked two jobs—cleaning houses and waitressing. She worked all the time. Emma remembered when June soaked her feet at the end of a long day, so sore, so weary. And that after just losing her husband.

"How'd you end up with Richard Compton?" he asked.

"Oh, the usual way. I met him when I was out with friends. In a restaurant. I was in the bar with my girlfriends and he was having dinner with clients. We had a nice conversation. He was clearly interested, which was flattering. He asked for my number and I wouldn't give it to him. I took his business card but he intimidated me, so I didn't plan to call him. A few weeks later he showed up in the store where I worked—he'd been back at that restaurant and one of my friends told him where I worked. I made him work really hard for a date, but honestly? I was completely smitten. Richard was very handsome, very classy. So charming. You don't weasel people out of a hundred million dollars by being an asshole. He could charm the pants off anyone.

"I didn't know how rich my husband was when I married him. I mean, I knew he was successful and lived well, but I didn't know much more than that. I certainly didn't know he was getting rich illegally. Had I known, do you think I could have stayed with him? But it's not like I ever saw a tax return. I didn't have a key to a safe-deposit box or anything. I didn't know there was a safe in his study. I guess because there was another larger and visible safe, the police never expected it, either. It was hidden behind a bookcase. Richard was not what you'd call transparent."

Adam frowned. "Didn't you sign the tax return?"

She shook her head. "We filed separate returns—Richard took care of it. There was a prenup, a generous prenup that would settle me with more money than I'd ever know what to do with. Of course I came to understand about his wealth, that he could afford almost anything. He never questioned what I needed."

In vitro, Emma? What the hell. Knock yourself out.

But, Richard, you'll have to have a few tests...

No problem. I'll schedule us with the best doctor in the city.

"This is a whole new world," she said. "No one is

going to pity me, learning how to live on two hundred a week after nine years with a Manhattan apartment and a vacation home in the islands. But… Well. Once I get a second job or a decent first job, things should be easier."

Adam smiled at her. "I'll keep my eyes open," he promised. "If you find something around here and need a strong letter of recommendation…"

"You're going to say you're pretty sure I'm not a bad person?" she asked.

"I'll say I've known you almost my whole life and have always known you to be strong, smart, honest and reliable." He pulled his wallet out of his back pocket and withdrew a card. He wrote something on the back and handed it to her. "My cell number. I don't very often find myself at the Burger Bomb in south Santa Rosa. Call anytime."

She turned it over and saw it was a business card. Kerrigan Cleaning Services. Industrial, business, residential. Riley Kerrigan, President and CEO.

Emma looked up into his eyes with a question.

"The work is hard but she pays over minimum wage and promotes from within the company. She's a good leader." He shrugged. "If desperation for rent and food ever take precedence over bad feelings about the past."

"Never gonna happen, Adam," she said, handing back the card.

He closed his hand around hers, refusing to take it. "The first thing you're going to have to learn about scrabbling to get back on your feet—never turn your nose up at an opportunity. Especially for pride's sake."

"You're reading me all wrong," she said. "I don't have any pride left. But I do have to protect myself in the clinches."

"As you should. And know this—my sister has done a lot for women, women like you who are trying to get on their feet, start over, build a functional life and their self-esteem, usually out of the ruins of divorce or being widowed."

"You're proud of her," she said.

"Oh, yes. Riley amazes me. Keep the card. It has my number on the back."

She slid it into her purse, thinking it would be a cold day in hell before she'd ask Riley Kerrigan for help.

The very next day the mean little tyrant at Burger Belch fired her.

Four

Riley Kerrigan ran a tight ship and an efficient workplace. She kept her office in Santa Rosa, for easy access to Marin County, San Francisco, Davis, Napa Valley. It had been her goal from the start to service companies and individuals who could afford the best. The fact that this demographic was also the most difficult to please, the greatest challenge, was irrelevant to her. She was confident she had the best service providers.

There were only two full-time office staff: Riley, and her secretary, Jeanette Sutton. She had had five rooms—a spacious office for herself, a front reception area for Jeanette, an office for Brazil Johnson, the CFO and numbers woman, a conference room for meetings and a small lunchroom and restroom. Brazil was rarely in the office; she worked from home whenever she could. Riley's director of operations, Nick Cabrini, worked in the field, but there was space for him in the office if he needed it, either in Brazil's office or the conference room. Makenna Rice was the head housekeeper and trainer; she used the conference room occasionally.

Riley kept an office because customers responded

to it, particularly business clients, although some home owners also liked to see her base of operations. It gave her credibility. Nick drove one of the company cars; he dressed sharp, carried a computer in his expensive briefcase and when he gave estimates or checked on cleaning crews he looked professional. She had two hundred employees, most of them part-time by choice. Some of her full-time employees took care of the same properties on a regular basis. She had night crews who cleaned office buildings, day crews in residences and crews on call for emergencies like fire or flood damage—regular hazmat duty. Her liability was high and well managed, her income was in the mid hundred-thousand range, her business net worth was now extremely high, her mother's house was paid off, her retirement savings gaining strength, Maddie's college fund nearly maxed and her state of mind—excellent.

It had been a long time coming. Many years of eighty-hour weeks.

When Riley was eighteen and a new high school graduate, she took a few classes at the community college that very summer and helped her mother with her housecleaning jobs. Back then they worked for cash, under the table, and too often they were treated like they belonged under the table, out of sight. Customers would take last-minute trips or vacations and forgo housecleaning service for a couple of weeks, not paying them. Clients complained about the cost; they added duties without making preparations in advance, without asking or offering to pay extra. "Oh, June, I have to run a couple of errands. You don't mind keeping an eye on little Eric, do you?" or "June, I'm way behind on the laundry, can you pitch in?" and "Junie, darling, looks like it's time for a good window washing." And as far as Riley knew, her mother hadn't had a raise in at least ten years.

"We have to fix this business," Riley had said. "Even some of your oldest customers take complete advantage of your good nature."

"I think of some of these people as my friends. I just like to help when I can," June always said.

"Well, they don't think of you as a friend. They treat their friends with far more respect, so don't be fooled. And none of them are worried about your retirement. We're going to find a better way to get it done and earn a decent living. And maybe a little security."

Riley set up a business plan at the age of eighteen, recruited a couple of college girls who were going to school part-time just as she was, got a business license for two hundred dollars and went looking for more clients. She called her company Kerrigan's Kleaning and had business cards printed. At first, she didn't have any overhead except the personal time it cost to do paperwork because Riley was paying taxes, social security, salaries and issuing 1099 statements to employees. Within months Kerrigan's Kleaning was humming along and even growing.

Then she got pregnant.

What a dark, terrifying time that was. Emma abandoned her, which came as no surprise, and Jock was suddenly MIA. He offered to give her money for an abortion, then he offered to marry her, but he had a black eye in the suspicious shape of Adam's fist. She turned down both offers. She did threaten to sue him for support, however, because in all areas she had a mind for business. She remained at home with her mother, brother and grandparents, where she had loving support.

She continued to work with her cleaning service. The bigger she got, the more she thought she'd better make this idea work because there was certainly no man waiting in the wings to take care of her. In fact, not only were Jock's support payments spotty at best, he didn't even show up at the hospital when she went into labor. Adam and her mother were with her, her grandparents waiting in the hall.

Jock came much later, after her family was gone, and though she tried to forget it, the image of him crying as he held the baby was forever burned into her mind. But she wasn't falling for his malarkey again.

The whole pregnancy was emotionally difficult and Riley felt she'd ruined her life with one terrible choice. But when she saw Maddie's perfect little face, everything changed. She might've had regrets, but now she also had purpose. And she worked like a demon because she had a daughter, and her daughter was going to have a devoted family, a good home and opportunities.

Jock started coming around after Maddie was a few months old, and the hurt and anger were almost too much for Riley. How dare he pretend to act like a father now! Every encounter was a strain; they fought and sniped at each other and not to be left out, Adam got into it, threatening Jock. Maddie was about nine months old when they had a blistering fight because Jock wanted to take her to his mother's house so his family could meet her, and Riley said she'd be damned if he was taking her anywhere.

"Stop!" June said. She took the baby from Riley, passed her to Grandma and sat the three of them at the table. "Don't anyone say a word if you value your life. That child is a happy baby who will live to be ninety if I have my way. But if all she hears from her parents and her uncle is fighting, what do you think that will do for her self-esteem?"

"We don't have any joint custody thing going on here," Riley snapped.

"You have money for a lawyer?" June asked Riley. She turned to Jock. "Do you?"

"If he wasn't responsible enough to take care of the mother, what makes you think he's responsible enough to take care of a baby?" Adam nearly shouted.

"Do you want this little girl to grow up wondering who her daddy is?" she asked Adam. "Or wondering why her mother and uncle kept him from her? This stops here and now. We don't raise voices around her, and Jock deserves a chance to grow into a good father. Part of that is spending time with his daughter. And if you two keep bullying him the only one who will suffer will be Maddie."

"I just want to do the right thing," Jock said.

"Too late!" Riley and Adam said. And then they both said, "Sorry," as they saw June's black scowl.

"Of course you can take the baby to your mother," June said. "First you have to learn the car seat, and I'd make you show me you know how to change a diaper but since your mother will be there, I think we're safe. I'll make you up a bottle and I want you to have her back in three hours. After today there has to be notice, Jock. Riley's a good mama and she is not the least bit flexible. Planning will be the key. We will all be cooperative and the number one priority will always be Maddie."

"If he'd planned before, Maddie wouldn't be here," Riley hurled.

"Was that a thank-you?" Jock asked.

"I'm warning you..." June said.

After that confrontation, things went a bit more smoothly with Jock but it was at least a couple of years before Riley's resentment of him calmed into a tense acceptance. This was not the life she had planned—a baby with a reluctant father who had no real love for her. And the fact that she had loved him, however briefly, only made her shame burn brighter.

Her mother had said one more thing to Riley. Privately. Knowing her daughter so well. "That pride will be the end of you," June said. "Try to put your focus on Maddie, not your injured pride. Please."

She built herself up one emotional brick at a time, becoming a tough, professional businesswoman. Her residential service grew. When she scored her first office building cleaning contract, she celebrated. She also provided what they called a mover's special—the cleaning of empty houses to get them ready for new occupants. That was a tough job that paid well and sometimes she, her mom and Adam would put in twelve- or fifteen-hour days to get it done. Sometimes Jock would babysit... at June's house.

Then she started researching industrial cleaning services, instinctively knowing the real money was there—mold, water damage, fire damage, sewage and odor removal. The only things she left alone were harmful chemicals and crime scene cleanup. She contracted one team, giving them the lion's share of her profits. But then she had them train a second team of industrial cleaners and they became *hers*. She ran her business from her mother's dining room table while spooning strained peas into Maddie's mouth and later, while helping Maddie with her spelling words and math exercises.

As a family, they had a bit of a setback when her grandparents passed, but she found that as long as she stayed ahead of the personnel and contracts, the company functioned very well. June worked part-time for Riley's company, a few jobs a week. The rest of the time she helped raise Maddie. When Maddie was ten, just five years ago, Riley changed the name of her company to Kerrigan Cleaning Services, rented office space and *cleaned up.*

From that home pregnancy test to here was a long and difficult passage. But she had people she knew who, barring death, would never desert her, would always forgive her, love her as unconditionally as she loved them. Maddie, her mother, Adam. Since Jock, she had not been in a romantic relationship.

Nor had she had another best friend.

Today was a fairly typical day. She started with a meeting with Brazil and Jeanette, going over office matters. She approved billing, answered emails, took a meeting with a man who was looking for a full-time domestic for a 14,000 square foot house. He'd already been given an estimate and offered a contract by Nick but was seeing the owner, Riley, because he balked at the idea that it would require a contracted team who would be paid by the hour when additional out of contract duties came along, chores such as, "Clean up after this wedding reception held in our house and courtyard." He could spend ten million on a house but wanted upkeep cheap. She stood firm. She let him go. He would be back.

She visited three teams on-site, found two to be managing well and one to be having some internal difficulties. It was a team of three housekeepers, two of whom had created a bond of friendship, probably behaving meanly to the third, an older woman she'd known a long time, who had been a team trainer and team leader. She'd been down this road so many times—the team leader was undeniably trustworthy with extremely high standards. The younger women wanted to get their eight hours done in six, probably cutting corners. They could take advantage of the trainer's skills, letting her take the detail work, but apparently they were shortsighted. She could have a meeting with them, counsel them, give them pointers on working together effectively. Instead, she said, "I'll create a new team for you, but for the rest of this week work together with no friction."

Then she turned it over to Nick Cabrini, her director of operations, with instructions to redistribute them. All three of them. Those two snotty women who abused the older cleaner weren't getting away with this.

The women loved Nick; her few male employees respected him. In fact, *she* loved Nick. He was young and personable but very rigid about their policies. He was never too harsh, that she knew of, but he was always firm. He was also bilingual. He had a good education and hoped to start a company of his own in another specialty—he wanted to get into transportation, limo and car service. But his best quality? His mother taught him to clean like a wizard. He could spot a smear or speck of dust at fifty yards.

His counterpart was Louis Spinoza, a retired firefighter who headed up their industrial restoration division. Louis had tons of hazmat experience, had worked construction on and off and, as many firefighters did, had worked a second job for years—in cleanup.

Riley grabbed a chicken salad on her way back to the office and ate it at her desk. Just when she was starting to feel that afternoon lull, who should show up but Adam. He gave a couple of raps on her door and stuck his head in.

"Is madam busy?" he asked.

She pushed her salad aside. "I'm always busy, but you're so welcome to come in. Out of school early today?"

"Nah, I just don't have any other duties."

"Good, I'm dying to hear about Maddie's driving test from an objective person. She says it took her fifteen minutes and she aced it."

He grinned. "Twenty minutes and she missed one, but she challenged it and even showed them the page on which her answer was located. I'd have given it to her."

"You'd give her a kidney," she said, laughing at him.

"Well, true," he said, sitting in the chair in front of her desk. He balanced an ankle on the opposite knee. "There is something we should talk about. I ran into Emma yesterday after the driving test. I met her later for a drink."

Riley frowned. "Oh?" she said. "Ran into—"

"We stopped for a hamburger on the way home from the test and guess who was working there? Little paper cap, apron and all."

"Maddie didn't say anything…"

"She teased me a little bit on the way home. I just told her Emma was an old friend we went to school with." He took a deep breath. "You're going to have to tell her, Riley. You're going to have to explain about Emma and Jock. And you."

"Why?" she asked quickly. Defensively.

"Because it was a thing around here. I don't know everything that went on, all I know is Jock was going steady with Emma when suddenly you were pregnant with Jock's baby. And had a huge blowout with your best friend. A couple of families were thrown into a tail-spin, all kinds of agony and grudges resulting. Riley, Maddie has a best friend. A couple of them. She needs to know what happened to you."

"That has nothing to do with Maddie," she said. "Maddie was born into a loving family, she knows the facts about who her father is, she spends plenty of time with him, especially when sports are involved. Maddie is secure."

"Secure with the sanitized version of this story? First of all, someone is going to tell her someday that there was a whole lot of cheating and hard feelings going on. Probably when people who have known us almost our whole lives notice that Emma is back in town—that might bring the whole drama to mind. It'll get so much more interesting to add that Emma left California permanently, probably at least partly because of that, and ended up married to an internationally famous con man. And second, we've never been that kind of family—the kind that short-sheets the truth."

"What does it matter?" she asked in a voice that verged on desperation. "It might not have been tidy but it wasn't complicated. Emma was gone, we were left behind, spent a lot of time together. Do I regret it? Not when I look at Maddie. But I wish Jock had been someone else's boyfriend!"

He leaned toward her. He was patient. His handsome eyebrows tented with concern. "Riley, what you don't want is for the question to come up. You want to make the circumstances clear to Maddie. Because of this—there were a series of unfortunate misunderstandings and events that caused some anguish, but I'd like to think things always work out in the end. I hope things can work out for Emma—she's been through hell. I think things worked out for you. At the end of the day, things worked for me—I have a beautiful, brilliant niece. I hope Maddie has the life she wants even though she has this mixed-up family of a lot of single parents. There's a sweet spot somewhere, Riley—that place where the good outweighs the bad. Know what I mean? That tender truth. The honest truth."

"You don't know what you're suggesting..."

"You've become a very successful woman, Riley. You have everything to be proud of. There isn't a single one of us who doesn't have to own a questionable decision or two but very damn few can show how they took that one misstep and turned it into pure gold."

"And if Maddie loses all respect for me?"

He shook his head. "Not possible. Maddie admires you more than anyone. Except maybe me," he said, grinning. "I think I'm your biggest fan."

She softened her expression. Adam was all goodness. All goodness wrapped up in the most beautiful package.

"What was she doing working at a fast-food restaurant?" Riley asked.

"As she tells it, it was the only job she could get. She wasn't sure if it was the fact that she hadn't had a job in ten years, outside of being married to a millionaire, or if it was because she was married to a notorious thief.

She suspects the latter and I'm inclined to agree. People won't take a chance on her."

"Why would she tell anyone? She should have changed her name!"

"She goes by Emma Shay, but she's not disguised. Employers are pretty savvy nowadays. They look up their applicants. They check Facebook and Twitter, just like you do. And she looks exactly as she did fifteen years ago."

"Sixteen," Riley said uncomfortably. Her fingers ran through her short, shaggy blond hair at her temples, smoothing it over her ears.

"Aw, Riley, you've always worn this thing like a hair shirt. We should've talked about this years ago but you were busy self-flagellating. Emma belonged to me and Mom, too, you know. She immediately knew who Maddie must be. Listen, even though you didn't confide everything in me, I know the whole thing wasn't entirely your fault. Last night I told her you and Jock weren't even together when Maddie was born and she was surprised. Surprised and disappointed in Jock. This should've come out years ago, not last night. That's how little communication she's had with this place."

Riley felt tears threaten to rise. "I tried to tell her—she wouldn't speak to me. Lyle could've told her, but he was determined to stay out of it. Besides, she was busy, Adam. Flying all over the world in that private jet…"

"I have no doubt she'd have walked away from that had she known what was really going on there. I thought you'd be sympathetic. She was lied to. Everyone abandoned her."

"And so now she's been struck down again? Poor Emma, she just keeps picking the wrong guys."

"Was that sarcasm?" he asked.

"I apologize. I'm feeling a little like a cornered animal. Oh, God, why am I apologizing to you? Emma doesn't know I was flippant about her troubles!"

"I gave her your business card. I told her you paid more than minimum wage."

"You can't be serious," she said, astonished. "She couldn't make in a year what her fresh-flower budget was."

"*Was* being the operative word. You might hear from her. She's having a hard time getting by."

"Lyle hasn't said anything," she said.

"Lyle has always been Switzerland where you two were concerned, which is why Emma knew so little about you and Jock. But get ready—one way or another, you're going to run into her. Because I'm planning to see her again."

"What? What's that about?"

"If you two can't reconcile, that's your deal. I'm not angry with Emma or with you. And I want to see her again."

"You act like you have a thing for her or something," Riley said.

"I told you, she was my friend, too. I'm a little worried about her. It's important to me to make sure she's all right." He stood up.

"Do you have a thing for her, Adam?" she asked directly. Her brother, so handsome, such a wonderful man, was rarely in a relationship even though women sighed as he passed. She had even once said, *It's okay if you're gay, you know.* And he had replied, *And it's okay if you are.*

"You want to date her, is that it?" Riley asked.

"We had a glass of wine together," he said. "It was good to see her. We talked a little bit about Maddie, about her return home after that sideshow back east, the difficulties of finding work. She asked about Mom, about Grandma and Grandpa. Except for Lyle and the old widow she rents from, she's pretty much alone, but we had a nice hour or so together and I was really happy to see her again. While all that mess was going on in New York with her husband, then his suicide, I thought about her a lot. I checked in with Lyle now and then to make sure she was okay. Lyle was talking to her almost daily at the end—he was her sole emotional support. I should have called her. I think Lyle would've given me her number, but I didn't ask. I decided to wait awhile, see how things shook out, then there was the suicide and feds all over her possessions. I think what she endured must have been unimaginably painful, worse than most things I can envision. You know that Emma, like you and I, was left orphaned when her dad died, except we had Mom and who did she have? Rosemary, that cold-hearted bitch. So yeah, it was nice to see her, talk to her, get reacquainted. I offered her a letter of recommendation. I gave her your business card. She probably won't ever call you or ask you for work, but I'm the one that gave her the card so don't be surprised. And if you don't mind me saying so—I think you owe her."

"Oh, God, don't lay that on me! I begged her forgiveness for Jock, which she did not give me, and I can't even repeat the horrible names she called me. She didn't leave here a broken woman, she—"

"Girl," Adam said. "She was just a girl." Then more quietly he added, "And so were you. You were girls."

"Don't do this, Adam. Don't get involved with her.

I bear no grudge but after what happened, please don't bring her around. Please don't tell me I owe her. Not now. I know things turned out badly for her but try to remember that while I was scrubbing floors and trying to hold it together to raise a baby alone, she went from sorority princess to New York socialite, and never sent a word of forgiveness to me."

"Everything is past now," he said. "She's no longer a sorority princess or socialite and you're no longer scrubbing floors and struggling to take care of your baby."

She rubbed her temples with her fingertips and groaned. "It's over and I don't want it all coming back. Not now. Please, Adam."

"You can't erase the past any more than she can. But we can all live with it decently. If she calls you, you better do the right thing, Riley."

He was really deep down a kind person, and since he was just a boy had felt most comfortable when the whole family was together. He didn't like loose ends; he was a protector. He'd been like a father to Maddie since she was born. And there was no question, Riley would be lost without him.

"She will never call me," she said.

"Don't be too sure. It's really time to lay this thing between you to rest."

"I have no jobs but cleaning jobs. She'd have to get her hands dirty."

He laughed. "You don't think she got dirty in that New York life?" He was moving toward the door. "I'm just giving you warning."

When they were kids, people were used to seeing them together. They were known as Beauty and Brains.

They were both smart and pretty, but very different. Emma was a tall, slender brunette with rosy lips and eyes more commonly seen on a doe—large and dark. Riley was blonde, four inches shorter with a tight little body and crystalline blue eyes. Both were incredibly popular. And while they seemed inseparable, they spent time with other friends, as well. Emma was a cheerleader and participated in gymnastics; Riley was in choir, was a pom-pom girl and the star in the school musical—*Grease*. Emma was the homecoming queen and Riley, the valedictorian.

There was another difference between them that Riley was extremely conscious of—she was the poor one. Emma protested that her family was not rich and privileged, just that her father, being a CPA, was extremely good with money. Plus, his business certainly paid better than cleaning houses.

When they were in grade school at St. Pascal's, Riley knew she looked shabby. By the time she was in eighth grade, thanks to a lot of babysitting and clever shopping, she was pulling herself together quite well. But Emma grew up in a five-bedroom house on a half-acre lot while Riley lived in a small, old three-bedroom, one-bath house that held five people. She and her mother shared a room. If Riley wanted Emma to spend the night, which was quite often, Adam would take the couch and say, "Only if Mom sleeps in my room because you would get into my stuff!" His *stuff*, as Riley recalled, wasn't all that interesting.

Even that hadn't driven a wedge between them. But Riley was only ten when she said, "My family isn't always going to be poor, you wait and see."

In all the years Riley and Emma were best friends,

they had about three memorable fights. One was in seventh grade when Riley was invited to the first boy/girl party in their class and Emma was not. In fact, Emma was most deliberately excluded by some jealous girls. It was melodramatic and tragic and there were many tears. They were estranged for a long, painful month.

In their junior year Emma was asked to the prom by a senior and virtually abandoned Riley for the older crowd. She did her dress shopping with senior girls who were part of the new guy's clique. Riley was crushed and sat home on prom night playing Scrabble with her mother and brother. And Emma's prom night was a disaster—the guy got drunk and pressured her for sex, so she called her father for a ride home. At nine o'clock.

Both girls were miserable and sad. They sulked and avoided each other for a couple of weeks.

Then Emma's father was killed in a car accident—a drunk driver.

Of course Riley and her whole family went to Emma at once, embracing her, propping her up. The girls made up and swore they'd never let such differences divide them again. Emma was so sorry she put such stock in those prom friends, and Riley was devastated that she'd begrudged her best friend good times and was so sorry things went so badly. They bonded over Emma's grief. After all, Riley had lost her own father at an early age. She knew the pain of it too well.

Emma was left with that tight-ass evil grump, Rosemary, and her two nasty sisters whom she didn't feel were her sisters at all.

Then came college. Emma got a partial scholarship; her stepmother said she would be able to help a little. She bought new clothes and excitedly prepared for a whole new life. Riley and Emma parted tearfully and for the first two weeks called each other constantly, missing each other desperately. Then Emma settled in, became busy, got a part-time job. She had awesome roommates, was pledging a sorority, she was overwhelmed by her classes, loved the many social events and the surrounding rush. Also, Emma, being a vivacious young beauty, was getting hit on by the college guys. Even older college guys. She confessed to Riley that she was doing a little harmless hanging out with guys, a little innocent dating that she didn't want Jock to know about. Of course her secret was safe with Riley.

Getting acclimated to community college wasn't nearly as exciting. Riley found it to be very much like high school, except they didn't take attendance. Big whoop. It didn't take Riley long to begin to feel lonely.

As Emma settled into campus life, making new friends and experimenting with her newfound freedom, she wasn't in touch as much. She wasn't picking up when Riley or Jock called; she wasn't answering texts or returning calls right away and when she did, she didn't have much time. She was always rushing off somewhere or it sounded like there was a party in the background. All she wanted to talk about was herself and all her cool new experiences. A week, then two, then three went by with hardly any contact and what contact they had was brief—just long enough for Emma to relate all the fun things she was doing. By early October she'd already made plans to spend Thanksgiving with one of her new classmates and her family in Astoria, Oregon, rather than coming home to Santa Rosa. "I saw pictures of her house, Riley," Emma said excitedly. "I think they're incredibly rich!"

"We never talk at all anymore," Riley complained. "It's like you're too busy to be bothered with me."

"No, of course not! Well, maybe we're growing apart a little bit," Emma said. "On account of going to different colleges. But we'll always be best friends."

Riley, who used to talk to her best friend every day, several times a day, was lost. Jock, not one to go long without a girl, was calling and hanging around Riley a lot. He said it made perfect sense for them to be going out. "You can't tell me she's not," he said to Riley. "I'm not sitting home until Emma decides she has time for me."

Looking back, Riley remembered she'd felt deserted. Abandoned. Was it too much to expect her best friend to talk to her every couple of days? Twice a week? For more than three minutes? And maybe ask her about herself once in a while?

She and Jock were commiserating a lot. Jock was always around, calling her, taking her out for pizza, inviting her to join him for their high school's homecoming game and subsequent parties with old classmates. They were pals in their shared loneliness.

"Be careful of him," Adam had said to Riley. "He's been known to take advantage of girls."

"We're just friends," she said.

But Riley was growing very fond of Jock. She looked forward to every call, every casual date. They stopped commiserating so much and started laughing and having fun. They met friends at pizza parlors and on the beach. One crisp fall night they drove over to the coast and had a few beers by a beach fire, just the two of them. It was amazing how much they had to talk about—Emma's name never came up. Riley was astonished to find she was feeling far less abandoned.

She was falling for him.

"I think I might be way into you, too," he said. "Damn, I never saw this coming! I'm starting to think it probably should've been me and you from the start."

"We have to tell her, Jock. We have to tell Emma exactly how this happened. We couldn't get her on the phone for five minutes, we started hanging out, we got closer—at first because we were both missing her. But then because we have something. I don't know…chemistry?"

He laughed. "You think Emma cares? Go ahead—leave her a message. She'll get back to you in a week or two."

Then it went too far. Riley never meant for it to happen. At least not until she had thought it through much more carefully. Not until they came clean with Emma. She was telling herself it wasn't the worst thing in the world to spend so much time with Jock, to kiss and fondle and whisper in the dark of night, but then things got out of control and before she knew it, her shirt was pushed up, her jeans were around her knees and they'd gone all the way. Before they'd been honest with Emma.

"Oh, God, I wanted us to tell Emma before something like that happened."

"Baby, Emma could care less."

"But I think I'm falling in love with my best friend's boyfriend!"

"Whoa, whoa," he said. "Riley, let's just slow down here…"

"Aren't we in love?" she asked. "All those things you were saying, that you couldn't get through this without me and I'm the best thing that's happened to you and you probably should've hit on me first…"

"Hey, shoot me for being nice, huh? Of course I care about you—who said I didn't? That was totally up to you. You were totally into it. Just don't say anything, all right? You don't have to make an announcement, for God's sake. I won't tell her. I just don't know if I'd call it love. Yet."

"You have to break up with her. Tell her about us. You're the one who started things with me, not the other way around. Aren't you breaking up with her?" Riley asked.

"I don't think I'm going to have to," he said. "I think she broke up with me about three months ago. She's partying her ass off in Seattle."

"And there's no grass growing under your ass, now, is there?" she threw back at him.

Four weeks later, right before Emma came home for Christmas break, she told Jock she was pregnant. She'd taken the home test and it was positive.

"You sure it's mine?" he said. "I used a condom."

"I haven't been with anyone else," she informed him hotly.

"But I don't know that for sure, do I? Since I wasn't with you every minute. And like I said, I had protection."

"What am I supposed to do?"

"I don't know. I guess what anyone would do. You need a little money?"

She was so filled with shame, disappointment and rage she wanted to die, but she lifted her chin and said, "Go to hell, Jock."

But really, when it happened, she had thought she loved him. And she struggled with that feeling, on and off, for a few years after that.

* * *

Adam left Riley in her office and got in his car. He thought he'd drive by his mother's house and ask if there was anything she needed him to do, see what her plans were for the evening. He might tell her about Emma, but he hadn't decided yet. Those dozen or so times he had gotten in touch with Emma before she got married, when she was in college and then living in New York in the city, well, he never mentioned that to his family. Or to Lyle. And it seemed as though Emma hadn't talked about it, either. But maybe it hadn't left that much of an impression on her.

What's that about? Do you have a thing for her?

Oh, yeah. He had since she was about fifteen. That summer she'd gone from fourteen to fifteen—man, that was the pivotal summer in a young woman's life—and Emma had gone from the little sister to a woman of interest.

I see the way you're looking at Emma, his mother had said. *Do not touch that girl, do you hear me? She's like a daughter to me, like a sister to you and Riley and you're eighteen. She is off-limits. At least until you're both adults. This is non-negotiable. Her evil stepmother would love to throw you in jail!*

But not long after she passed her eighteenth birthday, she was gone to Seattle. Soon after that Riley was expecting Jock's baby. There was a significant part of Adam's heart that was very happy Jock was no longer Emma's guy, but he was smart enough to know that until Emma recovered from her broken heart, he'd better not step forward.

The next six years were a blur. Emma didn't return to Santa Rosa except for very brief visits and he didn't see her. He worked two jobs and went to school, his grandparents both died, he was helping his mother and Riley as much as he could. He grew very attached to Maddie, and Emma moved to New York. He always thought, one of these days…

While he was thinking that, she got married. And not to just anybody, but some internationally known millionaire.

All that had changed. And she was back.

Five

Emma didn't qualify for unemployment, as hers had been a part-time job. She did qualify for food stamps, which weren't called food stamps anymore. Although she had applied online, she had to invest four hours in the county welfare office, completed forms in hand. It was now a debit card that would come in the mail. Soon, they said—in about thirty days. If things went well. After her application was approved.

She judged herself against the great throng of people gathered in the county welfare office. She'd heard her husband rant about how many undeserving and entitled people took advantage of the welfare system, got all this free money without hardly trying. She felt like one of them and wondered if she deserved help. Probably not. She'd been married to him, after all. She also wondered where all that free money was and where those people who worked the system were. She'd always had visions of slick con men sauntering in and with the flick of a form, walking out with money or some other assistance. Most of the people in the office were women, more than half with small children hanging on their legs or sitting on their laps. At least half were Hispanic but as she'd read in the guidelines, they had to be documented to qualify. None looked like the type she expected. And no one looked at ease or comfortable about being there. As for Emma, she felt a little ill. Demoralized and ashamed, like further proof she'd done something wrong. But she looked better than anyone in the place. She still had some good clothes, expensive shoes and a couple of nice handbags, unlike everyone else there.

Her clothes didn't fit so well these days. It hadn't taken long for the extra pounds she'd gained from Burger Hell to fall off. Job searching, the stress of it and the sheer calisthenics of tromping all over hell and gone ate up a lot of calories. Not to mention the worry that she'd never be able to support herself again.

There seemed to be a lot of hair in her hairbrush these days. Was she losing her hair? She'd been grinding her teeth at night for a couple of years and she dreamed about losing her teeth. Awake, she worried about falling apart one batch of cells at a time.

She wondered what Rosemary, Anna and Lauren thought she was doing right now. How did they not have the slightest concern that she might be struggling? None of them reached out or asked her how she was getting by. When she'd been comfortable, before Richard's investigation began, they were always front and center, her *family.* They'd wrangled first class trips to New York on Richard's dime and just to save himself the annoyance of having them about, he'd put them up in a suite at the Plaza Athenee. It quickly became expected. Rosemary, the woman who couldn't even have been bothered to take her shopping when she was a girl, called and in her sweetest voice would say, "It's time for our annual trip to the city, dear. Will you book it for us?" And Emma had given them such generous, beautiful birthday and holiday gifts. They never even thanked her. They thought it was nothing to her. They probably thought one of her servants bought and shipped them.

The only jobs she seemed to qualify for were laborer's positions. Waitressing paid far less than minimum wage because of the tips, which waitstaff were obligated to report to the IRS. In the end she did better for herself by not mentioning her degree; she said she was educated through high school. Stealing a little bit from Riley, she said she'd cleaned houses for work and the only reference she had was Adam Kerrigan because she hadn't lived around here since high school.

So she took a job on the housekeeping staff of a hospital in Petaluma. After four days of training she began on the day shift, punching in at 7:00 a.m.

She made a decision, an easy one. She wasn't about to tell anyone her story. She'd like to at least pay her bills for a while. She kept it simple. She had been married to a man named Rick—no one had ever called Richard *Rick*—they didn't have children, he died of a brain injury. Hospital people took that to mean stroke or aneurysm, not a bullet. She never mentioned New York; she said they'd lived in Ohio. On the line that asked for her last address, she made up a completely fictitious address in Akron. She decided to come back to California where she grew up, where she had a few friends and some sparse family. It was a little dicey when people asked, in a friendly way, "Who are your friends? Who do you hang around with?" At which point Emma began to have secret, imaginary friends.

"Oh, my girlfriend Mary Ann who I went to school with and a cousin, Jennifer, who's married with two kids. Then there's Ruth, my favorite aunt who's only four years older—I'm close to them."

The women on the housekeeping staff she worked with were exceptionally friendly, reaching out to her, warning her about the supervisor who was a dragon lady named Glynnis Carlson. Glynnis was short, wore a forty-year-old hairstyle with one silver slash in front, came upon them like an unexpected storm and without even raising her voice threatened their very lives for having a cell phone out, for disposing of soiled linens wrong, for leaving streaks on the floor or porcelain, letting their carts get overladen or worse, understocked. And that was nothing compared to the way she berated people who weren't keeping up with their assigned area, which was very hard because nurses and aides were constantly summoning housekeeping. They didn't help with cleaning up beds or patients, of course, but anything that hit the floor was passed on to the housekeeping staff. There were a lot of messes that hospital staff didn't handle. The horrid ones.

"Be glad you're not in the ER or the operating room. Wear a mask and never work without gloves, just change them out," advised Barbara, one of the cleaning staff who had been around for years. "Wrap as much mess as possible in the linens, careful not to get any plastics or papers in them, get them down the chute fast as you can. Let it be laundry's problem. They transfer it all with big sticks and hooks."

There was a lot of that in a hospital. The doctors passed it off to the nurses, who passed it to the orderlies and aides, who passed it to housekeeping, who passed it to laundry.

It was hard, ugly work, but steady and among decent people. Emma had never been shy of hard work and she was growing confident and a little bit happy. She had work. She had just enough money and didn't require much to live on. Life in her tiny bungalow was compact and uncomplicated. Not only were her coworkers nice to her but the patients and their visitors were also pleasant, and under the direst of circumstances—illness. Cleaners weren't allowed to have traffic with patients—they weren't trained for that. But there was nothing preventing them from being cordial, going for an extra water jug for flowers, calling nurses when they saw a problem. "Just don't touch them," the dragon lady said. "Not even if one of them falls. Switch on the emergency light and stand by."

"Not even if they fall?" Emma asked, aghast.

"All you need is to help someone off the floor and break their neck or something. You'll lose your job and the hospital will get sued. You never move an accident victim. You let the professionals do that."

"Makes sense, when you put it that way," she said.

"Think of them all as accident victims," Glynnis said. "Just get their bathrooms clean."

But despite these terrifying warnings, Emma warmed to the patients, particularly the elderly. Little old people were so vulnerable when ill and she found she couldn't turn away. The old women loved her and the old men loved her more, and she just couldn't stop herself from offering the occasional sip of water to someone who was struggling with the tray table or a glass. It pleased her to hand a wet washcloth to someone who needed it. She even stayed late and read to an eighty-five-year-old blind woman, though she was careful to ask the dragon lady for permission first.

"I'm not allowed to help you to the lavatory," she told the woman. "I'm so sorry. But I'll get the nurse."

"I hate the nurse. I'd rather it be you."

"Oh, I'd be happy to, but the housekeeping staff has been threatened with dire consequences if we break the rules, even just slightly. I'm not trained in patient care. Let me get that nurse and I'll stay with you until she comes."

She started thinking about possibly training as a nurse's aide.

She had three very blissful weeks in her hospital job, though it was the hardest work she'd ever done. She didn't care; she went on break with coworkers, she ate lunch with her new friends, heard about their marriages, their kids, their aging parents, their car problems and vacation plans.

Emma began to have fantasies of a normal life. It wouldn't be a rich life for sure, but at this point a rich life only represented disaster and danger to her. She was looking for stability, nothing more. She had her food debit card, she handed out Halloween candy with Penny, the leaves finished turning, November came in wet and cold. She got together for wine with Lyle and Ethan, who was almost starting to believe she wasn't a bad person. She spoke to Adam on the phone a couple of times when he called to see how she was doing. She had a light dinner with Penny on TV trays, watching *Madam Secretary* with her, just like normal people. Penny invited her to join her with her girlfriends Susan, Marilyn and Dorothy for a potluck one evening and to her delighted surprise, these old girls liked martinis! Susan's son was the chauffeur for Susan, Marilyn and Dorothy. "I told him I was completely capable," Susan said. "But it's just as well he wants to drive us. That way we can have two!"

"William is such a nice boy," Penny said of Susan's son.

"That *boy* is fifty-nine years old," Susan said. "Before long I'll be chauffeuring him!"

At two weeks until Thanksgiving, Emma had more than one offer for the holiday feast. Lyle and Ethan were going to Ethan's sister's house and had graciously included her. She might've gone but for the fact that Penny and a couple of her widowed girlfriends who were sharing the feast also invited her—and they were to dine at Penny's little house. She dearly wanted to join them.

"Being one of the new kids at the hospital, I'm sure I'll have to work that day," Emma said.

"We took that into consideration," Penny told her. "We'll be ready at about four—that should give you time to get home, shower, come over for some pre-turkey poo-poos and wine."

"Let me pick up the wine," she said.

"You're absolutely welcome to."

"And I'll visit Lyle's shop and see if he'll give me a break on a centerpiece," she added.

"Try your best, darling, but be warned—he's going to gouge you! I've been looking for a discount for years. I guess I can't complain," she said with a smile. "He gave me you."

Emma was having a life. She had friendly acquaintances at work, a paycheck large enough to cover her most immediate expenses, friends apart from the hospital, two invitations for a holiday dinner, a comfortable place to live. It didn't even bother her that her own family hadn't so much as called to check on her much less ask her to join them for Thanksgiving dinner. In fact, she was relieved.

Just as she was beginning to relax, something weird happened. One of the older nurse's aides was glowering at Emma for no apparent reason. Clarice seemed angry about something. Angry or on edge. Some others seemed to be following suit. It appeared to be an unhappy day on the ward. There was a static in the air and Emma knew something was wrong. There had been a couple of emergencies; maybe that was setting everyone on edge.

The static turned to an electric crackle. Emma tried not to notice but she was beginning to feel paranoid by the behavior around her.

It didn't last long. It was two in the afternoon, about an hour until shift change. A patient had been discharged and the room was ready for a terminal cleaning. Emma got her cart, mop, linens, gloves and went to the room. Standing there beside the now empty bed in a room with no other patients was Clarice.

"How much do you have stashed away?" she asked, her voice hard.

"What?"

"You heard me. How much do you have stashed away? Enough to take care of my elderly mother? Because Hugh and I can't afford her and she has to live with us now since her entire savings was stolen."

"What are you talking about?" Emma asked, fearing she knew.

"I know who you are, Mrs. Compton. We all know

who you are. My mother's name is Roberta Sinclair and you took everything she had and I think you can find a way to get it back."

Oh, no! Even though she'd been over every possible scenario, now Emma didn't know what to say. She just shook her head. "There's nothing," she said. "I have nothing."

"You have assets in your name," Clarice insisted.

Emma shook her head again. "There's nothing in my name. Everything was in Richard's name and the few things that weren't, I surrendered. All our possessions were auctioned—I surrendered those, as well. Do you honestly think I'd be scrubbing floors in a hospital if I had anything?"

"For a while, yes," she said. "You'll lie low for a while, then when the talk has died off, you'll tap into your hidden money. I read the book!"

"The books are wrong! The internet is wrong! Everything is gone—my wedding ring, my wedding gown, wedding gifts—I gave it all back. I'm not lying low—I'm using my legal name. I haven't even colored my hair! I didn't know what was going on, Clarice. I had nothing to do with Richard's business."

"What about offshore money? One of the books says he was about to give the SEC account numbers when—"

"Gone. He was trying to negotiate a smaller sentence, but… There's nothing that I know of, nothing left to me, I swear."

"The book says you retained 1.4 million and a lot of valuable property…"

She was getting dizzy, shaking her head. "I kept a few thousand so I could drive back here and rent a small space. The US Marshals sold everything at auction. Everything. I kept some sheets and towels, a few dishes and pots. I gave most of my clothing to women's shelters. There's nothing. Do you think I want to be tied to that hideous crime? I was told that investors got roughly thirty-two cents on the dollar. I couldn't do anything more."

"You're lying," Clarice said. "You had lawyers! My mother didn't have a lawyer, she couldn't *afford* one! And she didn't get that much. She borrowed against her house to invest with Compton!"

That was not exactly how it worked, as Emma knew from the trial. Richard Compton worked with a number of financial managers and brokers who represented smaller investors, and it was they who invested in his company. Richard didn't talk anyone into mortgaging their house; he talked hedge fund managers into investing with him and he neither knew nor cared where they got their money. Large sums. Many collections of smaller investors. Richard was big-time. He had a minimum requirement, probably a hundred times the value of Mrs. Sinclair's mortgage.

"My lawyer was assigned by the court and he wanted me to keep enough to live on since finding work would be hard, but I didn't keep anything. I'm sorry," Emma said. "I'm so sorry. I would never have let something like that happen if there was anything I could do to prevent it."

"You're *lying*!"

Clarice picked up a bedpan that sat on the now vacant bed and hurled it at her. Emma blocked the missile with her forearms but that did little good. The damn thing was full. Since she knew the patient just discharged was ambulatory, Clarice must have looked high and low through the whole ward for just the right bedpan. Or more likely, she emptied catheter bags into one. The splatter threw Emma off balance. She stumbled backward, hit her tailbone on the pail on her way down and cracked her head on the metal door handle. She was covered in the filth.

When she tried to stand, the world was spinning and she ended up scooting across the floor, escaping out of the room into the hallway.

"Oh, my God," one of the other housekeepers said, running to her. "What happened? Are you hurt?"

Clarice walked out of the patient room and, lifting her chin in the air, walked past Emma. She went down the hall to the nursing station.

"Can you get up?" the other housekeeper asked.

"I don't know," she whispered. "Ugh. Oh, God, this is awful."

"How did this happen?"

"She threw a bedpan at me. Apparently she was swindled by… My late husband was guilty of… But I didn't know," she said, turning imploring eyes to her friend. "I swear I didn't. I would never. And he's dead now."

Two of the RNs on staff came running down the hall. One said, "Dear God." The other one said, "Clarice has lost her mind." They tried to get Emma on her feet but when she swayed and threatened to fall again, they went for a wheelchair and took her to the ER. She tried to briefly explain the problem, but it didn't come out well. She tried to tell them she'd been married to a bad man, a thief, but she didn't know it and it seems Clarice was one of his victims but Emma didn't know…

I should have done something, she thought. *I should*

have done something when I wondered why lawyers negotiated our prenup but Richard had hired both of them. I should have asked questions when this fabulously wealthy man wanted to marry me, but I didn't! I should have done something when the SEC started investigating him. I should have looked through his papers or found a way to hack his computer when I realized something was wrong, but I didn't know. I should have known. How could I not have known? I should have talked to the people who worked for him, the people who eventually testified against him. I should have found out how they were going to carry on—they got deals from the prosecutors. Everyone got deals—even his mistress!

When everything was so murky, so mysterious, I should have looked into it! Maybe I should have hired a detective or something. Maybe I should have run!

"Clean her up and get a head CT," the ER doctor ordered. "Listen, you might have a concussion, Emma. Can you get a ride home today and a ride back for your car tomorrow?"

"I don't know," she said, thinking *I'm covered in urine! Who wants to drive me home?*

"Well, you can think about that. We're going to get you some clean scrubs, stand you in the shower and wash you off—Mandy will go with you and make sure you don't faint or fall in the shower. And while you're having your CT, think about who you can call. If there's no one, someone from the hospital can either take you home or put you in a cab. You can't drive for twelve hours, at least. And Mrs. Carlson is waiting to see you, but let's get you cleaned up first."

Glynnis! Glynnis was going to fire her!

She was taken to a shower, her smelly uniform was put in a plastic bag and a set of scrubs provided. "I think your shoes are fine," Mandy said from right outside the curtain.

"My shoes are fine because it hit me in the head and got in my hair," Emma said with a hiccup of emotion.

"Just to be safe, throw the shoes in the washer when you get home. Or spray clean them with some disinfectant cleaner."

"You can wash those?"

"I do it all the time—they're just running shoes. Canvas and that little bit of leather."

If I'd been doing my own laundry and cleaning instead of hiring people to do it, I'd probably know that, she thought.

Emma was given a comb and had a little lip gloss in her purse. By the time the doctor looked at her head CT, her hair was almost dry and completely mangy-looking. Without some product, a brush and a blow dryer, she looked a wreck. It was a relief to be clean, but she wasn't feeling much better about the whole thing. They gave her a list of symptoms to watch for and she had a very large bump on the back of her head, but that didn't hurt nearly as much as her tailbone where she'd hit the metal bucket on the way down. She was given some ibuprofen.

The doctor was insistent that she not drive herself. Emma thought about just ignoring the instructions. Then her wiser self intervened and reminded her that all she needed was to pass out while driving and kill a family of four. She couldn't bear the thought of calling Lyle and having Ethan snigger to learn that her past was kicking up trouble. She didn't want to call Penny;

she didn't want her landlady having second thoughts about her decision to rent to her.

She texted Adam.

I fell and had a little accident at work and need a ride home from the hospital in Petaluma. Are you available? If not, I'll look around for someone who will give me a lift.

He responded immediately.

School's almost out so I'll come for you ASAP. It'll take about an hour to get there. Are you all right until then?

I'm okay. Text me from the parking lot and I'll come out. And thank you.

She went to Glynnis Carlson's office and sat outside her door, holding the plastic bag with her work clothes in it. It was a few minutes before the dragon lady opened her door and motioned Emma to come in. She indicated the chair in front of her desk. Then Glynnis folded her hands on top of her desk.

"Would you like to tell me what happened?"

"I'll try," Emma said. "My husband was Richard Compton. Do you know the name?"

Glynnis nodded. She explained that Clarice claimed her mother was a victim, but Emma had only met a few of Richard's clients socially; they were typically big investors or multimillionaires. She had seen a few in court and was surprised there was anyone from California, especially surprised to learn it was Clarice's mother, but the crime was Richard's. Not hers.

"You should have told me," Glynnis said.

"You wouldn't have hired me."

"I might've hired you and put you on the night shift. Well, spilled milk. Now, you have the prerogative of calling the police and filing assault charges. The nurse's aide who attacked you will be disciplined, possibly fired, but you can still—"

Emma shook her head. "It would be a mistake to draw attention to it. Plus, I do understand her anger, I really do. Thing is, I can't help her with this. I surrendered everything. I didn't want anything Richard had gotten by swindling people. There isn't anything."

"Why does she think there is?"

"There were a couple of books written about Richard's crime, lots of articles, news stories and internet posts speculating that I had some of his money hidden away. False, of course."

"Emma, you can't work with the public even though you've been exonerated of wrongdoing. Not for a long time. Do you understand that?"

"I'm trying to keep a low profile," she said.

"I'm applying for workers' compensation for you, Emma. I've taken you off the schedule. You should take two weeks and then my recommendation is that you resign and find something else. You'd do better in hotel housekeeping—less contact with the public."

"I'm not hurt that badly," she said. "I don't need two—"

"This isn't the place for you right now, Emma. You should take the time. You're entitled to it."

"But you're not going to fire me?" she asked.

"As far as I know you haven't done anything wrong. But I want you to think about whether this is the right job for you. I can put you on a different shift from the aide who beaned you with the bedpan, but I'm sure she has friends. Word will travel. Life could be difficult."

She almost laughed. "I might not have any choice…"

"While you're recovering, check out the hotels in the area. That's an option. You'd be working alone, not with a lot of other employees. You'd rarely come into contact with guests. Or…wait a second." She reached into her drawer and began to shuffle through business cards. "This woman has an excellent service—domestic, business, et cetera. But for God's sake, tell her the truth from the start. And if you need one, I'll write you a letter of recommendation. You've done a good job here in your brief employment."

Emma looked down at the card. Riley Kerrigan. Lord, she was everywhere. "Yes, ma'am," she said. The only advantage she could see was that she wouldn't have to explain her circumstances.

"Think things over. Call me with your decision, please."

"Yes, ma'am."

Emma went from Glynnis Carlson's office to the restroom. She took several deep breaths. Glynnis had been kind. Fair and kind. But Emma had to face facts; people would blame her. If they didn't blame her as a co-conspirator, they'd blame her for not taking action or for not testifying against Richard. They'd never believe she had nothing to say, nothing to add.

Keep your head, she told herself. *It's only been six months. This could go on awhile. You knew it wouldn't be easy, no matter where you went, no matter what you did.*

Then she put the bag holding her soiled work clothes in the trash can. She went to the locker room in the basement where they clocked in and grabbed her jacket. She wasn't going to wait around for Adam where other employees might pass her on their way to their cars. There was a nice little courtyard behind the emergency room. It was primarily there for those die-hard smokers left in the world, but no one was there at the moment. The sun was shining. It was a beautiful fall afternoon. She sat with her back to the door and talked to herself a little more.

It's only been six months. Some of his victims will be angry for the rest of their lives. Many will feel his death wasn't punishment enough. And there would always be those who believed she had some of that money, that she had a plan, that she was just waiting to emerge like a phoenix, rolling in dough, living the high life. *It's only been six months so don't cry.*

But silent tears streamed down her cheeks.

A few minutes had passed when she heard the door behind her open. She heard a little rustling, some footsteps, then a man walked past her. He was carrying a cellophane-wrapped bouquet, hanging down at his side. That was the rustling she'd heard—the cellophane. He walked all the way to the end of the courtyard then turned back toward her. He glanced at her briefly and sat on a bench several feet away and didn't meet her eyes. He was looking at his knees.

She gave her eyes a little wipe.

He looked up. "Bad day?" he asked.

She nodded. "You?"

"A little disappointing, but it'll all work out. What happened to you? You're a doctor?"

She shook her head. It was the scrubs, she realized.

"Ah. Nurse. I guess nurses can have all kinds of bad days."

She didn't respond because it wasn't required, except that she had this real problem with deception. No one would believe that, of course. She imagined almost everyone thought she was a liar.

Her cell phone chimed in her pocket. She took it out and saw Adam's text. "I have to go, my ride is here," she said. "I hope your day gets better."

He actually stood and she realized he was very handsome. Also tall and broad-shouldered. "I hope yours does, too. Here," he said, holding out the bouquet. "Take these. They'll go in the trash otherwise."

"Can't you take them home to your wife?"

"No wife."

"Your mother? Daughter? Sister?"

He smiled, improving his looks even more. "Nah. Here. Enjoy." She just stood there. "Come on, someone just did something nice for you. Take them."

She did. She said thank you. She went to Adam's SUV in the parking lot and climbed in the passenger seat.

He eyed the flowers. "Parting gifts?" he asked. And she burst into tears.

Six

Adam knew something was wrong. Something more than "I fell at work." He wasn't sure how he knew, but he knew. He stopped on the way to the hospital and picked up a couple of large mocha coffees with heavy cream. When he asked Emma what had happened, there was a lot of incoherent blubbering and he decided it was probably best to drive rather than sit in the parking lot while she emoted. And emoted.

He picked up a few things—someone had identified her, recognized her, threw a ripe bedpan at her head. There was a lot of whimpering about how she hadn't known, hadn't been complicit, everyone thought her a gold digger, a liar. She ended with some incoherent bawling about the disgusting state of her hair, comments that caused his eyes to widen in shock. What did this have to do with hair?

He found a nice park and pulled into the lot in the shade of a colorful tree. He handed her some tissues and after she'd made use of them, gave her the coffee. And the world slowed down and she began to just talk about it.

Adam had a feeling he was going to hell for this, but he wanted her to get this issue resolved, in her mind, at least emotionally, because he just couldn't pursue her the way he'd like to until that happened. She just wasn't ready. She wasn't moving on yet. Everything was so unsettled for her. And that had more to do with what Emma thought of *herself* than the people who might think badly of her.

"Thank God I ran into you at the burger joint," she said tearfully. "Just take me home, please, Adam. I didn't mean to unload on you."

"Nah, we're not going home yet. You're going to have some coffee, calm down and we'll just talk awhile."

"I'm sure you don't need all this chaos clogging up your mind…"

"My mind is fine," he said. "I'm a little worried about yours. It seems like maybe you're still feeling confused, out of control. Vulnerable. Victimized."

"Wouldn't you?" she returned defensively.

"Probably. But I want you to think about something, Emmie. Lack of power comes from lack of knowledge. Unless I'm totally off base here, you're still completely confused about what happened to you, how it happened, what to do about it now."

"I don't know what you're getting at," she said.

"Have you seen a counselor?" he asked.

"What kind of counselor?" she asked.

"Okay, I'm just guessing here, but I think you're still in shock. Maybe you have a little PTSD because you're not advancing beyond the shock."

He actually smiled slightly when he noticed she was looking at him with wide, startled eyes.

"PTSD isn't limited to war veterans, Emmie. Anyone

who's been through a trauma qualifies. With a war veteran it might be a car backfiring that sends them into a series of PTSD symptoms—anger, sleeplessness, fear, panic, phobia, so on. For the victim of emotional abuse it might be facial expressions, certain comments, another's rage or threat. You should check this out, see a counselor."

"Listen," she said earnestly, scooting forward in her seat and turning in his direction. "I don't have the money for a counselor and I have health insurance for emergencies, but no one, I mean *no one*, is ever going to offer me discounted therapy because I suffered through kissing goodbye to millions of dollars after living like a queen for years."

"Victim," he said. "You are a victim. And you were probably a victim then, not a queen. You need some help. I'll check around. I might find someone, you never know. I know everyone—I've been teaching half their kids for fifteen years. But while I look, you might want to do some reading. From what you say, you still have so much mystery about what happened to you, you can't even figure out how you ended up in this mental-emotional minefield and there must be some kind of explanation. If there's not a clear explanation, there might be enough information out there to help you draw some conclusions. Hit the library. Read those books written by other people who think they've drawn conclusions. Find out who *they* think you are. And who they think your husband was."

She was shaking her head. "You have no idea what you're suggesting, how painful that is. Just the little excerpts are horrible."

"I know."

"You know? How do you know?"

"I read about it all," he said with a shrug. "Lots of theories about your late husband. About you. Varying theories."

"Why?" she asked softly. "Why would you read that trash?"

"Emmie, I'm a science teacher. We investigate. We look shit up." Then he gave her a wan smile. "I'm just suggesting, since you can't escape it, maybe it makes sense to face it."

"I thought I'd been facing it for the last several years," she said. "I was in the apartment when Richard blew his brains out, after all. I had to hide from angry plaintiffs. I had to watch the house stripped of personal possessions. I—"

"You wanted it behind you, and who could blame you. Now that the whole fiasco is part of your identity and you have to live with it, would it help to understand it better? Like, what kind of man was he, really? Because you don't actually know, do you? You've said that had you known, you would have run for your life. So what do you know about sociopaths? Because that's my guess. He was a sociopath."

"What do *you* know about sociopaths?" she asked.

He shook his head. "Just a little bit, but I admit to being fascinated. I think when they were passing out consciences they missed a few people but they gave the surplus to me—my conscience seems to work overtime." He reached for her hand. "If you understood, at least as much as possible, could you be at peace?"

"I don't know."

"Find out," he suggested. "I'll help if I can. I love

research. And I love talking to you. But first things first. You need a few days of rest and ice on your head."

"And my butt," she added.

"Did they x-ray that part?"

"No. They said if it remains painful to come back in, but it's already better from just a couple of Advil."

"Then let's keep moving forward. It's time to call Riley and see if you can get a job. It doesn't have to be a long-term job. But you have to have something..."

"Oh, Adam..."

"She'll protect you, Emmie. She knows how hard it is to start over, to rebuild your life after you've hit bottom."

"I can't believe she'd actually help me," she said.

"Sure she would. In fact, if she doesn't that would mean I don't know my sister at all. And that's not possible."

"Does she know we've been in touch lately?" Emma asked.

"She knows I ran into you at the burger joint. She knows we had a glass of wine and I gave you her business card. That's all she knows. In fact, I never mentioned we'd talked after you and Jock broke up, after Maddie was born..."

"It was more than a few times," Emma said. "And why didn't you tell her?"

He took a moment. "I didn't call you all those years ago for Riley and if I'd told her we talked, she would have asked a lot of questions about how you felt about her, how you felt about your situation, your feud, for lack of a better word. It would've been all about her and her relationship with you. That's not why I called you.

You were around my house for years, all your growing-up years. I called you for *me*."

"Oh, Adam," she said softly.

"And same goes for you. Every time I called, it didn't take long to get around to Riley. Riley and Jock. Riley and you. Even after years had passed. I'll say one thing for you and Riley—you have some amazing stamina, keeping that tired old feud alive this long. It's still got some energy—you got tears in your eyes when I introduced you to Maddie."

"No," she said, shaking her head. "I mean, yes, that's true, I almost cried. Can you keep a confidence? What am I asking, of course you can. You haven't even told Riley how much we've talked since I've been back. It wasn't because Maddie should've been my child. Not at all, even though anything would have been preferable to where I landed in the end. Lord, what would I have done, pregnant with only Rosemary to lean on? No, it was because on top of everything else I went through with my husband, my marriage, it turns out I'm also infertile."

Well damn, Adam thought. It was his turn to be shocked speechless.

Three days later Emma was introduced to Lucinda Lopez, family, marriage and individual counselor. "It's the first time Adam has ever asked a favor of me," she said. "He was my first friend in teaching, a great teacher. I was not such a great teacher but I think I'm a good counselor."

"You didn't like teaching?" Emma asked.

"It paid the bills and I did an adequate job. I know I did all that was required of me. But there are some teachers, like Adam, who instinctively know how to inspire. He might've grown some real scientists. So—he tells me you're on a very limited income but in need of counseling. I haven't read your intake form yet—does that describe you?"

"I'm on workers' comp right now and looking for a new job because… Well, that job isn't going to work out. And the reason for that is the same as the reason I need counseling."

"All right, we'll get right to it. But before we take a lot of time on the story, tell me what you can afford. It's very important that you pay something for your counseling, that you make it in some way a priority. At any time you might decide it's not working for you, and that's entirely up to you, but please understand—if it's free, you won't value it. Make an effort, please, not for me—I'm not in need. For you. Your results will be better if you stretch yourself. If you commit."

"I don't know. I don't know how often I'll be seeing you. Can you help me with it?"

"The cost of the session? Sure. I provide a sliding scale based on income. Here's the graph," she said.

Emma looked at it. She was taken aback by the numbers there, which ranged from thirty-five dollars for a one-hour session to one hundred twenty-five. Presumably, she'd try to meet with the counselor at least twice a month. Even seventy dollars cut deeply into a budget as tight as hers.

"We better get right to it," Emma said.

"I'm ready whenever you are," she said.

Emma launched into her story, the condensed version. That took fifteen minutes, interrupted by a few questions from Lucinda, merely for clarification. It took only that long for Lucinda's face to begin to seem soft and accessible to Emma. She was a very pretty Mexican woman with just the slightest threading of silver in her pitch-black hair, the deepest black eyes, the softest smile. Her voice was likewise soft, but very confident and gracious.

When Emma had brought Lucinda up to the present, the counselor said she'd like to go back in time a bit, to before Emma met her husband.

"How far back?" Emma asked.

"I'm flexible," Lucinda said. "Take me back to a time that seemed pivotal in your life. A time of change, maybe? A time that required a great deal of you? A period of adjustment and a shift in your priorities. Does anything stand out?"

She thought for a moment. Then she said, "The year after high school. When I went away to college. A year after my father died."

"Good. Try, if you can, to tell me not just the events that you think caused a major change in your life, but how those significant events made you feel then and how remembering them makes you feel now."

"We may run out of time," Emma said.

"And try, if you can, not to worry about the time. We don't have to do it all today. In fact, a great deal is achieved in counseling when you leave me with things you'd like to think about. Because, Emma, I'm not going to solve your problems. You are. I'm just here to direct the traffic."

When Emma left, she hugged Lucinda. "Do you think I'm completely crazy?" she asked.

"I think you're remarkable. I'm so glad we met. Be sure to thank Adam for me."

* * *

Emma called several hotel chains to ask about job availability and each one invited her to fill out an application and possibly be called back for an interview. No one she talked to seemed interested in hiring. She looked in all the newspaper ads and online for employment opportunities, as she had been doing since the day she returned, and nothing promising turned up there, either.

She tried to bolster herself to call Riley and ask for help.

Sometimes words fade over time, sometimes they fester, blister, even swell. Burned into Emma's mind was when she screamed at Riley, "I don't ever want to speak to you or see you again in my life!"

"We can find a way to get beyond this! We said we'd never let a guy get between us!"

"Yeah, until he was *my* guy! Well, he's all yours now! I wouldn't take him back if he begged me. Not with your stink on him!"

"You'll be sorry you let this ruin us! You know you'll never have a friend like me again in your life!"

"I hope to God *not*!" Emma had hurled.

And now she was going to ask Riley for a job.

"I'm so sorry," the receptionist said. "We don't have any openings right now. But if you'd like to leave a name and number, I can call you as soon as something opens up."

"Sure," she said. "I'm Emma Shay and..."

"Oh, Ms. Shay, I reserved an appointment for you. Can you come into the office to meet with Ms. Kerrigan Thursday afternoon at two?"

"Um. Sure," she said. Was that a good sign? Adam

had said Riley would help her, but what if he was wrong about that?

Sixteen years ago, right after screaming she hoped she'd never have a friend like Riley again, Riley had screamed at her, "Emmie, *please*! Please try to understand! I didn't mean for this to happen and I'm sorry. I can't lose your friendship!"

With a sneer, Emma shot back, "So get Jock to be your friend. Slut!"

Of course, Emma hadn't known Riley was pregnant but would knowing that have softened her words? Nah. It probably would have made her even more hateful. Emma didn't think she'd ever forgive Riley for what she'd done. But if she were Riley, she would never be able to forget those cruel words.

Why would Riley help her now?

She wore the same conservative but stylish skirt and sweater she'd been wearing to every interview. They were Chanel, brown wool with a little pleat in the front of the skirt right on her knee and a soft mauve sweater set. She wore hose and pumps, carried a matching Dooney & Bourke bag. Would she think Emma had obviously survived quite well, dressed so? The Riley she had known had never had such nice clothes.

Walking into Riley's office was one of the hardest things she'd ever done. She reminded herself that she'd walked down the steps of the Federal Court Building to the flashing of cameras; she'd walked from a grave site to her car through a clot of photographers. She opened the outer office door and the secretary looked up. She smiled at the young woman. "Hello. I'm Emma Shay and I have an appointment with Ms. Kerrigan."

"You can go on in," Jeanette said. "She's expecting you."

Emma gave a couple of courtesy taps and opened the door. Riley was concentrating on her computer screen. Without looking up she said, "Come in. Sit down. Give me a second."

Emma sat in one of the chairs facing the desk. She held her purse on her lap and crossed her legs at the ankle, her legs angled to her right. When Riley did look at her, her eyes rested for a long time on the purse.

Riley turned the screen away, folded her hands on the desk and focused on Emma. "Hello, Emma. How are you?" Riley asked.

"I'm all right, thanks. You?"

"Very well, thanks. Am I to understand you're looking for a job?"

"Yes."

"You do understand this is a cleaning company? Housekeeping?"

"Yes. I can provide a letter of recommendation. My last supervisor offered. She's the head of housekeeping at the hospital in Petaluma—Mrs. Carlson."

Riley's eyes grew round. "That carries some weight around here. I've known Glynnis for years. Why are you leaving the hospital?"

Emma was surprised then realized she shouldn't have been. Adam was very tight-lipped. "I had a fall. Actually, an angry person who claimed to be a victim of Richard's fraud threw something at me and I fell. I'm not hurt. I was checked in the emergency room. But Mrs. Carlson took me off the schedule, put me on workers' comp and suggested I get another job."

Riley was frowning.

"If you don't want to take a chance on that happening while I work for you—"

"That won't happen in my company. I know which of my customers know each other, so I know where gossip travels. We have a policy that our crews, while polite and helpful, do not become enmeshed with the client—that's how they get taken advantage of. Our crews take only first names into the jobs, and the majority of the time the client isn't home and if they are, they stay out of the way. There should be no reason for much conversation that isn't germane to the work. We have a pretty strict contract so that additional work is arranged with the company in advance and an hourly charge is made. But what's easy about this system is—everything goes through me or my director of operations, Nick. That way you're never put upon to argue with the homeowner or business owner. You're going to have to be trained. Can you make it till the Monday after Thanksgiving? Because I don't have training on my schedule until then."

"I can start anytime. I went through a rigorous training at the hospital."

"You'll be trained again," she said firmly. "The last time I skipped training because the housekeeper was qualified I ended up buying a new microwave because she took steel wool to it. Besides, the culture of the company is as important as the policies and I want you to understand."

"Maybe I should clean offices…" Emma suggested.

"I don't have any openings in offices. Those are night jobs and they're pretty precious—a lot of my staff prefer them. They pay a little more and many of them have two jobs and children to take care of. All I have is residential. It's very hard work."

"I know how to work hard," Emma said.

"I'm going to put you with Makenna Rice for training. She's young, tough, not particularly personable, has impeccable standards, can handle anything that comes along and will work you hard. But at the end of the day you will be proud of the job you did."

"Thank you."

"Fourteen dollars an hour to start. If you're still around after ninety days, you'll get a two-dollar raise. I provide training, uniforms, sometimes transportation—I have a few company cars and vans—and health insurance. Not the greatest health insurance, but competitive with most corporate plans. You won't need it but I have a deal for a discount with a day care provider—a lot of my workers have small children not yet in school. Any chance you speak Spanish?"

Emma shook her head. "Some very rusty French."

"A shame. A lot of my workers are Mexican, here with work visas. But don't worry—I have plenty of bilingual workers and my director of operations speaks Spanish." She looked at her squarely. "You won't get any special treatment. Are you sure you want to do this?"

"Yes, I'm sure. I'm very grateful."

"I'll give you a job," Riley said. "But that's all."

"I don't expect anything," Emma said. "I didn't even expect this much. Really."

"Jeanette will get you started on the paperwork. It should only take twenty minutes. Then I'll next see you the Monday after Thanksgiving, this office, seven a.m. Bring a tote or backpack that holds your lunch, water or energy drink, snacks. Jeanette will tell you where to go to get your uniform. I'll pay for one per year."

"Thank you," Emma said again.

Riley stood. "Come into the conference room to fill out your application and accompanying paperwork."

"Riley, I didn't do it," she suddenly said. She shook her head. "I had nothing to do with Richard's fraud. I was too stupid to know what he was up to, but I wasn't involved."

"Of course you weren't. Anyone with a brain knows he started building his Ponzi empire ten years before he met you. Come with me." She opened the door on the right wall of her office, exposing a shiny table and eight chairs. "Have a seat. I'll get Jeanette."

Emma sat down and waited. The interview wasn't exactly comfortable but it wasn't as bad as it could've been. It must have given Riley great pleasure to have Emma crawling back, begging for work. A lot of people who didn't even know her would feel the same way—the uppity young trophy wife, paying the piper every day. Every hour. Every minute.

Riley's clothes weren't baggy and worn anymore, she thought. In fact, she looked wonderful. She was obviously buying her clothes in San Francisco. That was a Marco de Vincenzo suit, a little young and short for Riley, but she wore it well. If Emma was a betting woman she'd think Riley pulled that one out of the plastic just for her.

She finished filling out her forms and went back into Riley's office, knocking before opening the door. Riley was on the phone but gestured her in, pointing to the chair. While she waited, Jeanette peeked in. She was wearing her coat and had her purse strap over her shoulder, obviously leaving. She gave Riley a wave and Riley waved back.

Now it was just the two of them.

Riley finished her phone call and focused on Emma. "Any questions?"

"Not that I can think of. Thank you again."

"Not at all," Riley said in a businesslike manner. "See you on your start date. On time."

"Absolutely." She rose to go.

Emma was almost out the door.

"Emma?"

She turned back.

"Now we're even," Riley said without looking at her. "I have no more debt to pay to you."

Emma was stunned and frozen, speechless for a moment. She finally found her voice. "Do you think I'm keeping score? You didn't have to do this. You didn't have to hire me just because of something… We were *children*!"

"We're not anymore," Riley said. "We're not going to be friends but this thing between us… I'm done with it. But stay away from my brother."

And she was completely refocused on her computer screen.

Emma slowly closed the door behind her. But then she opened it again. "Wait a minute," she said. "Are you angry with *me*? Because I said some awful things to you and I regret it, but I think you have to bear responsibility for what you did."

"It's over," Riley said.

"Obviously not!" Emma shot back, rather more hotly than she intended.

"It was all regrettable," Riley said. "And I'm sure there's plenty of blame to go around."

"It might be helpful if I knew exactly what blame I'm expected to carry," Emma said.

"I'd rather it be over," Riley said, standing to face Emma. "Let's call it done."

"Oh, no, you don't—you started this up again. Riley, I didn't sleep with your boyfriend behind your back! What is your grudge? Because of those terrible things I said to you out of anger? If that's it—"

"That's not it," she insisted loudly. "I guess you were entitled. I understood why you'd be furious."

"Then what?"

"You wouldn't forgive me!" she said. Riley's eyes glistened and she held her lips in a tight line.

Emma was struck silent. She said the only thing that came to mind. "I was too hurt. Too angry."

"Over Jock?" Riley demanded. She gave a short laugh. "You hadn't even returned our calls in weeks! It's so hard to believe your broken heart was serious enough to sustain such a grudge. We were best friends for ten years!"

She shook her head. "I got over Jock in a few months. I let it go so long ago," Emma said.

"And it never once occurred to you to send a note or even a text saying let bygones be bygones?"

"Riley, I… No, it never did. I figured we were best parting ways. That was one helluva fight."

"Yes," Riley said softly. "And I begged. I groveled. I sent a dozen notes, left messages. You wouldn't respond. You wouldn't even hear my side of the story. And you lifted your nose in the air and walked away to a better life, better friends."

Emma shook her head. "Not for long," she said. "Is that really what's up your butt? That I didn't say you're forgiven? Didn't listen to your story? Want to tell me now?"

"Hah! Now I don't even want to think about it, but it sure as hell had staying power!"

Emma laughed hollowly. "We should've both been furious with Jock, not each other!"

"I was. I still am some days, but he's Maddie's father and I'm stuck with him. You, I'm not stuck with."

"No, you're not. I don't need your charity. Well, I do, but I wouldn't take it if I were starving. But are you still giving me a job?" Emma asked.

"Yes, and by God you better not fuck up. I built this company and it means a lot to me. You mess up and I'll fire you in a New York minute."

"I'll do my job," she said, turning to go. She turned back. "Really, I might not have said anything, I was a little busy, but I forgave you a long time ago."

"And until I saw you, I didn't think it still mattered. I thought I'd learned never to let down my guard."

"What's this about your brother? What did you mean by that?"

Riley took a breath. "I'm happy to give you a job as long as you pull your weight and earn your paycheck. But I don't think it makes any sense for us to try friendship again. Obviously irreparable damage was done. That being said, I don't need to run into you at family gatherings."

"I see. I guess it could be problematic."

"Just don't put me in an awkward position with my family."

"Of course," Emma said. "We didn't exactly kiss and make up, but can we lay this to rest now? Start over as employee and employer?"

"Absolutely. Starting a week from Monday. Seven a.m."

Emma exited, softly closing the door behind her. But glutton for punishment that she was, she opened the door again. "You should probably thank me," she said. "If you hadn't been so pissed off at me and scared to death, you probably never would have built such a successful company."

"Don't hang your hat on that idea," Riley said. "I had a good start on it before Jock messed up my plans."

And that actually made Emma smile at her. "You were so much better off without me. Who knows? If we'd remained friends, I might've convinced you to let Richard help you invest your money."

Then she closed the door and left.

Riley sat at her desk for a long time, just still and quiet. The phone rang twice, she glanced at the caller ID that appeared on her computer monitor and let it go to voice mail.

Well, that was dirty, she thought to herself. It took them about ten minutes to be thrown back in time and fight like a couple of junkyard dogs, just like they had when they were thirteen. Only when they were teenagers their fights would be high and hot and over in ten minutes. That wasn't going to happen this time.

Well, that had only been about ten minutes. And it felt remarkably over. In fact, she felt a little tired, like coming down off a good run. She folded her arms on her desk and put her head down. That was the hardest thing she'd ever done, and she'd done some hard things. It wasn't fighting with Emma or giving her a job that was so difficult. It was seeing her, talking to her, taking her in, reconnecting with her, all the while knowing it could end up hurting her again.

Their history was so convoluted, so complex. From treasured childhood friends to bitter enemies, through a maze of anger, guilt, envy, pity. For the longest time Riley only wanted Emma to forgive her or at least join her in blaming Jock. She went through periods of terrible emotional pain and sadness. Then periods of such anger—if Emma loved Jock so much, why hadn't she even returned his calls in weeks? And when she saw a picture of Emma in her designer wedding gown in a carriage in Central Park, as beautiful and regal as any duchess while Riley was getting by scrubbing floors and balancing the books late at night, she wondered how Emma could still be mad that things didn't work out with Jock. Emma seemed to always land on her feet.

Then she witnessed, from afar, Emma's monumental fall. And it ripped her to shreds. But she didn't reach out. No, she had too much pride for that. Emma hadn't reached out when Riley was struggling and feeling so alone.

I was hurt at least as much! Can't she see that? That it was all so hard?

They had always been there for each other, until that first semester of college. *You didn't have to be so mean*, she said to herself. But Riley wanted to be clear—this was her company, her business; it was a job, not an invitation to reconcile or renew the friendship. She would never beg again.

But at long last, she'd gotten it out. She said her piece. She saw Emma's surprise and remorse painted on her face. Emma said she was sorry and that she'd forgiven Riley long ago—it was done. It was really done. Neither of them would go back but maybe now they could really move forward.

Riley shut everything down, switched the phones to forward to her cell, grabbed her purse and headed for the parking lot.

Seven

Riley went to Starbucks, a place that saw her at least once a day.

She rarely sat around inside. She was usually in and out and on her way—always so much to do. There were those who camped in Starbucks for hours, doing their emails or writing something or studying. People who didn't have to be somewhere every minute. Not Riley. She never relaxed.

She bought a newspaper on her way inside. She had a lot to process, something she could do while hiding behind a newspaper, the great barrier.

It was such a cold November day—a hot coffee with heavy cream sounded good. And there was a nice little table by the window that looked out on the patio that Starbucks shared with the deli. She smiled at a couple of people she didn't know but saw in there a lot. Then she settled behind the paper.

Women, she thought. Difficult, complex, emotional creatures. She should know. Not only was she difficult and complex, she also had far more women employees than men. She had those teams of three or four females who found issues they couldn't get beyond just because of something that was said or a look they didn't like or maybe a little power struggle. She had to mediate all the time. Or Nick did. Nick was only good at getting results because he didn't get what was going on with the women so he just scared them. "Can you work this out? Or do I separate the whole unit and scatter you around on different crews? Because you might not like your new crewmates any better. If you can't get along, then do your job and don't talk to each other, but you'd damn well better communicate on job issues. Are we all clear?"

She smiled thinking about that. A typical father-to-little-girls approach. He might as well say, "Since I can't understand what you're all upset about, just stop it."

Nick took problems getting the job done properly a lot more seriously than he regarded bickering. But women, ah, they could dig in. Grudges between women could last centuries. And they were very personal—a woman who wasn't usually annoyed could be deeply offended by an offhand remark about the choices of her teenager. "If you'd tell that lazy kid of yours he's not getting free rent anymore, I bet he'd get off his ass and get a job or go to school." *Pow.* Instant feud.

Sexist as it was, this sort of thing happened less often with men. Oh, they had their fights and their feuds, no question about it, and were even less likely to have dialogue that worked it out. They might blow up but they were less prickly and it was rare for them to obsess.

Riley, tough and smart and successful, had obsessed about Emma for years. She felt wedged between two extremes—being furious with Emma and feeling guilty over what she'd done. She'd tried so hard to make up with Emma, to beg her forgiveness! And Emma turned her back. Now, when Emma was down and out, Riley was supposed to be the benevolent one? Looking at both of their lives, from that point till now, things had just been…awry. Off. Emma had hooked up with a bad man and Riley? No man. At. All.

"Excuse me," a male voice said. "Is this chair taken?"

What perfect timing, she thought. A man. She lowered her newspaper, trying to think how she would politely say she didn't want to share the table or have a conversation.

"Hey," he said, smiling handsomely. "It's you."

"I…ah…"

He put out a hand and didn't let her finish. "Logan. Logan Danner. We've never officially met, but we've run into each other at the grocery store at least five times, which means you either live or work around here."

Don't do it, she told herself. She took his hand. "Riley. I, ah… I work not too far from here and am addicted to coffee that costs seven dollars a cup. Bad habit."

He laughed and sat down. "I guess it could be worse. We could run into each other at a crack house… Now, that would be bad."

"Look…"

"Oh, I'm sorry," he said. "You weren't looking for company, my mistake. I'll just make this a to-go cup and catch you someday at the deli counter…"

"No, I'm sorry," she said with a heavy sigh. "I was just trying to shake off a problem I had at work. Go ahead. Take the chair. But I might not be very conversational."

He didn't hesitate. "I'm a good listener, if you feel like talking."

"No, thanks. Let's stick to the price of melons."

"I'm also a good talker, if you'd rather not. Or we can pass the time as if we're alone." He reached down and pulled a small laptop out of a canvas shoulder bag. He put it on the table and opened it up. He turned it on. He sipped his coffee. He peeked at her around the screen.

She laughed lightly. "You're being very obvious."

He gazed over the screen. "In what way?"

"Are you trying to get my attention? Interest me?"

"I am," he said. "How'm I doing?"

"You're actually terrible at it," she said, laughter in her voice. "You verge on annoying. More to the point, we keep running into each other. Are you stalking me?"

"That would be rude," he said. "Not to mention a felony. Well, it becomes a felony if it's threatening, but it's a misdemeanor when it's just rude."

"And you know these things how?"

"I'm a police detective."

She started to laugh. "Oh, man, the only pickup line that works better than that is being a Navy SEAL."

He shifted his weight around and pulled out his wallet. He flipped it open. Sure enough, badge and ID. "Hold on, there," she said. She reached into her purse and pulled out her phone, poising over the open wallet to snap a picture.

He put his hand over hers, redirecting the phone lens. "Does this mean you're going to find out if I'm real before you go out with me?"

She shrugged. "I might find out if you're real before I give you advice on melons again or warn you off the macaroni salad in the deli. A date has never occurred to me. Or interested me."

He let go of the phone, allowing her to take the picture. "You're brutal. Knock yourself out."

She snapped the picture. "What kind of detective are you?" she asked.

"Property crimes."

"And that is?"

"Be careful about making friendly conversation, Riley. You might be acting less like a meanie and more like a girl. Property crimes, burglary. Someone stole your computer and your diamond ring and I'm going to get them back for you. They did not rob you—robbery is when there's a weapon involved."

"A deadly weapon?" she asked, intrigued.

He raised one brow. "Any weapon could be deadly. A spoon could be deadly if you know how to use it. Property crimes is property stolen from private property—your house, your business, your car, your person, without the spoon, of course." He grinned stupidly.

"And why do I keep running into you?"

"This little shopping center is between work and my house. And I'm in the field a lot. But running into you all the time is one of the perks. So—what do you think? Dinner? Hike? Bike ride? Conventional date?"

"Coffee," she said. "We're having coffee. I don't date."

"I didn't see a ring..."

She shook her head. "Not married, just not dating."

"You have to have a reason," he informed her.

"No," she said. "I don't."

"Do you mind if I ask—what do you do?"

"I do mind, but I'll tell you, but only because I think

you really are a policeman. I own a small business. Plus, I'm a single mother and have an elderly mother. So you see, very busy."

He closed the computer and leaned an elbow on it. "Look, I admit I've been hanging out at the grocery store a lot since you advised me on produce. Can't this be any easier? I'm overstocked in melons. What do you like to do besides work? Maybe we could go for a run? Play catch in the park? Meet for coffee a lot?"

"Why?" she asked.

He tilted his head. "I'm attracted to you?"

"Was that a question?" she asked.

"I haven't been out with a woman in a while. Well, haven't had a date with a woman. My partner is a woman, married to a great big firefighter, three little kids. My sister and ex-wife are best friends and believe me, their attempts at fixing me up are miserable…"

"Oh, God, that must be interesting! Your sister and your ex-wife?"

"It's awful. But see, I'm interesting," he said, triumphant. He looked around. "Would you like something to eat? Doughnut?"

She laughed at him because he was so ridiculous. Also, undeniably cute. "So it's true—cops and doughnuts."

"I was thinking of you. I've had my quota today. Come on, Riley. Let's just plan something. It can be public, daylight, completely safe and platonic. I'll show you my gun," he said, lifting his eyebrows, Groucho Marx style.

She laughed again. "No," she said. She stood up. "See you in produce," she said, walking out.

It took him a moment to get his computer put away in

his canvas bag and grab his coffee, following her. "Hang on," he yelled. He caught up with her and handed her a business card. "This will make your mission easier."

She looked at it. *Sgt. Logan Danner, Santa Rosa Police, Property Crimes.* Along with a phone number and extension.

"Would you like my cell number?" he asked.

"No."

"It's on the card anyway. Come on, Riley. I bet we'd have fun."

She turned before getting in her car. "No. And if you follow me, I'll call your boss. I'll tell on you."

"Hey, no worries. My boss likes me," he said.

Riley headed for home. But she smiled the whole way. He was handsome in a very hot way and adorably funny. He was tempting.

Whoa, Riley, she thought. *Really? Tempting? Now that's a first.* It wasn't as if she hadn't been flirted with or asked out on a date before. She'd actually been out a few times—nothing to write home about. Definitely no relationship stuff. It wasn't frequent since she hung out at work, at home, with Maddie and her mom, shopping for food and clothes, taking the occasional run…

Did he know about the running? Oh, if he'd been watching her, she was going to turn him in to his boss *and* tell Adam. Adam was *very* protective.

But for the first time in many, many years, she was feeling like maybe a casual friendship with a man might interest her. She wondered if seeing Emma and having that first confrontation behind her had anything to do with her change of mood.

But really, did he know about her running? Because if he did, she was going to deal harshly with him.

Still, she chuckled to herself. And I have his badge number.

She'd done the right thing with Emma. She'd had it out with her and given her a job. From now on she'd be nice; she'd be professional; she'd keep a safe space between them.

And maybe really get on with her life.

At last.

So Riley had drawn her line in the sand, Emma thought. It was clear—there were still some hard feelings, some resentment. Emma sulked for a minute, fighting melancholy. There was something about women and friendship that could run so deep, so personal, it was almost harder to say goodbye to a relationship like that than it was to break up with a man. She missed that friendship with Riley, so intimate and trusted. She grieved that it was forever gone.

But then she began to lighten up. She'd been beaned with a bedpan, for God's sake. Let Riley be a little superior—she'd survived better than Emma had. They weren't going to be friends. But Emma had a job. A decent job. And she had no doubt that tough little Riley wouldn't let anything happen to her. *That won't happen in my company!*

Once she settled that in her mind, she found herself almost breathless with excitement about her new job. There was no question in her mind, it would be physically demanding and dirty and she was ecstatic. She was sure it wouldn't be long—only days, perhaps—before this pink cloud would burst and the reality would settle in—she had signed on for hard work. But in the moment, it felt good on so many levels. She *wanted* hard work; it would help her scour from her past the stain of all that excess she had indulged in but never deserved. It would prove she could take on tough work and survive. In a way it felt like the hard labor she had earned. Her penance, though she was innocent. She was not innocent of loving wealth, however. And she had made trade-offs along the way. Not amoral or unethical trade-offs, but she had accepted her busy, sometimes indifferent husband, accepted loneliness, made excuses, ignored red flags, and all along she'd wondered, secretly and silently, what was wrong. And wondered, if he'd been penniless, would she have reconsidered? For that alone she should atone.

It would be dirty work for a clean paycheck, beholden only to her effort. And it would be safe.

To her astonishment, Riley made her feel safe. Riley's self-righteous stubbornness alone smoothly and effortlessly guaranteed a secure and protected work environment and... Dear God. And... Emma *trusted her.* After sixteen years of lamenting she could never really trust again, who did she put her faith in but the very person she feared could betray her. The very person who didn't want her for a friend.

"She gave me a job," she said into the phone to Adam. Her voice was quiet and breathy, astonished and secretive.

"Of course she did," he said.

"You didn't even tell her how often we'd been in touch," she said.

"I told you—I'm not interested in trying to reunite the two of you. How about a glass of wine to celebrate?"

"Can we meet at that wine bar?" she asked.

He chuckled. "I think instead I'll bring a bottle and some fruit and cheese over to your place, if you'll let me. I have to work in the morning. It can't be a late night."

"I should get the wine and cheese," she said. "After all you've done to help me..."

"You can do it next time. I'll stop on the way over. You'll have to tell me where you are."

Emma had had many boyfriends and one husband, but she'd never had a man she could talk to like she could Adam. He had evolved in exactly the way she would have expected him to. Looks aside, though his hard good looks must melt female bones all over Sonoma County, he was also smart, mature and engaging. So well-spoken, as one would expect a teacher to be; when he began to talk, he had her complete attention. He was also funny, making her laugh. And earnest—that was paramount. If he talked about his family, about Maddie, Riley or his mother, both the seriousness and sincerity of what he was saying rang through. *Mom hasn't changed since you knew her. Family is still everything to her and it's obvious she's nervous about idleness, having always worked hard. Now that she's finally been convinced not to work all the time, she volunteers. She does meals-on-wheels almost every day and sometimes she fosters rescue animals until they find a permanent home.* And, *Riley takes her achievements in stride but she takes her failures, however small, way too seriously. She's the overachiever in the family.* And, *If there's anyone in our family who understands pure joy, it's Maddie. She loves everyone, all of us, including Jock, and without any effort, with such simple authenticity, makes sure each one of us knows it.*

I live in a family of women, which can take its toll but keeps me sharp. I can't get away with anything. They lean on me, crowd me, are overprotective of me and demanding of me. They're in my business all the time. And I find I like it that way.

Emma wondered what it must be like to live with a man as strong and sensitive as Adam. She couldn't stop looking at his hands, scarred with hard work, so beautiful and strong. She learned he had worked in the vineyards, scarring his knuckles on the rough, hard vines. Also construction, where he learned enough building and carpentry to do all the fixing up and renovation to both his own house and his mother's—that work had also taken its toll on his hands. Those hands represented to Emma that he hadn't ever taken the easy way, but only traveled the path that demanded stamina and hard work. Honest work, something that had come to mean everything to her.

She was so grateful for him. Just knowing he was her friend, that he was in her camp, gave her a feeling of peace and comfort she hadn't felt in so long. She adored him. But at the end of the evening, when he was leaving, when he leaned toward her, she jumped away from him. She just couldn't let him muddy his relationships and his sturdiness by getting too close to someone like her. "No, no…" she said in a whisper.

"Sorry, Emmie. That was insensitive of me," he said. "You're recently widowed…"

"No, it's not that, it's…"

"Shhh," he said, putting a finger to her lips. "I'm with you. We don't want to complicate our friendship."

"Right," she said, because she was at a loss as to how to explain herself. If she'd ever wanted to be kissed, it was now. And if she ever wanted a certain person to kiss her, it was him. But it wasn't friendship with him she feared complicating. It was hurting him just by being in his life. She couldn't bear the thought of being Adam's problem.

That's when he smiled, looked at his watch and said, "I've stayed way too late."

"No," she said, shaking her head. "Not at all. I hope we'll do this again very soon. Very soon."

"We will."

Then he was gone.

After having a conversation with Penny, Emma made some plans for her little bungalow. She was on a mission. She had very little time before starting her new job and she put it to good use. First of all, she bought a couple of cans of paint—a pale yellow, a pale blue and a nice supply of extra-light tan, a kind of heavy cream color. She wasn't exactly overconfident but she did feel she could spend a little on renewing her digs since she was absolutely determined she'd be able to keep her job indefinitely. As long as she stayed out of Riley's way.

She painted her bathroom to match the towels she'd brought with her. One wall in her tiny living room became yellow and the alternating walls the tan so light it was off-white. She was all over the small towns in Sonoma County on Saturday, haunting the garage sales, and found colorful throw pillows, a decorative blanket to cover the sofa back, small wicker shelves she could stack her bathroom towels on, a beautiful basket she could fill with fruit or gourds for the small table, a couple of bronze picture frames and a framed print for the bedroom wall. It was a Matisse and the frame was excellent. She found wood trays she loved and could use to serve wine and cheese because now she knew she'd have guests sometimes. She also found some beautiful wineglasses and dessert plates she didn't need but couldn't resist. And a distressed white denim jacket called out to her. "I gained weight," the lady who was selling it told her. "It's hardly been worn."

"Well, you look amazing and I lucked into a great jacket," Emma told her. So the woman threw in a navy blue scarf, a thin, soft knit that was almost pashmina quality.

The weather was perfect for walking the old-fashioned, tree-lined neighborhoods. Children still played in the street around here; there were a lot of front porches on old brick two-stories and people were out raking leaves, watching kids, chatting over fences. It was sunny, low sixties, and grocers put their late fruits and vegetables outside in large racks. She couldn't resist apples, zucchini, tomatoes, a couple of peppers, a fistful of green beans and a few onions. One of the things she had missed most in New York were the vegetable stands along the roads, owned and operated by the farmers who grew the stuff—it was as if you could taste the sunshine and hard work.

When she went home, she was pleased to see her little bungalow already had a newer, more cheerful look, more like the old Emma. She went back to the hardware store. She painted her little table bright yellow, one of the chairs bright blue and one Irish green.

It looked a bit like a summer house, she thought.

She invited Lyle to an antipasto and wine dinner so she could show off her new-old house, including the framed picture of Emma, Lyle and Riley, cutting up at a pep rally in high school.

"This is interesting," he said, picking it up. "Does this bode well?"

"I was saving this for our toast, but I can tell you now. Riley gave me a job in her company."

"Ah," Lyle said. "So at least one of you is open to reconciliation."

"Oh, don't get too excited. She was very cool, very professional and made it clear I wouldn't be getting any special treatment. We're not going to be friends. It's a job, that's all. But I'm very grateful. She'll be paying me almost twice per hour what I've earned since I've been back. Plus benefits."

Thanksgiving, possibly the last holiday she'd have off for a long time, was such a pleasure, such a breath of fresh air after the holidays she'd had the past several years, she wished it would never end. She not only bought wine for the meal at Penny's and had Lyle create a lovely centerpiece, she also spent the entire morning helping Penny clean the house, prepare the turkey and other food and appoint the table. It was so companionable, so stress-free.

"I wish I'd had a daughter," Penny said as they worked in the kitchen together.

"Do you have any children?" Emma asked.

"No," she said. "Bruce and I had a happy marriage, but we weren't blessed."

"When did he pass away?"

"Oh, it's been over twenty years now. It was awful hard at first, having no kids, you know..."

"I'm so sorry, Penny," she said. "You must miss him so much."

"Sometimes. But then I get ready for a celebration like this and I forget I was once married for thirty-five years and hardly did anything without him. We're all widows, in a way..."

"In a way?" Emma asked.

"Well, Susan is divorced from her second husband, a long while ago, but her first is now dying, hanging on by a thread, the old bastard. She never did get really free of him. Dorothy is divorced and her ex-husband finally kicked. Ew, he was a son of a bitch. Marilyn lost her darling husband a few years ago. They hadn't been married too long. Married late, had a good decade together. She's pulled it together pretty well. Not a one of us ever got a daughter. The injustice…"

Emma smiled. "I'll be your proxy daughter," she said. "I've been on the lookout for a quartet of hip mothers."

"We've been known to cause trouble," Penny said, grinning.

"Even better," Emma said.

Eight

Adam called Emma the Friday after Thanksgiving. He asked her if she'd like to drive up the road to Napa and have lunch at one of the vineyard bistros before she settled into her new job. "If you're free tomorrow," he said.

"That would be perfect," she said. "I'm anxious to hear about your Thanksgiving. And to tell you about mine!"

"Great. I'll pick you up around eleven-thirty."

He didn't linger on the phone. He was relieved by her cheerful mood, by her quick acceptance. He'd been worried that Emma might've been put off by his advances, concerned about what he wanted. He'd moved too fast, leaning toward her for a kiss. God, this was a whole new ball game! And so awkward. He was thirty-seven—he didn't think about things like this. First-date kisses were routine. Expected, even. A woman would think she didn't appeal to you if you didn't at least try... But Emma was different.

She wasn't even close to ready to entertain the notion of a man in her life and when she would be, there was no reason he should expect it to be him. He told himself that her husband hadn't been gone that long. He probably hadn't been a husband to her for at least three years, but her ordeal wasn't far behind her. She'd only been back in California for a few months.

He tried to remind himself: she'd come home, but she hadn't come home to him.

He intended to back off. She'd find her footing. He hoped she'd show signs of recovery pretty soon because he was dying to get his arms around her.

Amazing, how that feeling had come right back to him. The moment he saw her he was filled with it, like stepping back in time. When she'd finally come of age so many years ago, when it would finally be permissible to pursue her, there couldn't have been more complications if they were at war. She was in Seattle, he was struggling to keep up with work and school, then *bam*!—Riley was having Jock's baby. So he did what he had to do—he reeled the feelings back in.

But Emma never came home. She went from college in Seattle to New York. He'd just been working up his courage for a trip to New York to see her when she'd announced she was engaged. To the most wonderful man in the world.

He was hoping for a second chance, but Adam was realistic. This might be something he'd always wanted, but that didn't mean Emma did. Then he picked her up and she was absolutely alive with happiness to see him. She met him with a hug, her eyes glittering and her smile so beautiful. All the way to Napa, she chattered like a girl about what she'd been doing—painting, decorating, hitting all the garage sales she could find.

"I even bought this jacket," she said, laughing. "Used

clothing from a garage sale! I hope Richard is spinning in his grave!"

"Emma!" he said, laughing at her.

"Is it too much to hope he's being eaten by worms by now?"

"What's gotten into you today?" he asked.

"It's hanging out with those merry widows, I think. You should hear the way they talk, especially about departed and ex-husbands who were not the best. They're incorrigible and I love them. Penny and I played host for Thanksgiving and we had a blast. It wouldn't have had to be much to outshine the holidays of the last several years, let me tell you, but it was fantastic!"

"I hadn't even thought of that," he said. "I'm sure your life the last few years didn't include festive holiday celebrations."

"It didn't before, either," she said. "Before the indictments came down, holidays were rich family showcases—parties, celebrations and open houses meant to outdo each other. I got into that, you know? I'm a designer by trade. It was once my goal to design and decorate big hotels, which included ostentatious holiday themes. There wasn't anyplace better than New York for that. But memorable family holidays that filled a person with comfort and joy?" She shook her head. "Richard didn't even invite his family to our home. He was very strategic. He gave them first-class tickets to the islands so they'd be conveniently out of town."

When they arrived at the restaurant she stopped talking while they were led to a pretty table for two in a small arbor. It was a little chilly in the shade, but there were a few space heaters around the patio. Even though it was a holiday weekend, there weren't many for lunch. The tasting rooms seemed to be overflowing and plenty of people were visiting the valley, but the patio of the small restaurant was quiet. Adam couldn't have planned it better if he'd called ahead and asked for a special table.

Emma was so animated, enjoying herself so much, you'd think it was her first lunch date. Maybe it almost was, he thought. Once they'd ordered she wanted to know all about Thanksgiving at his house, every detail, down to the kind of stuffing June made. So he told her everything, including the fact that Jock dropped by to see Maddie and stayed for dessert.

"I'm so glad to hear that," she said. "Does he try to be a good father?"

"He's a good dad, I think," Adam said. "His parenting has been complicated by the fact he lived in Sacramento for a few years for work. Then there was a brief marriage to a woman with children, and that didn't always go well. But on the upside, he's never missed a birthday or holiday and when she plays soccer and basketball, he makes almost every game, even when he had to come over from Sacramento."

"Tell me about you, Adam. How can you be single? You're such a catch! Surely there have been girlfriends."

"If you want to know if I dated, the answer is yes. I even had a couple of near misses, relationships that lasted a couple of years."

"And yet you didn't marry? You, such a family man? Why?"

"I don't know. It just didn't feel right. I wasn't in love enough, I guess."

"I wish I'd thought of that," she said.

"But you loved him, Emmie," he said. "From the way you described him, he walked on water."

"I loved him," she admitted, growing serious. She put down her fork. "I was twenty-four when I met him. He proposed almost immediately. I realized much later, I was hand-picked. He was looking for an idiot who could pull off the millionaire-wife image, from haute couture to decorating to entertaining to social grace under pressure. And of course I had to be able to take orders." She finished her glass of wine. "I'd like to tell you something." But then she stopped.

"Another glass of wine?" he prompted.

"I think I'd like a cup of tea. When the waitress comes back, I'll ask her. But I wanted to say something. I might've misled you. About investigating Richard so I'd know how I ended up in this place. I've already read everything, Adam. If there's anything new, I don't need to know about it. For over three years I was completely addicted to the news. I was glued to everything that floated across the internet. The books and biographical pieces started turning up long before he even went to trial. I read every court transcript, although I was usually there, in the courtroom. I had my own lawyers. For a long time they were the only people who talked to me.

"It didn't take long before all the things I suspected proved logical. Richard had strong sociopathic tendencies. As far as I know he didn't murder the neighborhood pets, but according to old classmates he lied and cheated his way through school. He used people. He enjoyed getting away with things. He liked deceit and winning by any means and he had no empathy. The state and the feds might've been able to prove his fraud and theft, but there was only conjecture about most of the other things, the things having to do with his ethics, his personality disorder. It all became so clear before his trial was over."

"Emmie," he said sympathetically, touching one of her hands.

"I didn't know, yet I did know, Adam. I lived under the same roof with the man, after all. Even though we weren't close, even though I can't say we had a loving marriage, I lived in his house. I traveled with him. The first time I suspected there was a mistress we'd only been married a year. He smiled indulgently, kissed my forehead and said, 'Why in the world would I have a mistress? I have you, the most beautiful woman in New York City.' I bought it, of course. He was so confident and convincing. But there came a time I just knew something was off. I overheard things—he had employees and they were well aware of what he was doing, feeding his business from the bottom, paying out dividends here and there when it would bring in more capital. He referred to it as seeding... Seed money... Satisfied clients brought in more clients. We never discussed it, but after we'd been married a few years, I heard things like that when he was talking to someone who worked for him or when he was on the phone with a client. I heard him moving money around to offshore accounts. He thought I was an idiot, at least about financial matters. I never really knew anything, but I strongly suspected that my slick and sleazy husband would stop at nothing to make big money.

"And I came to know about the mistress. Andrea Darius. I met her for the first time before we were married. Beautiful woman, so beautiful. Smart, classy, very high-society type. She looked kind of like Katherine

Heigl—that stately, confident, above-it-all look. I'd suspected from the first time I met her. There was something in the way she looked at him, it was just there. She was an image consultant, a public relations expert who specialized in the financial sector. Lenders and investors are constantly scrutinized, especially private companies and hedge fund managers. But that was just a front. That was one of the first issues I faced when I looked the other way. I made excuses to make my existence more acceptable in my own eyes." She laughed hollowly. "While I'm a leper in Manhattan, Andrea is still a prominent figure in New York society. There's been speculation that she's a high-priced prostitute or even madam. Who knows? Who cares?"

The waitress came to their table, picked up some plates and took their beverage orders. Adam really wanted another drink but he asked for a coffee.

"See, I didn't have any proof of any kind, but things he said and did made me wonder why I didn't understand him better. Then one day I realized I was married to a man I didn't know, a man who had no conscience. But by then it was too late."

"Why didn't you testify against him?" Adam asked.

She shook her head. When her tea came she added milk and sugar and stirred slowly.

"I really wanted the whole thing to just go away so I could make my escape, which I fully intended to do. I have no real defense, but it is true that any testimony I might have given wouldn't do any good for the defense or the prosecution. It was suspicion, hearsay, speculation. Nothing, really."

"You were trying to have a baby with him?"

She winced. It was unmistakable.

"It was madness. I don't know what I was thinking. We hadn't been married that long, a couple of years, and I was still so young, but I knew something wasn't quite right in our marriage. I thought I could fix it. I thought we could be a family and he would become more...*conscious* of me." She shook her head. "How stupid was I? Anyone knows that babies don't fix things! And God knows nothing was going to cure what he had! It's a blessing I couldn't get pregnant. I finally realized what a catastrophic mistake that would be.

"So you see, Adam—it's not necessary for me to gather up all the things written about Richard and the case against him. Or me. I'm up to speed on all that. I very rarely watch the news now. And those bios?" She shook her head. "I don't know if they're half true. But they sound suspiciously as if they could be."

"I'm so sorry, Emmie," he said.

"I haven't really talked about this. I can trust Lyle and I dumped on him a little bit while I was going through it, but I didn't want to make his relationship with Ethan tense—Ethan thinks very little of me as it is."

"But Lyle..."

"The best," she said immediately. "So loyal, so wonderful and always there for me. And believe me, I put him through some drama." She sipped her tea. "I'm so grateful for Lucinda Lopez, who I've seen twice now. She's perfect. She makes telling it all so easy, and every once in a while she leads me to a perfect conclusion that explains everything, that makes me understand. Men like Richard Compton have a gift for finding the right sucker. He needed a girl who'd lost her parents, who had nowhere to go, who wanted someone who could make her think she was a fairy princess. Someone who wouldn't question his motives. And that was me to the core. Adam, I want you to know who you've gotten yourself mixed up with."

He frowned. "You think I didn't know most of that? I didn't know how you coped but I found out all that stuff—his scheme, his mistress, his lack of conscience, all the speculation from old acquaintances that he'd always been sociopathic. He was so narcissistic it's odd he killed himself."

"People think there's money hidden somewhere," she said. "I certainly don't know of any and I don't have any, but I think his suicide was part revenge and part *gotcha*. He didn't have much value for life, now did he? Not even his own."

"In the end, you were sure your conclusions about him were right?" Adam asked.

"Oh, yes," she said. "During our marriage, through the investigation, through all the depositions, he was one cool dude and we didn't discuss any of it. But in the end, when he'd been warned he was looking at anywhere from forty to seventy-five years in prison, he let the floodgates open and did some incredible lashing out. He proved to me and anyone within earshot that he was a beast with no remorse." She sighed. "There are things I just can't repeat, they're so vulgar."

They were quiet. She sipped her tea and he drank his coffee. The waitress silently refilled his cup and brought her more hot water, along with the check.

"It's okay, Emmie," he said.

"It's really not, Adam. You almost kissed me. You shouldn't do that. I'm damaged. I still can't believe what I allowed myself to be sucked into."

"You were twenty-four. And you were a great deal wiser by the time you were thirty. Give yourself a break."

"Rosemary always said, 'It's just as easy to fall in love with a rich man as a poor man.' She was full of sayings. After Richard's death, leaving me holding the mess of his crimes, leaving me the suspect, you know what my darling stepmother said? 'If you marry for money, you'll earn every cent.'"

"I never liked her," Adam said.

"She's got some great sayings, though."

"We're going to get through this, Emma," he said.

"I wanted you to kiss me," she said.

He had to work at keeping his heart from exploding.

"I wanted to be kissed and the only person in the world I wanted to kiss me was you," she said. "But, Adam, you shouldn't because I'm broken. I don't want to hurt anyone who gets close to me. We have to keep it friends. And Riley… Listen, she was totally professional, but she made it pretty clear… She wouldn't like the idea of us being close."

"You think I give a shit what Riley wants?" he asked.

"Well, I do. And you should. She's your family. I'm going to keep seeing the counselor for a little while. Maybe she's got a shortcut or two. I've got a few good years left and I'd like to live them happily."

He smiled. A few good years? She was all of thirty-four. She probably felt like she'd wasted a lifetime already. "We'll get through this, Em. You're starting a whole new life on Monday. Cleaning toilets and mopping floors. Wowser."

"I'm going to make Riley proud of me," she said. "Don't tell her I said that."

"I don't tell anyone anything."

* * *

Emma didn't necessarily feel better about laying all that on Adam, but she felt cleaner. More honest. He should know—she might not have been complicit in Richard's crimes but she was certainly a participant in ending up right where she was. She fell for every little trick he had. And before it was all over, he made sure she knew it. Snatches of their dialogue in the final weeks might echo forever, never leave her, might never give her peace.

Adam reached across the small table and held her hand. "One thing you're not going to do—you're not going to worry about taking care of me. I don't need you to protect me. All right?"

She knew he was strong. She knew he was smart. But was he wise to what association with a man like Richard had done to her? "I'm not innocent anymore, Adam."

"Not guilty, either. And you're a survivor. I know you are."

"Really?" she asked. "Is that so?"

He chuckled but not with humor. "Your father's death? Rosemary? God, a few years of her would damage anyone! You pulled yourself together after Jock. Picked up what you could carry and went to New York—one of the biggest, scariest cities in the country." He drank the last of his coffee. "I guess now I'll never see it."

"Why is that?"

"No way you're going back there," he said. "And I'm not going back there without you." He briefly looked at their check.

"I'm afraid you're already getting in over your head."

He laughed and pulled out his wallet.

"Let's at least split the check," she said.

"Forget it. I'm not in over my head, Emmie. You don't scare me at all. And you've been through a lot, but I know people who have been through worse. Hell, I know people who have served in combat several times. They have issues, just like you, and they're working on them. It's very tough, too."

She was feeling a little desperate. He was clearly forging ahead, not taking seriously how bad she might be for him, and she wasn't going to be able to hold him back. She adored him for wanting her still. And she feared for him. "When I asked him why he'd kept a mistress, he said he needed someone to fuck that he could talk to!"

"It's hard to believe how pathetic he was," Adam said, peeling off bills to put with the check. "The dumb shit," he added, shaking his head.

"I accused him of being a common thief and he slapped me and told me there was nothing common about what he'd done!"

"He *hit* you?" he asked, his green eyes darkening dangerously.

"Just the once," she said more quietly.

"I kind of want to dig him up and beat the shit out of him, but dead is dead. I bet he didn't get away with anything this time. I may not go to church much anymore but I still believe there's a heaven and a hell." He put his wallet away. "About ready, Emma?"

"Yeah," she said. "Sure."

Walking to the car, his hand on the small of her back, she gave it one more try. "Adam, you heard me, right? I'm coming out of a really dysfunctional situation. Beyond dysfunctional. Sick. Really sick. And it could follow me for quite a while. You don't want to be too close if—"

He stopped walking when they were almost to the car. He put his hands on her waist and looked into her eyes. "Emma, I've been waiting for you to come back for sixteen years. I'm not going to run scared now, just because some insane asshole did his best to leave you wounded. I told you—we can get through this." He leaned toward her and gave her lips a sweet kiss. "You don't have to warn me anymore. You didn't have to warn me in the first place. Now I'm going to take you home. And if there's a God, you're going to invite me in."

"I worry about the concept of us," she said. "I don't want you to be collateral damage when the detritus of Richard's crimes sprinkles down on me."

"I understand completely," he said. "Finished now?"

"Don't be a fool," she said.

"I won't."

All the way home from the restaurant, he talked to her softly of casual things, of the beauty of Napa, the way the cold drizzle of a Sonoma County winter had always made him crave soups and fires. She didn't have a fireplace of course, but he did. He was looking forward to showing off his house—it was over fifty years old in a quiet tree-lined neighborhood and he'd enjoyed renovating it. He'd done most of the work himself, tearing up old carpet and installing hardwood floors, texturing and painting walls. "I focused on the four most important rooms—living room, kitchen, master and bath. The new kitchen is so beautiful it almost makes me want to cook."

"Don't be hasty," she said.

He was seducing her with ordinary things, as if he knew how starved she'd been for a reality she understood—soups and fires, rainy days in a home that hugged her, the love of a good man.

After their lunch they went to her house. He held her hand the entire drive and when she let him into her little bungalow, he glanced around and said, "You've been busy."

"Just a little settling in," she said.

"Come here," he said, locking her door behind them and pulling her into his arms.

His lips came down on hers with an urgency and hunger she hadn't been prepared for. After one brief moment of surprise, she matched his passion with the surging need of her own. It wasn't just her need for intimacy because it had been so long but her need for it to be *him*.

Clothing was removed while they kissed. It seemed that it only took seconds for them to be in her bed, skin to skin, lips to lips. Emma hadn't felt the touch of loving hands in years. Adam's beautiful hands, his lips, his strong fingers, did the one thing she didn't think possible—took her away. Far away. She thought only of him, intoxicated by his scent, his taste, his body.

He was thoroughly beautiful. He had long, strong legs, muscled arms and shoulders, a smooth, hairless chest. With his thick brown hair, expressive brows, emerald-green eyes and strong jaw, he should probably be sculpted and put on display. For this moment in time he belonged only to her. And she to him.

She inhaled his breath, licked her way into his mouth, opened for him and welcomed him into her body. He was gentle and smooth, teasing her into a frenzy. He responded to her arousal with heat, finally taking her on a powerful ride that had her crying out his name as she came. And came. And came.

He joined her, softly whispering her name, his large frame shuddering, his mouth at her neck, his big hands in her hair. She trembled with the aftershock of orgasm and he chuckled, a deep rumble. He kissed her eyes, her ears, her chin, her lips. Her calm returned so slowly; he didn't leave her body, pushing into her softly, again and again. "Still worried about the concept of us?" he whispered in her ear.

"You drugged me," she accused.

He pushed into her again. "A little bit. Damn, woman, I knew we'd be great together, but I didn't have enough imagination to know how great."

They continued kissing, soft and deep and lovely. He moved inside her, filling her, rocking with her in a smooth, deep motion. It didn't take long before she was clutching at him, pushing against him, begging for more.

"I can't say no to you," he whispered. "I have a feeling I'll never be able to say no to you. God, why would I even want to?"

"I didn't say no, either, did I?"

"More it is," he whispered, pounding into her until they were both rising again, reaching for another mutual climax. The moment she started to clench and tremble around him, he went off like a rocket, a powerful blast that made her almost whimper in pleasure. And she finally collapsed under him.

Again he kissed her eyes, her cheeks, her lips, running his work-roughened hands all over her.

They were quiet for a while as their breathing evened and their bodies began to cool. He reached down to pull the duvet over them. Rolling onto his side, he brought her with him, gently holding her against him.

"Are you going to stay inside me forever?" she asked.

"Would that be inconvenient?" he asked. "Because it really feels like exactly where I should be."

"Funny," she said. "Feels that way to me, too."

"Friendship with you has perks," he said.

She was quiet for a moment. "Good," she finally said.

He laughed. "I don't want to be friends, Emmie."

"You don't?"

"Of course not. I don't share that with friends. There was nothing casual about that and you know it."

"Oh?"

"Wasn't a friendly fuck for you, either," he said. "That was some of the finest love I've ever made. Might be the absolute best ever."

"You think?"

"I know," he said.

She smiled. "I'm glad to hear that, even though it was probably not a good idea."

He raised up, looking down at her. "I think it was the best idea I ever had."

She couldn't keep from touching him, tenderly running her fingertips over the planes of his face. "I guess you're not going to come to your senses anytime soon…"

He shook his head. He gently brushed her hair back from her face. "You know how I feel. I think you've always known. Do you think you can talk me out of it?"

"Well, I thought I could…"

"You can't…"

She bit her lip and just looked into those fierce green eyes. She sighed. "Thank God," she said.

He smiled at her.

"Could be problematic that I just slept with my new boss's brother…"

"None of Riley's business who I sleep with. None of her business who you sleep with, for that matter."

"Do you think she'll agree with that?"

"Do you think I care?" he asked, raising a brow in question. "Come on," he said, pulling her closer so she was nuzzling into his chest. "Enjoy the moment. You'll have plenty of time to worry later."

She let herself be cuddled. "I do feel considerably more relaxed than I did a couple of hours ago."

"There you go," he said with a laugh. "God knows I do." After a few minutes of silence he asked, "You going to sleep?"

"No. I'm afraid I'll wake up and find out it was just a dream."

He kissed her forehead. "Nothing like that's going to happen. The bad dreams are over. The good dreams are just beginning."

The rest of the weekend was ideal, the kind of perfect Emma had given up on. After lying around in bed for a couple of hours, Emma showered and primped. When she came out of her bathroom, Adam was puttering comfortably around her little kitchen, making tea and checking out the refrigerator, taking inventory. He wore his jeans, his shirt hanging open over that gorgeous chest, socks on his shoeless feet. He looked so delicious like that she wanted to take a bite out of him.

"If you want to go out for dinner, I'll take you out,"

he said. "If I can talk you into staying in, I'll go get us something."

"You want to stay in?"

He grinned at her. "Oh, yeah."

Then his phone rang. He pulled it out of his pocket, looked at the ID and picked up. "Hi, Mom." He listened for a little while, nodding as though his mother might hear it. "You need me to fix that now?" A pause. "You did? I wish you wouldn't do that. I know it was irritating but what if you fell? All right, all right, I didn't mean to offend you, but really… Don't do it again, all right? Well, thanks, but I'm actually going out tonight so tomorrow I'll have errands and have to get ready for school. Oh, nothing too exciting." He winked at Emma. "Just having a glass of wine with a lady friend. I don't think so, which is how I'd like to keep it for now. Listen, if you need me to help with those Christmas decorations… Jock is? Okay, I appreciate the pass and I'll get the lights up after school one day this week, so no ladders. Talk to you tomorrow? Great."

He put the phone back in his pocket. "Her smoke alarm was beeping because the battery was dead and she climbed up on a stepladder in the stairwell and changed the battery. She's perfectly capable, but I hate thinking of her up on a ladder. That's what I'm for." He made a face. "I change them regularly to keep her off the ladder."

"You mentioned Jock?"

"He's pulling out the big boxes for Maddie and Mom. Maddie must have asked him. Gives them a chance to hang out for a while."

She shook her head. "She asked who you were going out with…"

"She just asked, 'Do I know her?'" His smile was devilish. "I'm going to get a shower before I go shopping."

"Adam, they can't know," she said. "I'm sorry, but Riley can't know..."

"I wasn't planning to tell her," he said. "But I wasn't planning to keep it a secret, either." He frowned. "Is that your plan?"

She bit her lower lip as she nodded. "Until she decides it's okay I'm back, until I prove to her I'm an asset as an employee, please—let's keep it between us."

"You're afraid she'll be angry," he said.

"Of course. She isn't too sure of me yet. She was very clear—giving me a job had nothing to do with making up or being friends. She isn't ready for me in her life. You are a huge part of her life."

"Do you want to stop this right now? Me and you? Because I can leave. I wouldn't like it, but if you need more time..."

"I can let you go but, heaven help me, I don't want to give you up. Not if you want to stay. Not even for Riley." She smiled a bit tremulously. "You should really think about this."

He smiled at her. "I'm going to take a shower, go to the store and stay as long as you'll let me. And if it's important to you that we keep it from Riley for a while, I can do that. I want you to feel safe."

"Thank you. I just need a little time to settle into my job. Not only do I need the job, I also want to prove to Riley that I don't expect any favors, that there's no debt to settle."

"If that's the way you feel."

"It is."

"Then that's how it will be," he said.

"Can I go shopping with you?"

He smiled at that. "So you're not hiding us from the world, just from Riley. Just for now."

"That's about right. Can you live with that?"

"It's okay, Emma. I know the ground still feels pretty shaky. But I think everything is going to be okay."

She hoped so. But she knew things would only become more difficult if Riley and Adam were pitted against each other because of her. And that would be terrible.

An hour later they were back at home with potato-cheese soup, mini ham sandwiches and antipasto from the deli, plus a nice bottle of wine. They ate on the couch in front of the TV then curled around each other for a while before going to bed. Adam didn't ask if he could stay; he just stayed as long as she didn't ask him to leave. She hung on to him all night long as if lost at sea, and rather than try to shed her clinging arms, he held her firmly to him.

In the morning they had bagels and cream cheese with their coffee and then went for a walk through the quiet town. Then back to Emma's place for more cuddling on the sofa.

"So this is normal, is it?" she asked, relaxed and blooming under his touch.

"You'll get used to it," he said.

Nine

After Thanksgiving dinner, Riley checked on a few of her cleaners, but only by phone. Of course they had clients who couldn't even wash their own dishes on a family holiday. Some people entertained on Thanksgiving, and while she found the fact that they hired help away from their own families on such an occasion somewhat tacky, it was also profitable. Riley made it profitable for her employees, too. And from what her people in the field said, all went smoothly.

It was a tradition for Riley and Maddie to help June decorate the house the day after Thanksgiving. Riley dropped Maddie off at June's then went out to run a few errands. By the time she got back to her mother's, Jock was in the garage, getting out boxes for Maddie and June.

"I didn't expect to run into you today," she said. "Isn't the store busy?"

"Worse than busy. I was there for a couple of hours this morning when they opened the doors to the crowd. And I'm going back later to work tonight. It'll be a zoo all weekend."

Black Friday was sale day and nothing sold like electronics. Computers, TVs, everything from headphones to cell phones. Jock was the manager now at least and had a little more control over his schedule, and though she hated to have to admit it, he put in some hard weeks.

She went into the house. She didn't like to look at him. He was still so good-looking that it kind of pissed her off. Couldn't he at least age badly? But he was still drawn to sports, worked out, played a little football, a little basketball, golf—and he was as fit as he'd been in high school. He still looked like the guy who'd stolen her heart and then broken it.

June was in the kitchen getting out all her Christmas cookie cutters. "I didn't expect to see him here," Riley said.

"I think Maddie asked him to come," June said.

"Why didn't she just ask Adam?"

June sighed in some aggravation. "Because Jock is her father, I suppose. And much as it galls you, they enjoy each other."

"It doesn't gall me," she lied. "What can I do?"

"Do you want to help go through the decoration boxes in the garage?" June asked with a sly smile.

"What can I do in here?"

"As soon as they find it, you can put the garland up on the bannister, string it with lights and hook up the extension cords."

"Fine," she said, heading for the coffeepot.

When Maddie was a baby, Jock spent time with her more often at June's house than anywhere. When he wanted to take her to his parents' house, he talked to June rather than Riley because June was more accommodating. When Maddie was in grade school, he pushed his presence more forcefully, but still cautiously. He insisted on being notified of school activities, from parent-teacher conferences to carnivals. He couldn't make them all, but he wanted to at least be told. "I'd rather not ask the teacher, Riley." Riley most often asked her mother to let Jock know.

Then there was that time when Maddie was ten that Jock suggested to Riley that they revisit the idea of joining forces. "I think we should get together, just you and me, maybe leading up to a date," he said. "Let's get to know each other again, see if we can remember what it was that brought us together in the first place."

"You've completely lost your mind, right?" she said.

"Not at all. I know you don't like it but I consider you and Maddie my family. Since there's no getting around it, we could explore it."

She was appalled. "I wouldn't even consider it," she said. "And why would you? You've dated a lot since Maddie was born. I don't consider you my family! Get someone else to take a chance on you."

"I hardly ever date," he said. "You really don't know anything about me."

"I think I probably know enough," she said. "Aren't you the guy who talked me out of my clothes and then dumped me?"

"You have a real blind spot when it comes to me, don't you, Riley? I apologized a hundred times for being a stupid eighteen-year-old when that happened but I really cared about you. I just got scared off. Mostly by you!"

"And what makes you think I'd be willing to take that kind of risk again?"

"Maybe because I'm not eighteen anymore and we have a daughter together?"

"Even more reason I should be cautious!"

And of course their conversation had deteriorated from there. They often did. She'd push his buttons, she'd get pissed off all over again and before they knew it they were sniping at each other.

So Jock married someone else, a young woman with two sons. The ink was barely dry on the marriage license when he was back on his own and the woman was back with her ex. And Riley felt vindicated—Jock was not capable of a committed relationship.

Starting in junior high, Jock began to communicate directly with Maddie and Riley would run into him at everything from car washes to softball games. And now she never knew when she'd run into him at her mother's house.

On Saturday Riley had worked for a couple of hours and Maddie had girlfriends over for the night, so she was trapped at home. On Sunday afternoon Maddie and June were going through the recipes and planning their Christmas baking. Riley was there by four o'clock to share a family dinner of Thanksgiving leftovers with them. All but Adam, who had begged off because he was busy. He'd told his mother he was running errands and getting his schoolwork done since he'd been out with a friend Saturday night. "Oh?" Riley had asked. "What friend?"

"He said I don't know her," June said.

It was hardly noteworthy. Adam was known to date, though circumspectly. As a rule, he didn't introduce a woman he was dating to the rest of the family until it had been weeks or months, proving they stood the test of time.

Riley met Monday with some excitement, some trepidation. Emma was starting work. She'd begin her training with Makenna Rice at 7:00 a.m. and Riley thought Makenna might scare the life out of Emma. Riley had made a secret pledge—no arguing or fighting. It was one thing to clear the air upon their first meeting—they had been alone in the office. But from now on they were only employer and employee and they'd be professional and courteous or Emma would have to go. "It's my company," Riley kept reminding herself.

Riley was at the office at six-thirty and, unsurprisingly, Makenna had beat her there. She already had her training manuals and supplies scattered around the boardroom.

"Well, good morning," Riley said. "Getting an early start, I see."

"I don't want us to be late for our first job. That would set a bad example."

Riley laughed. "Can I get you a coffee?"

"I'm all set, thanks. I didn't start the pot in the kitchen, knowing you'd be bringing your Starbucks. I guess I'd better put on the coffee, huh? Ms. Shay might need a cup."

"I'll do it while you set up here," Riley said.

Makenna was an interesting character, one of Riley's first employees. She was tiny but strong. She had spiked orange hair and dark brows, plenty of piercings on her ears and a couple of eyebrow piercings, a few colorful tattoos that had expanded over the years. The only one that showed while she wore her work uniform was a serpent that wiggled up the back of her neck. She reminded Riley of a biker chick but she was a straight arrow. She was a single mom like so many of Riley's employees—one fourteen-year-old son who towered above her already. And she was a strict mom. As far as Riley knew,

Curtis didn't give her any trouble. Hell, Riley was afraid to give her trouble.

All the doors between the offices and conference room were standing open, the front door unlocked, the coffee brewing, and at six-fifty Emma arrived, ten minutes early. *Good.* She carried a tote that presumably had her drinks and lunch for the day, her uniform was new and pristine and she looked far too good to be cleaning houses. But that was the look Riley wanted her employees to have because that was how her clients wanted the hired help to look.

"Good morning," Riley said.

"Good morning," Emma replied.

She blushed just slightly. It was almost imperceptible, but she glanced briefly away.

Was that about the words they'd exchanged when Emma was interviewed and hired, or something else? Did Adam really have errands? Errands my ass, Riley thought.

"How was your weekend?" Riley asked.

"Very nice, thanks. I had the best Thanksgiving. The lady I'm renting from and her girlfriends, all widows a bit beyond a certain age, had dinner and included me—it was fantastic."

"Good. What about Rosemary?"

"Didn't you know? Rosemary and her third husband, Vince, moved to Palm Springs years ago. I haven't heard a word from Lauren or Anna. I'm not even sure if they're still around here. With any luck, Rosemary and I are finished. I haven't heard from her since...since Richard's death."

Riley made a face. "With any luck," Riley muttered

under her breath. She led Emma to the conference room. "Makenna is ready for you. Makenna, this is Emma Shay."

Emma put out her hand. "Pleased to meet you. And thank you. I'll try to be your star pupil."

"They all say that. Get yourself a cup of coffee if you like. We're going through the handbook first. Coffee's in the kitchen."

Emma reached into her bag. "I brought my coffee," she said, pulling out a large thermal cup.

"Save it for later. Get office coffee while you can. Meet me in here."

"Thanks," Emma said, heading for the kitchen.

Riley went to her desk. No, surely not, Riley thought. Surely Adam wasn't spending more than a little time with Emma. He wouldn't get romantically involved with her, would he? Weren't they all conflicted enough without that?

I will fire her, Riley thought.

Emma eyed the handbook—a large spiral notebook two and a half inches thick.

"We're going to start with some important company rules and guidelines. I have a notebook like this for you to borrow. You can make copies, take notes, memorize, whatever works best for you, and you can have it for two weeks. There is always a book in the office. Nick Cabrini, director of operations, has this book on his computer and phone. I have one at all times and you can stop by here or call any of us with questions. Let me put that more clearly—if you have a question, please check the book to make sure you're acting within company policy before doing anything."

Emma frowned. "Like?"

"I'm going to tell you." Makenna flipped open the

book. "Nick or Riley give the estimates and unless there are special conditions, the client contracts for our basic house or office cleaning services, which are very thorough. We'll go over the basic in a few minutes. Extra duties must be approved by Nick and he will make a charge, so please don't quote prices to the client. Extras include things like windows, refrigerator/freezer cleaning, garage cleaning, patio and outdoor furniture cleaning, cupboard clearing, laundry, special-event cleanup—like receptions, holiday entertaining, et cetera. We don't provide child care or care of the elderly or infirm. We're not plumbers—we don't unplug toilets. If they can't figure it out, we have subcontractors—plumbers, electricians, pool service, chimney sweeps, landscapers and gardeners and so on. There's a very long list, right here." She tapped a page in the book. "It's routine for our clients to ask for more without considering the time and expense, so we have a standard. We never use the client's cleaning supplies—only ours are approved. They've been known to come up with weird concoctions that stain, damage or create noxious fumes. They can damage their own possessions. Likewise, you will learn about materials and cleaning agents and will not take the homeowner's cleaning advice—for your own protection. When the lady of the house says, 'Just use a little bleach on this Oriental rug,' you will explain that doesn't match your instructions and offer the services of our in-house expert, Nick, who will be happy to consult before we have to buy her a new rug. And if you think clients haven't tried to dupe the poor, stupid cleaning lady into ruining something so it can be replaced for free, you're unbearably naive. For breakage, which is going to happen, we have insurance with a high deductible. The company will cover each team member for the first fifty dollars—that's the odd wine-glass, ashtray, soap dish or plate.

"We use only the front powder room if the need for a bathroom arises and if there is no powder room, we'll designate an appropriate restroom in the home. We don't eat in the client's house but a drink of bottled water—our own—is appropriate. We don't accept new or used gifts or clothing. Under any circumstances. If they want to tip you in cash, it's acceptable. Individual cleaning teams cannot offer discounts or additional work without being approved. We don't develop personal relationships with our clients—be cheerful, helpful and courteous. If someone wants to discuss problems, if they're not cleaning problems, explain that you're not at liberty to offer advice or act as a confidante. We have a policy that individual employees not make arrangements with clients to work on the side. And there is a non-compete agreement that you will be asked to sign that states you will not work as an independent house cleaner or maid until you have been separated from Kerrigan's Services for six months.

"Our clients have an expectation of privacy and confidentiality. We understand that it is unrealistic to suggest cleaners never chat among themselves, but we do have an ironclad rule that no employee of this company discuss clients' personal matters outside of the company. It goes without saying—if you're accused of stealing, you will be investigated by the police. It has happened and I am proud to report, it has rarely been true. So if you have any legal issues, wants or warrants that will be complicated by a law enforcement intervention, best to say so now." She gave Emma a chance to say so. After a moment's silence Makenna cleared her throat and went on. "And if you run into burdensome issues you can't quite manage, please bring them to me, Nick or Riley. Believe me, we've seen it all."

Emma frowned. What kind of confidential things might she witness? "I'm almost afraid to ask…"

"Inside of two months, you won't have to ask, but I'll save you some time. Obviously, you're not going to be picking through drawers or closets, reading correspondence, diaries, or studying papers on desks. We don't look at personal papers or property, we dust it.

"But you're going to see things. Mrs. X, the cheapest client we have, one who has never tipped or given a holiday bonus, has a checkbook balance of one-point-five-million and a monthly credit card bill over twenty-five thousand dollars. She leaves these papers in plain sight, very hard to miss. Mr. and Mrs. Y carelessly leave out objects of intimate pleasure." To Emma's expression of consternation, Makenna said, "Sex toys, Emma."

"Ew," Emma said.

"Gloves," Makenna said. "And Mr. Z is knocking the shit out of Mrs. Z. She thinks no one knows."

"Oh, my God! And you don't do anything?"

Makenna glanced down at the pages of the employee manual. "Mrs. Z said someone made an anonymous call to the police department and they were visited by someone from the domestic violence unit, but I'm sure I wouldn't know anything about that."

"So—we don't get involved, even if someone's health and safety is at risk?"

"That would be one of those issues you're going to want to take to Nick and Riley. Very important that you do so, Emma. If a member of the household we service is at risk, we're at risk. If you have reason to believe someone is breaking the law, it's important you tell your supervisor. There are examples of difficult situations in this manual. The book was compiled by Riley over years. When a new situation arises it is not only added to the handbook, a confidential memo is also sent to team leaders so they can advise their crews." Makenna peered at Emma. "Are you going to be able to ignore the obvious? Look the other way?"

Emma almost laughed. "Oh, you have no idea," she said. "It's a skill of mine."

Makenna cleared her throat. "Now, let's go over some important issues—cleaning supplies, techniques, basic chemistry so you don't mix bleach and toilet bowl cleaner and end up a 911 call..."

The lecture was intense and fast-paced. Makenna put all of her supplies out on the table with corresponding color photos and explained how each cleaning implement was to be used and which cleaning chemicals were provided.

"I don't expect you to remember all of this, Emma. You're going to be trained on the job this week—I'll be watching you and helping you. To that end, I'm taking you to some of our more challenging homes. You'll have to learn to do it well, fast, not be distracted by your chatty home owner, cooperate with your team and employ all the smart moves—safety first. Don't lift anything over forty pounds, use your legs, not your back. We have knee pads in the van if you want them, as well as smocks and aprons, and do protect your uniform as much as possible. You're bound to get dirty, but avoid bleach marks or grease stains if you can." Then the little pixie smiled and said, "Ready?"

"Oh, God," Emma said.

"Good! Help me put this stuff away."

And with that they gathered up all of Makenna's training aides and headed out of the office, getting in the van. Two other team members—Shawna and Dellie, short for Delilah—were already there and ready to roll. Shawna held a clipboard.

"Okay, first house I have linens and dusting, Dellie has the kitchen and hardwood floors, the newbie Emma is passing the vacuum—do not forget the stairs! Do not slam the vacuum into walls or furniture! And it is with vengeful pleasure I give the bathrooms to Makenna."

"You don't scare me," Makenna said.

"You scare me," Emma said.

"Make nice tracks with that machine, Emma," Shawna said. "The clients like the tracks. The little things keep us popular."

"Is dusting the primo job?" Emma asked.

They all laughed. "It's the least difficult," Makenna said. "But there are blinds, high shelves, ceiling fans, plants, light fixtures, wooden furniture, books—it's endless. It's hard to be fast and keep breakage down. It takes practice. The vacuum is hard but safe."

"And the bathrooms are the worst job?"

"Sometimes, depending on the client," Shawna said. "Some of them aren't, how should we say it…?"

"Clean," Makenna supplied.

"Kitchens are hard. You never know what's happened in the kitchen this week. It could've been a big dinner out or a takeout week or there could have been a lot of cooking. Greasy, splattering, nasty cooking. People with regular cleaning service get a little lazy about a thorough cleaning after cooking. They never oil their cabinets or wash the floors. I hate cleaning kitchens," Shawna said.

Then it seemed like in minutes they were there.

"Let's do it," Makenna said. And they hit the ground running.

Emma was home in her little house at six. She walked in and collapsed on the sofa. It wasn't until she was in that position that she realized she still wore her knee pads—the last house of the day, she got the bathrooms. Six of them. Every one had been *thoroughly* used. If possible, the sinks were the worst she'd ever seen. The family must have been the hairiest family on the planet. They were obviously descended from the Yeti. The toilets... She couldn't think about them.

When she got some energy, she would call Adam. He had texted sometime after three that he couldn't wait to hear about her day. There hadn't been a moment yet. She went from the cleaning company's van directly to her car and straight home. Her carry pouch was empty of drinks and snacks, she was famished and she was sure there wasn't anything left in the house from her weekend with the bottomless pit, Adam. He'd bought plenty of food to sustain them during their "honeymoon" and he'd eaten all of it.

There was a knock at her door. It was unrealistic to expect it was a huge takeout order. Possibly it was Penny. She lifted her head. "Please be the pizza delivery boy," she called out weakly.

"How was your day, dear?" Adam. He stood over her, smiling.

"Oh. God." She struggled to sit up. He was holding bags. "Oh, you brought sustenance."

"Knee pads," he said, grinning like a fool. "Nice touch."

"What's in the bags?" she said, frowning at his attempt at humor.

"Food. Stuffed salmon, rice, Italian beans, bagels and muffins for morning, milk for your coffee, a couple of sandwiches for you to take to work tomorrow."

"Oh, you are a perfect man."

"You're hungry?"

"Starving. But these hands cannot go near food. My hands have been places..."

"Never mind," he said. He put his parcels on the table and went to sit on the chair facing her. "I've worked for Riley. A hundred and twenty teenagers every day is like a paid vacation." He touched the hair at her temple. "I also brought wine."

"Can you uncork it and just pour it straight down my throat?"

"Tougher than Burger Hell?"

"She was right, I was worked hard."

"She used to say, 'People have dirty lives and we clean them up.' I don't have to stay for dinner. I won't be offended."

"Oh, stay," she said. "Can I take a shower first?"

He nodded. "I'm not staying late tonight. I promise."

"What if I want you to stay late?" she asked.

"Just get your shower. I'll set up dinner."

"Nothing sexier than a man who brings dinner."

"If you had a real kitchen, I'd cook you dinner, but..."

"You provided. That's everything." She struggled off the couch but had trouble straightening. She groaned.

"Don't forget to take off the knee pads before you get in the shower," he said.

A few minutes later when she came out of the bathroom, the table had been set, the wine uncorked, the ibuprofen bottle sitting beside one plate.

"I hope this is a casual dinner," she said, indicating her pajamas.

He held a chair for her. "Madam?"

She took her seat and he poured her a small amount of wine. She sipped. "Well, your sister is amazing, Adam. Her business is impressive. Complex, well thought, practical, no detail omitted. It's brilliant what she's done. I have an employee manual I can barely lift, spent the day with a trainer..." She sipped again. "I had a personal trainer in New York. I was not worked nearly as hard by him."

Adam chuckled and served their food. "I know Makenna," he said. "She's a little demon, isn't she?"

"Depends on what you mean by *demon*. She's quite the handler. Five feet of brute strength and fearsome threats. I guess Riley hired her when there were no mob bosses or biker gang enforcers available. Where'd Riley find her?"

"I can't remember," he said. "She's been around forever. She's a fixture in the company. Riley keeps trying to move her into a management position and Makenna wants nothing to do with it. She likes her work and she's good at it. She agreed to work as a supervisor and trainer so it would be done right."

"I met Nick," she said. "He seems nice."

"Stay on his good side," Adam advised. "Some of the women make the mistake of thinking they can sweet-talk him. There are two people who can sweet-talk Nick and the first is his mother."

"And Riley?" she asked.

"You've been away from Riley too long. She doesn't

sweet-talk anyone. The other, oddly enough, is Makenna. Though she rarely tries. Makenna eats nails for breakfast. And she don't need no *steenking* man."

"Hmm. This morning she had me instead of the nails," she said. She sampled the salmon. "Ohhh, Adam. I think I'm getting turned on."

He laughed at her.

When he was seated across from her on the green chair, she went after her dinner in earnest, trying not to gobble. "I didn't make a single mistake," she finally said. "I did everything right. Well, Makenna inspected my carpet tracks, my shining bathrooms, my oiled hardwood and made a few comments—nothing much. Clearly it was good enough. Better than good enough. Those women are workhorses."

"They're good," he agreed.

"Makenna indicated I was with an exceptionally good team this week but they weren't all this good. She also said sometimes there's a weak link, but she didn't say how she knew who that was. Do they tattle on each other?"

"Sometimes, but that's not how they do it. They measure client complaints and watch for similarities. Then Nick and Makenna get involved with the team. Often they'll split them up and move them around. Once they figure out who's not getting the job done, they try training, counseling, observing. They almost never have to fire someone for not working. It's other stuff."

"Like what other stuff?"

"Absenteeism, tardiness, breaking policy. The most irresistible is taking used clothing from clients. Obviously most of Riley's employees aren't well-off and those high-end clothes are tempting."

"I never found out why that's not allowed," she said.

He chewed thoughtfully. "The risk that they'll be accused of stealing them is too high and there's no way to get to the bottom of it. The safe course is just forbid it."

She put down her fork. "Did Riley come to all these conclusions by trial and error or did she take some class or read some book about how to set up a business like this?"

"She read everything, took a few business courses and learned a lot through experience. It's really an amazing little company. The employees who work hard and honestly have excellent perks and benefits. Discounts at child care agencies was very hard to negotiate and worth a lot to a working mother. Not many companies help working mothers."

"Takes a working mother to know about that," she said.

She asked about Adam's day. He had a lab—that was always fun, especially if no one blew anything up. Test review for a couple of classes. He flipped a homeroom and study hall for a friend who wanted to go to the OB with his pregnant wife to see the sonogram of the baby. That had him finished at 2:30 so he went to his mother's and put up one row of Christmas lights across the front of the house for her. Then he cleaned up and stopped at the store on his way over to her house.

"Sounds like such a perfect, almost leisurely life," she said.

"I'll get out of your hair as soon as I help you clean up the dishes. I know you're tired," he said.

"If I'm not *that* tired?" she asked.

He left at 5:00 a.m.

Ten

Riley was very observant during Emma's first week on the job. The feedback was excellent. She was surprised, but shouldn't have been; Emma had always been a hard worker. Riley just couldn't get beyond the image of Emma riding through Central Park in a carriage on her wedding day, decked out in Vera Wang, no less. When Riley thought of Emma on her hands and knees scrubbing around the base of a toilet, she wondered what her budget for housekeeping had been in her Manhattan apartment.

She shouldn't have been surprised because when Emma wanted something, she had never been afraid to go after it. She was diligent. Determined. She wondered what Emma had done to land herself a millionaire. But in order to find out, she'd have to be on friendly terms with her and that just wasn't happening. Employer and employee—that was who they were.

Emma had always had to be enterprising. Her childhood had been tough. Her father's sudden death left her essentially alone, alone but for Riley and the Kerrigans. Somehow, Emma got through the worst of it with grace.

She always managed to work hard, get by, put a good face on it. Like she was doing now, acting like it was her lucky goddamn day she got a job cleaning.

Really, she'd survived so much. Riley felt sorry for her. But she was also feeling something else. Trouble. Unease. Distrust. Maybe envy? Why would you envy someone who'd had so many bad knocks?

Because she was the beautiful, strong and tragic princess. No one would ever see Riley that way. Riley was the tough poor girl who made good. For that she'd get applause. But Emma? In her mind she saw that news clip of her on the courthouse steps, broken and crying, then rising stoically, lifting her regal chin and slowly descending as if she were on the red carpet, damaged shoe notwithstanding. Even in her most devastating moments, always chic. Always poised. In fact, Emma could wear devastation like a crown.

Friday night after work Riley dropped in on her mother. June was puttering around in her old kitchen. June was always cooking. She would never stop working even though Riley and Adam had convinced her to retire. So now she volunteered. At the church, in the neighborhood, at the animal shelter.

A mangy-looking dog wandered into the kitchen, walking slowly as if her feet hurt.

"And who is this?" Riley asked.

"This is Beatrice. Isn't she lovely?"

Riley gave a short laugh. "Actually…she's pretty ugly."

"Shhh. Be nice now—Beatrice has had a rough time of it. She's going to need a little time to regain her former beauty. But she's a lovely lady and needs a place to relax until she has her forever home."

"If the whole world were as kind as you…"

"Where's Maddie tonight?"

"Hanging out at Kylie's house. Studying, she said."

"Ha," June laughed. "On Friday night? What do you suppose they're really doing?" Beatrice wandered over to the doggie bed in the corner of the kitchen and June told her she was a good girl.

"Eating junk, calling boys, practicing dance steps, plotting things… But Kylie's mother is home tonight so they can't get into too much trouble." She smiled as she looked at June, her *elderly* mother. June was sixty-three, kept her short hair a dark auburn color, still wore a size ten and her eyes sparkled with mischief. She'd worked hard all her life and it had kept her in excellent shape, except her feet gave her fits; she'd used them well, cleaning and waitressing, and sometimes they screamed in protest, but she was in excellent health and fitness otherwise. She looked her years, but beautifully so. She would be termed a handsome woman. "What are you building over there?" Riley asked from her place at the breakfast bar.

"I'm making a meat loaf," June said. "I'm so bloody sick of turkey. Aren't you?"

"God, yes. But you got a lot of mileage out of it," Riley said. "Why don't we have a glass of wine?"

"Perfect idea," June said.

"So… Adam's coming to dinner?"

"Not tonight. He stopped by after school yesterday to put the trash on the curb because apparently I'm too feeble to get it there." She laughed, washed her hands and wiped them on the towel.

"What are you going to do with that meat loaf, then?"

"Well, I'm going to eat some. With mashed potatoes. I could share some with you, if you're interested. Then I suppose I'll freeze it, but I'm damn sure not eating another bite of turkey. At least until Christmas. But obviously I haven't had enough of mashed potatoes yet." She opened the refrigerator and pulled out a chilled bottle of white, already opened. "It's not as fancy as your preferred label but will this do?"

"Certainly," Riley said. June poured them each a glass and Riley took a sip. "Has Adam seemed to be awfully busy lately?" she asked June.

"I don't know," June said. "I talk to him almost every day. I haven't needed him for anything. Just the lights, which he finished this week. I hate doing the lights…"

"I've hardly talked to him," Riley said.

"Do you need him for something, Riley?"

"Well, no… But we usually talk longer than a minute. He hasn't been to dinner since Thanksgiving."

"He took some leftovers on Friday night, I think. He said that should do it for him."

"I think something is going on with him," Riley said. "And I should probably tell you—" She took another sip of her wine. "Emma's back in town."

"I know," June said. "She got back a few months ago, right?"

"I gave her a job," Riley said.

"Good for you! I hope to see her one of these days. I haven't gone looking for her—I'm sure she needs time to adjust to being back. I'm so glad she's free of that terrible mess. Does she seem well?"

"Oh, yes, beautiful as ever," Riley said, though the

words did curl her lip. “Listen, I suspect Adam might be seeing her.”

“Oh? And why do you suspect that?”

“He’s seeing someone and he’s mysteriously silent about it. And completely unavailable.”

“Well, then…”

“Well, then?”

June put down her wineglass. “Riley, I want you to leave Adam alone.”

“So he *is* seeing her!”

“Riley, you’re not going to interfere. You’re going to say nothing, do you hear me?”

“You can’t tell me what to say!”

“I just did and I don’t think you want to mess with me on this.”

Riley slammed her fist on the breakfast bar. “Why are you in the middle of this? You seem to know what’s going on well enough that you’re telling me what to do! What to say!”

“I know about as much as you do. When Adam wants us to know more, he’ll fill us in. Until then, you’ll leave it alone.”

“Did he tell you he was seeing her?”

June shook her head. “He told me she was back, that he ran into her and had a glass of wine with her one evening, gave her your business card and even though there’s a good chance you’d work her to death, he hoped Emma would call you about a job. He had all faith you would do right by her. She’d be in a good work environment with fair pay. And I have absolutely no doubt that’s what you did.”

“I don’t want her with Adam!”

“I think if you voice your opinion to Adam, you’re

going to get nothing but trouble. Telling him who he should or shouldn't date is overstepping your rights as a sister. You'll piss him off. You'll piss me off, for that matter."

"I don't entirely trust her," Riley said.

"Then you'll keep your distance. What the rest of us do is up to us, not you. Besides, what makes you think Emma is ready to be seeing any man? Hasn't she been through enough with a man?"

"Well, of course," Riley said. "But why are you acting like you know if you don't know?"

"I said he didn't tell me," June said. "Of course I know. I've always known."

"Known *what*?" Riley demanded, getting pissier by the second.

June took a breath. "Adam has been in love with Emma since she was fifteen. I threatened him with murder if he went near her before she was eighteen. You were too busy minding your own romances to even notice, which I considered a good thing. But Adam did all he could to steer clear of Emma. And we both remember what happened when Emma was eighteen—she went away to college. And never came home."

"And you think—"

"That my son hasn't found a woman who makes him completely happy in all that time? I've met a dozen perfectly nice women in the last fifteen years. A couple of them seemed to be around for a long time. That Natalie, remember her? She was looking at bridal magazines, but Adam was barely intrigued. No, Riley, in fifteen years, he hasn't said a word and I thought he was just going to live out his days as the bachelor uncle. Then he told me Emma was back and I saw a spark. He didn't say much after that and I didn't ask but I know my son. The woman he's wanted since he was a boy is back. And if you say one word, I'll make you sorry."

Riley was struck silent. "Well, jeez," she finally said. "Mama bear."

June narrowed her eyes. "He's entitled to take his time and have his privacy. We both owe Adam that much. He's been wonderful to us."

"Does he really need your protection?"

"He has it. And so would you."

"I can't remember a time you ever—"

Riley stopped talking. Of course there was a time. When she came home pregnant and needed the support of her family. Her mother didn't demand complicated explanations, didn't ask a lot of questions, didn't force her opinion. She asked Riley what she wanted to do and stood firmly beside her. Her grandparents' first reaction was that she'd better get married and take her lumps, but June protected her, kept her safe from the opinions of others, didn't judge her. June had done everything in the world to help her.

"Never mind," Riley said.

"Indeed," June replied.

"Am I supposed to be happy Adam has someone even if she's someone I can never have as a friend?"

"You should be very quiet in your speculation because you don't know and neither do I. I haven't seen Emma in many years. Who knows if she feels affection or just friendship? In fact, who knows if Emma is the one he's—"

"Oh, it's Emma," Riley said. But then she stopped herself from saying more. In her heart she knew that shy little blush was related to Adam. Because that's the kind of luck she had where that woman was involved. And also, she could still read Emma. And Emma could no doubt read her. Just like when they were young.

"I just hope I'll see her before too much longer," June said. "I can't tell you how often I've thought about that girl, worried about her. I practically raised her. For a while there I thought she'd lassoed the moon, but that didn't last long, did it? It nearly crushed the life out of her." She tsked, shook her head, took a sip of her wine. "I think your splitting up with Emma was as hard on all of us as it was on you."

I was a pregnant eighteen-year-old—nothing was as hard as that, she thought. "Always poor little Emma," Riley said meanly. "Do you think… I mean, is it at all possible… Honestly, you think Adam has been *waiting* for her? All these years?"

June thought about that. She shook her head. "Not deliberately," she said. "And yet…"

They sipped their wine quietly. After a long spell, Riley broke the silence. "We're going to remodel this old kitchen. Get all new appliances."

"I like my appliances and I'm comfortable in this kitchen. It's like my skin."

"We're going to do it anyway. For resale value."

"When I'm dead," June said.

"I think that will be too late," Riley said.

"But not for me," June replied.

"I'm going to have to pass on the meat loaf. I have other plans."

"Oh?" June said.

"Since Maddie's going to be at Kylie's, I can grab a salad on the way home, get in my softest pajamas and read. I'm in the middle of a really good book."

"You haven't finished your wine," June said.

"I'm anxious to get out of these panty hose..."

"You want to ditch me so you can think about all this. Listen, don't think too much, Riley. Adam tends to act on instinct—just kind of feeling his way. You know things happen for a reason."

Not always, she thought. But yes, sometimes. Whether this was one of those times was still an unhappy mystery.

She stood. "I'm not going to think. I'm going to read and relax and enjoy a quiet evening. I hope I haven't disappointed you."

"I'm fine. I've become very happy about my own quiet time."

Riley kissed her mother's cheek. "I won't say a thing. I won't even make a face. I'll have to concentrate, however."

"It will go better that way, I promise."

Riley slipped into her coat, went to her car, drove to the nearest grocery parking lot and sat for a few moments. Thinking, of course. And letting her eyes well up with tears before she made herself stop. It was so crazy, thinking that Adam had, for all these years, thought of Emma, wanted Emma. Pined for her. To the point that the second she turned up, he was cooked. Done for.

Riley's hurt was deep. In all those sixteen years, Riley had felt such loneliness and guilt. And her family was now so happy, so relieved to have Emma back! Riley hadn't had the courage to trust a friend since Emma left.

She'd done everything she was determined to do in the last fifteen years. She'd focused on her business and her daughter, taking care of her mother, as well. Her best friends were the women she worked with and her family. In all that time, while other people had forged and ended relationships, sometimes moving on to loving unions that lasted, Riley had preferred not to be distracted or tempted. Even Jock, who she had once secretly wished would come to her and beg forgiveness and say he'd always loved her, had married and divorced. The only exception was her mother, and June claimed to be happy as she was; she had family and good friends and apparently no interest in romance. But Riley assumed that happened to old people.

Here was Riley, thirty-five and alone. No interested man. No partner. Sitting in a damn parking lot at night, crying because her friend had let her go sixteen years without forgiving her for that one little... Okay, that one major mistake.

She had a sudden vision of herself making meat loaf for charity, taking in old ugly dogs and watching movies alone for the rest of her life. Whimpering because Emma would never again be her friend. And it was her own fault.

She dug around in her purse until she found a business card. She flipped it over and found the cell number. She texted:

Are you completely out of melons already?

What came back was:

??

She texted:

I'm going to have some dinner at the Chinese Palace. Have you eaten? Riley.

When four minutes had passed, four of the longest minutes she'd ever endured, during which she could feel extreme embarrassment about texting him, she was ready to go into the grocery and get a salad. Then her phone pinged with a text.

On Wayside and Bayshore?

That's it.

Ten minutes or less.

I'll get a table.

Riley kept telling herself it was an experiment, just to see if she had any game left after all these years. She'd had the most uncomfortable feeling in her chest when she realized that not only had Adam managed to brave a relationship, but Emma had somehow bounced back, too, after probably the most destructive relationship of all time. So who better to try this out on than a guy who intrigued her and was as safe as dating a member of the Royal Guard. He was a cop. If he gave her the least trouble, she'd call the police chief, whom she'd met on several occasions at community functions. The only thing that could make this better would be if one of her teams cleaned the chief's house.

While she waited for Logan Danner, she ordered wine and pot stickers. This might take more than one wine. Would he give her a breath test before she got in her car?

Her pot stickers had barely arrived when he came in the door. And she got instant nerves. He was attractive; he wore jeans, a beige sweater over a white shirt, a leather jacket. His light brown hair was just a bit too long. Not shaggy, but no buzz cut for this guy. And he had a bit of a beard growth. That sexy I-have-just-too-much-testosterone growth.

He slid into the booth across from her and grinned. "Date night!"

"Don't get frisky," she said. "This probably won't work out to be anything."

He shook his head. "What an attitude." The waiter came over and he asked, "Have you ordered dinner, Riley?"

"Just the pot stickers."

"Great. Bring me a Tsingtao," he said to the waiter.

Riley had a look of confusion on her face.

"Beer," he said, smiling. "In the end, you asked me out. How's that for a major upset?"

"This isn't really a date. It's two people sitting in the same booth, eating dinner."

"So you just couldn't stop thinking about me, is that it?" he asked.

"That is not it at all," she said.

He put his napkin on his lap. "So tell me about your day. That's how most dates start out. Which, by the way, is usually two people sitting in the same booth, eating dinner."

She leaned her head into her hand. "I knew I'd live to regret this…"

He laughed at her. "Okay, we'll start with my day. I was off today. I had stuff to do. I went to the gym, stopped by my mother's office—her car has a weird warning light so we swapped cars and I took hers to the shop. I did some laundry and ran the vacuum around the house, a couple of things I do every month like clockwork." He stopped talking to check her expression. "I was starting to think about dinner but I had something more lively in mind."

"Like a bar?"

"Yes. I have a foolproof system. When I'm flying solo I go to a noisy place where there will be people, some I know, some new to me. When I have a date, I pick a quiet place like this. Want to know what's different about tonight? I'll tell you—usually if I have a date and pick a quiet place like this, the woman talks my leg off and I don't have to work very hard to seem interesting and charming."

"Huh," she said. "I really don't date."

He sat back against the booth's padded seat. "I guess that makes me pretty special."

"I guess it does," she said. "It also makes you the only person I know who has any interest. Besides my brother, that is."

"I'll try to elevate my status," he said. His beer arrived and he took a drink. "Just out of curiosity, why isn't anyone interested? Or am I going to understand why in another ten minutes?"

"It's a long story, really…"

"Maybe you could give me the bullet points," he said.

"Okay, let's see. I'm a single mother. When my daughter was little…very little… I was so focused on working, staying one step ahead of the bills. I absolutely did not consider a date. I probably wasn't very…"

"Nice?" he asked, lifting his brows.

"I was going for another word. Like *receptive*."

"So you were so not receptive that before you knew it, you gave off a vibe?" He cocked his head and waited.

"And this is your interesting, charming side?" she asked. She sighed. "Let's just order," she added, opening her menu.

"Vibe," he said under his breath.

She lifted her hand and the waiter was back at their booth.

"I'll have the chicken and broccoli with rice and egg drop soup and…" She looked at him. "Need a minute?" she asked.

He didn't even open the menu. "Shrimp lo mein, garlic chicken, another beer."

"You already knew what you wanted?" she asked.

"I've been here before. I live about two miles down Wayside. So—how old is your daughter?"

"Fifteen," she said, taking a sip of her wine, regretting more with every moment what she'd done and completely at a loss as to why she'd done it.

"And I'm your inaugural reentry into the world of men and women?"

She shrugged. "Time flies."

"So now we're going to have to try to unlearn a few things, right?"

"Like?"

"Like having dinner out with someone of the opposite sex can be fun. Getting to know someone new is like… Well, making a new friend who has had experiences you haven't had can be stimulating. I can tell you lots of things about police work if you're interested, and you can tell me lots of things about…about…" He indicated her with his hand.

"Cleaning house," she supplied.

"You clean houses?" he asked.

"Sometimes, but mostly I own a company that provides housekeeping services and other stuff. I bet you're fascinated."

He shook his head. "This is going to take longer than I thought," he muttered.

"What makes you such a know-it-all?" she asked. "Didn't you say you're divorced?"

"That wasn't my idea," he pointed out. "But we parted on very good terms, attesting to the fact that I'm an extremely amiable guy with lots of patience and am very nonjudgmental."

"Then why'd you get divorced?"

"Now, that's a long story," he said.

Elbow braced on the table, she leaned her chin in her palm. "The service here is slow. Give me the bullet points."

He sighed. "My wife wasn't cut out to be married… To a man…"

"Huh?"

He looked trapped. "She's playing on the other team, okay?"

"Are you serious?"

"As a heart attack," he said, making fast work of his beer.

Riley started to laugh. She covered her mouth, but then she just couldn't keep it in.

"I'm sure you're going to tell me what about that's funny…"

"Riley?"

She jumped at the sound of her mother's voice, tipping her wine over. She and Logan went after the spilled wine with their napkins. "Mom?" she said, looking up.

June had changed clothes. At least some of them. She wore a crisp white shirt with her jeans, covered by a blazer. She'd fluffed up her hair and put on lipstick.

"Mom?" Logan asked, sliding out of the booth.

"Hello," June said good-naturedly, smiling at him.

"Mom, what are you doing here?"

"I ordered some takeout," she said.

"But what about your meat loaf?"

"I lost interest so I put it in the freezer. My goodness, Riley, when you said you couldn't wait to get out of your panty hose, I had no idea—" She put out her hand to Logan. "I'm June Kerrigan."

"Pleasure to meet you. I'm Logan Danner. Would you like to join us?"

"Not on your life," she said with a laugh. "Have you two been seeing each other long?"

He gave a short laugh and looked at his watch. "About fifteen minutes now, as a matter of fact, though we've bumped into each other at the grocery store and Starbucks a dozen or so times."

"Isn't that nice," June said. "We'll visit more another time. I'm going to grab my dinner and head home. Have a nice time. Try to keep the drinks upright."

"Definitely," Logan said. He waited for her to pass their table before sliding back into their booth. "Your *elderly* mother, I presume?"

"She was a lot older last time I saw her," Riley said.

"This is going to be more fun than I thought," he said, his smile very wide. "You're going to need some training in dating..."

"You sure you're the one to do it?" she asked.

"Oh, yeah. I'm the guy."

Eleven

After Riley's mother departed and Logan got her another glass of wine, the whole mood of the date lightened and they laughed together like old friends. Riley told him all about her family, how she came to Santa Rosa to live with her grandparents after her father's death, her brother the schoolteacher, her mother—not elderly at all but very hip and cool and someone who'd helped her so much with her daughter, she couldn't have survived without her.

"What about Maddie's dad?" he asked.

"Oh, he's around. He came by on Thanksgiving to see her. It was my mother and grandparents who got me through the pregnancy and early years and I really hated Jock for his negligence, but we were eighteen, for God's sake. He was useless, his support was erratic and insufficient, but he was just a kid. Immature. He grew up over time." Then she laughed. "Not a lot, but he did grow up. He's good to Maddie. He loves her. He's very proud of her."

"Does he still love you?" Logan asked.

"He never really did," she said with a laugh. "I've been over him a long, long time."

"What does he do?"

"He's a manager in a big electronics chain. You know the guy—short-sleeved dress shirt, bad tie, khaki pants, sort of athletic-looking and he watches over the nerds who help you find just the right phone or laptop or speakers. He's very personable. Kind of perpetually happy. A little bit like a puppy. Now that I'm over being pissed off at what a lousy boyfriend he turned out to be, we get along all right. What about you and your ex?"

"I think I told you—she's my sister's best friend. My sister's married..." He paused and grinned. "To a man—they're not that kind of best friends. And my ex is a nice person, a real nice person. I admit, it threw me, but that was years ago. I'm over it. She's happy, she has a good life, she's successful..."

"But you took some heat?"

"I'm a cop, what do you think? There are some good women in the department but it's still mainly a guy's shop and yes, they didn't let up for a long time. They still give it to me from time to time. But they also like my ex. Because she's..." He shrugged. "Likable. But it's mostly over now."

"Mostly?"

"Well, there's that odd first date when you have to explain your wife left you because she's a lesbian..."

"I'm sorry, I was very rude. I shouldn't have found humor in it."

"You laughed your ass off," he pointed out.

"Well, just before that revelation, you'd been way too confident. So what does she do? Your ex?"

"Nurse practitioner. We dated a year, were married a year, been divorced eight years, still see each other all the time because she hangs out with Bernie, my sister."

"It sounds kind of nice. Family-like." She smiled at him. "Let's have coffee," she suggested.

Before Logan knew what was going on, over two hours had passed and he'd had one of the best first dates he'd had in a long, long time. He found Riley to be funny, cute, sexy and smart. He was intrigued by how she built her business. He loved hearing about the way she grew up, the family's struggles, the family's close relationship.

She never once mentioned Emma Shay and he grew hopeful that there was no strong connection between them.

"Why am I telling you so much?" she said, well into her second cup of coffee.

He shrugged. "I'm a detective. I know how to ask the right questions. I know when to ask them. But hey, I play fair—this is a date, not an interrogation. I'll tell you anything."

"Anything?"

"Pretty much. I can't talk about cases I'm working on but you'd find that boring anyway. Riley," he said seriously, "this turned out really nice. I think your mother catching you having a date broke the ice."

"I think you're right," she said. "And I'm never going to hear the end of it."

"Are you ever going to tell me why it was me?" he asked. "And why tonight was the night?"

She wore a mysterious smile. "Maybe next time," she said. "Or the time after that."

"That's what I wanted to hear."

* * *

Logan wasn't allowed a kiss that first night, but she did make plans with him for the next day. She agreed to meet him Saturday afternoon for a movie and early, casual dinner. He took her to see a disaster film—a violent earthquake took out the entire west coast—and if it had been a test, it was a very successful one; she loved the movie and it had her nearly sitting on his lap through the whole thing. And then during a dinner of pizza and beer he was more than happy to tell her his life story.

Logan's parents had divorced because his father cheated on his mother when Logan was at a very vulnerable age of thirteen. Although his father never remarried and his parents seemed to have made their peace with each other, Logan wasn't over it. "I'm thirty-eight, my dad has always stuck around, made amends as best he could, I get along with him as well as possible but the truth is, I'm still pissed."

"That's a powerful grudge," she said. "Remind me not to make you angry."

"Funny thing is, I don't think I'm that kind of person, not really. I didn't stay mad at my wife, did I? My sister's fine with him. But we just rub each other the wrong way. And the rest of the family gets chronically annoyed with both of us. Maybe we just don't like each other that much."

"Did you like him once?" she asked.

"I worshipped him," Logan said.

"And there's the problem," Riley said.

If that had been a second test, she passed with flying colors. She was good to talk to—perceptive and sensitive. Intelligent and compassionate.

"Might be time to let that little boy in you grow up," she said.

And she made him laugh. For Logan, a laugh was almost as good as a kiss.

Almost.

On Sunday they went to brunch in Bodega Bay then drove to a hilltop that overlooked the Pacific. Once there, Logan got his kiss and it was so excellent he helped himself to several more. He got the message Riley was just as pleased because in no time they were making out like teenagers. And it was good. She tasted good, felt good, responded to him in a lush and delicious way.

She stopped him. "Whew," she sighed. "I'm not ready for more than that."

He smiled and kissed her nose. "That's fine. You're probably the smart one here. But you have to admit—we have ourselves a very nice start."

"Meaning…?"

"Three dates in three days, good food, good talk, excellent making out…"

"Yes… And now the workweek starts and…"

"And?" he asked.

"I have long hours, family obligations… I don't usually have this much time to play around."

He hugged her close. "I'm not playing, Riley. And I understand about schedules, work, family. How about if I call you? How about we stay in touch? In close touch? Let's work out when we'll get together again."

"I guess…"

"You sound a little cautious," he said.

"It's been a long time," she said. "But yes, let's talk."

"When is too soon to call you?"

"Fifteen minutes after we say goodbye today," she said.

He laughed. "You read me, all right. I'll call tonight."

Then they kissed a little more.

Logan hadn't been looking. Well, he was always looking, but he hadn't been expecting to find anyone. This woman was a surprise—as pretty as any woman he might be physically attracted to, as smart as any he could be serious about, as sexy as anyone he could be completely into. It took him a little by surprise, but damn.

This one, he sincerely believed, had some outstanding staying power. A few things would have to be managed, however. Like the case he was working on. And the fact that Riley had only crossed his path because he'd been watching Emma Shay.

They talked late Sunday night, too late. That quiet, intense, getting-to-know-each-other, coming-on-to-each-other kind of talk. He had dreams. Fantastic dreams. He went to work early Monday morning tired with a love hangover.

"We got a break in the Compton surveillance," his partner Georgianna Severs said. "Her relationship with the Kerrigans flared—she took a job from Riley Kerrigan and it appears her casual friendship with Adam Kerrigan has been upgraded. I reviewed a week's worth of her phone log and she calls the brother at least three times a day. She took a job with Riley and she's boinking the brother, Adam. We've got her on tape referring to both Adam and Riley Kerrigan multiple times. I guess we know why she's back here."

Logan felt the shot to his gut. His suspect was involved with his new girl…

Logan slid down in his desk chair and said, "Fuck."

"What?" Georgianna asked him. "We knew they knew each other."

"Everyone knows everyone around here. She went to school with half the town but she hasn't been in touch with them. The word was they were estranged, hadn't talked in years. In four months we had one text to the brother's cell. One! They weren't in touch!"

"That we know of," Georgianna said. "Our warrant is limited to her phone and her banking. We don't have her under surveillance."

"We've been watching her," he said.

"Hit and miss, not surveillance. We're not sitting on her."

"I thought we'd be cutting this loose pretty soon..." He shook his head miserably.

They occupied a little cubicle, but it was early. Not too many people around. They wouldn't even have their morning briefing for another half hour.

"What did you do?" Georgianna asked.

"I'm hooked up with the friend. Riley Kerrigan."

Georgianna was silent. It took her a long time to speak. "Why?"

"Why? Why?" he asked incredulously. Then all the wind out of his sails, he put his head in his hands. "The flesh is weak," he muttered.

"Oh, my Jesus," she said tiredly. "What were you thinking?"

"What do you know?" he asked. "You were born married. You were seven the last time you were tempted. She's beautiful, all right? She's funny in a ridiculously arrogant sort of way—she thinks she knows everything, like all women, as you should understand. Besides, this just wasn't that much of a case. I thought she might accidentally give me some useful information and probably never even know it and *poof*—the warrants would expire, it would be over and—"

"And we agreed it certainly would be a major case if we caught her transferring money from a hidden account. In which case it would be a career maker. And there was probable cause for the warrant."

"Very thin probable cause that had nothing to do with Riley Kerrigan," he argued.

He got up from his desk and went for coffee.

A little over six months ago, shortly before the suicide of Richard Compton, Emma Shay Compton's cell phone had gone missing. So she claimed. It was not recovered, but in the interim the FBI monitored calls and there had been two placed from that number to Aruba where the Comptons had owned a beachside estate—their winter place. Based on the suspicion that Emma might have offshore funds in the islands, money set aside from her husband's estate for her to access, a judge had granted a warrant for surveillance of phone and banking records for six months. The six months would be up in February and if there wasn't any new probable cause, it would not be renewed.

It was a soft case now with Compton dead, everything either liquidated and auctioned or held by US Marshals for auction. The apartment in Manhattan and the estate in Aruba had been sold. Emma Shay had been thoroughly investigated and if no new incriminating evidence turned up before the expiration of the warrant, it was likely the case would be closed. The FBI was being assisted by local detectives Danner and Severs, but after the expiration of the warrant the local police would be off the case and it would be up to the FBI to sniff around Emma to see if she suddenly started living large or if she bought airfare to another country where she might access her nest egg without the interference of the US Government.

Law enforcement could investigate her forever if they chose to, but they couldn't access her property, phone records, banking records or other personal property and space without a warrant.

Logan and Georgianna had been watching, listening, and there had been nothing to indicate the former Mrs. Compton had access to illegally received money. And they had other cases to work. They were actually property crimes cops but both had had some previous experience in intel and fraud and it served a purpose to have them working in a division that didn't normally deal with white-collar crime. No one would suspect them of investigating Emma Shay.

Logan went back and sat at his desk. Their desks were pushed together, back to back so the partners faced each other. There were two computers, two phones, a couple of bulletin boards, a couple of shelves where spiral notebooks and loose papers were constantly stacked. George had pictures of her kids, parents and her framed awards on her side of the cubicle. Logan had a picture of his last dog, a German shepherd named Suzanne after an ex-girlfriend he hadn't had a great experience with. The accoutrements in the room were heavy on George's side.

"It's not going anywhere and we know it," he said.

"You have to tell Mike," she said.

Mike was the captain in charge of the fraud unit.

"When there's something to tell him, I'll tell him," Logan said.

"There's something to tell him now," she insisted.

"Are you going to get in my business here?"

"He's going to ask you to either drop and hand off your investigation or make yourself available to detectives for questioning. He's going to ask you, 'Do you want to work this case, which could be a career making case if you find something, or do you want to fall in love?' Because you can't have both. If you want to work it, then you're now undercover and everything you do with Riley Kerrigan is subject to examination, but you can't have both."

"I can if she's not in any way involved in a conspiracy to receive or help someone receive stolen money or property."

"But you won't know that unless you're undercover. I have no problem passing this to another team and…"

"And dropping it after months of work? What do we have—a surplus of bored detectives around here looking for extra work? By the time the warrant is expired we'll know what we're dealing with!"

"And you'll be in over your head," she pointed out. "You'll screw it up."

"No. I. Won't." He took a breath. "I know how to keep my work and my personal life separate. I've done it for fifteen years."

"Well…" she said.

"Okay, once or twice I might've blurred the line a little, but I'm not exactly famous for it."

She leaned on her hand, looking at him earnestly. George was beautiful. She was five-ten with shoulder-length bronze hair, big brown eyes, a knockout body and a drop-dead intelligence that she'd completely betrayed by marrying and reproducing with a big, burly firefighter. Cops had a love-hate relationship with firefighters. The smoke-eaters always got the girls and it just wasn't right. If Logan had seen George first, he might've married her, but unfortunately he'd been married to someone else back then. But he drew her as a partner and in that got one of the smartest detectives he'd ever known. He knew he should probably listen to her now, take her advice.

"I got it, George," he said.

"Why don't you go ahead and tell me how you justified this in your tiny little brain," she said.

"I was befriending her! I never would've gotten interested if I thought she could possibly be involved with our suspect! But then… I just found out, okay?"

"You've had five minutes, which is about all the time you give matters this important. Go ahead. Tell me."

"It's not going anyplace. So they know each other, so what? Everybody knows everybody—it's her hometown, that's why she's back. That doesn't spell conspiracy or fraud or anything. It's too soon anyway. If I'd been married to a multimillionaire who got all his money through fraud and if I had a little of that stashed somewhere I wouldn't tap it in six months. I'd wait a few years till there was no scent on the money. If she wanted some money, why didn't she take the settlement she was offered?"

Georgianna pulled a face. "Because she looks better this way and what she's got stashed is more."

"Then why didn't she take the settlement, move to the islands or something and have both? We talked about this. One of two reasons—either she's afraid she won't be able to travel because she'll end up extradited and prosecuted or maybe, just maybe, she's not guilty of anything."

"Danner, here's what you don't get—they were *married.* They lived together. They slept in the same bed. He probably talked in his sleep. They socialized with his employees and his clients. Do you really think he pulled off a Ponzi and she never thought something was weird? Really?"

"And here's what you don't get, George—not everyone is married like you are. Most of the cops in this shop don't tell their wives what happens at work and their wives don't ask. Not all married couples talk. Al's wife has these huge bills and he doesn't want to ask her what she's spending the money on and for that matter Al has a little issue with the slots, so he's not into sharing. Not all couples have that whole transparent thing going on like you and Mr. Universe."

Georgianna smiled. "He likes that you call him that."

"Great. Then I'm going to stop."

"So let me tell you another thing you don't get. If she didn't communicate with her husband, then if she has a secret of any kind she'll tell her girlfriend. Guaranteed."

"Shit," he said, knowing she was right.

"So what do you want, Danner? A new squeeze or a case?"

"Leave me alone. I can do this."

"I'm watching," she said.

Here's what was going to happen, Logan thought. He was going to work the case with George—they were considered a dream team because they were smart, instinctive and experienced. He'd listen to phone tapes and scrutinize bank records. He would gladly tell George anything he learned from Riley that had anything to do with a possible conspiracy and pointed a finger at Emma Shay. He would not share the personal and intimate details he hoped to achieve with Riley Kerrigan, and very soon. He would keep those two parts of his life separate.

If he learned from Riley that her girlfriend Emma was coming into money or had hidden money, then Logan would do the right thing—he'd tell George and they would hand over the case and report it to the FBI. Logan wouldn't break the law. Not even for his own mother.

But he was going to have something with Riley because he was irresistibly drawn to her. He thought he caught her scent several times through the day and night even though she wasn't anywhere nearby. He thought they could have one of those unique give and take relationships that was part fun, part intense, part sexual. He was into her, that's all. He might be an idiot about women, but he was into her and he was going for it until it worked or flopped.

He might've noticed Riley at first because he was checking out some of Emma's old friends, but that connection faded fast and he kept finding her because she appealed to him. And there was nothing illegal about that.

The second week in December was bitterly cold, with frost on the ground, dark clouds overhead, fires in every home with a hearth. But in Riley's heart there was a special warmth that she hadn't felt since her youth.

She laid her plans carefully. She left work early,

went to the grocery store, picked Maddie up after cheer practice and took her home. Then she got busy in the kitchen. With her mom and Adam always ready and eager to plan family dinners, it wasn't necessary for Riley to cook very often. Of all of them, her hours were the longest. Adam was usually done at school by four at the latest, June was busy but liked to deliver her meals early in the afternoon—her elderly clients liked to eat early and looked forward to her visits. She was always finished before five in the afternoon. When they weren't eating at June's, Riley and Maddie often grabbed takeout, something for which her daughter was usually grateful.

Tonight she was making corn chowder, salad and biscuits. She set the table even though they usually ate in front of the TV. A fire blazed in the family room. She even refreshed her lipstick.

"I have some things to talk to you about," Riley said when her daughter joined her in the kitchen.

"Wow," Maddie said. "Must be deadly serious. Fancy spread."

"It's not. I mean, I think it's important but… Well, I just wanted to tell you—I met someone. A man."

Maddie grinned. "And you're finally going to tell me?" Maddie said, dipping a spoon in her soup and blowing on it.

"What does that mean? Did Grandma say something?"

"Well, she did, but only a couple of days ago. Really, Mom? You think I haven't heard you whispering into your phone late at night? And giggling? Or that I haven't noticed how nice you've been lately?"

Riley stiffened. "I'm not usually nice?"

"Sure you are. In a very businesslike way."

"Wow," Riley said. "I thought we were very close."

"We are. I know you love me. Now tell me about this guy. We don't want to waste this cozy setting." Then she smiled prettily.

"Hmm," Riley said. "Well, I met him accidentally several times—grocery store, Starbucks—he lives around here. He's a police officer in Santa Rosa so I saw an opportunity to ask him to check on you and make sure you're not getting into any trouble and if you were, to tell me."

"You wouldn't dare!" Maddie said, outraged.

"Touché," Riley said, smiling. "He is a police officer, though. And I got a kick out of him—he's cute and kind of funny—and I thought, if I want to have a date again, maybe a cop would be safer than someone who had no ties to the community. Know what I mean?"

"You checked him out," Maddie said.

"Well, I'd have checked out any man before dating him…"

Maddie laughed. "Oh, Mom."

"What? I don't meet them in school, you know!"

"I think it's great. Do I get to meet him one of these days?"

"Sure. Yes. Of course. There's something else I wanted to tell you. It's about an old friend of mine. Emma." She took a deep breath. "Emma Shay. We were best friends all through school and when she went away to college in Seattle, your dad was actually her boyfriend. But…" She shrugged and looked into her soup. "Emma kind of lost interest in him and, well, we started going out."

Riley looked up and Maddie was staring at her patiently. Waiting.

"I got pregnant. I suppose that's why things didn't quite work out with your father and me. He'd actually been Emma's guy. But…well…"

"I know all that. You and Daddy weren't really a couple but you got together and—bingo."

"You know all that?"

"Uh-huh. Daddy told me. A long time ago. At least a couple of years ago. Maybe more. He said it was all his fault and the biggest mistake he ever made."

"Well, that was delicate of him…"

"Not because of me! Because it screwed things up with you, Mom. He said the biggest mistake of his life was not begging you to marry him." She slurped a little soup. "I think he's still kind of in love with you."

Riley was momentarily stunned. "Well, that's news to me. He certainly has an odd way of showing it."

"He's kind of stupid that way," Maddie said. "But he's a very good guy."

"Well… So there's a reason I wanted to tell you about Emma. She's been through a really hard time. She married after college, had a miserable marriage, her husband committed suicide and Emma came home. She's had a struggle. So I gave her a job, of course. Grandma was also close to Emma when we were kids and can't wait to see her again, so I guess she'll be around. Also, I think Adam might be dating her, but I haven't asked, it's just that I have a good nose. So I wanted you to have all the information so you wouldn't be completely shocked if you actually meet her. There are lots of connections and complications there."

Maddie stabbed some of her salad. She pulled it off her fork with her teeth and chewed. "I know all that, too."

"Oh, really? And who explained all that?"

"Well, Uncle Adam wanted to give me a heads-up—he has a girlfriend and he hasn't brought her around yet because you're Emma's boss and she has history with the family, not all of it good. I figured out she's the one who used to be your friend and Daddy's girlfriend. And Adam suspects you might still be enemies."

"Huh," Riley said. "Is there any reason for me to be here right now? Anything I can tell you that you don't already know?"

Maddie took another bite of salad, chewed and swallowed. "I seriously doubt it," she said.

Riley put down her spoon in exasperation. "What did Grandma tell you?"

"Hmm." She stalled. "Well. She said after all these many years you and Adam were starting to get your stuff together. She didn't say *stuff,* but you know Grandma can swear sometimes. And so do you, and yet I will be punished if I— Okay, so she said after all these years it appeared Adam might have a serious love interest and she caught you finally on an actual date. With a decent-looking guy who was nice and polite and kind of interesting…"

"She doesn't know anything about him!"

"You sure about that?" Maddie asked. "Who knows what she knows? This is really good soup." She slurped a little more. "I like these talks, Mom. When am I going to meet your friend Emma?"

"Aren't you more interested in the guy?" Riley asked.

"I want to know about you and Emma, like when you were kids. And when you were teenagers," Maddie said.

"What do you want to know?" Riley asked.

"Everything," she said. "Uncle Adam said if I wanted to know all that I had to ask you. I asked him was there secret stuff? Was that why I had to get it from you? And he said it wasn't because it was secret. It was because it was special. Really special."

Riley thought for a moment. "It was," she said. "She was the first friend I had here. We were nine…"

Riley told her daughter all the details, from nine to nineteen, and Maddie understood it all because she had best friends—the laughter, the fights, the trouble, the way they'd always helped each other through dark times. Although it was frightening, Riley also told about the end. She didn't quote Emma or herself, but she admitted there were hateful things said.

"Mom," Maddie said. "Mom, you're crying…"

Riley wiped at her cheeks. "I didn't realize," she said. "I didn't think it was still so real. It was such a hard thing… And then there was you, and you made it all worth it. Because I had you, my regrets were gone. I was sorry I hurt her, though. And I said so, I really did."

"Is she still mad?" Maddie asked.

Riley shrugged. "I don't think so. We haven't had that talk. We nibbled around the edges of it. She said she got over it a long time ago and I said that I'd begged her to forgive me and she never did. But then we left it without a real talk."

"Are you going to?"

"I'm her boss now so I don't know," Riley said.

"You better," Maddie said. "Know why? Because I don't think I've ever seen you cry before."

"Oh, Maddie, I've cried so much!"

"Not around me," she said. "And you know what? You're more real when you cry."

Twelve

Emma had to concentrate very hard just to keep up with the rest of her team so for the first two weeks in her new job she saw very little besides the dust and dirt she was waging war on. It wasn't just important that she be flawlessly thorough, but also fast. Clients had an expectation of not only a perfect job, but an on-time job, too. In most of the houses no one was home and it was usually planned that way; people didn't like being underfoot while the house was being cleaned.

Nick came by a couple of times as she was working to check on her. He was a happy and energetic guy in his early thirties, and two things were immediately clear—all the women liked him and he had eyes only for Makenna. He joked with her, complimented her, asked her a lot of questions, but she kept moving and gave him mostly short answers. Emma was amused by the way she tried to ignore him. Makenna was much friendlier with the women, though she was their superior. If Emma knew her better she might tease her, but she really didn't dare.

In fact, there wasn't much she dared. She very much

wanted to prove she could clean as well as she could supervise a household staff. That first week, she didn't notice much, but there was one thing that drew her attention. The trash in the wastebasket of a fifteen-year-old girl. It appeared she'd thrown away some clothing. Emma didn't mean to inspect her trash, but she couldn't help but notice the price tags still on the clothes. She pulled them out—two pair of pants, three tops, a scarf, a blazer—all stuffed into the trash can. A wad of gum was stuck to a brand-new Free People long-sleeved knit top that sold for eighty-five dollars. There were designer labels on the other items. Prada. BCBG. Christian Lacroix.

She smoothed the clothes out on the girl's bed.

"What are you doing?" Makenna asked.

"She must have made a mistake," Emma said. "She threw away brand-new, very expensive clothing—these still have the tags on."

"It's not a mistake," Makenna said. "They're in the trash."

"But..."

"And please, don't talk to Dellie about the clothes in the trash. Dellie has three daughters, no spousal support and seeing this careless treatment would be hard on her heart."

Emma frowned. "But why?"

"Because her ex is an asshole, why else?"

"No—why are these things in the trash?"

"Some of that stuff we don't see, Emma. Her parents are never around, her mother's assistant buys the clothes, Bethany doesn't want them. In fact, she resents them and does it out of spite. But they can't end up on an employee's daughter. Who knows how much trouble that could create."

"Shouldn't her mother know?"

"Do you know her mother?" Makenna asked, lifting her dark brows.

"Well, no, but if I—"

"Don't project. Don't extrapolate. Telling her mother might only create bigger problems for us."

"How?"

"She'll fire us and hire a new service merely because we looked too closely and presumed to know more about her family than she does. Trust me. Or, to keep from getting in trouble with her mother, sweet little Bethany will claim we stole the clothes."

"Doesn't she care?" Emma asked Makenna.

"I don't know. And neither do you." And with that, Makenna stuffed the beautiful clothes back into the trash can and handed it to Emma.

Emma did as she was supposed to do and emptied that trash can into the big plastic bag she was carrying from room to room. She so hoped she'd see some of those expensive new things on a homeless person. "If she were mine..."

"I'm sure you'd care enough to take her shopping, listen to her likes and dislikes and be a perfect mother. Congratulations to you."

"I bet there are some homeless people who'd like to know where the best trash cans are," she muttered when she was out of Makenna's earshot.

She didn't say another word but she could begin to see how you could become hard, cynical. If the dirt the clients left behind wasn't enough to turn you, the private lives they thought no one could see might.

"We need to be invisible," Makenna reminded her.

"We can't afford to be enmeshed with the client. It's not good for business."

Emma was surprised no exposé had been written by a member of her Manhattan household staff. Had she and Richard been more clever in concealing how obscene their private lives were? Looking back she thought she'd been a very decent mistress of the house but it was true; she didn't remember the names of all the people who served them. She knew the housekeeper, the driver, the cook, her part-time assistant. The cleaning people changed regularly, the florist's delivery people were always different, she'd had seven different personal shoppers in five years.

They had been invisible to her.

At the end of the second week on Friday afternoon, she went with Makenna back to the office to pick up her car.

"Here's your schedule for next week. Meet your team here. You can take a van to your appointments. And Riley asked me to tell you she'd like to see you if you have some time."

She was the boss. How could Emma not have time?

When she got up to the second floor, Jeanette was gone for the day and Riley's door was ajar. There was laughter coming from inside. Emma tapped lightly.

"Come in, come in," Riley called. "Well, you look pretty decent for a Friday night."

"I do?"

"You do," she laughed. "Emma, this is Brazil Johnson, our accountant and CFO. We go way back. Brazil, this is Emma Shay and we go back even further—we first met in fourth grade."

Brazil, a tall, lanky African American woman in jeans and crisp blouse with a scarf tied around her head, stood and put out a hand. "Emma," she said. "I like that. Emma. Is it short for anything?"

Emma shook her head. "No, and I wasn't named for anyone that I know of."

"I used to clean houses with Brazil," Riley said. "We were almost the original team."

"I'm happy to meet you," Emma said.

"Come in and sit," Riley invited. "Brazil isn't around the office too much and when she is I like to take advantage of her stories."

"My mother is an invalid now," Brazil explained. "I work from home as often as I can so I'm there for her. Most days she drives me out of my mind. But it's very good practice for me—might make me conscious of what it's like and keep me from burdening my daughter with the same." She shook her head. "Woo-eee, Denise wouldn't put up with a tenth of what Mama gives me!"

"Denise is an attorney," Riley said. "Also a single mother. So many of us."

"Do you have children?" Brazil asked Emma.

"No," she said, shaking her head. "It's just me."

"Well, your old friend Riley has created a company that welcomes single parents and makes it easy for them to work at a decent wage. She should get a medal."

"I'm thinking a statue in the town square," Riley said with a laugh. "How's work going? Any problems or revelations?"

Emma was a little uncertain. She bit her lip for a moment. "Work is fine. Is there a suggestion box around here?"

Riley's eyebrows were raised in question. "You have a suggestion? Already?"

"Just a thought," Emma said with some trepidation. "I understand why it's a bad idea to accept used clothing from clients..."

"It can be disastrous," Riley said.

"I was wondering, if it was managed and there was a receipt from the donor so there wouldn't be any misunderstanding..."

"I don't think it's a good idea to have our clients think we're needy, Emma."

"I understand, but the client doesn't have to know where donated clothing goes. In fact, we could send out a notice to clients saying that if they choose to donate to a variety of worthwhile outlets from shelters to dress for success organizations that help to clothe people for job interviews..."

"The clothes you were forced to throw away wouldn't have made it into donation, Emma," Riley said. "That screwed up fifteen-year-old girl's clothes wouldn't have been donated. She was making a statement when she put them in the garbage."

"You know about that, huh?" Emma said.

"There's very little I don't hear about," Riley said. "I'm sorry, Emma. I think it's a bad idea."

"If someone came to you and said, 'Would you like to donate these nice clothes?' what would you think?" Brazil asked. "You'd think, 'Why's that cleaning woman picking through my trash?' that's what."

"Our clients want to think their cleaners don't need charity. They like thinking we don't see their castoffs, that we don't notice things like that."

"Tempting though, ain't it?" Brazil said.

"It is," Emma said.

"Look the other way, Emma," Riley said. "Anything else on your mind?"

She shook her head.

"I'm glad it's going well for you. Makenna tells me you're doing a very good job."

"Thank you," she said. "The team does a very good job. They're good girls. Women."

"That's all I have for you," Riley said. "I just wanted to check in with you. And here's your check," she added, handing Emma an envelope. "From now on Brazil will have your pay deposited in your account and Nick will give you the stub showing your deductions. Welcome aboard."

"Thanks," she said. And took her leave.

Emma had been in touch with Adam every day without fail. On those few nights they weren't together, they talked on the phone. Tonight Emma was going to Adam's house for dinner. When she was there, which had only been twice so far, she put her car in his garage so that if Riley drove by she wouldn't see it. When she arrived, he was busy in the kitchen, slicing and dicing, garlic being sautéed in the pan on the stove.

"It already smells wonderful."

"I have something to tell you," he said. "My mother asked me if I happened to have a phone number for you. She's planning to call you. I gave her the number. I hope you're okay with that."

"Will she tell Riley?" Emma asked.

"You can ask her not to, Emma. I don't think Riley finding out we're seeing each other will be as much of a problem as you think."

"It will be a problem for her, I guarantee it."

"I hope you're wrong, but we'll do things your way. My mother wants to see you. She knows Riley has your number and she didn't ask her."

"I don't know what's going to piss her off more—us being together or hiding it from her."

Every time Emma's phone rang, she jumped. She looked at the caller ID and it was either Adam or Lyle. Then on Wednesday while she was working, her phone vibrated in her pocket and she didn't dare answer it, even though the home owners were not home. When they took their break between houses, she listened to the message.

"Emma, it's June Kerrigan. Adam gave me your number and I've been looking for a time I could ask you to dinner when it would be just us so we could talk, catch up with no interference from eavesdroppers or others. Maddie is having a sleepover Friday night so her mother will have to stay home with them. How I got out of sleepover duty, I'll never know, but finally the house is my own. Can you come to dinner? At about six? When you were a little girl you loved my fried spaghetti—it was your favorite and your little feelings were hurt if we had it without you. If I make fried spaghetti, will you come? I think I've waited long enough!"

Tears came to her eyes and she sniffed loudly enough that Shawna turned from the front seat and asked, "You okay, girl?"

"Yes, sorry. I just got the sweetest message from an old friend…"

"It your birthday or something?" Shawna asked.

"No," she said, laughing. "She's going to make my

favorite dish from when I was a little girl—fried spaghetti with pesto, black olives and pepperoni."

And both women oohed and ahhed.

On Friday afternoon, immediately after work, she went to the flower shop. She'd called Lyle and asked him if he'd make a Christmas centerpiece for her to give to someone special. When she got to the flower shop the guys were both there. With the holidays upon them, they were keeping the shop open a little later and Lyle hadn't gotten around to her centerpiece.

"Who's getting my masterpiece?" Lyle asked.

"You have to promise not to tell," she said. "June called me and invited me to dinner, just the two of us. Adam gave her my cell number."

"Adam?" Lyle and Ethan said in unison.

"Yes, Adam—and you have to keep him a secret, too. It started out that he was a very nice and helpful friend. You know, a little glass of wine, a cell number in case I needed a hand with anything, lunch at a vineyard bistro, then..."

They were leaning toward her. "Then...?"

"It got a little...you know...romantic."

"OMG, she's doing Adam, the love of my life," Ethan said, swooning into Lyle.

"Get a grip," Lyle said. "He's straighter than my hair."

"He actually is," Emma said. "Could you get on my page here? I'm reuniting with June tonight and I need a centerpiece. A lovely centerpiece. One that says I'm grateful for everything, for accepting me without questioning about Richard's crimes, for missing me, for welcoming me back, for still loving me."

"I've had a crush on Adam since the first day I met him," Ethan said.

She looked at Lyle. "What's going on here? Is Adam his hall pass?"

"It's completely meaningless," Lyle said. "Adam couldn't be less interested in Ethan. Come on back to the playroom, Emmie. You can supervise my creation."

"I'd love that," she said.

"And why are we keeping Adam and June secret?" Lyle asked.

"Riley is my boss and until Riley invites me to join her and the family, I'm staying back. She's keeping me at arm's length. Maybe someday, but not someday soon. But I so miss June."

"Understandable. Take your time. And tell me all about the job," he said.

"I told you," she said, finding a seat on a stool.

"Not really," he said, digging around for the tools of his profession—clippers, tape, scissors, foam, wire. "You did some groaning and whining about how exhausted you were but no details."

"We're not supposed to talk about details—the client, I am told, has an expectation of privacy."

"You aren't supposed to name them, Emmie, but you can tell tales to a person you can trust. That's me." He grinned. Then he stepped into the refrigerator and gathered up some stems, fern and baby's breath. "What's it like?"

"It's the hardest work I've ever done—and remember, I helped decorate a seventy-thousand square foot department store for holidays, on my feet, lifting and hauling and climbing for sixteen hours a day. I was a lot younger then, too. It's the hardest I've worked and

I'm learning that to work for Riley is to get the best pay available for cleaners. Apparently clients cancel their contracts all the time and get cheaper cleaners but, because Riley and her two bulldogs, Makenna and Nick, keep everyone's standards really high, they end up returning and paying the money to get the good work. We do good work," she said, giving her head a shake. "Wow, do we do good work. And fast. I am appalled to note that there are so many jobs that pay better and have far less impact on the quality of life for a family. Families," she added. "You get a feeling for what family life is like in a house right away, which homes are run by the kids who have every possession imaginable and others don't even have family games. There are houses we clean where the wife hovers and inspects and says, 'My husband likes it this way or that way,' and houses I've cleaned four times and have yet to meet a home owner. You can pick out their nesting spot right away, the places that are used—a favorite chair, desk in the office, bathroom counter. We have one client who lies on the sofa watching TV until we get to that room, then she shifts to the bedroom. She eats all day and I've never seen her dressed in anything but loungewear. Some kids' rooms have awards and pennants and group pictures, some show no sign of any siblings or friendships or group activities. Some children's rooms are very, very sad."

"What makes a sad room?" he asked while he laid out a sheet of paper, placing baby's breath on it. The little ball inside the spray paint can bounced when Lyle shook it and with a quick, deft hand, he painted the baby's breath red.

"That's amazing, what you just did there," she said.

"Christmas colors. What's a sad room?"

"Well, there's a teenager's room that's so pristine it hurts. It's like a ghost room, but someone lives in it—there's evidence of living—trash in the bin, books moved, linens slept in, laundry in the hamper, towels in the bath have been used. When I moved the desk blotter to dust I saw something carved in the wood, something her mother would never see because her mother works long hours and doesn't clean or look at her daughter's things. She carved, *I miss her every day.* I assume she carved it. They're rich. They wouldn't have purchased a damaged piece of furniture."

"Wow," Lyle said, stopping his arranging. "Who do you think?"

"I don't know," Emma said. "Could be a sibling. There are no other children's rooms or family pictures anywhere. Maybe a friend? Grandmother? I have no idea. And you know what else, Lyle? I never realized this when I had help of my own but I realize it now. We're invisible. I always thought of myself as very tidy but now I wonder if I prepared for the cleaning staff—did I wipe the bathroom mirror? Clean the sink? Flush? Because now I see that some people don't."

"Ew," he said. "I certainly know I do those things."

"I think I did. I hope I did. But a hard truth for me is—I don't know the names of the ladies who cleaned our apartment. They changed regularly. But still..."

"My God, you're learning volumes about yourself. About people you don't know."

"It's humbling," she said.

"Are you humbled by who you are? Or who you were?"

"Both," she said.

* * *

She was so nervous. Anxious and nervous. She carried her centerpiece up the walk to June's front door and knocked. The door opened immediately and there she stood, looking only a little older.

"Emma! At last," June cried, embracing her at once.

Emma was left to balance the centerpiece in one hand and return the hug with the other.

"How I've missed you," June said. "I thought of you, prayed for you, hoped you'd come back to us. It's been so long."

Emma closed her eyes against tears. June's skin on her cheek was so soft, just as she remembered. She smelled faintly of Ivory soap, something so basic, clean and memorable. And she could smell clean sheets—June used to iron the pillowcases, and the smell of hot linen that filled the room gave Emma such comfort. The arms that held her were the same, just strong enough but not overwhelming. June knew just how to cradle a person.

"June," she whispered.

June backed away a bit and looked at her. "You've held up so well," she said, wiping Emma's cheeks with her thumb. "Shall we stand here in the doorway and cry or will you come in?"

"I've been so excited and so nervous," Emma said.

"Now, stop that," June said with a little laugh. "From the very first day we knew each other we knew we'd be friends. Close friends."

"This is for you," Emma said.

"Ah, our Lyle hasn't lost his touch at all, has he? He's getting even better. Thank you, it's so beautiful. Come in, come in."

There was a small noise, a little whine, and Emma looked down to see the oddest-looking dog.

"Emma, this is Beatrice. She's staying with me for a while until she can recover from her last owner. She's a rescue and I'm afraid she was quite mistreated. I'm a foster mother for the animal shelter. Beatrice was once very beautiful and will be again after a little love and attention."

"She's so sweet," Emma said, reaching out.

But Beatrice just skittered away, going back to her bed in the kitchen.

"She usually needs a little time to get used to new faces, new smells." June carried the centerpiece into the kitchen where she had the table set with two places, candles and wineglasses. She put the flowers in the middle.

"Speaking of new smells… I haven't had fried spaghetti in so long. Since I was last at your house, I think."

"It's ready and in the warmer," June said. "We're going to light the candles, have a glass of wine and just talk for a while. Are you starving? I made us some crab rolls, just a little snack."

June busied herself getting the rolls, the wine, lighting the candles, then she sat down in the place next to Emma. She lifted her glass. "To your return, darling Emma."

Emma burst into tears.

It took her a moment and a couple of napkins to compose herself. June was the nearest thing to a mother she'd had and whether she'd admitted it to herself or not, she'd been afraid she'd never be reunited with her.

"Riley might not be okay with our private party," Emma finally said with a hiccup of emotion.

"Well, Riley's stubborn sometimes, but that's all right.

Her pride and stubbornness probably got her through the tough times. She's a good woman. She's also logical and usually comes around eventually. And—I haven't mentioned this to her but not because I'm keeping secrets. Because she'd want to be here. And we need this time. I want you to tell me everything."

"Oh, June, you don't want to—"

"Yes, yes, I do. We always had the most important talks. About the hardest things, too. Tell me, Emma, did you love him?" she asked in a soft voice.

"I did," she said in a whisper. "I thought I was the luckiest girl in the world. In the universe. Richard was sophisticated and smart. He treated me as if I was some kind of precious gift. I loved him. I didn't think he was capable of doing anything terrible, of hurting people." She shook her head. "A couple of times I was selfish or demanding or complaining and he would just frown and say, 'Emma, Emma, this childish behavior doesn't suit your image at all. Don't you know how powerful you are? How many people watch you?' If I asked for something he would just say, 'Of course.' I thought he was kind. A few times I overheard him say things that were mean or harsh and if I questioned him he'd say he was sorry I had to hear that, that sometimes in business he had to be strong. Firm."

"Things like what, Emma?"

"Once I heard him on the phone, saying something like, 'That old bastard doesn't know what to do with his money anyway—he'll never miss it. Push on him a little bit harder and if you need me to, I'll call on him.' When I questioned him he said one of his clients was questioning his investment strategy, that he'd brought in more money in six months than the client's last broker had brought in over six years. And of course, he was sorry I'd seen him in such a negative light. June, he was so *nice*. Everyone loved Richard."

"You never knew what was happening," June said.

"But I did," she said in a secretive whisper. "I wouldn't let myself believe it. He had this PR person, Andrea. She'd worked with him for a long time before we got married. If he was having a relationship with her, why would he marry me? But they were together often. Sometimes she traveled with us. Sometimes with him—it was work. But I saw looks between them. Reckless, steamy looks. So I asked my husband—was he involved with Andrea? And he did what he did best—he calmed my worries, reassured me, said that was absurd. And later, much later, I learned Andrea was his mistress all along. Andrea was the one to tell him, 'It's time to marry for your image.' I wonder if he married me because I was too stupid to see what was in front of my face."

"No, no," June said. "He must have been that good at fooling people."

"But I let him fool me."

"What happened, Emma? What caused it to unravel?"

"The perfect storm. A couple of big clients didn't get good returns on their money and pulled out. There were flaws in the statements. Rich people have lots of CPAs running around, double-checking everything, and Richard made a few mistakes. Not mistakes—irregularities. There was a banking and investment corporation crisis and people were pulling their money out everywhere—no one wanted to be the last one holding the bag. Richard's funds were not insured or guaranteed. People were losing money everywhere else but not with Richard. Investments across the board were crashing like crazy, but not Richard's. A reporter from the *Washington Post* started sniffing around, angry and paranoid investors complained to the SEC, an investigation began..." She shrugged helplessly. "And I began to see a whole new Richard."

"Oh, Emma, was it terrible?"

"It was terrible," she said. "Want to know why I stayed? Why I went to court? Because it was the only way I was going to find out the truth. He wasn't going to tell me. I was making assumptions, I was guessing, I was reading the papers, financial journals, watching the news—and they got so many facts about me wrong, I couldn't be sure they were getting facts about him right. But at the trial there was evidence. I wanted to know who he was and what he'd done. I probably should have left. But I wanted to know."

June straightened. "That's what I would have done."

"You would?"

"Absolutely. Ignorance isn't really a happy place, it just seems like it for a while. I would have wanted to know."

"He thought he was a god, June," she whispered. "He thought he could do anything to anyone, that he was the most important person alive. He used people, lied to people, laughed at them."

"Emma, what was it like to be rich?" she asked.

"It was isolating," Emma said. "Most of the time I felt like I was just visiting my own life. Then I'd remember, I was hired to play a part—the part of the great Richard Compton's wife. I'd always wonder how many others were pretending to be who they were. When you have a big pile of money, it should mean security. Safety. It didn't. All our friends were rich and they worried about having the most, spending the most, trying to figure out how it could make them the best. They trusted no one. You know that silly saying, he who dies with the most toys wins? I think for a lot of people it's actually true."

"For a little while were you happy? Did you think you'd been crowned?"

"Looking back, not for very long. Two days into our honeymoon, Richard got a phone call that sent him hurrying off to Dubai and he couldn't take me—it was business. He worked long days, had business dinners, business trips. I was like a happy little girl whose daddy had finally come home when he spent an evening at home. He took employees along on vacations. He never rested. June, I loved him because I didn't know him. I didn't know him at all. By the time he was convicted I wondered how I'd been so easily duped. How I managed to stay blind—that's the part I don't get. How can I ever trust myself again?"

Thirteen

Emma and June talked for hours, talked over dinner and then a cup of coffee. It reminded Emma of those times when she was a girl and she had issues or heartaches and she and Riley would sit on June's bed and talk it all out. When her father died and her stepmother and sisters weren't very comforting, June was there. Then it was worse when Rosemary remarried less than a year later, bringing home a man they didn't even know. A creepy man who made Emma so uncomfortable just by the way he looked at her. She was always at Riley's house and Rosemary didn't miss her at all. And June was constant, always there for her, no matter how tired she might've been. Even when Emma and Riley fell out, June wrote Emma a lovely letter saying she hoped one day they could make amends, but no matter, June would always love her like a daughter. "You are the daughter of my heart, Emma, and no matter what happens, I will always embrace you. If you need me, just call me."

It was ten o'clock when June nearly pushed her out the door. "I'm afraid to leave," Emma said. "I don't know when we'll ever have another chance to do this, to talk like this."

"There will be many chances, Emma. I promise. Maybe you'll invite me to your little house."

The second the cold night air hit her face, Emma realized she was emotionally exhausted. Wrung out. She was glad Adam's house wasn't too far away; she was so happy he invited her back tonight. She hadn't packed a bag or anything but she was going to impose on him, steal one of his T-shirts and curl up next to his big warm body and sleep forever, maybe till Sunday.

"Emma?"

She nearly jumped out of her skin at the sound of a man's voice. She shrieked and crossed her arms over her chest.

"Oh, Jesus, sorry. I didn't mean to scare you."

"What are you *doing* here?" she asked, panting a little out of fear as who should come out of the shadows but Jock.

"I was waiting for you. I thought maybe we could talk. Just for a few minutes?"

"About what? And why are you waiting around here in the dark? How did you know where I'd be? Are you *following* me, Jock?"

"Oh, hell no, Emma. Maddie told me you'd be visiting June tonight. In fact, I think Maddie helped plan it."

"Huh? What are you talking about?"

"Maddie and her grandmother," Jock said. "You gotta watch those two. They're co-conspirators." He rubbed his hands together and stomped his feet, freezing.

"Why didn't you just call me?" she asked.

"Because Maddie didn't have your number. And I wasn't going to ask Adam or Riley." He snorted with laughter. "Oh, that would be interesting, like either one of them need another reason to be pissed off at me." He blew on his hands. "Hey, could we just sit in the car for a few minutes? I won't take too much of your time."

"Why didn't you just tell Lyle you wanted to talk to me?"

"Because he might not have given you the message and even if he had, you might not have wanted to talk to me. Come on, Emma—it took me forever to get up my nerve. And I'm freezing!"

"Have you been waiting outside all this time?"

"I didn't think you'd be in there so long. And I didn't want to miss you. Look, I only want to apologize. Explain and apologize."

She shifted her weight to the right foot. "I don't know if that's wise, getting into the car with you, late at night, isolated like—"

He laughed. "Seriously? You think I'd hurt you? When did I ever hurt anyone, huh, Emma? My little girl told me where you'd be tonight. You think I'd do that to my little girl? For the love of—"

"All right, all right… But hurry up. I'm so tired I could lie down in the street right here and fall asleep!"

He put his hand on her elbow to steer her toward his SUV. "I know I'm a fuck-up, but I thought this was the right thing," he said, handing her into the car. He went around to the driver's side and got in. He started the car for heat and rubbed his hands together. "So, Emma, this isn't going to come as news to you—I cheated on you."

Emma couldn't help herself, a short burst of laughter escaped her. Then another laugh and another, until she had to put a hand over her mouth.

"I didn't think it was that funny," Jock said.

"I might be feeling a little emotional," she said, wiping tears of laughter off her cheeks. "I know, Jock. You were slightly unfaithful. Your daughter is now fifteen."

"Well, I pretty much screwed up everything. I'm sorry I hurt you."

"What about Riley?"

"I'm sorry I hurt her, too. But what I'm really sorry about is that I didn't get my shit together in time to be a real father to Maddie. I mean, I'm a real father, don't get me wrong. I'm crazy proud of that girl. She really did get the best of me and Riley—she's beautiful and smart as her mother, she's fun and athletic. She's going to set the world on fire. I don't know what she's going to do—I bet a doctor or scientist or something. If I'd done the right thing fast enough, we'd be together, but hell, I was a stupid kid. I didn't know what I was doing. I didn't know how I felt. Plus, even if I did know, I couldn't put it into words. Or actions."

"No, Jock," Emma said, shaking her head. "We wouldn't be together. It didn't take me very long to come to that conclusion. We were falling apart right away. We were too young to hold together a long distance—"

"Not you and me, Emma. Me and Riley and Maddie. It's my fault, I get that. I didn't step up like I should have. To tell the truth, it scared me to death. I had a part-time job at a gym, for God's sake. I mostly picked up towels, wiped down equipment, showed people how to use the weights, checked IDs and got to work out for free. And that was right before I got a part-time job at the store—in shipping. I was in school, showing everyone how stupid I was, mostly. When Riley said we should tell you, I couldn't face it, couldn't face you. Couldn't face her family—you know how tight they are. Sheesh. So I was too late. When I did go back to her and suggest we get married, she told me to go to hell." He shrugged. "Can't say I blame her, but I never got another chance."

Emma was a little stunned. "You cared about her?"

"Of course I did, what do you think? Okay, I was an idiot and I thought maybe me and Riley would be friends with benefits for a while till I was ready, you know. But I was eighteen. And let me tell you about those Kerrigans…" He whistled. "You don't have five minutes to think with them, know what I'm saying? Riley's grandpa went straight to my dad and threatened to lock me up, for what, I don't know—we were over eighteen. Adam coldcocked me and told me to never set foot near his sister again or he'd kill me. Riley—Riley said I'd ruined her life, caused her to lose her best friend and I'd be lucky if she ever even let me *see* my child. And you never came back. I was so screwed. I couldn't win."

Emma was frowning. "You really cared about her?"

"I was a little slow, okay? I admit it—I didn't speak up fast enough."

"And Maddie told you where to find me tonight? What does Maddie know about it?"

"Everything," Jock said. His expression was composed and confident.

She tilted her head to look at him. He hadn't changed too much, actually. His hair was still a little shaggy but he had that handsome square jaw, pretty blue eyes and brows a little thick and bushy. And the lashes. Whew, girls would sell their mothers for some of those lashes.

"Everything?" Emma asked.

"I'm real close with Maddie. 'Course Maddie's real

close with everyone. She's got a kind of gift. She knows how to make people feel okay about themselves. I told Maddie the truth a long time ago. I told her her mama was embarrassed about it all, maybe still upset about it. And I told her it was my fault because it was. But I wanted her to know—I really cared about her mom."

"But, Jock—you didn't even go to the hospital when she was born!"

"Yes, I did. I just waited for the Kerrigan clan to clear out. No point in getting my blood all over the maternity ward! But I went. I went a lot. The nurses knew the family was pissed—they let me in after hours. And I snuck over to her house when Adam and Riley weren't around. Took me a year to get Maddie to my house so my mom could fuss over her. In the end, Riley's fair. Plus, there was June. June put a stop to all the fighting and stuff, for Maddie's sake."

"Well," Emma said. "You didn't carry a torch long, did you? You got married, didn't you?"

"Yeah, I'm so brilliant—that was me showing just how smart I am. Maddie was around ten or so and I figured Riley had no reason to hold off on us getting together. I thought it all through—I'd been helping with Maddie, keeping her sometimes, giving Riley whatever I could for support—I know it wasn't much but I didn't have much of a job back then. So I worked it all out in my head and ran it by Riley—we could be a family. Something about the way I did it really pissed her off. I mean *really* pissed her off. She said, 'In your dreams, Jock.' So I did the most rational thing I could think of—I married this woman I worked with. She had two kids, she was crazy about me. I wanted to have a home. It didn't take me long after Riley shut me down to realize once I grew up a little bit, I wanted to be a family man. Turns out she wasn't crazy about me for long. But you know me, Emma—I'm such an idiot, I think there was a part of me that was gonna show Riley—See, someone wants me. I actually thought Riley might be a little jealous. So trust me, I learned my lesson."

"My God, you have to tell her all this, Jock! You should tell Riley you screwed up when you were eighteen but you really care about her."

"Nah, that ship has sailed," he said. "I'm not good enough for her anyway. You know how smart she is? I'm just lucky we don't fight anymore. We get along okay. Maddie's happy. Maddie—she's incredible. You know Maddie's even proud of me? *Me?* I don't do much to brag about but I play some mean softball and Maddie comes to my games. All my friends and their families know her." He laughed. "Riley even came to a game once. She left like her pants were on fire, but hell—she did come."

"You used to play some serious football, as I recall," Emma said, her voice soft.

"Only for fun after high school," he said. "I've been with Mackie's Electronics for a long time and I do all right now. To tell the truth, I do better than all right—I have the management of a store. I have a mortgage. A house and a mortgage. Riley won't take support money anymore so she said just put some aside for Maddie for college. I'm sure Riley thinks I just ignored her, but I didn't. I think Maddie can pick any college by now. Not that she's going to need tuition—she's the smartest kid in school. Like her mom was. Riley was valedictorian."

Emma laughed. "Yeah. I was there."

"So I'm sorry, Emma. Sorry I cheated on you. I

should've broken it off with you when we stopped talking, when I started hanging out with Riley. If I'd done that one thing..."

"Well, it's all behind us now. You were forgiven a long time ago."

"You okay, Emma? I heard about how bad things got for you. Anything I can do?"

"Nah. I have a job. I'm back in a town I know. I have a few friends."

"Maybe you could count me as a friend," he said. "No ulterior motives," he said, holding up his hands. "But if you need anything..."

"That's very nice, thanks. Right now I have to go. I worked all day and seeing both you and June... By the way, Riley doesn't know I had dinner with June."

"I know. Maddie said we're not exactly keeping secrets, but we're not talking about it."

Emma laughed. That was what keeping secrets was. She made a decision—she was going to tell Riley about dinner with June. If it made her angry, she'd have to get over it. Emma was relatively sure Riley wouldn't fire her. In fact, she might have to tell about Adam, too. Now for that, Riley might fire her.

Jock was right. Those Kerrigans could really close ranks. But what should you expect from a family that had to stick together to survive?

She shook hands with Jock, wished him luck, thanked him for making amends. By the time she got to Adam's house it was almost eleven. The front door was unlocked. He had a fire going and was nursing a drink.

"I had almost given you up for lost," he said.

"For a little while there I thought I was lost. My night started with your mom and Beatrice..."

"I know Beatrice," he said with a chuckle.

"And ended with Jock waiting for me so he could apologize for cheating on me—sixteen years ago."

Adam was tempted to beg for every moment of time Emma would spare him, to keep her close, to possess her. Hold her. But he knew she had to untangle her life. And he was part of it. She said, very clearly, she needed to try to build her life as a woman before she thought of herself as part of a couple.

Last night in the glow of the fire she'd asked him, "Were you too hard on Jock? Did you scare him too much? Discourage him too much? Because it turns out he always cared for Riley. I mean, I think he loved her. And he adores Maddie."

"He was an irresponsible idiot," Adam said. "*Then.* Back then, I mean. I know he's gotten better over time. And don't kid yourself, he's not afraid of me!"

"He did a lot of stupid things," she said.

"That's an understatement."

"So did I," she said. "So did Riley. You appear to be the only perfect one."

But he'd lost his temper with Jock. He'd hated Jock. He didn't hate him anymore but he wasn't crazy about him.

Emma went home to help Penny rake up some dead leaves in her garden, to shop for her lunch supplies for the week, to launder her uniform. But she did invite him to share a pizza and a movie later. He knew that meant he'd somehow manage to spend the night. So he planned to spend some of his Saturday checking on his mother and buying another big box of condoms.

He'd had plenty of sex in his adult life. Great sex, as a

matter of fact. But he'd never had a woman who wanted him like Emma wanted him. She unfolded like a rose in full bloom when he touched her. She said his name with a kind of breathy awareness that turned him on so much, he was completely helpless. He'd always thought of himself as a man with great control, but he lost that with her. He teased her until she became a little wild and then he was done for—he went crazy with her and they blew up together. He thought he knew why it was that way with them. He was in love with her.

After the weekend, Emma found herself actually looking forward to work on Monday morning, even though it was getting particularly difficult cleaning with Christmas approaching and all the decorations littering the houses. She'd never seen her own Christmas decorations looking shabby or dusty! She now realized she must have had an excellent cleaning crew.

Makenna had no trainees this week so in addition to working with Emma, Dellie and Shawna, she was visiting other teams at either Riley or Nick's request. Makenna was part of quality control. "The fabulous four rides on," Shawna said of their team. "I'm glad they haven't moved you to another team, Emma. I like working with you."

"Why?" she asked before she could think.

"You're a hard worker and stay in a good mood," Shawna said.

"She's still happy she got work," Dellie said. "She'll turn into one of us before you know it."

"If I have to push someone along all day..." Shawna made a face. "It just puts me in a temper." Then she launched into a litany of shortcomings about team members who didn't meet her expectations, everything from laziness to lying.

In ten minutes they pulled up to their first house, the Christensens'. They cleaned here twice a week but it hardly needed once. Mrs. Christensen, Makenna had informed them, knew if they missed a piece of lint or a hair on the bathroom countertop. They were here every Monday and Thursday. Emma hoped she wouldn't get the vacuum cleaner—those tracks had to be perfect. The house was huge.

This was where Bethany, the fifteen-year-old with the carved-up desk lived.

"How long have you been cleaning the Christensens' house?" Emma asked.

"I don't know," Shawna said. "I've been on it a year, I think. Dellie, how long?"

Before Dellie could answer, Makenna jumped in. "The company's been in that house four years now, but we've changed teams a few times. A couple of times Mrs. Christensen found the cleaning unsatisfactory and the other times it was just time for a schedule change. New people on the job usually freshens things up."

As luck would have it, Emma was assigned the dusting, vacuuming and linens upstairs. This time she meant to take a closer look in the bedrooms. Maybe there was a mystery to unravel. Maybe she'd spy some evidence of a visiting grandmother or another child. She'd like to at least see a picture of Bethany, the girl who threw away the expensive new clothes.

The bathrooms and kitchen in this five thousand square foot custom home were usually fast work—Mr. and Mrs. Christensen had very demanding jobs and long hours. They didn't seem to do much cooking, and the only even slightly challenging bathroom was the master bath. There wasn't even much kitchen trash. Since they weren't contracted to clean the refrigerator, it was against the rules to look in it but Emma had an aching desire to know what kind of food was there.

She went to vacuum and dust Bethany's room first, fiercely curious. As she started ripping off the linens she found that the lump in the bed was Bethany. The girl shrieked and Emma jumped back, crying out.

"Oh, my God, I'm sorry! I didn't know you were in bed!"

Bethany grabbed for her covers. "I stayed home today."

"Oh, honey, are you sick?"

"Sort of," she said, burrowing back into her bed. "Sick of school."

"Oh. Can I get you anything? Call someone to look after you?"

"I'm fifteen! I look after myself!"

"Right," Emma said. "Would you like me to skip your room?"

"Yes. Just go. And look…" She talked from under the covers. "Just…don't say anything."

She's frail, Emma thought. Thin and pale and completely miserable. Who does she miss every day?

She moved on to the parents' room. Why did they have a cleaning service at all? They were immaculate. She stripped the bed, applied new linens, began dusting the furniture and heard Dellie in the bathroom, cleaning. She leaned against the door frame. "Skip the girl's bathroom," Emma said softly. "She's home, sick in bed, asked me to leave her room."

"All rightie," Dellie said. "I bet she's cutting school."

"No, she's sick," Emma said. Then she wondered why she was protecting the girl. She went back to dusting the bureau. A drawer was ajar an inch and impulsively, irrationally, she pulled it open a bit. Then a bit more. And there it was—the thing that was the root of all the pain and forced order in this house—a family portrait in a frame, hidden from sight, lying atop folded clothes. Mom, Dad and Bethany. A plumper, slightly younger Bethany who smiled as if the very sun was inside her. They were a beautiful, happy family a few years ago. Bethany was robust, rosy, healthy. That Bethany was gone now and in her wake, terrible pain.

She closed the drawer and felt her face catch fire. Her hands shook a little while she tried to concentrate on her dusting. If anyone knew, she would be fired. She would *have* to be fired.

What had happened to this family? Why was the only picture in evidence hidden in a drawer?

Then, later, as she pushed the vacuum around the room, she realized something significant—it was the father's drawer. How strange that seemed. She could envision the father demanding all the pictures be removed and the mother clinging to one. But it was the father holding on...and the mother's assistant was buying Bethany clothes.

Emma knew without even thinking about it that the next time they cleaned, the next time she had vacuuming and dusting, she would look in the mother's drawer. Look for a picture.

Then she thought of her stepmother. Rosemary dispensed with Emma's father's personal effects quickly, and the pictures soon followed because less than a year after his death Rosemary remarried. Emma kept pictures, however. So had her little sister, Lauren.

The next house was a filthy mess. It took too much of their time but it removed all that conjecture about Bethany and her family from Emma's mind for a while.

Makenna left them for a while to go with Nick and check a few crews. The next house wasn't bad, but messier than usual. The lady of the house was at home because her arm was in a sling. "Fell and dislocated my shoulder and might've injured my rotator cuff, but I had X-rays and it will be fine," she explained. "I'm just resting it and the doctor said to keep in immobilized for a few days." Then she laughed and said, "I could have gone to work, I just can't fix my hair with one arm!"

Then she stayed out of the way. When they were finished and back in the van, they took a break to eat a little lunch. "Fell my fine ass," Shawna said. "That's about her fifth fall this year!"

Emma almost choked on her drink. So—that was one of the households they knew too much about.

"It's possible she's clumsy," Emma said. "Isn't it?"

"Humph," was the answer. "She's being kicked around. Know how I know? Because I see it in her eyes and I've seen it before. When I looked in the mirror."

"Oh, dear God, Shawna," Emma said.

"Don't waste pity on me—I found the way out, even if you never get all the way out. If he isn't still out there posing a threat then he's in here," she said, tapping her head.

"Don't you worry none about Shawna," Dellie said. "Her boys are as big as he is and they take good care of their mama."

"They do. Now we're gonna get over to Ms. Fletcher's... She's the clumsy one."

"I think I might know what makes her so clumsy," Dellie said. Then the two of them cackled madly.

"What?" Emma asked.

"She's a wino," Shawna said. And they giggled some more.

It had taken her a while, but now Emma figured it out—she was hearing all this gossip because Makenna wasn't with them. Makenna was part of the executive trio with Riley and Nick, the holders of the holy grail, the policy manual. Violation of the policies got you fired.

"What's up with the Christensen house?" Emma bravely asked.

Shawna shrugged. "Career couple."

"Someone's got a little OCD going on there. I vote for her."

"Could be him," Dellie said. "We wouldn't know, they're never home. It's an easy house."

"Not a speck of dust anywhere."

"You gotta wonder why they hired a cleaning crew," Shawna said.

"For the carpet tracks," Dellie said.

"You gotta wonder why they had a kid," Emma ventured.

"Yeah, poor kid. Typical."

"Typical?"

"All they think about is work and money. Everything has to be perfect," Dellie said.

"I like it that way better than the Brewsters—those boys have every toy and gadget ever invented, they're sloppy, with no manners or respect and—" Shawna said.

"And I bet they already got accepted to Harvard even though the oldest one is twelve."

"That is a hard house," Emma agreed. Dirty, messy, cluttered with stuff. If she'd had a child, she would have taught him to put away his things, even if they had household help. When she dumped the trash in the master bath it was full of the lady's outrageous price tags. She smiled to herself. Those numbers hadn't always seemed outrageous to her.

How many of her cleaning staff saw her price tags? Well, hardly any of her things *had* price tags as they were designed specifically for her. But there was the odd outrageously expensive purse purchased at Neiman's…

She had an urge to unburden herself to her new friends, new friends who would never understand. She'd like to tell them what she knew—that those people with all their possessions could wake up one day to discover they'd been living a lie, that the identity they thought they had was gone and they would have to figure out all over again who they were.

Of course she couldn't. This was why she'd come back. There were a few people here who knew her before and after, who knew who she had been growing up and who she was again.

Only Emma was having a hard time getting a fix on her identity.

Emma had a message on her cell phone from Aaron Justice so she called him back before leaving the parking lot after work.

"I just wanted to wish you a pleasant holiday," he said. "And to tell you—we're working on an accounting of your father's estate according to his will. It should be ready after the holidays. I don't want you to get your hopes up but I anticipate a late Christmas present for you."

"Thank you, Aaron. And don't worry about my hopes. Just seeing you again has been an enormous treat. I wish you a lovely holiday."

"I'll be with my sons and grandsons. One of them is talking about making me a great-grandfather!"

"What a fantastic Christmas present for you! Thank you, Aaron, for trying to help me. Your friendship is so valuable to me!"

"Your father would be proud of you, Emma."

Proud? She wasn't sure about that. She'd made some pretty bad choices in the last decade. But she hoped she was making better choices now.

"I hope so," she told Aaron.

Fourteen

Riley was very much out of practice with the whole dating thing, but one thing she knew she wanted to do—she wanted to introduce Logan to her daughter. Their relationship had always been honest and up-front with those few little exceptions Riley had held back, like that whole Riley/Jock/Emma thing, which was now mostly out there. So she nervously asked Maddie if she'd like to meet Logan and have dinner with him.

"Dinner? Wow, we're going all out, I guess. Will Gramma and Adam be coming, too?"

"I thought we could just be the three of us. You know, we've got Christmas in a couple of weeks—Logan has a family, I have my family, we'll all be busy. We might see each other but I'm not planning on merging families over an important holiday like Christmas. So I thought I'd cook something simple, invite him over, let you get to know him a little..."

"What about Dad?" she asked.

"No, I definitely won't be inviting your dad," Riley said. "Maddie, I'm dating Logan. Sort of."

"Sort of? You're dating him for real, Mom. You giggle on the phone. Even I haven't had a boyfriend like that yet!"

"What about that Brian Breske?" she asked. "Wasn't he a boyfriend? You invested a lot of time in him."

"That was seventh grade. Kid's stuff."

"Oh," Riley said. "Well, I haven't quite elevated Logan to boyfriend status yet."

"So you're not sleeping with him yet?" Maddie asked.

"Oh, my Jesus, you did not really ask me that!"

"Of course I did." She grinned. "Is there anything we should talk about before you get in over your head?"

"I thought I'd cook," Riley said.

"Ew, you don't want to scare him away, do you?"

"It's cold. I could make chili and corn bread muffins."

"Are you going to actually make it?" Maddie asked.

"Possibly."

Maddie laughed herself stupid.

"Listen, I want you to be nice to Logan," Riley said. "I've met men for a drink or coffee over the years but I think I've been out to dinner twice since you were born. Really, the men out there are dismal. Logan is kind of fun. He's interesting—he has cop stories. His partner is a woman. He says she's the smartest cop he's ever known. There probably won't be time for more than one dinner like this until after the holidays so let's pretend we're very excited to have him over. Very happy to meet him. Hmm?"

"I can do that," she said. "Will he bring his gun?"

"Lord, I hope not!"

"Well, what fun is that?"

Riley was used to Maddie's humor, her teasing. But she sincerely hoped Maddie could put a good image forth and impress Logan a little bit.

On the day they had chosen, just over a week before Christmas, the house was decorated a little bit. No point in going crazy with decorations when they'd spend most of the holiday celebrating at June's house where the decorations were over the top, complete with outside lighting. Riley did have a tree, however. You can't be a single mom and ignore the tree!

She told June what she'd be doing and June deftly pulled a big bucket of her best chili out of the freezer and handed it to Riley, telling her to just dump it in the Crock-Pot. June whipped up some corn bread muffins—it took her under thirty minutes. "Are you going to be able to throw together a green salad?" June asked Riley.

"Of course!" she said indignantly.

Riley stopped at the grocery store on the way home and worked her way around the salad bar in the deli section, looking over her shoulder the whole time, hoping not to get caught.

Then she saw him. There he was, standing in the check-out line with a bunch of flowers and a bottle of wine. She just shook her head and chuckled to herself. She went and stood behind him.

He jumped in surprise and attempted to hold the flowers behind his back. But when he saw her holding the salad, he relaxed and returned her smile with his own.

"So this is how working people date," she said.

"Do you like these?" he asked, holding out the cellophane-wrapped bouquet. "If you want to pick something you like better..."

"I like them very much," she said. "Want to follow me home?"

"I've wanted to for weeks now."

* * *

The chili and muffins were exceptional—June liked her chili with a little kick to it, something she didn't share with the elderly on her meal route. But Logan thoroughly enjoyed it. Since they'd run into each other at the store, Riley told him the truth, that it was her mother's chili, and it was a good thing she did because Maddie wasted no time in selling her out.

Riley and Logan started off with a glass of wine and she arranged the flowers. The table was set, the chili was in the Crock-Pot, she put the muffins in a basket to warm in the microwave. The house was, as usual, immaculate.

"How was your day, dear?" Logan said.

"Perfectly ordinary. Yours?"

"It was a day full of reports, meetings, paperwork and no fun stuff."

"What's the fun stuff, I'm afraid to ask?"

"Chasing bad guys. Haven't done hardly any of that lately. George and I have been on this task force with feds and we've been sorting through a lot of paper. Feds love their paper."

"What kind of task force?"

"I'm not allowed to talk about it yet, but give it a few more weeks and when it's behind me and closed, I'll tell you all about it. It will help you sleep. It's boring."

That's when Maddie came into the kitchen, was introduced to Logan and poured herself a Diet Coke.

"Wow," she said, eyeing the table. "Fancy. Watch out, Logan—when she sets a fancy table it usually means something serious is coming down."

"Is that right?"

"That's affirmative," she said, mocking police lingo.

"My Gramma made the chili because my mother really doesn't cook much."

"I'm a pretty good cook. I just don't have a lot of time and Gramma loves to cook so we eat over there a lot," Riley said. She put the flowers on the table and they all sat down.

"Will Gramma be making Christmas dinner?" Logan asked.

"Oh, most definitely," Maddie said before Riley could open her mouth. "She'd be brokenhearted if we changed tradition. And so would my dad!"

"Your dad?" Riley asked.

"We always spend quality time together around the holidays and he usually comes over to my Gramma's at least for dessert. He was there on Thanksgiving. We're kind of a close family."

"We are?" Riley asked.

"My parents might not be married but they get along very well. What do you do on holidays?" she asked Logan.

"Go to my mother's," he said. "I have a sister, brother-in-law, niece and nephew."

"And are you divorced?"

"Maddie!"

"What? It's a getting-to-know-you dinner, right?"

"That's okay, Riley. I am divorced. Eight years and yes, we're still friendly. No kids."

"Do you wish you'd had kids?"

Logan leaned toward her. "I have an unmarked police car. Want to go outside and press the button for the lights and siren?"

"Gee, tempting as that is, I'll pass. Mom, want me to help you dish up?"

"I thought we'd visit a little first and then I'll serve, Maddie," she said slowly, measuring each word. What was this? Riley wondered. Asking about his divorce?

"So tell me all about the family, Logan," Maddie said. "Mom, Dad, sister, et cetera." She leaned her head on her hand, waiting.

And so it began. Maddie interviewed Logan. Logan did great at avoiding and evading and punctuating with his own questions because he was, after all, a detective. But Riley was soon horrified. Maddie managed to insert lots of information about Jock, making her dad look like he was extremely desirable and quite accomplished.

My dad is in electronics. He has a business degree. He works for Mackie's. It's a national chain and he's the manager of one of their biggest stores. Oh, my mom and dad still spend a lot of time together—they go to all my games and meets together and they chaperoned the homecoming dance together. My dad was all-conference in high school and he's still as athletic as ever—are you interested in sports, Logan?

"Yes," Logan said to that last question, beginning to look annoyed. "I'm very athletic. I frequently throw very large men over the hood of my unmarked car and cuff them. And I often chase bad young men *and* women who have committed crimes and I always catch them."

"I'm going to put on the coffee," Riley said. "And I have cheesecake. Store-bought."

"May I be excused?" Maddie asked.

"Absolutely," Riley said.

"Thanks," she said. "Really great to meet you, Logan."

"Likewise," he said. "Please tell your gramma the chili was outstanding."

There was no sound in the kitchen but the dripping

and bubbling of the coffeepot and then, the closing of Maddie's door. Riley and Logan let out their collective breath.

"Logan, I'm sorry about that. That was the last thing I expected."

"Don't worry about it. I think I can get her a job if she's interested in grilling hardcore criminals."

"You handled it great, but I have no idea what she's talking about—that I spend a lot of time with her dad. I don't. At least, I sure don't feel like I do. We try to coordinate plans so I know where Maddie's going to be on a given—"

"I don't think that had anything to do with her dad," Logan said. "But I think we got a close view of her preference."

"It makes no sense," Riley said. "She was excited to know I was finally dating someone."

"Then come here," he said, pulling her chair closer, putting his hands on her waist. "Date me a little." He leaned toward her for a kiss and she obliged. "She's not quite ready," he said very quietly. "She's going to need a little more time. And apparently I'm going to have to prove myself in athletics, electronics and a few other things."

"I've never felt a stronger urge to spank my daughter."

"I think you better talk to her instead. See what's going on. But for now, kiss me better."

"Are you wounded?"

"Nah, not too bad. I'm having a talk with myself right now. Families are complicated and I'm going to be patient. You know why? I want us to work, that's why. I think it's going to be okay but it's Christmas, and Christmas has a way of stirring things up, so I'm taking my lead from you. I want to be together as much as you want to be—you're going to have to drive this train. Can you do that, Riley?"

"Are you kidding? It's one of my most serious flaws—I like being in charge." She wiggled away from him and poured two cups of coffee and dished up two slices of cheesecake. Then she sat back down, closer to him than necessary. She put a little cheesecake on her fork and fed it to him. "The only part of this dinner I made was the coffee."

"Modern women turn me on," he said. "I have a feeling this first Christmas of ours isn't going to include our families, but that's okay. We're still new, there's lots of time." He fed her a bite from his plate. "So my busy season is here," Logan said. "And not because I'll be partying. More burglaries, domestics, drunk driving—it all adds up to overtime. But maybe we can sneak in our own little Christmas. I want you to think about it, tell me when you have time, help me decide what kind of day or evening you'd like."

"I'm sorry about Maddie. She's really not like that. She's one of the most accepting, generous, warmhearted people I know. And I don't think she got it from me."

"Who'd she get it from, then?" he asked.

"My mom I think. My mom is like that."

"Can I help with the cleanup?" he asked, feeding her another bite.

"No, no. Cleanup is my specialty. My profession."

They finished dessert and coffee, then Riley treated Logan to a very nice, deep, meaningful kiss and some heartfelt caressing by the front door. Riley was starting to ask herself why she'd avoided this kind of contact for so long. No one had interested her, true. But why had no one interested her? Was it because after Jock she fasted?

She cleaned up the kitchen very slowly and quietly. She had a dishwasher but sometimes she liked washing and drying the dishes by hand. When she was finished and the kitchen was perfect and shining, she went to Maddie's room. She knocked before going in.

Maddie was in her pajamas—ballerina and heart pajamas, perfect for a five-year-old girl, but her girl had long blond hair, blue eyes and was five foot eight.

"You want to tell me what that was about?" Riley asked.

"What?"

"Don't pretend you don't know, Maddie. I've never seen you act like that. Didn't you like him?" She came into her daughter's room and sat on the bed.

"Yeah, I liked him. He seemed nice. He's even kind of hot. What kind of cop is he?"

"That's kind of up in the air, I think. His business card says property crimes but he says he's doing some special project at the moment. Now, why were you going on and on about your dad? That's not really true, all that stuff you said."

"Sure it is. I talk to him every day, he's never missed a game or meet, he always comes by on special occasions even if we're at Gramma's, he takes me to my other gramma's, though not as much, and he's around you a lot because of me. He's nice and he's handsome, too."

"But, Maddie, your dad and I couldn't work things out—I explained all that."

"Not really. He did a better job of explaining than you ever did. And when I told him you were dating some guy, it made him so sad." She shrugged. "I think he's lonely. And he still loves you."

"Maddie, I don't think he ever loved me. And Lord knows he wasn't ready to be a father."

"Well, no kidding! That would be like me being a mother! But he's older now."

"Maddie, you have to be realistic. Your dad has been married. He loves you very much but he doesn't have any feelings for me."

"I know. He's pretty embarrassed about that marriage. He didn't know what he was thinking. He said he should've known better. But he said he's always loved you and always will."

"Because I'm your mother," Riley said. "That's all it is."

"No, Mama, that's not all. But it's okay. Logan is nice. And he's nice to you. That's what matters, right?"

"Right. Are you going to be nicer the next time he's around?"

She nodded, but bit her lower lip. "You know, you never went out on a date. I thought maybe you and Daddy still might have a thing for each other."

"Listen, I had a couple of dates. A few, actually. I never said anything."

"You probably said you had meetings…"

"Probably. But I was asked out. I met a couple of guys for coffee, went to a couple of happy hours, went out to dinner a couple of times, but it just wasn't the right time, I guess. I was bored. I figured if it was right I'd get a little excited."

"Does Logan get you excited?" she asked.

"I don't know. But he makes me laugh. I'm comfortable with him. I feel good about myself when we're together and it seems like we have a lot to talk about. But, Maddie, it's not serious. It's friendly. It could get serious, but I've only known him a few weeks. Relationships take time. And I'm in no rush. Now, is there anything else you need to know?"

"One thing. I hope you'll tell me the truth…"

"Maddie, I always tell you the truth!"

"Okay. Did you ever love Daddy? I mean, really?"

It was the oddest thing—Riley felt tears in her eyes. She blinked a little wildly, willing them away. She cleared her throat. She wiped her palms on her slacks. "Yes," she finally said, her voice soft. "Yes, I did."

"Really?" she asked.

"Painfully so," Riley said.

Emma steadfastly refused to announce to Adam's family that they were officially seeing each other, though everyone but Riley knew. "Let's not push our luck," she said. She didn't want any trouble or friction from Riley and mostly she didn't want a brother and sister at odds over her during Christmas. "Riley has to be the one to invite me back into her life, even as just an acquaintance. We'll never be good friends, I get that, but I don't want to push my way into your family before she's ready."

"You know I don't give a damn what Riley thinks about this," Adam said.

"That's exactly what worries me."

"Why are you so intent on having it the hard way?"

"Is that what you think? Oh, you're wrong. I want it the peaceful way. Especially now—my first Christmas home, with a nice place to live, a decent job, a great fella. I'm going to invite your mom over to see my little place and host her for a couple of hours. I'm going to spend some time with Lyle and Ethan, bring them a nice bottle of wine and some Brie and caviar, wriggle my way into Ethan's good graces. I'm spending an evening with Penny and her girlfriends—they have a little Christmas party every year and I'm now officially part of the club."

"And me?" he asked.

"I'm sure we'll have lots of quality time together."

"How about Christmas Eve?" he asked.

"I'll wait up," she said.

She wanted to enjoy the days leading up to Christmas. She didn't have much to spend on her few friends and she enjoyed it more that way. She found a lovely pashmina shawl for Penny, a couple of small but pretty tree decorations for the other ladies, and for Lyle and Ethan, a Christmas serving platter. For June, a decorative Christmas table runner that was lovely and on sale. For Adam, a soft, cuddly navy blue sweater with a white button-down shirt, a pair of delicious slippers because she had noticed he didn't have any and a book, a Nelson DeMille novel. She had studied his bookcase—he loved that particular author and although he had an e-reader, he liked to read paper.

She bought herself a few modest decorations for her little house. Adam still came to her place, though she knew he really liked his house and was so happy when she was there with him. "It's going to be a long time, Adam, before I'm good for more than this, than what we have right now. I'm working through everything but it's slow. Everything that came before us is weighty."

"Is Lucinda helping?" he asked.

"I think so, but I'm not seeing her again until the

New Year. I'm feeling almost secure," she said. "I'm afraid to blink."

"I'm not going anywhere," he said.

The holiday decorations in the homes they cleaned were a beautiful pain in the ass—difficult to clean and tidy around. Still, Emma enjoyed them as never before. It was entertaining to see what each family had done—the Douglases with the three spoiled boys had enough presents under the tree to take care of all the children in an orphanage. The Nesbitts had grown children and grandchildren, and they kept the number of gifts reasonable, yet decorated lavishly, many of the things meant to be fun for the children—advent calendar, talking Rudolph, nutcracker soldier. The Parkers had no presents under the tree—they'd be spending Christmas in Maui.

She was looking forward to seeing what the Christensen family had done. The last time she was there nothing had been done to decorate and she feared nothing would be done. But voilà! Just in time for Christmas the decorations had appeared and they blew her mind—it was a decorator's dream. She knew the cost of many of the ornaments and tabletop decorations. A nativity painted in gold and draped in Swarovski from Bergdorf's, crystal reindeer from Tiffany's, a stunning wreath—surely those weren't real diamonds, but it was copied from the real one created by Pasi Jokinen-Carter. Their tree and staircase garland were decorated by a professional, she could tell. The few packages under the tree were wrapped in expensive paper that matched some of the glass balls; fancy ribbon was coordinated with the home furnishing colors. There were silver candelabra with red candles, fresh Christmas flowers in the dining room and foyer, an expensive tapestry hung on the staircase landing and a garland to end all garlands, fresh and adorned with balls and ribbons that matched the tree.

Dellie and Shawna gasped when they saw the house.

"Stay away from the tree and garland," Emma told the girls. "Most of those ornaments came from jewelers, not Target."

Both of them backed up fearfully. "How do you know that?" Shawna asked in a whisper.

"This isn't my first rodeo," was all Emma said. "In fact..." She got out her cell phone. She called Makenna. "We're at the Christensen house and you might want to check this out. The Christmas decorations are worth more than the van. No one wants to dust them. We'll wait for you."

They started upstairs. As usual, nothing was disturbed except for a damp towel in the hamper, which Emma scooped up and put in the laundry bag for pickup. The laundry and dry cleaning was picked up and delivered twice a week, expertly timed for the moment the Kerrigan cleaners were finished cleaning.

Bethany had left her diary open on the table next to her bed, the bed she meticulously fixed in the morning even though it was cleaning day, clean sheet day. There was only one sentence written on the page and Emma couldn't stop herself. After all those years of not noticing things, now she was a damn runaway train!

I just wish there was someone to talk to.

It clutched at Emma's heart and before she could reason with herself, she picked up the pen and wrote a note. *Talk to me.* She wrote her cell number. Then her cheeks flamed so red she thought she might pass out. This house, this family was going to kill her and she was going to end up getting fired over it. She quickly passed the vacuum, leaving perfect tracks. *I am totally fired*, she thought.

She wasn't even done with the vacuum when Makenna was at the house and with her, Nick. They took one look at the decorations and called Emma down.

"Good call," Makenna said. "How'd you know?"

Makenna didn't know about her past? Riley hadn't told her closest coworkers their complicated history, Emma's spectacular and horrifying past? She was stunned. "I…ah…this isn't my first fancy house. Believe me, you don't want to break anything at Christmastime around here."

"Doesn't it just give you that warm, fuzzy holiday feeling?" Makenna said. "Stay away from all the ornamentation. I'll take care of this."

Emma wondered if there was any way to sneak upstairs to Bethany's room and remove her note from the diary. But of course it was written in pen. The only option was to tear out that page, and she couldn't bring herself to do it.

Makenna and Nick seemed to be outside conferring, talking on their phones for a long time. They sat in the company car for a while, talking. And then without saying another word, they were gone. Before leaving the house, Emma called Makenna. "What's the verdict on this house and the ornaments?"

"Riley will be discussing it with Mrs. Christensen. Clean around them the best you can. Riley agrees we'll need a release of liability on the care and cleaning of apparently priceless knickknacks. Leave everything."

"Who *are* these people?" Emma asked.

Makenna sighed. "Olaf Christensen owns an import-export business and his wife is the CFO. They're very successful, very driven, both perfectionists."

"Import-export," Emma said. "Well, that explains some of these precious decorations. They're in the buying-and-selling business. We already dusted around," Emma said. Then to her partners she said, "We're on the road again, girls."

The next house was messy and dirty, which put them a bit behind schedule, but this was the way things went during the holidays, what with all the partying and clutter. The last house of the day was the Andrewses and they were a bit late. Mrs. Andrews had had her arm in a sling last week but this week no one answered the door.

"Going to fight the damn cat hair," Shawna said. "I hate cat hair."

There was a sudden but definite commotion inside, the sound of a man shouting and a woman's voice. Emma rang the doorbell again and a third time.

"This ain't no good, trust me," Shawna said. "Time to go make another call to Makenna."

"Wait," Emma said. She leaned her ear up to the door. She couldn't hear what he was saying but he was barking, yelling, and she was wheedling, maybe whimpering. "I'm worried about her," Emma said. "I can't leave her in there with him."

"We call Nick now," Dellie said.

"Open it," Emma commanded.

"Now, that's something we don't wanna do," Dellie said.

Emma leaned her ear against the door again and suddenly it popped open and she fell inside, right onto a skinny, smelly, worked-up man. He growled and pushed her off him with surprising strength and stood up. He muttered something then walked briskly to the car that sat in the drive.

Dellie and Shawna lifted Emma to her feet.

"See what I'm talking about?" Dellie said. "We don't need any part of that!"

Emma was still frowning after the man. He was balding, short and ugly. His ears were big, he had a beak for a nose and she was sure she saw a sizeable wart on it. He cast a mean look over his shoulder; the three of them stood on the front walk with their supplies—dusters on extenders, a big plastic carrier with all their chemicals, vacuum, bag of rags, knee pads and gloves.

He spit on the ground, got in his Mercedes and drove away.

"We're not cleaning this one today," Shawna said. "She'll pay her bill, don't worry about that."

But Emma walked into the house. She found Mrs. Andrews on the floor in a crumpled heap, crying. She still had her sling, all askew, and she held her arm as if it hurt. There was a fresh slap mark on her cheek and her neck was very red, like he'd been choking her.

Dellie and Shawna followed Emma slowly. Cautiously. Working together, they lifted Mrs. Andrews to the couch. "Someone get Mrs. Andrews some ice. I'll just be a minute," Emma said.

"What are you going to do?" Shawna asked.

"Today I'm working on getting fired, it seems," she said. She walked to the front door and standing just outside she called the police.

Fifteen

Riley's heart was heavy. Every time she thought about her conversation with Maddie she felt both confusion and regret. Confusion because she couldn't exactly remember her explanations about herself and Jock the way Maddie remembered and wondered if she'd fed her daughter a series of excuses. And regret because now that she looked back on it, she had probably glossed over things so it wouldn't sound like what it was. After about sixteen years even she didn't remember it as accurately as she should because she'd been trying to blot out some truths—that she'd fallen for her best friend's boyfriend, that she'd loved him, slept with him, expected him to stand by her from that moment, but instead she lost them both.

Sex for girls is a defining moment; sex for guys is sex.

She shook her head as if to clear the memories. After Jock had said no, he wasn't in love with her, after she had groveled and begged Emma to forgive her, after finding herself completely alone except for her mom, there was just no going back. She was completely damaged, felt like a fool, was not about to be hurt like that again.

No one could ever know how much it tore a woman apart, to trust your heart and be completely wrong. For Riley, nothing was quite as hard as being stupid.

The one thing she hadn't counted on all these years of ignoring Jock, just putting up with his attempts to be a family man, was that all that time he was talking to Maddie. Apparently honestly. From the heart. Expressing his own regrets. Who knew Jock was even capable of that! Maddie seemed to think he still wanted them to be a family.

As usual, Jock's timing couldn't be worse. Riley had only just met someone she actually liked. A smart guy with a career.

Jeanette had left the office early to do a little last-minute Christmas shopping and Riley turned back to her computer. She'd write Jock a letter. She'd never send it, of course, but she could get her thoughts and questions all lined up in her head by writing a letter. This was something she did with regularity—she often wrote letters to demanding and obnoxious clients, then hit delete.

Dear Jock,

I've been talking to Maddie and it comes to me that my perception of our history is very different from yours and I need to know—did I miss something? Was I sleepwalking through that whole time, not catching the innuendo? I'm sure I was conscious when you panicked because I said I loved you. I believe I was paying attention to detail when you said, "No—wait a minute—we can't call that love! That was consensual sex, not love." And I was pretty pregnant when you said, All right then, let's get married. I apologize if that didn't sweep me off my feet, but there you have it. I wasn't convinced it would be a marriage worth having. When you married and divorced so quickly... Ah, well, you must understand why I wasn't convinced of your good judgment. But to tell Maddie this silly thing, that you always loved me, that you wanted to get married but I was too angry, that you probably wouldn't be worth a damn to another woman, that you'd resigned yourself that this was all you were going to get... Now, how does all that make me look? You lamebrain, you dipshit, you mental midget, you—

That was typical of her write-but-don't-send cathartics. She was reduced to name-calling. Sometimes that helped, too. *Jock, you stupid idiot, I loved you! You cast me off. I'd betrayed my best friend for you and you left me high and dry. The next years were so unbearably hard...*

"Riley?"

"Eeek," she squeaked and jumped about a mile. She grabbed her chest. She wasn't talking out loud, was she? "Logan! Dear God—"

He chuckled. "Whatever you're writing, you were really in the zone there, I guess. Your door was open."

She cleared the screen and actually blushed. "I was… I mean… A proposal… An itemized…"

"I didn't mean to scare you," he said.

"Come in, come in. What are you doing here?"

He walked into the room and sat in one of the chairs facing her desk. "I was in the area and hadn't seen you in a few days…"

"We talked," she said, feeling a little defensive.

"Not quite as much fun. Listen, I have a crazy week

coming up and you probably do, too. Can I take you to dinner tonight? Might be the only chance we get for a while."

"Oh, gee, that would be…" She folded her hands on top of her desk. "We didn't really talk about this, about Christmas. I'd love to have you come over to my mom's either Christmas Eve or Day, but I figured you have to see your family. And I don't know if you want to meet everyone in my family for the first time on a holiday."

He just grinned at her.

"But if you'd like to—"

"It's okay, Riley. My debut with Maddie didn't go all that well."

"I'm sorry, that was so unexpected. I guess that's what I get for never dating. But I don't think it would be that awkward at my mom's house."

"I think I'll just take care of my own family for the holidays. I can spell my partner so she can have time with her husband and kids. And God knows, I want to be available for my ex-wife—I'm sure she'll be at least stopping by. And my father." He rolled his eyes. "But dinner tonight would be excellent. Or tomorrow night. How about it?"

"That sounds like a great idea. Where would you like to go?"

"How about Riviera Restorante?"

"I love that place!" She glanced down at herself. She was wearing pants and a blazer today. "Am I dressed all right? So I don't have to go home?"

"You look perfect." He looked around. "I wondered about the office. This is really nice, Riley. Very—"

The outside office door opened and a moment later

there was a light tapping on Riley's door. Emma peeked in the door.

"Oh. Sorry. When you're finished…" she said, beginning to pull out.

"Come in, Emma. This is a friend of mine, Logan Danner. We were just making plans for dinner. Logan, can you give me five minutes with Emma?"

"Of course," he said, standing.

"Oh," Emma said. "It's you! From the hospital."

He frowned slightly. "The hospital?"

"I was waiting for a ride. I was a little upset. You gave me your flowers," she said.

"That was you?" he asked, peering at her. "Huh, that *was* you! You said you were having a bad day."

"That was the last day I worked at that job. I was in hospital housekeeping. I came here immediately after that. That was nice of you—the flowers."

"I was visiting a coworker who had checked out. I wasn't going to take the flowers to her house. I saw that as problematic." Then he grinned.

"You two know each other?" Riley asked.

"We never met, actually," Emma said. "We both happened to be waiting outside of the ER and I looked like I felt—at the end of the line."

"I told her to take the flowers or they were going in the trash," Logan said. "Just a spontaneous gesture. I could have left them with the nurses but…" He shrugged.

Emma looked at Riley. "It's all right with me if he stays. It's going to take about one minute." Emma took a breath. "I did something today that was against policy. In our last house, the man was beating his wife and

I know I'm supposed to call you or Nick or Makenna with issues, but I called the police."

"Oh, my Jesus," Riley said. "Sit down, Emma."

"I'm sorry, I know our policy is not to see the client's personal stuff but I just couldn't look the other way."

"Emma, that wasn't personal, that was assault. Against the law! That's not the stuff you're supposed to pretend not to see. That Reverend Douglas likes to wear his wife's lingerie is what we don't see, not crimes."

"Reverend Douglas wears his wife's lingerie?" Emma and Logan said at the same time.

"I didn't say that," Riley said. "I wish you had called me, but not because I'd ignore something like that. Because I'd file the complaint, drive out to the scene and wait with you for the police and hopefully Mr. and Mrs. Andrews would blame me and not you. Hopefully they'd forget you had anything to do with it."

"That wasn't going to happen," Emma said. "I was listening at the door to see if I could hear her crying for help and he opened the door suddenly. I fell on him. *Splat!* The mean little squirt." She huffed a little. "I wish he'd taken a hand to me!"

"Was she badly hurt?" Riley asked.

"I don't know how badly but they took her to the hospital in an ambulance, and that took some convincing. I have a feeling they've been there before. He might've broken her arm. And he tried to strangle her."

"Oh, my God!" Riley said. "Okay, listen, Emma—this isn't the first time we've faced an abusive situation. When we enter their homes and clean their personal space, we enter their lives in ways even they don't comprehend. If you ever suspect abuse or unlawful behavior, please don't hesitate to say something to me. Or if you're not able to reach me, call Makenna or Nick. We've been doing this longer than you have."

"I just couldn't wait," she said. "I'm sorry."

"No need to apologize," Riley said. "I would have done the same thing. You did fine. I just like to take my employees out of the equation when possible, if possible. They'll discontinue our service, there's no question—we saw too much. Good riddance." Riley smiled. "And I heard about your call on the Christensen home—smart move."

"I was afraid to breathe," Emma said.

"I can't wait to hear what that's about," Logan said.

"Go ahead. Tell him," Riley said.

She looked confused for a moment. Tell him what? "Well, in a previous life I had some experience working with decorators and I recognized the Christmas ornaments and decorations in one of the homes were very expensive. And very fragile. Even the most careful housecleaner can upset an ornament—these were balls from Wedgwood, from jewelers, crystal from high-end stores like Tiffany's and Waterford."

"What's expensive?" he asked.

"One Waterford ball—couple of hundred. A couple of Tiffany reindeer statuettes, fifteen hundred. A Swarovski wreath. Everything was high-end."

"Wow," he said. "You must have had a lot of experience handling that stuff."

"A little," she said. "I didn't want me or my team getting stuck with a big bill just for dusting."

"Mrs. Christensen has decided to have her decorator come in and make sure all her priceless decorations are shiny clean. We're going to leave that stuff alone,"

Riley said. "Thanks for stopping by to explain, Emma. I'll follow through."

"Thank you," Emma said, noting the meeting was over. She stood. And so did Logan.

Logan reached in his pocket and fished out a card. "If you ever have a problem or need some advice on police matters, don't hesitate. Use the cell—I'm in the field a lot. I'm only in the office a few hours a day."

"You're a police officer?" she asked.

"Yep. And if I don't know the answer to your question, I can get it. I worked some battery domestic and assault as a patrol officer and I have friends in those specialized units. We're not a huge department."

"Well, thank you, Mr. Danner…"

"Just Logan, Emma."

"I appreciate that," she said. She looked at Riley. "Hopefully the rest of the week is a little less exciting."

"Things always get a little wacky during holidays. Have a good week."

"Thanks," Emma said.

She's very pretty, Riley thought. *Even at the end of a difficult day.* Wouldn't it be tidy if Logan took to her? He seemed to light up a little bit when he saw her.

And why would you think that? she asked herself.

Emma's mind was really working as she drove. The domestic battery was so disturbing, so in-your-face horrid. The first thing she told herself was that her situation had never been as bad as that! She'd never been abused like that. Never.

But then how many of her New York household had noticed that her husband didn't hold her, that the troop of worker bees who often traveled with them were not all for work, that he had such a developed sense of entitlement he had a mistress right under her nose and bilked his clients for a hundred million dollars. No, she'd never been abused, nuh-uh. Her life had been ruined by the very man who vowed to love and protect her.

Mrs. Andrews must ask herself those same questions every day. How did I marry that man? How did I trust him with my life, my future? And now she was undoubtedly asking herself how she could get away from him.

Emma didn't have to go to Riley's office. She could have just called Makenna and Nick and chances were one of the other girls had after it was all over. But Emma wanted to look Riley in the eye as if to say, *Here's your chance. I blew it. I didn't follow the rules—fire me.*

But Riley stood up for her. Supported her. Wanted to protect her. Emma didn't kid herself that it was because she was Emma, it was because she was an employee. Adam had been so right about his sister—she ran a good company, provided a safe work environment, took good care of her people, was steadfast. Riley could ignore the fact that she really didn't want to be around Emma and see the situation professionally and fairly.

She sighed. Ah, what did it matter? She didn't want a new best friend. She just wanted to work, live, enjoy a simple peace that helped her heal. That was all.

Her cell phone rang and it picked up in her car. She didn't recognize the number. "Hello," she yelled into the speaker.

"I know who you are," said a very timid, female voice.

Emma was right in front of a side street and made an abrupt turn, no signal involved, earning her a blast from a car behind her. She pulled over.

"Hello?" she said again. She pulled her cell phone out of her purse and turned off the car. "Let me get you on my cell. Okay. Here I am."

"I know who you are," she said again. "The cleaner."

"Oh. Uh. I'm sorry I read your page. I'm not supposed to."

"I know. I left it where you would see it."

"Oh," Emma said. "You want to talk?"

"I go to the counselor twice a week to talk and that hasn't done any good."

"Oh, I'm glad, you have someone. Why isn't it any good?" Emma asked.

She was met with silence and she thought, *I'm an idiot. I should have apologized, asked her not to tell, confessed to Riley again and—*

"Because they don't want to talk to me, they have to. They're paid to."

"Ah," Emma said. "I understand."

"Now I think you're doing it. You some kind of spy?"

"No," Emma said, laughing a little in spite of herself. "I'm a cleaner who's going to get in big trouble for touching your personal property. I apologize."

"Why'd you do it, then?"

"Well… Well, there have been times I had no one to talk to. Really, no one. And I had a lot on my mind. A lot of worries and no one to listen and I know how that feels."

"Like when?"

"Well…when I was sixteen, my dad died in an accident. I didn't have a mom. I felt kind of alone then." It was a lie. She had the Kerrigans, though she was still shot through with pain and grief. Emma was trying to understand what this girl might be up against.

"Did you have a sister?" she asked.

"Ah… I had a stepsister. And a stepmother. It was a dark period." She cleared her throat. "Do you have a sister?"

"No. They figured out after me that there couldn't be more kids," she said. "My mother is dead. And I have a stepmother. I hear she's wonderful."

"Oh? You don't sound like you believe it."

"I guess," she said. "My stepmother says this family is getting back in the groove." She laughed. "How'm I doing getting back in the groove so far?"

Emma bit her lower lip. She knew nothing about this sort of thing. She'd never even been to a counselor before Lucinda. June and Riley were the nearest things to counselors she'd ever had.

But she'd had a stepmother. "Do you like your stepmother?" she asked.

"I want to. She's a good person. But I try and I can't."

"Why?"

"Really? Really, why?"

"Only if you want to say," Emma said. "You can talk about something else if you—"

"She wears my mother's clothes."

Emma felt her stomach cramp and her throat closed. She couldn't speak. No one was that insensitive. No one. Not the stupidest person. Even Rosemary had been more subtle than that.

"She asked if she could," Bethany said. "We said yes. My dad and me. But my mother's dead and she's wearing her clothes."

"What did that counselor say?" Emma asked.

"The counselor asked me if I thought she was trying to replace my mother and that's why I was upset."

"But you told the counselor why you were upset, right?" Emma asked.

"I was upset because she was wearing my mother's clothes!" she said, her voice suddenly strong. "They'll be worn out pretty soon and she'll have to get new ones. I hope, but I don't think so."

"Did you tell your dad it bothers you?" Emma asked.

"My dad is…you know…he's not the same. I can tell even if he smiles all the time and acts like we all just got tickets to the Ice Capades, it's all fake. Inside he's just so sad. He can't do anything."

Emma's cheeks were wet with tears. "You should tell him, though. You shouldn't just hurt inside without anyone to talk to. Your dad wouldn't want you to do that."

"I have you," she said.

"But—"

"Except I don't know your name or anything."

I should call Adam tonight and we should have a good dinner and maybe two bottles of wine and a long night in each other's arms because I'm going to be looking for work very, very soon.

"I'm Emma," she said. "And I've been alone and sad, too. But I'm not right now so I can talk to you. Except I'm not allowed to use my phone during work—during the day. I'm off at five. And on weekends."

"This weekend is Christmas," she said sadly. "It's a little harder at Christmas."

"I know, honey."

"I need to go," she said. "I'll call you sometime."

"Okay. And you can leave a message if I'm working. Or in the shower or something."

"Or text?" Bethany asked.

"Sure. But hey. Let's talk. Okay? It's what you want to do."

"Yeah. I think. Don't tell them, okay?"

"I'm not telling them." *I hope. I might have to, but let's see.*

"This Emma seems like an interesting character," Logan said.

Riley smiled. They were at the restaurant, chatting about nothing at all. "You made it all the way to the antipasto," she said.

"What? Did I say something wrong?"

"Not at all. I've been expecting you to say something. You kind of came to life when Emma showed up."

"Did I? I think I came to life when she recognized me but I didn't really remember her. Could the world get any smaller?"

"This is a small place. And Emma is very pretty," Riley said. "Unforgettable."

"She did the right thing, you know," he added.

"When there's trouble of some kind, I like it if they go through me. Or Nick. Nick is brilliant with situations like that. He's not a big guy—he's a short, stocky Italian—but he manages to seem six foot six if he has to. To the women who work for us he's a sweetheart until they push him too far, try to take advantage of him, then he's great at getting serious and making his point firmly. Not meanly, but firmly. With the men, he's one of the guys until they try to take advantage and then he's clearly the boss. No one wants to mess with Nick. He's got a look. A scrappy look. Often a potential client will get an estimate from Nick and then come to me, looking to sweet-talk the lady boss into a better, cheaper deal." She laughed and shook her head. "It hasn't worked even once.

"I'd have liked it if Nick had been there when the police came," she went on. "I'd have liked it if Nick and I were both there when the police confronted Mr. Andrews, but that's asking for a miracle."

"I'm sure they found him," Logan said. "He'll turn up at work or a bar or come to the hospital to try to offer up some lame excuse for beating the shit outta his wife."

"What will happen to him?" she asked.

"He'll go to jail," Logan said, spearing an artichoke heart with his fork.

"His wife might think to make peace by denying—"

"There was a witness and evidence of a beating. You think the police don't know what she's up against? They know what she'll say, what she'll do and they've heard it all before. By now she's as messed up as he is. There are two lawbreakers who can't make bail—battery domestic violators and drunk drivers. They get to spend the night. In the first case so their victim has time to get away if he or she will do so and in the second case, to sober up."

Riley thought about that. "That's very clever of the police," she finally said. "Here I thought abusers and drunks could get away with stuff all the time."

"They do, even with all the stops in place. But we're awful smart. We know how they think and act."

"You are smart," she agreed with a laugh.

"So tell me about Emma," he said.

"Why do you want to know?" she asked.

"Because you're friends," he said.

Riley scooped some more greens from the salad on her plate, focusing on the antipasto and not him. "We're not friends, actually. I've known her for a long time but she has only recently come back to Santa Rosa after being away for years. She needed a job. That's pretty much it."

"Oh, no, it's not," he said, laughing. "You two have some kind of important relationship that goes beyond work."

"Is that so? And how would you know that?"

He shrugged. "Experience. Body language. Tone of voice. Eye contact. The way you two respond to each other. There was a lot of chemistry in your office for a little while."

"Sassy," she said, lifting her eyebrows. "You're a smarty-pants, aren't you? We were friends, in younger years."

"I thought so."

"We went to school together. But Emma went away to college, moved away after college, got married and just recently returned. After the death of her husband."

"Aw," he said, chewing. "She's young. That's sad."

"I gather it was a bad marriage."

"Abusive?"

"Why would you ask that?" Riley wanted to know.

"It would explain her sensitivity to that woman being abused."

"Huh," she said. "And I thought I was intuitive. But I don't know if the marriage involved that kind of abuse. Her husband was not a good man, I hear. And he killed himself. As soon as she buried him and sorted out her affairs, she came back here. I suppose she feels comfortable here where she still has a few friends."

Logan whistled. "Suicide. That's ugly."

"I suppose that would be hard to deal with even if you hated the guy."

"Yeah. I hope he left her something..."

"I doubt it. If he'd left her anything, would she be cleaning houses?"

"Were you and Emma close friends in younger years? Because even though you're the boss and she's the employee, I detected something—like an element of familiarity. Intimacy."

"Intimacy?" she asked, aghast.

"Not sexual intimacy. Or maybe it was trust."

"From her?" Riley asked, a bit incredulously.

"Well, from both of you. If you looked anything alike, I'd make you out to be sisters. There was that familial give and take, like sibling love/hate. You know what I'm talking about, we all have it. I can call my sister a bitch but no one else can. There was... You know each other very well."

She smiled at him. "We were good friends as kids. But that was a long time ago. We haven't even been in touch in over fifteen years. Don't you love the Riviera antipasto? Isn't it the best there is? We should have gotten the bruschetta, which is also the best there is."

He put his elbows on the table, leaned forward and smiled at her. "If there's something you'd rather not talk about, you can just say so."

"When I'm on a date, which I so rarely am, I'd rather not talk about another woman," Riley said. "Besides, if your secret motive is that you'd like to date her, I believe she's taken. And I'm not one bit happy about it, either."

His eyebrows shot up and his eyes were as round as saucers. One look at him and she knew he wasn't going to let that one go.

"Do not be a tease," he said.

Riley sighed in defeat. "I suspect she's seeing my brother. Adam said he ran into her, that it was really great to see her again after so many years. They went out for a glass of wine and he passed on one of my business cards. I said she'd never call me for a job, never work for someone she'd felt kind of competitive with when we were kids. Not nasty competitive, not rivals, nothing like that, but still… Adam's been curiously busy and stupidly happy lately…"

That made Logan smile. "Why Riley, you little witch."

"Well, she works for me! Do you think I want to see her at every family function? That would be a little complicated, don't you think?"

The waiter was just passing by and tried to snatch the antipasto platter and Logan stopped him. "We're still working on this, but I'll have another beer and I think the lady will be ready for more wine in a few minutes. Thanks." Then to Riley he said, "I think there's more to it than that, but I don't want to screw up the rest of our date. I like the way our dates end—slowly with lots of personal contact. So… How about those Lakers?"

"I didn't want to give her a job *and* my brother," she said.

He reached for her hand. "I thought she was a good-looking woman and have absolutely no interest in dating anyone but you. You're a showstopper, Riley. And I want to make out with you like mad."

"I might be falling out of the mood," she said.

"Drink more wine," he urged. "We're going to be on hiatus over Christmas and by the time we get to— Hey, should we make plans for New Year's Eve?"

"Maybe," she said. "Can I check with my daughter first? I want to be sure she's not on the loose while I'm partying with you."

"Fair enough," he said. "Here comes dinner. And save a little room for the tiramisu. Damn, does that look good or what?" He gave her hand another squeeze. "Come on, baby. Let's get in the same canoe here. Tonight's about us. I want to impress you with my manners, good taste, brilliance and sexual allure."

She laughed at him. "I don't want to hear another word about your sexual allure. Especially in front of the waitstaff."

"Killjoy. Some women find the spectacle of a man willing to make a fool of himself in public very titillating."

"Do they, now?"

"You know they do, Riley." And he winked.

Logan had learned something tonight, like what an idiot he could be. First of all, a detective with a working brain would have waited for her to bring up Emma before homing in on her and their friendship. And second, whatever was in their past was enough to take Riley to another place and nearly ruin the evening. Maybe he wasn't smart enough to balance a budding relationship and a case because he was hot for Riley. He liked her in a way he hadn't liked a woman in a long time.

By the time the conversation got around to Emma possibly dating Riley's brother, she was shutting down, moving away. Riley didn't seem to mind talking about the fact that Emma was pretty, that she'd had a bad marriage, but she didn't want to talk about Emma and her relationships with men.

After dinner he managed to persuade her to do a little kissing beside her car. He even talked her into getting in the car for a little more. But when he asked her to come to his place for an hour or so, she was too smart for him. "I'm afraid not, Logan," she had said. "I'm not ready for that next step." And he said he was ready whenever she was and she replied, "I know. I can tell. I'm so smart that way."

So now they were driving home to their own houses in their separate cars and he had the feeling something had changed. Instead of going forward, they were moving back. And this had something to do with Emma even though Riley had no idea of his interest in Emma.

His cell rang and the number popped up on the dash screen in the car. Georgianna. He pressed the connection for the hands-free. "What?" he said.

"Hello, dear," she said. "You're late for dinner again."

"What do you want? What if she'd been in my car?"

"Didn't you say you'd be meeting for dinner? Why would she be in your car?"

"Because she drank too much wine and I had to drive her to my house, which I very much tried to do. But she left most of her second glass and declined my invitation. And I'm a little unhappy so why don't you just leave me alone."

"Did you learn anything?"

"No. Not anything useful."

"Why don't you go ahead and tell me, huh? I'm much more objective than you are."

He took a breath. She was right. "There's some significant history between the girls but it's obviously complicated. When I started to ask about their history, using all of my brilliant detective skills, she mentally moved away from me. That's when I lost her. She was fine talking about Emma coming back here, needing a job, getting over a bad marriage—generic on the bad, no details—but when I asked what their relationship was like when they were young, she shut down. Oh—and she thinks Emma might be seeing her brother."

"She doesn't know?" George asked.

"Not for sure, I guess. How firm is that?"

"Every night."

"How do you know?" he asked.

"The only conversations they have are about what's for dinner and when will you be here."

Logan thought Adam Kerrigan was getting a lot luckier than he was. "I don't get it," he said. "They're one nice big happy family. I saw Riley and Emma today, working through a tense situation, supportive of each other, friendly. The brother and the mother obviously like her. But Riley's smart. She's scary smart. You think she knows something and doesn't want her family mixed up in it?"

"Possible," George said. "If you don't have anything interesting to tell me, I'm going to kiss the kids and hit the sack. Bruno's on shift."

Bruno was not his real name. Mr. Universe's real name was John.

"Good. Don't call me anymore."

"You know it's probably a good thing you didn't get laid…"

"Shows what you know. That's almost never a good thing."

"Oh, I can think of a ton of circumstances when getting laid would be a really bad—"

He hung up on her.

Sixteen

Emma received her second phone call from Bethany two days after the first, again while she was driving home from work. She learned that Bethany's mother had died from a freakishly terrible case of the flu almost two years ago. She got sick, then got sicker, was admitted to the hospital then to the ICU. It was the kind of thing that usually happened to the extremely frail, chronically ill or elderly, but it got Danielle Christensen, taking her life in a week. The family was, understandably, wrecked by it.

Then Olaf Christensen brought home a woman he had worked with for a long time, a CPA in his import-export company. There were many such businesses in the port city, the Bay Area, and the Christensens' was successful. Danielle had only been gone a couple of months, but it seemed to help him a great deal to be seeing this woman. Liz was forty and had never married, had no children and before six months had passed, they were married. Everyone loved her—she was good at her job, active in her church, popular at work, laughed a lot and showered attention on Bethany's father. But she never laughed with Bethany, only with Bethany's father and other adults.

Before they even married, Bethany's stepmother was taking over the house. She fired the cleaning lady who'd been with them for years and hired Riley's company. She made every meal or ordered something she could pick up on the way home or booked reservations. The once comfortably lived-in house became spotless and sterile. Danielle's clothes were moved to a guest room closet and chest of drawers, then little by little they moved back to the master bedroom. The family pictures were removed. Liz said, "They're certainly not helping our situation, these constant reminders." Bethany was told to clean her room to Liz's specifications and if she didn't, Liz went in her room, put things away and tidied up. In order to keep Liz out of her room, Bethany followed the instructions. When Bethany just wouldn't stop acting depressed, Liz found her a therapist.

"I heard her saying I should be put in a hospital or boarding school but my dad didn't agree. Maybe I should. I would be away from them."

Bethany told Emma she took a bunch of drugs from Liz's medicine chest and had to have her stomach pumped last Christmas.

Emma gasped. "Oh, sweetheart, how terrifying! Please tell me you'll never do that again!"

"No, I won't. It was horrid. It turns out Liz doesn't have any good drugs," Bethany said.

"Well, I guess that's a point in her favor," Emma said. "I know Christmas is hard, Bethany, but if you start to feel terrible will you please tell a school counselor? Or teacher? Or someone?"

"I could try, but I think I'm just going to ask my dad

and Liz if I can be a foreign exchange student. My dad wants everything to be all right. But I think Liz would be happy to see me go."

"Do you have pictures of your mother?" Emma asked. "Pictures you can look at to give you comfort?"

"I have some in my drawer."

"Bethany, what about your grandparents?"

"My grandma is in assisted living. She was so good but when my mom died… She just got so old, so fast."

"And what about your friends from school?"

"I have friends at school, but they don't want to hang out anymore. I think I make them sad or something. And Liz makes them nervous. She's too much."

Emma was almost surprised to hear the sound of her own laughter. "Okay, I wasn't going to tell you this but I have a stepmother. And she's too much, too."

"No way," Bethany said.

"Rosemary. I remember when my adviser in high school told me I was so lucky to have a mother like Rosemary who was strict and made sure my homework was done and had a strong set of values. She said I'd appreciate it someday. Rosemary was kind of scary. Her smile was fake, if you know what I mean."

"I know what you mean," Bethany said. "My stepmother doesn't like me. She pretends in front of my dad, but it's not real. Sometimes I can hear her complaining and crying to him, saying I don't appreciate her. Maybe it's just because she's not anything like my mother, I don't know. It's like we don't live in the same house anymore."

"Tell me about your mother," Emma said.

"She was so sweet. Not that she couldn't get mad—she chased me with a mop once, yelling her head off.

But she couldn't catch me and then she laughed her head off. She was kind of messy. She left her clothes on the closet floor all the time and our cleaning lady, Mary, she used to grumble and mutter and complain and my mother would laugh and say, "Come on, Mary! I'm such great job security!" But my mother could cook and bake! The house always smelled great. And she loved to go to my school things. She worked at my dad's company, too, but she'd take off to help at school, to go on field trips, to watch my concerts and programs and stuff. And she used to…" Bethany's voice slowed and stopped. Emma could tell she was crying. "We used to get in bed together and talk and rub each other's backs and heads and laugh and fall asleep in a pile."

Emma struggled to find her own voice. "I love your mother," she finally said.

"Thank you for saying that because I believe you, and you don't even know her. I wish I could be with her."

"She's with you in your heart and I believe she's watching over you. You're going to be like her, you know. Maybe not tomorrow or next week, but you're going to have a great life and make your house smell like great things are baking and laugh with your children and fall asleep in a pile. You will, Bethany. I grew up and moved away from my stepmother and you'll move away from yours."

"Did you move away and have a great life?"

Emma bit her lip. It wasn't really a lie if she thought about where she was now. "Yes, I have a lovely life. A happy life."

"Cleaning houses?"

"Yes. And meeting wonderful people."

When they hung up, Emma drove the rest of the way home, crying all the way. Was she helping by taking these calls from this poor, grief-stricken, lonely girl?

She remembered when her life was at a point like that, when she'd lost her father, when she was just sixteen. But she had Riley. And Riley hadn't been afraid to hang out.

The twenty-third of December fell on Friday and that was the day Penny and her girlfriends chose for their little Christmas party. The girls had decided that everyone would bring substantial hors d'oeuvres and Marilyn agreed to make two desserts. They were going to have a cocktail party and ornament exchange.

Earlier in the week Emma had helped Penny bring in her tree and put her decorations up. She brought another centerpiece and wine; her wrapped presents were under Penny's tree. She'd been looking forward to this holiday for weeks, her first Christmas as a free woman. And especially her evening with the girls, Penny, Susan, Dorothy and Marilyn. But all the while, it was hard for her to shake off Bethany's call.

Their wine was poured, their cocktail plates were loaded, they were comfy in Penny's little living room and someone toasted, "Another year gone to hell." They all said *Here! Here!* with laughter.

"You're not quite as perky as usual, Emma," Marilyn pointed out. "You haven't had another pan of pee tossed at your head, have you?"

Emma shot wide eyes to Penny. "You *told*?"

"Way to keep it to yourself, Marilyn," Penny scolded.

"Well, I don't have to keep it from Emma, do I?

You haven't had a falling out with that lovely Adam, have you?"

"No, he remains lovely. Really, Penelope, I can't believe you told about that! I'll see Adam late tomorrow night after he has his dinner and celebration with his family. I have the littlest work problem, that's all."

"Do tell!" three of them said at once.

"I shouldn't. I don't believe you're entirely trustworthy," Emma said.

Dorothy laughed. "Don't worry about that, angel. No one listens to us anyway. What happened at work?"

She sighed. Truthfully, she was dying to talk to someone and these old biddies were good listeners. As long as she didn't name names. "I've gone and done the dumbest thing."

"What? Tell us at once!"

"But it's not a happy story," she apologized. "I don't want to cast a pall on our party—I've been looking forward to it."

"Pah, we love trouble and misery. We can take it!"

"Indeed," Emma said with a frown. "It's quite sad, really."

They had no trouble talking her into it; she was more than ready to unload. She started with the new clothes in the trash, the scarred desktop, then the diary and her bold move in leaving her number.

"Oh, bless you, little darling!" Susan said. "You're all mush, aren't you?"

Then Emma explained Riley's rules and Bethany's two calls.

"Oh, my dear, you did absolutely the right thing!" Penny said. "Someone has to talk to that child!"

"But what can I do to help?"

"I'm sure listening helps, love," Dorothy said. "Where is that girl's grandmother?"

"I asked, as a matter of fact—apparently she went downhill fast after her daughter died and is now in assisted living. I don't know the details, but I gather she can't be of much help in her condition."

"Some of us are frail," Marilyn said. "Not *us*, mind you. *We* turned into leather. Tough old broads who have outlasted way too many friends. You can give her our numbers, Emma. There's no group of grannies who know more about the pain of loss and the way to move on than we do."

"I bet you would be good for her," Emma said.

"What about that woman, the new wife. Wearing the dead woman's clothes! That should be against the law. I'm calling my lawyer after Christmas. I'm going to give him a list of names of those approved to be seen in my clothing after I'm gone," Marilyn said.

"Save your dime," Penny said. "No one wants your old-lady clothes."

"It is awful, though, isn't it?" Emma asked. "She made a point of saying she asked them, but what's a young, grief-stricken girl going to say?"

"Sounds like she can't help herself," Susan said. "She's probably a well-meaning idiot. Trying to make her new husband happy, keeping the house immaculate to impress anyone who's watching that she's a caring mother, getting expensive clothes for the girl, rather than giving time and understanding…"

"They put her in counseling," Emma said.

"So what? I have an ex-sister-in-law who was a counselor!" Susan exclaimed. "Worst fucked-up piece of work I've ever seen."

"Nice language," Dorothy said. "You know what you should do, Emma? You should talk to that nice Adam about this. You said he's lovely with teenagers."

"With his niece, I've seen a little of that. But I'm working for his sister. I broke the rules. I wonder if he'd feel obligated to tell her. Because it wouldn't be the first time I've broken the rules. Not long ago I called the police on one of our clients…"

They all leaned toward her as one. Their eyes were wide and hungry. "I don't believe you mentioned that, darling," Penny said.

"I'm going to need another glass of wine," Marilyn said. "Don't tell about it until I've gotten reloaded here."

"A man was assaulting his wife. Beating her," Emma said, going through the story, explaining she was supposed to call her directors or Riley but she just called the police.

"Good for you!" everyone said.

"I thought strong women had died off, but look at you go!" Dorothy added.

"I might've chased him with a tire iron, the bastard!" Penny said.

"Exactly why I carry," Susan finally said.

"I just wish I could've seen them arrest him," Emma said. "Say…" She looked around the room. "Penny, just how much have you told them about me?"

"Well, there was that story about the bedpan. Slowed down the bridge table a bit, that one. And of course that little bit about the Ponzi…"

"You told them all that, did you?" Emma asked.

"You wouldn't want them to be caught off guard," Penny said.

"I say good riddance," Marilyn said. "Thank goodness he had that Saturday night special in his office!"

"It was a Glock, you dolt," Susan said. "At least keep your weapons straight."

Emma was shaking her head.

"What's the matter, darling?" Penny asked.

"You're incorrigible," she said. "There is no logical reason why I should want to be exactly like you. Yet…"

They all giggled and lifted their glasses. "To women with balls," someone said.

If Riley was asked by a client to provide holiday housekeeping service, she charged double and offered the jobs to her senior housekeepers. There were always at least a few eager for the extra money and they would arrange their holiday celebrating accordingly. She was careful which jobs she accepted and who she sent because Nick and Makenna shouldn't be asked to supervise. And Riley wanted to be called only in an emergency, which shouldn't happen with a skilled crew.

Christmas was a holiday she'd dearly loved since Maddie was born. They did most of their celebrating at June's house and Maddie wouldn't have it any other way. Jock had joined them for dinner a few times, usually showed up early Christmas morning to watch Maddie open gifts, even stole Maddie away for a few hours to spend time with his family. He was always very cordial and respected Riley's wishes, not pushing too much. He still spent most of his major holidays with his mom, dad, brother and sister. Once he'd asked if Maddie could stay over so they could have Christmas at his mom's. Riley had known that wasn't asking too much. But she'd said no, and he had come to June's instead.

Riley loved helping her mother with the meals, Adam was always there Christmas Eve and Christmas Day, and over the years there had been the occasional extra guests—a girlfriend of Adam's or friends or coworkers who would otherwise be alone. Now that Maddie was a teenager, Christmas morning wasn't such a big deal and they'd do their gift opening later in the morning while the turkey roasted. June cooked all day, talking, laughing and singing carols when the spirit moved her. Riley spent the whole day with her mother and daughter. Adam was in and out because he liked delivering gifts and good tidings to his friends at their homes, just as friends and neighbors stopped by June's house, knowing there would be eggnog, coffee and cookies. It was always warm, cozy, low-key, and made Riley feel secure. After all, she'd drawn the blueprint for this life.

She had a feeling everything was about to change. She could smell it in the wind.

Maddie was getting older, more mature. She was asking the questions Adam had predicted, and then some. She wanted to know how she came to be. Did her parents love each other? If they did, why did they stop? Riley could no longer live in denial—Jock was a pretty good dad and Maddie loved him.

And Adam, he would never leave them, but he wasn't going to belong to them anymore. It was the elephant in the room—Emma had come back and Adam was different. Emma had come back and Riley had lost fifteen years, feeling thrown back in time. She wanted to ask where Emma was today but she wouldn't. Surely Lyle would look after her. Or her landlady would.

Riley tried to savor the two days, to fill up on them, as if they'd have to hold her for a long time. The presents were a success and dinner was slowly being prepared. She stood at the stove and sink with her mother, got out the Christmas dishes and set the table. Maddie came into the dining room, her cell phone to her ear. "Put an extra plate on. Daddy is coming to dinner."

"Does he know it's at four?" Riley asked.

"He knows. He's glad. He'll have to go to work early tomorrow."

Because Mackie's would be a madhouse, Riley thought. People would be returning and exchanging all their gifts. He'd worked for Mackie's full-time since getting his degree. Which took him over five years to accomplish, she reminded herself.

But he'd been there for fifteen years—part-time at first while he went to school, steadily working his way up. It wasn't a big job but it was solid.

He wasn't the senior partner of a law firm or chief of neurosurgery, but he worked hard, long hours in a tough, competitive business and his employees loved him. *So when are you going to give him a break, huh*? she asked herself.

He arrived, wearing the ugly Christmas sweater Maddie had gotten him, thrilling her and forcing a laugh out of everyone, even Adam. And too soon it was coming to a close and Riley had a sinking feeling the Christmas holidays she'd known since Maddie was born would never be the same. Maddie was growing up. She was so smart they were already looking at colleges. Riley, though still young, was staring in the face of a different life. June would age, Adam would leave her, Maddie would build a life of her own.

Riley's phone rang and she fished it out of her purse.

"I just wanted to call to wish you a merry Christmas," Logan said.

"And merry Christmas to you!" she replied cheerily. "We're just sitting down. Can I give you a call after we eat?"

"Perfect," he said. "I am blessedly finished with my family. I'm home."

"I'll call in a little while," she said.

Jock and Adam both left while Riley and June were cleaning up the leftovers and washing the dishes. Maddie was on the phone planning a big shopping day with Gramma and two of her girlfriends for tomorrow bright and early. Riley would go to the office. The Monday after Christmas was always a busy day for her crews.

That left only tonight. Maddie was staying overnight with Gramma, and Riley was alone. She felt a little guilty that seeing Logan hadn't even come to mind. It was only seven and Christmas was over.

It was a dark, cloudy night and she drove to Jock's house. He'd lived in this house for three years now. It was small and one of the newer houses in Santa Rosa, a new construction. He was proud of it. Riley had never been inside but she knew where it was because she'd dropped Maddie off there to visit many times. Maddie hadn't spent the night very often; her life was still mostly with her mom and gramma and girlfriends. Jock didn't push any kind of custody arrangement. He didn't dare. Riley scared him, she knew that.

She sat in her car out front for a while, just thinking. She wasn't sure what she was going to do, but here she was. She was driven by some sentimental force she didn't understand. After ten minutes or so, she walked up to the front door and rang the bell.

Jock threw open the door and looked at her in shock. "Riley?" he said. "You need Maddie to stay over?" he asked, looking over her shoulder.

He had gotten rid of the sweater and wore an old sweatshirt—Seahawks. His jeans were old, torn here and there and looked like a beloved garment and in absolutely poor taste. He was in his stocking feet and held the TV remote in his hand. The TV was muted but there were football players paused like statues on the screen.

"You shouldn't just open the door like that," she said. "I could've been a home invader or something."

"In Santa Rosa?"

"We have crime here, you know."

"Would you like to come in?" he asked.

"I don't want to interrupt. I just had something on my mind and… Maddie's growing up so fast."

He stepped back and held the door open. "I'm having a cup of coffee. Would you like one?"

She absently rubbed her tummy. "I've had too much of everything today. But I wondered if we could have a little talk."

"Something wrong?" he asked, walking back into his living room.

"No, I—" She stopped talking and looked around. He had a tan velour sectional, a tall dining table surrounded by stools—looked like a poker table. There was a wall unit and a big-screen, but it looked like someone had actually helped him decorate. There were female touches—throw pillows, a marble bowl on the table, a couple of framed prints on the wall, shelved books, a shadow box with pictures of Maddie from childhood. "This is very nice, Jock."

"Would you like to see Maddie's room?" he asked.

"Sure," she said.

He led the way and she was stunned to see an actual girl's bedroom. The furniture matched, the bulletin board was covered with pictures, there was pretty bedding, a couple of her trophies were on the bureau, there was a desk and chair, and her pom-poms from seventh grade were hanging up on the wall. On her bedside table was a professionally done portrait of Jock and Maddie. It was beautiful. She walked over to it and picked it up.

"When did you have this taken?"

"Last year. We'd have given you one but I was pretty sure that wouldn't work. My mom has one."

"Why didn't Maddie tell me?" she asked.

"I suppose because she thinks you don't like it that I'm her father," he said.

"Oh, nonsense," she said defensively, with the slightest blush. "I'm surprised by all this. Maddie doesn't stay over here very often."

"She has, though. Did you think I put her on the couch? She knows she has a room here whenever she wants it or needs it. I bet she has a room at Adam's…"

"No," Riley said. "No, of course not. But if Mom and I were both going somewhere and needed a babysitter, he wouldn't mind coming over to my house. Or Mom's house. But this is so nice. Thanks."

"She doesn't use it that much," he said. "Come on, Riley. What do you want to talk about? You never want to talk."

She turned and went back to the living room. "We talk," she said as she went. She sat at the end of the sectional, as far from where his coffee cup sat as she could get. She put her purse down on the floor beside her but didn't even open her coat. "We talk," she said again.

"Not really," he said, sitting down. "You're very businesslike."

"Well, I suppose that goes with the territory. I run a business and I'm used to being that way."

"And tonight?" he asked.

She sighed deeply. "I don't know why, but it just struck me—things will be changing again. Maddie's growing up. She's a woman now."

"I wouldn't go that far," he said. "She's still a young lady to me."

"Jock… I did a good job, didn't I?"

"Huh?" he said, obviously completely confused.

"A single mother, barely holding it together, living with her mother and brother… Maddie seems to be remarkably well-adjusted. Don't you think?"

"She's fine, Riley. She's amazing."

"She's been asking me difficult questions lately."

"Really? Like what? She hasn't had anything new for me," he said.

"She said you two have talked a lot about back when… When we were so briefly together."

"I wouldn't say a lot," he said. "I think she was about twelve when she asked me why we weren't married. I figured that'd be coming. So I told her."

"But what did you tell her?"

"I told her that getting pregnant was an accident, that we weren't careful about preventing it, about birth control. Mostly my fault. And I issued a warning—teenage boys and young men are idiots, do not trust them. So—we were pregnant and we talked about marriage but didn't think it would work for us. We were too young, for one thing. But we both wanted her—I made sure to tell her that. My mom always said that kids want to know two things—that you love them and wanted them."

"You offered to give me money for an abortion," Riley reminded him.

He shook his head sadly. "Look, I did what I thought men did, what I thought they were expected to do. I didn't think it through. Thank God you didn't want that. Thank you for that, Riley. You've always been the smart one."

"You didn't tell her about that, did you?"

"Of course not," he said. "That wouldn't do one single positive thing for Maddie and I'm so damn grateful for her, you will just never know. I did tell her that as far as stupid eighteen-year-olds go, I was the dumbest. I told her I had a lot of regrets but none had anything to do with her. She made me the luckiest dimwit alive."

"She wants to know things, like did we love each other," Riley said. "I told her I loved you."

"That was good, to say that. She should think that her mom and dad loved each other when she was made."

"Jock, I *did* love you. I told you I loved you and you said, 'Whoa, wait a minute…'"

He rested his elbows on his knees and briefly hung his head. Then he looked at her. "Riley, there's no way I'm ever going to be able to go back in time and fix mistakes like that. I never should have done that. I never should have talked that way. I'm telling you, I was a stupid boy and I was scared to death. I didn't know how I felt. I just didn't know what to do."

"You wouldn't tell Emma…"

"Yeah, the list just gets longer and longer. Riley, I'll be the first person to admit it took me way too long to grow up, to know my mind, to figure out that life was handing me a gift and there was no way I was ever going to deserve it. But I admit I'm a damn lucky man and really, I'm so grateful. And I made my peace with Emma. I finally got to see her and tell her I was sorry that I did that to her, that I cheated on her."

"Huh," Riley huffed.

"I should have called her and told her we were together. Things might be a lot different if I'd just done that."

"You saw her?" Riley asked.

"Well, yeah." He laughed ruefully and shook his head. "That daughter of yours, Riley. She's fifteen going on fifty, you know that? After I told her I was someone else's boyfriend when I fell for you, she started asking me if I ever said I was sorry to Emma. Of course I hadn't. I'm too clumsy for that. It would've meant finding her number in New York and we both know she was in a bad place—she didn't need to hear from me. Then Maddie told me she was back. She'd met her. I guess she was with Adam and they ran into her. Maddie isn't sure but she thinks Adam likes her. And Maddie told me Emma would be having dinner with your mother so I hung around and waited for her to leave so I could..."

"Wait! What?"

"What what?" he asked, looking confused.

"Emma had dinner with my mother?"

"Yeah. A week or two ago, I think. You didn't know?"

"No," she said, feeling her blood pressure rising. "And Adam is seeing her."

"I don't know. She didn't mention..."

"He is," Riley said, angry. "I can tell. And my mother

is having dinner with her behind my back and not telling me. And you're seeing her, too. Making up with her?"

"Sort of making up. I just wanted to say I was sorry about all that, sorry that it hurt her, not sorry it happened because we're very lucky to have Maddie and—"

"So everyone has personal private stuff going on with Emma and no one finds it necessary to mention any of this to me!"

"Holy Jesus, maybe if you weren't so mad all the time!" he fumed. "Don't you ever get tired of people walking on eggshells around you?"

"Why aren't people at least honest with me?" she demanded.

"I don't know, Riley! Could it be because you get so freaking *angry*?"

She stood up. "So you said you were sorry you cheated on her. Did you ask her for another chance?"

Jock stood, as well. "Oh, for the love of God, of course not! I don't want another chance! Why are you so upset?"

"Oh, I don't know, Jock. Could it be because everyone is keeping stuff from me? My daughter, my brother, my mother, you! But who gave her the job? Me! Why am I always the one picking up the pieces?"

Jock just stared at her in shock. "Is that what you think? That you pick up the pieces? Not June or me or even Adam? Aren't we the A-Team? I know no one counts on me much but you all can. I do everything any of you asks. You weren't left alone, goddamn it! You had all of us! All of us doing it the way you wanted it done! And here you are, your girl is almost grown and you found someone, she tells me. You finally found someone who deserves you. Well, good for you. And I said I was sorry every way I could so you can get over it now and move on. I never stood a chance with you anyway."

"You didn't want a chance with me!"

"I asked you to marry me! More than once!"

"To be with Maddie! To be with your daughter!"

"No! To put our family together the way it should be! To be with you! But you never got over blaming me for all your problems. Me and Emma. So let me clear that up right now—we all make our own messes and as messes go we got real damn lucky. We got ourselves a beautiful fifteen-year-old mess who's going to do great things with her life in spite of us."

"You didn't want me," she said. "You were married six months later!"

"Yeah, another brilliant move of mine. I was so hungry for someone to love me, to want me, I married the first woman who convinced me I was trusted, that I was desirable. It lasted less than a year but it was over in a day."

"Bullshit. Women have always wanted you!"

"Just not the right one! Don't you get it, Riley? I did my best. My best has never been good enough."

"Now you're just feeling sorry for yourself. Maddie's proud of you."

"Kids will do that."

"She nearly ruined the first dinner we had with Logan. All she did was brag about you. It was very uncomfortable."

Jock smiled. "I'll have to thank her. She run him off?"

Riley raised her chin. "No. He doesn't scare easily, I guess. I'm going to go," she said, feeling exhausted.

"The next time you want to talk, give me about forty-eight hours advance warning, okay?"

Seventeen

After leaving Jock's, Riley had herself a hard cry, something she hadn't done in quite a while. It felt as though everyone was showering love on Emma and just not acknowledging how this might affect her, how she might feel like the bad girl, being punished all over again. Left out and unloved. Damn Emma! Had she come back and taken over Riley's support group?

She felt like a thirteen-year-old girl. A baby. An ogre who tried to prevent Adam and her mother from embracing their old friend. Tried and failed and now they knew how selfish and mean Riley could be.

At midnight she heard her phone chime with an incoming text. It was Logan.

Just wondering if everything is okay?

Crap! She'd never called him. Although she was in bed and had a stuffy nose, she called him.

"I'm so sorry," she said. "I'm fine. I got caught up in a difficult family discussion. You know how those things can sneak up at holidays."

"Oh, yeah," he said with a laugh. "My dad and I usually entertain the family by acting like assholes. We did pretty well this year. We stayed on opposite sides of the room and there wasn't too much friction.

"It's funny, here we are, twenty-five years later and I'm still a pissed-off little boy. Everyone else has forgiven him and let him back in the family. My mom and dad are as close to being a couple without being one as you can get. They're not remarried or anything, but he's at every family thing. I think he should be shunned."

"Gee, only twenty-five years?"

"You're probably not going to believe this, but I'm actually a pretty easygoing guy. I think. I wouldn't have a problem in the world if my mother just hated him."

"Sadly, I understand completely. Let's talk tomorrow," she said. "I've had such a long day."

"Sure," he said. "And, Riley? We have a new year ahead of us. Let's make it a good one, okay?"

"Absolutely, Logan."

What a nice guy, she thought. She snuggled back into the covers. But she didn't think about Logan. She wanted to. A smart woman would make something positive out of that relationship.

Why do people do these things on the holidays? she asked herself. Why couldn't Jock have saved his outburst for another time, another day?

Jock's outburst? her conscience mocked her. *You started it! You always start it!*

Maybe she should start to admit it if only to herself. She was so scared and hurt, felt so alone even though she had Adam, her mother and her grandparents for a little while after Maddie was born. When she wasn't crying she was bitching. In the beginning, when she was pregnant, Jock didn't come around much. When Maddie was born he only came around when he felt safe, when Adam wasn't around. He often visited Maddie when June was watching her because June might've been unhappy with Jock but she was never mean. Though he didn't come to see the baby on a schedule or often, he did come regularly. And he called. He called Riley until he could just call Maddie.

It seemed like forever that every time she saw him her heart ached and her throat burned with tears she wouldn't shed. But she got over it. As she grew older and met more and more women who were raising children on their own, she learned how to bear it.

But it left her hardened and somewhat bitter. She didn't want to be that way. Here she was, the mother of a beautiful and brilliant daughter with everything in the world to be grateful for and she could behave in the most ungrateful manner sometimes.

It had had the opposite effect on Jock. Having Maddie had sweetened him. Mellowed him and made him more mature.

I made one mistake, she thought wearily. *And it was the best thing that ever happened to me. Yet I've managed to suffer for it for years. How do I stop it? How has Jock moved on with grace?*

How has Emma?

Just before falling asleep she remembered, *I fell for you*, he had said. *I was never good enough for you*, he had said. Was that what he'd said? She must've misunderstood.

Emma wasn't at all unhappy with the quiet way she spent the holiday weekend. On Christmas Eve she went with Lyle and Ethan to Ethan's sister's house for dinner. Given that Lyle and Ethan had their own flower shop, a centerpiece wouldn't do, so she borrowed Penny's kitchen and recipes and made crab croquettes and a cheese ball. It was a rather hectic and noisy evening; Ethan's sister was pregnant and his niece was two. Emma enjoyed the two-year-old for about an hour and then started to wonder how young mothers did it—the toddler was tired, cranky, hungry, restless and generally bad. One of her first rebellious acts was to pitch the cheese ball at their Labrador retriever.

"Yeah, this is about ninety percent of the time these days," Ethan said.

"I don't think I was prepared for how fast a two-year-old can move," Emma said.

"Watch your valuables," Lyle said. "She swallowed Mommy's diamond engagement ring about six months ago."

"It's okay, I got it back," Ethan's sister yelled from the kitchen.

"Ewww," Emma and the two men said together.

When she got home at nine that night, Adam was waiting for her. She regaled him with stories of dinner and the fate of her cheese ball. She insisted he open his gifts; she wanted him to try on his new slippers. He liked the book and sweater and had a gift for her, a very big box. Inside was a black waterproof trench coat, a very stylish maxi length with a belt. She told him to wait right where he was. She took it to her little bedroom to try it on and when she came back he admired the sleek design with her pumps. Then she untied the belt, opened the coat and flashed him with her nakedness. Although they roared with laughter, it only took a minute for it to be replaced with the sound of kissing and panting, the new coat on the floor on one side of the bed, Adam's clothes on the other.

On Christmas morning she woke up to see Adam raised up on an arm, watching her. "I've made a decision," he said. "I've decided to wake up like this every Christmas morning."

"Ah. Will Santa approve?"

"I'm very nice," he said. "And you're a little naughty. Sounds perfect to me."

While Adam did his family thing, Emma relaxed, gathering her strength in the quiet of the day. She'd been warned that the week following Christmas was sheer hell at work. Some of their clients had been out of town over the holidays but many more had extra people in, company from out of town, lots of refuse from the gift exchanging, greasy and splattered kitchens from the constant cooking and baking. School was still on break until after New Year's, which meant general messiness everywhere and a tougher time cleaning while stepping over people.

And there were a few things she was eager to find out. First, was Bethany okay? She hadn't called since before Christmas, but the Christensen house was one of the first on her schedule for Monday. When they arrived, she ran right up the stairs, tapped quietly on Bethany's bedroom door and when the girl told her to come in, she stuck her head in. "Okay?" she asked quietly.

Bethany gave her a sheepish smile. "Okay," she answered.

"Was it a nice Christmas?"

She nodded. "And I saw my grandparents. I'm just so glad it's over. I feel so much more in control now."

"Life will be easier now, I think," Emma said. "Holidays are always a bit tough when you've had losses. You have my number."

"I do. I'll call you."

When Emma was pulling the door closed she turned and came face-to-face with Shawna, who was frowning. "You're gonna make trouble for yourself," she predicted.

"It'll be all right," Emma said, because that's what she'd been telling herself.

The Christensen home reminded her a little bit of her own New York apartment—spacious, pristine, the furnishings rich and carefully chosen, and while it was filled with warm colors and dark wood, you could almost feel the emptiness. It was too quiet. Homes were made to be filled with conversation and laughter and even arguing from time to time. It was too clean, too orderly. It felt so lonely here.

Emma, Shawna and Dellie got busy and as predicted, there was more cleaning than usual. Mr. and Mrs. Andrews had not canceled the cleaning service. Nick caught up with them on Tuesday to tell them he was sending a different crew and he would be watching closely to be sure there wasn't any trouble. He wouldn't allow Emma's crew to return to that volatile house. "For two cents, I'd cancel them," Nick said. "For now I'll be keeping a very close eye on that house."

At the end of the week when they were nearly finished with the last house, Riley texted Shawna and asked that the three of them stop by the office when they returned to turn in the van. They found a full staff gathered—Nick, Makenna, Riley and her young assistant, Jeanette.

"Come in, please," Riley said. "Something terrible

has happened and I wanted to tell you. You'll hear about it tonight if you watch the news. Mr. Andrews is dead. It appears Mrs. Andrews shot him. The police have taken her into custody." Riley cleared her throat. "Our crew let themselves in and found them."

Emma actually swooned against Shawna. "Dear God," she whispered.

"Here, sit down," Nick said.

"That man probably got what he had coming," Shawna said. "He was beating that woman."

"Has anything like this ever happened before?" Emma asked.

"We've had a delicate situation or two over the years. One of our clients was found unconscious—he had a stroke and went to the hospital and from there into a special care home. Nothing like this. People don't just have dust and dirt," Riley said. "They have complex personal lives. Some of them have serious problems. And we're in their private space. We have to be vigilant and blind—it's a very difficult balance. I'm sorry this happened."

"The other crew," Emma said. "Are they okay?"

"Not at all," Nick said. "It was Cora, Maria and Connie—and they're shook up. They're going to take Monday and Tuesday off and if they need to see someone, like a counselor, we'll find someone."

"Was it horrid?" Dellie asked.

"One bullet in the back of his head," Nick said. "He still had the TV remote in his hand. Looked like it might've happened much earlier or even the night before."

"Ew, that ain't gonna play good for her," Shawna said.

"Had he been beating her again?" Emma asked.

Everyone shrugged.

"I'm sure we'll get more information as time passes. I just wanted to be sure to tell you personally since you know the couple and had some dealings with them and the police. Everyone okay?"

"Sure," Dellie said. "They have kids, you know. Grown kids in their twenties."

"I know. Emma?"

"Yes. Fine." She shuddered, remembering Richard. Remembering the cruelty of his suicide. The horrific sight. The smell of blood and gun powder. His open eyes and gallons of blood. The smell of death and all its atrocities. "Fine," she said again, standing.

"Then I think we're finished here. Nick, you'll let me see that memo before you send it out to our crews."

"Definitely."

"Thanks, everyone."

Emma lingered as people slowly left, talking among themselves. When Riley was alone behind her desk, gathering up her purse and briefcase, she approached. "Um, excuse me. When would be a good time to talk? There's something I should tell you."

"Is it going to upset me?" Riley asked.

"Probably."

Riley hesitated. "Sit down. Let's get it over with."

Emma told Riley about Bethany's house, Bethany so frail and pale, Emma leaving her phone number and Bethany calling it. "You have got to be kidding me," Riley said.

Emma shook her head. "And I don't regret it. She sounds better since the holiday is past, but I have no idea how to help her. The family situation sounds so sad—her stepmother wearing her dead mother's clothes? My God, I don't know what to say or do. I just know that it won't help her if I cut her off, if I don't take her calls. Mostly I just listen. Are you going to fire me?"

"You've put me in a terrible position here," she said. "You know perfectly well I can't fire you. My family will only come down hard on me if I do that. My mother, who I have learned you've been seeing, my brother, who is your current champion..."

"Adam has been a good friend. He's the one who suggested your company, which, by the way, I happen to like." She laughed and shook her head. "I actually look forward to work. The girls I work with are fantastic. The clients range from difficult to weird to sweet. Some of them I would actually miss."

"Employees with a high school education and citizenship usually stay with this company for an average of nine months. And I am stuck with you."

"I should think it would give you great satisfaction," Emma said. "But tell me truly, Riley. Just for a second put aside whatever differences we've had and tell me—if you'd been in my position and saw that note, would you have done something? Anything? You have a fifteen-year-old daughter—what if she were that lonely? And had no one? Would you wish someone had answered her call, even if it was a lowly cleaning lady?"

"First of all, cleaning ladies are not lowly. Haven't you learned yet? We know more about our clients than they know about each other! Second, I don't know that I'd have done *that*!"

"Oh, you would, too," Emma said. "Just as you'd have called the police on Mr. Andrews."

"I wouldn't have left my number," Riley asserted. Then her own phone chimed. She looked at it and pressed a button, sending it to voice mail. "I admit I would have watched. Waited. Tried to think of a solution. A counselor…"

"She has a counselor," Emma said. "A counselor who asks her if she's jealous of the new stepmother."

"Dear God, what an imbecile! I knew of Mr. Christensen's marriage. When he filled out his contract, we always ask them to list the family members and pets in the household and I knew he had a teenager and was engaged to be married. But I didn't know he'd been widowed."

Riley's phone rang again. Again she looked at it. "She really wants me. I'm sorry," she said before clicking on. "Yes, Maddie?"

"Mom! We were in an accident! Someone hit us. We're taking Daddy to the hospital. Mom, he's hurt! He's hurt!"

"Slow down, Maddie," Riley said. She completely forgot about Emma as she put the cell phone on speaker so she could gather her purse, keys, coat. "Are you hurt?"

"No. Not really. But they couldn't get Daddy out right away and they wouldn't let me go in his ambulance because they needed the room to work on him. Oh, Mom, what if he dies?"

"He's not going to die," Riley said. "What hospital are you going to?"

Maddie asked someone. "Petaluma."

"Are you sure you're all right?"

"A couple of bumps, that's all."

"All right, I'm coming. I'm on my way."

Riley ran around her desk, past Emma and out the door. Two seconds later she ran back in and said, "Jock and Maddie were in an accident."

Emma grabbed her tote and ran out with Riley. "I'll come. Lock the door, I'll be right behind you. You might need me."

For just a moment Riley was thinking, *Why would I need you?* But she didn't say anything, she just locked the door without bothering to check the office, turn off the lights or anything. She bolted for her car and without looking back at Emma, she jumped in and flew out of the parking lot and down the road.

She still had Maddie on the line. "Okay, I'm driving. Tell me how you are," she nearly shouted into the phone.

"We're here! I'm going in with Daddy! No more phones!"

Riley growled as they were disconnected.

It took thirty minutes to get to the hospital and Riley ran from the parking lot into the ER. She asked for Jock Curry or Maddie Kerrigan and was directed to the waiting area. "But are they all right?" she asked in a booming voice.

"Mom?" a voice called. "Mom?"

Ignoring all protocol, Riley pushed people aside to go into a treatment area where a series of beds were enclosed by curtains. "Maddie?" she called.

"Here!" Maddie said.

Riley found her sitting on a bed, holding an ice pack to her forehead, tears running down her cheeks. She embraced her and squeezed her too tight.

"Mom, Daddy is hurt. They took him upstairs to see if he needs surgery. I had to call Gramma and Grandpa because I'm not old enough to make decisions for him."

"Maddie, is he conscious?"

"He was talking a little. He has pain in his shoulder and stomach and he got a cut on the head that bled everywhere and he said he was bruised all over. He says he's fine. But the doctor says he's not fine and needs X-rays and stuff and to be checked for internal injuries and a head injury, so he's gone upstairs."

"Have you been checked over?"

She nodded. She took away the ice pack to reveal a contusion. "I might've hit his head. Someone just ran into us—*kabam*! She hit Daddy's side of the car and they could hardly get him out!" Then she burst into tears. "Mom, what if he isn't okay?"

"Shh, Maddie. He was talking and conscious—that's a good sign. They'll take good care of him."

Adam jogged into the front entrance of the hospital and Emma was there, waiting for him. "How are they?" he asked.

"Maddie is fine and they've taken Jock to surgery, but they're not sure they're going to operate on him. He has some kind of spleen injury that they might be able to manage with medication, but they'll have to watch him, keep him. His parents came right away. Maddie and Riley won't leave until he's completely out of the woods. And I knew you'd want to see them."

"Where are they?"

"They're all in the third floor waiting area outside of surgery. Quite the group."

"Okay," he said, grabbing her hand.

"Ah… I'm going to go. Will you call me if you need me? If there's any change?"

"You don't have to go, Emma."

"I think I should. I'm not family and I'm not family of family. I just wanted to be here until everyone arrived, just in case…well, in case Riley needed me."

"I'm going up there," he said. He leaned toward her and kissed her on the forehead. "Thank you. I'll call you the second I know something."

"I'll be around. Go take care of your girls."

Emma was glad to be leaving, though she was worried about Jock. She had a soft spot in her heart for the guy after his amends. If they kept him in the hospital for the weekend, she'd swing by and pay him a visit.

Her phone chimed with a text and she saw it was from Lyle.

Can you call or come by the shop before we close?

She got in her car and turned it on for a little heat, but she sat in the parking lot while she called Lyle. "What's up?"

"You might want to hear this in person. Are you far away?"

"Half hour, I suppose. Just tell me. It's been a crazy day."

"Well it's about to get crazier. Lauren Shay stopped by the shop today."

"My sister?"

"She wanted me to get a message to you. Rosemary wants to see you."

"Well, that's going to be pretty difficult as I can't go to Palm Springs," Emma said.

"She's back. She's ill, Lauren says. She's back in the family home with Lauren and Anna and…" He took a breath. "She's in hospice care."

"Wow. What about her husband?"

"I didn't ask. I have no idea what this is about, just

that she's back and she's apparently dying and she wants to see you. I have Lauren's number if you need it."

"I don't know," she said. "You know I'm afraid of Rosemary. She's mean. Do you suppose she's thought of one last mean thing to do to me before she dies?"

"I'll go with you," Lyle said. "You might want to call Lauren and get more information before you walk into the lion's den."

"Are you almost ready to close the shop?" she asked. "Can we grab a glass of wine? I have a bottle in the refrigerator at home."

"Won't you be with Adam?" he asked.

"Not for a while. See, Jock and Maddie were in a car accident and Adam's at the hospital. Maddie's all right but Jock isn't—they might have to remove his spleen. The call came while I was in Riley's office. We were having a little meeting because one of our clients murdered her husband and a cleaning crew found them."

"And you want a glass of wine?" Lyle asked. "If I'd had that kind of day I'd just hook up a nipple to the bottle and go to town."

"Want to come over and watch me unwind? I'd like to talk out this situation with Rosemary."

"I'll be there in about thirty minutes. Don't start without me."

Adam found Riley alone in the waiting room and she jumped up when he came in.

"How did you know to come?" she asked. "I was going to call you and Mom in a little while, but I didn't want to scare you. Maddie is okay."

"Emma called me. Where's Maddie?"

"She's in Jock's room. She won't leave him. She's

fine, but it really scared her to see her dad all banged up and medical people rushing around him."

"What happened?"

"A young woman ran a light and T-boned him on the driver's side. Her airbag deployed so she escaped injury. But both cars are likely totaled."

"Maddie wasn't driving?"

Riley shook her head. "Thank God."

"Emma said his parents are here."

"They went down to the cafeteria to get coffee. Mrs. Curry is a little shaken. I think they're going to call Jock's brother and sister. There could be a crowd soon and he's in a holding room being monitored so they can take him into surgery if they have to. Apparently he has some internal injuries. He said he feels like he's been thrown down a flight of stairs. He's in a lot of pain and they have him medicated. The bruises on his face are starting to show up." She winced. "He looks awful."

"Are you trying to get Maddie to leave? Go home?"

"No, we're going to stay. I might run home and get her a change of clothes—she has blood on her clothes from Jock's head. Not much of a cut but it sure bled a lot."

"And Maddie? Anything at all?"

"Goose egg." She touched her own forehead in the spot. Then her eyes filled with tears. "I had words with Jock Christmas night."

Adam frowned. "I thought the two of you did fine," he said.

"Not at Mom's. I drove to his house. I wanted to talk to him about… Oh shit, about nothing, really. Just that Maddie's growing up so fast and she'll go off to college and get married and have children and… How are we going to balance all that?"

"Divorced couples do it all the time," Adam said with a shrug.

"I'd never been in his house," she said quietly. "He has a nice house. He has a room for Maddie."

"What's the matter, Riley?"

"I was mean to him. I kind of picked a fight with him. And he said he did his best but it was never good enough. You know I'd never even been in his house?"

"You said that already," Adam pointed out. "It's okay. The only relationship you had with Jock was the parenting of Maddie and you both do that pretty well."

"He implied I never gave him a chance," she said.

"Riley, what the hell is this?"

"I don't know, I don't know," she said. She went for the purse she'd left sitting on the chair and dug around for a tissue. She dabbed her eyes and blew her nose. "I think I've made so many mistakes."

Maddie came into the waiting room with a doctor; the doctor had a bolstering hand on Maddie's shoulder. "We're going to take Mr. Curry into surgery. I think he's going to have to part with that spleen, after all, and while I'm in there I can look around for any other problems."

"Can I talk to him?" Riley said, looking suddenly panicked.

"He's being prepped," the doctor said. "He'll be in surgery about an hour then in recovery." He turned to look down at Maddie. "When he wakes up in recovery you can see him, but then you should go home for the night. He's going to be groggy and it would be best for him to sleep."

"I'll be quiet," Maddie said. "I'll sit with him and be quiet."

"If I thought he needed someone to sit with him, believe me, I'd put an RN at his bedside. But he's going to be monitored, checked regularly and we're going to take good care of him. If there's any change in his condition, I'll call you personally."

"But I'll see him after surgery?" she asked.

"Absolutely. I've got this."

"Okay," she said meekly.

Adam waited around for the two and a half hours it took for Jock to have surgery, regain consciousness in recovery and see Maddie. During that time more of Jock's family showed up, all wanting to see him. Adam had called June and she came. He stepped outside a couple of times to text Emma and was relieved to know she was home and having a glass of wine with Lyle. When the doctor was finally ready to kick the whole lot of them out, June left with Jock's parents, holding Jock's mother's hand and reassuring her.

Maddie seemed to be exhausted. Adam walked them out to Riley's car. "Would you like me to follow you home? Feel like talking about it?"

"What is there to say?"

"Well, I think maybe you have something heavy on your mind. Mistakes, Riley? I've always felt like you do everything right."

She looked at him with a weak and rueful smile. "Shows what you know."

"I'm coming over," he said. "You can put Maddie to bed and we'll talk a little bit."

"No offense, Adam, but I don't feel like talking right now." She stopped walking and looked in her purse, patted her pockets and said, "Nuts. No cell phone. It must be in the waiting room. Adam, take Maddie home please? I'll be right behind you."

"Sure. I'm parked right over here, Maddie. Let's get you home so you can get out of those bloody clothes and get a shower."

"Yeah. I guess," she said, leaning on Adam.

He put his arm around her and opened the passenger door for her, settled her into his car.

"Thanks, Uncle Adam, for coming to the hospital."

"Everyone came. It was like a party." He reached across the console and patted Maddie's knee. "You feeling a little better now that he's out of surgery?"

"I guess so. It's just that I know so many people who lost a father when they were still young, and just the thought… Two friends at school, and even you, Uncle Adam." She sniffed back tears. "I want Daddy to have a chance to be happy, that's all."

"Your dad seems pretty happy to me," Adam said.

"He says he's fine, that he's happy, that he's proud of me. But one time when we were talking he said his one biggest regret was that he couldn't get Mom to marry him so we could be a real family. But he doesn't blame her. He said he made mistakes."

"Mistakes," Adam muttered. "Lots of talk about mistakes these days. You know what I think? I think I'm tired of hearing about mistakes. It would be a lot more productive to leave the mistakes behind and just think about the future."

"Don't you have any regrets, Uncle Adam?"

"Everyone does, Maddie. But I think my life has turned out exactly the way I meant for it to. And it's a good life. Our family might be a little different, a little chopped up here and there, but last time I checked, we were all feeling pretty lucky with what we have."

"Maybe till tonight," she said. "I'll feel a lot better when I know Daddy's all right."

"See what I mean," Adam said. "He's a lucky man."

Riley got off the elevator on the third floor. She pulled her cell phone out of her coat pocket and glanced at it. Four missed calls from Logan. She had texted him about the accident, told him everyone was fine but she was tied up and would call him later. Then she'd turned her phone off.

And she knew where her cell phone was all along.

She was relieved to see that none of Jock's family remained in the waiting room. She went into the recovery area where she'd seen Jock not ten minutes ago and there he was, sleeping off his anesthesia and pain meds, mouth open slightly. She felt tears threaten again. She walked over to his bed and gently touched his forehead. "Oh, Jock," she whispered. "I'm the screwup. Not you."

All those years of being angry, of being awash in pride and determined to keep Jock from ever hurting her again, she held him back, held herself back. She put her head down and worked like a maniac, single-minded in aiming to succeed in business and show them all—*I am not a bad person, am not a disloyal, betraying friend.* "All I wanted to do was keep myself safe," she whispered to him. "To keep Maddie safe. To prove to the world I could make it without trusting anyone."

He opened one eye and she sniffed.

"You're right about me, Jock. I was always angry. And scared. I never gave you a chance."

He lifted his hand to where hers rested on the bed

rail. "It's okay, Riley," he rasped out. "It's going to be okay."

"What if you'd been killed in that accident? What if I never got to say I'm sorry?"

"Shhh," he said. "It's okay."

"It's not really," she said with a hiccup of emotion. "But maybe when you get better… If you think you can give me another chance, I'd like us to be friends."

He smiled sleepily. "Okay," he said, letting his eyes drift closed. "Boy, you really make a guy work for it, don't you?"

A huff of laughter escaped her. "It wasn't my intention."

"What about the other guy? The new guy?" he asked, not opening his eyes.

"Not much going on there, Jock. But listen, let's not say anything to Maddie. I don't want her having fantasies about us."

"Okay," he said. He gave her hand a little squeeze and she bent over and put a soft kiss on his forehead.

Suddenly there was an orderly and a nurse at the bedside, interrupting them. "We're going to take Mr. Curry to his room now. You can follow us if you like, Mrs. Curry. But then you should let him sleep and come back in the morning."

"I'm not… Okay," she said. "I'll follow you so I know where to find him in the morning."

Eighteen

Adam and Emma stayed in for New Year's Eve. Emma parked her car in his garage in case Riley or June drove by. "I think the point of this discretion is just about moot," Adam said as he was taking her coat. "My mother has guessed, I think Riley has guessed and Maddie wouldn't care."

"Still, until Riley assures me there are no longer any hard feelings between us, we will be discreet. One of the last things she said to me just before her phone chimed with Maddie's call was that she was stuck with me because of her family. She's not ready. By the way, where is Riley spending New Year's Eve?"

"She and Maddie took some snacks and a couple of board games to the hospital to spend it with Jock. I'm pretty sure they won't be allowed to stay until midnight but they're keeping him company tonight."

"Aw, that must make him very happy. He'd probably risk another car accident to get this much attention from Riley."

"Now, why would you say that?" Adam asked.

"I think he cares for her very much. I think he might

love her. The way he talked about Riley and Maddie, about how he screwed up with Riley… It just sounded like he has deeper feelings than he lets on in front of you." She put her arms around Adam's waist and looked up at him. "Do you ever think about ways things could've been different?"

"Like how?" he asked, really wanting her perspective.

"Well, Jock could've started dating Riley in the first place. Then I think we would all have remained friends. But Riley might not have built her business—I get the impression she did it out of survival. Or I could have come back here after college and fallen in love with you ten years ago."

He stroked her cheek with the back of his knuckles. "Are you in love with me now?"

She nodded. "Pretty much. It all hangs on what you feed me tonight."

"If I'd known that I would have tried harder. I have a big assortment of finger foods—your favorite crab balls, stuffed mushrooms, a cheese ball and no dog present, spinach/artichoke dip and a veggie tray."

She put her arms around his neck. "My absolute favorites. You're a shoo-in. But, Adam, when do you think you'll fall in love right back?"

"Emma, I've been in love with you since I was eighteen. I'm just waiting for you to get your life back so you can share it with me."

"Well, I didn't expect this, you know. I thought I'd be spending my Saturday nights with my gay boyfriend and his jealous partner, looking for work all the time and trying to forget the debacle that was my marriage."

"I don't know if you'll ever forget it," he said. "We

can move on in spite of it. Are you finally over the idea that being with you will hurt me?"

"I'm still worried that it might, but I'm now convinced I couldn't change your mind if I tried. There has been yet one more complication, one more piece of unfinished business I have to deal with. I'm going to see Rosemary tomorrow. She asked Lauren to get in touch with me. It seems Rosemary can't die in peace without seeing me and she's come back to Santa Rosa to die. She's in the house that had belonged to my father."

"And you're going to do it?" he asked.

"I am. Maybe I'm crazy but I'm hoping that since she asked for me, staring death in the face has made her kinder. But honestly? I'm scared to death. Our last words weren't very nice."

"Let me go with you," he said.

"You are my champion," she said. "That's what Riley called you, 'my champion.' Lyle also offered, but I told him no. You I might take along. I always feel a little braver with you around."

The house Emma grew up in was now about forty years old and because it was a custom home built on a large lot, it had held up handsomely. It was, she remembered, one of the best homes in the area, at least in the parish where her Catholic school was located. Compared to some of the homes Emma had cleaned lately, it seemed ordinary, but it wasn't. It was a large five-bedroom, three-bath home decorated in Country French style. With its huge kitchen, spacious master bedroom and bath, and twelve-foot ceilings, it had been considered very much upscale forty years ago. The curb appeal was still there; the house was very attractive with its well-maintained lawn, shrubbery and a couple of formidable trees, sitting on a wide street with well-spaced homes.

Of course Emma didn't have many good memories of the place. She was not Rosemary's child. Rosemary introduced Anna and Lauren as her daughters, Emma as her stepdaughter.

"I've never been in the house," Adam said.

"Never? How is that possible?"

"If I came to fetch Riley and walk her home, I waited on the stoop."

"I never noticed. But that doesn't surprise me. Let's get this over with."

At first Emma wasn't sure which of her sisters opened the door as they looked very much alike and she hadn't seen them in a few years. It took her a moment to realize it was Lauren for not only did she look tired and ashen but she'd gained about a hundred pounds. And then right behind her was Anna, thirty-seven now and morbidly obese. They both looked entirely miserable, but how should they look, knowing their mother was dying?

The house was cluttered and held a strange smell. Dust, chemical cleaners, perhaps death.

"Happy holidays," Emma said, presenting Lauren with a gift basket filled with salami, cheeses, olives, wine and other goodies, like chocolate.

Lauren didn't thank her but took the basket and left it on the table in the foyer. "Come with me," she said, turning so they could follow.

They went in the direction of the master bedroom where Rosemary lay in a hospital bed rather than the bed that had been in there. Rosemary had always been heavyset but now she was shockingly thin, her color a bit jaundiced and her hair extremely sparse. All that sudden weight loss left her face sagging. There were bottles and vials on the dresser, an IV hooked up to her arm, and the room was messy with medical supplies. Her bible lay on the bed beside her. Rosemary's eyes were closed.

"Rosemary?" Emma said, merely breathing her name.

She opened her eyes. "Oh. It's you."

"Lauren said you wanted to see me."

"Yes. Who is that? Another man so soon?" Rosemary asked weakly.

"It's Adam Kerrigan. You remember him. Riley's brother." She looked around the room. "Rosemary, where is Vince?"

"Vince isn't here. He didn't sign on for this."

Emma actually grimaced. She hadn't liked Vince at all but hadn't they been married quite a long time for him to bail out on her like that?

"So, you turned your lawyer on me," Rosemary said.

"No," Emma said, shaking her head. "Mr. Justice was my father's lawyer and helped him with his will. He offered to—"

"I am the trustee of my late husband's estate and I want you to know what to expect. Your father left some money in a trust. It was left up to me to distribute with discretion. I have my own lawyer. He'll tell your lawyer if there's anything to distribute, but I highly doubt it. Then we have no further business. And I forgive you."

Emma's mouth hung open. "You forgive me for *what*?"

"For being an ungrateful brat. For bringing shame on our family with your scandal. For never appreciating your good fortune. I'm going to die in peace, knowing I did everything I could and more than necessary."

Emma had to bite her lip to keep it from trembling. So, Rosemary had seized one last moment to be cruel. "And the house?"

"It belongs to my daughters now."

"My father's house," Emma said weakly. It was not a mansion by any means but California real estate was valuable. Just guessing, she would think a custom home this size on such a generous piece of property would go for a great deal of money.

"It became my house," Rosemary said.

"You've never mentioned money before," Emma said. "You said there wasn't any."

"It was a modest amount. There was no reason to discuss it," she said. Then she winced as if in pain. "I was given discretion to use it for the children responsibly, and I did."

"You didn't use any on me," Emma pointed out.

"You were married to a millionaire!" Rosemary screeched, which sent her into a coughing fit. Lauren came rushing to her side. She held her mother up until she recovered. Then she gently lowered her again.

"I was sixteen when my father died," Emma said. "I paid for college with scholarships, part-time work and loans. You remarried…"

"You don't need it now," Lauren said bitterly.

"My father built this house," Emma said.

"He left it to me and it has been transferred into my daughters' names. I want you to tell your lawyer this business is finished, that we have nothing more to discuss. I want to be at peace with this. Please tell your lawyer that you're satisfied everything is settled and stop pursuing this idiocy. Leave my poor girls what little I left them and go away. Don't be picking my bones like a selfish brat."

"Stop," Adam said. "Stop it right now. I'm sorry for your ill health, Rosemary, but I think you've abused this woman enough. It's over." Adam turned Emma around. "We should leave. There's nothing more to discuss here."

"I just want to leave peacefully knowing you won't visit your vengeance on my daughters," Rosemary said.

Emma just shook her head. "Why would I?"

"Knowing you, you think you deserve everything. You've always been haughty, miss homecoming queen. Don't steal what I left for my daughters."

Adam just shook his head. "Let's go, Emma. You wouldn't want this house. The meanness has seeped into the walls by now." He looked at Rosemary with a frown.

Adam took Emma's hand and pulled her away. "Don't listen to her anymore, Emma. These people are poisoned with envy. Come on."

She let him pull her to the car and help her inside.

She sat still, saying nothing, stricken. He started the car and began to drive away and still she was silent. A good five minutes passed before she spoke. "I thought I was beyond being surprised by them. I thought I was beyond being hurt. She must hate me so much. Why does she hate me so much?"

"I think Rosemary might hate a lot of people. At the least, I think very few people are cherished by her. Emma, you can walk away from them knowing you were very kind. More kind than I would've been. I think that woman stole from a grief-stricken child. I wouldn't want to be where she's going."

"She might meet Richard where she's going—his values were similar, I think."

The following week Emma finally met with Lucinda Lopez again.

"It's been over two weeks," Lucinda said. "Your first Christmas in your hometown in at least ten years."

"More than that," Emma said. "More like a dozen. It didn't take me too many years after my father's death to see that my stepmother and sisters didn't really want me to interrupt their celebration. But it's a whole new life now—a simpler, quieter life. There was a little excitement here and there." Emma told Lucinda first about Bethany and how she seemed much brighter and stronger now that the holiday was past.

"That's very kind of you to take the time to listen to this troubled girl," Lucinda said. "Would you do something for me? If you think she trusts you, will you please promote the idea of her talking to her counselor? And if her counselor isn't helping her, suggest she ask for a new one or talk to someone at school. Kids that age who have suffered loss are feeling isolated and fragile. And they're very unpredictable. I don't want you to find yourself up against a situation you can't handle. The loser could be the girl."

"Yes," she said. "Yes, of course. Can I suggest you?"

"You can suggest me, sure. In fact, you're welcome to tell her you're seeing a counselor. Sometimes that has a positive effect. I just worry when someone who has been depressed suddenly becomes cheerful."

Emma then told her about her visit with Rosemary and her plea that Emma leave her daughters and their inheritance alone. "My father's been gone for eighteen years and while we were comfortable, he wasn't a rich man. I can't imagine there's much, if anything. And I'm not going to stir up the curious press by going after money. In fact, I don't want to hear the word *money* associated with my name in any way."

"You'll do whatever makes you comfortable, Emma. I would like you to think about one thing. What your father had in his will was his ardent wish. If he willed something to you, he meant for you to have it."

"I understand that. But it was meant for college. He told me when I was just a little girl that he was saving for college. Well, college was paid for a long time ago."

"And you just had a very simple, very quiet holiday. Much different from what you've experienced the past decade, I suppose."

"I spent Christmas Eve and Christmas morning with Adam, who is more wonderful than you can imagine. He had dinner with his family at his mother's house then came back to my little bungalow, bringing the best leftovers. I had to work the next morning but he's off—Christmas break. He gave me a beautiful trench coat and I gave him a sweater and slippers. Lucinda, it was perfection. So peaceful. All the stress of the world was somewhere else for a change. No flashy baubles, no fancy parties."

"None of that filthy lucre," Lucinda joked. "After some of the Christmases you've experienced in past years, how did it compare?"

"I've never felt richer," Emma said.

Jock was released from the hospital after a few days but would not be cleared for work until after his next visit with the doctor ten days post-surgery. His mother wanted him to come home with her but he flatly refused. His mother said she would stay with him at his house and he said, "Oh, just shoot me." Riley witnessed all of this as she and Maddie were at the hospital visiting at the time.

"Don't worry, Mrs. Curry," Riley said. "We're close.

We'll check on him frequently. And we're just a phone call away if Jock needs anything."

After his mother left to pull her car to the front of the hospital, Jock said, "Thanks, Riley. But there's nothing to worry about. I'm finally going to have time to watch all those golf tournaments I recorded. I'm not going to need help with anything. I'm not going to be moving furniture."

"You're just going to camp on the couch, right?"

"That's my plan."

"Maddie's back in school so we'll swing by after school tomorrow and we won't stay long."

"Stay as long as you like. Or you can just drop Maddie off if you feel like it."

But she didn't feel like it. She wanted to take stock of his refrigerator, make sure his house was tidy because he couldn't do it; she even put fresh sheets on his bed because there was no telling how long it had been.

She left Maddie with Jock and went to her mother's house. She asked for some of her plentiful stock of frozen meals she had prepared for her volunteer meal service. For Jock, she explained.

"This is interesting—you going to such trouble for Jock," June said.

"Did you see how frightened and upset Maddie was when he got hurt? Had surgery? I knew Maddie was close to Jock but for some reason I thought it was no closer than she is to Adam. But I was wrong—she's very close to Jock. I'm going to have to try harder to get along with him."

June gave her a dubious look and said, "Of course."

She didn't take the meals to Jock's house. She took them home and put them in her freezer before going to collect Maddie. Then the next day at around noon she retrieved them and dropped in on him.

He answered her knock looking a little rumpled, scruffy and slightly stooped because his incision was still sore.

"Riley?" He looked over her shoulder, looking for Maddie.

"It's just me. I brought some of Mother's meals for your freezer. And I also have some milk, orange juice, eggs, bread, lunch meat and veggie salad from the deli."

"You didn't have to do all that," he said, but he let her in. "Aren't you working today?"

"Uh-huh," she said, loading things into the refrigerator and freezer. "I took a long lunch. These meals are all frozen, thaw in just a few hours and they're labeled. You have meat loaf and mashed potatoes, mac and cheese, lasagna, that meatball concoction she makes…" She raised her head and listened. There wasn't even a TV on. "Were you napping?" she asked.

He indicated the kitchen table where his laptop was set up next to a cup of coffee. "Paying bills," he said.

"Oh, Jock, are you going to have financial issues because of the accident?"

"Not serious ones," he said, shaking his head. "I won't get what I need on that car, but I guess the lady—a girl, really—was charged with running the light so maybe her insurance company will step up." He chuckled. "At least she has insurance. The last guy who rear-ended me didn't."

Riley frowned. "Did someone rear-end you?"

"Ten years ago. Maddie wasn't in the car. She was still in a car seat back then, wasn't she? She wasn't in my car very often."

Because Riley had avoided that as much as possible. Not because Jock wasn't a safe driver. Because she liked having control. Especially over him. She shook her head a bit mournfully. Maddie obviously adored him. And Riley had tried to give Jock as little time with her as possible.

"Have you had lunch?"

"Not yet. I'll graze around in there when you're done. And thank you. That was nice of you."

"I'll make you a sandwich and some salad. Go ahead and finish with your bills. Do you have more coffee?"

"Right there," he said, nodding toward the counter.

She was a little uncomfortable and she could tell Jock was both confused and suspicious. But she had to start somewhere. So he went back to his computer and she got out what she needed—knife, fork, plate, bread, mayo. She was impressed to see he was very tidy. His refrigerator was clean as a whistle—that was a good sign. "Nice," she said. The refrigerator was always one of the last things to get scrubbed. He had lettuce and tomatoes, so she added that to the sandwich.

She bravely dished up a little salad for herself as well as him then delivered the plate to him. She made herself a cup of coffee and joined him at the table.

He looked at her for a long moment. "You're joining me for lunch?"

"Just a bite of this salad," she said. "If that's okay."

"It's okay. So you meant it. You want to be my friend?"

"Listen, if you'd rather I leave…"

"You want to just tell me what this is about?"

She put her hands in her lap, her salad and coffee untouched. "Right," she said. "First of all, I felt bad about Christmas night, about the argument we had, and I couldn't stop thinking about it. You nailed it, Jock—I've been angry. It's true, and I thought I had every right to be angry. But then when you got hurt and I saw how terrified

Maddie was, it hit me hard that you'd always tried with me, even if it didn't go very well most of the time, and I didn't really try with you. And our daughter loves us both."

"Yes, she does."

"And you've had a very close relationship with her, one that I was barely aware of. It seemed you didn't see her that often."

He shrugged. "You weren't easy about that and there was no reason to make life tough for Maddie by pushing you too hard. So I got her a phone and—"

"She was much too young for that phone!"

Jock waited patiently for her to get over that little outburst and she did. There she was again, jumping to conclusions, controlling things. She twisted her lips a little. "Ach," she said, chagrined.

"I got her a phone and a laptop so we could communicate and we stayed in close touch. I went to all her school things, when I could. My hours weren't always good—I had the store a lot of nights. But we were able to talk. She's so smart, Riley. Like you."

Riley felt her cheeks grow a little hot, flushing. "You're smart," she said. "She definitely got your legs."

He laughed. "Yeah, you've been looking up at her since she was thirteen. She's a beauty."

"I didn't know you'd told her about Emma. I didn't know a lot of the things you talked about."

"I told Maddie it wasn't a good idea for her to carry stories about me to you and about you to me. I told her that would cause more friction between us. And she didn't want that."

"I don't know where we start," Riley said. "We've been kind of at each other's throats for a long time."

"Not really. Not always," he said. "I really pissed you

off a few times but around Maddie we were always nice to each other. At least tolerant, thanks to June. But there is one thing that kind of grates on me. I don't know if I dare talk about it."

"Maybe you better," she said. "Let's get it all on the table."

"You have to promise not to scream or throw things. I'm recovering from major surgery."

"I have never..." She stopped herself because her voice had become shrill. "I've never thrown anything."

He smiled. "You seemed angriest with me when I tried to tell you I cared about you. I wanted us to have a chance. I thought I could be a decent husband and I liked being a father. I knew I'd screwed it up completely in the beginning, I knew I wasn't really good enough for you, but I—"

"We didn't get off to a good start..." she said.

"My fault," he said. "I don't have any excuses. I take that back—I have nothing but excuses. I was young and dumb, terrified, confused, not to mention I felt completely incompetent. I wanted to do the right thing and I was pretty sure I wasn't capable of it. I had no education, no money, just a shitty little part-time job—"

"It wasn't all your fault," she said. "Look, there's no way you can understand this, but I had a lot to overcome. I was a poor kid. A poor fatherless kid. I'd cheated on my best friend with her boyfriend and she hated me, which she was bound to. I was ashamed and angry and pretty desperate. It gave me a little satisfaction to blame you for all my problems. Then I started my company and I was afraid to look up for at least twelve years. When you asked for another chance, I couldn't hear you."

"I asked a few times..."

"You married Laurie..."

"I thought it might fix what was hurting. I shouldn't have done that to her."

"But she dumped you!"

"We knew right away it wasn't working, but I'll be honest with you—I was going to stay. I wasn't going to fail twice. But if you think our relationship is complicated? Jesus, Laurie's life was a train wreck. She's back with her ex. They probably never should've divorced in the first place. And they fight twenty-four-seven."

"Is it even possible for us to pick up the pieces after all this time and be friends?" she asked. "Do our grudges just run too deep?"

"I don't have any grudges, Riley. I've made peace with my screwups. I have a great family, a beautiful daughter, a good job, a few friends and a decent life. If we can be friends, I'll be a happy man."

"Did we bicker too much in front of Maddie?" she asked.

He laughed a little bit. "No more than your average married couple," he said. "You take one look at Maddie and know—she's pretty normal for a daughter of mine. You're a wonderful mother. And you're not the poor kid anymore, that's for sure."

She sighed. "You can't imagine the kind of desperate ambition that took. I've craved a nap for fifteen years." She gave him a long look. "Don't you ever get...lonely?"

He shook his head. "Hardly ever. Sometimes I go too long without seeing Maddie, but I can always talk to her. But lonely? Not so much. Do you?"

She nodded. "Even though I have good people in

my life, too. Sometimes it feels like there's something missing."

"Now, *that* I understand. So—is the new guy going to be okay if you're friendly with your daughter's daddy?"

"New guy?" she asked. Then she remembered. "Oh! Logan, the police officer. Um, I'm not sure that's going anywhere. He's a great guy. But..." She bit her lip.

"Riley, he's the first guy you've dated since we split," he pointed out.

"Nah, I went out a few times," she said. "Nothing ever clicked."

He just smiled. "So here we sit. Two people who had a child together, raised a little girl together, bickered like cranky old married people and could never find anyone else to fill the gap. Doesn't that make you a little curious?"

"Let's be very careful here, Jock. If we screw up again, we might end up hating each other."

"If I screw up again, you might end up hating me, but I'll never hate you. I never have. I've gotten a little pissed here and there, but I've always loved you. I just didn't know how to behave. I was a boy."

He's not a boy anymore, she thought. "Go slow," she said.

They ate their lunch, talked about Maddie, then Riley cleaned up the kitchen and said she had to go back to work. He walked her to the door. Then he turned her toward him and put a gentle kiss on her forehead. "Be very careful, Riley," he said. "I love you. I always have. But I'm not going back and forth. If being with me doesn't work for you, that's it. I don't want to experiment," he said. "You're not the only one with feelings."

"I know. I know."

Nineteen

All the way to Aaron Justice's house Emma was anxious. She was looking forward to seeing him again but a little worried about how to pay him for the work he'd done when it turned out there was no money left in that estate. She should have called him and told him to stop whatever he was doing—he'd already invested valuable time. She'd find a way to pay him eventually. And she'd made up her mind—she wouldn't try to take that house away from her sisters. Really, it wouldn't make her happy anyway.

Aaron now kept a small office in his house, the home he'd shared with his late wife. It was a lovely house that Emma had never been to before.

"Emma, how good it is to see you. Come in, I've made us tea."

He invited her to sit down. "I'm not sure how many details you recall from our visit when we went over your father's will immediately after his death. You were so young and in a state of grief. I encouraged you to call me, but you never did."

Emma shrugged. "I didn't see the need," she said. "I

remember that you said there should be a little money to help with school, should I go to college. And Rosemary did send me spending money sometimes."

He frowned. "Let's go over the conditions of the will just to refresh your memory."

The assets John Shay had accrued were to be split in two—half to Rosemary, his wife, and half to be divided by the children. Rosemary was the executor of the will. She was also the trustee, which meant the inheritance held in trust for the children couldn't be spent on some young boyfriend. Emma almost laughed out loud—*as if!* The will included all three children, even though Anna was not John's biological child. And his plan had been to distribute the proceeds over time—half of their portion when each child reached the age of thirty, the second half at the age of thirty-five. Those assets, however, were available for certain reasonable expenses—welfare—as in the cost of housing and such, education, down payment on a home, extraneous medical expenses not covered by health insurance, etc.

"I paid for my own college," Emma said.

"I know," Aaron said. "As I told you, Rosemary got herself another lawyer soon after your father died. A few years after that she changed lawyers again. She asked her new lawyer to write her a new will, which she was entitled to do. But the money your father set aside for you and your sisters was part of an irrevocable trust, meaning that if she withdrew any of it on your behalf for things like college, she had to have records. And she was to inherit the house, as well—it was not held in trust. Emma, did you receive anything from your father's estate?"

Emma shook her head. "Rosemary said that just

maintaining the house and raising three girls to the age of independence had been all she could afford. I counted myself lucky to get an allowance while I was in school. Small, but it helped."

"She had receipts for tuition and housing…"

"She asked me for receipts. For records, she said."

"When you were thirty, you were due some money."

"Wow," Emma said. "I didn't know that. Or maybe I just didn't remember. My father was a pretty simple guy. I knew there might only be enough to get Rosemary through the difficult period of getting three daughters into adulthood."

"Rosemary's attorney has provided an accounting of the trust. I have a balance due you that might be grossly inadequate, given the house, the funding that was misdirected, small details, and I recommend a good forensic accountant. You should challenge the trustee."

Emma let out a huff of rueful laughter. "Aaron, the trustee is dying. I saw her. She has very little time left and she wasn't pleasant. She asked me to leave her daughters alone—said that she's leaving the house and whatever money there is to them. I'm not going to challenge them. I'm not ever going back to court."

"Unfortunately for Rosemary, she can't redirect the terms of the trust. The sum left to you is grossly inadequate. You're entitled to more. I'm afraid she was irresponsible."

She shook her head. "I'll take whatever it is and I'll pay you, but I'm not going to pursue this—she can take the burden to eternity with her. Those mean girls who got the house and the bulk of my father's life savings and insurance can choke on it. I've learned a few things about money, Mr. Justice. It can turn sour in your mouth."

"You should think about your future, nonetheless…"

"And challenge a will? Oh, wouldn't the newspeople love that. No, if there's a thousand bucks left, I'll pay you. Otherwise, the idea of going after my father's money just holds no appeal at all. I know, you'd think I'd be more pragmatic, but I watched what that whole thirst for money can do to a person. I'm cleaning toilets for a living, Mr. Justice. I have a boyfriend who's a schoolteacher, a wonderful schoolteacher. I feel richer now than I did when I was married to Richard. I don't need anything more. I'm good."

He was speechless for a moment. His hands were folded primly on his desk and he looked at her earnestly. "Emma," he said. "It's more than a thousand dollars."

"Well, how lucky for me," she said with a laugh. "And here I thought Christmas was over. How much then?"

"This would be half—what you were due at age thirty, with another payment due quite soon, when you're thirty-five. Before even doing an audit to see if there's more buried in there, it's $463,072."

Emma's mouth hung open and she stared at him in shock. Then her eyes rolled back in her head and she fainted, falling off the chair and hitting the floor with a thud.

Sitting at his desk Logan felt frustrated by his failed attempts to get Riley alone at all over the holidays. First came family, he understood that. And she had explained that people didn't cancel housekeeping services, unless of course they were out of town and the office cleaning arm of the business stayed steady.

And then there was her ex's car accident. They might never have married but there was no disputing he was the ex. And although Riley insisted it was for Maddie's peace of mind and not hers, she was spending an awful lot of time with the guy.

But now the holidays were past, Maddie was back in school and the ex was cleared to go back to work. Everyone could get on a normal schedule and by the end of next month he and George would be closing out the surveillance on Emma Shay. Six months of watching and listening, no one had talked about money, the banking was tight as a drum, Emma was still cleaning houses and all seemed right with the world. It was possible the federal judge could extend the warrant, but it wouldn't be based on anything George and Logan had discovered. No calls to Aruba, no suspicious dialogue, no funny money.

"Good news," Georgianna said. "We caught a break. She's moving money."

"Huh?" he asked, dumbfounded.

"Large sums, too. We got a wire transfer for almost a half million."

"No shit?" he said, stunned. "We know where it came from yet?"

"We'll know soon. We just have to exercise the warrant. And I think we notify the feds and offer to open an investigation."

"We can notify the feds and let *them* open an investigation," he suggested.

"It's our investigation," she reminded him.

"It doesn't have to be."

"Is this you making the easy choice?" she asked. "You skipping out so you don't mess things up with the girl? Should we pull you out of this investigation for conflict of interest?"

"There's nothing to indicate Riley had anything to do with Emma Shay's financial situation."

George sighed, took a deep breath. "Emma's tied into the Kerrigan family in a big way. A bigger way than I think you realize. She works for Riley Kerrigan, she's sleeping with Adam Kerrigan, she's socializing with June Kerrigan, and the other guy? Your girl's ex? That was her boyfriend in high school and they've rekindled their friendship. She's referred to him in conversations with Adam. And there's another twist that makes me uncomfortable and suspicious. Emma Shay is having serious dialogue with a teenage girl she calls Bethany and I'm asking myself if that could be Maddie Kerrigan with an alias or a close friend of Maddie's. Emma and the girl are close. They seem bonded over something and I'm not sure what. The girl complains about her stepmother sometimes and Emma commiserates. Is it possible that it's Emma's child, given up for adoption? Could that be her motive for hiding money? A child?"

"What?"

"Just a thought. A guess, really. Quite a coincidence that Maddie Kerrigan is fifteen and this Bethany, whoever she might be, is fifteen and troubled. That aside, just with the money transfer we have enough probable cause. We'll get the okay, we'll get a little more traction on this then bring her in for questioning."

He winced.

"There's a reason we don't get involved with our suspects."

"Riley isn't a suspect!"

"She's a person of interest with a close relationship to our suspect."

Logan knew this was not going to bode well for their relationship. Riley was not dumb. She was going to have no trouble connecting the dots. He didn't simply come upon her in the deli section, innocent of agenda or intention. He knew Emma had some connection to the Kerrigans and stumbled across Riley and then damn! She was just the kind of woman he wanted. Somehow, he thought he could get the skinny on Emma without damaging his budding relationship with Riley.

"This is why we don't shit where we eat," George told him.

He knew why. He just didn't want it to be true this time.

It was the second week in January by the time Riley finally got around to having lunch with Logan. She invited him. They met at a small, quiet restaurant on a Sunday. Riley was already having a glass of wine when he arrived. He smiled a little sadly as he sat down at her table. "This is a little obvious," he said.

"What do you mean?"

"I'm in a barely populated restaurant at a somewhat isolated table on a Sunday so you can give me some bad news."

She sighed heavily. "Come on," she said. "Let's have a glass of wine. Let's talk. Let's have lunch."

"I'll join you for the wine but I reserve judgment on the lunch." The waiter was there immediately, taking his order. "You don't have to wait for the wine. Go ahead. Lay it on me."

"What exactly do you think is going to happen here?" she asked.

"I think you're going to break up with me."

"First of all, I hadn't considered us steadies," Riley said. "And second, I know I've been hard to reach the past couple of weeks—since Maddie's accident—but that's exactly the sort of thing I hate about dating. Just because we have a few nice dates and fun conversations you have this expectation of some priority when I have a daughter, a business—"

"And an elderly mother?" he asked. "Don't spoil it, Riley. Men are clumsy assholes who just don't call when it doesn't work out the way they wanted. Women are completely different. They feel the need to be honest, to explain, to iron out all the details and make sure everything is smooth. Fixed." His wine was delivered and he took a sip. Then he tapped her glass. "Do it. Do what you came here to do."

"Wow, you make it seem horrible. I think from now on I'm going with the not-calling route."

"Nah, this is classier. I'm ready to hear it. I think I know but I'm ready to hear."

"What do you think you know?"

He shook his head. "No way. It's your show."

"I'm sorry. I'm going to put our dating adventure on hold. Maybe for a while, maybe forever, time will tell. It seems I have some old issues to sort through. Some baggage. I'm as surprised as you are."

"The ex," he said.

"You shouldn't really call him that. He's Maddie's father."

"And the accident made you realize how much you care about him," Logan said. It was not a question.

"Not exactly, but close. We all spent Christmas dinner at my mother's, which is pretty typical unless Jock could convince me to let him take Maddie to his mother's house. And afterward I dropped by his house to talk about Maddie. Nothing urgent, just the fact that we're moving into a new phase in this co-parenting. She's growing up and we'll be visiting colleges next year! I realized I had never seen the inside of his house. I didn't know Maddie had a perfectly lovely room there that she hardly ever uses. I was a little shocked to realize how difficult and distant I'd been where Maddie and Jock are concerned and… Well, the next thing you know, there's an accident and he's seriously injured."

"And you realized you nearly lost your chance?"

She shook her head. "No, it was Maddie. She verged on hysterical. She was so shaken and terrified—her father means a lot more to her than I realized. How could I have been so dumb? So I'm trying to help out a little—visiting him in the hospital, with Maddie of course, taking him some meals while he's recovering and most of all just talking to him."

Logan looked down.

"My daughter is almost sixteen years old, Logan. And I've spent the last sixteen years being mad at Jock for being the idiot to screw up everything. More than once! And he's the first to admit he made some incredibly immature mistakes. I've been very pigheaded. I thought maybe it's time to know the guy now that he's grown up. I don't have any expectations—you'd think if we were meant to be a couple it would've happened long before now. But I want to explore the idea of us being friends, if you can understand that. One day we'll be grandparents to the same grandchildren."

"And we can't date while you're working on getting along with your ex for the sake of the grandchildren?" he asked. "You're not fooling me, Riley. You want to be open to something more than friendship. Deny it, go ahead. Because I already know you don't lie."

"Then you also know I don't move very fast," she said. "And you're moving a little fast."

"I don't have fifteen years."

"I certainly wouldn't suggest you wait that long for someone like me," she said. "Will you still have lunch with me?"

"Why? Is there more?" he asked.

"Please, Logan. I like you. I like you very much. I think our timing is a bit off and I'm being completely honest when I say that I'm not sure where this thing with Jock is headed. Is it possible you and I can remain friends?"

"Let's order lunch," he said, opening his menu.

"Yes, let's," she said, opening her menu. They made their choices, ordered and she said, "Thank you."

"Don't thank me yet," he said. "We're going to have lunch. And then I'm going to tell you—I don't really want to be friends. I was falling in love with you and I think you know it. And I also think maybe you're afraid of that. I was willing to wait, to put up with being third or fourth on your list. I was willing to take chances for you. So we're going to have lunch, talk a little then say goodbye. And if you're ever ready to pick this up where we left it, which was pretty close to the next level in the man-woman equation, you have my number. But I'm not waiting around while you check out your ex."

"I don't think you understand at all," she said.

"Oh, yeah," he said. "I understand. You might intend to just get to know him so you can be grandparents together but I guarantee you, that's not how he's going to see it."

"How do you know that?"

"I'm a guy, Riley. That's how I know."

It turned out that John Shay was the millionaire next door. An unpretentious, hardworking man of sensible but excellent taste. He and his first wife built themselves a solid house in a good neighborhood and he saved and invested all his life. Emma didn't come along until he was thirty-five and he lost his wife to diabetes-related kidney failure a year later. He had accrued a nice little nest egg by the time he died, and insurance paid off the house, which was valued at a million and a quarter.

John bought good cars and drove them until they died of old age, did all his own yard work and could have indulged in European vacations or maybe had a summer home, but instead he saved and invested. His second wife had worked, his children were always well dressed and he insisted on a good mattress. They never scrimped on food; they ate good, healthy meals. Emma would have expected her father to have left a reasonable sum that was meant to cover his retirement but she was completely unprepared for the estate to be worth several million dollars.

It was obvious that Rosemary did what she always had done where Emma was concerned—she took what was Emma's and gave it to Anna and Lauren, two young women who had inherited their mother's anger and bitterness. For a little while Emma was sad that those two had her father's house but then she thought about the two of them living there together in old age and her sadness turned to pity. She had no idea if either of them had a significant relationship or love in their lives but they seemed far too unhappy for that. But then Rosemary was a stiff and negative woman and she'd been married three times.

Emma gave Aaron her banking information and he arranged to have the money she was entitled to transferred into her bank account—she wasn't sure what she was going to do with it yet. After her experience with Richard she wasn't eager to turn it over to a broker or money manager so she thought maybe she'd study a little about investments herself, do something that felt safe. She was her father's daughter, after all.

Rosemary died and Emma paid her respects. Adam was her escort. She went only to the visitation and had a very large floral arrangement delivered. There weren't many people present, mostly friends of Anna and Lauren's, and Emma didn't stay long.

She told no one about the money, not even Adam. When he noticed she was a little melancholy she made the excuse that the final goodbye to Rosemary and probably her sisters had left her feeling a little let down. But it was the money. It bothered her. Worried her. She decided she had to get that off her back and planned to explain to Adam that she'd been blown away by an uncomfortably large sum.

She asked if she could cook dinner for him at his house on a Friday night. It was the end of January and he was thrilled by the offer. She wasn't much of a cook—so little practice over the years—so she made an extra-large pot of spaghetti and meatballs, bought prepared garlic bread that only needed a few minutes in the oven and threw together a simple salad.

"Perfect," Adam said.

"I made a big batch so we can have fried spaghetti tomorrow night. If I'm invited back."

"I want to be with you every night you'll have me," he said.

"Adam, I have something to tell you. I've been keeping something from you. Just for a couple of weeks, but I have to tell someone and you're the only one that really matters."

"I thought something was wrong," he said. "I've been worried."

She explained about the will. She didn't tell him how much she'd received but she said it was substantial.

"Emma, that's fantastic! But how in the world did Rosemary think she'd hide it from you?"

"I'm not sure, except that she managed the trust. The lawyer, who was my father's friend, said there was more, especially a third of the value of the house, if I wanted to fight for it. Adam, I put the money in the bank and I hope I don't regret it, but I asked Aaron not to pursue this any further. There's another check due when I'm thirty-five and I'll put that in the bank. My sisters…my lonely, angry, heartbroken sisters might be very rich but I won't challenge the management of the trust. I'm done. Just having more than ten thousand dollars in the bank makes me uncomfortable."

He laughed. "Something for you to talk to Lucinda about," he said. "But you have a little savings, Emma. The sky isn't falling anymore."

"Why does having anything make me feel bad? Guilty?"

"And why does that surprise you after what Richard did? Listen, if you can't beat the guilt even with therapy, you can always give it all to charity."

"Would you?"

"Oh, hell no," he said with a grin. "I've been working my whole life for a savings account. I'm thirty-seven, have an IRA, a little money socked away, a schoolteacher's pension and my mortgage will be paid off in ten years because I always throw a little extra at the principal. Mom is taken care of, Riley is very successful, Maddie's college tuition is in the bank… We're in great shape. If someone dumped a bunch of money in my lap, I wouldn't feel guilt unless it was stolen."

"But I bet you'd use it to help people," she said.

"Emma, I help people every day. My mom helps people and animals. Riley thinks she's just working herself to death but look at what she's built and how it caters to the single mothers she employs. For most people helping people is either a way of life, or it's not."

And she thought, *he is so right. I will just be still and quiet for a little while and I'll know exactly how to make my father's legacy help people.*

"One of the best ways to help the world is to never be a burden to it. Give money, give time, give love, and make sure you give yourself a little to spare so you're not the one in need."

"You are so wise," she said.

"Poor boys work harder to be wise," he said. "I'm very grateful not to be a poor boy anymore. And I'm really grateful for this spaghetti. And to know you have no real reason to be sad."

They talked late into the night. They kicked back and forth many ideas of what it meant to really live well, to live in the moment, to be present and aware and to be grateful. What was plenty, really? Emma had been up and down the financial spectrum so many times—she should know. She'd been one of the well-off girls in school, struggled in college and almost didn't have enough money to join a sorority. Her first years in New York were awfully tight, but also filled with like creatures and great fun. Then there were the years with Richard during which she often felt like a visitor in her own life. And here she was in the arms of a good, honest man and everything seemed so real to her. So rich.

In the morning she began to stir when she heard him moving around. He got up, started the coffee, got in the shower. When she heard the shower shut off she went to the kitchen for coffee and the second her feet hit the floor she felt strange. Her stomach was upset. Her knees were a little weak.

She got to the kitchen and was overtaken by instant and powerful nausea and she dashed for the sink to be sick. She retched and choked, not that there was much there. She felt Adam come up behind her, take hold of her hair and gently rub her back. She ran the water, rinsed her mouth, reached for a paper towel and slowly, shakily, turned to face him.

He lifted one brow. "That spaghetti worked fine for me," he said.

"I have no idea what's wrong," she said. She sniffed. "I feel completely fine now. That coffee even smells good."

"Emma," he asked. "When did you last have a period?"

"Oh, shit," she said.

It was next to impossible to get an immediate appointment with an OB, especially if you were a woman about four weeks pregnant. What they routinely did was give you vitamins and see you for the first time at a couple of months, maybe three months. But Adam taught with a man whose wife was an OB and called in a favor because Emma was worried. She was afraid she'd gotten a positive pregnancy test because something was terribly wrong. After all, she'd been through a little over a year of infertility tests and treatments.

"I can't see that anything is wrong," Dr. Winnet said. "And you are definitely pregnant. Due in the fall."

"But I was told my only hope was in vitro!"

"I'll request the records from your specialist and do a little blood work, but if you were infertile, you're not anymore. And you appear to be in excellent health."

Her records were electronic and therefore transferred from Dr. Grimaldi in New York within a couple of days. Dr. Winnet called her. "I'm a little confused. You say he did a fertility workup? Because all I find in your chart is regular exams, birth control medication, one cyst removal."

"No, no, not birth control pills. I was taking hormones to stimulate ovulation. I was x-rayed for blocked fallopian tubes. We were getting ready to harvest eggs for in vitro when..." She stopped. *When Richard said, "I don't have time to deal with this while I'm consumed with the investigation. They're demanding records constantly. Just let me get through this and we'll give it a go."*

"Maybe I can find better records at the hospital or surgical center where the procedures were performed."

Emma took a deep breath and tried to think clearly. It couldn't be that it had all been a lie. "Dr. Grimaldi had his own surgi-center." And she had gone with Richard after-hours because of Richard's impossible schedule.

"I'll call them, ask if they have records for your procedures."

But there were none.

"Could the records have been lost?" Emma asked.

"Possible, but unlikely," Dr. Winnet said. "It has happened, though it's rare. But all that aside, your blood work is good, your physical was excellent and you have no reason to worry."

Emma would never know for sure, but she strongly suspected she'd been pulled into the web of Richard's many lies yet again. When she first suggested a baby, he didn't like the idea because of his age. When she pestered him, he made an appointment with Dr. Grimaldi—early evening when there was only one nurse present and no other patients. Emma had felt, as she often did, that she was given special treatment because of Richard. She was flattered to be seen by such an important doctor after the office was closed. Dr. Grimaldi had seemed thrilled to help Richard with this little problem. And now she thought Dr. Grimaldi had probably been very well paid for his fraud.

"I'd bet my life on it," Emma told Adam. "He pulled off things I never could have dreamed of."

"Well, the only thing I want to pull off with you is a child. I didn't think I'd ever be a father."

"You don't have much choice now, do you?" she said.

"You're going to have to come clean with Riley," he said. "We can do it together, you can do it your own way, you can enlist June to help, but it has to be done. Like it or not, we're all family now."

"I'm sorry for the surprise, for the shock," Emma said.

"I'm not," he said. "I wasn't sure how I'd ever convince you to give me a chance. I couldn't be happier about it. And all I want to do is make you happy. Think you can live with that?"

She smiled and touched his sweet face. "I'm sure I can."

Twenty

Maddie had a date for the Valentine's dance. It was her first official date, the kind where a boy formally asks a girl for a special occasion, when a perfect dress has to be found. But, there were three sophomore couples going together, not a sixteen-year-old among them, thank God. So they were chauffeured by parents. And Jock came over to Riley's house to see Maddie all dressed up and picked up by her date.

He didn't act like one of those caricature dads who growled and threatened the skinny young man, and Riley was so proud of him for that. He was completely comfortable, complimenting Maddie, grinning at the kids, taking a few pictures and texting them to his side of the family. And when they were gone, off to the dance, Riley opened a bottle of wine and poured them each a glass.

She clinked his glass in a toast. "That's going to be hard to get used to—watching her go off with a man like that."

"That wasn't a man," he said. He pulled her down

on the couch beside him. "She's going to figure us out real soon, you know."

"I think she has no idea it's you I've been talking to at night."

"It's probably none of my business, but what happened to the other guy?"

"We parted on friendly terms," Riley said. "I invited him to lunch, told him that many circumstances combined to make me realize I wanted to get to know my daughter's father better. He was pretty civil about it."

"*Pretty* civil?" Jock asked.

"He's a very nice guy and I suggested we stay in touch, remain friends, and he said no, thank you."

"Smart man," Jock said.

"What are we going to do if we don't work out?" Riley asked.

"You mean if it doesn't work for you? It's working pretty well for me."

"I don't want Maddie traumatized," Riley said. "You know she'll be thrilled to think of her parents romantically involved. What if we hit a wall, fight, split apart again? What if that happens?"

He smiled and just shook his head. "Couples argue sometimes. People disagree." He put his arm around her and pulled her closer. "It's okay if that happens. But those things that kept us apart as teenagers—we don't have those things to wrestle with anymore. At least I don't. I'm not scared and immature anymore. And you and Maddie are my family. You think I won't do anything under the sun to protect that?"

"How long have you been like this?" she asked him.

"I don't know. Look, I'm not the smart one. But my mother says I have good common sense."

"There hasn't been anyone for me," she said. "No one."

He chuckled. "I wish I could say the same, but I made a few women completely miserable, looking for someone to love."

"It is positively ridiculous that we've loved each other for all these years and couldn't get together on anything."

"I think Emma has something to do with it."

"Emma?"

"Riley, you've been hung up about Emma for sixteen years. Feeling guilty, angry, lonely. You blamed yourself for so much. You blamed her when you couldn't blame yourself anymore. Then she came back, wounded after all she went through, and you saw that she was just a hurt little girl willing to do whatever she had to do to get her life back. Just like you had been. The two people who had failed you in the worst time you'd ever faced—me and Emma—are back, hoping for another chance to be there for you."

"I get that you are, but Emma?"

"Emma. Working for your company, following your rules, staying away so she doesn't crowd you, visiting your mother in secret so she doesn't anger you. Just coming back, she reminded you that all our mistakes were so, so long ago. And some of them turned out to be real gifts. She wants to be your friend again, Riley. And I want to be your man."

"After all this time," she said.

"I couldn't get close to you before now," he said. "It wasn't your fault. I don't blame you. I was such an asshole. But we have what it takes now."

"Ever since you lost your spleen, I've been very satisfied."

"Nice to be a little older, isn't it? The backseat of a car or a sandy beach sure can be a challenge. Maddie can't come home early without calling one of us for a ride. Let's go to bed and take our time, huh?"

It amazed Riley that her old passionate feelings for Jock when she was so young could feel just as fresh and new now. But vastly improved. Now she couldn't help but be aware that his every touch was meant simply to please her. They had only renewed this part of their relationship about a week before and already they were like seasoned lovers, like old pros. He worked her body like he'd been doing it for years. The Jock she'd been so angry with had been replaced by a tender and unselfish man. The Jock she always thought of as an idiot was actually a very funny, intuitive man. And the man who had been such a giving father to their daughter proved he could be trusted.

She curled up to him and whispered, "I think you are a wonderful lover."

"Or you are and it makes me look good," he said, kissing her.

Pressed up against his warm body, she drifted back in time for a while. They didn't have the tools to make it when they were kids. Nor the wisdom and patience. But they had those things now.

It seemed that only seconds had passed when the sound of the front door opening woke them. Riley looked over Jock's shoulder at the clock. It was midnight. "Oh, God, what are we going to do?"

"Mom?" Maddie yelled.

"I think we're coming out of the closet," Jock said. "Unless you have a better idea."

"Mom? You went to bed? I thought you'd wait up to

hear about the—" She stood in the doorway. Her mouth hung open; her eyes were big and round. "Dad?" she asked, confused. "What are you *doing*?"

"Hmm. Well, we couldn't find the Scrabble game…"

Late Sunday morning, Riley went to Emma's little bungalow. She knew the address from her employment records and she wasn't going to do what she had to do at work. She immediately thought it was so cute, sitting on a street with a lot of little houses, big trees and old people—not a child in sight. She parked on the street and recognized her brother's SUV in front of the house. Hmm. That should make things easy. Sort of.

She tapped on the door and Emma opened it wearing jeans and a sweatshirt, her hair pulled back in a ponytail. She jumped in surprise when she saw Riley.

"Sorry for the shock," Riley said. "Sorry I didn't call ahead. I didn't want you worrying about what I wanted. I didn't want you to waste a lot of energy trying to prepare yourself. Can we talk?"

"Adam's here," Emma said almost shyly.

"I saw his car."

Then there he was, right behind Emma, his hand on Emma's shoulder. And he was frowning. "Riley?"

"I just wanted to talk to Emma for a moment. And you, also. Okay?"

"Sure," Emma said. "Of course. I just fixed a cup of tea. Would you like one?"

"That would be nice. If you're sure it's all right…"

"Come inside, Riley," she said, holding the door open.

"I'll get that tea," Adam said.

Riley looked around the pleasant little room and

smiled. It was very understated, comfortable and homey. "You must really like it here," she said to Emma. "But what a difference for you."

"A very positive difference. Riley, I wasn't intentionally keeping my relationship with Adam a secret. It felt as if… Well, as if you really didn't want to know."

"One of the many things I probably should work on—that control thing. Emma, we've worked well together…"

"Despite the fact that I can't seem to follow the rules…"

"I'm not here about that. A long, long time ago I did you wrong and I'm sorry. I wasn't just being a terrible girlfriend, an untrustworthy friend. There was a bit more to it—I fell for Jock. I don't blame you at all for being furious, for ending our friendship. It's what I would have done."

"It was a long time ago," Emma said. "My feelings were hurt and I was angry, but if I'm honest I have to admit, I'd already moved on from Jock. I think I kept up the grudge for so long because I'd lost you."

Adam handed Riley a cup of tea, but she put it on the small sofa table in front of her. "I think we were all collateral damage. Jock and Adam and Mom, too. A couple of girlfriends, friends for life, fell out over a guy and there were dead bodies everywhere. I'm here to tell you again, I'm sorry for what I did to you. And I'd like another chance."

"Of course," Emma said. "Why now?"

"Because Jock and I are back together. After sixteen difficult years."

Emma actually stood up from her chair. "Really?" Then she slowly sat. "Really?"

"Jock's always been a good father to Maddie, when I'd let him. And when he was in the accident and I saw how terrified Maddie was I decided I'd waited way too long to have a closer look, to make an effort with Jock. He loves Maddie so much. He's not the same kid who messed up our friendship, Emma. He's a good man. And I find I still care about him."

"Oh, that's so sweet," Emma said. "What could be better? Yes, of course we should give ourselves another chance. But don't worry—I will remember you're my employer when we're at work."

"I'm not worried about that. I have a feeling you won't work for me much longer. You have too much talent..." Riley took a breath. "So? You two are official?" she asked of Emma and Adam.

"More than official," Adam said. "We're pregnant."

"Are you kidding me?" Riley said. "Does Mom know?"

"We have to take care of that," Adam said. "Easier now that you know."

"And you're getting married?" Riley asked.

"We're still kind of in shock, but probably."

Riley got a little teary. She felt the emotion welling up inside her. "We should've worked on this a long time ago, let go of the baggage and grudges—"

There was suddenly a hard knocking at the door and they all froze. There was something about it that signaled it was not an ordinary visitor. Certainly not Penny. Adam opened the door and was met with two badges. "We're looking for Emma Shay."

Riley stood. "Logan?"

"Riley," he said with a nod. "Ms. Shay, we've met. I'm Logan Danner. This is my partner, Georgianna Severs. We have some questions for you and would appreciate your cooperation."

"What kind of questions?" Adam demanded.

"Yeah, what kind of questions?" Riley chimed in. "What are you doing here?"

"Just some questions, Ms. Shay. We'd like you to come to the station to be interviewed."

"About…?" Emma said.

"About the disposition of your late husband's estate."

"My late husband didn't have an estate," she said. "Am I under arrest?"

"At this point it's just an investigation."

"She's not going anywhere with you," Adam said.

"Wait a minute here," Riley said. "Is this a coincidence? You wanting to question Emma?"

"Ms. Kerrigan, we don't have any reason to detain or question you," Georgianna said. "Ms. Shay?"

"No, wait," Riley said. "Have you been investigating Emma?"

"Ask me whatever you like," Emma said. "Just make it quick."

"We'd like you to come to the office so that we can record and have a record of our interview."

"I wonder if my lawyer would approve of that idea…"

"We're not filing any charges at this point. We're not going to be reading you your rights. If you'd just answer those questions you can, we'd very much appreciate it. No one wants to arrest you."

"And this is in regards to…?" Emma persisted.

"Large sums of money appearing in your accounts, ma'am," Georgianna said.

"Ah," she said. "So you've had a warrant, the only way you could legally watch my account. I see. I'll drive myself to your office and I'll answer your questions—with my lawyer present."

"No, Emma," Adam said, taking her elbow in a soft grip. "I don't want you to do this. There's no reason."

"Yes, let's get this over with," she said. She looked at Logan. "Is the warrant for banking records?" He nodded. "And what else? Have you been in my house?"

Logan shook his head.

"What else is your warrant for?" she asked.

"Banking and phone. Let's do this, Ms. Shay. You're eventually going to have to answer our questions. We don't want to ask for an arrest warrant."

"And I don't want you to," she said. "I'll call my lawyer and drive myself over. I'm not going to take off." She grabbed her purse and jacket. "This must be exciting for you," she said. "It's Sunday morning."

"And you knew exactly where to find her," Riley said.

"They've always known, Riley," Emma said. "They've been watching me. They want to know if I have some secret hidden money from my husband. They're going to watch me forever. And they're not going to find anything because there isn't anything." She looked at Logan and Georgianna. "Let's get this over with."

"I'm going with you," Adam said, grabbing his jacket.

"I'm going, too," Riley said.

Three hours later Emma and Aaron emerged from the interview room to find Adam and Riley waiting. By quick consensus, they decided to go to a nearby Mexican restaurant to talk and order something to eat and drink. Aaron excused himself from the group. Riley beat them inside and secured a booth. The waitress was beside them right away.

"I think we're going to need three wines. Any preference?" Riley asked.

"I'm having tea," Emma said. "Just any hot tea, please. Milk and sugar."

"I'll have hers. Chardonnay," Riley said.

"I'll have a beer, whatever's on tap. And how about some nachos?" Adam asked.

When they were alone again, Riley was the first to speak up. "I think that bastard dated me because he was watching you."

"They were very nice," Emma said. "Tiresome, but polite enough. I was warned this might happen. When we settled up in New York the lawyers told me there would be victims and law enforcement who would find it preposterous that I'd surrender everything, right down to my engagement ring. I didn't want anything that had come from Richard. But I did recently come into some money. My father's estate, which Rosemary always claimed was hardly worth talking about, actually had something in it. Rosemary, God rest her soul, failed to let me know. She clearly meant for her daughters to have it. But my father's lawyer followed through and some money came my way. He showed them a copy of the will along with all the financial information. It's all completely legitimate."

"Is this going to keep happening?" Riley wanted to know.

Emma shrugged. "Until there's nothing to notice, I suppose."

"But you were already investigated and cleared," Riley said.

"And I remain a curiosity to some. The best way to handle it is to be cooperative, show them the quickest route to the information they want or need."

"Emma, how have you stood this kind of treatment?"

"I've found that if I just put myself in their shoes, I get it. And it's best to just be honest and forthcoming. I learned right away, refusing to answer just intensifies the whole process. According to Logan, they'll make their report to the FBI Fraud division and it will probably be over. Not to say it can't start up again in the future." Her tea was delivered along with the drinks for Riley and Adam. "I've made peace with that. I understand why they want to be sure I'm not a part of his crimes."

"You are a brave soul," Riley said, lifting her glass to Emma. "I still want to punch Logan. The bastard."

"Go easy, Riley. He has a job to do. And I'm just guessing but I don't think he had to date you to do it." Then she smiled. "Even so, the best news I've had lately is that after all this time you and Jock will find a way."

"Jock," Adam scoffed. "What the hell kind of name is that, anyway?"

"You know he was named for his grandfather. Are you going to start being nice to him now?"

He took a drink from his beer. "I guess I'll have to."

"Emma, do you need a day off to recover from Dragnet?" Riley asked.

"Nah, I'll be fine. Let me catch my breath and then I think we should tell June she's going to be a grandmother again."

Despite the stressful police questioning, Emma was feeling euphoric. Her world was coming into focus and she had so much to look forward to. She had Adam's perfect love, something she never for one second anticipated when she was making her way home to Sonoma. Riley had finally come around and it looked as though they all might not just be friends but family, as well. June was so happy about the baby she cried. Even Maddie and Jock were excited.

She was anxious to tell Shawna and Dellie, but there were a few details to work out before she went public. A date to get married and merge households would help.

Adam, as protective as when they were kids, asked her to quit work, at least working that hard. His income was modest, but he'd been a teacher for a long time and he could support a family. She said no. She wanted to work.

She spent more time with Riley, a little while after work most days. They had so much to catch up on. "Will you be my maid of honor?" Emma asked her.

"Yes, absolutely! And will you wear a mask while you clean so you don't inhale bleach? I don't want my nephew to have two heads."

So Emma carried a mask in her pocket and discreetly slipped it on when she was using bleach in the bathrooms. But Riley's concern gave her deep happiness.

And then a text came from Bethany.

I'm sorry, Emma, but it's just too much. There's no laughter. There's just no love here and I've had enough.

Emma was cleaning another house but because it was Bethany, she read the text and responded immediately.

What's too much?

The girl had been mostly cheerful since Christmas. Emma had hoped her feelings of sadness and helplessness were starting to wane.

No reply. If that had been Adam or Riley, she'd have waited until she was between houses, but she smelled an ill wind.

Bethany, where are you?

No reply.

She tried calling, but it went directly to voice mail.

She went to Dellie; Dellie had daughters and there was something about teenage girls, even those not in crisis, that was so terrifying, so filled with drama. "Dellie, Bethany texted me this," she said, showing her the phone. "I can't reach her."

"She's just wanting some attention, probably."

"What if she's not? She took a bunch of her stepmother's pills a year ago or so and it just knocked her out for a while, but that's something to think about. What if this means she's given up? What if she's suicidal?"

"You don't even know where she is," Dellie said. "She might be on top of the Golden Gate Bridge."

"I think I have to go to her house," Emma said.

"We're not done here!"

"I'll call Riley. I'll go check and come right back. I'll even stay late and help if we get behind."

"You're getting sucked right into this girl's drama," Dellie said.

"I guess so. But if anything is wrong and I don't check on her, I'll never forgive myself."

"Oh, Lord, you're gonna be the death of me. Shawna!"

she yelled. "We gotta go check something and come right back!"

"You don't have to," Emma said.

"Better we all stay together. That house ain't so far from here. Don't pack up. We'll be back here in half an hour."

"Thank you," Emma said.

While Shawna drove, grumbling about how this day was gonna get long, Emma called Riley. She had to leave a message. She called Makenna and Makenna said, "Do not do this! I'll call her parents but you just stay out of it!"

When Emma disconnected, Dellie wanted to know what Makenna said. "She said go ahead and good luck." Then Emma swallowed hard.

When they got to the house, Emma looked up and down the street. All the houses were separated by trees and shrubs, sitting back on huge lots. Running to the neighbors would take too much time. She took the keys and went to open the front door, but it wouldn't open. There was a security lock that could be used at night, locked from the inside. So she banged on the door and rang the bell. She pulled out her small notebook, looked at the key code for the garage and punched in the numbers. The garage door slowly rose and she ran inside, trying the door to the house. It was bolted, as well.

She was frozen. What if Bethany wasn't even in there? She called Makenna. "Did you reach her parents?"

"No," Makenna said with a sigh. "I said it was important but I haven't gotten a call back."

"Listen, I'm sorry, but I'm scared," Emma said. "She's fragile. She's been talking to me and she's…

She has good days and bad days but her mother died, her stepmother moved right in and... She's fragile..."

"Oh, crap, you're involved..."

"She needed someone..."

"Emma, you are *at least* on probation!"

So Emma called the police. Once they established that there was no missing person, no cry for help, no family member seeking a welfare check, they said they'd send a patrol by when they could.

She dialed another number.

"Logan Danner," he said in answer to her call.

"Logan, it's Emma. Listen, I have a situation. I've been talking to a fifteen-year-old girl from one of the houses I clean. She's troubled. She's maybe suicidal. I might be suicidal in her situation. It's complicated, it's—"

"Bethany Christensen?" he asked.

"How did you know?" she asked.

"I listened to your telephone conversations," he said. "We were a little confused about that one but it didn't seem to have anything to do with the transfer of funds."

"I'm at her house. She left me a suspicious text—it's all too much, she said. She said she's had enough. And the doors are bolted from the inside."

"Did you call the police?"

"They weren't impressed. I'm calling to tell you to get out your handcuffs because I've decided to break in. I really want to be wrong...but I'm going to break in..."

"Can you wait for me? I'm not far away."

"I can't wait for you. I'm sorry, but I can't let anything terrible happen. Her parents aren't returning calls, no one cares about this girl. No one." She hung up the phone.

I am clearly insane, Emma thought. *I don't know that much about her but I'm completely involved, totally sympathetic, terribly scared for her.*

There was a workbench in the garage that, like the rest of the Christensen home, was far too clean and tidy. She eyed a hammer, a big screwdriver, a crowbar. She took the crowbar and wedged it into the tight space right where the doorknob was and started prying with all her might. She was at it for a good five minutes when she heard a car pull into the drive. She looked over her shoulder. Shawna and Dellie were standing in the driveway behind her, staring in wonder. Logan strode toward her.

"Give me that," he said. "If we're going to do it, let's do it."

"Thank you," she said, rubbing her upper arm.

It took him three powerful tugs with the crowbar, some splintering wood and a great big kick and the door opened. Logan was inside first. "Bethany!" he shouted.

"Look through the downstairs," Emma said. "I'll check the upstairs bedrooms."

Their feet pounded through the house, each of them shouting the girl's name. Emma went immediately to Bethany's bedroom and found the room undisturbed, the bed made as usual. She checked her bathroom—it was spotless. She called out, checked the master bedroom—again, everything in order. The master bath was clean as a whistle and she thought, I've made a terrible mistake…again!

She heard a soft moan and opened the door to the large, walk-in closet and there, in a little pile on the floor was Bethany, covered in blood. "Logan!" she screamed. "Up here! Help me!"

She rolled Bethany to the side and it seemed the blood was coming from her thin, pale wrists. "Oh, God, Bethany! No!" She put her fingers to Bethany's neck and felt a faint pulse. "In here!" she shouted again.

"Is she alive?" he asked.

"Yes, but unconscious and her pulse is weak."

Before Emma even finished talking, Logan had grabbed a white shirt from a hanger, bit a tear in the hem and ripped it into a couple of strips. He tossed one to Emma. "Pressure," he said, ripping the shirt again and again. "Nice and tight."

When that was done he got on his cell and called for paramedics.

Over the next fifteen minutes, the master bedroom began to fill with people. Emma and Logan stayed beside Bethany, Emma holding her gently, rocking her, telling her she must be all right, *must.* First Dellie and Shawna were there, watching. Then Makenna, followed quickly by Riley. Both of them were stunned and angry that this poor girl could have suffered so much and there seemed to be no one to help her. Finally paramedics arrived and by that time Bethany was moaning and whimpering weakly. After an IV was started and the gurney stood ready to take her to the ambulance, Olaf and Liz Christensen appeared. Liz gasped and covered her mouth while Olaf rushed to his daughter.

As the paramedics transferred Bethany, Olaf Christensen faced Emma. "Who are you? And how did you know my daughter was in trouble?"

"I clean your house, Mr. Christensen. And she reached out to me. I wanted her to reach out to you, but she didn't think you could handle it. She's been in a lot of pain since her mother passed away."

"But I got her a counselor!" Liz Christensen said.

"Yes, and you also cleared out all the family pictures and started wearing her dead mother's clothes. How you thought that was going to be okay, I'll never know."

"I asked," she said defensively, looking a bit confused. "I asked permission! From Bethany! And the pictures… I didn't think that was helping us become a family!"

Emma took out her phone and revealed the text. "Bethany lost her family. She told me when her mother was alive they laughed a lot, they hugged and laughed and fell asleep together. She told me your assistant bought her birthday and Christmas presents. She was so, so lonely."

Olaf Christensen read the text. "God," he said. "I just wasn't looking, was I? I don't know how to thank you for finding her. I don't know how you knew she would need you."

"Well, I've looked the other way at times in my life when I shouldn't have. I won't ever do it again."

Epilogue

June Kerrigan threw a nice party for her family and friends two days before Christmas. It was a buffet featuring her favorite dishes. Her house was decorated to such an extent it made her shudder to think about the taking down and putting away. She may have gone a little overboard, but this was a very special holiday to her.

Emma Shay Kerrigan no longer cleaned houses for Riley. Now she was a full-time student and mother. John Shay Kerrigan was born in October, a little early but a good size, while Emma was supposed to be in a lecture at UC Davis where she was studying toward a masters in counseling. Now at his first Christmas, John was being passed around to every person present.

Adam was married and a new father, something June had nearly lost hope for. Riley and Jock were married, too. Riley had just announced that Maddie would be getting a little brother or sister in the spring.

Penny Pennington had been invited and had spent a lot of time in the kitchen with June and was busily monitoring the buffet table to make sure fresh hors d'oeuvres were always available. Ethan and Lyle were literally waiting in line for their shot at John. Aaron Justice had come, bringing a huge wreath with him. Beatrice, the particularly ugly rescue dog, had found her forever home with June, though she had not gotten very much prettier. And Bethany, Liz and Olaf Christensen were there, together, laughing at all the old Kerrigan family stories.

But the nicest thing—June saw Riley and Emma lifting their glasses in a secret toast. Smiling. Emma had her favorite wine and Riley had sparkling cider. They were friends again.

They'd been each other's maid and matron of honor and would be raising their children together. After all.

* * * * *

Acknowledgments

Many thanks to my readers for the continuous outpouring of support and encouragement. You make my pursuit of creating good fiction such a joy.

Special thanks to Kurt A. Johnson, Esq., for showing me the path through the complex world of wills, trusts, and miscellaneous estate details and laws.

To my favorite financial wizard, Kayla Koeber. Thank you for helping me understand the many mysteries of the world of finance. You are so patient and wise.

Any errors or alterations in the technical aspects of the story are not the fault of my adviser but mine, most often license to create a strong story, and I appreciate the reader's indulgence.

Thank you to a very hardworking PR machine: Michelle Renaud of Harlequin, Nancy Berland of Nancy Berland Public Relations and Sarah Burningham of Little Bird Publicity. I would be so lost without you!

My deepest gratitude to Craig Swinwood, Loriana Sacilotto, Margaret Marbury and Nicole Brebner, my Harlequin Dream Team. Every day of working with you all is a privilege.

To Dianne Moggy, thank you for that special day eighteen years ago when you said yes to a submission from me, changing my career path and my life. I am so grateful for the opportunities that started right there.

To my agent, Liza Dawson, thank you for your dedication and loyalty through the years. It's been quite a wonderful trip and an honor to call you my friend.

Turn the page for a sneak peek at Robyn Carr's emotional new novel, The View from Alameda Island, *available soon from MIRA Books.*

One

Today was Lauren Delaney's twenty-fourth wedding anniversary and there wouldn't be a twenty-fifth. To many it appeared Lauren had a perfect life but the truth was something she kept to herself. She had just been to see her lawyer and now she needed a little time to think. She headed for one of her favorite places. She needed the solace of a beautiful garden.

Divine Redeemer Catholic Church was an old church that had survived all of the earthquakes since the big one—the San Francisco earthquake of 1906. Lauren had only been inside the building a couple of times, but never for mass. Her mother had been Catholic, but she hadn't been active. The church had a beautiful garden where parishioners often walked and there were several benches where you could sit and pray or meditate. Lauren was on her way home to Mill Valley from her job at Merriweather Foods and she stopped there, something she did frequently. There were no brochures explaining the genesis of the garden or even the fact that the church sat on such a generous plot of land for Northern California, but she'd happened upon an old priest once and he'd told her one of the priests in the early 1900s was a fanatic about growing things. Even though he'd been dead for decades, the church kept the garden going. They even preserved a large garden behind the beautiful flowers for fruits and vegetables, which they donated to food banks or used to feed hungry people in poorer parishes.

Divine Redeemer's parish just outside of Mill Valley, California didn't have many hungry people. It was an upper-class area. It was where she lived.

She was very well off. Richer than she'd ever imagined by her family's standards, yet her husband ranted about his low pay. He was a prosperous surgeon raking in over a million a year but he didn't have a yacht or a plane, which irked him. He spent a great deal of time managing and complaining about his finances.

She would be leaving him as soon as she could finalize the details. She had spent an hour with her attorney, Erica Slade, today. Erica had asked, "So, is this going to be it, Lauren?"

"The marriage was over many years ago," Lauren said. "All that's left is for me to tell him I'm leaving. I'm getting my ducks in a row."

They would be spending the evening at a charity auction and dinner. For that she was so grateful. There would be no staring at each other over a starched white tablecloth searching for things to say, no watching Brad check his phone and text all through the meal. As he was fond of reminding her, he was an important man. He was in demand. She was nothing.

If she ever received a call or text, it was from one of her daughters or her sister. But if they knew she was out, they wouldn't expect a response. Except maybe her eldest daughter, Lacey. She had inherited her father's lack of boundaries and sense of entitlement—it was all about her. Her younger daughter, Cassie, had, perhaps unfortunately, inherited Lauren's cautious and reticent nature. Lauren and Cassie didn't like conflict, didn't step on toes.

"When are you going to stand up for yourself, Lauren," Brad had been known to say to her. "You're so spineless." Of course, he meant she should stand up to anyone but him.

Oh, wouldn't Brad be surprised when she finally did. And he'd be angry. She knew people would inevitably ask, *Why now? After twenty-four years?* Because it had been twenty-four *hard* years. It had been hard since the beginning. Not every minute of it, of course. But overall, her marriage to Brad had never been a good situation. She spent the first several years thinking she could somehow make it better, the next several years thinking she probably didn't have it so bad since he was *only* emotionally and verbally abusive, and the last ten years thinking she couldn't wait to escape once her daughters were safely raised. Because, the truth was he was only going to get more cantankerous and abusive with age.

The first time she'd seriously considered leaving him, the girls were small. "I'll get custody," he said. "I'll fight for it. I'll prove you're unfit. I have the money to do it, you don't." She'd almost done it when the girls were in junior high. He'd been unfaithful and she was sure it hadn't been the first time he'd strayed, just the first time he'd been caught. She'd taken the girls to her sister's cramped little house where the three of them shared a bedroom and the girls begged to go home. She returned and demanded marriage counseling. He admitted to a meaningless fling or two because his wife, he said, was not at all enthusiastic about sex anymore. And the counselor cautioned her about throwing away the father of her children, explained that the repercussions could be very long term. She found another counselor and it happened again—the counselor sympathized with Brad. Only Lauren could see that Brad was a manipulator who could turn on the charm when it suited him.

Rather than trying yet another counselor, Brad took the family on a luxurious vacation to Europe. He pampered the girls and ultimately Lauren gave the marriage yet another chance. Then a couple of years later he gave her chlamydia and blamed her. "Don't be ridiculous, Lauren. You picked it up somewhere and gave it to me! Don't even bother to deny it."

She'd told him she wanted a divorce and he had said, "Fine. You'll pay the price. I'm not going to make it easy for you."

Knowing what was at stake, she moved into the guest room instead.

Days became weeks, weeks became months. They went back to marriage counseling. In no time at all Lauren suspected their marriage counselor had an agenda and favored Brad. She helped him make excuses, covered for him, pushed Lauren to admit to her manipulative nature. Lauren suspected him of sleeping with the counselor. He told her she'd become sick with paranoia.

By the time Lacey was in college and Cassie was applying to colleges, Brad was worse than ever. Controlling, domineering, secretive, verbally abusive, argumentative. God, why didn't he want her to just leave? Clearly, he hated her.

But he told her if she left him he wouldn't pay college

tuition. "No judge can make me. I can be stuck with some alimony but not support payments. And not tuition. When they're over eighteen they're on their own. So go then," he'd said. "You'll be responsible for cutting them off."

The last few years had been so lonely. She had spent a lot of time worrying that by staying with a man like Brad she had taught her daughters a dreadful lesson. She'd done her best with them but she couldn't make them un-see how their own mother had lived her life.

She'd taken a few hours from work to meet with the lawyer, laying out plans, creating her list and checking things off. The lawyer had said, "He's had you running scared for years. We have laws in this state. He can't cut you off and freeze you out. I'm not saying it will be easy or painless, but you will not starve and your share of the marital assets will be delivered."

It was time. She was finally ready to go.

Lauren inhaled the smell of spring flowers. This was one of the best times of year in Northern California, the Bay Area and inland, when everything was coming to life. The vineyards were greening up and the fruit trees were blossoming. She loved flowers; her grandmother had been a ferocious gardener, turning her entire yard into a garden. Flowers soothed her. She needed a garden right now.

Lauren heard the squeaking of wheels and looked up to see a man pushing a wheelbarrow along the path. He stopped not too far from her. He had a trowel, shovel and six plants in the wheelbarrow. He gave her a nod, and went about the business of replacing a couple of plants. Then he sat back on his heels, looked at her and smiled. "Better?" he asked.

"Beautiful," she said with a smile.

"Is this your first time in this garden?" he asked.

"No, I've been here a number of times," Lauren said. "Are you the gardener?"

"No," he said with a laugh. "Well, yes, I guess I am if I garden. But I'm just helping out today. I noticed a few things needed to be done…"

"Oh, is this your church?"

"Not this one, a smaller church south of here. I'm afraid I've fallen away…"

"And yet you still help out the parish? You're dedicated."

"I admire this garden," he said. He rotated and sat, drawing up his knees. "Why do you come here?"

"I love gardens," she said. "Flowers in general make me happy."

"You live in the right part of the country, then. Do you keep a garden?"

"No," she said, laughing uncomfortably. "My husband has very specific ideas about how the landscaping should look."

"So he does it?"

Get dirt under his nails? Hah! "Not at all. He hires the people who do it and gives them very firm orders. I don't find our garden nearly as beautiful as this."

"I guess you have nothing to say about it, then," he said.

"Not if it's going to create conflict," Lauren said. "But it's kind of a secret hobby of mine to find and visit gardens. Beautiful gardens. My grandmother was a master gardener—both her front and backyard were filled with flowers, fruits and vegetables. She even grew artichokes and asparagus. It was incredible. There was no real design—it was like a glorious jungle."

"When you were young?"

"And when I was older, too. My children loved it."

"Did your mother garden?" he asked.

"Very little—she was a hardworking woman. But after my grandparents passed away, she lived in their house and inherited the garden. I'm afraid she let it go."

"It's a hereditary thing, don't you think?" he asked. "Growing up, our whole family worked in the garden. Big garden, too. Necessary garden. My mother canned and we had vegetables all winter. Now she freezes more than cans and her kids rob her blind. I think she does it as much for all of us as herself."

"I would love that so much," Lauren said. Then she wondered how the residents of Mill Valley would react to seeing her out in the yard in her overalls, hoeing and spreading fresh, stinky fertilizer. It made her laugh to herself.

"Funny?" he asked.

"I work for a food processor. Merriweather. And they don't let me near the gardens, which are primarily research gardens."

"So, what do you do?" he asked.

"I cook," she said. "Product development. Testing and recipes. We test the products regularly and have excellent consumer outreach. We want to show people how to use our products."

"Are you a nutritionist?" he asked.

"No, but I think I'm becoming one. I studied chemistry. But what I do is not chemistry. In fact, it's been so long..."

He frowned. "Processed foods. A lot of additives," he said. "Preservatives."

"We stand by their safety and it's a demanding, fast-paced world. People don't have time to grow their food, store it, make it, serve it." His cell phone rang and he pulled it from his pocket. "See what I mean?" she said, his phone evidence of the pace of modern life.

But he didn't even look at it. He switched it off. "What, besides flowers, makes you happy?" he asked.

"I like my job. Most of the time. Really, ninety percent of the time. I work with good people. I love to cook."

"All these domestic pursuits. You must have a very happy husband."

She almost said nothing makes Brad happy, but instead she said, "He cooks too—and thinks he's better at it than I am. He's not, by the way."

"So if you weren't a chemist cooking for a food company, what would you be? A caterer?"

"No, I don't think so," she said. "I think trying to please a client who can afford catering seems too challenging to me. I once thought I wanted to teach home economics but there is no more home ec."

"Sure there is," he said, frowning. "Really?"

She shook her head. "A nine- or twelve-week course, and it's not what it once was. We used to learn to sew and bake. Now there's clothing design as an elective. Some schools offer cooking for students who'd like to be chefs. It's not the same thing."

"I guess if you want homemaking tips, there's the internet," he said.

"That's some of what I do," she said. "Video cooking demonstrations."

"Is it fun?"

She nodded after thinking about it for a moment.

"Maybe I should do video gardening demos."

"What makes you happy?" she surprised herself by asking.

"Just about anything," he said with a laugh. "Digging

in the ground. Shooting hoops with my boys when they're around. Fishing. I love to fish. Quiet. I love quiet. I love art and design. There's this book—it's been a long time since I read it—it's about the psychology of happiness. It's the results of a study. The premise that initiated the study was what makes one person able to be happy while another person just can't be happy no matter what. Take two men—one is a survivor of the Holocaust and goes on to live a happy, productive life while the other goes through a divorce and he can hardly get off the couch or drag himself to work for over a decade. What's the difference between them? How can one person generate happiness for himself while the other can't?"

"Depression?" she asked.

"Not always," he said. "The study pointed out a lot of factors, some we have no control over and some are learned behaviors. Interesting. It's not just a choice but I'm a happy guy." He grinned at her.

She noticed, suddenly, how good-looking this man was. He looked like he was in his forties, a tiny amount of gray threading his dark brown hair at his temples. His eyes were dark blue. His hands were large and clean for a gardener. "Now what makes a volunteer gardener decide to read psychology?" she asked.

He chuckled. "Well, I read a lot. I like to read. I think I got that from my father. I can zone out everything except what's happening in my head. Apparently I go deaf. Or so I've been told. By my wife."

"Hyper focus," she said. "Plus, men don't listen to their wives."

"That's what I hear," he said. "I'm married to an unhappy woman so I found this book that was supposed to explain why some schmucks like me are so easy to make happy and some people just have the hardest damn time."

"How'd you find the book?"

"I like to hang out in bookstores..."

"So do we," she said. "It's one of the few things we both enjoy. Other than that, I don't think my husband and I have much in common."

"That's not a requirement," he said. "I have these friends, Jude and Germain, they are different as night and day." He got to his feet and brushed off the seat of his pants. "They have nothing in common. But they have such a good time together. They laugh all the time. They have four kids so it's compromise all the time and they make it look so easy."

She frowned. "Which one's the girl? Oh! Maybe they're same sex...?"

"Germain is a woman and Jude's a man," he said, laughing. "I have another set of friends, both men, married to each other. We call them the Bickersons. They argue continuously."

"Thus, answering the question about gender..."

"I have to go," he said. "But... My name is Beau."

"Lauren," she said.

"It was fun talking to you, Lauren. So, when do you think you might need to spend time with the flowers next?"

"Tuesday?" she said, posing it as a question.

He smiled. "Tuesday is good. I hope you enjoy the rest of your week."

"Thanks. Same to you." She walked down the path toward her car in the parking lot. He steered his wheelbarrow down the path toward the garden shed.

Lauren made a U-turn, heading back toward him. "Beau!" she called. He turned to face her. "Um... Let me rethink that. I don't know when I'll be back here but it's not a good idea, you know. We're both married."

"It's just conversation, Lauren," he said.

He's probably a psychopath, she thought, *because he looks so innocent, so decent.* "Yeah, not a good idea," she said, shaking her head. "But I enjoyed talking to you."

"Okay," he said. "I'm sorry, but I understand. Have a great week."

"You, too," she said.

She walked purposefully to her car and she even looked around. He was in the garden shed on the other side of the gardens. She could hear him putting things away. He wasn't looking to see what she was driving or what her license plate number was. He was a perfectly nice, friendly guy who probably picked up lonely women on a regular basis. Then murdered them and chopped them in little pieces and used them for fertilizer.

She sighed. Sometimes she felt so ridiculous. But she was going to go to the bookstore to look for that book.

Lauren was in a much better mood than usual that evening. In fact, when Brad came home in a state—something about the hospital screwing up his surgery schedule and flipping a couple of his patients without consulting him—she found herself strangely unaffected.

"Are you listening, Lauren?" Brad asked.

"Huh? Oh yes, sorry. Did you get it straightened out?"

"No! I'll be on the phone tonight. Why do you think I'm so *irritated*? Do you have any idea what my time is worth?"

"Now that you mention it, I don't..."

"Isn't it lucky for you that you have a husband who is willing to take care of details like that…"

"Oh," she said. "Lovely."

"It might be nice if you said something intelligent for a change."

"It's the odd night when you're not taking calls," she said. "Were you hoping for a night off?"

"Obviously! Why do you imagine I brought it up? I've told them a thousand times not to get involved with my schedule. They're going to cause patients unnecessary anxiety, not to mention what they do to me! But they think I'm at their beck and call, that I serve their pleasure, when I'm the money-making commodity. Even when I very carefully explain exactly how they should manage the schedule, can they figure it out? I'm paying a PA, a very overqualified PA to schedule for me, my clinics and my surgeries, and the hospital brings in this high school graduate who took a six-week course and gives her authority over *my* schedule…"

Lauren listened absently and fixed him a bourbon, watered, because they had to go to that fund-raiser tonight. She poured herself a glass of burgundy. This was her job, to listen and let him rant, to nod and occasionally say, *That must make you so angry.* While she did that, he paced or sat at the breakfast bar and she unwrapped some cheese and crackers and grapes for him to snack on.

But while all this was going on she was thinking about the man with the easy smile, the tiny bit of gray, the dark blue eyes. And she fantasized how nice it would be to have someone come home and not be a complete asshole.

"We might think about getting ready for the dinner," she said. "I'd like to look at the auction items."

"I know, I know," he said. "I bought a table. We shouldn't be too late."

Of course people would expect him to be late, to rush in at the last minute. "I'm ready. Do you need a shower?"

"I'll be down in five minutes," he said, leaving and taking his bourbon with him.

"Happy anniversary," she said to his departing back.

"Hmph," he said, giving a dismissive wave of his hand. "Nice anniversary," he grumbled. "My schedule is all fucked up."

The charity event was for the local Andrew Emerson Foundation supporting underprivileged children. They came to be known as Andy's kids. Tonight's event would raise money to provide scholarships for the children of fallen heroes. Professional athletes, businesses, the Chamber of Commerce, hospitals, veterans' groups and unions from San Francisco and Oakland supported the charity with fund-raising events such as this dinner and auction. Andy Emerson was a billionaire software developer in San Francisco; he was politically influential and admired by people like Brad. Brad never missed an event and claimed Andy as a friend. Brad was a fixture at the golf tournaments and donated generously. The children of military men and women and first responders disabled or killed in the line of duty could apply for the scholarships generated tonight. To be fair, Lauren had a great deal of respect for the foundation and all that it provided. She also happened to like Andy and Sylvie Emerson, though she was not so presumptuous as to claim them as friends. This event was a very popular, well-organized dinner that would raise tens of thousands of dollars.

Brad and Lauren attended this and many other similar events; Brad's office and clinic staff were invited and he usually paid for a table. This was one of the few times during the year that Lauren visited with Brad's colleagues. And while Brad might be primarily fond of Andy's assets, Lauren thought the seventy-five-year-old Emerson and his wife of almost fifty years, Sylvie, were very nice people. It's not as though Brad and Lauren were invited over to dinner or out for a spin on the yacht—the Emersons were very busy, involved people. However, it was not unusual for Brad to get a call from some member of the Emerson family or a family friend with questions about an upcoming medical procedure or maybe looking for a recommendation of a good doctor.

Just as she was thinking about them, Sylvie Emerson broke away from the men she was chatting with and moved over to Lauren. She gave her one of those cheek presses. "I'm so happy to see you," Sylvie said. "I think it's been a year."

"I saw you at Christmastime in the city," Lauren reminded her. "You're looking wonderful, Sylvie. I don't know how you do it."

"Thank you. It took a lot of paste and paint. But you're aglow. How are the girls?"

"Thriving. Lacey is doing her post-grad study at Stanford so we see her fairly often. Cassidy graduates in about six weeks."

"UC Berkeley, isn't it?" Sylvie asked. "What's her field?"

Lauren chuckled. "Pre-law. She's scored beautifully on the LSAT and is bound for Harvard."

"Oh my God. Are you thrilled for her?"

"I don't know yet," Lauren said. "Don't you have to be a real tiger to take on law? Cassie seems so gentle natured to me."

Sylvie patted her arm. "There is a special place within the legal system for someone like her. I don't know where, but she'll find it. And no one chose medicine?"

Lauren shook her head. "I'm a little surprised about that, since I have a science major as well. Though it's been so long ago now that—"

She was distracted by a man who had been pressing his way through the crowd with two drinks and suddenly stopped. "Lauren?" he said. Then he smiled and those dark blue eyes twinkled. "I'll be damned."

"Beau?" she asked. "What in the world are you doing here?"

"Same as you, I suppose," he said. Then he looked at Sylvie and said, "Hi, I'm Beau Magellan. I just recently ran into Lauren at church."

Lauren laughed at that. "Not exactly, but close enough. Beau, this is Sylvie Emerson, your hostess tonight."

"Oh!" he said, sloshing the drinks. "Oh jeez," he mumbled. Finally, laughing, Lauren took his drinks so he could shake Sylvie's hand.... after wiping his hands on his trousers. "It's a pleasure, Mrs. Emerson. I'm personally indebted to you!"

"How so, Mr. Magellan?"

"My sons have a friend whose dad was killed on the job, Oakland police, and she received a scholarship. Now I'm a big supporter of the cause."

"Magellan," Sylvie said. "Why does that sound familiar?"

"I have no idea," he said, chuckling. "I'm sure our paths wouldn't have crossed. Magellan Design is my company. It's not a big company..."

She snapped her fingers. "You designed a rooftop garden for my friend, Lois Brumfield in Sausalito!"

He beamed. "I did. I'm very proud of that, too—it's incredible."

Sylvie looked at Lauren. "The Brumfields are getting up there... Aren't we all... And they have a single-story home in Sausalito. They didn't have any interest in a two-story anything, their knees are giving out. So they put the garden on the roof! And they have a lift! They sit up there any evening the weather will allow. It's gorgeous! They have gardeners tend their roof!" Sylvie laughed. "They have a patio on the ground floor as well, nice pool and all that. But that rooftop garden is like their secret space. And the house is angled just right so it's private. From there they have an amazing view."

"There's a hot tub," Beau said. "And a few potted trees in just the right places."

"Really, if the Brumfields had more friends, you'd be famous!"

"They have you," Beau said.

"Oh, I've known Lois since I was in college. She's outlasted most of my family!" Then she looked at Lauren. "Church?"

Lauren laughed. She put Beau's drinks on the table she stood beside. "I stopped to see the gardens at Divine Redeemer Catholic Church—they're beautiful. And they're right on my way home. Beau was replacing a few plants. I thought he was the groundskeeper." She made a face at him.

"I love the grounds and I've known the priest there for a long time," Beau said. "I gave them an updated design and got them a discount on plants."

"Do you have a card, Mr. Magellan?" Sylvie asked.

"I do," he said. He pulled one out of his inside jacket pocket. "And please, call me Beau."

"Thank you," she said, sliding it into her slender purse. "And of course, I'm Sylvie. Lauren, the weather is getting nice. If I give you a call, will you come to my house, have lunch in my garden? Just you and me?"

"I would love that," she said. "Please do call! I'll bring you a plant!"

"I'll call. Very nice meeting you, Beau. Excuse me please. I have to try to say hello to people."

And that fast she was gone.

Lauren looked at Beau. "What am I going to do with you? Met me at church, did you?"

"In a manner of speaking," he said. "Seeing you here is even more startling."

"We're big supporters," she said. "See that bald guy over there? With Andy? My husband."

"Hm," he said. "He's friends with the host? Andy Emerson?"

"He believes so," she said. "Like I said, big supporter. Do you play golf?"

"I know how," Beau said. "I don't know that you could say I play, in all honesty."

"That's right," she said, laughing. "You read psychology. And fish. And garden." She glanced at the drinks. "Should you get those drinks back to your table?"

"They weren't dehydrated last time I looked. They're signing up for auction items."

"It's possible we have friends in common," she said. "My brother-in-law is an Oakland cop. I remember a fatality a couple of years ago."

"Roger Stanton," Beau said. "Did you know him?"

She shook her head. "Did you know him?"

"No, but the boys know the kids. You'll have to ask your brother-in-law…"

"Oh, Chip knew him. Even though it's a big department, they're all friends. It was heartbreaking. I'm so glad his daughter is a recipient." She nodded toward the drinks. "You should probably get those drinks back to your wife…"

He shook his head. "She's not here tonight. I brought my boys, my brother and sister-in-law and a friend."

"But not your wife?" she asked.

"Pamela finds this sort of thing boring and the friend I brought is a guy. But I don't find things like this boring. So tell me, what are you doing Tuesday?"

"What are you doing?" she asked.

"I'm going to check on the plants, maybe hoe around a little bit. H-O-E," he specified, making her laugh. "I'm going to put some bunny deterrent around. See how things are doing. I like the plants to get a strong hold before summer. Do you think you'll want to be uplifted by flowers?"

"You're coming on to a married woman," she said.

"I apologize! I don't want to make you uncomfortable. I'll get out of your space," he said, picking up the drinks.

"I might check out the plants," she said. "Now that I'm pretty sure you're not a stalker or serial killer."

"Oh Jesus, do I give off that vibe?" he asked, sloshing the drinks over his hands again. "I'm going to have to work on my delivery!"

"You sure don't give off the waiter vibe," she said, lifting a napkin from the table to assist him.

Just then, Brad was at her side. "We're down in front, Lauren. Don't make me come looking for you."

"I know. Brad, this is Beau Magellan, a landscape designer. A friend of Sylvie's."

Brad's black eyebrows shot up. "Oh? Maybe we'll have you take a look at ours." He put out a hand to shake, once he heard there was an Emerson connection, but Beau's hands were full of drinks. They were wet besides.

"Oh. Sorry," Beau said, lifting his handfuls clumsily.

"Okay," Brad said with a laugh. "Another time. I'll save you a seat," he said to Lauren.

"Sure. Be right there." She looked back at Beau, a mischievous smile playing at her lips.

"You're a liar, Lauren," Beau said.

"I'm sorry." She laughed. "It was irresistible. I hope we run into each other again, Beau. Now if there's anything left in those glasses, get them to your table."

* * * * *

The View from Alameda Island
by Robyn Carr
Available April 30, 2019,
from MIRA Books.

ROBYN CARR

36916	THE SUMMER THAT MADE US	___$8.99 U.S.	___$10.99 CAN.
33118	ANY DAY NOW	___$8.99 U.S.	___$10.99 CAN.
32931	WILD MAN CREEK	___$7.99 U.S.	___ $9.99 CAN.
32899	JUST OVER THE MOUNTAIN	___$7.99 U.S.	___ $9.99 CAN.
31978	WHAT WE FIND	___$8.99 U.S.	___$10.99 CAN.
31914	SUNRISE POINT	___$7.99 U.S.	___ $9.99 CAN.
31890	REDWOOD BEND	___$7.99 U.S.	___ $9.99 CAN.
31854	FOUR FRIENDS	___$7.99 U.S.	___ $8.99 CAN.
31787	A NEW HOPE	___$8.99 U.S.	___ $9.99 CAN.
31772	ONE WISH	___$8.99 U.S.	___ $9.99 CAN.
31763	BRING ME HOME FOR CHRISTMAS	___$7.99 U.S.	___ $9.99 CAN.
31749	WILDEST DREAMS	___$8.99 U.S.	___ $9.99 CAN.
31742	PROMISE CANYON	___$7.99 U.S.	___ $8.99 CAN.
31733	MOONLIGHT ROAD	___$7.99 U.S.	___ $8.99 CAN.
31724	THE HOUSE ON OLIVE STREET	___$7.99 U.S.	___ $8.99 CAN.
31702	ANGEL'S PEAK	___$7.99 U.S.	___ $8.99 CAN.
31697	FORBIDDEN FALLS	___$7.99 U.S.	___ $8.99 CAN.
31620	THE PROMISE	___$7.99 U.S.	___ $8.99 CAN.
31599	THE CHANCE	___$7.99 U.S.	___ $8.99 CAN.
31590	PARADISE VALLEY	___$7.99 U.S.	___ $8.99 CAN.
31459	THE HERO	___$7.99 U.S.	___ $8.99 CAN.
31452	THE NEWCOMER	___$7.99 U.S.	___ $9.99 CAN.
31447	THE WANDERER	___$7.99 U.S.	___ $9.99 CAN.
31419	SHELTER MOUNTAIN	___$7.99 U.S.	___ $9.99 CAN.
31415	VIRGIN RIVER	___$7.99 U.S.	___ $9.99 CAN.

(limited quantities available)

TOTAL AMOUNT	$ ______
POSTAGE & HANDLING	$ ______
($1.00 for 1 book, 50¢ for each additional)	
APPLICABLE TAXES*	$ ______
TOTAL PAYABLE	$ ______

(check or money order—please do not send cash)

To order, complete this form and send it, along with a check or money order for the total above, payable to MIRA Books, to: **In the U.S.:** 3010 Walden Avenue, P.O. Box 9077, Buffalo, NY 14269-9077; **In Canada:** P.O. Box 636, Fort Erie, Ontario, L2A 5X3.

Name: ______________________________

Address: ______________________ City: ______________

State/Prov.: ____________________ Zip/Postal Code: __________

Account Number (if applicable): ______________________

075 CSAS

Harlequin.com

*New York residents remit applicable sales taxes.

*Canadian residents remit applicable GST and provincial taxes.

MRC0419BL